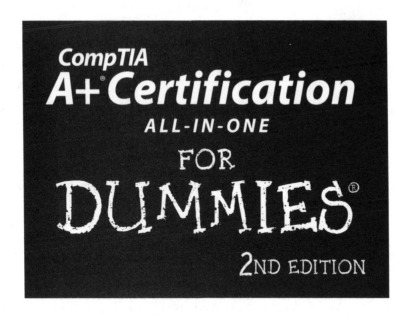

CompTIA
A+ Certification
ALL-IN-ONE
FOR
DUMMIES
2ND EDITION

by Glen E. Clarke and Ed Tetz

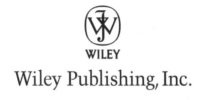

WILEY

Wiley Publishing, Inc.

CompTIA A+® Certification All-in-One For Dummies® 2nd Edition

Published by
Wiley Publishing, Inc.
111 River Street
Hoboken, NJ 07030-5774

www.wiley.com

For general information on our other products and services, please contact our Customer Care Department within the U.S. at 877-762-2974, outside the U.S. at 317-572-3993, or fax 317-572-4002.

For technical support, please visit www.wiley.com/techsupport.

Wiley also publishes its books in a variety of electronic formats. Some content that appears in print may not be available in electronic books.

Library of Congress Control Number: 2009935238

ISBN: 978-0-470-48738-9

Manufactured in the United States of America

10 9 8 7 6 5 4 3 2 1

WILEY

About the Authors

Glen E. Clarke (MCSE/MCSD/MCDBA/MCT/MCTS/CEH/Security+/Network+/A+) is an independent trainer and consultant, focusing on network security and security auditing services. Glen spends most of his time delivering certified courses on A+, Network+, Windows Server, SQL Server, Exchange Server, Visual Basic .NET, and ASP.NET. Glen also teaches a number of security related courses covering topics such as ethical hacking and countermeasures, vulnerability testing, firewall design, and packet analysis.

Glen is an experienced author and technical editor who has worked on fourteen certification books. Glen designed and coauthored the award nominated *A+ Certification Bible* and has worked on certification titles involving topics such as Windows certification, CIW certification, Network+ certification, and Security+ certification. Glen is also author of *The Network+ Certification Study Guide, 4th Edition*.

When he's not working, Glen loves to spend quality time with his wife, Tanya, and their four children, Sara, Brendon, Ashlyn, and Rebecca. You can visit Glen online at www.gleneclarke.com, or contact him at glenclarke@accesswave.ca.

Edward Tetz graduated in 1990 from Saint Lawrence College in Cornwall, Ontario with a degree in Business Administration. He spent a short time in computer sales, which eventually led to a computer support position. After several years of providing system and LAN support to small and large organizations, in 1994 he added training to his repertoire.

Some of the certifications that he holds include A+, ITIL Foundations Certificate in IT Service Management (IT Infrastructure Library), Microsoft Certified Trainer (MCT), Microsoft Certified Systems Engineer (MCSE), Microsoft Certified Database Administrator (MCDBA), and Chauncey Group's Certified Technical Trainer (CTT). Since 2002, he has been a full-time consultant for a value added reseller in Halifax, Nova Scotia. Over his years of work experience, he has supported Apple Macintosh, IBM OS/2, Linux, Novell NetWare, and all Microsoft operating systems from MS-DOS to Windows 2008, as well as hardware from most of the major vendors.

He welcomes comments from his readers and can be contacted at ed_tetz@hotmail.com, or if you are not trapped by the junk mail filters info@edtetz.net.

Dedication

To my wife, Tanya, who once again has shown amazing support.

— Glen E. Clarke

I would like to dedicate this book, with love, to my wife, Sharon, and my children, Emily and Mackenzie. They have always shown support in all of my endeavors, at a cost of time with them. If I owe anyone my gratitude for having this book written, it is them.

— Edward Tetz

Acknowledgments

There are so many hard working people that are needed to write a book and these people never get the credit they deserve — so I will attempt to show my appreciation. I want to thank the people at Wiley for their hard work and continued support. A special thank you to acquisitions editor, Katie Feltman, for asking Ed and I to do the second edition of this book and for her patience as I worked through the chapters. I also want to thank project editor Blair Pottenger for his patience and quick responses to any questions I fired his way! Much appreciation goes to copy editor Teresa Artman for an outstanding job on the editing of the chapters — thank you! I also want to thank Dan Lachance for his feedback as the technical editor and a job well done!

Over the years I have developed friendships through my work, and one of my favorite people to work with is the coauthor of this book - Ed Tetz. I want to thank him for the long hours he has dedicated to this book and for once again doing an amazing job! I also want to thank the folks at Tim Horton's for not kicking me out when I occupy a table for hours at a time and for keeping the coffee *always fresh*!

A special thank you goes to my four children, Sara, Brendon, Ashlyn, and Rebecca for giving me the time to sit down and participate in kids play with them — it makes me realize what is important in life. A needed thank you goes to my wife, Tanya, for all her support — you have made great sacrifices with this project as well. Thank you for all that you do!

— Glen E. Clarke

I would like to thank Katie Feltman, our acquisitions editor, for inviting Glen and I to take on this project, and to both Katie and Blair Pottenger, our project editor, for keeping this book on track, which I am sure was an effort for them, and thanks

for that. I cannot forget Teresa Artman, our copy editor, and Dan Lachance for their work of ensuring that what I wrote made sense, was accurate, and in many cases, making my words sound better than when I originally wrote them.

In addition to them, I would like to thank the rest of the staff at Wiley Publishing who worked behind the scenes taking care of many of the details that are required to get this book into print, and I am sure that due to their hard work, this will be a successful book.

— Edward Tetz

Publisher's Acknowledgments

We're proud of this book; please send us your comments at http://dummies.custhelp.com. For other comments, please contact our Customer Care Department within the U.S. at 877-762-2974, outside the U.S. at 317-572-3993, or fax 317-572-4002.

Some of the people who helped bring this book to market include the following:

Acquisitions, Editorial, and Media Development

Project Editor: Blair J. Pottenger

Senior Acquisitions Editor: Katie Feltman

Senior Copy Editor: Teresa Artman

Technical Editor: Dan Lachance

Editorial Manager: Kevin Kirschner

Media Development Project Manager: Laura Moss-Hollister

Media Development Assistant Project Manager: Jenny Swisher

Media Development Associate Producer: Shawn Patrick

Editorial Assistant: Amanda Graham

Sr. Editorial Assistant: Cherie Case

Cartoons: Rich Tennant (www.the5thwave.com)

Composition Services

Project Coordinator: Katie Crocker

Layout and Graphics: Samantha K. Cherolis, Ronald Terry, Christine Williams

Proofreaders: John Greenough, Christine Sabooni

Indexer: Broccoli Information Management

Special Help: Anne Sullivan

Publishing and Editorial for Technology Dummies

 Richard Swadley, Vice President and Executive Group Publisher

 Andy Cummings, Vice President and Publisher

 Mary Bednarek, Executive Acquisitions Director

 Mary C. Corder, Editorial Director

Publishing for Consumer Dummies

 Diane Graves Steele, Vice President and Publisher

Composition Services

 Debbie Stailey, Director of Composition Services

The logo of the CompTIA Authorized Quality Curriculum (CAQC) program and the status of this or other training materials as "Authorized" under the CompTIA Authorized Quality Curriculum program signifies that, in CompTIA's opinion, such training material covers the content of CompTIA's related certification exam.

The contents of this training material were created for the CompTIA A+ Certification exam covering CompTIA certification objectives that were current as of 2009.

CompTIA has not reviewed or approved the accuracy of the contents of this training material and specifically disclaims any warranties of merchantability or fitness for a particular purpose. CompTIA makes no guarantee concerning the success of persons using any such "Authorized" or other training material in order to prepare for any CompTIA certification exam.

How to become CompTIA certified:

This training material can help you prepare for and pass a related CompTIA certification exam or exams. In order to achieve CompTIA certification, you must register for and pass a CompTIA certification exam or exams.

In order to become CompTIA certified, you must:

1. Select a certification exam provider. For more information please visit http://www.comptia.org/certification/general_information/exam_locations.aspx.

2. Register for and schedule a time to take the CompTIA certification exam(s) at a convenient location.

3. Read and sign the Candidate Agreement, which will be presented at the time of the exam(s). The text of the Candidate Agreement can be found at http://www.comptia.org/certification/general_information/candidate_agreement.aspx.

4. Take and pass the CompTIA certification exam(s).

For more information about CompTIA's certifications, such as its industry acceptance, benefits or program news, please visit www.comptia.org/certification.

CompTIA is a not-for-profit information technology (IT) trade association. CompTIA's certifications are designed by subject matter experts from across the IT industry. Each CompTIA certification is vendor-neutral, covers multiple technologies and requires demonstration of skills and knowledge widely sought after by the IT industry.

To contact CompTIA with any questions or comments, please call 1-630-678-8300 or email questions@comptia.org.

Table of Contents

Introduction

The A+ Certified Professional certification is a well-recognized certification, and having this certification will serve as a basic foundation for a number of other certifications that you might pursue. The exams test your knowledge of hardware and software used in today's computer world, and the certification is one of the most popular certifications that IT professionals attain to prove their hardware and software knowledge.

About This Book

A+ Certification All-in-One For Dummies, 2nd Edition is designed to be a hands-on, practical guide to help you pass the A+ certification exams. This book is written in a way that helps you understand complex technical content and prepares you to apply that knowledge to real-world scenarios.

I understand the value of a book that covers the points needed to pass the exams, but I also understand the value of ensuring that the information helps you perform IT-related tasks when you are on the job. That is what this book offers you — key points to pass the exams combined with practical information to help you in the real world, which means that this book can be used in more than one way:

- ✦ **An exam preparation tool:** Because my goal is to help you pass the A+ exams, this book is packed with exam-specific information. You should understand everything that is in this book before taking the exams, but to help identify key points that you *must* know, look for icons named *For the Exam* to help you prep for the A+ exams.

- ✦ **A reference:** Rely on my extensive experience in the IT industry not only to study for (and pass) the exams but also to help you perform common computer-related tasks on the job. I hope you find this book a useful tool that you can refer to time and time again in your career.

Conventions Used in This Book

Each chapter in this book has different elements that help you prepare to pass your A+ exams. Each chapter holds the following features:

- ✦ **Labs:** Lab exercises offer the opportunity to get your hands dirty with a particular topic with real-world experience performing specific tasks. The labs for the chapters are located on the CD-ROM in a file called Labs.pdf in the Author directory.

✦ **Icons:** Look for the icons used in each chapter to draw your attention to information needed for the exams or in the real world. For more details on the icons I use, check out the later section, "Icons Used in This Book."

✦ **Getting an A+:** Found at the end of each chapter, the "Getting an A+" summary covers key points you should remember for the exams.

✦ **Prep Test:** Following each chapter's "Getting an A+" section, you can find example questions to help review the chapter content and prepare you for the A+ exam. Be sure to do the review questions with each chapter! Then, after you complete the book, check out the practice exams on the companion CD-ROM, which is designed to function like the real exams, with the same level of difficulty.

Foolish Assumptions

I make a few assumptions about you as a reader and have written this book with these assumptions in mind:

✦ **You are interested in obtaining the A+ Certification.** After all, the focus of this book is helping you pass the exams.

✦ **You have a computer to work on.** To perform the labs on the companion CD-ROM, you need a computer that you can take apart and install a copy of Windows on. I recommend downloading a copy of Microsoft Virtual PC to do the installation of the different operating systems.

✦ **You will study hard and do as much hands-on work as possible.** There is a lot of content on the A+ exams, and you will most likely need to read over the information a few times to ensure that you understand the content. You should also experiment as much as possible after you read a particular topic. For example, after you read about how to add a hard drive on a computer, you should get a second hard drive and add it to your computer. Or if you are reading about Windows utilities, try each one to be sure you are comfortable with what the utility looks like and what it can do.

How This Book Is Organized

Like all *All-in-One For Dummies* books, chapters are organized into mini-books. The chapters in each minibook are related by a specific theme or topic. For example, Book IX — "Securing Systems" — contains all security-related content needed to pass the A+ exams.

The following sections outline what you can find in each minibook.

Book I: Setting the A+ Groundwork

In this minibook, you discover what A+ certification is all about and what you will be tested on when taking the exam. You also find out some basic safety guidelines and general "soft skills," such as how to communicate with customers.

Book II: Inside the Box

In Book II, you find out about the inside of a computer and what makes it tick. You venture into the innards of your computer, such as motherboards, memory, and processors; and also see how to install and upgrade these components.

Book III: Outside the Box

Book III discusses topics related to what goes on outside the computer. You find out about the different ports on the back of the computer; how to install devices, such as video cards, sound cards, and network cards that give you output (think sound and video).

Book IV: Maintenance and Troubleshooting

The maintenance and troubleshooting minibook discusses how you care for the computer to prevent problems or hardware failure. This minibook also discusses how to troubleshoot different hardware components and how to diagnose the problem.

Book V: Operating System Basics

Book V is a special minibook because it makes the transition from hardware topics to operating system topics. In this minibook, you find out the purpose of an operating system and which major files an OS needs in order to run. You also discover how to install and upgrade Windows.

Book VI: Managing the Operating System

In this minibook, we discuss and demonstrate in a hands-on way how to manage aspects of the Windows operating systems. You find out how to load drivers and how to install and support applications and start using a number of troubleshooting tools available within Windows.

Book VII: Recovering Systems

In this minibook, you discover which core files are needed to start up a Windows computer and how to fix computers that fail to boot up. You also find topics related to system recovery, such as how to back up the system and perform a restore operation.

Book VIII: Networking

The A+ exams test your knowledge of basic networking concepts and ensure that you know how to network two computers. This minibook gives you the networking background you need to pass the A+ exams. You discover the basics of networking technologies and figure out how to troubleshoot systems on a TCP/IP network.

Book IX: Securing Systems

This final minibook covers topics related to securing your environment. In this minibook, I cover fundamental terms related to network security and also how to perform such tasks as creating user accounts, setting permissions, performing virus scans, and updating Windows.

Appendixes

Appendix A gives you an overview of what you can find on the CD-ROM that accompanies the book. Please have a look at this section to get the scoop on valuable resources on the book's companion CD-ROM, such as the lab exercises.

Appendix B is an exam objective mapping table that lets you know where in the book each of the exam objectives can be found. This is very useful when you are preparing for the exam to make sure you know each point in the objectives.

Icons Used in This Book

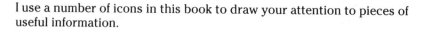

I use a number of icons in this book to draw your attention to pieces of useful information.

This icon gives you a heads-up on information you should absolutely know for the certification exams.

Information that would be helpful to you in the real world is indicated with a Tip icon. Expect to find shortcuts and timesavers here.

This icon is used to flag information that may be useful to remember on the job.

Information that could cause problems to you or to the computer is indicated with a Warning icon. If you see a Warning icon, make sure you read it. The computer you save may be your own.

Detailed information that is not needed for the exams or that is a step above the knowledge you absolutely need to know for the exams is indicated with a Technical Stuff icon.

This icon lets you know when you can find accompanying information or supporting documents on the CD-ROM. For example, there are a number of lab exercises written for the book — when a topic has a related lab, it is indicated with this icon.

Where to Go from Here

The A+ Certification is the most popular certification for individuals new to the IT industry and the certification world. After you pass the A+ exams, you might want to continue your certification path by studying for the following certifications from CompTIA:

+ **Network+:** A vendor-neutral certification that ensures the candidate understands networking technologies.

+ **Security+:** After passing the Network+ certification, you may want to continue on the network topic with a certification that proves your network security knowledge.

Book I

Setting the A+ Ground Work

The 5th Wave By Rich Tennant

"Wait! Wait! Wait! You've got a lung and
two eyeballs in there! I thought you said
you were A+ Certified?"

Contents at a Glance

Chapter 1: The 2009 A+ Exams

In This Chapter

✔ **Understanding A+ Certification and its benefits**

✔ **Looking at the exams and their objectives**

✔ **Preparing for the exams**

✔ **Arranging to take the exams**

✔ **Test day**

So, you are interested in taking the CompTIA A+ Certification exams? This chapter introduces you to the exams and gives you a good idea of what you can expect when you go to take them. Knowing what to expect in regard to the exam procedures and format will remove that uncertainty from you, which can weigh on your mind. Read through the procedures here; then you will be able to focus on the exam facts, which will help you breeze through the exam.

I hope that this chapter helps remove some of that normal fear of the unknown by giving you information about the actual test-taking process. This chapter will also help you develop good test-taking skills.

CompTIA A+ Certification and Why You Need It

The benefit of the CompTIA A+ Certification is proof that you know and have validated the hardware and software knowledge necessary to troubleshoot and repair computers. The CompTIA A+ Certification can be presented to employers and clients alike as proof of competency and skill in this area. This certification never expires.

Formed in 1982, CompTIA was originally named the Association of Better Computer Dealers. It is a company focused on providing research, networking, and partnering opportunities to its 19,000 members in 100 countries. In 1993, in response to the need for vendor-neutral, entry-level PC certification, the company created the A+ Certification.

Prior to CompTIA creating the A+ Certification, there were many places where a person could get hardware and software certifications. However, such training was often very expensive, difficult to get, and not designed for accessibility for most people. Microsoft, Novell, IBM, and other software

companies offered software certifications, but these were specifically focused on teaching high-level support skills for these products, were difficult for average users or support people to attain, and lacked relevance for most day-to-day work.

IBM, HP, Compaq, SUN, and other hardware companies offered hardware repair and maintenance certifications, but again, these were specifically focused on their hardware — and more on the peculiarities of their own platforms, and not always covering the basics of configuration and maintenance. CompTIA stepped in to fill the gap that a majority of users fell into, which is a hardware and software neutral certification that covered all the basics required by a support person. This certification can then be followed by vendor-based certifications, if desired, but the A+ Certification by itself proves a firm grasp of the basics.

An A+ Certification gives employers confidence that existing employees or new recruits have a level of knowledge with which they can do their jobs efficiently. It also gives employers a yardstick against which recruits and employees can be measured. And an A+ Certification also allows clients to rest assured that the person they hire to fix their computers has the knowledge to do so without blowing up equipment or deleting valuable data. This provides clients with peace of mind and increases repeat business. In the end, with the CompTIA A+ Certification on your side, you have more opportunities open to you in your career path.

Checking Out the Exams and Their Objectives

You have to take two exams to get your CompTIA A+ Certification. Both exams are required. The first required exam is the CompTIA A+ Essentials Exam (220-701), which focuses on the terminology and concepts. The second required exam is the CompTIA A+ Practical Application Exam (220-702), which focuses on practical knowledge required to work in a challenging IT environment.

Revised exams for CompTIA A+ were released in 2009. You have 90 minutes to complete each exam; Table 1-1 contains the number of questions and passing score for each exam. CompTIA is releasing the exams as linear format exams — standard timed exams — taken on a computer. After CompTIA gathers grading statistics, it might re-release the exams as adaptive exams (what CompTIA has done in the past), but there are no current plans by CompTIA to do so. If the exam you take is adaptive, these limits will change. In this adaptive exam, you will be asked a minimal number of questions (usually about 15), and then asked additional questions based on any incorrect answers. The exam adapts to your wrong answers by choosing additional questions for you from the area where you are weaker.

Table 1-1	A+ Exam Information	
Exam	*Number of Questions*	*Minimum Passing Score*
A+ Essentials (220-701)	100	675
Practical Application (220-702)	90	700

If you are taking an adaptive exam, you will pass or fail based on the number of wrong answers you get. For instance, if on a standard, timed exam, you are asked 50 questions and you need a score of 75% to pass, you need 38 correct answers. For the same exam in an adaptive form, however, you would fail if you get 13 questions wrong. As soon as you get to that level, your test would be over, even if you were asked only 13 questions because after that point, it is then statistically impossible for you to pass. After an initial set of questions, if you have few enough wrong answers, you will pass.

The CompTIA A+ Essentials Exam

The CompTIA A+ Essentials Exam (220-701) covers the basics of computer maintenance and support across the CompTIA A+ *domains,* or exam areas. Table 1-2 provides a breakdown of the exam areas that are covered on the CompTIA A+ Essentials Exam. This exam puts heavy emphasis on personal computer components and operating systems.

Table 1-2	CompTIA A+ Essentials Exam (220-701)
Domain	*Percentage of Examination*
1.0 Hardware	27%
2.0 Troubleshooting, Repair & Maintenance	20%
3.0 Operating System and Software	20%
4.0 Networking	15%
5.0 Security	8%
6.0 Operational Procedure	10%

The CompTIA A+ Practical Application Exam

In addition to the CompTIA A+ Essentials Exam, you have to take a second exam. This exam is the CompTIA A+ Practical Application Exam (220-702), which is designed to measure skills required to maintain and support

computers and small networks or enterprise environments. The breakdown of the exam components is covered in Table 1-3. Based on the domain breakdown, this exam has the widest breadth of topics for a well-rounded IT.

Table 1-3	CompTIA A+ Practical Application Exam (220-702)
Domain	*Percentage of Examination*
1.0 Hardware	38%
2.0 Operating Systems	34%
3.0 Networking	15%
4.0 Security	13%

Using This Book to Prepare for the Exams

Exams are stressful events for most people, but if you are well prepared, your stress level should be much lower. If you read and understand the material in this book, you should have no problem with any of the exams. The review questions, sample exams, and exam test engine on the companion CD are all designed to prepare you for what lies ahead. There is substantial overlap between the topics covered on the CompTIA A+ Essentials Exam and the CompTIA A+ Practical Application Exam, so this book takes a holistic approach to studying for the exams. Review all the material found here, and then you will be prepared to go and take either of your exams you choose because they can be taken in either order. I recommend taking both of your exams in a short timeframe to avoid forgetting the information you have learned.

Examine the objectives for each chapter before diving into the content so that you can use them as a guide to which sections you might need to focus on. After thoroughly reading the content of the chapter, attempt the Prep Test section at the end of the chapter. If you do poorly on the Prep Test, go back to the objectives to see where you need more effort. When you re-read the chapter sections, try to examine the content from another viewpoint to help you associate the information with the questions and the objectives. For example, a differing viewpoint might be that of a computer user, a help desk employee, or a desktop support technician. After you can complete the Prep Test in each chapter with an 85% or better score, move on to attempt the exams on the companion CD. If you are unable to achieve a mark of 85% or better, you should continue to review the areas in which you are weak.

Making Arrangements to Take the Exams

The A+ Certification exams can be scheduled at Pearson VUE or Prometric testing centers. For more information about scheduling your exam, check the CompTIA A+ Certification page on CompTIA's Web site at

```
http://certification.comptia.org/a/default.aspx
```

The cost to take the A+ exams is $168 (US) per exam while CompTIA members will receive a discount. To become a CompTIA member, you must hold a valid CompTIA certification and pay a membership fee. If you are reading this book, you probably do not have your A+ Certification, but you might hold a Network+, Linux+, or some other CompTIA certification. If so, you can become a CompTIA member. Details on this process can be found on CompTIA's IT Pro Web site at

```
http://itpro.comptia.org/default.aspx
```

The Day the Earth Stood Still: Exam Day

Knowing what to expect on the day of the exam can take some of the pressure off of you. The following sections look at the testing process.

Arriving at the exam location

Get to the exam location early on the day of the exam. You should arrive at the testing center 15 to 30 minutes before the exam starts. This keeps you from being rushed and gives you some temporal elbow room in case there are any delays. It is also not so long that you will have time to sit and stew about the exam. Get there, get into a relaxed frame of mind, and get into the exam.

When you get to the test site, before you sign in, take a few minutes to get accustomed to the testing center. Get a small drink of water. Use the restroom if you need to. The test will be 90 minutes, so you should be able to last that long before another break. You might want to check the center's policy for bringing a beverage with you; some centers will allow it, and others will not.

Now relax. Getting to the exam site early gives you this privilege. You didn't show up early just to stew and make yourself more nervous.

If you feel prepared and are ready to go, you might want to see whether you can start the test early. As long as a testing seat is available, this is usually not a problem. When signing in, you will usually need two pieces of ID, with at least one of them being a photo ID. After signing in, you are taken to the testing room.

You will not be able to take anything into the testing room. You will not be allowed electronics, paper, and so on. They will provide you with something to write with and to write on, which they will take back at the end of test.

Taking the exam

In the testing room, and depending on the size of the testing center, there will usually be as many as eight computers set up. Each computer represents a testing seat.

Because the exam consists of multiple-choice questions, take it slow — or at least pace yourself. Trying to complete the questions too quickly will no doubt lead you to errors. When you are about to start the exam, you will see onscreen how many questions there will be, and how long you have to complete the exam. Be sure to read the onscreen exam instructions at the start of the exam; they do change from time to time.

Based on the number of questions and your exam time, figure out how long you can spend on each question. On average, you have slightly more than one minute per question. Take your time, but be aware of your time for the exam overall. Think of it this way: When you have completed 25% of the exam, you should have used only 25% of your allotted time.

Read the entire question and try to decide what the answer should be before looking at the answer choices. In most cases, you will find a few key words that are designed to remove any ambiguity in the question, as well as a few distracters and useless information designed to throw you off. If you do not notice these key words, the question will seem vague. If this is the case, reread the question and look for the key words. Exam questions are written by many authors, so the style of writing for each question could differ.

Don't overcomplicate the questions by reading too much into them. Besides the key words and the distracters, the question should be straightforward. In some cases, the question might ask for the best choice, and more than one answer might seem correct. Choose the one that is *best* — the quickest, most likely to succeed, least likely to cause other problems — whatever the question calls for. The best choice is always the right choice.

After identifying the key words and distracters, follow these additional steps:

1. **Eliminate choices that are obviously wrong.**

 Most questions will ask you to choose one of four answers. Some questions will ask you to choose all that apply and have as many as eight choices. You should be able to immediately eliminate at least one

choice — perhaps two. Now the odds of choosing the right answer have gotten substantially better. Re-read the question and the remaining choices carefully, and you should be able to locate the correct answer.

2. **If you don't have a clue which of the remaining choices is correct, mark an answer.**

 On a standard timed exam, you can review your answers. Not answering a question is automatically wrong, so if you at least *have* an answer, it might be right. You might also find information on other questions in the exam that triggers the correct answers for questions you were not sure of.

3. **Make your choice and leave it.**

 Unless you have information that proves your choice is wrong, your first instinct is usually correct.

The adaptive exam delivers a series of questions to you. If you answer a question incorrectly, you get additional questions in that category. You can't review or change your answers on the adaptive exams like you can with standard timed exams. Because skipped questions are automatically wrong, with no ability to change them, you must provide an answer to the question before moving to the next question. You are allowed to attempt to answer a finite number of questions (known only by CompTIA) before the test "decides" that you really don't know what you need to know to pass the test. If you exceed the allowed number of wrong answers (again, known only by CompTIA), the exam ends; you fail. (But that won't happen to you because you bought this wonderful book!)

If you get all the initial category questions correct, you can pass the exam in relatively few questions. If you get an initial category question wrong in a category in which you are weak, though, you will find the adaptive format very difficult. You won't know exactly how many questions you have to answer to complete the exam, so the end of an adaptive exam will always come as a surprise — hopefully, a good one.

If you are taking the nonadaptive exam, you are allowed to mark questions and come back to them later. However, I recommend selecting an answer for every question, even if you are unsure about it, because you might run out of time before you can review previous questions.

Your first choice is usually correct — don't second-guess your first choice! Change your answer only if you're absolutely positive it should be changed.

Regardless of which type of exam CompTIA has available for you when you take your exam (adaptive or standard timed), you are given a Pass/Fail mark right on the spot after completing the exam. In addition, you get

a report listing how well you did in each domain. If you don't pass (or even if you do), you can use this report to review the material on which you are still weak.

How does CompTIA set the pass level?

CompTIA uses a scale score to determine the total number of points that each question on the exam will be calculated from. Your final score will be between 100 and 900. In any case, the passing score (not a percentage, due to the scale) varies from one exam to the others. The scale score system allows the number of points assigned to questions to vary between each copy of the exam, which makes it harder for test candidates to compare scores across exams.

CompTIA has a retake policy. If you do not pass on the first attempt, you can take the exam again at any time, but you have to wait at least 30 days before your third or subsequent attempts.

Chapter 2: A+ Soft Skills

Exam Objectives

✔ Knowing your troubleshooting techniques

✔ Communicating effectively and professionally

As a CompTIA A+ Certified Professional, you will often need to trouble-shoot systems as well as deal with customers or clients. For you to complete these tasks, you need good troubleshooting skills, and you also need to develop good customer-relation skills.

This chapter examines the basics of troubleshooting. These basics are not based on specific hardware components, but rather on basic methodology that is used to solve problems. This methodology will not change even though the underlying technology might change. Troubleshooting specific components is covered in Book IV, Chapter 2.

When solving problems for customers — internal or external customers — you will likely need to talk to them. This chapter takes a look at communication skills that help you maintain a high level of professionalism.

Using Troubleshooting Procedures and Good Practices

Many people say that troubleshooting skills cannot be learned, but this is not true. If you are methodical or just very curious, you will probably have an easier time troubleshooting. However, anyone can learn the practical order to follow when troubleshooting problems. Follow the steps in this chapter, and you should have an easy time when it comes to troubleshooting.

The two main sections of troubleshooting are hypothesis generation and hypothesis evaluation. In other words, based on the symptoms that you see, you create a list of things that might be wrong and then test to see whether any of them are actually the problem. Figure 2-1 shows a rough outline of general troubleshooting procedures.

On the exam, some of the CompTIA terminology might vary from what I use here, but the general guidelines and approximate order will remain the same.

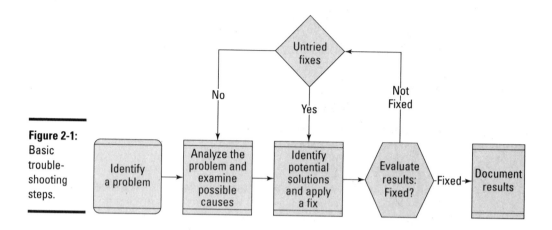

Figure 2-1:
Basic trouble-shooting steps.

To troubleshoot any system, you need to know how that system is supposed to function and what options can be changed or might fail. This information allows you to quickly assemble a list of hypotheses. The better you know the system, the easier this phase will be. You then need to test these hypotheses. Testing might involve using tools appropriate to the system to test the condition of certain components, or it might involve changing a series of configuration settings and rechecking to see whether the problem has been resolved at certain stages.

Identifying the problem

The first task is to identify the problem. The first step to identifying the problem is to question the system's user. This shouldn't be a police interrogation, nor should you accuse the user of causing the error. You might discover, after all is said and done, that the user actually *did* cause the error, but you should never assume that upfront, or you will quickly become an adversary instead of an advocate.

The information you gather from the user helps you set the scope of the problem. Many users start with the simple, "It's broke!" It is up to you to figure out how "it" is "broke," and you do that by asking simple questions: "What issues are you having with it? What is it not doing? Does it always happen or only at certain times?"

Even if the user gives you a better starting point, you will likely still need to ask some questions to refine the scope of the problem. Here are some things to keep in mind while you try to identify the problem:

> ✦ **Identify changes to the computer.** Some errors are caused by the user or his surroundings. The user should always be asked upfront, in much the same way a doctor will ask whether his patient's lifestyle has changed or whether he is on any medication. Ask the user whether he

made any changes to the computer by installing software, changing hardware, or changing the computer's location. This often provides you with an early lead to the possible problem.

✦ **Break big problems into smaller pieces.** Continuing with my doctor analogy (see the preceding bullet), the "I feel sick" statement causes a doctor to ask questions and build a list of symptoms. That list of symptoms (sore throat, headache, runny nose, gaping hole in abdomen) might be easier to deal with if broken down into groups of symptoms rather than being treated as a whole. The doctor might then treat each group of symptoms individually. The same applies to the computer problems. That "broke" computer might be malfunctioning because of a variety of smaller problems: insufficient RAM, a fragmented hard drive, malware, Trojans, and poor networking protocol configuration. If the problems are broken down instead of being treated as a whole, you can approach each item separately.

✦ **Prioritize problems and decide in which order they should be tackled.** With your list of problems, decide which are the most critical and should be approached first. For instance, if the hard drive is corrupted *and* you need to reinstall or upgrade the operating system, fix the issue with the hard drive before performing the software upgrade.

In most cases, you prioritize the issues based on the impact to the user and the impact of other fixes implemented at a later time. One rule I live by is, "Fix the business problem first." For example, if you are working for a stock trader, she needs her stock trading program working immediately, but she might be willing to wait for a fix to the word processing program.

Analyzing the problem and potential causes

For each problem that you work on, decide the scope of the problem. This can be done by testing. The initial tests that you conduct determine the scope of the problem. Say you go to a doctor for an upset stomach. She asks stomach- and food-related questions and then probably runs some basic tests to determine whether the problem is an ulcer, an allergy, or just some bad sushi.

The same is true with computer issues. You ask questions and then perform rudimentary tests to determine the scope of the issue. For example, after being told that a printer does not print, you might verify that its cables are in place, it powers up, it has toner or ink, and it accepts commands from the computer. These rudimentary checks allow you to see how large the problem is; from there, you can perform additional analyses. For example, if the printer is passing paper but the pages come out blank, your list of potential causes can be reduced because it is not a power issue. Rather, the problem is either with the transfer of the printing material — the ink or toner — or with the interpretation of the commands from the computer. With this narrowed list of potential causes, you can move on with addressing the problem.

The basic troubleshooting process

With your list of potential causes in hand, move on to figuring out potential solutions. In some instances, you might approach the problem starting at a general level and then work down to specific components. Conversely, you might look at entire systems, like the power system, in a sequential manner. In most cases, your potential causes can be placed on an imaginary line that forms a resolution path. The resolutions path forms a sequential chain of possible causes for the issue, starting at one point and moving to another. For instance, if a computer does not power up, you can start testing at the electrical socket; move to the power supply, power supply connectors, power switch, motherboard; and then move to the devices. This process moves through the sequential chain along the possible path that power would flow. Following a possible resolution path from one end to the other is sometimes referred to as the *layered* or *linear approach*.

The term *layered* is often used when discussing networking issues because the layers in the networking model are easily definable and are often referenced. For more information about the layered network model, see Book VIII, which discusses networking.

Most systems that make up computer systems and networks can be broken into layered models, and troubleshooting can move through these layers. Another example of layered troubleshooting is a gasoline engine, with its two major systems: the electrical system and a fuel supply system. The electrical system has layered troubleshooting starting at a power source (say, a battery) through power supply cables, a distributor, and finally to a spark plug. The fuel supply system starts with fuel storage, supply lines, a pump, and filter, and then ends at a combustion chamber. In the event of a problem, both systems can be reviewed and tested from end to end, in a linear or layered manner, until the problem is located.

The following sections take a close look at some suggestions for implementing potential solutions.

Back up any settings or files that you need to change

You don't want to introduce more problems to a system than it had when you started. Before changing any basic input-output system (BIOS) or application settings, record the original settings — or back them up. For instance, if an application that you are troubleshooting stores its configuration in a text or binary file, copy that file so you can quickly restore it to the initial state if your solution doesn't work.

Some computers allow you to make a backup copy of the complementary metal-oxide semiconductor (CMOS) configuration or back up the existing BIOS prior to overwriting it with an upgrade. Some things cannot easily be

reversed, like the application of a Service Pack, so care should be taken when doing those tasks, such as setting a restore point or making a full system backup.

Test one configuration change at a time

This step is required to know what the fix actually is. If you change five things and the problem component now works, you don't know which change made the difference. In some cases, you might incur monetary cost. For instance, if the computer starts to blue screen on boot and you suspect a hardware fault, you could change the disk controller, hard drive, RAM, CPU, and power supply. After that, if the problem no longer exists, what was the solution? Are you going to replace all five components the next time you have the issue? By substituting one item at a time and testing at each step to re-create the issue, you will know which change you implemented corrected the problem.

Don't discount the obvious

When I get the messages Missing Operating System or NTLDR not found, the first thing I do is look for a floppy disk that was left in the system. For power problems, is it plugged in? For network problems, is the cable plugged into the correct jack? These simple first steps are often over-looked by the user. Just because it is obvious to you does not mean that it is obvious to the user. If the solution is not obvious, go back to your layer approach — it will not let you down.

Research to find potential fixes

If you run out of ideas for a specific problem, do a little research. The "Documentation resources" section, later in this chapter, gives you some ideas about where to begin.

There is nothing wrong with you, as a CompTIA A+ Certified Professional, not knowing the solution to a particular issue with a specific product. What is important is that you know where you can find the answers — quickly.

Prioritize potential fixes for the problem

After you spent time researching the symptoms, now you have a long list of items to check and possible solutions to apply. And, you must prioritize them. You can put the most likely fix at the top of your list, or you can put the quickest and least disruptive fix at the beginning of the list. In most cases, you will likely do the latter.

For instance, a good fix for many software-related problems is to reimage the computer or reinstall the application. Although this often fixes the problem, it can be time consuming for you and disruptive for the user.

Reinstallation often involves checking for local files that need to be backed up, backing them up, verifying application settings, restoring the computer operating system, restoring backed-up user files, and reapplying settings. This usually leaves a lot of settings that the user needs to reset when she runs the application(s) for the first time after reinstallation. Because this is time consuming and disruptive, it should be left toward the end of the list of options. Rather, the list should begin with items such as verifying application settings, testing new-user profiles, and other quicker and less-disruptive fixes.

Test related components

Sometimes, a symptom in one area is caused by a problem in another. The classic example with computers is being asked to look at a computer that is reported as slow, and has an extremely active hard drive. You can test the hard drive and related cables, use diagnostic utilities to test its health, swap it with another, only to not find a solution. Then you have to take a step back and evaluate other system components, such as memory. In many cases, a lack of RAM can cause excessive paging, which causes high disk activity. So, the solution to the problem might be to add RAM to the computer and not do anything with the hard drive. If you did not look at the related component (RAM), you would not have been able to solve the problem with the active hard drive. In some cases, you might need to do some research to know what components of the system are related. Don't just go for the obvious: Test related systems as well. That might be where the actual issue is.

Evaluate results

At each step of the analysis and application of potential fixes, evaluate the results. By evaluating often, you will know what is working, what is not, and what additional problem you might have caused. At any time, the results might cause you to change your initial hypothesis and choose to pursue a different path. Changing your hypothesis should be done only if there is sufficient proof that your initial statements were in error, or you might find yourself running in circles.

Document findings, activities, and outcomes

The philosopher George Santayana said, "Those who cannot remember the past are condemned to repeat it." To remember it for the long term, write it down or otherwise record it. If you do not document your findings, you might find yourself repeating the same troubleshooting steps in the future to solve a similar problem, when the process could have been abbreviated.

I recommend using a personal or a corporate knowledge base to record troubleshooting activities. Some companies have a formal help desk or trouble ticket system, with the main goal of documenting their problems and solutions. Having a technician close his trouble tickets with "Problem resolved" might be fast for the technician, but it is not the purpose of the application. One of the application's goals is to build a database of problems and resolutions. The more detail that is included in the resolution documentation, the more helpful it will be in the future.

After the trouble ticket database has enough information, it becomes more than a place where the information is stored: It also becomes a place where solutions are found. The larger the database, the more likely it will be able to provide your solution. When a problem is reported, you can search the database to see whether the problem has previously happened for that person (or another person), and you might be provided with a solution. Testing a few known solutions is faster than starting the troubleshooting process at the beginning.

Documentation resources

CompTIA A+ Certified Professionals aren't expected to know every answer, but they should have a good list of resources at their disposal to find an answer. Here are the most common resources:

✦ **Vendor manuals:** Gone are the days of an IT department filled with bookcase upon bookcase of manuals for every application that the company owns. In many cases, manuals are now shipped on CD in PDF format or are available for download from vendors' Web sites. Many of these manuals have specific sections detailing product installation, options to watch during the installation, and diagnostics or troubleshooting. Looking up a computer's symptoms in this guide can lead to concise, quick solutions.

✦ **Service documentation:** In addition to general user manuals, some companies offer additional service documentation that can be obtained by owners of the product. In some cases, this will be available to you only if you are certified on the product or you are employed by the manufacturer. Check whether this technical documentation is available to you because it often has detailed configuration and troubleshooting information.

✦ **External knowledge bases:** In the same way that your organization can create its own internal knowledge base of problems and solutions, many vendors have compiled their knowledge base, and they make this data available and searchable on their Web sites. If the manuals seem to be

lacking, see whether the vendor has a searchable online knowledge base. In some cases, vendors ignore the manual when they maintain a good knowledge base. Again, if your problem is found in the database, you likely have a quick solution that you can apply.

✦ **Training:** Knowledge is half the battle, and one of the best ways to get quick knowledge is to attend vendor training on the products that you are working on. In many cases, you will find out a product's *gotchas* — those common but hard-to-solve problems that are unique to the product. If you don't walk away with this, you should at least leave the training with a complete picture of how the product is supposed to work, which can reduce your troubleshooting time.

✦ **Other Internet resources:** In addition to the vendor Web sites as an official support tool, additional discussion forums and Web sites might have answers to your specific problems, even though the Web site or forum is geared toward a general industry area. For instance, you might be having issues with a specific sound card; if the vendor's Web site does not provide you with the answer, you might find the answer on a site that covers all computer audio cards and issues. Your favorite search engine is a good place to start looking for these sites.

With these documentation resources and the basic troubleshooting guidelines in your arsenal, you should be able to approach problems and troubleshoot them in a methodical, organized way.

Additional troubleshooting processes for specific hardware components are covered in other sections of this book, with much of it in Book IV, Chapter 2.

Professionalism and Communication

Whether you are an internal or external support professional, you have customers. For the external support professional, it is easy to identify your customers. For the internal support professional, the people for whom you provide support are still your customers, and you still need to provide them with service. To provide this service, you will be required to communicate with them, and this communication should remain professional in its tone and manner. The best way to maintain the right level of professionalism is to respect the customer; whether the customer is right or wrong, you should still give him respect. You can still show him respect while you educate him, work with him, or explain to him that he is wrong.

The professionalism and communication section of the A+ exam should be common sense for most readers. The exam questions will present a wide range of responses to given scenarios; the answer will usually be the one that illustrates good communication skills and respect for the client. Verbally abusing the client and hanging up will not be the correct answer!

Good communication skills

What we've got here is a failure to communicate.

—Cool Hand Luke

A breakdown in communication can be blamed for many of the problems that exist in our world today. It is often a source of conflict that begins with a misunderstanding. To avoid this conflict with your customers, always make sure that you use good communication skills. Here is a list of things to keep in mind when communicating with a customer:

✦ **Listen to the customer and don't interrupt.** One of the best abilities of a good communicator is the ability to listen. All too often, in today's society, the emphasis is on speed; and for the sake of speed, people tend not to listen. Part of "not listening" is completing other peoples' thoughts or sentences. This is a problem that can be resolved by resisting the urge to just jump in. Put yourself in the listener's position while you let the person tell you the problem and how it is affecting her life. "Not listening" can extend to e-mail. I have written e-mails to vendor support addresses, detailing a problem and the steps already taken to solve that problem, only to receive a stock reply from the vendor support person saying, "Try this," which was already tried, or does not address the problem. At times like that, I usually reply to the e-mail, stating the fact that he failed to read the message and rather suggested a solution based on the subject line or the first line of the message.

✦ **Clarify statements and repeat what you have heard.** One technique that helps to clarify any misunderstandings is to repeat to the user what he told you. This reinforces for the user that you are listening and are not daydreaming. It also verifies that you understand what the user said. When you repeat it, you may substitute terms or give additional examples of what the client described to you.

✦ **Use clear, concise, and direct statements.** Translation: Don't be long-winded. Many people like to hear themselves talk; resist any temptations to verbosity you might have. Don't use a $10 word when a 25¢ word will do. Keep your statements direct with clearly focused points.

✦ **Avoid tech talk.** As a CompTIA A+ Certified Professional, you are constantly exposed to technical terms and abbreviations that you slowly incorporate into your vocabulary. However, not everybody in the general public is familiar with *RAID, asynchronous, MTBF, SCSI,* and a whole slew of other terms that can confuse clients who refer to the computer as being composed of a monitor and a hard drive. Whenever possible, try to gauge the user's knowledge level and use an appropriate level of terminology.

Professional behavior

Always try to conduct yourself with professionalism. Doing so generates respectability in the eyes of your clients and supervisors. The following list contains some aspects of professionalism that should be practiced:

+ **Positive attitude:** It is often said that animals can smell fear on a person. The same is true of users: They can smell a negative attitude right away. You should approach each client and each job with a positive attitude and a feeling of confidence. If you do, you will get more satisfaction from your job. Regardless of your position, there will likely be some aspects of your job that you don't enjoy, but don't let these things bring down your attitude.

In most cases, you deal with clients who have problems that might put the client in a foul mood. If you seem happy to see a client, he will likely lighten his mood, and you will both have a more positive experience. Win/win.

This could go in reverse if you let it: The client's negative attitude could dampen *your* mood. Don't let this happen. Stay positive.

+ **Proper dress:** Professionalism likely includes appropriate attire as well as attitude. When choosing what to wear, plan around the jobs that you are doing. Client meetings might dictate formal business attire; if you are expecting to pull cable through crawlspaces, though, something more casual would fit the task.

Regardless of the job, your clothes should be clean and well-kept. To a client, a shoddy appearance indicates shoddy work.

+ **Privacy, confidentiality, and discretion:** It's surprising what information clients are willing to let you see on their computers. In many cases, you have access to their most private documents. In corporate environments, this can include confidential employee information. When doing retail bench work, this can include private financial information. In both cases, a client's computer often holds information that you should not be seeing — and, in normal circumstances, you would not be allowed to see. In most cases, you will know what you should and should not be looking at. If there is a reason to open a file to verify accessibility, then sure — you will need to do that. However, you should ignore the information you find when you're done.

As an outside consultant, I am amazed by the number of clients who freely offer up administrative credentials for their network, granting access to all areas of the network and to all kinds of information. Take care to ensure that these credentials are not misused by you or put in a place where they could be used by another person without your knowledge.

✦ **Respect:** People with different cultural backgrounds will have different means of showing respect, and you should use techniques appropriate to your local region or culture. In general, the techniques listed here are fairly universal. Respect should be thought of as a two-way street. In most cases, if you show appropriate respect to your clients, they will return that level of respect.

If the client doesn't show you any respect, don't lower yourself to his or her level — stay calm and continue to be respectful. Ask the client to calm down, let him know that he is not acting appropriately, and that you will not be able to help if he does not give you the information you need. This is a tough situation to call because when people are told that they are not acting appropriately, they either calm down or become defensive and more disrespectful. While you tell them that they should calm down, make sure to reinforce that you want to help them. The logic of the situation might finally sink in.

Some steps or actions you can take to show respect are

- *Don't argue or be defensive.* The client might be in a foul mood. You would likely be as well if technology got in the way of your job or you thought that you had just lost several years of personal data or photos. A client might have many reasons to be upset when you start dealing with him.

 To some clients, you represent the technology they're having issues with. Their frustration often gets vented all over you. Don't take this personally or get upset by users' actions. Do what you can to relieve some of their stress and remind them that you're not part of the problem. Rather, you're part of the solution.

 If you argue with the client, the entire issue will become ugly. Avoid arguing at all costs.

- *Don't belittle or minimize problems.* In most cases, the problems that users face are serious to them. Even though you might not share their view of the importance of the problem, do not dismiss the issue. By claiming that the problems are trivial, you suggest that the clients' feelings are trivial. If the clients were not upset before this point, they will be if they think you are trivializing them.

- *Don't be judgmental.* Any biases you have should be checked at the door when you come to work. That way, you will likely reserve your judgments on issues until you have seen all the facts. This point goes very nicely with the previous one: namely, that if you pass early judgment on a user, you might be more inclined to trivialize her issues.

- *Avoid distractions and interruptions.* When dealing with a client, try to reduce distractions for yourself. If you are working a help desk, you should not be carrying on conversations with those around you when you are on a support call. If you are working a retail repair bench, you should deal with one client at a time and not try to multi-task among them or take phone calls. If you are visiting a client, you should silence your mobile phone.

 In all cases in which you are physically with a client, maintain eye contact. This will be taken as a sign that you're paying attention. If you don't maintain eye contact, the client will think that you are not paying attention. There is also a chance that you might become distracted by something you see. If you maintain eye contact, you will not get distracted by other events, and you will tend to have a better understanding of what is being said to you.

- *Property is as important as people.* Respecting the person extends to respecting his or her property and privacy. For many clients, you will be working in their office, very possibly at their desk. When you're waiting for a reboot or for software installation, you will be tempted to look around. Don't do it! You should always respect your client's privacy and possessions, from the computer to the Marvin the Martian action figure.

- *Don't bad-mouth other clients.* Respect for a customer extends beyond the time you spend fixing his computer. Don't be disrespectful of any client in front of current ones. If the client sees you lack respect for others or hears you say negative things about other clients, she will think that you are going to say similar things about her to your other clients.

- *Be culturally sensitive.* With the globalization of IT services, as well as the multicultural makeup of so many countries, you will invariably be working with people from different backgrounds and ethnicities. Some care should be taken to avoid offending the people you will be dealing with, either as customers or fellow employees.

 With the wide range of customers that you may encounter, this may not be possible all of the time; many of our colorful expressions that we have grown up with may be a little taboo. Some of the remarks we make can sometimes be thought to be too colorful, and it is easy to cross the line — in some cases without ever planning to. I once ran into a problem describing a problem where only one control process should talk to a system and used the expression "Too many chiefs . . .," which I stopped there, realizing that I was working with a group of Native Americans; I have not used that express since, opting instead for "Too many cooks . . ." and fewer hurt feelings.

Getting an A+

In this chapter, I discuss general skills that will make you an effective troubleshooter, as well as how you present yourself to and treat the clients that you deal with. The following points are covered:

✦ Create a list of possible problems based on the information that is provided to you, and then follow that up with testing to locate the true cause.

✦ When troubleshooting problems, work through systems sequentially from general to specific or from beginning of a system to its end. That way, you won't miss items that may be involved in the solution.

✦ Back up user or system files and any configuration files or settings that may be lost or changed during troubleshooting.

✦ Document issues, solutions, and any other items that are important.

✦ Follow basic principles for respecting other people, which will answer most exam questions related to professionalism and communications.

Prep Test

1 Which of the following is not a step in the basic troubleshooting process?

 A ○ Document findings
 B ○ Respect client property
 C ○ Evaluate results
 D ○ Identify the problem

2 Where should you go/what should you do to get a complete list of problem symptoms?

 A ○ Product documentation
 B ○ Internet search engines
 C ○ Question the user
 D ○ Analyze the problem

3 Which of the following should you find out when questioning the user?

 A ○ Recent changes to the computer
 B ○ The last time the computer was shut down
 C ○ How the computer is connected to the building electrical system
 D ○ The location of resources to document your outcomes

4 When making configuration changes during the troubleshooting process, what practices should be followed? Choose all that apply.

 A ○ Apply one configuration change at a time
 B ○ Discount the obvious
 C ○ Back up any settings or files that you need to change
 D ○ Test related components

5 When looking for information related to the problem, which of the following is not considered to be a good source?

 A ○ Vendor manuals
 B ○ Service documentation
 C ○ Internet Web pages related to the product
 D ○ Competitive knowledge base

6 **Which of the following is not a good communication skill?**

A ○ Let the customer talk; don't interrupt
B ○ Have a positive attitude
C ○ Make concise statements
D ○ Avoid jargon

Answers

1 **B.** Respecting client property is part of good communication skills, not the troubleshooting process. *See "The basic troubleshooting process."*

2 **C.** The best source for finding out what the symptoms are, and a description of what appears to wrong with the computer, is directly from the user. *Review "Identifying the problem."*

3 **A.** The user should be questioned about changes that have been recently made to the computer. In some cases a user may not know or may not want to tell you. *Check out "Identifying the problem."*

4 **A, C.** Before applying any changes to the system, relevant files and settings should be backed up so that the changes can be reversed or critical files can be restored if anything goes wrong. You should apply only one change at a time so that you will know what change actually resolved the problem. Although testing related components is part of the overall troubleshooting process, it does not necessarily apply to making configuration changes. You should not discount the obvious. *Peruse "The basic troubleshooting process."*

5 **D.** When looking for an answer related to a vendor's product, you might find some information on a competitor's knowledge base, but this is not typically going to be a good source of reference for you. *Take a look at "Documentation resources."*

6 **B.** Having a positive attitude is part of professional behavior and not a communication skill. *Peek at "Professionalism and Communication."*

A+ Soft Skills

Chapter 3: Protecting Yourself and Your PC

Exam Objectives

✔ Gathering the tools of the trade

✔ Understanding ESD and EMI

✔ Recognizing high-voltage equipment

✔ Disposing of components

✔ Understanding ergonomics

Before addressing how to install computer components such as memory, processors, or a hard drive, you want to make sure that you understand the risks that are involved every time you take the cover off the computer. On the A+ exams, CompTIA will be sure to test your knowledge on how to safely handle a computer's electronic innards and how to safely and legally dispose of broken or obsolete parts.

In this chapter, I discuss topics such as ESD (electrostatic discharge) and EMI (electromagnetic interference), as well as concepts such as what high-voltage equipment is and why you should stay away from these components. I also show you how to dispose of computer components, and then introduce you to ergonomics.

Gathering Tools of the Trade

When plumbers or electricians come to your house to do some work, they bring a toolbox containing what they need to fix most problems that might arise while on the job. As an A+ Certified Professional, you need to do the same thing: Keep a PC repair toolkit of all the tools — software and hardware — that you need to do your job.

The following sections discuss the hardware and software tools that you need to perform your job well.

Hardware tools

Of the myriad pieces of hardware you need to repair computers, the most popular is the humble screwdriver. You can purchase a PC repair toolkit (shown in Figure 3-1) at your local computer store, but you should be able to get away with a multihead screwdriver for most jobs.

Figure 3-1:
A typical
PC repair
toolkit.

The following is a list of tools that you might need from time to time to fix most of your computer repair problems:

✦ **Screwdrivers:** Most toolkits come with a variety of screwdrivers that have a variety of tip shapes and sizes — flat-head screwdrivers with a flat tip, Phillips screwdrivers with a +-shaped tip, and TORX screwdrivers with a star-shaped tip. I usually use a multihead screwdriver instead of choosing from a mass of different screwdrivers.

Be sure that you don't use a magnetic screwdriver on the computer because you could erase your data!

✦ **Tweezers:** PC repair toolkits typically come with a set of tweezers, which are a lot more useful than they might seem. You use tweezers to work with smaller items in the computer, such as jumpers. (For more information on jumpers, check out Book II, Chapter 1.)

✦ **Chip extractor:** A lot of PC repair toolkits come with a *chip extractor,* which you use to remove a chip from a board. For the most part, you won't need this tool because most of the chips today are on a card or module instead of being attached directly to the board: You can remove the entire module by hand.

✦ **Chip inserter:** PC repair toolkits also come with a *chip inserter,* which you use to push a chip into a socket. This tool is just as useful (or useless) as a chip extractor.

✦ **Canister:** A number of premade PC repair toolkits include an empty canister, which seems really silly at first but becomes very useful. You can use this canister to store additional screws or jumpers. Before throwing away any old computer parts, I usually take the screws and jumpers off and put them in my canister. You never know when you might need them!

✦ **Multimeter:** You can use a multimeter (shown in Figure 3-2) to verify that the wall outlet is supplying the correct voltage and that your power connectors to the hard drive and CD-ROM drives are supplying the correct voltage as well. This is a useful tool to have around if you suspect the power supply isn't doing its job.

Figure 3-2:
A digital multimeter can be a valuable tool when trouble-shooting power problems.

Software tools

Most technicians think of hardware tools when they think of tools of the trade, but software tools are important, too. I give you in-depth information about the software tools you need in your PC repair toolkit in Book VI, Chapter 4, but I want to introduce them here so you get a more complete listing of the tools you will use in the field:

✦ **Windows boot disk:** A Windows boot disk contains the core boot files that are needed to boot a Windows operating system. If those files go missing off the hard drive, you can boot the operating system from the boot disk.

✦ **Windows CD:** The Windows CD can help you fix boot problems with Windows when a file goes missing. You can also use it to recover from some basic disk problems by using the Recovery Console.

✦ **Live CD:** *Live CD* is the general term used for booting and running the operating system from CD. There are Live CD versions of Windows and Linux, and you can use them to help retrieve your data when the operating system will not boot.

These are just a few of the software tools that you can use. You find out more about troubleshooting utilities found in Windows by checking out Book VI, Chapter 4.

Avoiding the Dreaded ESD

In this section, I discuss the dangers of servicing a system without taking precautions as to not damage the computer or yourself. Be sure to take this section very seriously!

ESD means electrostatic discharge (not extrasensory deprivation)

When you walk around on carpet, scuffing your feet, you build up a static charge. You walk over to your best friend, touch his or her hand, and zap! — an explosive shock! You feel that static shock because you have a higher static charge than your friend. When two objects with dissimilar charges touch, the excess electrons are transferred to the object with the lesser charge. This is when you feel the shock.

Here comes the important part: *That little shock is more than enough to kill a computer chip.* So, had you touched a computer component instead of your friend, you would most likely kill the poor little computer chip.

The scary part about all this is that in order for you to feel and hear the shock, you must have a charge of approximately 3,000 volts (V), but only about 200V are needed to kill a computer chip — and just 30V can do long-term damage to a chip.

Transference of static charge to another object — *electrostatic discharge (ESD)* — is responsible for damaging or killing computer components, such as computer chips. It is your job as an A+ Certified Professional to make sure that you eliminate ESD by following ESD best practices.

Preventing ESD

You can reduce ESD, but because ESD occurs naturally, you can never completely get rid of the static buildup you carry with you. To reduce your chances of damaging a system when servicing a computer, follow these best practices:

✦ **Grounding strap:** One of the most popular solutions for preventing damage to computer components is to wear a grounding strap (shown in Figure 3-3), also known as an *ESD wrist strap*. The grounding strap goes around your wrist and contains a *resistor* that absorbs any static electricity. The wrist strap then clamps to the metal *chassis* — the casing — of the computer. This gives you constant grounding while servicing the computer, eliminating any static buildup.

Figure 3-3:
An antistatic wrist strap, also known as a grounding strap.

If you don't have a grounding strap to connect to the chassis of the computer, be sure to constantly eliminate any static electricity that has built up on yourself by touching the chassis before touching any computer part.

✦ **Carpet spray:** You can use a specialized carpet spray on the carpet around your work area to help reduce the static electricity, but it won't eliminate the static entirely. Don't rely on antistatic carpet spray as your *only* source to eliminate static electricity.

✦ **Antistatic bags:** When carrying computer components from one place to another, it's a good idea to carry the components in an antistatic bag to protect the components from static electricity. For example, if you are going to carry some memory to a user's workstation, carry the memory in the antistatic bag.

✦ **Humidifiers:** You can use humidifiers to place moisture in the air. Your goal is to get the humidity level to about 50 percent. Overly dry environments help create static electricity while overly humid environments could create unwanted moisture.

Watching Out for EMI

A number of people confuse ESD with *electromagnetic interference (EMI),* which involves computer equipment receiving electrical interference from an outside source, such as another electrical device or a piece of machinery.

Be sure to know the difference between ESD and EMI.

Although ESD often causes permanent damage (if you fry a computer chip, it is damaged permanently), EMI is, for the most part, temporary. For example, if you notice that your monitor display is distorted because you are getting interference from an outside source, moving the monitor away from the external source should get the monitor back to normal.

That being said, EMI exposure for a long period of time *can* cause permanent damage to computer components.

Recognizing High-Voltage Equipment

High-voltage equipment can cause serious injury if you touch it — it might even kill you. You will not typically service these two major computer components unless you have special training or certification beyond the A+ Certification exam:

✦ The power supply unit

✦ The monitor

The danger in servicing the power supply and a cathode ray tube (CRT) monitor is that both devices use capacitors that hold an electrical charge even after the component is unplugged. The electrical charge is enough to cause severe shock or electrocution. Beware!

High-voltage equipment usually bears a warning label that indicates that you shouldn't open the component — and, that if you do, you could be severely hurt. Bottom line: You're playing with fire (all right, electricity) if you open these components. Have them serviced by a certified electrician or someone with special training.

Power supply unit

The *power supply unit (PSU)* is responsible for taking alternating current (AC) from the wall outlet and converting it to a direct current (DC) that is usable by computer components.

The power supply usually takes 120V of alternating current from the wall outlet and supplies the power to computer components by converting the 120 volts AC into 3.3V, 5V, or 12V of DC.

The power supply contains a charge even after it is unplugged, so servicing a broken power supply is not recommended. If your power supply is broken, just replace it.

For the exam, remember that a power supply is high-voltage equipment that you should keep your hands — and tools — away from.

Monitor

The part of the monitor that you need to be aware of is the cathode ray tube itself. Creating the images on a CRT monitor takes a lot of power — typically 50,000V, which is enough to cause yourself serious damage, if not kill yourself. Remember that this charge is held even when the monitor is unplugged from the wall: As a general rule, do not open the monitor unless you are a qualified professional (and remember that passing the A+ Certification exam doesn't qualify you to work with CRTs).

As a general rule, you should never open up the monitor! Send it to a qualified professional. Because of the risk of the potential seriousness of injury, opening a monitor is not recommended unless you know what you are doing.

For the A+ exams, you need to be familiar with the general steps to discharge a CRT. You would discharge the CRT if you were going to perform some work on the monitor (which I do not recommend unless you are qualified). If you decide to open a monitor, you will notice a heavy wire running along the side of the CRT — this wire supplies the 50,000V. Be sure *not* to touch this wire! If you are going to work on a monitor, first discharge the high voltage. To discharge the CRT of a monitor, you need a *shorting probe*. Follow these steps to discharge a monitor's CRT:

1. **Unplug the monitor and open it up.**

2. **Clip the wire on the shorting probe to the metal chassis of the computer.**

3. **Slip the end of the shorting probe under the rubber grommet (looks like a little rubber flap).**

 Make sure that you don't touch any other metal parts. You should hear loud popping noises as the high-voltage equipment is discharged.

4. **When the popping noise has stopped, you may remove the probe.**

Note that the general steps to discharge a CRT are here for A+ exam preparation purposes only. It is not recommended to open a monitor for any reason unless you are qualified.

Disposing of Components

When you replace an old part from a computer, you have a responsibility to dispose of the old part properly. You are not permitted to dump certain computer components in a landfill because they are hazardous to the environment. For example, the chemicals in a battery could leak into the water supply and contaminate the drinking water. In this section, you find out how to dispose of certain computer components that can be dangerous to the environment.

Federal and local laws regulate the disposal of hazardous materials; if you break these laws, you could be fined. If you're unsure how to dispose of a certain component, contact your state or province environment regulator office to find out how to appropriately dispose of it.

You can also contact the U.S. Environmental Protection Agency (EPA) for proper procedures and guidelines on how to safely dispose of computer components. These guidelines are also published on the EPA Web page at `http://www.epa.gov/epawaste/conserve/materials/ecycling/index.htm` .

Batteries

Because batteries contain metals that are environmentally harmful (such as nickel and cadmium), federal, state, and local laws prevent people from dumping their batteries in trashcans and throwing them to the curb destined for a landfill. The federal government passed the Battery Act in 1996 to ensure that the public properly disposes of rechargeable batteries and batteries that contain mercury. You can find information about the Battery Act by checking out http://cfpub.epa.gov/compliance/resources/policies/civil/ba/.

Each state has different regulations and rules that deal with the disposal of batteries, and you should be sure that you follow these rules when disposing of old batteries. Contact your state's environmental regulatory office for more information on disposal of batteries and other computer components.

CRTs

Because CRTs contain harmful components, they cannot be dumped in landfills. You can donate old monitors that are still in working condition to public schools, churches, and other charities. With any donation, you can get a tax benefit! If the monitor doesn't work or is so badly damaged that it can't be given away, you can contact recycling companies that will take it off your hands and use it for spare parts.

Toner kits and cartridges

A number of vendors offer a small discount if you turn in old toner kits or cartridges when you buy new ones. Even if they don't give a small discount, at least they'll take the old toner off your hands! These vendors typically send the old toner kit or cartridge back to the manufacturer to be recycled.

If the vendor you purchase from doesn't take the used toner kits and cartridges, you should contact the manufacturer and find out how you can dispose of them. If you don't want to contact the manufacturer, you can always check with your state's environmental regulatory office.

Material Safety Data Sheet

A *Material Safety Data Sheet (MSDS)* contains information about hazardous chemicals present in different materials. The MSDS contains the composition of these materials and includes their ingredients so that you will know what makes up a particular material.

The MSDS also contains information on the proper handling of materials and the lethal doses for each material. You can obtain information on MSDS by visiting www.osha.gov and running a search for "MSDS" and your material.

A great Web site to find out more on how to donate or recycle computer parts is www.computerhope.com/disposal.htm.

Exploring Ergonomics

Computers do a lot of great things. They crunch thousands of numbers and process data at phenomenal rates; they perform tedious, repetitive actions without complaining; and they allow a thousand-page book like this one to be written, edited, and proofread without using a single sheet of paper. Unfortunately, working on a computer can cause health problems. *Ergonomics* is the study, or science, of designing equipment that reduces discomfort for the user and reduces or prevents repetitive strain injury (RSI).

RSI is an injury to the muscles and tendons in the neck, shoulders, arms, wrists, and/or fingers caused by the poor posture and frequent repetitive movements that accompany long hours in front of a computer. Some common examples of RSI are carpal tunnel syndrome, tenosynovitis, and tendonitis. Here are some recommendations you can follow to help reduce discomfort and RSI:

✦ **Maintain good posture.** Be sure to keep good posture when working on the computer (see Figure 3-4). Put your feet flat on the floor; your thighs and back should be at a 90-degree angle from each other; your forearms should be on the table, parallel to the floor.

Figure 3-4: Having good posture when working on a computer helps prevent injuries to your neck and back.

✦ **Use a comfortable keyboard and mouse.** Try to keep the keyboard and mouse at a comfortable position so that you can keep a relaxed posture and not have to stretch too far to do your work. If at all possible, use an *ergonomic keyboard,* which has a left and a right half set at comfortable angles to help reduce the strain put on your wrists, arms, and fingers.

✦ **Monitor at eye level.** Keep the monitor at eye level so that you don't have to bend or stretch your neck to look at it. Keep your monitor two feet away from you because of the rays older monitors emit.

✦ **Take frequent breaks.** It is so important to take time out in the day to get up and stretch your legs and arms. Staring at the computer screen too long can also hurt your eyes, so give them frequent breaks as well. It's great for the mind, too!

✦ **Care for your eyes.** If you are working at the computer for long periods of time, be sure to blink your eyes frequently and try to give them a break by focusing on a distant object for a few seconds every 15 to 20 minutes. Computer users have dry eyes because they don't blink as often as someone not using the computer all day. Have some eye drops handy when working on the computer for long periods of time.

✦ **Use a wrist rest.** If you do a lot of typing and mousing on the computer, use a wrist rest for the keyboard and mouse so that you don't put unnecessary strain on your wrist because of bad positioning.

✦ **Invest in a good chair.** If you're going to be sitting for a while, you might as well invest in a good chair. Buy a chair that has an adjustable back and adjustable height and that provides lower-back support.

Getting an A+

This chapter highlights a number of safety issues surrounding the servicing and using of computer systems. The following is a quick review of some of the key points to remember from this chapter:

✦ ESD can kill computer chips, so make sure that you do your best to protect computer components.

✦ Always use a grounding strap when servicing a computer.

✦ EMI is electrical interference from an external source.

✦ Recycle computer parts or donate them to charity whenever possible.

✦ Power supplies and monitors are high-voltage equipment that holds a strong electrical charge even after unplugged, so send them to a qualified technician to be serviced.

✦ Be sure to maintain good posture and use a supporting pad for your wrist if you're doing a lot of typing.

Prep Test

1 Which of the following is considered high-voltage equipment? (Select all that apply.)

A ❏ Printers

B ❏ CRTs

C ❏ Power supply units

D ❏ Hard drives

2 Computer components can be destroyed with as little as

A ❏ 3,000 volts

B ❏ 200 volts

C ❏ 500 volts

D ❏ 900 volts

3 ESD stands for

A ❏ Electrostatic discharge

B ❏ Electrostationary discharge

C ❏ Electrostatic disruption

D ❏ None of the above

4 What does EMI stand for?

A ❏ Electromagnetic interference

B ❏ Electric motor interference

C ❏ Electromechanical interference

D ❏ Emits magnetic interference

5 EPA stands for

A ❏ Environmental Protection Association

B ❏ Environmental Protection Agency

C ❏ Environmental Preservation Agency

D ❏ Environmental Preservation Association

6 **RSI stands for**

 A ❏ Restive strain injury

 B ❏ Repetitive self-injury

 C ❏ Restrictive system injury

 D ❏ Repetitive strain injury

7 **The static shock one commonly feels is typically about how many volts?**

 A ❏ 3,000

 B ❏ 200

 C ❏ 10

 D ❏ 5

8 **You can prevent damage from ESD by**

 A ❏ Keeping the air dry

 B ❏ Using a multimeter

 C ❏ Using a grounding wrist strap

 D ❏ Using a static meter

9 **A grounding wrist strap contains a**

 A ❏ Surge protector

 B ❏ Capacitor

 C ❏ Voltmeter

 D ❏ Resistor

10 **The risk for electrostatic discharge is the greatest at**

 A ❏ Daytime

 B ❏ High humidity

 C ❏ Low humidity

 D ❏ Nighttime

Answers

1 **B, C.** Examples of high-voltage equipment are CRTs and PSUs. *See "Recognizing High-Voltage Equipment."*

2 **B.** Computer chips and components can be killed with about 200V. *Review "ESD means electrostatic discharge (not extrasensory deprivation)."*

3 **A.** Electrostatic discharge, or ESD, occurs when two objects carry a charge of different amounts, and the charge is transferred from one object to another to balance the charge. *Check out "ESD means electrostatic discharge (not extra-sensory deprivation)."*

4 **A.** EMI — *electromagnetic interference* — is electrical interference from an external source. *Peruse "Watching Out for EMI."*

5 **B.** The Environmental Protection Agency (EPA) provides guidelines on how the components should be disposed of. *Take a look at "Disposing of Components."*

6 **D.** When you continuously work with your computer for prolonged periods of time, there is a chance of developing a repetitive strain injury. *Peek at "Exploring Ergonomics."*

7 **A.** The shock we give one another is typically 3,000V. *Look over "ESD means electrostatic discharge (not extrasensory deprivation)."*

8 **C.** You can prevent damage from ESD by using a grounding wrist strap. *Study "Preventing ESD."*

9 **D.** An ESD wrist strap contains a resistor. Refer to *"Preventing ESD."*

10 **C.** The risk for electrostatic discharge is greatest at low humidity. *Examine "Preventing ESD."*

Chapter 4: An Overview of System Components

Exam Objectives

✔ Introducing the basic components that make up personal computers

✔ Identifying the fundamental principles that apply to personal computers

This chapter defines basic terminology and provides a brief overview of many topics that will be covered in this book. By the time you finish reading this chapter, you should have a good understanding of the major components of the personal computer, from the motherboard to the monitor.

In preparation for the rest of the minibooks, I give you an overview of the major elements that make up the modern computer. As an A+ Certified Professional, you must be aware of these components, be able to service and manage these components, and be able to explain computing concepts to other people.

What Is a Computer?

Computers are a major element of our society, and they exist in so many places that we tend to forget that they are there. In simple terms, all computers are made up of four basic functions:

+ Data input
+ Data output
+ Processing
+ Storage

These functions, along with their related devices, are illustrated in Figure 4-1. In this chapter, I briefly introduce each of these functions and devices, which are covered in depth in Book II, Book III, and Book VIII.

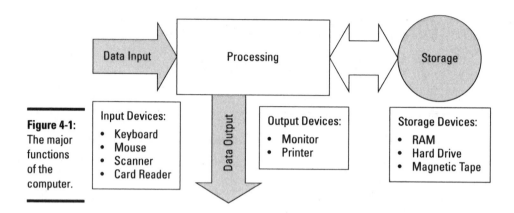

Figure 4-1:
The major
functions
of the
computer.

Although the packaging of these functions takes very different shapes, from personal digital assistants (PDAs) and digital video recorders (DVRs) to routers, laptops, and tower computers, they all share these functions at the most basic layer. The CompTIA A+ Certification exam focuses on the common arrangement of devices performing these four functions — typically called the *personal computer* — and not the more obscure arrangement of devices (such as the automobile engine idle controller). The rest of this chapter guides you through the major components in the personal computer.

Looking Inside the Box

Most of the processing and storage devices show up "inside the box." This section gives you a look at the major elements that you will find inside the system housing, or case.

Processor/CPU

The *processor* (also known as the central processing unit, or CPU) is the "brains of the organization," so to speak. It is designed to do very few things, but to do them extremely quickly. The processor performs a limited set of calculations based on requests from the operating system and controls access to system memory. Processor speed is measured in several different ways, including clock cycles or megahertz (MHz), and millions of instructions per second (MIPS). Any of these measures gives you an estimate of the processor's speed/power.

The speed of early processors ranged from 4 MHz to 8 MHz, but today's processors have broken the multigigahertz (GHz) mark. With the advent of multiple core processors, the processors speed is usually represented as a "per core" value.

You can find processors covered in detail in Book II, Chapter 2.

Storage devices

Storage devices on your computer are responsible for storing data, such as the operating system, applications, and actual output of applications or user data. Depending on the amount and type of data, the five basic types of devices to work with are

+ **Floppy drives,** including some of the high-capacity formats (such as 120MB SuperDisks)

+ **Hard drives,** including some of the removable cartridge drives (such as SyQuest drives)

+ **Optical drives,** including CD-ROM and DVD drives

+ **Magnetic tape drives,** which come in a variety of capacities and are usually used for archiving data

+ **Flash drives,** which store data in a variety of nonvolatile memory chips

Any one of these formats enables your computer to store and retrieve data. Each of these storage options is considered to be long-term or permanent storage, but either descriptor is relative because each media format has a limited lifespan.

When dealing with storage devices, the four major technologies used to connect hard drives to motherboards are

+ IDE (Integrated Drive Electronics) or ATA (Advanced Technology Attachment)

+ SATA (Serial ATA)

+ SCSI (Small Computer System Interface)

+ SAS (Serial Attached SCSI)

An ATA controller allows the 40-pin IDE connector to accept a wide variety of devices while maintaining full backward-compatibility with traditional IDE drives or devices. In most cases, IDE and ATA are used interchangeably, while the current systems are technically using ATA technology. There has been a long, ongoing battle for speed and performance between IDE (or ATA) and SCSI; in general, SCSI provides faster and more reliable transportation, and IDE has been the low-cost alternative. SATA is IDE's younger cousin, and helps in IDE's fight to challenge the benefits of SCSI, which has had its support bolstered by SAS.

Do not forget that ATA and IDE terms are used interchangeably, but you do not want to confuse these terms with Serial ATA, which uses different technology.

Within a computer, a *bus* is a mechanism that is used to move data between devices of the computer, much like how a city bus is used to move people between bus stops in the city. Hard drives are manufactured as ATA, SATA, SCSI, or SAS devices, and they are usually connected to the motherboard through the high-speed PCI (Peripheral Component Interconnect) bus. However, being internal devices, they cannot be easily transported between computers. The USB, IEEE 1394 (or FireWire), and PCMCIA (PC Card) buses provide fast-enough data transfer to allow hard drives to be attached to a system using these technologies, and are designed to be used with external devices. Many manufacturers have products that allow standard ATA or SATA drives to be connected using these buses. Because of the higher cost and the difference in technology, SCSI drives are not normally used.

Although SATA is usually thought of as an internal technology, there has been a rise in popularity of eSATA (External SATA), which provides an external connector to the SATA bus. Some external USB hard drives also support eSATA connectors.

The type of drives that you can attach to your computer depends on the types that are supported by your motherboard and I/O (input/output) cards.

You can investigate what you need to know about hard drives and storage devices for the A+ exam by going to Book II, Chapter 5.

Memory

Memory is a *solid-state* (that is, no moving parts) storage medium. It can take many forms, such as RAM (random access memory), flash RAM, ROM (read-only memory), or EPROM (erasable programmable ROM). Access time for RAM is measured in *nanoseconds* (one-billionth of a second). When memory is discussed, it usually refers to RAM, which is the computer's primary working memory. RAM is a form of storage, albeit typically temporary storage. Many people might not think of RAM as a storage medium because it is volatile and loses its information when power is removed, but temporary storage is still storage.

RAM is always temporary and requires power to retain information. When you put your computer into a hibernation state, the contents of RAM are written to a file and then retrieved when you power up your computer.

An analogy that I often use when talking about RAM is that of a tabletop (RAM) and a filing cabinet (hard drive or magnetic tape). People will not argue the point that a filing cabinet is a storage area for my papers, but they might dispute that a tabletop is a storage area. When I want to work with my papers, I take them out of the filing cabinet, and place them in temporary storage on my tabletop, where I am able to read the papers and make changes to them. When I am done, I will place the papers back in the permanent storage of the filing cabinet. I know some people who would use their tabletop as a form of permanent storage. Just like with RAM, my tabletop has a limited space, so when it becomes full, I will find that my work gets slower as I have to shuffle papers about. When the OS loads, it loads into RAM; when applications load, they load into RAM; when you open documents, they load into RAM; and when you need to send output to your monitor, the output is loaded into RAM before it appears on your monitor.

In addition to working memory, RAM is used in many areas of your computer. In most situations, it is used for caching data or dedicated to specific subsystems. Most video cards will have dedicated RAM on the video card, and processors and hard drives have special high-speed RAM for caching.

To be able to answer all of the memory questions on the A+ exam, read through Book II, Chapter 3.

System boards

The term *system board* describes any number of circuit boards that make up the internals of your computer, but it is used most often to describe the motherboard. The *motherboard* is the main board in your computer that contains the BIOS chips, RAM, I/O ports, and CPU. This board maintains the electrical pathways that enable all other components to communicate with each other.

Some service manuals use the term *daughter board* to describe a secondary board that contains motherboard functions, such as disk or I/O control. A *daughter board* is a board that contains some of the chips that could have been put on the motherboard but were not — perhaps because of space limitations or for other reasons. It is common to see them used in laptops and other mobile devices.

Motherboard information required for the A+ exam can be perused in Book II, Chapter 1.

Power supply

The *power supply* does exactly what its name suggests: It supplies power to the rest of the components in the computer. The power supply takes 120 or 240 volts (depending on the country you are in) of alternating current (AC)

from your electrical outlet and converts it to 3.3V, 5V, and 12V of direct current (DC). It contains a number of leads that supply different voltages for different types of devices (such as floppy drives and hard drives).

Book II, Chapter 6 provides you with all the information you need to answer the power supply questions on the A+ exam.

Adapter cards

Adapter cards allow you to adapt your computer to another role (such as controlling assembly line robots) or to add specific functionality to your computer (such as printing). The most common adapters are now integrated into most motherboards. These components include display, network, keyboard controller, mouse controller, serial ports, parallel ports, FireWire ports, and USB ports.

When the first computers came out on the market, most of the elements (if not all of them) were added to the motherboard by using the adapter slots, such as ISA, PCI, PCI Express, and AGP (well, ISA anyway, because the other slots did not exist).

Cooling system and fans

As electricity moves through any circuit, heat is generated, which is illustrated by looking at a simple circuit that contains an incandescent lightbulb. As electricity moves through the bulb, the filament heats to glowing. Heat is also generated while electricity moves through the integrated circuits that are contained in most of the components of the computer. In addition to these fixed integrated circuits, hard drives contain moving parts that generate heat from friction. These components generate a large amount of heat, which needs to be removed from the critical components to prevent them from failing early in their careers.

To remove heat from computer systems, there has been a steady increase in the use of fans, vents, and other heat-dissipation units. Heat sinks with fans are commonly placed on processors and critical chipsets. *Heat sinks* are made of heat-conductive metals (usually aluminum or copper), with a solid side in contact with the chip that they are protecting and thin fins on the other side, thus putting greater surface area with the air, which helps dissipate or transfer heat to the air. The use of a fan with the heat sink allows more cool air to flow through the fins. Case vents and fans bring cool air into the computer housing, and also vent and pull out hot air.

Faster processors produce more heat. As processors have become faster, more methods for pulling the heat away from the processor have been developed, such as liquid cooled devices.

You will find answers to A+ exam questions related to cooling processors in Book II, Chapter 2; and for overall systems in Book IV, Chapter 1.

Firmware and chipsets

People like to keep their world in a perceived state of order to give themselves a sense of control. This is often seen by how we classify everything we see or work with into categories. Many of these categories seem very distinct until something comes along to challenge our opinions, and then the waters become murky.

One of these murky areas is the distinction between hardware and software, which at one point were thought to be distinct and separate. *Software* is programming code that is stored on your disk or on some other form of media. *Hardware* refers to the physical components — boards, peripherals, and other equipment — that make up your computer.

Firmware fills in a middle ground between software and hardware, where the distinct line begins to disappear. *Firmware* is programming code (software) that is contained in or stored on the IC (integrated circuit) chips (hardware) on your computer. This combination of hardware and software makes up the BIOS on several different devices, with settings stored in CMOS or flash RAM. This firmware is tied to the function of the IC chips that it is working with; in the case of a network card, firmware would manage network or PXE (Pre-eXecution Environment) boot functionality of the card.

Most modern motherboards have a series of IC chips and firmware that work together to control the integrated functions of the motherboard. The compatibility of these chips and the code that ties them together is provided by a single supplier, and this group of chips is referred to as a *chipset*. Intel and VIA Technologies produce popular chipsets.

BIOS

BIOS is short for *basic input-output system*. The BIOS is actually software that is stored on a ROM chip on the motherboard. Most systems today use a flash EPROM to store the BIOS so that the user can update the programming code in the BIOS.

The BIOS is responsible for controlling or managing low-level but extremely important processes like the *POST (Power-on Self-Test)*, the boot process, and the interaction of components on the motherboard.

Book II, Chapter 4 provides you with all the facts that you will need to answer BIOS questions on the A+ exam.

CMOS

CMOS (complementary metal-oxide semiconductor) is the type of manufacturing process that creates most integrated circuits. This development process is used to create the following:

✦ High-density DRAM (dynamic RAM)

✦ High-speed processors

✦ Low-power devices for mobile use

The term *complementary* refers to the fact that these chips use negatively and positively charged transistors (which complement each other) to store information. Most RAM chips rely on CMOS technology to store information, but when discussing CMOS, you will probably be referring to the hardware configuration settings that are saved between reboots of your computer. These settings include

✦ Which hard drives and floppy drives are present

✦ How much memory is installed

✦ Whether a keyboard is required to boot

✦ The type of mouse installed (PS/2 or serial)

✦ What are the reserved resources (such as IRQ [interrupt request], I/O addresses, and DMA [direct memory access] channels)

✦ What is the power-on password and whether it is required to boot up the system

✦ The date and time

✦ Whether ACPI (Advance Configuration Power Interface) is enabled and what devices it applies to

To be ready for your A+ exam, review the CMOS information, such as common settings, in Book II, Chapter 4.

Remember that BIOS stores programming code, and CMOS stores settings for the BIOS options.

Checking Outside the Box

Now that you have looked at what is inside the box, you will want to see what gets added to the system — *outside* the box.

Casing and form factors

Part of the outside of the box is the box itself. There are many different form factors for the box, some of which dictate the form factor of the motherboard going into the case. Cases come most often in tower or desktop form factors, but are also found in forms that make them attractive for entertainment units and in extremely small forms for specific uses.

Input and output devices

Computers use many different kinds of input and output devices (also called I/O devices), which connect to the computer via one of the computer's ports. In the following sections, I give you an overview of the most common input and output devices.

Monitor

The different types of buses that can provide video services include

+ **ISA (Industry Standard Architecture),** which runs at 8 MHz.

+ **PCI (Peripheral Component Interconnect),** which runs at 33 MHz and 66 MHz.

+ **PCIe (Peripheral Component Interconnect Express),** or PCI Express, is a high-speed serial bus, so its speed is measured differently than the others, which are parallel buses. PCIe has between 1 and 16 channels (1x–16x).

+ **PCI-X (Peripheral Component Interconnect Extended),** which runs at 133 MHz.

+ **AGP (Accelerated Graphics Port),** which runs at 66 MHz (but can be increased to 8x the base speed, or 528 MHz).

You have probably already guessed that the faster the bus speed, the faster your video card is likely to function. The AGP bus was designed specifically for video and is being replaced by PCIe. In addition to a fast bus speed, video performance and color depth are provided by RAM or video RAM. This RAM is found on the video card itself. Some high-end video cards also have a small processor to handle some of the work of displaying information on your monitor instead of letting the computer's main processor do all the work.

The processing done by some video cards can require that the card receive additional power from the power supply, rather than relying solely on the power provided by the bus. This is why some power supplies have a special 12VDC connector for your video card.

Video cards traditionally allow for color depths that include

+ 4-bit or 16 colors
+ 8-bit or 256 colors
+ 16-bit or 65,000 colors
+ 24-bit or 16 million colors
+ 32-bit or 4 billion colors

Standard screen resolutions are (in pixels)

+ 640 x 480
+ 800 x 600
+ 1024 x 768
+ 1152 x 864
+ 1280 x 1024
+ 1600 x 1200

Modern video cards follow the SVGA (Super Video Graphics Array) standard, but all support at least VGA. The VGA standard is output in 16 colors at 640 x 480.

Review Book III, Chapter 3 to fully understand monitors and video.

Modem

Modem is short for modulator/demodulator. *Modulation* refers to the conversion of a digital signal to an analog signal, and *demodulation* reverses this process. Your computer is digital, and phone lines that you want to communicate over are analog. In order to allow the digital signal to be passed over the analog lines, you must use a modem.

Modems allow computers to communicate with each other if they are placed where there are phone lines. Prior to modems, there was no low-cost means of connecting distant computers; your only choice was an expensive, dedicated, leased phone line from the telephone company. The speeds at which modems operate have been increasing since their invention. They started with transfer rates of 300 bps (bits per second) and have moved up to 115 Kbps.

Today, where modems were traditionally used, they are often replaced by other remote connectivity options, such as ADSL (Asymmetric Digital Subscriber Line), ISDN (Integrated Services Digital Network), and broadband

cable. Each of these systems has a device — a modem — to connect your Ethernet network card to the data network. ADSL and broadband cable send the signals over analog networks and modulate your data signal to previously unused frequencies. ISDN is digital on both sides of the connection, so there is no modulation taking place. The correct term for this device would be a TA (terminal adapter) and not a modem.

Standard modems connect to your computer through the serial port and can be synchronous or asynchronous. Most modems that are purchased for a computer are asynchronous.

To prepare yourself for modem questions on the exam, read through Book III, Chapter 2.

Ports

Sailing ports provide a location for ships to load and unload goods from one location to another. On your computer, *ports* act as connection points for cables, which allow for the transfer of data between your computer and another device. Several different types of connectors and cables are used to join devices. Although the list of devices that communicate through the different types of ports is limitless, some of the basic types of ports and their uses are listed in Table 4-1.

Table 4-1	Basic Types of Ports
Port	*Use*
Serial	Connects serial devices, such as modems, to your computer.
Parallel	Connects parallel devices, such as printers, to your computer.
Video	Connects a monitor to your computer.
USB	Connects various types of devices to your computer. Devices that used other ports in the past are increasingly being converted to use USB ports. Devices that use this port include printers, modems, mice, keyboards, and scanners.
Keyboard	Connects a keyboard to your computer.
Mouse	Connects a mouse to your computer.

Reading through Book III, Chapter 1 will give you a full appreciation of all of the types of ports, cables, and connectors that are used by computers.

Getting an A+

This chapter provides an overview of the major components found in a computer system, including

✦ *System boards*, which contain most of the computer circuitry

✦ *Power supply*, which converts a building's AC to usable DC for the computer

✦ *Processor/CPU*, which efficiently executes instructions for the OS

✦ *Memory*, which holds working data and application code

✦ *Storage devices*, which are long-term or short-term storage areas

✦ *Monitor*, which displays data from the computer

✦ *Modem*, which communicates with other devices

✦ *Firmware*, which is a cross-breed between hardware and software

✦ *BIOS*, which are low-level internal communication routines

✦ *CMOS*, which is a storage area for configuration settings

✦ *Ports*, which are used as connection points for other devices

Prep Test

1 Which of the following components is not usually found on a motherboard?

 A ○ BIOS chips

 B ○ USB drives

 C ○ Memory

 D ○ I/O ports

2 What type of memory loses its contents when power is turned off on your computer?

 A ○ CMOS memory

 B ○ RAM

 C ○ ROM

 D ○ EPROM

3 A standard North American power supply converts 120V AC to which of the following? (Select all that apply)

 A ❑ 3.5V DC

 B ❑ 3.3V DC

 C ❑ 6V DC

 D ❑ 12V DC

4 What is the primary purpose of the processor?

 A ○ To convert digital signals into analog signals

 B ○ To process signals so that they can be displayed on your monitor

 C ○ To carry out instructions from the operating system

 D ○ To convert 16-bit data into 8- or 32-bit data

5 What unit is used to measure RAM speed?

 A ○ Milliseconds

 B ○ Gigaseconds

 C ○ Picoseconds

 D ○ Nanoseconds

6 Which two of the following represent hard drive architectures?

A ☐ PCI

B ☐ IDE

C ☐ CMOS

D ☐ SCSI

7 What standard do most current monitors follow?

A ○ VGA

B ○ SVGA

C ○ CGA

D ○ FLAT

8 Modems are usually attached to a computer through what type of port?

A ○ Serial

B ○ Sequential

C ○ Parallel

D ○ Modem

9 Firmware is composed of which of the following? (Choose two)

A ☐ Software

B ☐ Middleware

C ☐ Hardware

D ☐ Componentware

10 The programs that allow the POST to take place are stored in what?

A ○ BIOS

B ○ CMOS

C ○ RAM

D ○ POSTOS

11 What does CPU stand for?

A ○ Core predetermination utility

B ○ Complementary provider unit

C ○ Central processing unit

D ○ Co-primary uniprocessor

12 **What does CMOS stand for?**

A ○ Complementary metal-oxide semiconductor
B ○ Co-management of operating system
C ○ Configuration management and option semiconductor
D ○ Configuration memory option system

13 **What does SCSI stand for?**

A ○ Serial Component System Interface
B ○ Small Component Serial Interface
C ○ Serial Computing Storage Interface
D ○ Small Computer System Interface

Answers

1 **B.** The motherboard will include I/O ports or connectors for a variety of devices, but will not typically include the devices themselves. It will include the ATA controller and also a connector to attach the ATA drive, but not the drive itself. The same would be true of USB drives; the motherboard will include the controller and connector for the USB bus but not the actual device. *See "System boards."*

2 **B.** RAM memory is *volatile,* or nonpermanent, because it loses its contents when power is turned off on the computer. *Review "Memory."*

3 **B, D.** Power supplies have leads that supply 3.3V, 5V, or 12V. *Check out "Power supply."*

4 **C.** Processors carry out instructions that they receive from the operating system. *Peruse "Processor/CPU."*

5 **D.** The normal measurement for RAM is nanoseconds, or billionths of a second. *Take a look at "Memory."*

6 **B, D.** Hard drive architectures used with computers are IDE (or ATA), Serial ATA (SATA), SCSI, and Serial Attached SCSI (SAS). *Peek at "Storage devices."*

7 **B.** Super Video Graphics Array (SVGA) is the current graphics standard that monitors follow. *Look over "Monitor."*

8 **A.** Modems are serial devices, and as such are attached to the serial port. *Study "Modem."*

9 **A, C.** Firmware consists of programming code or software that is contained within a hardware component such as a ROM chip. *Refer to "Firmware and chipsets."*

10 **A.** BIOS contains the programs that allow the POST to take place. The BIOS is stored on a ROM or an EPROM. *See "BIOS."*

11 **C.** Central processing unit. *Review "Processor/CPU."*

12 **A.** Complementary metal-oxide semiconductor. *Check out "CMOS."*

13 **D.** Small Computer System Interface. *Peruse "Storage devices."*

Book II

Inside the Box

Contents at a Glance

Chapter 1: Knowing Your Motherboard

Exam Objectives

✔ Distinguishing motherboard components

✔ Recognizing types of motherboards

✔ Identifying bus architectures

*O*ne of the major replaceable components in your computer is the *system board,* also known as the motherboard. The *motherboard* is the big green board (that might not be a technical description, but I think that looking inside your system will demonstrate that it is an accurate one) connected to the computer case. It is the motherboard that holds your RAM, processor, and a number of other components in place.

Think of the motherboard as the glue that connects all the other PC components. For example, you can see how the hard drive is connected to the motherboard by following the IDE ribbon cable from your hard drive to the motherboard. If you do the same with the IDE cable that connects to the floppy drive, you can see that the floppy drive also connects to the motherboard. The memory sockets and the processor socket are likewise located on the motherboard.

In short, all the components that work together (to make the computer functional) connect to the motherboard. If you take a close look at the motherboard, you can see wires embedded on the board that form little pathways that span the system. Think of these wires as the highway system that data signals use to travel from one location to another.

In this chapter, I introduce you to the different types of components found on the motherboard. After identifying the motherboard components, you find out about the different types of motherboards. Finally, you explore what an expansion bus is and discover the different bus architectures.

Finding Out What's on a Motherboard

When you look at the motherboard inside your computer, you notice that a number of different items connect to it. The memory sockets, CPU socket, and BIOS chip are all located on the motherboard. In this section, I identify the different components that are interconnected via the motherboard.

The terms *system board* and *motherboard* are interchangeable.

Processor

One of the easiest items to identify on the motherboard is the *processor,* also known as the *central processing unit* (CPU). The processor is usually the largest chip on the motherboard and is one of the few chips with a heat sink or a fan on top of it, as shown in Figure 1-1.

Processor

Figure 1-1:
A processor
on a
mother-
board.

The motherboard has a socket that the processor is inserted into. Today, this socket is implemented as a *zero insertion force (ZIF)* socket, which means that the processor chip can be removed or added to the socket with very little effort. ZIF sockets (shown in Figure 1-2) typically have a lever that you pull to pop the processor out of the socket.

When the Pentium II processor was developed, Intel used a different type of packaging, known as the *Single Edge Contact (SEC)*. Motherboards had to implement a different type of "socket," known as *slot 1,* to hold this proces-sor. The cartridge would drop into the slot, as shown in Figure 1-3. For more information on processors and sockets, check out Book II, Chapter 2.

Socket 7 ZIF Socket

Figure 1-2:
A ZIF socket
on the
mother-
board.

Figure 1-3:
A Pentium
II, using SEC
packaging.

Remember that classic Pentium chips are inserted into socket 5 or socket 7, whereas Pentium II processors are inserted into slot 1. With newer Pentium processors, such as Pentium III and Pentium 4, Intel has moved away from SEC. The Pentium III is placed in Socket 370, and the Pentium 4 is placed in Socket 423 or Socket 478.

SIMM/DIMM sockets

When you look at a motherboard, one of the first items that should stand out is the processor; the next things you will usually notice are the memory slots used to install RAM into the system.

There are typically two types of sockets for installing memory: *single inline memory module (SIMM)* sockets and *dual inline memory module (DIMM)* sockets. Original Pentium systems typically have either four 72-pin SIMM sockets or two 168-pin DIMM sockets to install memory, and newer motherboards today use DIMM sockets and no SIMM sockets. There are no rules as to how many SIMM or DIMM sockets a motherboard manufacturer may use, as you can see with Figure 1-4. Figure 1-4 shows a motherboard with four 72-pin SIMM sockets *and* two DIMM sockets used to hold memory. SIMMs have been phased out and are only available on older motherboards.

Two 168-pin
DIMM slots

Four 72-pin
SIMM slots

Figure 1-4:
SIMM and
DIMM
memory
slots on a
mother-
board.

When installing SIMMs on Pentium motherboards, you have to install them in pairs. When installing DIMMs, though, you can install them individually. The reason for the difference is that when installing memory, you must fill a memory bank, which is the size of the processor's data path. That is, if you install 72-pin (32-bit) SIMMs onto a Pentium (64-bit) motherboard, you have to install two modules to fill the 64-bit data path of the processor. DIMMs are 64-bit memory modules — the same number of bits as the data path of the CPU — which is why you can install only one at a time. For more information on memory banks and installing memory, check out Book II, Chapter 3.

Cache memory

Cache memory increases performance by storing frequently used program code or data that can be later accessed by the processor. Cache memory is much faster memory than normal RAM and, as a result, is more expensive. The system stores data accessed from RAM in cache memory when the data is accessed the first time, making subsequent requests to the same data faster because the data is accessed from cache (faster than RAM) for subsequent calls.

All processors today have integrated cache memory, which is known as *level 1 cache. Integrated cache* is cache memory that is built into the processor, while *nonintegrated cache* — known as *external cache* — is built outside the processor, typically on the motherboard. The types of cache are as follows:

✦ **L1 (level 1) cache:** Cache integrated within the processor

✦ **L2 (level 2) cache:** Cache located outside the processor, usually on the motherboard

Older motherboards implemented cache memory as rows of DIP (dual inline package) chips placed directly on the motherboard. This area was sometimes even labeled "cache." Unfortunately, you can't expect a motherboard to be well labeled; if you find labels (in English), consider it an added bonus! For more information on chip packages, check out Book II, Chapter 2.

Other systems have implemented the cache as a memory module, so you might see an empty slot on the motherboard that looks like a SIMM slot but will really hold a cache module. A lot of times, this is labeled as "cache" on the motherboard. Figure 1-5 shows L2 cache on an older motherboard.

L2 Cache

Figure 1-5:
L2 cache
located on
a mother-
board.

L2 cache is usually located on the motherboard near the processor. That way, data travels over a shorter distance from cache to processor, thus increasing overall system performance. Also, today's processors implement both L1 and L2 cache in the casing of the processor. For more information on cache memory, refer to Book II, Chapter 3.

Motherboard chipset

Each hardware component in the system has circuitry responsible for managing a specific hardware part. This circuitry is the *controller* for that specific piece of hardware. For example, access to memory is controlled by the *memory controller,* the hard disk is managed by the *hard disk controller,* and the keyboard is managed by the *keyboard controller.*

The combination of computer chips that hold the logic for these controllers is the *motherboard chipset.* Together, the computer chips make up the chipset control communication from the CPU to each of the hardware devices in the system.

Two chips that make up a big part of a motherboard's chipset are the North Bridge and the South Bridge. The *North Bridge* chip is responsible for communication from the CPU to memory, the CPU to the PCI Express bus (more on PCI Express later in this chapter), and the Advanced Graphics Port (AGP) device (more on AGP later in this chapter). The *South Bridge* chip is responsible for communication between the CPU and other devices, such as PCI, ISA, and IDE devices. These two chips contain the bulk of the logic that allows a CPU to communicate with other hardware. Figure 1-6 displays the relationship between the processor and the North Bridge and South Bridge chips.

Figure 1-6:
The
relationship
between
the CPU
and the
mother-
board
chipset.

Locating the North Bridge and South Bridge chips on a motherboard can sometimes be challenging. The North Bridge chip is typically the second largest chip (after the processor) and also typically contains a heat sink or a fan on top of the chip to keep it cool. The North Bridge chip is typically located between the processor and the AGP slot, and the South Bridge is normally located farther from the processor — usually beside the PCI slots, as shown in Figure 1-7. Notice in the figure that the North Bridge chip bears the manufacturer name "AOpen" on it, and the South Bridge is the chip above the PCI slots.

North Bridge South Bridge

Figure 1-7:
The North
Bridge
and South
Bridge
chips on
an AOpen
mother-
board.

BIOS chip

The *basic input-output system (BIOS)* is the low-level program code that allows all the system devices to communicate with one another. This low-level program code is stored in the BIOS chip on the motherboard.

Locating the BIOS chip on the motherboard is easy; it is usually rectangular and generally features a label with the manufacturer's name and the year the chip was manufactured. Some of the popular manufacturers are AMI, AWARD, and Phoenix.

The BIOS chip is a *read-only memory* (ROM) chip, which means that you can read information from the chip, but you can't write to the chip under normal circumstances. Today's implementations of BIOS chips are *EEPROM (electrically erasable programmable ROM),* which means that you can get special software from the manufacturer of the BIOS to write to the chip.

Why would you want to erase the BIOS? Suppose, for example, that your BIOS is programmed to support a hard disk up to 200GB in size, but that you want to install a new, larger hard disk instead. What can you do about it? You can contact the BIOS manufacturer and get an update for your BIOS chip, which is usually a software program. (In the past, you generally had to install a new chip.) Running the software program writes new instructions to the BIOS to make it aware that there are hard disks bigger than 200GB and provides instructions for dealing with them. But before new instructions can be written, the old instructions need to be erased.

The BIOS chip also contains code that controls the boot process for your system. It contains code that will perform a *Power-on Self-Test (POST),* which

means that the computer goes through a number of tests, checking itself out and making sure that it is okay. After it makes it past the POST, the BIOS then locates a bootable partition and calls on the master boot record, which loads an operating system. Figure 1-8 shows a BIOS chip on a motherboard. For more information on the system BIOS, refer to Book II, Chapter 4.

ROM BIOS Chip

Figure 1-8:
A BIOS chip
located on
the mother-
board.

Battery

The computer keeps track of its inventory in what is known as the *complementary metal-oxide semiconductor* (*CMOS*). CMOS holds a listing of system components, such as the size of the hard disk, the amount of RAM, and the resources (IRQs and I/O addresses) used by the serial and parallel ports.

This inventory list is stored in CMOS RAM, which is a bit of a problem because RAM loses its content when the power is shut off. You don't want the computer to forget that it has a hard disk or forget how much RAM it has installed. To prevent this sort of problem, a small watch-like battery on the motherboard maintains enough energy that CMOS RAM doesn't lose its charge. If CMOS RAM loses its charge, CMOS content is lost. Figure 1-9 identifies a battery on the motherboard. For more information on CMOS, check out Book II, Chapter 4.

CMOS battery

Figure 1-9:
The battery
(on the
mother-
board) used
to maintain
a charge to
CMOS RAM.

Expansion slots

Most motherboards have one or more *expansion slots,* which add functional-
ity to the computer. For example, assume that your computer doesn't have
sound capability: You can install a sound card into the expansion slot to
add that capability to your system.

Expansion slots come in different varieties, and it is extremely important
to understand the benefits of each type. I discuss these issues later in the
chapter, in the section titled "Understanding Bus Architectures." For now, I
just want you to be able to identify the expansion slots on the motherboard.

If you look at the motherboard, you can see a number of expansion slots.
There are probably some white, narrow PCI slots on the board, as well as a
tan-colored AGP slot (used for video cards). You might also see some larger
black slots; these are ISA slots used by older devices. Most motherboards
today do not have ISA slots, or might have only one. Figure 1-10 displays
ISA, PCI, and AGP expansion slots used to add expansion cards to the
system. For more information on expansion slots, see the "Understanding
Bus Architectures" section, later in this chapter.

AGP slot ISA slots

PCI slots

Figure 1-10:
Expansion
slots (AGP,
PCI, and
ISA) on a
mother-
board.

Ports and connectors

A number of *ports* on the back of the motherboard connect the keyboard,
mouse, printer, and other devices to the system. This section identifies
those ports. Figure 1-11 displays a number of built-in *input/output* (I/O) ports
on the back of an ATX motherboard.

Figure 1-11:
Built-in
ports on the
back of an
ATX mother-
board.

Serial ports

Most motherboards have serial ports integrated directly into the board.
The *serial ports* are also known as *communications (COM) ports*. They are
called *serial ports* because they send data in a series — a single bit at a time.
If eight bits of data are being delivered to a device connected to the COM
ports, the system sends the eight bits of data, one bit at a time, in single file.
Typically, there are two COM ports — COM1 and COM2 — on each system.

The official standard that governs serial communication is known as *RS-232*, and you might see serial ports referred to as *RS-232 ports*.

You usually connect an external modem or a serial mouse to a serial port. Each device is used for communication. For example, a modem allows your computer to talk to another computer across phone lines, and a serial mouse allows you to communicate with the system. Figure 1-12 shows two serial ports connected to a motherboard.

Figure 1-12:
Integrated ports on the back of an ATX motherboard.

Serial ports on the back of the motherboard are one of two types:

✦ **DB9-male:** A serial port with 9 pins

✦ **DB25-male:** A serial port with 25 pins

Parallel port

Another type of connector on the back of a motherboard is the *parallel port,* also known as the *printer port,* or *LPT1.* The parallel port gets its name by being able to send information eight bits at a time. Whereas serial ports send only one bit at a time in single file, parallel ports can send eight bits in one operation — side by side, rather than single file. Refer to Figure 1-12 to see a parallel port connected to a motherboard.

The parallel port, known as *DB25-female,* has 25 pin holes and is located on the back of the motherboard. Looking back at Figure 1-12, you can see the parallel port located above the two serial ports.

Do not confuse a serial port with a parallel port. A serial port is a *male* port (the port has a number of pins in it), whereas a parallel port is a *female* port (contains pin holes).

You connect the parallel port to a printer by using a parallel cable with a different type of connector at each end. On one end of the cable is a DB25 connector that attaches to the parallel port on the back of the computer. The other end of the cable (the end that connects to the printer) has a 36-pin Centronics connector.

A standard printer cable has a different type of connector on each end. One end has a DB25-male connector with 25 pins, and the other end has a 36-pin Centronics connector.

Video adapter

In the past, a motherboard came with a built-in *video adapter,* sometimes called a *video card* or *video controller.* The video adapter converts digital data from the processor and prepares the information to be displayed onscreen. Figure 1-13 displays a video adapter port, which you can identify by the three rows of five pins. The video port is a 15-pin female port.

Video adapter

Figure 1-13:
A video
adapter
port.

Because many systems today use the ATX motherboard form factor, they have an AGP or PCIe slot to hold the video adapter. This means that the video adapter is not integrated into the motherboard like it was in the past.

Figure 1-14 shows how information flows from the computer system to the monitor. The following steps mirror the numbers in Figure 1-14.

1. The video adapter is responsible for receiving digital data from the processor, which instructs the video adapter on how the images are to be drawn on the screen.

2. The video adapter stores the information about drawing the images in its memory and starts converting the information into analog data that the monitor can understand.

3. The data is sent in analog format from the video adapter to the monitor.

Figure 1-14: How information flows from the processor to the display.

Keyboard/mouse connectors

The mouse and keyboard connectors on motherboards today are most likely PS/2 style connectors or USB connectors. Focus on PS/2 connectors for now. A *PS/2* connector is a small, circular six-pin connector. In Figure 1-15, you can see the keyboard and mouse connectors on the left side of the diagram.

Figure 1-15:
PS/2
connections
for a
keyboard
and a
mouse.

Keyboard connector

Mouse connector

Older motherboards might have a *DIN keyboard connector*, also known as an *AT connector*, which you can see on AT and Baby AT motherboards. These systems did not have any other ports on the back of the system, so you needed to insert an I/O card for other ports (such as serial and parallel ports).

Sound

Most motherboards today have built-in sound capabilities, allowing you to connect speakers and a microphone to the computer. Figure 1-16 shows the integrated sound ports on a motherboard. The three different ports on the integrated sound card are

✦ **Line-in:** The line-in port (typically blue) allows you to connect many audio sources to the system.

✦ **Line-out:** The speaker port (typically green) allows you to connect speakers to the computer.

✦ **Microphone:** The MIC-in port (red) allows you to connect a microphone to the system for recording.

Network interface card and modem

A number of systems today have built-in network support via an integrated *network interface card* (NIC), or network card for short. These systems might have a built-in modem as well. The built-in network card has an RJ-45 port on the back of the system that looks like an oversized telephone jack, as shown in Figure 1-17.

MIC-in

Line-in

Line-out

RJ-45 port

USB ports

Universal Serial Bus (USB) is a high-speed serial technology that transfers data at 12 Mbps (USB 1.0), 480 Mbps (USB 2.0), and up to 5 Gbps for USB 3.0. One of the major benefits of USB is the fact that all USB devices use the same type of connector, so you won't have to guess which ports to connect the mouse, keyboard, or scanner to. If they are all USB devices, they connect to the same type of port on the computer!

Because USB 3.0 is still fairly new, the popular USB standard used today is still USB 2.0, but that will change quickly. USB 2.0 has a transfer rate of 480 Mbps, which is much faster than the original USB 1.0 standard. When using USB 2.0 devices, be sure that you also have USB 2.0 drivers installed to leverage the performance benefits of your USB 2.0 devices.

USB devices also support *daisy chaining.* For example, you can connect Device A to the back of the computer and then connect Device B to Device A, and so on. You can connect as many as 127 devices to a system using USB. Figure 1-18 identifies the USB ports on the back of an ATX motherboard.

Figure 1-18:
USB ports
on the back
of a mother-
board.

USB ports

A USB device that connects to the computer and then has other devices
connected to it is considered a *hub device*. If you do not have a USB device
that can act as a hub device, you can purchase a specific USB hub that
allows you to chain four or more other devices off it. With a USB hub, you
can easily increase the number of USB ports your system has by connecting
USB devices to the hub and then connecting the hub to the back of the com-
puter. Figure 1-19 shows a USB hub.

Figure 1-19:
A USB hub
with four
ports.

FireWire (IEEE 1394)

When USB 1.0 was introduced, it ran at 12 Mbps. This was a fairly good
speed for most types of devices but was a little too slow when it came to
multimedia devices, such as digital video cameras. Typically, these types
of devices use a *FireWire* connection, which has a transfer rate of up to 400
Mbps and supports 63 devices in a chain. This is a huge jump compared
with the USB 1.0 standard.

The official standard that defines FireWire is known as the IEEE 1394. Be
sure to remember that for the exam!

Just like USB has different versions with faster transfer rates, so does FireWire. The second version of FireWire is defined as the IEEE 1394b standard and transfers data at 800 Mbps! This second version of FireWire is also known as FireWire 800. Figure 1-20 shows a digital video camera being plugged into a FireWire port.

Figure 1-20: A digital video camera being connected to a system by the FireWire port.

For the exam, remember that the original version of FireWire runs at 400 Mbps and is known as IEEE 1394. The second version of FireWire, FireWire 800, is also known as IEEE 1394b but runs at 800 Mbps. Also, FireWire supports 63 devices in a daisy chain.

For more information on common ports and connectors — such as keyboard, mouse, serial, parallel, USB, and FireWire — read Book III, Chapter 1.

Power connectors

All the devices connected to the motherboard need to get power from somewhere, so the power supply is connected to the motherboard, which supplies power to the board and its components. The following sections discuss power connectors on older and newer motherboards.

Older motherboard power connectors

Figure 1-21 shows power connectors on an older motherboard. There are power cables coming from the power supply to connect to the motherboard with very unique connectors on the end. These power connectors coming from the power supply that connect to the motherboard may be labeled as P1 and P2; or on some systems, P8 and P9.

Motherboard power connector

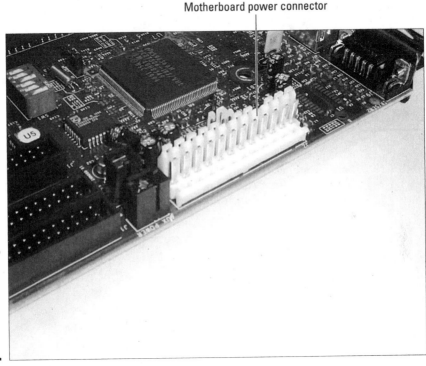

Figure 1-21:
Power
connectors
on an older
mother-
board.

You have to be extremely careful to make sure that the connectors on the cable coming from the power supply to the motherboard are inserted properly, or you could damage the motherboard. Often, these connectors are *keyed* (meaning that they can go in only one way) so that you cannot put both of the connectors in the wrong way. These older power connectors supplied power in 5 volts (V) and 12V.

ATX power connectors

Newer ATX motherboards use a different power connector than the one shown in the preceding section. The ATX power connector supplies 3.3V, 5V, and 12V. The ATX power connector, shown in Figure 1-22, is typically labeled as P1.

ATX power connector

Figure 1-22:
The ATX power connector on an ATX motherboard.

Some systems, like ones that use the Pentium 4 boards, use an additional power connector (the P4 connector), which supplies an additional 12V to the ATX board. Figure 1-23 displays the P4 power connector.

Figure 1-23:
The P4 power connector on an ATX motherboard.

For more information on power supplies and their connectors, check out Book II, Chapter 6.

Drive connectors

You need to be able to identify the different types of connectors that link hard drives to your system. As you might already be aware, the hard drives are used to store information permanently on the computer, but to access that information the drives have a physical connection to the system via the motherboard.

The four major types of drives in systems today are IDE (Integrated Drive Electronics), SATA (Serial Advanced Technology Attachment), SCSI, and floppy drives. Each type of drive has its own type of connection on the motherboard. Before you purchase a hard disk to add to the system, you need to be aware of what types of drives your motherboard supports.

IDE connections

IDE drives have been around since the 1980s, and although the technology has improved from a performance perspective, IDE drives connect to the system the same way they always have. If your motherboard supports IDE, you will have two IDE connectors that are made up of 40 pins each, as shown in Figure 1-24.

Book II
Chapter 1

Knowing Your
Motherboard

Figure 1-24: IDE connectors on the mother-board.

You connect the drive to the connector on the motherboard by using a 40-wire or 80-wire IDE ribbon cable. This ribbon cable typically has two connectors on it — one end connects to the drive and the other end connects to the motherboard. You can also find IDE ribbon cables with three connectors that allow you to connect two drives to each IDE connector on the motherboard. This means that you can have up to four IDE devices on a system. Figure 1-25 shows an IDE ribbon cable connector.

Figure 1-25:
A 40-wire
IDE ribbon
cable.

When connecting the IDE ribbon cable to the drive and motherboard, the colored wire on the ribbon cable connects to pin 1 on the connector. This is the *pin-1 rule*. Pin 1 is normally labeled on the motherboard and drive. If it isn't labeled, see whether the manufacturer has labeled pin 40 — if so, pin 1 is at the other end!

IDE controllers is a popular term used in the computer industry for the IDE connectors. Although in theory, these are not controllers, this term is used in the industry to describe the IDE connections on the motherboard. The *actual* IDE controller — the circuitry located on the circuit board on the drive itself — is responsible for controlling the flow of information to and from the drive.

SATA connections

Limitations of the IDE architecture have kept its data transfer rate around 150 MBps. As drives become more powerful, a new standard is needed. The first new standard to replace IDE — SATA — is the popular drive technology in desktop and laptop computers. SATA can reach transfer rates of up to 600 MBps! This is quite a bit (450MB, to be exact) faster than the 150 MBps offered by high-end IDE drives.

SATA uses its own unique four-wire cable to connect to the motherboard. Figure 1-26 shows a SATA cable connected to the SATA connector on the motherboard. Notice that the cable is quite a bit thinner than the IDE ribbon cable; this allows for better airflow in the system and improves overall temperature control of the computer.

Figure 1-26:
A SATA
cable
connected
to the
mother-
board.

Unlike IDE drives, you cannot connect more than one SATA drive to a con-
nector. For example, if your motherboard has two SATA connectors, you
can connect only two SATA drives to the system unless you purchase a
SATA card that has additional connectors.

SATA is a hot-swappable technology that allows you to remove and add
drives while the system is still running. This adds huge benefits over IDE
solutions.

eSATA connections

eSATA (External SATA) allows for external drives to connect to a system via
a SATA port instead of the typical USB or FireWire port. In the past, external
drives were enclosures that held SATA drives, but the interface to connect
the enclosure to the computer used USB or FireWire. This created overhead
because the SATA interface is translated to USB or FireWire, which is slower
than SATA. With eSATA connections on the motherboard, you can connect
to the external drive using eSATA to leverage SATA speeds with no transla-
tion drawbacks!

The eSATA device, which requires its own power source because it is an
external device, can have an external SATA cable length of two meters. The
eSATA cable is a special cable designed to help prevent electromagnetic
interference (EMI). The eSATA cable has also been designed to handle more
than 5,000 insertions and removals of the drive; the current internal SATA
cable is suited for only 50 insertions and removals.

If your motherboard does not have an eSATA port, you can purchase an
expansion card to add to the computer, providing the eSATA ports.

SCSI controller

Some high-end machines, particularly those designed for use as servers, might have a controller on the motherboard with 50 pins on it. This is the footprint of a *SCSI (Small Computer System Interface) controller*. Because SCSI devices outperform IDE devices, SCSI controllers are extremely popular for servers (which have greater hard disk access and storage needs than regular desktop computers). To connect a SCSI drive to the 50-pin SCSI connector on the system, you use a 50-wire ribbon cable.

IDE uses a 40-pin connector that a 40/80-wire ribbon cable connects to, and an internal SCSI connector has 50 pins that connect to a 50-wire ribbon cable.

Lab 1-1 and Lab 1-2 will help you identify the major motherboard components on the motherboard. Lab 1-1 and Lab 1-2 can be found in the Labs.pdf file in the Author directory of the book's companion CD-ROM.

Floppy disk connectors

Located very close to the IDE connectors on the motherboard, you should see a smaller floppy drive connector that contains 34 pins instead of the 40 pins found with the hard drive IDE connectors. The floppy drive connector on the motherboard is used to connect the floppy drive to the motherboard using a 34-wire ribbon cable.

When connecting the floppy drive to the system, notice that the wires on one end of the ribbon cable are twisted. This twisted end must be connected to the floppy drive. The opposite, untwisted end connects to the motherboard. Also note that one wire of ribbon cable is colored, usually red, which indicates wire 1. Like the IDE drives, you need to connect wire 1 to pin 1 on the motherboard and on the floppy drive.

To find out more information about IDE, SATA, SCSI, and floppy drives, check out Book II, Chapter 5.

Jumpers and DIP switches

A *jumper* is a set of pins that have a plastic cap enclosed over them to create an electrical connection. The plastic cap contains a piece of metal that makes contact with the pins and creates the electrical circuit. The circuit that is created enables a feature on the motherboard. Most motherboards (and older expansion cards) use jumpers to implement different settings. Figure 1-27 displays a jumper on an expansion card.

Jumper

Figure 1-27:
Identifying
a jumper.

Notice in the figure that the jumper has three sets of pins that the cap may be placed over. The idea behind the three sets of pins is that each set of pins would enable a different setting. For example, looking at Figure 1-27, the three different sets of pins might be used to assign three different interrupt requests (IRQs) to the card. You choose which IRQ is assigned to the card by setting the jumper over a set of pins. Keep in mind that you no longer assign IRQs with jumpers; that was something was done years ago. (For more information on IRQs, check out Book III, Chapter 4.)

Today, you find jumpers on motherboards, hard drives, CD-ROM drives, and DVD drives. Many different features can be enabled or disabled on a motherboard by using jumpers. For example, there usually is a jumper on the motherboard used to clear the CMOS password of a system, to change the voltage supplied to the processor socket, or to change the speed of the motherboard. To know what jumper to set, check the documentation for the motherboard.

Another popular component of a motherboard or expansion cards in the past that was used to enable or disable different features is the dual inline package (DIP) switch. A *DIP switch* (as shown in Figure 1-28) is a set of switches that can be turned on or turned off to enable functionality on the board. To know what to set for on/off combinations, consult the documentation for the board.

Figure 1-28:
A DIP
switch.

Identifying the Types of Motherboards

Now that you understand some of the major components of the mother-board (system board), it is important to mention the different motherboard form factors. A *motherboard form factor* just describes the dimensions of the motherboard and the layout of the motherboard components.

You need to understand the different motherboard form factors because you can't just take *any* motherboard and place it in a computer case. For example, you must put a full AT motherboard in a full AT case, a Baby AT board in a Baby AT case, and an ATX board in an ATX case. Figure 1-29 shows the three major types of motherboards to give you an idea of size and shape differences between the three types.

Full AT Baby AT

Figure 1-29:
Looking at
different
mother-
board form
factors.

ATX

Full AT

The full AT motherboard — 12" wide and 11" long — is easily recognized by the fact that it has only a keyboard connector on the back of the motherboard and that it contains no other I/O ports.

The full AT suffers from a problem with accessing some items on the motherboard because the drive bays hang over the motherboard. This configuration makes installing and troubleshooting motherboard components very difficult.

Another problem with the layout of the full AT board is that the expansion cards, after having been inserted into the systems, cover the processor. This situation leads to cooling problems because ventilation is insufficient to keep the chip from overheating. Figure 1-30 displays a full AT motherboard being installed in a full AT case.

**Book II
Chapter 1**

**Knowing Your
Motherboard**

Figure 1-30:
A full AT
mother-
board in a
full AT case.

Baby AT

The *Baby AT* motherboard form factor had been one of the most popular motherboard types until recent years. The Baby AT board is 8.5" x 10". You can easily identify this motherboard because it usually has a *DIN* (multipin, round) keyboard connector on the top-right corner of the board. This keyboard connector is the only I/O connector on the back of the motherboard.

92 Identifying the Types of Motherboards

A Baby AT board is about two-thirds the size of a full AT board and typically incorporates a Socket 7 ZIF slot for classic Pentium processors. The Baby AT board usually has a mixture of ISA/EISA and PCI slots located on the motherboard and includes a Plug and Play BIOS. Figure 1-31 shows a Baby AT motherboard and identifies the popular components.

Figure 1-31: Baby AT mother-board components.

Take a minute to consider some of the key components on the Baby AT motherboard. You can see the Socket 7 ZIF slot at the bottom of the motherboard where the processor is to be installed. Also notice the SIMM and DIMM sockets (on the right side of the motherboard); these house the

system memory. To the left of the SIMM and DIMM slots are the primary and secondary EIDE connectors (sometimes called *controllers*) for connecting the hard drives to the board. To the left of the EIDE controllers are the types of expansion slots that are used: here, four PCI slots and three EISA slots. Above the PCI slots is a silver circle, which is the CMOS battery.

LPX/NLX

In an effort to allow computers to take up much less space, a slimline desktop system was designed with a smaller motherboard. After the era of the Baby AT came the LPX (low profile extended), which was then replaced by NLX (new low profile extended) motherboard. Both motherboard types served the same purpose — to create low-profile computers.

The NLX motherboard is identifiable by the I/O ports along the back of the motherboard. This motherboard is unlike the full and Baby AT because they incorporated only the keyboard connector. Comparatively, the NLX provides a keyboard and mouse connector, serial and parallel ports, and a video connector.

The NLX form factor — 9" x 13.6" — uses a riser card to house the bus architectures. The riser card typically connects to the side of the motherboard and is then secured along the side of the case. Figure 1-32 shows an NLX motherboard with a riser card. (I cover bus architectures in the section, "Understanding Bus Architectures," later in this chapter.)

Book II
Chapter 1

Knowing Your Motherboard

Figure 1-32: An NLX form factor motherboard.

ATX

In 1995, Intel wanted a motherboard that would support the Pentium II processor and the new AGP slot, so the ATX form factor was built (shown in Figure 1-33). The ATX board — 7.5" x 12" — has most of the I/O ports integrated directly into the board, including USB ports.

Pentium II AGP video adapter card

Figure 1-33:
The position
of the I/O
ports on an
ATX mother-
board.

I/O ports

The ATX motherboard incorporates the I/O ports and includes an AGP slot for high-performance video cards. Figure 1-33 displays the ports on the back of the ATX motherboard. Note how they are clustered in the left corner of the board and do not spread across the length of the board like they do with the NLX form factor.

The ATX board introduced a 100 MHz system bus and has been increased to speeds of 533 MHz and higher. The ATX motherboard has one AGP slot for the video card, which means that the built-in I/O ports on the back of the board do not have a built-in video card like the NLX. The ATX board also has *soft power support,* which allows software developers to create software that controls the startup and shutdown of the system.

The ATX form factor rotated the Baby AT components by 90 degrees so that any cards inserted into the bus architectures would not cover the processor and prevent proper cooling. Figure 1-34 shows an ATX motherboard.

Figure 1-34 also highlights some of the common components on the ATX board. Notice, for instance, slot 1, where a Pentium II chip can be inserted. Newer versions of the ATX motherboard use a ZIF socket to house the processor. Notice also, in the top-right corner, the BIOS chip with a white label on top of it. At the top of the figure, you can identify the EISA and PCI slots, and located in the center of the board is an AGP slot. The hard drive controllers are located on the left side beside the three slots that hold the DIMM memory.

Figure 1-34:
The ATX mother-board is very popular in today's systems.

EISA slots

Chip set

ROM BIOS

PCI slots

AGP slot

Secondary
EIDE connector

Primary
EIDE connector

Floppy drive
connector

AGP chip

Serial 2 port

Parallel port

Serial 1 port

(2) USB ports

PS/2 keyboard
& mouse

DIMM
sockets

ATX power
connector

CPU slot I
(Pentium II)

Parallel

microATX and FlexATX

Smaller versions of the ATX motherboard are the microATX and FlexATX. The microATX motherboard form factor is 9.6" x 9.6" and can fit in either a micro-ATX case or a normal ATX case, known as a full ATX case. Measuring 9" x 7.5", the FlexATX is smaller than the microATX but can fit in an ATX or a microATX case. FlexATX is not as popular because the size of the motherboard limits how much you can expand the system. Figure 1-35 shows a microATX board.

The important point to make here is that when you purchase a motherboard, you must ensure that it fits your case. For example, if you have an ATX case, you know that an ATX or microATX motherboard can fit in that case.

Another motherboard form factor that was designed to replace the ATX form factor and create smaller, low-profile systems is the Balanced Technology eXtended (BTX) motherboard form factor.

Figure 1-35:
Compare
ATX mother-
board size
(left) with a
microATX
mother-
board
(right).

ATX motherboard microATX motherboard

Lab 1-3 will help you summarize distinguishing features of popular mother-
board form factors. Lab 1-3 can be found in the Labs.pdf file in the Author
directory of the CD-ROM.

Understanding Bus Architectures

The motherboard has a number of expansion slots that can expand the com-
puter's capabilities. When the system is first purchased, a computer has
only so many capabilities. The nice thing is that you can expand on those
capabilities by purchasing cards to add to the expansion slots, or bus slots.

Expansion slots, um, expand what the computer can do. The problem is
that there are different types of expansion slots in the system, so when you
purchase a sound card or network card, you have to make sure you get the
right type. In the following sections, I show you the different types of expan-
sion slots and also compare their characteristics.

Another term for the expansion slots is *bus slots.* A number of different bus architectures have been developed over time. You need to be able to identify the differences between each of these architectures and also to know which ones are more popular today.

ISA

The *Industry Standard Architecture (ISA)* was the first major expansion bus architecture. It was originally developed as an 8-bit architecture and then evolved into a 16-bit architecture. The ISA bus architecture has a speed of 8 MHz, which is extremely slow by today's standards. Figure 1-36 shows two 16-bit ISA slots; note that the ISA slots are the black slots in the system.

Figure 1-36: Identifying ISA slots on the system.

ISA slots

One of the reasons why you still see 16-bit ISA slots in some earlier Pentium or Pentium II systems is because companies typically had a number of ISA network cards in the office from previous systems. When a company upgraded to the Pentium or Pentium II, it was nice not to have to purchase new network cards because earlier Pentiums had ISA slots. Most systems today, though, no longer have ISA slots. Figure 1-37 shows a 16-bit ISA network card.

Figure 1-37:
A 16-bit ISA network card.

MCA

One of the major downfalls of the ISA bus architecture is its performance. It runs at only 8 MHz, and it is only a 16-bit architecture. That was fine years ago, but everything evolves, and new and improved standards arise.

The *Micro Channel Architecture (MCA),* developed by IBM, is a 32-bit architecture. The MCA architecture runs at 10 MHz and is not compatible with ISA. You usually find MCA slots in high-end IBM machines, such as those that might be used as a server.

ISA is an 8-bit or 16-bit technology that runs at 8 MHz. MCA transfers information in 32-bit chunks and runs at 10 MHz.

With MCA, IBM came up with a feature called *bus mastering.* Bus mastering works like this: Devices in the bus don't have to send information through the CPU if they want to talk to one another — they just send the information directly. This takes some of the workload off the processor and allows it to perform other tasks. Bus mastering became an important feature in future bus architectures. Figure 1-38 shows an MCA card.

Figure 1-38:
An MCA network card.

EISA

In 1988, the industry standard for expansion cards was still ISA, but bus architectures had already been created that performed better. So a number of companies got together with the goal of extending ISA while maintaining backward compatibility so that companies could use their existing ISA cards.

As a result, the *Extended Industry Standard Architecture (EISA)* was developed as a 16- and 32-bit architecture. The big advantage to EISA is that it maintains support for the ISA cards that some companies already have in large quantities, and it also supports 32-bit EISA cards. EISA also included the major advancement in expansion bus technology that MCA created — *bus mastering.* Because both ISA and EISA cards fit into the same slot, they keep the same speed of 8 MHz.

The bus architecture holds both 16- and 32-bit cards because the EISA slots have two levels. The EISA cards have very deep edge connectors that fill the two levels (32-bit) of the slot, but ISA cards fill only the top level (16-bit). Figure 1-39 shows an EISA slot and the two different levels in the slot: one level for the ISA card to fill and the other level for the EISA card to fill.

Figure 1-39:
How a EISA slot is organized.

VESA

In 1992, the Video Electronics Standard Association (VESA) developed a bus architecture that outperformed ISA. *VESA* is a 32-bit architecture that supports bus mastering and runs at the same speed as the processor, which, when VESA was created, was around 25 to 33 MHz. Because the bus runs at the speed of the processor, developers called this *VESA local bus,* or *VLB.* • VESA slots are typically used for video cards.

Remember that EISA is an extension on ISA and is a 16-bit or 32-bit technology. For backward compatibility, EISA runs at 8 MHz. VESA is a 32-bit architecture that runs at the processor's speed. It is generally used for video adapters.

VESA slots are extremely easy to identify because they are tan and because they act as an extension to the ISA slot. You will notice the black ISA slots; right beside them might be a tan slot. The VESA card fills the entire ISA slot and the additional extension to make the full 32-bit path for VESA. This allows an ISA card to be inserted into the slot for backward compatibility. Or, with the extension slot, the VESA slot can hold a VESA card. Figure 1-40 shows a VESA slot.

ISA slots VESA slot

Figure 1-40: A VESA slot, which is an extension of an ISA slot.

PCI

Peripheral Component Interconnect (PCI) has two flavors: 32-bit cards and 64-bit cards. When Pentium systems hit the market, their motherboards featured both ISA/EISA slots and PCI slots. When buying a new card today, you would most likely buy a PCI device for one of the PCI slots in your system.

The 32-bit version of PCI has a speed of 33 MHz, and the 64-bit version of PCI runs at 66 MHz. PCI also supports bus mastering. One of the other major benefits of PCI is that it is a Plug and Play architecture. If you are running a

Plug and Play operating system, such as Windows, and your computer has a Plug and Play BIOS, the system resources (such as IRQs and I/O addresses) are dynamically assigned for PCI components.

PCI slots are easily identified on the motherboard as the small white slots, usually located alongside the AGP slot. Figure 1-41 identifies PCI slots on a motherboard.

Figure 1-41:
Installing a card into a PCI slot on a motherboard.

PCI slots

PCMCIA

Personal Computer Memory Card Industry Association (PCMCIA) is a unique type of expansion bus architecture because of its small size. PCMCIA is popular in laptop computers. After all, how can you get a big network card like the one in a desktop computer into a little laptop to add network support? The answer is that you can't; you have to purchase a PCMCIA network card for the laptop to add network support. *PCMCIA cards,* also known as *PC Cards,* are a little bit larger than a credit card and can fit into your back pocket (although I don't suggest that you put one there). Figure 1-42 shows a PCMCIA network card.

Figure 1-42:
A PCMCIA
network
card.

PCMCIA network Card Canadian quarter

PCMCIA (say that five times fast!) is a 16-bit architecture that runs at 33 MHz, supports Plug and Play, and is also a *hot-swappable* technology. That is, you can insert and remove PCMCIA cards without first shutting down the system. PCMCIA has three different types of slots: type 1, type 2, and type 3.

Table 1-1 shows the different PCMCIA slot types and the types of devices you can find in the different types of slots.

Table 1-1	PCMCIA Slot Types	
Slot Name	*Thickness*	*Types of Devices*
Type 1	3.3mm	Memory cards
Type 2	5.0mm	Modems/network cards
Type 3	10.5mm	Removable drives

Type 1 cards were originally used to add memory to laptop computers or personal computers. This is where the "personal computer memory card" part of the PCMCIA name comes from.

PCI is a 32- or 64-bit technology, runs at 33 MHz, and supports Plug and Play. PCMCIA is the expansion bus architecture used by laptop computers and is a 16-bit architecture that runs at 33 MHz.

AGP

Advanced Graphics Port (AGP) has been around since the Pentium II processor appeared in 1997. It's a 32-bit bus architecture that runs at 66 MHz, which is twice the speed of the PCI bus. Many older motherboards have one AGP slot to hold an AGP video card. The performance gain from the AGP port comes not only from the increase in speed, but also because the AGP bus has a direct path to the processor so that information travels quickly from the processor to the AGP card. Figure 1-43 shows an AGP slot beside some PCI slots.

Figure 1-43:
An AGP
card in an
AGP slot.

AGP slot

AGP can run in different modes, and the different modes dictate the speed of the bus. 1x mode runs at 66 MHz (266 MBps), 2x runs at 133 MHz (533 MBps), 4x runs at 266 MHz (1.07 GBps), and 8x runs at 533 MHz (2.2 GBps)!

PCI-X

One of the newer bus architectures to arise on the market over the last few years is the Peripheral Component Interconnect Extended (PCI-X) bus architecture. Because PCI-X uses the same connector style as PCI, it is totally compatible with PCI in the sense that it can hold PCI cards. So, a motherboard with PCI-X slots can also house older PCI cards — and that is a great feature!

Like PCI, PCI-X is a 32-bit and 64-bit bus architecture and is available in four different speeds: 66 MHz, 133 MHz, 266 MHz, and 533 MHz.

PCI Express

PCI-X is compatible with PCI by being able to hold PCI cards and also sending data in parallel (multiple bits at one time), but the PCI Express (PCIe) bus architecture takes a totally different approach. PCIe is a serial bus that does not support existing PCI cards. The PCIe slot, shown in Figure 1-44, is the smaller black slot and is much smaller than a normal PCI slot, so it can't possibly house a PCI card.

PCI Express slot

Figure 1-44: A PCI Express slot on a mother-board.

PCIe uses data lanes to transfer the information within the bus architecture. A data lane delivers an amazing transfer rate of 250 MBps per lane. PCIe has different implementations, each of which has a different number of lanes identified by a multiplier. For example, PCIe with only one lane is known as x1, and a PCIe bus with eight lanes is known as x8. PCIe can thus reach fast transfer rates by implementing additional lanes. For example, current graphics cards for PCI Express have 16 lanes that provide a transfer rate of 4 GBps (16 x 250 MBps) — which is twice the rate of AGP 8x, which runs at 2 GBps.

Most motherboards today have a combination of PCI and PCI Express slots. You can find systems with PCI Express at x1, x2, x4, x8, x16, and x32. The PCI Express slot gets bigger with each multiplier. For example, Figure 1-44 shows a PCI Express x1 slot: the black slot, about 1" long.

AMR and CNR

Audio/Modem Riser (AMR) is a newer bus architecture that adds a modem and audio card to the system. AMR allows the two components to be incorporated into a single card to reduce cost. Figure 1-45 shows an AMR slot on a motherboard.

Communication and Network Riser (CNR) is another bus architecture that has come out in recent years, used to implement LAN, audio, and modem functionality all in one.

Figure 1-45:
An AMR
slot on a
mother-
board.

AMR slot

As far as the "real world" and the exam are concerned, you need to be extremely strong in the area of bus architectures. A big part of servicing computers is installing network cards, sound cards, and video cards. These components come as PCI, PCI Express, or AGP cards today. You need to know how to look at a system and say, "We are going to buy a PCI network card for this system."

Lab 1-4 will help you identify the different performance characteristics of each of the standard bus architectures. Lab 1-4 can be found in the Labs. pdf file in the Author directory of the CD-ROM.

Performance Considerations

When you want to improve a motherboard's performance, one of the first things you should do is check the motherboard speed. For example, some systems today have 600–1500 MHz motherboards. To find out the speed of the motherboard, check the board documentation. You can get a performance increase from a faster motherboard.

Another performance consideration occurs when you add expansion cards to the system. You should first evaluate what expansion slots are free and then purchase a card that will give you the best performance. For example, when you need to buy a network card, start by looking at what expansion slots are free. If only two slots are free — say, an ISA slot and a PCI slot —

your choices are then obviously limited to an ISA network card or a PCI network card. Because PCI outperforms ISA, however, you would be better off purchasing a PCI network card.

You can also get a performance increase from motherboards that have more cache memory. Look at the motherboard to see whether there is a place to install some Level 2 (L2) cache. L2 cache can dramatically increase performance because it is generally closer to the processor than the system memory (RAM) and is a faster type of memory than the system memory. Bottom line: The more cache memory you install, the better the motherboard's performance.

Getting an A+

This chapter introduces you to a number of key components of the motherboard and different motherboard form factors. The following is a list of the key points to remember when dealing with motherboards:

✦ The *motherboard* (or *system board*) is the computer component that interconnects all other components.

✦ Serial (COM) ports come in two flavors: DB9-male and DB25-male. Parallel ports come in only a DB25-female port.

✦ The two main types of cache memory are L1 and L2 cache. L1 cache memory is integrated into the processor, and L2 cache is contained outside the processor but in the processor casing or on the motherboard.

✦ IDE supports two devices in the IDE chain, whereas EIDE has two channels with two devices in each channel (a total of four devices).

✦ A number of major motherboard form factors are available: Full AT, Baby AT, NLX, and ATX, to name a few. Motherboard form factors differ in the size of the board and the layout of the components stored on the board.

✦ You may add components, such as a sound card or network card, to the computer by inserting an expansion card into one of the expansion slots in the system.

✦ ISA was the popular bus architecture for years, but because of its limitations (16-bit architecture and a speed of 8 MHz), it has been replaced by the PCI bus architecture. PCI is a 32-bit/64-bit architecture with a speed of 33 MHz.

✦ AGP and PCI Express are the common bus architectures used to insert a video card in today's systems.

✦ You may increase the performance of the system by using a faster motherboard or by purchasing better-performing expansion cards.

Prep Test

1 What was the original motherboard speed of the ATX board?

- **A** ○ 33 MHz
- **B** ○ 60 MHz
- **C** ○ 66 MHz
- **D** ○ 100 MHz

2 Which bus architecture supports 32-bit/64-bit cards and transfers information at 33 MHz?

- **A** ○ ISA
- **B** ○ EISA
- **C** ○ AGP
- **D** ○ PCI

3 Which motherboard component is responsible for charging the CMOS RAM so that CMOS can maintain its data?

- **A** ○ Battery
- **B** ○ BIOS chip
- **C** ○ CMOS chip
- **D** ○ Power supply

4 How many pins does a standard IDE controller have?

- **A** ○ 33 pins
- **B** ○ 40 pins
- **C** ○ 50 pins
- **D** ○ 20 pins

5 Which of the following best describes a Baby AT motherboard?

- **A** ○ Uses slot 1
- **B** ○ Runs at 100 MHz
- **C** ○ The only I/O port is a keyboard port on the back.
- **D** ○ Incorporates AGP

6 How many devices are supported in a USB chain?

A ○ 10
B ○ 27
C ○ 127
D ○ 255

7 How many pins does a standard floppy drive controller have?

A ○ 34 pins
B ○ 40 pins
C ○ 50 pins
D ○ 75 pins

8 Which bus architecture might be found in older IBM servers?

A ○ ISA
B ○ MCA
C ○ VESA
D ○ EISA

9 What type of cache memory will you find on a motherboard?

A ○ L1
B ○ L2
C ○ SDRAM
D ○ SRAM

10 Which type of memory module supports 32-bit data chunks?

A ○ DIMM
B ○ Cache
C ○ SIMM
D ○ Video

11 Which bus architecture runs at 8 MHz and supports 16-bit ISA cards?

A ○ MCA
B ○ AGP
C ○ PCI
D ○ EISA

12 What is the bus architecture used in laptop computers?

 A ○ PCI

 B ○ PCMCIA

 C ○ EISA

 D ○ ISA

13 Which of the following best describes AGP?

 A ○ AGP slots have a direct path to the processor to help increase performance of AGP devices.

 B ○ AGP cards run at 33 MHz.

 C ○ AGP runs at 66 MHz and gets access to the processor through the PCI bus.

 D ○ AGP stands for Advanced Graphics Port and is used to install additional video memory.

14 Which PCMCIA card type is used for modems?

 A ○ Type I

 B ○ Type II

 C ○ Type III

 D ○ Type IV

15 Which port is typically used for a modem?

 A ○ USB

 B ○ LPT1

 C ○ COM1

 D ○ LPT2

16 When connecting a floppy drive to the system, which end of the ribbon cable connects to the floppy drive?

 A ○ The end with a red stripe

 B ○ The end with a twist

 C ○ The end with a blue stripe

 D ○ The end without a twist

17 What are the labels given to the power connectors that supply power to the motherboard?

 A ○ P1 and P2

 B ○ P22 and P2

 C ○ PT1 and PT2

 D ○ PS1 and PS2

18 How many pins are in the end of a parallel cable connector that connects to the computer?

A ○ 36
B ○ 40
C ○ 25
D ○ 33

19 Which port sends information 8 bits at a time, side by side?

A ○ COM1
B ○ LPT1
C ○ COM2
D ○ USB

Answers

1 **D.** The ATX board had an original motherboard speed of 100 MHz. Older boards, such as the Baby AT, had motherboard speeds of 60 and 66 MHz. *See "ATX."*

2 **D.** The PCI bus architecture is a 32-bit and 64-bit architecture that runs at 33 MHz. AGP runs at 66 MHz, and both ISA and EISA run at 8 MHz. *Review "PCI."*

3 **A.** The battery is responsible for maintaining a charge so that the CMOS RAM doesn't lose its information. The BIOS chip stores the core system code that allows all the devices to communicate. *Check out "Battery."*

4 **B.** An IDE controller has 40 pins to allow a 40-wire ribbon cable to connect a hard disk or CD-ROM to the motherboard. A floppy controller uses 33 pins, and 50 pins are used by internal SCSI devices. *Peruse "IDE connections."*

5 **C.** The Baby AT motherboard uses a DIN connector as the keyboard connector and is the only I/O port found on the Baby AT and the full AT motherboards. Both slot 1, which is the processor slot for Pentium II processors, and the AGP slot that is used by video cards, exist on the ATX board. *Take a look at "Baby AT."*

6 **C.** A computer can support up to 127 USB devices in a USB chain. *Peek at "USB ports."*

7 **A.** A floppy drive connector has 34 pins, and an IDE connector has 40 pins, and internal SCSI devices have 50 pins. *Look over "Floppy disk connectors."*

8 **B.** In the past, you were likely to see MCA in older IBM servers because IBM developed the MCA bus architecture. *Study "MCA."*

9 **B.** Level 2 (L2) cache is the type of cache memory that is found on motherboards, whereas Level 1 (L1) cache is found in the processor. Choices C and D are not types of cache memory. *Refer to "Cache memory."*

10 **C.** 72-pin SIMM modules are 32-bit modules, but a DIMM is a 64-bit memory module. *Examine "SIMM/DIMM sockets."*

11 **D.** The EISA bus architecture runs at 8 MHz and supports ISA cards. MCA does not support ISA, AGP runs at 66 MHz, and PCI runs at 33 MHz. *See "EISA."*

12 **B.** The bus architecture used in laptop computers is called PCMCIA (Personal Computer Memory Card Industry Association). The other three choices are bus architectures available to desktop computers. *Review "PCMCIA."*

13 **A.** The AGP slot runs at 66 MHz and has a direct path between the slot and the processor so that information will not have to travel through one of the slower buses. AGP stands for Advanced Graphics Port and is used to install a video card, not video memory. *Check out "AGP."*

14 **B.** Type II cards are used for network cards and modems. Type I cards are used for memory upgrades, and Type III cards are used for removable drives. *Peruse "PCMCIA."*

15 **C.** COM1 is a serial port that is typically used for modems or serial mice. LPT ports are parallel ports that are generally used to connect printers. *Take a look at "Serial ports."*

16 **B.** The floppy ribbon cable has one end that is twisted; that twisted end must be connected to the floppy drive. *Look over "Floppy disk connectors."*

17 **A.** P1 and P2 are the typical labels given to a motherboard's power connectors. *Study "Power connectors."*

18 **C.** A parallel cable has a different style of connector at each end of the cable. The end that connects to the computer has 25 pins, and the end that connects to the printer has 36 pins. *Refer to "Parallel port."*

19 **B.** Parallel ports send information in 8-bit chunks, side by side; LPT1 is the only parallel port listed. The other three ports are serial ports that send information 1 bit at a time. *Examine "Parallel port."*

Chapter 2: Picking Your Processor

Exam Objectives

✔ Understanding CPU characteristics

✔ Identifying popular CPUs

✔ Identifying sockets

✔ Installing a processor

Although all components of the computer function together as a team, every team needs a leader — someone who gives instructions and keeps everyone working toward the same goal. If any PC component were considered the team leader, it would probably be the *central processing unit (CPU)*, also known as the *processor.* The key word here is *central,* which implies "center" or "focus." The CPU can be considered the focus of the computer because it controls a large number of the computer system's capabilities, such as the type of software that can run, the amount of total memory that the computer can recognize, and the speed at which the system will run.

In this chapter, you get a look at some of the features of the CPU that are responsible for regulating the capabilities of the computer system. This chapter also discusses the importance of the CPU and its role as a PC component, and also identifies some of the main characteristics that make one CPU better than another.

When preparing for the A+ exams, it is important that you are comfortable with terms like *MMX, throttling,* and *cache memory.* You also want to be sure that you are comfortable with the differences between various processors. For example, what makes a Pentium 4 better than a Celeron? Which AMD processor competes with the Celeron? All these are questions you should know the answer to before you take the A+ Certification exams, and this chapter helps you find out the answers. Good luck!

Understanding Processor Terminology

In this section, I cover some basic terms that describe characteristics of different processors, past and present. The exam might not ask for the specific definition of each term, but understanding the terms will help you answer the related questions in this topic area.

Processor speed

Processor speed is how fast a processor executes its instructions or commands. This speed was originally measured in millions of hertz, or megahertz (MHz), per second. A *hertz* is also known as a clock cycle, and a processor can execute code at every clock cycle. Thus, a processor operating at a measly 1 MHz per second can execute one million tasks every second. Processors today now measure their speed in gigahertz (GHz) per second. A *gigahertz* is one billion clock cycles per second — so the CPU can execute tasks a billion times per second!

Original CPUs had a speed of 4.77 MHz, and systems at the time of this writing are running over 3.0 GHz. Although processor speed is not the only factor affecting performance, in general, the faster the processor, the faster the system.

Data bus

A city bus is responsible for transferring people from one location to another. In the world of computers, a *bus* is responsible for delivering data from one location on the PC to another. *Data bus* is the term used to define the pathway between the processor and memory. Because the processor accesses information from memory so often, an entire bus — the data bus — is dedicated to this action. The larger the data bus, the more data can be carried from the CPU to memory in one clock cycle.

Here's an illustration. Say 50 people needed to go from one end of the city to the other, but a city bus had only 25 available seats. The solution? The bus would make two trips. Hmm. Wouldn't getting a larger bus be more efficient? If you upgraded the bus to 50 seats, the bus would have to make only one trip to transfer the 50 people from one end of the city to the other, which increases the efficiency of the public transit system.

The data bus works the same way, only it transfers data in the form of bits. A single bit is either a one or a zero. All data processed by the computer is in the form of bits. The data bus has a full capacity point at which it cannot handle any more bits of data, just like the bus system in the city has a full capacity point (measured in seats).

If a processor has a 16-bit data bus, it can deliver — at most — 16 bits during a single clock cycle. If the same processor needs to deliver 32 bits of information, it has to take two trips: sending 16 bits during the first clock cycle and the remaining 16 bits during the next clock cycle. Taking that same 32 bits of information and processing it on a 32-bit processor means that the information will be delivered in one trip — one clock cycle — as opposed to two, which increases the overall efficiency of the system.

Address bus

Figure 2-1 shows how system memory is organized like a spreadsheet, in rows and columns. These rows and columns make up blocks that can be written to and read from. If you want to store information in one of the blocks, you have to reference the location by address. For example, you may store data in cell B2.

Figure 2-1:
How system
memory is
organized.

	A	B	C	D
1				
2				
3				
4				
5				

To store information into system memory, your processor has to give an address that points to a particular storage location, only the address doesn't look like B2. It looks something like 10, or maybe 11, which are two completely different memory locations. As a result, the data would get stored in two different blocks.

Your processor accesses memory locations through the *address bus*. If, for example, the address bus is two-bit, the processor has two address lines from the processor to system memory. The *address lines* carry signals that specify locations in memory, each with an on/off state. A 1 represents an on state, and 0 represents an off state. The combination of the on/off states of both address lines at any given time is how a reference to an area in memory is made. The left side of Figure 2-2 illustrates a processor making a reference — or *call* — to address 10. The left side of the figure shows a reference to address 11. These two address calls reference completely different locations in memory.

If you add another address line to the address bus, the processor can access even more possible addresses because the processor has more variations with three bits than with two. A two-bit address bus can make a reference to four possible memory addresses (2×2), but a three-bit address bus can make a reference to eight possible memory addresses ($2 \times 2 \times 2$).

Therefore, the address bus dictates how much physical memory the processor can access. For example, an old 80286 processor has a 24-bit address bus, which means that it can access 16,777,216 (2^{24}) memory addresses, or 16MB of system memory. Newer processors have 36-bit address buses, which allows them to access 68,719,476,736 memory addresses, or 64GB of memory.

Figure 2-2:
Accessing
two different
memory
addresses
with the
address
bus.

Registers

Registers are storage areas within the processor used to store data tempo-
rarily for manipulation later. They are used to store and process data and
perhaps write back the result of the processed data. The benefit of stor-
ing this information in the registers — instead of in memory — is that the
processor contains the information and does not have to retrieve it from
memory, which takes time. It is as if information to be processed were in
your pocket, rather than across a room, where you would have to walk all
the way over and pick it up. Having information in your pocket means it can
be accessed much more quickly, saving time and increasing performance.
Registers give a processor quicker access to data; the more registers a pro-
cessor has, the more data it can store.

Registers are measured in bits. A processor with 16-bit registers has 16
containers into which a programmer can choose to store information.
Comparatively, a processor with 32-bit registers has twice as many contain-
ers that it can use to store information.

Cache memory

The processor accesses information that resides in system memory, which
is a slower process than if the information is stored in the processor's own
special high-speed memory, known as *cache memory.* When the information
is sitting in system memory and the processor sends a request for that infor-
mation, the request goes to the *memory controller,* which manages data in
memory. The memory controller finds the data in memory, retrieves it, and
delivers it to the processor. Throughout this entire process, the processor
is simply waiting around for the information. Thus, many newer processors
include their own special high-speed memory within the processor's chip.

When the processor retrieves information from slower system memory, it then stores it in the high-speed cache in case the processor wants to access the information a second time. The benefit is that the second time the data is needed, it is sitting in the high-speed memory located on the processor chip. The processor does not need to sit around and wait for the data to come from system memory — again, increasing overall performance.

Cache memory is integrated right into the processor's chip and is made up of *static RAM (SRAM)*. For more information on SRAM check out Book II, Chapter 3. Cache memory is very expensive because it is much quicker than regular system memory. As a result of this extra memory being integrated into the processor chip, the processor becomes more expensive than a processor that has less or no cache memory.

The two types of cache memory are *Level 1 (L1) cache* and *Level 2 (L2) cache*. L1 cache is built into the processor, whereas L2 cache resides outside the processor. In the past, L2 cache resided on the motherboard, but newer processors have a bit of L1 and L2 cache in the chip package. If you upgrade the cache memory on your computer, you are adding L2 cache to the motherboard — you wouldn't be able to upgrade the L1 cache on the processor. Because L1 cache is built into the chip, you can't upgrade it without replacing the entire processor.

The integration of cache memory into processor chips didn't come to market until the 80486 chips were developed in 1989. Generally, 80486 chips had 8K of L1 cache, and the Pentium chip increased that amount to 16K. In fact, many newer processors have increased the L1 cache to over 16K and have also included large amounts of L2 cache. The more cache memory a processor has, the quicker (and more expensive) the system will be.

Math co-processor

The *math co-processor,* also known as the *numeric processing unit (NPU),* is the processor's sidekick. Systems with math co-processors can well outperform systems that do not because the math co-processor takes some of the workload off the CPU. For example, it performs many of the large calculations that applications may require, such as floating point arithmetic. Overall system performance increases because the CPU can focus on logic functions while the math co-processor executes complicated mathematical functions.

If you have large spreadsheets or use large graphics applications, you might find that applications run very poorly or not at all on systems without a math co-processor. If you are running a system that does not have a math co-processor integrated into the CPU, you can add one to the motherboard, or perhaps upgrade the main processor.

In earlier computers, the processor was one chip, and the math co-processor was a separate chip on the motherboard. For example, years ago, a 386 computer used an 80386 chip on the motherboard as the processor, but you could add an 80387 chip to the board to act as the math co-processor. All processors since the 80486 computer, including Pentium-class systems, have a math co-processor integrated into the processor's chip, so you will not be adding a math co-processor to the system.

Real-mode versus protected-mode

A *real-mode* processor sees memory as a whole unit and deals with it as a single entity. In other words, if you have 512MB of RAM, the real-mode processor sees that as one block of memory. This is limiting because to run multiple programs at the same time, each program has to be assigned its own independent block of that 512MB — something that real-mode processors cannot do. As a result, real-mode processors don't have any *multitasking* capabilities — the capabilities to divide memory into multiple parts and run different applications or tasks in each part.

Protected-mode processors support the segregation of system memory into different parts and assigning a different application to each part of memory. Therefore, protected-mode processors support multitasking and multitasking operating systems, such as Windows and Linux.

Protected-mode processors also support *virtual memory*, which is the process of using hard disk space as emulated memory. This means you could increase your 512MB of RAM by using 768MB of hard disk space as "pretend" RAM. In this case, as far as the applications that are running are concerned, the system has 1280MB of memory — the combination of true memory plus virtual memory.

MMX

After the Pentium was developed, Intel introduced a feature called *MultiMedia eXtensions*, or *MMX*. MMX added 57 new instructions that were built into the processor and told the system how to work with audio, video, and graphics. If these instructions were not built into the processor, the processor would have to retrieve them from somewhere else.

When MMX was developed, both home and business users seemed to be heading toward the world of multimedia, and it made sense to enhance the processor and make it "multimedia aware." Running any kind of multimedia application on a processor that supports MMX gives you a major performance increase over a processor that doesn't support MMX technology.

Hyperthreading

Hyperthreading is a feature designed by Intel that was placed in the Pentium processors. *Hyperthreading technology,* or *HTT,* allows a processor to logically act as two different processors by being able to execute simultaneous threads. A *thread* is a part of an application that executes at any given time. For example, when running Microsoft Word, one thread accepts keystrokes, and another thread runs the spell checker while you type. Thus, two parts of the application run at the same time.

For a system to truly be able to take advantage of multithreaded applications, you normally need a system that has multiple processors — one processor to run one thread at a time. With hyperthreading, one processor can run more than one thread at a time, increasing performance by 15 to 30 percent.

Multicore

A *multicore* processor combines a number of independent processors and the L1 cache from those processors onto a single processor chip. The benefit of a multicore processor is that it can execute multiple threads at the same time without hyperthreading because you essentially have multiple processors in one chip package.

A multicore processor has the benefit of having multiple processors' core features — such as superscalar execution, pipelining, and threading — all packaged into one physical processor. The core features also include each core having its own L1 cache memory. Multicore processors also have a block of shared L2 cache between the two processors in the multicore chip.

A huge benefit of being only one chip on the motherboard is that the one multicore chip draws less power than two separate processors would. Figure 2-3 shows the logical view of a dual-core processor.

A number of different flavors of multicore processors are available today, such as dual-core, triple-core, and quad-core processors. Here are the differences between the three:

✦ **Dual core:** Has two cores in one chip package, with each core typically having 128K of L1 cache and 512K of shared L2 cache.

✦ **Triple core:** Has three cores in one chip package with each core typically having 128K of L1 cache. Most triple-core processors also have 512K of L2 cache per core and share a block of cache memory, known as L3 cache.

✦ **Quad core:** Has four cores in one chip package with each core typically having 128K of L1 cache. Most quad-core processors also have 512K of L2 cache per core and share a block of L3 cache (2MB–6MB).

Figure 2-3:
Looking at the logical structure of a dual-core processor.

Throttling

Throttling (a feature built into a lot of newer processors today) involves the CPU sensing when it is going to overheat and then reducing its speed to lower the heat to an acceptable range.

Processors that support throttling have a built-in *thermal sensor* (a high-tech thermometer) that monitors the temperature of the processor. When the processor detects that it is going to overheat — maybe, because of a fan failure — the processor drops its speed so that the temperature drops to an acceptable range.

Overclocking

Overclocking, a big feature for PC enthusiasts, involves running a piece of hardware faster than the speed at which it is rated. A number of devices can be overclocked, such as video adapters and (of course) processors.

Although you might be able to overclock the processor, it is not recommended because overclocking can result in an unstable system or even hardware failure.

VRM

The *voltage regulator module (VRM)* is responsible for regulating the voltage that is delivered to the processor. The VRM is located on the motherboard (or appears as its own device in the system) and provides the correct running voltage to the processor.

Some VRMs use a jumper on the motherboard to determine how much voltage is supplied to the processor, and other VRMs sense what the processor needs on startup. Typically, VRMs on the motherboard sense what voltage the processor needs and then supply that voltage.

Chip packaging

Chip packaging refers to how the chip is constructed and delivered to the consumer. The chip package defines the appearance or form factor of the chip. Many chip packages have been used over the years.

The chip packages you should be familiar with for the A+ exam are as follows:

Book II
Chapter 2

✦ **Dual inline package (DIP) chip:** A rectangular chip with two rows of 20 pins. Pin 1 is located at the end of the chip that has a square notch carved into it. It is important to identify pin 1 because when you add a DIP chip to the motherboard, you have to match pin 1 on the chip with pin 1 in the chip socket.

Older processors (such as the 8088) and many math co-processor chips use the DIP chip style. Although they are no longer used for CPUs, DIP chips are still used for cache memory and BIOS chips on motherboards. They are also found on memory modules. (See Book II, Chapter 3, for a discussion of memory modules.)

✦ **Pin grid array (PGA) chip:** One of the most popular processor chip packages in use today, the PGA chip is a square chip with an array of pins filling up the shape of the chip. In general, the PGA chip uses hundreds of pins. You can locate pin 1 on the PGA by identifying the corner of the PGA chip that has the corner cut off — that corner is where pin 1 is located. Figure 2-4 compares a DIP (right side) with a PGA (left side) chip type.

Figure 2-4: Comparing a DIP chip package (right) to a PGA package (left).

PGA chip DIP chip

Today's implementation of the PGA chip fits into a *zero insertion force (ZIF)* socket. The ZIF socket is ideal for upgrading processors (especially compared with the days before ZIF sockets were used) because

the ZIF socket has a lever (on the side of the socket) that you lift to raise the chip from the socket. Because the chip is automatically raised out of the socket, you can simply remove the chip out of the socket with little effort! Before ZIF sockets were used, you had to pry the chip out of the socket while trying to ensure that you did not damage the chip or the pins. With the ZIF socket, after the processor is raised, you can replace the old chip with a new one. In the past, not all boards used ZIF sockets, so you had to get some special extractors to pull the chip out (carefully!). Figure 2-5 shows a ZIF socket.

Socket 7 ZIF socket

Figure 2-5:
A ZIF socket
on the
mother-
board holds
a processor.

✦ **Single Edge Contact (SEC) chip:** A chip package type that was popular with the Pentium II processors, the SEC chip is a huge cartridge surrounded by a plastic casing. The newer version, SEC2, is implemented as a card that is inserted into a slot on the motherboard and doesn't have the big plastic casing around it. It is important to stress that the SEC and SEC2 are inserted into a slot and not a socket. For more information on slots and sockets, read the next section. Figure 2-6 shows an SEC chip package along with some PGA chip packages.

SEC chip

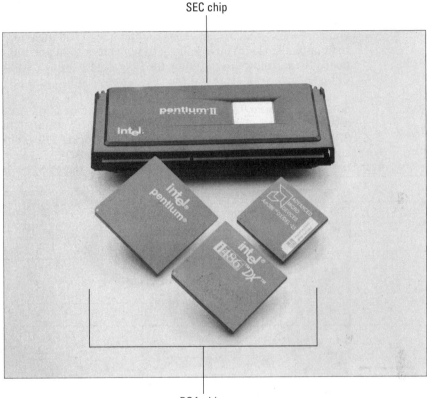

Figure 2-6:
An SEC chip
package
along
with some
PGA chip
packages.

PGA chips

Be sure to remember the different chip package types for the A+ exams. The
Pentium II processor used the SEC. Newer processors, such as the Pentium
4, are using the PGA.

Identifying Socket Types

Intel decided to develop a new standard for upgrading a processor on moth-
erboards, beginning with the 80486 chips and continuing with the Pentium-
class processors. This standard — a processor socket designed to hold a
specific processor chip with the appropriate number of pins — enabled
Intel to develop new chips with compatibility of a particular socket in mind.
For example, if a socket is developed with 321 pins, Intel could develop a
new processor that has 321 pins and know that the processor will work with
any motherboard that has the right socket. This allows the consumer to
upgrade a processor much easier than in the past. Intel could design a new
chip for an old socket so that customers could update their computers by
dropping the new processor in the compatible socket.

Original Pentium processors supported mainly Socket 5 with 320 pins or Socket 7 with 321 pins. Thus, to add a Pentium processor to a motherboard, you determine what socket exists on that board and then purchase a CPU to fit in that socket. You also have to remember to match the voltage of the board to the voltage required by the CPU. Figure 2-7 helps you identify a CPU socket in your system.

Sockets are normally labeled by type along the side of the socket. For example, in Figure 2-7, the socket is labeled as PGA 370, meaning that it is Socket 370 and will hold any processor designed for Socket 370. (Socket 370 is a socket that holds a processor containing 370 pins.)

Figure 2-7:
Identifying
a processor
socket.

Table 2-1 lists the different types of sockets and the processors that are placed in the sockets. For more information about the processors, read the sections "Looking at Popular Intel Processors" and "Don't Forget Non-Intel Chips," later in this chapter. Table 2-1 also shows the number of pins associated with the different types of sockets and slots.

Table 2-1	Processor Socket Types and Slots	
Socket	*Processor*	*Number of Pins*
Socket A	Later Athlon, Duron, and Athlon XP	462
Socket 1	80486, 80486DX2, 80486DX4	169
Socket 2	80486, 80486DX2, 80486DX4	238

Socket	Processor	Number of Pins
Socket 3	80486, 80486DX2, 80486DX4	237
Socket 4	Pentium 60/66	273
Socket 5	Pentium 75-133	320
Socket 7	Pentium 75-200	321
Socket 8	Pentium Pro	387
Socket 370	Celeron and Pentium III	370
Socket 418	Itanium	418
Socket 423	Pentium 4	423
Socket 478	Later Celerons and Pentium 4	478
Socket 603	Xeon (Pentium 4 version)	603
Socket 611	Itanium	611
Socket 940	Opteron	940
Slot A	Athlon	242
Slot 1	Pentium II and Pentium III	242
Slot 2	Xeon	330
Socket 754	Turion 64, Athlon 64 , Sempron	754
Socket 775 or LGA775 (also called Socket T)	Pentium 4, Pentium D, Celeron D, Core 2 Duo	775
LGA1366 (also called Socket B)	Intel Core i7 processor	1366
AM2	Opteron, Sempron, Athlon 64, Athlon 64 X2	940
AM2+	Athlon 64, Athlon 64 X2, Phenom, Phenom II	940
AM3	Phenom II	941

<div align="right">

**Book II
Chapter 2**

Picking Your Processor

</div>

Know the socket types used to hold the Pentium 4, Celeron, Athlon XP, Athlon 64, Phenom, and Turion processors. You will not be expected to memorize the entire Table 2-1, but you should be familiar with the sockets used by today's popular processors.

Originally, the sockets were simply called Socket 1, Socket 2, and so on up to Socket 8. To make it easier to understand what processors went into which sockets, Intel started naming the sockets after the number of pins that existed on the processor that the socket would support. For example, Socket 370 holds a processor with 370 pins, and Socket 478 holds a processor with 478 pins. It is much easier now to identify what processors go into which sockets!

Now that you understand some of the characteristics of processors and you understand what a socket is, take a look at some of the popular Intel and AMD chips you are expected to know for the A+ exams.

Looking at Popular Intel Processors

In this section, I provide an overview of the Pentium-class processors and their characteristics, including data bus, address bus, registers, and the amount of cache memory supported on these processors. You will also be introduced to any new or unique processor features that each processor offers.

Pentium

The original Pentium processor, released in 1993, was developed at speeds of 60 MHz and 66 MHz. The Pentium processor was a PGA chip that was placed in Socket 5 or Socket 7. Soon after its release, Intel marketed Pentium processors in 75, 90, 100, 120, 133, 150, 166, and 200 MHz flavors, which were really just clock multipliers of the original 60 MHz or 66 MHz systems.

Clock multiplying is the concept that the processor will run faster than the motherboard that the processor sits in. For example, the original Pentium processor ran on 60 or 66 MHz motherboards. Say that the computer is marketed as a Pentium 90. Because you know that the motherboard runs at 60 or 66 MHz, you can determine that the 90 comes from 60×1.5 — meaning that the processor runs 1.5 times the speed of the motherboard. This is important because as a consumer, when you purchase a computer, you want to make sure you know what the motherboard speed is, too — not just the advertised speed of the processor.

From a consumer's point of view, clock multipliers become important when you take a look at computers such as the Pentium 133 and the Pentium 150. Which is faster? The obvious answer is the Pentium 150, the system with the higher megahertz speed. But is it really? The Pentium 133 is a clock double of the 66 MHz board, and the Pentium 150 is a clock double and a half of the 60 MHz board. My point being that the overall performance of the system is controlled by more than just the speed of the processor — you need to consider other components, such as the speed of the motherboard.

By looking at the motherboard speeds of the Pentium 133 and the Pentium 150, you could assume that the computer running the Pentium 133 might be able to keep up with (if not outperform) the one running the Pentium 150. Table 2-2 compares the speed of the motherboard and processor for the different Pentium systems.

Table 2-2	Pentium Clock Multipliers		
Processor	*Motherboard Speed (MHz)*	*Multiplier*	*Processor Speed (MHz)*
Pentium 90	60	1.5	90
Pentium 100	66	1.5	99
Pentium 120	60	2	120
Pentium 133	66	2	132
Pentium 150	60	2.5	150
Pentium 180	60	3	180
Pentium 200	66	3	198
Pentium II	100	4.5	450

The Pentium processor has a 32-bit address bus, 32-bit registers, and a 64-bit data bus. It also has 16K of L1 cache that is divided into two 8K channels. One channel is for data cache and the other for application code cache.

Before the Pentium came along, processors used one *instruction pipeline*. This meant that when an application executed, it would run each stage of the application job one step after the other. For example, if an application has three lines of code, as seen in Figure 2-8, each line of code can be processed only after the previous line of code is fully completed. This creates a delay, or wait time, which slows performance.

Figure 2-8:
Single-instruction pipelined processor executing application code.

The Pentium processor introduced a feature called *superscalar design*. The processor has two instruction pipelines, named U and V. Having two instruction pipelines enables the processor to execute two instructions at the same time. Thus, the three lines of program code, shown in

Figure 2-9, can be quickly executed on a Pentium processor because lines 1 and 2 are processed at the same time, causing line 3 to be processed that much sooner. Notice that lines 1 and 2 execute parallel to one another; therefore, *parallel processing* is taking place.

Figure 2-9:
Dual-instruction pipelined processor processing application code.

An application has to be designed to take advantage of two instruction pipelines. These applications are often labeled something like Pentium Aware or Pentium Ready.

Pentium Pro

In 1995, Intel released the Pentium Pro chip, which added a new level of performance to the Pentium processor. The Pentium Pro had all the characteristics of the Pentium processor — such as a 64-bit data bus and 32-bit registers — but it increased the address bus to 36 bits, which means that the Pentium Pro could access 64GB of RAM. The speed of the Pentium Pro ranges from 120 MHz to around 200 MHz.

The Pentium Pro included two additional features on its chip that helped it outperform the original Pentium. First, the Pentium Pro chip is really a two-chip team. One chip was the actual processor (with 16K of L1 cache, like the Pentium chip), but the other chip holds an extra 256K of cache memory. Because this cache memory is physically outside of the CPU, it is considered L2 cache.

The second feature that led to the performance gain of the Pentium Pro is *dynamic execution,* which has three stages: multiple branch prediction, dataflow analysis, and speculative execution.

✦ **Multiple branch prediction** is the idea that the processor will look ahead and predict a number of instructions that might be needed in the very near future.

✦ **Dataflow analysis** occurs when the processor looks at the instructions it has predicted will be needed next and then assigns them a logical order of execution.

✦ **Speculative execution** is the actual execution of a given instruction based on the prediction and the order of execution assigned.

The Pentium Pro chip, shown in Figure 2-10, was implemented as a PGA chip that was placed in Socket 8.

Figure 2-10:
The Intel
Pentium Pro
processor.

Pentium II

In 1997, Intel produced the Pentium II, which was really just an enhanced Pentium Pro with speeds ranging from 233 MHz to 450 MHz. The Pentium II had a 64-bit data bus, a 36-bit address bus (64GB of RAM), and 32-bit registers; and supported features such as MMX.

The Pentium II increased the amount of L1 cache that was integrated into the CPU to 32K, as opposed to 16K. The 32K of L1 cache was still divided into two equal channels: one 16K channel for data and one 16K channel for application code.

Intel packaged the Pentium II in the *Single Edge Contact* (SEC) — sometimes also referred to as the *Single Edge Contact Connector (SECC)* — that fits into Slot 1 on the motherboard. The SEC is a module enclosed in a casing or shell with two chips inside: one chip being the processor, and the other chip being the 512K of L2 cache. Refer to Figure 2-9 to see what a Pentium II processor, which uses the SEC, looks like.

Another enhancement that accompanied the Pentium II was single instruction multiple data (SIMD). To visualize how SIMD works, imagine five toddlers in a playroom, and that these toddlers are at the entertaining age of

two — the age, of course, when the toddlers are preparing for their teen years by answering "no" to everything you say. You walk into the playroom and see that the five toddlers have found your box of darts and are throwing them at the walls. You are faced with a choice: You can either walk around to each child and explain why throwing darts at your walls is not a good idea (which means you will have to explain the same thing five different times), or you can have a good scream at the top of your lungs, which means that all the children will stop immediately and listen. SIMD works on the same basic principle. With SIMD, the processor gives the instruction to multiple processes at once instead of having to give the same instruction multiple times. Thus, the processor saves time and creates a much more efficient way to work with information.

Celeron

The Pentium II processor performed very well, and with all that cache memory, it should! Unfortunately, that performance came with a price. If you were not willing to pay that price, Intel created a chip for you: the Celeron chip!

The Celeron chip is nothing more than a less-expensive version of the Pentium II processor with the built-in L2 cache either removed entirely or reduced. The first-generation Celeron chip was code-named the Covington; it has no L2 cache memory on it. The second-generation Celeron was code-named the Mendocino, and it contains 128K of L2 cache. Although this version of the Celeron does have L2 cache, it is dramatically reduced from the Pentium II's 512K so that it can be sold at a lower price.

The original Celeron shipped in an SEC package but also had a version that was packaged as a PGA, as shown in Figure 2-11.

Figure 2-11: Intel's Celeron processor was first implemented as an SEC package, but later had a PGA chip that was placed in Socket 370.

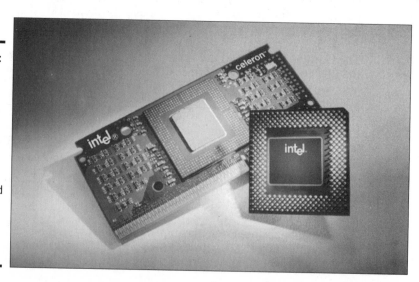

Pentium III

The Pentium III processor shares many of the Pentium II characteristics. It supports dynamic execution (as the Pentium Pro also did) and MMX technology, has 32K of L1 cache, and has either 256K or 512K of L2 cache. The Pentium III runs at a speed of 450 MHz to 1000 MHz (1 GHz).

The Pentium III chip offers 70 additional instructions that are integrated into the chip, enhancing the user's experience with 3-D graphic applications. The Pentium III chip also supports a number of low-power states to help conserve energy when the system is not in use. This processor is designed to run on either 100 MHz or 133 MHz motherboards.

Also note that there is a Pentium III version of the Celeron chip that runs as fast as the Pentium III processor but again has the L2 cache memory reduced. So now there are multiple versions of the Celeron chip — the PII version and the PIII version.

The Pentium III processor shipped in the SEC2 package (as shown in Figure 2-12) originally, but was then packaged as a PGA chip. The SEC2 goes in Slot 1, and the PGA chip is inserted into Socket 370.

**Book II
Chapter 2**

**Picking Your
Processor**

Figure 2-12: The Pentium III processor in the SEC2 package that lives in Slot 1.

Xeon

The Xeon processor is built on the Pentium II and Pentium III architecture — meaning that, like the Celeron, there is a PII version and PIII version of the Xeon. The Xeon chip is designed for higher-end systems, such as server-class systems, and contains more cache memory than the typical PII and PIII. The Xeon comes in flavors of 512K, 1MB, and 2MB of L2 cache.

The Xeon can also address 64GB of RAM and is designed for *multiprocessing systems:* that is, computers with a motherboard that supports multiple CPUs. The Xeon processor has been designed to coexist with two, four, or eight CPUs.

The Pentium II Xeon and Pentium III Xeon chips were originally packaged as an SEC (as shown in Figure 2-13) that was placed in Slot 2, but later versions use the PGA and are placed in Socket 603. The Xeon chip also contains a thermal sensor that shuts the processor down if it starts to overheat.

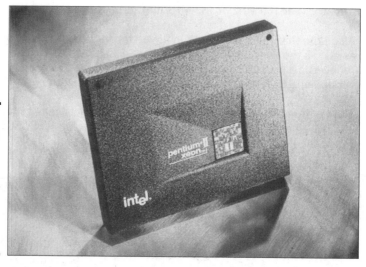

Figure 2-13:
The Pentium II Xeon processor was originally delivered in the SEC package.

The Celeron is a scaled-down version of the Pentium II or III processor, and the Xeon is a step up from the Pentium II or III. There are also PIV (Pentium 4) versions of the processors:

+ **PIV Xeon:** Designed to work with a multiprocessing system that uses one or two processors

+ **PIV Xeon MP:** Designed to work with a multiprocessing system that uses four or eight processors

Pentium 4

The Pentium 4 processor runs between 2 GHz and 4 GHz. The Pentium processor has 20K of L1 cache and 512K of L2 cache. The processor is shipped as a 423-pin or 478-pin PGA package, which means that the chip will be placed in Socket 423 or Socket 478 (as shown in Figure 2-14).

Figure 2-14:
Socket 478
can house
a Pentium 4
processor.

The Pentium 4 processor gets a huge performance benefit by being able to perform four data transfers in one clock cycle along the *front side bus (FSB)*, which is the bus that connects the processor to system memory. (See Chapter 1 of this minibook.)

Most Pentium 4 processors today are multicore processors and enjoy the performance benefits that multicore brings.

Itanium and Itanium 11

Intel created its first 64-bit processor in the Itanium and Itanium II processors and was marketed for server class–system or high-end PCs. Although the Itanium is a 64-bit processor and designed to run 64-bit software such as the 64-bit version of Windows, the Itanium can run some 32-bit code with the use of an emulator, but the code will run slower than if it were on a 32-bit processor. Special 64-bit editions of Windows can run on the Itanium processor, which enables you to take advantage of the 64-bit architecture. To learn more about the 64-bit editions of Windows, check out

www.microsoft.com/windowsxp/64bit/default.mspx

The original Itanium processor used a special packaging known as the *pin array cartridge (PAC),* which uses 418 pins. The Itanium II was packaged in *organic land grid array (OLGA)* — a variation of the PGA — but the chip is located on a *processor card* (a circuit board that holds the processor). The OLGA fits into Socket 611.

The Itanium processor runs at around 1 GHz and contains a large block of cache memory: 32K of L1 cache, 96K of L2 cache, and 2MB or 4MB of L3 cache. The L3 cache is an additional block of cache memory located in the chip packaging.

Moving from 32-bit processors and applications to 64-bit versions would truly benefit any user using applications that are memory intensive or calculation intensive. For example, a user who works a lot with multimedia-type applications would see an improvement in performance.

Pentium M

For years, laptop manufacturers have been asking for smaller processors to place in laptop systems, and they finally have their wish. A number of processors have come out with the M version, which stands for *mobile.* The mobile versions of the processors are smaller than the processors that go in desktop systems, so they fit better and also use a lot less power. The benefit of using less power also means that they run much cooler.

Because the mobile versions of the processors use less power, they also run a little slower than their desktop counterparts.

Some popular brands of mobile processors are the Intel Pentium III M and the Pentium M. Intel's big competitor, AMD, also has mobile versions of their processors: Athlon XP M and Mobile Duron. (Some manufacturers put the word *mobile* in the name of the processor instead of the letter *M.*) The next sections discuss more about AMD processors.

Intel Core 2

Intel designed the Intel Core 2 to be its 64-bit, multicore processor. The Core 2 comes in three flavors:

+ **Core 2 Solo:** Single-core processor

+ **Core 2 Duo:** Dual-core processor on the one chip

+ **Core 2 Quad:** Actually two chips, with two cores per chip, packaged in a multichip module

Core 2 processors range in speed from 1 GHz to around 3 GHz and fit into an LGA 775 socket, also known as Socket T. Core 2 processors come with either 2MB of L2 cache or 4MB of L2 cache.

Intel Atom

Intel has created a processor to run on the now-popular Netbooks. A Netbook is a laptop-like computer — but much smaller — that is used primarily for Internet usage. The Netbook is much smaller and cheaper than a regular laptop system and is marketed for e-mail and Web browsing features.

The Intel Atom has many characteristics of normal processors — it runs between 1 GHz and 2 GHz and contains 32K of L1 cache and 512K of L2 cache. Originally the Atom processor had one instruction pipeline, but there are versions with two instruction pipelines. There are also single core and dual core versions of the Atom processor.

Don't Forget Non-Intel Chips

One of Intel's major competitors is Advanced Micro Devices (AMD). AMD has developed a family of processors that compete with Pentium-class processors. In this section, I provide an overview of some of the characteristics of the AMD processors.

K6

The AMD K6 processor was designed to compete with the original Intel Pentium. The K6 has 64K of L1 cache, supports MMX technology, and has built-in branch prediction techniques. This processor has 321 pins, which means that it will fit into a Socket 7–supported motherboard.

K6-2

The K6-2 processor was designed to compete with the Pentium II chip. It has 64K of L1 cache and 256K of L2 cache. The K6-2 also supports dynamic execution, MMX technology, and superscalar design.

The K6-2 has added *3DNow!* technology, comprising a number of additional instructions integrated into the chip to improve 3-D graphics applications. The K6-2 chip also uses a 100 MHz motherboard speed, which is a big improvement over the 60/66 MHz motherboard speed that the original Pentiums used.

The K6-2 has 321 pins, which means that it will fit into a Socket 7–supported motherboard.

K6-III

The K6-III processor is designed to compete with the Pentium III chip. This chip shares many of the features of the K6-2, including a 100 MHz system bus. One of its features was the tri-level cache. Not only can it take

advantage of an L1 and L2 cache but also an L3 cache that can be included on the motherboard.

Athlon

The AMD Athlon chip has 128K of L1 cache and 512K of L2 cache. It supports improved dynamic execution, MMX technology, and 3DNow! technology. The Athlon chip runs at speeds of up to 1.2 GHz and is designed to run on a 200 MHz system bus speed.

Unlike the K6-2 and K6-III, the Athlon is not a PGA-packaged chip that supports Socket 7. It uses its own socket type — Slot A, so called because the processor is packaged as an SEC. The Slot A socket is not compatible with Intel's Slot 1, which means that users have to purchase a motherboard designed for the Athlon chip.

Later versions of the Athlon moved to the PGA package that has 462 pins. These PGA chips are placed in Socket A.

Athlon XP

After the Athlon chip was produced, Intel created the Pentium 4 chip. So AMD wanted to create a competing chip for the Pentium 4: namely, the Athlon XP. The Athlon XP is packaged as a PGA with 462 pins and is placed in Socket A. The Athlon XP runs at 2 GHz or more and contains 128K of L1 cache and 512K of L2 cache.

AMD markets these processors a little differently. Instead of labeling the processor with its speed, AMD labels it with its competitor's speed. For example, the Athlon XP 1800+ is rated at 1.6 GHz but runs as fast as the Intel 1.8 GHz processor.

Duron

AMD wanted to create a processor that competed with each version of the Intel processors. So, if the Athlon XP competes with the Pentium 4, what competes with the Celeron? You guessed it — the Duron.

The Duron has 128K of L1 cache and 64K of L2 cache. This processor is packaged as a PGA with 462 pins, which means that it, too, goes into Socket A.

Opteron

Just like the Duron was built to compete with the Intel Celeron, AMD created the Opteron to compete with Intel 64-bit Itanium processors. The Opteron runs at about 1.8 GHz and contains 128K of L1 cache and 1MB of L2 cache.

The Opteron is packaged with a micro-PGA, which is made up of 940 pins and is placed in Socket 940. One of the major differences between the Opteron and the Itanium is that the Itanium cannot run 32-bit applications. AMD decided that the Opteron would run in a 32-bit *or* 64-bit mode, thus allowing it to run 32-bit applications.

Athlon 64 and Athlon 64 X2

The Athlon 64 — the successor to the Athlon XP — is the AMD 64-bit processor for desktop systems. The Athlon 64, with 128K of L1 cache and at least 512K of L2 cache built into the processor, is designed to compete with the Pentium 4.

Although the Athlon 64 is a 64-bit processor, it has been designed to be backward compatible; it can run 32-bit code. The Athlon 64 X2 is the dual-core version of the Athlon 64. The Athlon 64 family processors fit into a number of sockets: Socket 754, Socket 940, and the AM2 socket.

Know that the Sempron processor is a low-end version of the Athlon 64 and has replaced the Duron as the AMD low-end processor. The Sempron was originally a 32-bit processor with reduced cache size, but current versions are 64-bit with the cache size reduced.

Phenom and Phenom II

The Phenom and Phenom II pick up after the Athlon 64 and are the AMD triple- and quad-core processors. The Phenom, designed for desktop systems, uses the code names Toliman for the triple-core version and Agena for the quad-core version.

The Phenom processor, which comes with 128K of L1 cache and 512KB of L2 cache per core, also has 2MB of shared L3 cache. The processor fits in the AMD AM2+ socket and runs between approximately 1.8 GHz and 2.6 GHz.

The Phenom II also sits in the AM2+ socket and increases the shared L3 cache to 6MB! There were issues with the Phenom running on Windows Vista, but those bugs have been fixed for the Phenom II. The Phenom II has a triple-core version, code-named Heka, that runs between 2.6 GHz and 2.8 GHz. The quad-core version that is named Deneb runs between 2.5 GHz and 3.0 GHz.

Turion 64 and Turion 64 X2

The Turion 64 processor is the AMD 64-bit mobile processor for use in laptop computers. The Turion processor used to be called the Athlon Mobile 64, but AMD has moved to the new label of Turion 64 for its mobile processors. The Turion 64 is a single-core processor, and the Turion 64 X2 is the dual-core processor.

Turion 64 processors come with 128K of L1 cache and either 512K or 1024K of L2 cache. Both the Turion 64 and the Turion 64 X2 fit into Socket 754, and the newer chips fit in AMD Socket S7.

Be sure to know the multicore processors for the exam. The Athlon 64 X2 is the AMD dual-core processor, and the Phenom/Phenom II have triple-core and quad-core versions. Also be familiar with the Turion being the AMD 64-bit processor for laptop computers.

Installing a Processor

Now that you understand some of the popular processors that exist today, take a look at how to install a processor. This section identifies installation decisions you have to be aware of before actually attempting to install the processor.

Will it fit in the socket?

The first thing you need to verify before you purchase a new processor for your system is what socket type you have on your motherboard. You want to make sure that you purchase a processor that fits in that socket. For example, if you have Socket A on the motherboard, what processors fit in Socket A? If you said Athlon, Athlon XP, and Duron, you are correct.

Also be sure you know how many pins the socket has because some processors support a few differently sized sockets. For example, Intel makes both Socket 423 and Socket 478 versions of the Pentium 4, so make sure you get the correct version of the Pentium 4 for your socket.

CPU voltage and transistor integrationAnother important CPU characteristic that you have to watch for when upgrading your processor is the voltage the processor requires. *Voltage* is the power that the processor draws from the main motherboard, which the motherboard receives originally from the power supply.

A processor is designed to run at a certain voltage. You need to ensure that the motherboard you are placing the processor into provides that voltage. If a motherboard supports more than one voltage, you can typically change a jumper on the motherboard, which will then control the voltage used by the processor. For more information on jumpers, check out Book II, Chapter 1.

Performing the installation

Because most systems today use ZIF sockets and PGA chips, I discuss installing a processor into the ZIF socket. After you verify that your new processor will work with your motherboard, you are ready to install the processor. To install the processor, first remove the existing one by pulling up on the lever on the ZIF socket. When you pull the lever on the ZIF socket, the existing processor should rise out of the socket a bit.

Be sure to ground yourself before touching the insides of a computer. Get an antistatic wrist strap and clamp it to the computer's chassis so that you have a constant ground. For more information on safety procedures, read Book I, Chapter 3.

With the processor a bit out of the socket, you can then gently lift out the processor (as shown in Figure 2-15). Be sure to lift the processor straight up so that you do not bend any of the pins.

**Book II
Chapter 2**

**Picking Your
Processor**

Figure 2-15:
Removing
the
processor
from its
socket.

After you have the old processor out of the socket, you can install the new processor by first finding out where pin 1 is on the processor chip. Pin 1 is located in one of the corners of the chip and is usually indicated with a gold line marked on the bottom of the chip that contains the pins. If you do not see a line indicating where pin 1 is, you will notice that one of the corners of the square PGA is cut off (see Figure 2-16) — this corner is pin 1.

Pin 1 indicator

Figure 2-16: The cut-out corner of the processor indicates the location of pin 1.

After you locate pin 1 on the PGA chip, you also need to figure out where pin 1 goes in the socket. Again, you can figure this out by finding the cut-off corner of the socket. This corner is where the cut-off corner of the processor goes, as seen in Figure 2-17.

After you match up pin 1 on the PGA chip with pin 1 on the ZIF socket, carefully place the processor into the socket and then push the lever down to lock it in place.

Just lay the chip into the socket; don't push it in. The whole point of a *zero insertion force* socket is that you don't have to risk damaging the pins by applying pressure.

Figure 2-17:
Identifying
the cut-out
corner
in the
processor
socket.

Pin 1 indicator

Keeping a Processor Cool

After you have the processor in the processor socket, you need to install
something to keep it cool, such as a heat sink or fan — or maybe even both.

Processors are made up of thousands, even millions, of transistors. A
transistor acts as a switch, permitting or prohibiting the flow of electrical
current. If current is allowed to flow through the transistor, some result is
generated. If the current is not allowed to flow through the transistor, a dif-
ferent result is generated.

A processor contains millions of transistors that each hold an electrical charge, causing the processor to run at very high temperatures. Therefore, it is important to keep the processor cool. The most common cooling mechanisms today are heat sinks and CPU fans, which are sometimes used in tandem.

A number of other cooling devices are on the market today, and they are a little more expensive than your typical heat sink or CPU fan. The following are other cooling techniques you may find in systems today:

✦ **Liquid cooling:** A liquid cooling system pumps a cooling liquid throughout the PC by using small hoses. The benefit of a liquid cooling system is the reduced noise, but its big drawback is the amount of space needed in the PC for the components of the cooling system — and, of course, the threat of a leak if the cooling system is not installed properly.

✦ **Temperature sensors:** A number of processors today come with a built-in thermal sensor (a high-tech thermometer). Temperature sensors allow the processor to identify that it is overheating and then shut itself down until the temperature drops to normal.

✦ **Thermal compound:** This liquid paste is placed between the processor and the heat sink to help draw the heat away from the processor and pass it through the heat sink.

✦ **Heat pipes:** A heat pipe is designed to transfer heat from a hot temperature source by vaporizing a form of coolant liquid that is then vacuumed away from the heat source to a cooler interface. The vapor can then be rerouted from the cool source to the heat source again as a liquid to perform the cooling process again.

Heat sinks and CPU fans

Because of the size of the Pentium processor and the number of transistors passing current, the chip can get so hot that it becomes unstable. Thus, many Pentium processors come with either a cooling fan or heat sinks. A number of processors today have a heat sink with a fan on top of the heat sink.

Heat sinks are a group of metal pins placed on the chip to draw heat away from it. A *cooling fan* is a small fan placed on top of the processor to pull away hot air, helping to keep the processor cool. Figure 2-18 shows a heat sink.

Installing a heat sink and fan

Some processors can get so hot that a heat sink might not be enough of a cooling device; in this case, you might want to place a fan on top of the heat sink. To install the heat sink and fan on your system, simply place the heat sink on the processor and then clamp it in place with the heat sink–clamping bar. After you have the heat sink in place, you can secure a fan on top of it by clamping the fan on the heat sink, as shown in Figure 2-19.

Figure 2-18:
Looking at a
heat sink.

Figure 2-19:
Placing the
fan on top
of the heat
sink.

The term *passive heat sink* is used for a heat sink that does not use a fan on
top, and the term *active heat sink* is used for a heat sink with a fan on top.

Increasing Performance

When it comes to processors, there are a number of different ways to increase the performance of your system. A first and obvious way is to buy the faster processor when upgrading; for example, upgrade a 1.8 GHz processor to a 3 GHz processor if possible. Also, get a processor designed to run on the faster motherboards. For example, back when Pentium II processors were popular, there were 100 MHz motherboards or 133 MHz motherboards. You get a faster system by having a 133 MHz motherboard.

You will have to look at other features of the processor, such as the L1 cache and L2 cache that reside in the processor packaging. Acquiring a processor with more cache memory can dramatically increase system performance.

Getting an A+

This chapter provides an overview of the key terms that are used to identify the popular processors and their capabilities. Some of the points you need to remember when preparing for the exam are

+ **Chip packages:** The three major chip packages are DIP, PGA, and SEC. PGA is the popular chip packaging used in today's systems.

+ **Processor speed:** Processor speed is measured in gigahertz (GHz) but was measured in megahertz (MHz) in the past.

+ **Cache memory:** L1 cache is cache memory integrated into the processor chip, while L2 and L3 cache are found outside the CPU chip.

+ **Sockets:** A socket is used to hold the processor in place on the motherboard. Be sure to be familiar with the sockets for the Intel Pentium III, Pentium 4, and Celeron chips. Also know about the sockets for the AMD Athlon, Athlon XP, and Duron chips.

+ **Chips:** Be sure to review the characteristics of different Intel chips and AMD chips.

Prep Test

1 Which of the following best describes superscalar design?

 A ○ The processor is designed using only 3.1 transistors.

 B ○ The processor predicts the next few instructions to be executed and then determines the optimal order for the execution of these instructions.

 C ○ The processor has two instruction pipelines, which enables multiple instructions to execute at the same time.

 D ○ The processor works twice as fast as the motherboard.

2 In what socket/slot would you find a Pentium II processor?

 A ○ Socket 5

 B ○ Socket 1

 C ○ Socket 7

 D ○ Slot 1

3 Which of the following are placed in Socket A? (Select all that apply.)

 A ❑ Pentium III

 B ❑ Athlon XP

 C ❑ Celeron

 D ❑ Pentium 4

 E ❑ Duron

 F ❑ Itanium

4 What chip type was the original Pentium processor packaged in?

 A ○ SEC

 B ○ PGA

 C ○ DIP

 D ○ Socket 5

5 Which of the following is a characteristic of protected-mode processors?

 A ○ Heat sink support

 B ○ Virtual memory support

 C ○ Run only one application at a time

 D ○ Encased in protective shell

6 How much L1 cache does a Pentium III processor have built in?

A ○ 32K

B ○ 64K

C ○ 8K

D ○ 16K

7 Which of the following acts as a storage container for information that will be processed by the processor?

A ○ Data bus

B ○ Address bus

C ○ Registers

D ○ Math co-processor

8 How much memory can a Pentium Pro address?

A ○ 128MB

B ○ 512MB

C ○ 4GB

D ○ 64GB

9 Which statement best describes the purpose of a math co-processor?

A ○ Performs all logic functions on behalf of the processor

B ○ Performs floating-point calculations on behalf of the processor

C ○ Runs all applications, and a processor runs the operating system in a multi-tasking environment

D ○ Allows for communication between devices

10 Which sockets/slots do original Pentium chips typically fit into? (Choose two.)

A ❑ Socket 1

B ❑ Socket 5

C ❑ Slot 1

D ❑ Socket 7

11 How much L1 cache memory does a Pentium II have built in?

A ○ 8K

B ○ 16K

C ○ 32K

D ○ 64K

12 **What sockets do Pentium 4 processors fit into? (Choose two.)**

A ❏ Socket 370
B ❏ Socket 423
C ❏ Socket 478
D ❏ Socket 920

13 **What is the major difference between a Celeron processor and a Pentium 4 processor?**

A ○ The Celeron has more L1 cache memory.
B ○ The Celeron has less L1 cache memory.
C ○ The Celeron has more L2 cache memory.
D ○ The Celeron has less L2 cache memory.

14 **Which of the following CPU characteristics determines how much total memory the system can access?**

A ○ Data bus
B ○ Address bus
C ○ Registers
D ○ Math co-processor

15 **In what chip package type was the Pentium II processor packaged?**

A ○ Slot 1
B ○ PGA
C ○ DIP
D ○ SEC

16 **Which processor is the AMD 64-bit processor designed for laptop systems?**

A ○ Core 2
B ○ Athlon 64
C ○ Phenom II
D ○ Turion 64

17 **What chip type uses a ZIF socket?**

A ○ SEC
B ○ DIP
C ○ PGA
D ○ Socket 5

18 **What is the name of the Intel processor that has four cores?**

A ○ Intel 64 X2
B ○ Intel 64 X4
C ○ Intel Core 2 Quad
D ○ Intel Core 2 Duo

19 **A Pentium 133 runs on what speed motherboard?**

A ○ 60 MHz
B ○ 66 MHz
C ○ 100 MHz
D ○ 133 MHz

20 **What type of cache is integrated into the Pentium processor's chip?**

A ○ L1 cache
B ○ L2 cache
C ○ Integrated cache
D ○ DRAM cache

Answers

1 **C.** Superscalar design is the idea that the processor has more than one instruction pipeline to process application code. Choice B describes a feature called *dynamic execution,* and choice D describes a clock double chip. *See "Pentium."*

2 **D.** The Pentium II chip comes in a package called the Single Edge Contact (SEC) chip package, which fits into Slot 1. Sockets 5 and 7 are used by original Pentiums, and Socket 1 is used by some 80486 chips. *Review "Pentium II."*

3 **B, E.** AMD Athlon, Athlon XP, and the Duron chip are placed in Socket A. *Check out "Don't Forget Non-Intel Chips."*

4 **B.** The original Pentium processor was packaged in the pin grid array (PGA) chip type, which fits into either Socket 5 or Socket 7. Socket 5 and Socket 7 are incorrect choices because they are not chip types; they are the names of sockets. Dual inline package (DIP) is an older type of packaging for processor chips, and SEC is the chip packaging used with Pentium II processors. *Peruse "Pentium."*

5 **B.** Virtual memory is one of the features of protected-mode processors. Choice C describes real-mode processors, the opposite of protected-mode processors. *Take a look at "Real-mode versus protected-mode."*

6 **A.** The Pentium III processor contains 32K of L1 cache. *Peek at "Pentium III."*

7 **C.** Registers are storage areas for information to be processed by the processor. The data bus is the pathway to system memory, the address bus controls how much memory can be recognized by the processor, and the math co-processor performs many of the complicated mathematical operations. *Look over "Registers."*

8 **D.** The Pentium Pro has a 36-bit address bus, which enables it to access 64GB of system memory. The original Pentium processor could address up to 4GB of system memory. *Study "Pentium Pro."*

9 **B.** The math co-processor performs many of the complicated math operations on behalf of the CPU, and the CPU itself performs the logic functions. *Refer to "Math co-processor."*

10 **B, D.** The Pentium processor is placed into either Socket 5 or Socket 7. Pentium II uses Slot 1, and some 486 chips use Socket 1. *Examine "Pentium."*

11 **C.** The Pentium II chip increased the L1 cache to 32K, which is broken into two 16K channels. One channel is used for application code, and one is used for data. 486 chips originally used 8K, and Pentium chips originally used 16K. *See "Pentium II."*

12 **B, C.** Pentium 4 processors have either 423 or 478 pins, so they are placed in either Socket 423 or Socket 478. *Review "Pentium 4."*

13 **D.** The Celeron chip is a cut-price Pentium chip. The L2 cache is decreased to save on cost. Celeron chips either have no L2 cache or 128K cache, and Pentium II, Pentium III, and Pentium 4 chips have 512K of L2 cache. *Check out "Celeron."*

14 **B.** The address bus dictates how much memory the CPU can address. The data bus is the pathway to system memory, and registers are storage areas for data being processed. *Peruse "Address bus."*

15 **D.** The single edge connector (SEC) was used for Pentium II processors. Slot 1 is not a chip package type, but a slot that holds the SEC. Newer processors now use the PGA format. Although DIP chips are no longer used for processors, it is still important to understand what the DIP chip looks like because most BIOS chips come in that format. *Take a look at "Chip packaging."*

16 **D.** The Turion 64 is the AMD 64-bit mobile processor to be used on laptop systems. *Peek at "Turion 64 and Turion 64 X2."*

17 **C.** PGA packaged chips can be placed in ZIF sockets. These sockets have a lever; when the lever is pulled, the processor chip pops out of the socket. *Look over "Chip packaging."*

18 **C.** The Intel Core 2 Quad is the Intel processor with four cores. It is made up of two chips, with each chip having two cores. *Study "Intel Core 2."*

19 **B.** The Pentium 133 is a clock-double processor. It runs twice as fast as the motherboard. Therefore, the motherboard speed is 66 MHz. *Refer to "Pentium."*

20 **A.** L1 cache is integrated into the processor, and L2 cache typically has always resided outside the CPU, usually on the motherboard. DRAM is a type of memory used for RAM. It is not used for cache memory. *Examine "Cache memory."*

Chapter 3: What to Remember about Memory

Exam Objectives
- ✔ Understanding memory terminology
- ✔ Identifying RAM types
- ✔ Understanding DRAM types
- ✔ Working with memory modules
- ✔ Identifying parity and nonparity memory

*F*inding out how much memory a computer has is one popular way to measure that computer's power and capabilities. Think about it: If someone asked you what kind of computer you have, what would you answer? Probably something like, "I have a Pentium 4 with 1 gig of RAM." But why do we measure the power of a computer based on the amount of memory it has?

In this chapter, you discover the purpose of memory and some of the different types of memory found in computers today. This chapter also discusses issues that affect installing memory in personal computers and laptops.

Understanding the Types of Memory

This section outlines different types of computer memory — anything that stores information either permanently or temporarily. Computers have two different flavors of memory: ROM and RAM.

From an exam perspective, make sure you fully understand the different types of memory and their uses because you are sure to see a few questions on memory.

Remembering the purpose of memory

Before you look at the different types of memory, you need to understand the purpose of memory. Think about your desk at home or in the office. Whether sitting at your home or office desk (working on a proposal or preparing for your A+ Certification exam), chances are good that your desk is covered with documents, books, and papers. This desk is your work area, and its size dictates how many documents you can work on at any given time.

System memory works the same way. You have documents and applications stored on the hard drive. When you want to work on these documents, you open them and place them in the computer's work area. The work area (or desk space) for a computer is *system memory*. When you want to work with any application or document, the computer must retrieve that information from the hard drive and execute it from memory.

Assume, for instance, that your computer has 512MB of memory (not a lot in this day and age). You start up your system, which is running Windows XP, and decide to run Microsoft Word and Adobe Photoshop at the same time. Assume that you open two very large files in each application. Assume further that you are using 480MB of precious memory at this point — a few MBs for the operating system (OS) to load, and a few for each running application. As you can see, your memory usage adds up quickly.

In this scenario, you are already using 480MB of memory, which leaves a scant 32MB of memory remaining. Assume that you are about to open up a Photoshop document and copy and paste information from one file to another. To put it simply, you are running out of desk space. You can solve the problem in one of two ways:

✦ **Do less work.** In other words, work in one application at a time. This is not an optimal solution, especially for business users who often need to run multiple applications simultaneously.

✦ **Get a bigger desk.** In computer terminology, install more RAM. When you install more RAM, you have a bigger desk to work on.

Now that you understand the general purpose of memory, it's time to dive into the different types of memory. For the A+ exam, you are required to know many different types of memory, which I outline in the following sections.

Read-only memory (ROM)

ROM is a type of memory that you cannot write to: hence its name, read-only memory. Information is written to ROM chips by the manufacturer, and this information cannot be changed. In the past, if ROM information needed

to be updated, you had to remove the original ROM chip and replace it with an updated ROM chip from the manufacturer. Today, you can update the ROM by running a special software program downloaded from the manufacturer's Web site. In essence, you do not really have a ROM chip but rather have an EEPROM (more on EEPROM in a bit).

Software written to a ROM chip is *firmware*.

One of the major uses for ROM is storing the system BIOS (Basic Input-Output System), which contains Power-on Self-Test (POST) routines and other routines that initiate loading the OS. The BIOS also contains the low-level code that allows the system to communicate with hardware devices.

You need to know that the POST is part of the BIOS code stored in ROM. The POST contains routines that initiate OS loading as well as routines that make communication between hardware devices possible.

EPROM

EPROM (erasable programmable ROM) is a type of memory that normally cannot be written to because it is a variation of ROM. An EPROM chip is a special ROM chip that the manufacturer can reprogram by using a special programming device that uses ultraviolet light.

EEPROM

A newer implementation of ROM is electrically erasable programmable ROM (EEPROM), or flash ROM. The manufacturer writes the software instructions into the ROM chip, but you can update these instructions by running a special software setup program provided by the manufacturer. The software setup program is usually available through the manufacturer's Web site.

EEPROM (better known as flash ROM) is a ROM chip that can be rewritten with special EEPROM update software provided by the manufacturer of the chip.

Using EEPROM has become the typical way to update your BIOS. BIOS code is designed to work with certain hardware. As hardware improves, you need to update your BIOS code so that your system is aware of these hardware improvements. Therefore, the manufacturer places BIOS updates on its Web site to download for computer users running its particular BIOS. You just have to download the BIOS update program and then run the BIOS update on your system. The update rewrites the BIOS instructions, making the computer "more aware" of today's hardware.

Random access memory (RAM)

Of the two flavors of memory (ROM and RAM), RAM is probably the more fundamental. As I mention earlier, ROM is permanent memory, or permanent storage of information. As the computer's primary working memory, though, RAM stores information temporarily. RAM is *volatile,* meaning that it needs constant electrical current to maintain the information that resides in its chips. If the electrical current is lost, RAM contents are erased. Likewise, when a computer is powered off, all RAM contents are flushed out.

The following sections discuss the different types of RAM. On the exam, you can expect a few questions about the different types of memory, so be sure that you are familiar with these different types of RAM.

DRAM

Dynamic RAM (DRAM) is probably the most popular type of memory today and the one that you are most often going to upgrade. When someone says to you, "I have 1024 megs of dynamic RAM," he or she is talking about DRAM.

Dynamic RAM gets its name from the fact that the information stored in DRAM needs to be constantly refreshed. Refreshing involves reading the bits of data stored in DRAM and then rewriting the same information back. *Note:* DRAM is *single-ported:* You can read and write to the memory but not at the same time.

Older implementations of RAM measured the memory's performance based on how long it took the CPU to access that data. This time is measured in nanoseconds (ns; 1 ns equals one-billionth of a second). If you have memory that is 50 ns and your best friend has memory that is 70 ns, your memory is presumably faster. Your CPU receives the information from memory after waiting only 50-billionths of a second, whereas your best friend's CPU waits 70-billionths of a second.

The lower the number of nanoseconds, the better the performance.

The speed of older DRAM ranges from 60 ns to 80 ns. Today's implementations of DRAM measure the speed of memory in megahertz (MHz), typically matching the motherboard speed. For example, my Pentium II system uses 100 MHz memory because it runs on a 100 MHz motherboard.

For more information on the types of DRAM, see the section "Identifying the Types of DRAM," later in this chapter.

SRAM

Static RAM (SRAM) — so-called because the information held in its memory cells doesn't need to be refreshed — requires less overhead than DRAM to maintain the information stored in memory.

With speeds running from 10 ns to 20 ns, SRAM is much faster than DRAM. Because SRAM is faster memory than DRAM, it is also more expensive, which is why people add DRAM to their systems more often than they add SRAM.

SRAM is typically used for *cache memory,* which stores frequently used data and program code after it is read from slower DRAM. Think of cache memory as a bucket that sits beside the CPU and stores frequently used information. After the system has searched through DRAM once for specific information, it can store that information in the bucket for easy access later. The next time the data is requested, it is read from cache instead of from system memory.

Because cache memory is much faster than DRAM, the CPU first tries to retrieve the information from cache: specifically, L1 cache first and then L2 cache. If the information is not located in cache, the system then tries to retrieve the information from memory. If the information is not located in system memory, it then is retrieved from disk. Attempting to retrieve the requested information from cache first reduces wait time if the information actually resides there because of how fast cache is compared with DRAM.

Cache memory (SRAM) stores frequently used data and program code. Because cache memory is faster than DRAM, retrieving information from cache means that the processor does not have to wait for the slower DRAM, thus enhancing system performance.

CMOS RAM

The *complementary metal-oxide semiconductor (CMOS)* is the area where the computer stores its configuration information, such as whether the computer has a floppy drive, the amount of memory installed, the date and time for the system, and the number and size of the hard drives that are installed. Think of CMOS information as an inventory list for the majority of components that are installed on the computer. For more information on CMOS, see Book II, Chapter 4.

Where is CMOS information stored? Is CMOS information stored on the BIOS chip, or perhaps another ROM chip? The answer is neither. In fact, if the information were stored on a ROM chip, you wouldn't be able to go into the CMOS setup program and change the configuration. Instead, CMOS configuration information is stored in a type of RAM called *CMOS RAM.*

CMOS RAM is a special, volatile RAM chip that stores the CMOS information. If power is lost, the information is wiped out. This could present a problem with regard to CMOS configuration because if CMOS RAM is wiped out, the computer forgets its inventory information and has to relearn it. To prevent this problem, computers have a small battery on their motherboards that maintains enough of a charge to prevent CMOS RAM from losing its data.

CMOS information is stored in CMOS RAM, which is volatile memory that maintains its information by using a battery stored on the system board.

Shadow RAM

Part of the boot process involves copying some of the BIOS instructions from ROM to RAM and then executing those instructions from RAM rather than from the ROM chip. Why? Because ROM is much slower than RAM, performance speed increases when executing the instructions from RAM instead of ROM. The process in which a copy of the BIOS instructions is shadowed, or copied, to an area of memory called "shadow RAM" is *shadowing*.

VRAM

Video RAM (VRAM) is most commonly used on video accelerator cards to store values of pixels onscreen for refresh purposes. VRAM is the favored memory for video because it outperforms the other memory types because it is dual-ported memory: that is, it can be read from and written to at the same time. Comparatively, DRAM is *single-ported,* which means that the memory can be written to and read from, but not simultaneously — only one direction at a time. VRAM, however, allows you to do both simultaneously.

WRAM

Window RAM (WRAM), also known as "Window accelerator card RAM," is a modification of VRAM and is also used for video display purposes. Like VRAM, WRAM is dual-ported memory but runs about 25% faster. In general, WRAM offers better performance than VRAM.

Identifying the Types of DRAM

DRAM is the most popular type of memory used in systems today. It is also the most popular type of memory that computer users add to their computers when upgrading memory. Therefore, you must understand the different types of DRAM and what types of DRAM outperform others.

Standard DRAM

Memory is organized into rows and columns, like a spreadsheet. Information is stored in the different cells, or blocks, that are created by the intersection of these rows and columns. With standard DRAM, the CPU requests data from the memory controller by sending the address of the row and the address of the column for every block of data that needs to be read. The memory controller then fetches the information from that memory location. Figure 3-1 shows two memory cells that hold data that the CPU wants to have.

Figure 3-1: Looking at how data is accessed in memory.

To access the information shown in Figure 3-1, the CPU follows these basic steps to request information from standard DRAM:

1. In the first clock cycle, it sends the row address (1).
2. In the second clock cycle, it sends the column address (2).
3. On the third clock cycle, the memory controller reads the information (Address 1-2).
4. In the fourth clock cycle, the row address for the second memory cell is given (1).
5. In the fifth clock cycle, the column address for the second memory cell is given (4).
6. In the sixth clock cycle, the second memory cell is read (Address 1-4).

Fast page mode

Fast page mode (FPM) improves the performance of standard DRAM by not requiring a row address for each request to memory, assuming that the next block of data is on the same row (which in most cases will be true). The following step list outlines the basic steps to access the same two blocks of data shown in Figure 3-1 via FPM memory:

1. In the first clock cycle, the CPU sends the row address (1).

2. In the second clock cycle, it sends the column address (2).

3. On the third clock cycle, the memory controller reads the information (Address 1-2).

4. In the fourth clock cycle, the column address is given (4).

5. In the fifth clock cycle, the second cell address is read (Address 1-4).

You can see in this example that it takes less time to read both blocks of data from memory with FPM DRAM. Therefore, FPM memory is a faster DRAM memory type than standard.

Extended data output

Extended data output (EDO) memory is about 10 to 15% faster than FPM memory and is usually found on 66 MHz motherboards. With EDO memory, the memory controller can read data from a memory block while listening for the next instruction. This capability increases performance because the memory controller does not have to wait for the next instruction after reading a block of memory; while it is reading one block of memory, it is receiving the next instruction. In contrast, with FPM DRAM, reading one memory block and listening for the next instruction are done in multiple steps.

Burst extended data output

Burst extended data output (BEDO) is a bursting-type technology. The word "burst" refers to the fact that when one memory address is requested and that address is retrieved, the system bursts into the next couple of blocks and reads those as well. The theory behind BEDO is that the system has already gone through the trouble of locating that block, and chances are that the next request will be for the next block, so why not take that information while the memory controller is already there? If that extra block is the next requested block from the CPU, the memory controller already has the data and can pass it to the CPU immediately.

BEDO is 50% faster than EDO. Because of lack of support from computer manufacturers, however, BEDO has not been used in many systems. It has been surpassed by SDRAM instead.

Synchronous DRAM

Synchronous DRAM (SDRAM) is memory synchronized to the system board speed. This synchronized speed means that the data stored in memory is refreshed at the system speed, and data is accessed in memory at the system speed as well.

SDRAM is one of the most popular types of DRAM found in earlier Pentium systems, such as the Pentium II. When you upgrade memory on your system and you determine that you need SDRAM, you then need to determine what speed of SDRAM. Because you are running at the system speed, you must match the DRAM speed with the motherboard speed. Thus, if you have a 100 MHz motherboard, you need 100 MHz SDRAM. If you have a 133 MHz motherboard, you need 133 MHz SDRAM.

As I mention, for a 100 MHz motherboard, purchase 100 MHz memory, which is typically labeled PC100. Be aware, however, that there is some flexibility when purchasing SDRAM. For example, I have a 100 MHz motherboard on an old Pentium II system. When I upgraded the DRAM on this system, I couldn't buy PC100 memory because PC133 (which is SDRAM that runs at 133 MHz) was the popular memory at that time. Not a problem! You can use faster memory than your motherboard speed as long as you are willing to accept that you have paid for memory that will not run to its full potential speed. In my example, the 133 MHz memory runs at only 100 MHz because of the speed limitations of the motherboard.

Rambus DRAM

When SDRAM was popular, a high-speed flavor of DRAM was on the market — *rambus DRAM* (RDRAM) — which runs at speeds around 800 MHz! RDRAM chips have a 16-bit internal bus width and are packaged together in a 184-pin, gold-plated memory module called a *rambus inline memory module* (RIMM). To take advantage of this type of memory, you need a motherboard and chipset that support RDRAM. Due to the cost of RDRAM, it lost the popularity contest to SDRAM and eventually DDR memory.

DDR

Double data rate (DDR) memory gets its name from the fact that it can transfer data twice during each clock cycle, compared with SDRAM that can transfer data only once per clock cycle. DDR memory ships in 184-pin DIMM modules (see the section "DIMMs," later in this chapter) for desktop computers and 200-pin SODIMMs for laptop systems.

DDR memory speed is measured in MHz, like SDRAM is, and is labeled to indicate the speed. DDR memory labeling might look obscure at first because it also indicates the bandwidth by taking the speed and multiplying it by 8 bytes of data (64 bits). Here's how to read DDR memory labeled as PC1600: Divide the 1600 by 8 bytes to get the speed of the memory. In this case, you are looking at 200 MHz memory. PC2700 runs at 333 MHz, and PC3200 runs at 400 MHz. When you upgrade memory on systems that require DDR memory, you need to know the speed of the DDR memory.

DDR2 and DDR3

Improvements to DDR memory have already started with DDR2 memory. *DDR2* memory runs at speeds 400 MHz and higher, which is where DDR memory left off. DDR2 memory uses 240-pin memory modules and runs at 1.8 volts (V), as opposed to 2.5V for DDR memory. This results in less power consumption for more memory, which is great for laptop users.

Popular modules of DDR2 memory are PC3200 (400 MHz), PC4200 (533 MHz), PC5300 (666 MHz), and PC6400 (800 MHz).

The newer form of DDR memory is DDR3, which offers twice the data rate of DDR2 memory. One of the goals of DDR3 memory is to reduce power consumption; reportedly, DDR3 memory reduces power consumption by about 30%.

DDR memory modules are 240-pin DIMMs for desktop PCs and 204-pin SODIMMs for laptop systems. (Read more on DIMMS and SODIMMs in the next section.) Like DDR2, DDR3 memory is advertised by the speed and transfer rate. For example, DDR3-800 (also known as PC3-6400) is 800 MHz memory that has a throughput of 6400 MBps. DDR3-1066 (also known as PC3-8500) memory has a throughput of 8533 MBps. Another example is DDR3-1600, which is 1600 MHz memory with a transfer rate of 12800 MBps.

How Would You Like Your Chips Packaged?

Whether you are purchasing or installing RAM, understanding the different types of memory packages available is important. The following sections identify different memory packages used in desktop computers and laptop systems.

SIMMs

Single inline memory modules (SIMMs) used to be one of the most popular types of memory modules, but they have been replaced by DIMMs (see the next section). A *SIMM* card holds a number of memory chips and has an edge connector containing a number of pins that make contact with the motherboard. This design makes it quite a bit easier to install memory than it was many years ago. In the past, you had to take a dual inline package (DIP) chip out of the system board and reinsert a new chip. Today, you purchase a card of chips (a SIMM) and install the SIMM into one of the SIMM sockets.

SIMMs come in two flavors — 30-pin and 72-pin — which describe the number of connectors that make contact with the motherboard. Before buying a SIMM, review the documentation for the computer or look at the system board to determine what size SIMM module you need. Figure 3-2 shows a 30-pin SIMM, a 72-pin SIMM, and a 168-pin dual inline memory module (DIMM).

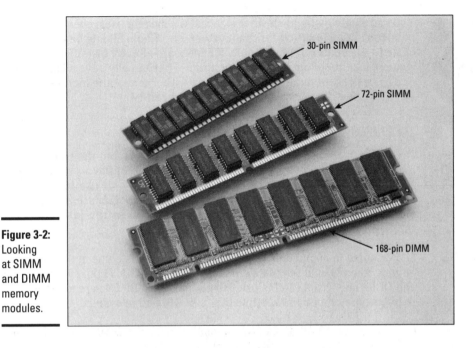

Figure 3-2:
Looking
at SIMM
and DIMM
memory
modules.

The 30-pin SIMMs have an 8-bit data path, meaning they supply information in 8-bit blocks. When installing memory into a system, you *must* install enough SIMMs to fill a memory bank. A *memory bank* is the number of SIMMs it takes to fill the data path of the processor. For example, if you have a system with a 486 processor, the processor is a 32-bit processor. Therefore, the processor wants to deal with information in 32-bit chunks. When using 30-pin SIMMs, you need to install four of them at a time to fill a memory bank because each 30-pin SIMM supplies only 8 bits of data (8 bits × 4 SIMMs = 32-bit chunks).

The 72-pin SIMMs supply information in 32-bit chunks. Therefore, if you are installing 72-pin SIMMs on a system using a 32-bit 486 chip, you need just one SIMM to fill a memory bank and the data path. If you are installing 72-pin SIMMs in a Pentium system, you must install SIMMs in pairs because the Pentium data path is 64-bit; to fill a bank on these systems, you need two 32-bit modules (72-pin SIMMs).

Remember the data path of the SIMM modules. You should also know how many SIMMs it takes to fill a memory bank on different systems. Remember that a memory bank is the number of memory slots needed to fill the data path of the processor.

In this day and age, you most likely will not see SIMMs in a system unless you are supporting older computers. If you see a system that uses SIMMs, it most likely conforms to the 72-pin format.

You can easily distinguish what size SIMM a system uses, even if you don't have the documentation for that system. The 72-pin SIMMs have a notch close to the center of the module. If SIMMs are already installed in the system, take them out and examine them. They usually have a label with a 1 or a 72, representing the pin numbers, at either end of the module. If you see a number 72, you know you have a 72-pin SIMM.

DIMMs

Dual inline memory modules (DIMMs) are like SIMMs, but they supply information in 64-bit chunks. DIMMs come in different flavors that have a different number of pins on the modules. Older DIMMs use 168 pins for SDRAM and 184 pins for DDR memory; and newer DIMMs use 240 pin modules for DDR2 and DDR3 memory. DIMM modules are a little larger than the 72-pin SIMMs. (Refer to Figure 3-2.)

SIMMs come in 30-pin and 72-pin flavors, but DIMMs come in different flavors. The original DIMMs were 168 pins. DDR DIMMs come with 184 pins, and DDR2 and DDR3 DIMMs use 240-pin modules. DIMMs are also the most popular type of memory module that you will find in systems today.

Consider the memory bank issue again. Because the DIMM supplies data in 64-bit chunks and the data path of a Pentium processor is 64 bit, you can install DIMMs singly in a Pentium system. On the other hand, you must install SIMMs in pairs in a Pentium system. Figure 3-3 shows what 72-pin SIMM and 168-pin DIMM sockets look like.

SODIMM

Small outline dual inline memory modules (SODIMMs) are memory modules that are smaller than normal DIMMs and are used in laptops. A SODIMM comes in three different-sized modules: a 32-bit 72-pin module; a 64-bit 144-pin module (SDRAM); and a 64-bit 200-pin module for DDR and DDR2 laptop memory. Figure 3-4 compares a SODIMM and a DIMM.

MicroDIMM

A *micro dual inline memory module* (MicroDIMM) is another memory module used in laptop computers. The MicroDIMM is smaller than the SODIMM and comes in a 144-pin module for SDRAM and a 172-pin module for DDR memory.

Four 72-pin
SIMM slots

Two 168-pin
DIMM slots

Figure 3-3:
Looking at
memory
sockets on
a mother-
board.

SODIMM DIMM

Figure 3-4:
Comparing
a SODIMM
and a
DIMM.

Understanding Error-Checking Memory

Two primary types of error-checking memory have been used in systems over the years. The following sections introduce you to these two types of error-checking memory. Be sure to become familiar with them for the exam.

Parity versus nonparity

Parity memory is a type of error-checking memory, which is memory that verifies the information stored in memory is what is actually read from memory at a later time. *Nonparity memory,* comparatively, is memory that does not perform any kind of error checking to ensure that the data written to memory is what is actually read when it is retrieved.

Here's how parity memory works. The two types of parity memory are odd and even. Both parity methods function the same way but differ in the sense of whether they look for an odd number of bits or an even number of bits. This discussion uses odd parity as the example.

With parity memory, for every byte (8 bits) of data written to memory, there is an additional ninth bit — the parity bit. When storing information to memory, the number of the enabled data bits (bits set to 1) written to memory are added up.

With odd parity, if an even number of data bits are enabled, the parity bit is set to 1 (enabled) so that there is an odd number of enabled bits in total written to memory. If the result of all the enabled data bits is odd, the parity bit is set to 0 (disabled) so that the odd number of enabled bits is retained.

After the parity bit has been set, the byte of data and the parity bit are written to memory. Even parity works the same way except that it looks for an even number of enabled bits; if the number of enabled bits is odd, the parity bit is enabled.

When the CPU requests data from memory, the data byte is retrieved along with the parity bit that was generated when the byte of information was stored in memory. The system looks at the data byte and calculates whether the parity bit stored in memory should be set to 1 or 0. It then compares the answer it has just generated with the value of the parity bit stored in memory. If the two match, the integrity of the information in memory is considered okay, the parity bit is stripped from the data byte, and the data is delivered to the CPU. If the two differ, you have a *parity error,* meaning that there is a problem with the integrity of the data stored in memory.

Parity memory cannot correct the error; it just reports that an error exists.

Parity memory has an extra bit (the parity bit) for every 8 bits of data. SIMMs with parity come in 9-bit (30-pin SIMM) or 36-bit (72-pin SIMM) flavors. Also, remember that a parity error indicates something wrong with the integrity of data stored in memory.

ECC memory

Error-checking and correction (ECC) memory is memory that can detect data integrity problems the way that parity memory can. (See the preceding section.) The difference between the two is that ECC memory can recover from the error and attempt to fix the problem with the data being read, whereas parity memory cannot.

Single Channel Versus Dual Channel

When installing memory today, you can install memory modules into a dual-channel configuration versus a single-channel configuration. A *single-channel configuration* (used for years) mandates a "single lane" used to send and receive information from memory.

With some of today's systems, though, you can install memory in a *dual-channel configuration,* which allows for two lanes to carry information to and from memory at the same time. This configuration increases overall performance by allowing for more input/output per operation, or clock cycle.

To take advantage of dual-channel memory, you first need to ensure that your motherboard supports dual channel. Dual-channel memory is a function of the memory controller. If your motherboard supports dual-channel memory, you will install the memory modules in pairs. For example, when installing 1GB of RAM, you install two 512MB modules. When you install these modules, install them into the same color slots on the motherboard. If the motherboard does not color-code the memory slots, you install the pair of memory modules in the odd-numbered slots or the even-numbered slots — but not an odd and an even.

To leverage-dual channel memory, you must install the same memory modules in pairs. You must use the same type (for example, DDR2 or DDR3) of memory for both modules and the same speed. The two modules must be able to keep up with one another when performing parallel IO.

You can purchase dual-channel memory kits to ensure that you are using the same type of memory and the same speed. You do not need to use these kits, but you are paying for the fact that someone has already tested the memory in a dual-channel configuration. Some benchmarks report that you

can achieve a 65% increase in memory performance by using a dual-channel configuration. You can use a program called CPU-Z (www.cpuid.com/cpuz.php) to check to see whether you are running your memory in a dual-channel configuration.

Single Sided Versus Double Sided

Memory modules are either single-sided or double-sided memory modules, but this characteristic does not mean that the memory chips exist on only one side of the memory card or both sides of the memory card (which is what most people think).

For *single-sided memory,* all the memory on the memory module is accessed at once by the system and is treated as a single "bank" of memory. It is important to note that the memory chips on a single-sided memory module may exist on both sides of the memory board.

For double-sided memory, the memory module (or memory board) is divided into two discrete chunks of memory (banks).The system can access only one bank at a time. Original double-sided memory modules were created by taking two single-sided memory modules and connecting them.

Working with Cache Memory

Cache memory stores frequently used data and program code after it is read from slower DRAM. Cache memory is made up of SRAM, which is much faster than DRAM. The average speed of DRAM is 60 ns, whereas the average speed of SRAM is 20 ns. If at all possible, you want the CPU's request for information to be serviced by cache memory for a quicker response. To help service these responses, the system has two major levels of cache memory: L1 and L2, which are popular; and also L3 cache, which is making its way on systems today.

L1 cache

Level 1 (L1) cache is "internal cache" integrated into the CPU. This memory is typically a small amount of SRAM integrated into the processor's chip, giving the processor instant access to this memory with no wait time. *Wait time* is how long it takes between when the processor requests information stored in memory and it actually receives that information.

Every pre-Pentium processor has L1 cache integrated into the processor chip, but the amount of L1 cache can vary. For example, the 486 chips had 8K of L1 cache, whereas the early Pentium processors had 16K of L1 cache. Newer processors have doubled that amount to 32K of L1 cache.

L2 cache

Level 2 (L2) cache exists outside the CPU, usually on the motherboard or just outside the processor but in the processor casing. Therefore, some delay occurs when the processor accesses the information in L2 cache because of the distance between the processor and the L2 cache.

L1 cache is SRAM integrated into the processor's chip, whereas L2 cache is SRAM located outside the CPU, usually on the system board or in the casing of the processor.

One of the selling points of different processors is the amount of cache memory that comes with the processor. Many processors today typically have at least 32K of L1 cache and 512K, 1MB, or 2MB of L2 cache inside the casing of the processor. The more cache memory a system has, the bigger the bucket to store more frequently used information.

When the processor retrieves information, it first checks whether the information it needs is stored in L1 cache (because L1 cache has no wait time). If the processor does not find the information in L1 cache, it checks L2 cache. If the information cannot be found in either L1 or L2 cache, the processor finally retrieves the information from RAM. Figure 3-5 shows the steps the processor takes to retrieve information.

Book II
Chapter 3

What to Remember about Memory

Figure 3-5: How the CPU retrieves information from memory.

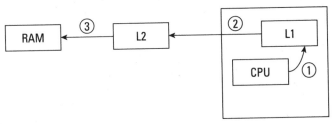

L3 cache

Because processors today provide a small amount of L1 cache *and* a large amount of L2 cache, some people are now using the term *L3 cache* to identify cache that resides on the motherboard.

If you are confused by L3 cache, I can see why — the terminology changed on you. In the past, L2 cache resided on the motherboard. However, now that processors include L2 cache on the CPU, the term for cache memory located on the motherboard is L3 cache!

Installing or Upgrading Memory

The discussion in this section focuses on issues related to memory upgrades. In general, upgrading memory is a simple task — assuming you purchase the proper type of memory for the upgrade. Factors that affect the proper type of memory are

+ Type of memory (FPM, EDO, SDRAM, DDR)
+ The speed of the memory
+ Pin connector type
+ Parity versus nonparity

The following sections discuss each of the factors that affect how you upgrade your system's memory.

Type of memory

The first thing you need to know to upgrade your computer's memory is which type of memory you need. You need to figure out whether you need to install a SIMM, DIMM, or SODIMM. Pentium II and later desktop computers usually need a DIMM; laptops use a SODIMM.

After you determine the memory module type, you need to determine the type of memory to install, such as SDRAM or DDR memory.

Speed

When you buy memory, you need to take into account the speed of the memory. Older memory, such as FPM or EDO memory, is typically measured in nanoseconds (ns) and ranges from 60 ns to 80 ns. With these types of memory, it is important not to mix speeds lest the system become unreliable. The speed of a SIMM is usually indicated on the chips themselves (displaying either a numeric value or a simple minus sign with a number). For example, a memory module running at 70 ns would show either 70 or –7 on the chips.

The speed of newer memory types, such as DIMMs and SODIMMs, is measured in MHz. When buying SDRAM or DDR memory, make sure to verify that you get the correct memory speed. For example, I recently upgraded the memory in the laptop I'm using to write this book. When I went to the store to buy a memory module, the first questions the in-store computer geeks asked were, "What type of memory?" and "What speed?" The system documentation can help you determine the speed of memory needed. If you don't have the documentation, be sure to look up the information on the manufacturer's Web site.

Connectors

Another important issue with regard to memory installation is with the metal used on the memory modules. You need to purchase memory modules that use pins plated with the same metal used in the memory socket on the motherboard. Memory modules use silver- or gold-plated pins. If the SIMM socket, for example, uses silver-plated connectors, the memory module you purchase must use silver-plated pins. If you mix metal types, you will eventually have an unstable system.

Today's preferred memory modules are gold-plated DIMM modules. Do not assume that you are using gold-plated DIMMs. Always ensure that you are installing the correct type of memory by checking the documentation for your system.

Using parity or nonparity?

The final issue with regard to memory upgrades is whether the system uses parity or nonparity memory. This information can be determined by checking the documentation that came with the system or by checking the system summary in CMOS. If you cannot find the information in CMOS or you misplace the documentation, try to find the information on the Internet at the vendor's Web site.

When you locate the information, use Table 3-1 to record the type of memory your system has so that you may refer to this when you perform a memory upgrade.

Table 3-1	Identifying Memory Used by Your System
Memory Type (SDRAM, DDR, DDR2, DDR3)	
Memory Speed (60 ns, 100MHz, 200MHz, 800MHz)	
Gold or Silver pins	
SIMM, DIMM, or SODIMM	

Installing memory on desktop PCs

After you purchase the correct type of memory — meaning the correct type at the correct speed with the correct number of pins — you are ready to install the memory.

Take off the computer's cover. You should see either SIMM sockets or DIMM sockets — and maybe even both types on an older system.

Look at the sockets and determine whether the memory modules will sit diagonally or vertically. This step is very important. I have seen many people struggle to install memory because they didn't understand how to correctly place the modules in the sockets.

If the socket is on a diagonal, lightly place the memory module vertically and then lay it back diagonally; it should just snap in. If the socket is vertical, place the memory module at a 45-degree angle and lightly lay it back to the vertical position; it should snap in. Figure 3-6 shows the installation of memory modules.

Figure 3-6:
Installing memory modules on a system board.

When you install the memory module, make sure you line up pin 1 on the memory module with pin 1 in the socket. To locate pin 1 on a SIMM, look for the cutout on the memory module (shown in Figure 3-7) and place it over the shoulder of the SIMM socket.

To locate pin 1 on a DIMM, simply look at the memory module; the pins are labeled. The DIMM cannot be placed in backward because it is *keyed* (with cutouts so that the memory can be inserted only one way). When installing the DIMMs, push down firmly on the module to place the DIMM deep in the socket.

Lab 3-1 and Lab 3-2 can be found in the Labs.pdf file in the Author directory of the CD-ROM. Use Lab 3-1 to practice finding out what type of memory you have; Lab 3-2 gives you practice installing memory on a desktop system.

Figure 3-7:
Locating
pin 1 on
a SIMM
memory
module.

Installing memory on laptop systems

Installing memory on today's laptop systems is just as easy as installing memory on a desktop PC. The first step is to make sure you buy the correct type of memory for the laptop. Again, check the laptop documentation before heading to the store!

To install your memory, flip the laptop over. You'll notice a door on the bottom of the laptop that can be removed (shown in Figure 3-8). This is where you add memory.

After the cover is removed, you can insert the SODIMM into an empty slot by lightly placing the SODIMM into the memory slot on a slight angle and then clamping it back into place, as shown in Figure 3-9. If you are replacing memory, first remove the old memory module by pressing on the clips on the side and then lifting out the old memory.

When you have the SODIMM locked in place, put the cover back on.

Use Lab 3-3 for practice finding out what type of memory is needed by a specific laptop. In this lab, you research the laptop on the Internet. Lab 3-3 can be found in the `Labs.pdf` file in the Author directory of the CD-ROM.

Figure 3-8:
Remove the
cover to add
memory to a
laptop.

Figure 3-9:
Inserting the
SODIMM
module into
the memory
slot.

Getting an A+

This chapter provides an overview of the different types of memory and installation of memory. The following points are touched on:

✦ *Read-only memory* (ROM) is memory that can be read from but not written to, and the information stored there is permanent.

✦ *Random access memory* (RAM) is volatile memory that can be written to and read from; information stored there is flushed out when power is lost.

✦ *Dynamic RAM* (DRAM) is memory that needs constant refreshing of its memory cells; it is also the type of memory that is typically upgraded on systems.

✦ *Static RAM* (SRAM) is static memory, meaning that it does not need refreshing as often as DRAM does. SRAM is also faster than DRAM. SRAM is typically used for cache memory.

✦ *L1 cache* is cache memory integrated into the processor, whereas *L2 and L3 cache* is cache memory that exists outside the processor's chip.

✦ Memory is installed with *memory modules.* Whereas 72-pin SIMMs were popular in original Pentium systems, DIMMs are now the popular memory module for desktop systems. Laptops use SODIMMs as their memory module type.

✦ You need to know the *type of memory* your system uses before you upgrade your system. For example, you need to note whether your system uses SDRAM or DDR memory. Also be sure to note the speed of the memory.

Prep Test

1 Which of the following types of memory is used for cache memory?

- A ○ SRAM
- B ○ DRAM
- C ○ EDO RAM
- D ○ SDRAM

2 How many bits make up the data path of a 30-pin SIMM?

- A ○ 12
- B ○ 8
- C ○ 32
- D ○ 64

3 Which type of cache memory resides on the system board?

- A ○ L1 cache
- B ○ DDR
- C ○ L2 cache
- D ○ SDRAM

4 Which type of memory must be constantly refreshed?

- A ○ DRAM
- B ○ SRAM
- C ○ VRAM
- D ○ L1 cache

5 Which type of memory is dual-ported (can read from and written to at the same time)?

- A ○ VRAM
- B ○ DRAM
- C ○ SRAM
- D ○ L1 cache

6 Of the following, which is the fastest memory?

- A ○ 30 ns
- B ○ 10 ns
- C ○ 120 ns
- D ○ 70 ns

7 How many 72-pin SIMMs make up a memory bank on a Pentium system?

A ○ 3
B ○ 1
C ○ 2
D ○ 4

8 How many pins does a DIMM have? (Select all that apply.)

A ○ 64
B ○ 128
C ○ 168
D ○ 32
E ○ 184
F ○ 196
G ○ 240

9 How many bits of parity information are found in a 72-pin SIMM?

A ○ 1
B ○ 2
C ○ 3
D ○ 4

10 If memory data is corrupted, what type of error is created?

A ○ File access error
B ○ Parity error
C ○ Disk error
D ○ DRAM error

11 When installing SIMM memory, what do you look for to identify Pin 1 on the memory module?

A ○ Square solders
B ○ Red ribbon wire
C ○ Blue ribbon wire
D ○ SIMM cutout

12 Which of the following best describes VRAM?

A ○ Memory that has video instructions burned to it by the manufacturer and that cannot be changed
B ○ Dual-ported memory usually found on video accelerator cards
C ○ Memory stored in the CPU and used for storing frequently used instructions
D ○ Memory that has video instructions burned to it by the manufacturer and that can be reprogrammed only by using special software

13 What type of memory is typically used for storing computer BIOS code?

A ○ DRAM

B ○ SRAM

C ○ RAM

D ○ ROM

14 Which of the following best describes shadow RAM?

A ○ An area of system memory where some of the BIOS functions are copied during the boot process

B ○ An area of system memory that stores the information twice so that if the system crashes there will be a backup copy

C ○ The process of having frequently used data stored in cache for quicker access

D ○ The same thing as SRAM

15 How many 30-pin SIMMs are required to fill a memory bank on an 80486 processor?

A ○ 1

B ○ 2

C ○ 3

D ○ 4

16 Which type of DRAM is synchronized with the system clock?

A ○ EDO

B ○ BEDO

C ○ FPM

D ○ SDRAM

17 How many DIMMs are used to fill a memory bank in a Pentium III system?

A ○ 1

B ○ 2

C ○ 3

D ○ 4

18 When a CPU needs to access data, where will it look for this data first?

A ○ L2 cache

B ○ RAM

C ○ L1 cache

D ○ ROM

19 **Which of the following best describes odd parity memory?**

A ○ When a byte of data is stored, the values of all bits in the byte are added; if the number is even, the parity bit is enabled to create an odd number. If all bits in the data byte total an odd number, the parity bit is turned off, leaving the total an odd number.

B ○ All data stored in memory is added; the answer is then stored in the parity bit.

C ○ When a byte of data is stored, the values of all bits in the byte are added; if the number is odd, the parity bit is enabled to create an even number. If all bits in the data byte total an even number, the parity bit is turned off, leaving the total an even number.

D ○ Every 8 bits of data are added, and the total is stored in the parity bit for that particular 8 bits of data.

20 **What is the purpose of CMOS RAM?**

A ○ On system boot, the contents of the BIOS are copied to faster CMOS RAM.

B ○ CMOS RAM is memory used to store the CMOS information. CMOS RAM maintains its information by using a battery found on the motherboard.

C ○ CMOS RAM is the amount of memory that is registered into CMOS.

D ○ CMOS RAM is read-only memory that stores CMOS information.

Answers

1 **A.** SRAM is used for cache memory. DRAM — known as system memory — stores data and program code that are running. EDO and SDRAM are types of DRAM. *See "SRAM."*

2 **B.** A 30-pin SIMM has an 8-bit data path. 72-pin SIMMs have a 32-bit data path, and a DIMM has a 64-bit data path. *Review "SIMMs."*

3 **C.** L2 cache memory is external to the CPU. This is the memory inserted onto the system board as additional cache memory. L1 cache is cache memory integrated into the CPU. *Check out "L2 cache."*

4 **A.** DRAM must be constantly refreshed. Other types of memory do have to be refreshed but not as often as DRAM. *Peruse "DRAM."*

5 **A.** VRAM, or video RAM, is dual-ported memory that can read from and written to at the same time. Because of the performance increase with this type of memory, it is the desired memory for video accelerator cards. The other types of memory are single-ported, which means that you have to read and write through the same port and can only go one way at a time. As a result, the memory is slower than VRAM. *Take a look at "VRAM."*

6 **B.** With nanoseconds (ns), the lower the number, the faster. Because it is measured in billionths of a second and determines how long it takes the system to access the information stored in memory, 10 ns is faster than the other choices. *See "DRAM."*

7 **C.** 72-pin SIMMs are 32-bit modules. Because Pentium processors have a 64-bit data path, you need two 72-pin SIMMs to fill the data path. *Look over "SIMMs."*

8 **C, E, G.** DIMMs come in different flavors: 168-pin (for SDRAM), 184-pin (DDR), or 240-pin (DDR2 and DDR3) memory modules. The other choices for this question are just common numbers used in the computer field, but there are no memory modules that use those numbers of pins. *Study "DIMMs."*

9 **D.** There is always 1 parity bit for every 8 bits of data. Because a 72-pin SIMM is a 32-bit module, it is made up of four 8-bit chunks, so it will have 4 parity bits. *Refer to "Parity versus nonparity."*

10 **B.** You'll receive a parity error if there are any problems with data stored in memory. *Examine "Parity versus nonparity."*

11 **D.** When looking at the memory module, you will notice that one side of the module is cut out. This indicates where pin 1 is located on the module. There are no ribbon wires on a memory module. *See "Installing memory on desktop PCs."*

12 **B.** VRAM is dual-ported video RAM, meaning that the memory can be written to on one port and read from on another port that is usually found on video accelerator cards. *Review "VRAM."*

13 **D.** A computer manufacturer's BIOS code is typically stored on read-only memory. Today's version of the BIOS chip can be reprogrammed by running special software to update the BIOS. *Check out "Read-only memory (ROM)."*

14 **A.** The term *shadowing* implies "making a copy" — more specifically, copying the BIOS instructions to system memory so that the functions can be executed more quickly. *Peruse "Shadow RAM."*

15 **D.** It takes four 30-pin SIMMs to fill a bank in any 486 processor because 30-pin SIMMs are only 8 bits wide, and a 486 processor's data path is 32-bit. A memory bank's data path should be the same as a processor's data path. If the SIMMs had 72 pins, you would need only one module because 72-pin SIMMs have a 32-bit data path, the same as a 486 chip. *Take a look at "L1 cache."*

16 **D.** SDRAM memory is synchronized with the system clock speed. If the motherboard runs at 100 MHz, you must buy the same speed memory for the board. *Peek at "Synchronous DRAM."*

17 **A.** Pentium IIIs have 64-bit data paths, and a DIMM has a 64-bit data path as well. Thus, you need only one DIMM chip to fill a bank in a Pentium system. *Look over "DIMMs."*

18 **C.** The CPU checks the L1 cache first because it is SRAM memory integrated into the chip and has no wait time. If the data is not in the L1 cache, the system checks the L2 cache, which is cache memory located outside the chip, usually on the motherboard. If the data is not in the L2 cache, the CPU checks in RAM. If the information is not found in RAM, it is then read from disk. *Study "SRAM."*

19 **A.** Odd parity memory stores a parity bit for every byte of data. The parity bit is enabled (set to 1) if the data bits total an even number, and is disabled (set to 0) if the data bits total an odd number. *Refer to "Parity versus nonparity."*

20 **B.** CMOS RAM is a small amount of memory that maintains the CMOS configuration information. Because this information is stored in a type of RAM, the memory has to have constant power; this power comes from the battery found on the system board. Choice A describes shadow RAM. *Examine "CMOS RAM."*

Chapter 4: Telling Your BIOS from Your CMOS

Exam Objectives

✔ Identifying the purpose of BIOS

✔ Upgrading a system BIOS

✔ Identifying the purpose of CMOS

✔ Identifying common settings contained in CMOS

A big part of system configuration is understanding what CMOS is and how the different settings within CMOS can help you troubleshoot a system. A wonderful talent to have as an A+ Certified Professional is the ability to understand CMOS and its functionality. Although CMOS doesn't seem like a place where you'd need to go every day, many PC-related problems can be solved in CMOS.

In this chapter, I introduce you to some of the common CMOS options that are found in modern systems. Keep in mind that these options might be labeled differently on your system or might not even exist on your system. The CMOS setup program is unique to each system. For example, the CMOS setup program on a Compaq system differs from that of a Dell even though the concept of CMOS remains the same.

In this chapter, I also make you aware of popular CMOS settings so that when a scenario arises that calls for such a change, you are comfortable with not only what you need to do but also how to do it.

The BIOS and Its Purpose

I can't start a discussion on CMOS without first comparing it against the system BIOS; the two are closely related and are often confused by many IT professionals.

BIOS — basic input-output system — is the low-level instructions used to communicate with the system devices. This is different than *CMOS* (complementary metal-oxide semiconductor), which is simply an inventory list for the system, containing information such as the hard drive space and amount of memory that exists on the system. CMOS is the inventory list; BIOS is the actual code that is run to communicate with those devices.

Originally, the BIOS was stored in a ROM chip on the motherboard. Because of this, you used to have to replace the entire chip with a new chip to update the BIOS. Today's systems, however, have the BIOS code stored in an EEPROM (electronically erasable programmable read-only memory) chip located on the motherboard. (For more information on ROM and EEPROM, check out the memory topic in Chapter 3 of this minibook.) The chip that contains the BIOS code is the *BIOS chip.* The BIOS chip should be easy to find — it's usually rectangular and clearly labeled, typically with the name of the manufacturer of the BIOS chip and the date when the chip was created. In Figure 4-1, the BIOS chip is the chip with the white label indicated with a number 1.

BIOS chip

Figure 4-1:
The BIOS chip (an EEPROM chip located on the mother-board) contains the BIOS code.

Along with the low-level code, the BIOS also contains the POST (Power-on Self-Test) and the CMOS setup program. The *POST* is a self-diagnostics routine that the system goes through each time it boots up. This self-diagnostic checks to see that each device listed in CMOS actually exists on the system. The POST also tests devices, such as I/O (input/output) ports and memory, to verify not only that they exist but also that they still function.

You use the CMOS setup program, which is stored in the BIOS, to navigate through the CMOS settings. However, the BIOS does not contain the settings themselves. As you find out in the upcoming section, "Understanding CMOS," the CMOS settings are maintained in CMOS RAM.

Upgrading the System BIOS

When your system was designed, its BIOS program code was designed to work with very specific devices. As you know, computer technology changes very quickly, almost overnight. So, what can you do if you have an older system and you want to update its capabilities?

The BIOS dictates a system's capabilities. For example, assume that the BIOS on my old Pentium is only aware of an 8GB drive, but I would like to install a 20GB drive into the system. I must first upgrade the BIOS so that the system knows how to refer to a drive of that size. As far as the current BIOS is concerned, there is no such thing as a drive larger than 8GB. Thus, I need an upgraded BIOS to make the system understand!

Another example of a good time to upgrade the BIOS code in hardware is with a wireless home router. A few years back, I purchased my first wireless router. I knew that I wanted to configure the wireless network to limit which Media Access Control (MAC) addresses (network cards) could connect to the wireless network. Unfortunately, there was no such setting in the configuration screens of the wireless router, so I went to the manufacturer's Web site and updated the BIOS in the router. After I completed the upgrade of the router, the setting I was looking for suddenly appeared on the configuration screens! The point is that it is extremely common to upgrade the BIOS on devices to make sure that the device is up to date with the current trends.

Performing the BIOS upgrade

In the past, with older systems, you would upgrade the BIOS by completely replacing the BIOS chip. Back then, BIOS was stored on a ROM (read-only memory) chip, which could not be written to. To "rewrite" the code, you needed to replace the entire chip!

Today's systems use a modified version of the ROM chip: an EEPROM chip. To upgrade the program code on an EEPROM chip, you do not need to physically replace the chip; you just run a software program that is designed to rewrite the program code.

To upgrade the BIOS, you need to get the update program from the manufacturer. You can usually find the program on the manufacturer's Web site (and it is usually downloadable), or you may be able to order a CD from the manufacturer. Be sure to follow the manufacturer's directions on how to apply the update to your BIOS.

For example, a few years back, a popular technique of updating a BIOS was to download the BIOS update program from the manufacturer's Web site to a floppy disk. After you downloaded the BIOS program to a floppy disk, you booted off the floppy disk, the update started, and you just followed the directions onscreen. The update program rewrote the program code stored in the BIOS chip that was typically read-only. Because you are writing to this ROM chip with a special program, they call the ROM a *flash ROM,* where *flashing* is the process of rewriting the program code.

Because today's computer systems are no longer shipping with built-in floppy drives, it is up to the manufacturer of the BIOS to decide how the BIOS update will be performed. Most manufacturers allow you to perform a BIOS update by running the update program directly by double-clicking the program in Windows after downloading it from the manufacturer's Web site.

Potential issues with BIOS upgrading

If you decide to perform a BIOS upgrade, consider these few words of caution:

✦ **Be sure you're applying the correct BIOS update for system.** You want to make sure that you are aware of the manufacturer for your BIOS before you look for an update. With this information, you can go to the manufacturer's Web site and download the update. You will not be able to mix BIOS codes between manufacturers. For example, you cannot update your Compaq system with a BIOS update from Dell.

✦ **Be sure that you not only have the BIOS update for the correct system, but also that the BIOS update you have is designed for your version of the BIOS.** Each BIOS has a revision number or version number. The developers of the BIOS update program might place a version check into the BIOS update, but you cannot be sure of that. So, as a result, be sure to double-check that the BIOS update you are running is for the *BIOS version* you have.

Installing the wrong BIOS version can cause the system to become dysfunctional. If you can't find a BIOS version number, use the BIOS date to decide which update to download. The current BIOS version or date can be located within CMOS or seen with the BIOS manufacturer on the screen during boot-up, as shown in Figure 4-2.

✦ **When you start a BIOS update, be sure that you complete it.** Rewriting only a portion of the BIOS code (whether as a result of an accidental shutdown or power loss during the writing process) can cause the system to become dysfunctional. The actual BIOS update should take only a few seconds, so try not to disrupt the BIOS update after it starts.

```
Phoenix BIOS 4.0 Release 6.0
Copyright 1985-1998 Phoenix Technologies Ltd. All Rights Reserved
Copyright 1996-1998 Intel Corporation.
404CL0X0.15A.0306.P02

Intel Celeron(tm) processor  333 MHz
128MB System RAM

Legacy Keyboard ... Detected
Legacy Mouse .......  Detected

  Fixed  Disk  0:  QUANTUM FIREBALL EX10.2A-(PM)
ATAPI CD-ROM:  MATSHITA CR-588-(SM)
ATAPI Removable Drive:  IOMEGA ZIP 100-(SS) ATAPI

Press <F1> to enter SETUP
```

Figure 4-2: Identifying the BIOS version by starting up the system.

TIP

As a way to prevent accidental writing to the BIOS code, some motherboards ship with a *jumper* on the board that must be removed to write to the BIOS chip. When you want to upgrade the BIOS and you have the correct BIOS update, you remove the jumper and then run the BIOS update. After updating the BIOS, you place the jumper back.

Now that you have an understanding of what the BIOS is used for and how to update the BIOS, it is time to move on to CMOS and the different computer settings that can be controlled through CMOS.

Understanding CMOS

As I mention earlier, *CMOS* contains the computer's inventory list and advanced setup options. It can be considered an inventory list because it contains a record of all the devices connected to the system, such as the floppy drive, the hard drive, memory, and so on. Not only does CMOS list the devices, but it also dictates their capacity — for example, whether the system has a 2GB or a 6GB hard drive.

During the boot process, the system compares its inventory list with what it detects during boot-up. If there are any discrepancies, the system typically gives you an error and takes you into CMOS right away, asking you to save the new change. For example, assume that your system has 512MB of RAM

and you add another 512MB of RAM. When you power up the system, the system compares what it had in inventory (512MB) the last time it booted with what it sees now (1024MB). Because there is a difference, CMOS reports a memory size error and gives you the opportunity to save the new changes to CMOS. CMOS doesn't know whether the difference is for the better; it sees a difference, so it reports an error. Because CMOS detected the new memory, all you have to do is save the changes to the inventory list and reboot.

Looking at the previous example, if you choose not to save the settings, you will get the memory size error the next time you start the computer. To prevent the error from appearing again, save the changes to CMOS. This way, the values that are detected are equal to what is stored in CMOS.

Before discussing the different CMOS settings, it's important to know how to enter the CMOS setup program. Figuring this out is difficult on some systems yet extremely easy on others. Some systems display a message on boot-up that indicates what keystroke (often Delete, F1, or F2) to use to enter the CMOS setup program. IBM systems typically use F1 (refer to Figure 4-2); Dell systems today typically use F2 or Delete.

Compaq systems typically use F10. In many Compaq systems, pressing F10 when you see a square cursor in the top-right corner of the computer screen when the system starts up lets you enter the CMOS program.

In some older systems, you enter CMOS by holding down multiple keys at the same time during boot-up — Ctrl+Alt+S or Ctrl+Alt+Insert, for example. Entering into these systems is a little trickier, so reviewing your documentation is helpful. (Note that it has been a long time since I have seen a system that uses these three-key combinations to enter the CMOS setup program.) Table 4-1 summarizes popular keystrokes used to enter CMOS, based on the manufacturer of the BIOS. (Remember that the CMOS setup program is stored in BIOS.)

Table 4-1	How to Enter CMOS Setup
BIOS Manufacturer	*Keystroke*
AMI	Delete
Award	Delete or Ctrl+Alt+Esc
Compaq	F10
Dell	F2 or Delete
HP	F1
IBM	F1
Phoenix	F1 or F2

CMOS information is held in *CMOS RAM,* which is volatile memory that can maintain its data during shutdowns or power loss by using a small battery located on the motherboard. Thus, if the battery on the motherboard loses power, the CMOS data is also lost. Figure 4-3 shows a CMOS battery on a system board.

Figure 4-3: The CMOS battery on the system board is responsible for powering CMOS RAM.

The CMOS configuration is stored in CMOS RAM. Because RAM loses its contents when the system is powered off, the motherboard has a small battery that maintains enough of a charge that CMOS RAM can maintain its data — thus allowing the system to retain the CMOS information between reboots.

Viewing Basic CMOS Settings

In this section, you find out about common CMOS setup options and their purposes. These CMOS settings are consistent with most systems and have become fairly standard settings to view or change when troubleshooting a system.

After you enter the CMOS setup program, you see an introductory screen, such as the one shown in Figure 4-4, displaying options that can be changed to control the system configuration.

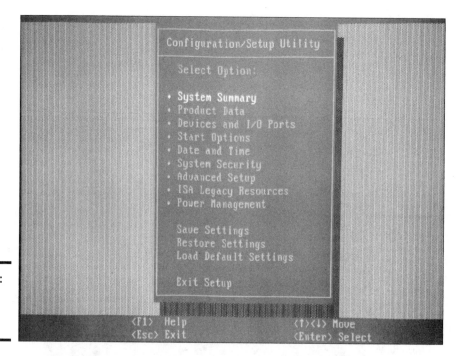

Figure 4-4:
A typical
CMOS
screen.

Hard drive

Within the CMOS setup program, you can find the size of the hard drive. CMOS displays the size of the hard drive based on what is detected during startup. The hard drive size is displayed in CMOS, as shown in Figure 4-5.

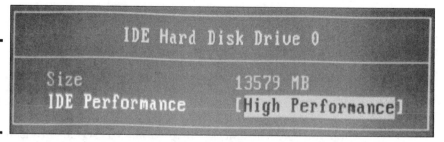

Figure 4-5:
Viewing
the hard
drive size in
CMOS.

The hard drives are typically displayed in today's systems as primary master, primary slave, secondary master, and secondary slave. Each entry shows the label of the drive; you highlight it in CMOS and then press Enter to view the details on the drive. The details can include the size of the drive, its geometry, and any settings for the drive.

On some older systems, you could change the CMOS from autodetect to manual so that you can specify the dimensions of the drive — overriding what was detected. Specifying the dimensions of the drive involves looking on the back of the drive to find out how many sectors, cylinders, and heads the drive contains — which dictates the size of the drive. When you know the dimensions, you can input these dimensions into CMOS (after switching from autodetect to manual). CMOS calculates the size of the drive based on the dimensions you input.

On older systems, you specify the hard drive size by specifying a *drive type,* which is a number representing a drive of a specific size. For example, a Type 2 drive might be 1.2GB in size, and a Type 10 drive might be 1.5GB in size. (The actual values of hard drive types vary from system to system and are usually displayed along with the type.) There is also a custom type on older systems — usually Type 47 — which enables you to specify the dimensions of the drive (sectors, cylinders, heads); CMOS can then calculate the size in megabytes for you after you input the dimensions.

Floppy disk drive

One option in CMOS lets you enable or disable the floppy disk drive. When the disk drive is enabled, its size is also specified and can usually be changed. If the disk drive is enabled but the wrong size disk drive is specified, you might not be able to access a floppy disk that has been placed in the drive. CMOS allows you to disable devices such as disk drives and USB ports so that companies can keep employees from copying proprietary data. Figure 4-6 shows the menu setting that allows you to change the size of the disk drive and even disable the disk drive.

Memory

CMOS indicates the total amount of memory installed on the system. Typically, this entry is not modified unless you add or remove RAM and the change is detected on boot-up. If you do add or remove RAM from the system, the system detects the change and modifies CMOS for you. All you need to do is save the modification once in the CMOS setup program. Some systems today inform you that the system has saved the change for you and don't require you to enter the CMOS setup program. Figure 4-7 shows the CMOS System Summary screen, which shows that there is 640MB of system memory installed on the system.

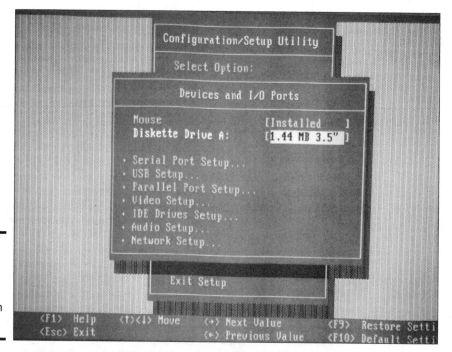

Figure 4-6:
Changing the size of the floppy disk drive in CMOS.

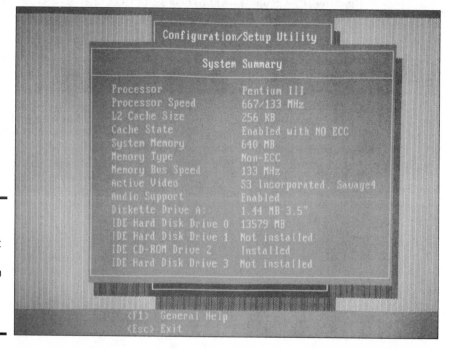

Figure 4-7:
Viewing the amount of memory installed on the system through CMOS.

The CMOS in some systems not only tells you how much memory you have installed but also informs you of the *type* of memory that is installed. These systems usually allow you to change the type of memory if the system supports different types of memory (for example, FPM, EDO, SDRAM, DDR; see Book II, Chapter 3 for more on memory types). For example, I have an old Pentium that supports either FPM or EDO memory, and CMOS displays the memory type being used.

Parallel port

CMOS offers the opportunity to configure your parallel port. This configuration allows you to either disable the port or change the mode the port runs in.

You might think that a parallel port does not require a lot of configuration, but think about this: Have you ever had problems with a scanner that plugs into your parallel port? Or more specifically, have you ever had problems with your parallel-port scanner plugging into your computer and the printer then connecting to your scanner? The problems might derive from the parallel port mode being misconfigured on the system. The *parallel port mode* dictates the capabilities of the parallel port. Table 4-2 lists the three parallel port modes that can be configured for your system.

<div style="text-align:right">**Book II**
Chapter 4

Telling Your BIOS from Your CMOS</div>

Table 4-2	Parallel Port Mode	
Mode	*Data Transfer Rate*	*Description*
Standard Parallel Port (SPP)	150 KBps	Supports communication in only one direction: from the computer to the device.
Enhanced Parallel Port (EPP)	2 MBps	A bidirectional port mode that enables communication in either direction: from the computer to the device and the device to the computer. This mode supports *daisy chaining*.
Extended Capabilities Port (ECP)	More than 2 MBps	Supports bidirectional devices.

If you're having trouble daisy chaining the scanner and printer off the parallel port on the computer, check to make sure that the proper port mode is selected in the CMOS setup program (shown in Figure 4-8). In this example, you want to make sure that EPP is selected because it supports daisy chaining.

Daisy chaining is the feature of connecting one device off another, such as connecting the printer to the scanner and the scanner to the LPT (line print terminal) port.

```
                Parallel Port Setup...

    Parallel Port                        [378h        ]
    Parallel Port Mode                   [Extended]
    Parallel Port Extended Mode          [ECP            ]
    Parallel Port Extended Mode DMA      [DMA 3 ]
    Parallel Port IRQ                    [IRQ 7 ]
```

Figure 4-8:
Configuring
the parallel
port mode in
CMOS.

The resources of the parallel port might also need to be configured if there
are conflicts with another device. Notice that the default IRQ (interrupt
request) for LPT1 is 7, and the default I/O address is 378-37F. You can read
about IRQs and I/O addresses in Book III, Chapter 4. For now, just make a
mental note that you can configure the IRQ and I/O address of the parallel
port in CMOS.

Serial ports

A typical system includes two serial ports — COM1 and COM2 — and CMOS
should have an entry for each of the serial ports. These entries enable you
to change the resources, such as the IRQ and I/O address used by each of
the serial ports, as shown in Figure 4-9. The CMOS shown in Figure 4-9 iden-
tifies the two serial ports as serial port A and serial port B. For more infor-
mation on IRQs and I/O addresses, see Book III, Chapter 4.

```
              Serial Port Setup...

    Serial Port A Address  [3F8h      ]
    Serial Port A IRQ      [IRQ 4 ]
    Serial Port B Address  [2F8h      ]
    Serial Port B IRQ      [IRQ 3 ]
```

Figure 4-9:
Configuring
the serial
ports in
CMOS.

Be sure to remember that the default IRQ for COM1 is 4, and the default IRQ for COM2 is 3. The default I/O address for COM1 is 3F8-3FF, and the default I/O address for COM2 is 2F8-2FF.

In the CMOS setup program, you can find not only an option to change the resources for the serial ports, but you can also disable the serial ports. Disabling the serial ports involves entering your CMOS program and switching a serial port to the disabled setting.

Date and time

The date and time each have an entry in CMOS as well, which is where the operating system (OS) gets its date and time information. Setting the date and time in CMOS sets the date and time for the OS. From a troubleshooting point of view, you know that your CMOS battery is dying when during startup, the system asks you for the date and time. During startup after a battery failure, all the other settings are detected again — which is why you don't specify the hard disk or the floppy disk. However, the date and time must be specified again.

Boot sequence

Take special note of the CMOS entry for boot sequence; it determines what devices the system will try to boot from and in what order it tries each device. For example, older systems are typically set up to boot off a floppy disk first; if a bootable floppy disk isn't present, the system then boots off the hard drive.

Newer systems let you boot off a CD-ROM device, or even off the network first; and then, if no bootable device is found in either of those spots, proceed to boot off the hard drive. Booting off a CD-ROM makes installing an OS extremely easy because most OSes today (like Windows or Linux) support booting off the installation CD to install the OS.

Most systems today are configured to try to boot from a floppy disk (if one exists), then a CD-ROM, then a hard disk, and finally a network. You determine the order to suit your needs, although typically, the floppy or CD-ROM drive is checked before the hard drive. If you like, you can disable devices, such as a CD-ROM drive, from being bootable. This is an important point because system security can be bypassed if a hacker can boot off his own CD containing his own copy of an OS. For security reasons, your company might consider disabling booting from floppy disk or CD-ROM. Figure 4-10 shows the CMOS menu where you can configure the startup order for your system's devices.

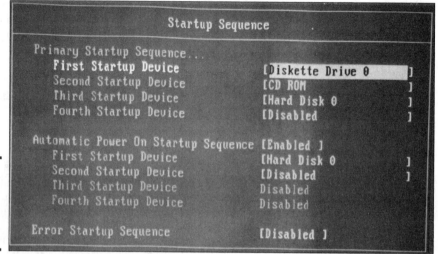

Figure 4-10: Configuring the startup sequence in CMOS.

Passwords

In general, two types of passwords can be set in CMOS: the power-on password and the administrator password. The steps to set the password are different per manufacturer, but you will usually find the password option under a security menu in the CMOS setup program.

The *power-on password* is required to power on the computer. It is part of the power-on process and occurs before the OS is loaded. Many people like to call it a *hardware password* because the OS (the software) won't have a chance to load unless the correct password is entered. The implementation of power-on passwords can be especially useful in environments where security is a significant issue.

You set the *administrator password* in the CMOS setup program. This password is required for anyone wishing to enter the CMOS setup program and make changes to the system configuration. It prevents unauthorized users from entering the CMOS setup program and changing the values that reside there.

When people get comfortable with computers, they start to explore the computer's options. Companies often end up spending time and money fixing problems that arise from the exploration of these options. This is why it might be useful to set an administrator password. The administrator password enables you to secure the workstation at the administrative level, and the power-on password allows you to secure the system at the user level — controlling who can use the system.

A question I often receive is, "What happens if you forget the CMOS password after it is set?" The answer is simple for desktops, but more difficult for laptops. First, check whether the motherboard has a jumper that can be removed to make CMOS forget the passwords (see Figure 4-11). After you remove the jumper to clear the password, put the jumper back on and power on the computer. Some systems have you place the jumper over specific pins in order to clear the password; check the documentation to find out how to clear the password for your particular system.

Password-clear jumper

Figure 4-11: A jumper that can be removed to erase the CMOS password.

If no such feature exists on your motherboard, you could remove the CMOS battery from the motherboard. Remember that CMOS RAM retains its information because there is a battery supplying power to the memory where CMOS data is stored. If you remove the battery, CMOS is erased, including the passwords (which is better than throwing away the system).

The only problem with removing the battery is that all the CMOS information is lost, including your hard drive, memory, and other device settings. The good news is that most of the information should be detected again on startup, such as the amount of memory installed or the size of the hard drive.

Earlier in this chapter, I mention that if your system asks you for the date and time when it boots up, this is usually an indication that your CMOS battery is dead or dying. As noted here, the date and time aren't the only things lost to a dying battery. If security is an issue and your system keeps asking you for the date and time at boot-up, replace the battery *immediately* and then reset the administrator password to keep others, malicious or benign, from altering the CMOS setup.

A third solution to a forgotten password — and the one I like — is to get a CMOS utility, such as the CMOS Save & Restore utility. CMOS Save & Restore backs up the CMOS information and then allows you to restore it when an emergency arises. This solution involves backing up CMOS *before* a password is set so that CMOS can be restored to a state without a password. These utilities are popular ones that can be found on the Internet, and they back up the CMOS information to a text file. An example of a CMOS save and restore program can be found at

```
http://mindprod.com/products1.html#CMOSSAVE
```

Plug and Play BIOS

Most systems today have a Plug and Play BIOS (PnP BIOS). The term *plug and play* refers to the idea that you can connect a new device to the system, and the system automatically detects and configures the device to work with your system. To have a Plug and Play system, three conditions are necessary:

- ✦ A Plug and Play device
- ✦ A Plug and Play OS
- ✦ A Plug and Play BIOS

If you are missing any one of these conditions, the OS cannot leverage Plug and Play and assign resources to a device on startup. On some older systems, you might see an entry in CMOS stating that it is a Plug and Play BIOS. All newer systems are Plug and Play BIOSes.

Viewing Advanced CMOS Settings

Many newer systems maintain the basic CMOS parameters mentioned in the previous section but are also supplemented by different advanced setup settings. This section examines the purposes and characteristics of some of these advanced settings.

Globally Unique Identifier (GUID)

The *Globally Unique Identifier* (GUID) is a 128-bit number, randomly generated for the system when it was built, and stored in CMOS. The GUID uniquely identifies the system from any other. It enables the identification of individual computers and ensures that this identification method is absolutely unique.

Many features in today's computers make use of the GUID. For example, one of the Windows installation tools (Remote Installation Services; RIS) allows the administrator to go into a client computer's CMOS, make a note of the

GUID, create a computer account within Windows Active Directory (AD) database for the workstation, and associate the GUID with the account. If the client computer is booting off the network when it starts, it contacts the RIS server and starts installing a Windows client OS. The client computer uses the computer name of the computer account found in Windows AD that its GUID is associated with.

Some systems have adopted the term *UUID* (Universally Unique Identifier) instead of GUID. You might see a UUID in CMOS instead of a GUID, as shown in Figure 4-12, but they are the same thing.

Figure 4-12:
Viewing
the system
UUID
and BIOS
revision
number
through
CMOS.

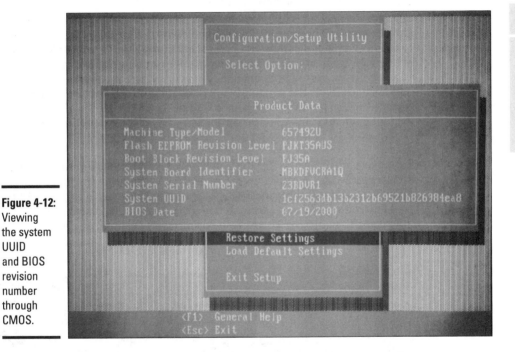

BIOS date and revision number

The date of your BIOS should be displayed somewhere in CMOS, usually under Summary Information. If you don't have a BIOS date, you might have a revision number or level. These entries in CMOS are important because you might be required to update your BIOS someday by going to the manufacturer's Web site and downloading the update. The first thing you will notice when doing this is that the manufacturer has built many different versions of BIOS for its systems. You need to make sure you get the proper update (the one for the date of your BIOS) by watching the revision number of your BIOS. For example, the site might instruct you to download BIOS update

1234 if you have Revision number R5.145. The big question is how to know what your revision number is. Check CMOS! Refer again to Figure 4-12. You can see the BIOS version, or revision number, identified by the label Flash EEPROM Revision Level.

To ensure that you downloaded the correct BIOS update for the system, always make a note of the revision number and the date of the existing BIOS. Both pieces of information are typically used to determine which BIOS you need to download from the manufacturer's Web site.

Universal Serial Bus (USB)

Universal Serial Bus (USB) devices have gained much recognition over the last decade. USB devices are high-speed serial devices that use a single connector style and can be chained together with a *USB hub device.* A USB hub device connects all USB devices together at a central point. The USB hub may be its own unique device, or it may be just another device in the USB chain that has the capability of connecting other USB devices to it. For example, a USB monitor may have a USB port to allow a mouse to connect to it. Some popular USB-type devices include digital cameras, scanners, mice, and keyboards. You can even find USB network adapters.

If you have any problems getting a USB device connected to your computer, make sure the USB port has been enabled in CMOS. Also, remember that you can disable the USB ports in CMOS (as shown in Figure 4-13) to help secure your environment. You might wish to do this to prevent a user on the network from using a flash drive to take home proprietary corporate data.

Figure 4-13:
Disabling
USB ports
prevents
using flash
drives
or other
USB-type
devices.

Built-in network adapter

Most systems today come with built-in network interface cards (NICs) that allow the system to connect to a network or the Internet. Because the card is built-in, you do not have to buy a network card for the system. However, built-in network cards (or any built-in device) sometimes become faulty, but

your system does not know that and always tries to use this built-in device anyway. Note that you can usually enable or disable the built-in network card through the CMOS setup program.

When your system includes a built-in network adapter, you usually have the option of enabling or disabling the capability to boot off the network as well. Unless this option is enabled, you cannot boot off the network, even if you specified a network boot in your startup order.

You need to verify three options in CMOS in order to boot off the network: that the network card is enabled, that your system has enabled booting off the network adapter, and then that the network device is located in the startup order of devices. To boot off the network, you probably want the network as the first boot device.

Virus protection

Some BIOS systems have built-in virus protection, which is (for the most part) a good thing. Some viruses attack the system by altering the *Master Boot Record* (MBR), which is the code that initiates the startup of the system and is located at the beginning of the hard drive. (For more information on MBR and hard drives, check out the next chapter in this minibook.) The virus protection built into the BIOS watches out solely for changes to the MBR and puts a stop to it!

Unfortunately, when you install a new OS, the installation modifies the MBR with its boot program files. As a result, the built-in virus detection in CMOS will see that "something" is modifying the MBR and will assume that it is a virus and stop the new OS from loading. In this case, you need to go into CMOS, disable the virus protection, and then restart the installation. After installation is complete you will want to enable the virus protection in CMOS once again. Figure 4-14 shows the startup options that indicate that virus protection has been disabled.

Onboard cache

In Book II, Chapter 3, I discuss the benefits of cache and the types of cache memory, L1 and L2. In CMOS, you typically find an entry indicating how much cache memory exists on the system, and you can configure CMOS to disable this built-in cache memory.

Sometimes cache memory goes bad and causes boot-up problems. If having cache memory enabled presents any compatibility problems with your system, you can try disabling the cache memory as a troubleshooting technique. Figure 4-15 shows the size of the cache memory and the option to enable or disable the cache memory. If the problem does not go away, there was no problem with the cache memory to begin with; enable the cache memory once again.

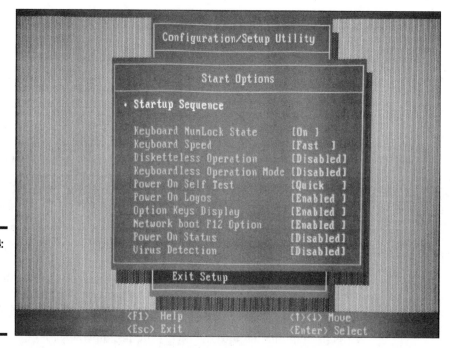

Figure 4-14:
Viewing
the virus
protection
setting in
CMOS.

Figure 4-15:
Disable
built-in
cache
memory in
CMOS to
troubleshoot
problems
with corrupt
cache
memory.

Reserve resources

Many systems let you reserve resources that have been assigned to legacy
devices in CMOS. *Legacy devices* are non–Plug and Play devices, such as
ISA (Industry Standard Architecture) cards, that have been added to the
system. The ISA non–Plug and Play devices are hard-coded with a particular
I/O address and IRQ, so you might need to configure CMOS to reserve the
IRQ so that it is not given to a Plug and Play device on startup.

Removing the IRQ will ensure that a Plug and Play system will not assign the resources that are hard-coded into older devices to Plug and Play devices, which would create a conflict. Most systems today are Plug and Play, so unless you are supporting older hardware, you will most likely not hit this issue. Figure 4-16 shows how to reserve a resource in CMOS by setting the resource to ISA — meaning it is being used by an ISA device, so the system is not to give this resource out to another device.

```
                    Interrupt Resources

        0:                  Timer
        1:                  Keyboard
        2:                  Interrupt Controller
        3:                  Serial Port B
        4:                  Serial Port A
        5:                  [ISA Resource            ]
        6:                  Diskette
        7:                  Parallel Port
        8:                  Real Time Clock
        9:                  ACPI
       10:                  [Available               ]
       11:                  [Available               ]
       12:                  Mouse
       13:                  Coprocessor
       14:                  IDE Drives
       15:                  IDE Drives
```

Figure 4-16:
Reserving
a resource
in CMOS
so that the
system does
not give the
resource
out.

Now it is time to get some hands-on experience by performing Lab 4-1 and Lab 4-2. Lab 4-1 and Lab 4-2 can be found in the Labs.pdf file in the Author directory of the CD-ROM.

Getting an A+

In this chapter, I introduce you to the common settings found in CMOS setup programs today. You discover the basic and advanced parameters in CMOS. The following points are covered:

✦ The BIOS is low-level code used by the system to communicate with the system hardware. The BIOS code is stored on an EEPROM chip located on the motherboard of the system.

✦ The BIOS is typically updated by downloading a BIOS update program and "flashing" the BIOS.

✦ You enter a system's CMOS setup program by using a keystroke such as F1 (IBM), F2 (Dell), or F10 (Compaq) when the system starts up.

✦ You can change the boot order of the different bootable devices.

✦ The three parallel port modes are SPP, EPP, and ECP.

✦ You can change the hard drive from autodetect to manual so you can input the drive dimensions.

✦ You can update your BIOS by downloading the BIOS update for your system from the BIOS manufacturer's Web site.

Prep Test

1 You have a USB camera from which you are trying to copy some of the pictures to the computer's hard drive. The computer does not seem to recognize the device. What should you do?

A ○ Check to see that the boot order is correct.

B ○ Make sure that the USB ports are enabled.

C ○ Make sure that the serial port is enabled.

D ○ Make sure that the operating system has not assigned the USB device resources to some other device.

2 The computer constantly prompts for the date and time. What does this indicate?

A ○ The date and time are wrong.

B ○ The time has fallen back by one hour.

C ○ The battery on the motherboard is losing its charge.

D ○ The time has increased by one hour.

3 On a Plug and Play system in which you have some non–Plug and Play devices, what should you do so that there are no conflicts with the legacy hardware resources and the resources assigned by the operating system?

A ○ Replace the BIOS with a non–Plug and Play BIOS.

B ○ Enable the Legacy Compatible option in CMOS.

C ○ Replace all Plug and Play devices with non–Plug and Play devices.

D ○ Go into the reserve resources area of the CMOS setup program and reserve the resources used by legacy devices.

4 Your manager is worried that someone will be able to start up any of the computers and view confidential information. What could you do to ensure that anyone starting the computer is supposed to be using that system?

A ○ Lock the computer case.

B ○ Set file permissions on the files that are confidential.

C ○ Set a power-on password in CMOS.

D ○ Use Microsoft Encrypting File System to protect the files from unauthorized access.

5 You are installing Windows on your computer, and you know that the Windows CD is a bootable CD. You have tried a number of times to boot off the CD, but you are unable to. What CMOS option should you look for?

A ○ You must delete the existing partitions so that you can boot off the CD-ROM.

B ○ Ensure that the CD-ROM device has been set up as the first device in the startup (boot-up) order.

C ○ Disable the hard drive in CMOS.

D ○ Disable the CD-ROM in CMOS.

6 You are worried that some of your advanced computer users on the network will start changing the settings within CMOS. What is the best thing you can do to protect these settings?

A ○ Set a power-on password.

B ○ Set an administrator password.

C ○ Set a Windows log-on password.

D ○ Ask the advanced users not to change any of the CMOS settings.

7 When looking inside the My Computer icon (or Computer icon in Vista), you notice that no floppy drive is listed. What should you check in CMOS?

A ○ Make sure that the floppy drive is listed as a bootable device.

B ○ Make sure that the hard drive is listed as a bootable device.

C ○ Make sure the floppy drive is configured correctly and enabled in CMOS.

D ○ Make sure the hard drive is configured correctly in CMOS.

8 Your built-in network adapter doesn't seem to be connecting you to the network. What is one of the first things you want to check for in CMOS?

A ○ That the built-in network adapter is enabled in CMOS

B ○ That the network adapter driver is loaded

C ○ That the resources are not conflicting

D ○ That the proper protocol is installed

9 You are trying to use Windows 2000 Server's Remote Installation Services, but the computer doesn't seem to boot off the network adapter. You have verified that the network adapter has been enabled in CMOS. What else should you check for within CMOS?

A ○ That the network card has been disabled

B ○ That the network adapter has been disabled

C ○ That the CD-ROM has been configured as a bootable device

D ○ That the network adapter is set up as a bootable device

10 You are experiencing a lot of problems running your customized software on some of the newer computers. What might you try disabling in CMOS to clear up the compatibility issue between the software and the system?

A ○ RAM
B ○ Cache memory
C ○ Hard drive
D ○ Floppy drive

11 You are having trouble installing a new operating system on your computer because the installation fails with each attempt. Which of the following CMOS settings would you disable to help the system make it through the installation?

A ○ Network adapter
B ○ Bootable CD-ROM
C ○ Antivirus
D ○ Bootable network adapter

12 Which of the following is a typical method for updating your system BIOS?

A ○ Replace the old BIOS chip with a new BIOS chip.
B ○ Run a BIOS update program from a diskette that flashes the BIOS with a new version of the BIOS.
C ○ Replace the old motherboard with a new one.
D ○ You cannot update the BIOS.

13 Which of the following best describes the difference between BIOS and CMOS?

A ○ BIOS contains the configuration information for the system, and CMOS is the low-level code that allows the devices to communicate.
B ○ BIOS is stored in RAM, and CMOS is stored in ROM.
C ○ BIOS is stored in RAM, and CMOS is stored in cache memory.
D ○ CMOS contains the configuration information for the system, and BIOS is the low-level code that allows the devices to communicate.

14 Which two of the following are typical keystrokes used to enter the CMOS setup program?

A ❏ F1
B ❏ Ctrl+Alt+Delete
C ❏ Alt+F10
D ❏ Delete

15 You are deploying Windows 2000 Professional computers by taking advantage of Remote Installation Services. What CMOS setting do you need to look up on the computer you are deploying the new operating system to?

A ○ GUID

B ○ Network adapter address

C ○ Serial number

D ○ ISBN

16 Where is the CMOS configuration information stored?

A ○ RAM

B ○ ROM

C ○ Cache memory

D ○ Floppy disk

Answers

1 **B.** In today's systems, many of the built-in devices can be enabled or disabled in the CMOS setup program. When experiencing problems with a built-in device, the first thing you should check is whether the device is enabled. S*ee "Built-in network adapter."*

2 **C.** The CMOS configuration information is stored in CMOS RAM. This special RAM chip maintains its information by using a small battery on the system board. If the battery loses its charge, the CMOS RAM is flushed out, meaning that it will prompt you for the information such as the date and time as the system boots up. *Review "Date and time."*

3 **D.** The newer CMOS setup programs allow you to reserve resources so that the OS will not give those resources away. If you reserve the resources, the system will not give those resources out. This way, when the legacy device initializes, the resource it tries to use is free. *Check out "Reserve resources."*

4 **C.** Choice C is the best answer to ensure that only authorized individuals are powering on the system. In order to use the system, someone will need to type the CMOS password. This password is not dependent upon any particular operating system because you are setting a hardware-level password. *Peruse "Passwords."*

5 **B.** Many computers are set up to boot off the floppy drive, then the hard drive, and finally the CD-ROM, which means that if the system can boot off the floppy or hard drive, the opportunity will never arise to boot off the CD-ROM. Changing the startup order so that the CD-ROM is the first bootable device means that you can put in the Windows CD-ROM, and setup will be invoked from it. Choice A would work, assuming that the CD-ROM device is listed anywhere in the bootable device order. Unfortunately, you have lost the contents of the hard drive because partitions have been wiped out, so Choice A is not the best answer. *Take a look at "Boot sequence."*

6 **B.** An administrator password is a password that must be provided to enter the CMOS setup program and change the settings. Choice A is not the right answer because you might not want to set up a password for when the computer turns on but only if a user tries to enter the CMOS setup program. *Peek at "Passwords."*

7 **C.** The floppy drive is a device listed in CMOS. Not only do you want to make sure that the floppy drive is physically connected correctly, but you also want to make sure that CMOS sees the device. Check to make sure that the floppy drive is not disabled in CMOS. *Look over "Floppy disk drive."*

8 **A.** One of the first things you want to do with a built-in device is ensure that the device has not been disabled in CMOS. If it has not been disabled, you should look at the other choices for the solution. *Study "Built-in network adapter."*

9 **D.** When taking advantage of Remote Installation Services, you need to ensure that the computer not only has the network adapter enabled, but also that the network adapter is signified as a bootable device, and maybe even the first bootable device. In this question, you have already verified that the network adapter has been enabled, so Choice D is the only possible answer. *Refer to "Built-in network adapter."*

10 **B.** Many systems today have built-in cache memory. Although it isn't that common, you might sometimes have problems with particular software not "liking the idea" of using information from cache instead of RAM. To test this, temporarily disable the cache memory. *Examine "Onboard cache."*

11 **C.** Viruses commonly attack the MBR of the hard drive, so virus software constantly watches out for applications that try to make a change to this area of the disk. Some systems today have built-in virus detection, and because the installation of a new operating system causes a change to the MBR, there may be incompatibilities between the OS installation and the virus protection built into the system. Disabling this virus protection in the CMOS will allow the installation to finish. *See "Virus protection."*

12 **B.** To update your BIOS today, you will download the update from the Internet and then run the update. In the past, you would have to replace the entire ROM chip. *Review "Performing the BIOS upgrade."*

13 **D.** CMOS is the inventory list of devices and their configuration, whereas the BIOS is the set of low-level instructions that tells these devices how to communicate. Choice B and Choice C are wrong because BIOS code is stored in ROM, not RAM. *Check out "The BIOS and Its Purpose."*

14 **A, D.** Typical keystrokes used to enter CMOS while booting are F1 and Delete. *Peruse "Understanding CMOS."*

15 **A.** When taking advantage of Remote Installation Services for Windows 2000, you will build a computer account in Active Directory and associate a GUID with the computer account. The GUID is located in CMOS and is a unique number associated with that system. *Take a look at "Globally Unique Identifier (GUID)."*

16 **A.** CMOS configuration information is stored in RAM, which maintains its information while the power is turned off by using a small battery located on the motherboard. *Study "Understanding CMOS."*

Chapter 5: Working with Storage

Exam Objectives

✔ Understanding hard drive terminology

✔ Discovering IDE devices

✔ Learning how SCSI works

✔ The serial ATA hype

✔ Using removable storage

✔ Working with file systems and partitions

*O*ne of the primary responsibilities of a PC technician is managing hard disks. This responsibility involves more than just partitioning and formatting disks; it also entails installing disks into the computer system and configuring the system to recognize the newly added disks.

In this chapter, you discover the skills that you need for installing, configuring, and troubleshooting hard disks. I introduce you to a new world of terminology related to hard disk installation and configuration, along with other types of storage like CD-ROMs and DVDs.

In this chapter, I also make sure that you understand the difference between IDE, SCSI, and serial ATA devices. You also see the steps required to install and configure IDE master/slave devices in a chain and the steps required to install a SCSI bus.

Understanding Hard Drive Terminology

If you took a martial arts class, the instructor would show you how to do some basic punches and kicks before letting you spar or compete. The instructor would be well aware that jumping into combat without the basics could do you more damage than good. PC repair works the same way: Before discussing the installation and configuration of IDE and SCSI devices, it is important to cover some basic terminology surrounding hard drives.

Disk geometry

The following sections introduce you to *disk geometry* — essentially the physical components of a drive that make up your data storage solution. You also find out some general terminology about hard drives and hard drive storage in this section.

Platters

A *platter* is a physical object (actually, a plate) inside the hard disk that is responsible for storing the data. A platter is similar to a music record (LP and '45 vinyl discs — remember those?), and a hard disk has many platters. Figure 5-1 shows the platters inside a hard disk.

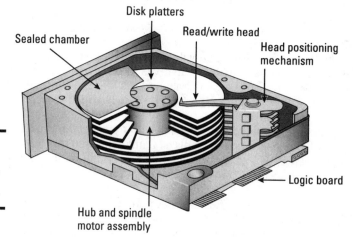

Figure 5-1:
The internals of a hard disk.

The platters are similar to records on a record player in the sense that they spin on a spindle that runs through the center of all the platters. Each platter has two sides for storing information, and each side of the platter has a unique ID. The ID for the first side of the first platter is 0, and each side increases by 1. For example, two platters are in the disk, the first platter has side 0 and side 1, and the second platter has side 2 and side 3. Figure 5-2 illustrates this concept.

Figure 5-2:
Sides of a platter.

Because each side of the platter has a writing mechanism, many people use the terms "head" and "side" interchangeably. The head is more accurately called the *read/write head* because it moves over the disk surface and reads from or writes to the disk. Like a needle on a record player, the read/write head moves over the surface of the disk with the help of an arm, called the *actuator arm* or the *head positioning mechanism.* Figure 5-1, shown previously, illustrates the read/write head on an actuator arm.

Each platter surface on the disk has its own read/write head. When information is written to the disk, the read/write head moves to the same track on all platters in a single movement and then writes the data across the same track on all platters. The actuator arm has multiple read/write heads on it.

Tracks

Just like there are grooves (tracks) on a music record, there are also *tracks* on each platter. These tracks are evenly spaced across the platter's surface.

Sectors

The platter is divided into pie-shaped slices, called *sectors.* Now the confusing thing about sectors is that where a track intersects with a sector, *sector blocks* are created — also known as sectors! Each sector (block) — 512 bytes in size — is the actual storage area for data. Figure 5-3 illustrates the tracks and sectors on a disk platter. Each pie-sliced sector has an address; the first sector is sector 1, the second sector is sector 2, and so on. The reason why the term sector applies to two different areas of the disk is because if you were to look at a sector (the pie slice), like the pie slice labeled in Figure 5-3 as "Sector," it might be sector 1. All sector blocks in that pie slice are considered sector 1 as well, but they differ in the track that they reside on.

So, each sector block has an address comprising the platter side number, the sector, and track number. For example, data can be saved to side 1, sector 2, track 4 — which is the address of a 512-byte sector block. Note that the term *sector block* is a term that I made up for this discussion; the term *sector* is also used to describe the 512-byte blocks.

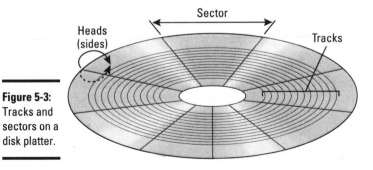

Figure 5-3:
Tracks and sectors on a disk platter.

Clusters

A group of sectors makes up a *cluster,* which is the allocation unit for a file — meaning where a file is saved. When a *partition* (a logical division of space on the disk; see the upcoming section "Managing Partitions and Volumes") is formatted, the file system determines the cluster size based upon the partition size. For example, a 2GB FAT partition uses a 32K cluster size. That same 2GB partition formatted as FAT32 uses only a 4K cluster size.

Having a partition use a 4K cluster size means that eight sectors make up a cluster. Keep in mind that after a file is saved to the cluster, no other file can occupy that cluster. For example, if you have a 32K cluster size and you save a 3K file to the hard disk, the file is saved to an empty cluster — but only 3K of that cluster is used, and the remaining 29K is empty. The remaining 29K is now considered unusable space; no other file can be saved to that unused 29K.

Cylinders

All platters in the hard disk contain the same number of tracks, but that number varies from one hard disk to another. These tracks are numbered from the outside in, starting with 0 (zero). For example, on a platter with ten tracks, the track closest to the outer edge of the platter is track 0, and the track closest to the center is track 9.

A *cylinder* consists of the same track on both sides of all the platters. In other words, when you reference track 0, you reference a particular track on a particular platter; however, when you reference cylinder 0, you reference track 0 on all platters.

If you know the number of cylinders, heads, and sectors per track, you can calculate the size of a disk. For example, if a drive has 4,092 cylinders, 16 heads, and 63 sectors per track, the size of the disk is 2,111,864,832 bytes (2.1GB). The formula to calculate the size of the disk is

cylinders × number of heads × number of sectors per track × 512 bytes per sector

Read/write process

Platters are divided into 512-byte sectors. These sectors are the area on the platter that data is written to. The platters have a magnetic coating applied that is extremely sensitive to magnetism. While the platters spin, the read/write head moves from track to track until it reaches the desired track. Then it waits for the appropriate sector to move underneath it, at which time the read/write head is energized to apply a magnetic charge to the particles in the disk coating. This changes the particle binary state from 0 to 1,

thus creating data. The same happens when the data needs to be read: The read/write head moves over the appropriate sector and reads the data that resides in the sector.

The read/write heads don't actually touch the surface of the disk platters; instead, they hover about 10 micro-inches (or millionths of an inch) above it. (That's not even enough space to place a hair between the read/write head and the platter's surface.) This design helps improve disk performance because a read/write head that makes contact with the platter causes friction, slowing down the rotation speed of the disk and creating extra heat.

Performance

Disk performance can be measured in terms of several important characteristics:

+ **Seek time** is how long it takes to move the read/write heads to the desired track. Seek time is a calculated average because the time it takes to move to the desired track differs from one instance to another. For example, if the read/write heads are on track 1, they will take longer to move to track 12 than to track 3. Seek time is measured in milliseconds (ms), or one-thousandth of a second. Figure 5-4 shows how seek time is measured.

+ **Latency** is how long it takes for the appropriate sector to move under the read/write head. Latency is measured in milliseconds.

+ **Access time** describes the overall speed of the disk. It is a combination of seek time and latency. The lower the access time, the better.

+ **Spin speed** is how fast the platters spin, measured in rotations per minute (rpm). The larger the rpm value, the faster the disk, which means less latency.

Master Boot Record

The *Master Boot Record (MBR)* is the first sector on the first track of the first side of the first platter; it holds the operating system (OS) boot code that controls the loading of the OS.

The MBR also holds drive characteristics, such as the partition table. During the boot process, the system has to find a primary partition that is active — it does this by looking at the partition table in the MBR.

In general, if anything goes wrong with the MBR, you will not be able to boot the system. Because the boot record is always in the same location on every disk, it becomes very easy for a malicious hacker to write viruses that modify or corrupt the MBR. This is one reason you should always run virus-detection software. See Book IX, Chapter 3, for more on virus detection and protection.

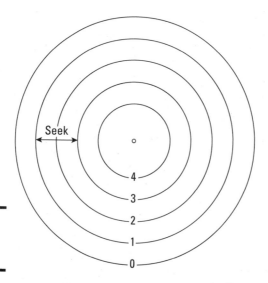

Figure 5-4:
Measuring
seek time.

LBA and ECHS

For the A+ exam, you need to be familiar with *Logical Block Addressing* (LBA) and *Extended Cylinder/Head/Sector* (ECHS) and their purpose. Essentially, LBA and ECHS perform the same goal: namely, performing *sector translation,* which is the hard drive controller lying to the BIOS about the drive geometry. LBA was developed by Western Digital, and ECHS was Seagate's solution to recognizing larger drives. Keep reading to learn why you need sector translation.

You need sector translation because the original BIOS code found on computers was limited to seeing only 1024 cylinders, 16 heads, and 63 sectors — which is a total drive size of 504MB ($1024 \times 16 \times 63 \times 512$). However, if you bought a 2.1GB hard disk, your BIOS would not recognize it because the geometry of the 2.1GB drive is too high for the BIOS. In this example, the geometry of the drive is 16,384 clusters, 4 heads, and 63 sectors. Look at Table 5-1 to see that the lowest value in each category is what will be recognized by the system.

Table 5-1	BIOS Limit Example			
	Cylinders	*Heads*	*Sectors*	*Total Size*
BIOS limit	**1024**	16	63	504MB
Hard drive (physical geometry)	16384	**4**	**63**	2.1GB
Detected	1024	4	63	132MB

Here's an example of why you take the lowest value in each category. If the hard disk supports only 4 heads, only 4 heads are detected. Although the BIOS supports a potential 16 heads, that doesn't mean that they are actually there.

So the problem is that you purchased a 2.1GB drive, but the system recognizes only 132MB! The solution to this problem is LBA or ECHS — again, both technologies offer the same solution. They were just built by different manufacturers.

An LBA-enabled BIOS can recognize 1024 cylinders, 256 heads, and 63 sectors — essentially being able to support more heads on the drive. As a result, the drive lies to the BIOS by using a *translation factor* of usually 2, 4, 8, or 16. The physical dimensions of the drive are taken and manipulated by the translation factor to calculate the logical dimensions reported to the BIOS.

Book II Chapter 5

Working with Storage

In my example, 16,384 cylinders are too many cylinders, so they are divided by translation factor of 16 to reach the LBA maximum number of cylinders supported. To make up for the loss in cylinders, the heads are then multiplied by 16, ensuring that the logical number of heads falls under the LBA limit of 254. Table 5-2 shows the solution — notice that the size of the drive (2.1GB) is what the LBA-enabled BIOS will recognize.

Table 5-2	LBA-Enabled BIOS Translation Example			
	Cylinders	*Heads*	*Sectors*	*Total Size*
LBA-enabled BIOS limit	**1024**	256	63	8.4GB
Hard drive (physical geometry)	16384	**4**	**63**	2.1GB
Translation factor	Divide by 16	Multiply by 16		
LBA-translated geometry	**1024**	**64**	**63**	**2.1GB**

To leverage larger size drives, your BIOS would have to support LBA or ECHS — which most BIOS do today.

Notice that an LBA-enabled BIOS can support only an 8.4GB drive — and we are way past that drive size today. Today's BIOS support the INT13 extensions, developed by Phoenix Technologies, which allow the systems to see drives past 137GB in size! The BIOS can recognize larger size drives because it simply identifies the drives by the number of sectors.

Discovering IDE Devices

In the following sections, you find out how to install and troubleshoot IDE devices. First, you get an overview of IDE devices and some of their features, and then you see a number of different configurations for installing IDE devices into a computer system.

IDE overview

The *hard drive controller* is responsible for converting signals made by the system CPU to signals that the hard disk can understand. These signals include instructions on where to find data and how to get to that data. The hard disk performs its task, and any data that needs to be returned is sent to the controller from the hard disk. The controller then converts the signals from the hard disk into signals that the system can understand.

In the past, the controller was on an expansion card, which was connected to the drives via ribbon cables. The goal of IDE was to make the installation of hard disks easier by including the controller on the hard disk, which is where the name comes from: *Integrated Drive Electronics* (IDE). So, today's drives have the controllers integrated into the drives themselves, meaning the drive is its own boss.

Originally, IDE was available only in the flavor of hard drives; you did not have any other type of IDE device, such as CD-ROM or tape drives. IDE hard drives had a maximum capacity of about 528MB. Another important limitation with IDE is that only two devices could be connected in a chain. Back in the day when IDE was first used, SCSI was better in that respect because it supported eight devices in a chain. (Read more on SCSI in the later section, "Learning How SCSI Works.")

Original IDE devices have a transfer rate of about 10 Mbps and may have cache on the drive itself. *Cache memory* is a small amount of memory for storing data frequently used to increase drive performance.

Because of its limitations, IDE has been replaced by *Enhanced Integrated Drive Electronics (EIDE)*. EIDE devices have a transfer rate of about 16 MBps. Four devices are allowed in an EIDE chain, with a greater variety available. For example, you may now add CD-ROMs and even Zip drives to an EIDE chain. Note that the capacity of the drives has been dramatically increased with EIDE — it now supports drives of over 200GB! Table 5-3 compares the features of IDE and EIDE.

Table 5-3	IDE versus EIDE	
Characteristic	*IDE*	*EIDE*
Size	528MB	200GB and higher
Devices in chain	2	4
Transfer rate	10 MBps	16 MBps and higher
Types of devices	Hard drives	Hard drives, CD-ROMs

On the A+ exam, you might be asked the number of devices that IDE supports. IDE supports two devices, and EIDE supports four devices. Although there have been improvements in the IDE technology, Table 5-3 displays some of the original specifications.

IDE has been around for quite some time now and has gone through some changes. The following sections outline some technologies and terms that describe the different versions of IDE. Be sure to know these for the exam.

IDE/ATA standard

A number of hard drive standards have been developed over the last two decades, the first major standard being the IDE standard. The IDE standard, which has been around since 1989, calls for an integrated controller on the drive to manage information entering and leaving the hard disk.

IDE drives attach to the motherboard by means of a 40-wire ribbon cable. The IDE standard also allows two drives to daisy chain, creating a master/slave relationship between devices. The master drive is responsible for sending and receiving information in the chain.

The IDE standard is also known as the Advanced Technology Attachment (ATA) standard, sometimes called the ATA-1 standard.

EIDE/ATA-2 standard

The EIDE standard followed shortly after the IDE standard. The EIDE standard allows four drives to be connected to a dual-channel controller. This is usually implemented as a motherboard with two connectors (also known as controllers) — one primary and one secondary. You could then connect two drives off of each controller, making a master/slave chain for each controller. Figure 5-5 shows a primary controller and a secondary controller on the motherboard. EIDE also supports larger hard disks than the original IDE standard; the original size of an IDE drive was approximately 528MB. The EIDE standard is also known as ATA-2 standard.

Figure 5-5:
Looking at the IDE/ATA connectors on the mother-board.

Most techies in the computing industry interchange *IDE* and *EIDE*. For example, if you have a newer motherboard that uses EIDE drives, most documentation and technicians simply use the term *IDE* even though the drives might be EIDE, or even an Ultra DMA (direct memory access) drive. Also note that most techies and documentation use the term "controller" for the connectors on the motherboard that you connect the drives to, but really the controller is the circuitry on the hard drive that controls access to the drive. My point is get used to people using the term *IDE* instead of *EIDE,* and *controller* instead of *connectors.*

ATAPI specification

Originally, IDE devices were implemented as hard drives, but an additional ATA specification allows other types of devices to exist on an ATA (or IDE) chain. This specification is the ATA Packet Interface (ATAPI), which allows devices like CD-ROMs and tape drives to exist on an ATA chain. Other types of ATAPI devices are CD writers, DVD devices, and Zip drives.

Ultra DMA

Ultra DMA drives have two major benefits over ATA drives:

✦ **Speed:** Originally, Ultra DMA devices functioned at twice the speed of regular IDE devices. IDE devices execute commands at 16.6 Mbps, whereas Ultra DMA devices execute commands at 33.3 MBps, or 66.6 MBps with Ultra DMA/66. Note that there have been improvements to Ultra DMA to include speeds of 133 MBps.

✦ **Reliability:** Ultra DMA devices implement error correction, which provides for increased data reliability compared with IDE, which does not implement error correction.

To take advantage of Ultra DMA technology, you need an Ultra DMA drive and an Ultra DMA–compatible BIOS. In addition, you need an Ultra DMA–compatible driver loaded in the OS that uses the device.

Ultra DMA technology is backward compatible with IDE and EIDE. For example, if you have a motherboard with Ultra DMA support, you can still plug an IDE or EIDE device into the controllers on the motherboard. You can also install an Ultra DMA drive on an EIDE board.

Ultra DMA/66 requires the use of an 80-wire ribbon cable, which contains the normal 40 wires of an IDE cable plus an additional 40 ground wires to reduce noise on the cable and thus increase performance. The 80-wire cable still uses a 40-pin connector on the end to keep compatibility with IDE.

Book II
Chapter 5

Working with Storage

Drive performance

The performance of the drive is determined by the Programmed I/O (PIO) mode or DMA mode it supports. The PIO mode or DMA mode is a protocol that determines the transfer rate of the drive. A number of different PIO modes and DMA modes are supported by devices, as shown in Table 5-4.

Table 5-4	PIO and DMA Modes	
Mode	*Runs At*	*Used By*
PIO Mode 0	3.3 MBps	ATA-1
PIO Mode 1	5.2 MBps	ATA-1
PIO Mode2	8.3 MBps	ATA-1
PIO Mode 3	11.1 MBps	ATA-1 and ATA-2
PIO Mode 4	16.6 MBps	ATA-1 and ATA-2
DMA 33	33.3 MBps	Ultra DMA drives
DMA 66	66 MBps	Ultra DMA drives
DMA 100	100 MBps	Ultra DMA drives
DMA 133	133 MBps	Ultra DMA drives

Be sure to know what a PIO mode is and also the transfer rates of Ultra DMA drives.

Installing IDE devices

In this section, I show you how to install an IDE device. Because all hard drives are different, I present only the most popular solutions for installing hard drives.

First, you want to open up the casing of the computer and find an empty bay for mounting the new hard disk. If you are removing the old hard drive, you can use the same bay. If you are adding a hard drive, find an empty bay and mount the drive there. Second, you slide the drive in the bay so that the power connector and ribbon cable connector face the motherboard. Figure 5-6 shows an IDE drive being placed into the mounting bay.

Figure 5-6: Mounting the hard disk into the drive bay.

IDE cabling

After you mount the drive in place, the third step is to connect the IDE connector on the motherboard to the IDE connector on the hard disk with a 40-wire IDE ribbon cable. Then connect a power connector to the drive. Figure 5-7 shows an IDE ribbon cable.

1st Wire

Figure 5-7: An IDE ribbon cable.

An IDE hard drive uses a 40-wire ribbon cable, and a floppy drive uses a 34-wire ribbon cable. Ultra DMA uses an 80-wire ribbon cable that contains 40 wires for data and 40 additional grounding wires.

One of the wires (wire 1) on the IDE ribbon cable is a different color than the others; usually, it's red, but it might be blue. Wire 1 must be placed over pin 1 when connecting the ribbon cable to the hard drive and motherboard — the Pin 1 rule.

The big question is how to determine which pin is pin 1. Hopefully, the manufacturer indicates pin 1 by placing a small 1 near it. If you look at the connector on the hard drive and on the motherboard, you might see a small 1 on one end of the connector. That's where you need to place wire 1 when connecting the ribbon cable.

Sometimes a manufacturer might not have enough space to indicate pin 1 and so does the opposite — indicate pin 40. This method gives you the same information, though: If you know what side pin 40 is on, you know that pin 1 is on the opposite side.

After you connect the IDE ribbon cable, connect the hard disk power from the power supply so that you can run the motor in the drive. (People often forget this step and then wonder why the drive doesn't work.) Figure 5-8 shows how to connect the ribbon cable and the power supply cable to the hard disk.

Figure 5-8:
Connecting
an IDE drive.

Master/slave configuration

If you are installing multiple IDE devices, you are creating an IDE chain. The chain will be made up of one 40-wire IDE ribbon cable with two drives connected to it. Most IDE ribbon cables today have three IDE connectors on them: one that connects to the motherboard and one for each of the two drives that can be connected in a single chain.

After the two drives are connected, configure the drives into a master/slave configuration. Use this type of configuration because each drive has a built-in controller that makes it act like its own boss. (Have you ever tried to work in an environment with two bosses? Not good.) The purpose of designating a master is to specify the boss of that chain — the controller responsible for communicating with the processor.

When setting up a multidrive system, you have two drives, each with a controller that can potentially send signals to and receive from the processor. To save confusion, one of the drives is designated as the *master,* which receives all signals from the processor and sends back any data on behalf of both drives. The other drive is designated as the *slave,* which passes any information it wants to send to the processor up to the master. The master then forwards that information to the processor. Figure 5-9 illustrates a multidrive system.

Figure 5-9:
One drive is configured as the master, and the other is configured as the slave.

Slave
(Hard disk)

Master
(Hard disk)

Motherboard

To configure the master/slave relationship, you have to configure the jumper settings on the drives. The idea of the procedure is similar for all drives, but because the actual jumper setting might be different for each type of drive, the best thing to do is review the documentation for the drive.

Most hard drives today have the jumpers labeled as Master and Slave. Configuring these drives is usually pretty straightforward. You place the jumper on the master setting for the drive you want to be the master of the chain (meaning that this drive will communicate with the processor directly), and you place the jumper to the slave setting for the drive you want to configure as the slave. The slave drive receives instructions from the master. Figure 5-10 displays master and slave jumper settings.

After you have decided which drive will be the master and which drive will be the slave you will need to adjust the jumper on each drive to set the appropriate setting. For the hard disk that will be master you will move the jumper to the master setting and for the drive that will be the slave you move the jumper to the slave setting. Also note that you will configure an IDE CD-ROM or DVD the same way — as either a master or slave device in the IDE chain.

Book II
Chapter 5

Working with Storage

Figure 5-10: Adjust the jumpers to set one drive as a master and the other as a slave.

Single drive

Drive 1 master

Drive 2 slave

Many times, configuring your drives in a master/slave setup might not be as easy as it looks. What do you do when you cannot see a specific master or slave jumper setting? Many manufacturers place documentation on the back of the drive telling you how to configure the drive for master and slave setups. Unfortunately, this was not the case on a drive I had to configure in the office one day. So I went to the manufacturer's Web site and found out that this drive had a jumper labeled J20; the Web site documentation stated

that if the drive was the only drive or was the master in a dual-drive configuration, the jumper (J20) should be set. If the drive was the slave in the dual-drive configuration, the jumper (J20) should be removed. Figure 5-11 shows the configuration for this example.

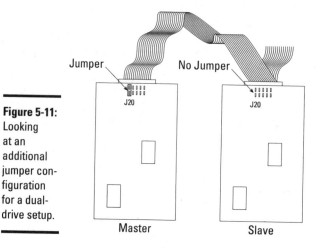

Figure 5-11: Looking at an additional jumper configuration for a dual-drive setup.

The moral of the story: If you can't find the jumper settings on the drives themselves, check out the drives' documentation or go to the manufacturers' Web sites.

Today, you are probably working with EIDE drives which, as I mention earlier, support up to four devices instead of two. These systems have two IDE connectors on the motherboard: the primary IDE connector and the secondary IDE connector. Each connector can have two devices configured in a master/slave relationship, for a total of four devices. Typically, the devices can be hard drives, CD-ROMs, or DVD devices. The steps are the same for configuring master and slave relationships for a hard disk, CD-ROM, and DVD because they are all considered IDE devices. Typically, you configure the CD-ROM or DVD as the slave, but you could also make it the master device on the second IDE connector.

After configuring the jumpers on the drive, power-on the system. The computer should recognize the additional drive and take you into the CMOS setup program. When you review the CMOS settings, you should notice the new drive. If you do not see the new drive, verify the master and slave settings, and maybe even switch the roles of the drives and try again.

Lab 5-1 demonstrates how to master and slave the drives. Lab 5-1 can be found the Labs.pdf file in the Author directory of the CD-ROM.

Learning How SCSI Works

In the following sections, I discuss a type of device more popular than IDE drives in high-end machines, such as powerful workstations or servers — SCSI devices.

SCSI overview

SCSI is an acronym for Small Computer System Interface. The important part of this term is *small computer*, meaning that SCSI has its own brain — the *SCSI adapter* — that handles the SCSI environment. This SCSI adapter (also known as a *SCSI card* or *SCSI controller*) is responsible for managing all SCSI devices and controlling the conversation on the SCSI chain.

SCSI technology has many advantages over IDE technology, such as

✦ **The types of devices supported:** SCSI supports a multitude of devices, including hard drives, CD-ROMs, scanners, printers, and tape drives, to name just a few. This is a huge benefit because originally IDE typically supported only hard drives and CD-ROMs.

✦ **The number of devices supported in a single SCSI chain (also known as a *SCSI bus*):** Original versions of SCSI supported as many as eight devices in the chain, but one of those devices is the SCSI card added to the computer to give you the capability to use SCSI.

IDE allows only two devices in the chain, and EIDE supports four devices. With SCSI, you are not only allowed to have more types of devices but also to have more of those devices!

Original SCSI supports as many as eight devices in the chain. However, if the exam asks how many devices can be *attached* to a SCSI adapter, the answer is seven. If the test asks how many devices can *exist* in the SCSI chain, the answer is eight because the card counts as one of those devices. Remember to watch the wording of the questions closely.

✦ **The performance of SCSI over IDE devices:** Original SCSI devices don't compare in the performance category with EIDE devices, but some of the later SCSI technologies, such as SCSI-2 and SCSI-3, can outperform IDE and EIDE.

I give details about transfer rates of the different types of SCSI devices in the "Types of SCSI" section, later in this chapter.

For the remainder of this chapter, assume that you are dealing with original SCSI, also known as SCSI-1. In the "Types of SCSI" section, I discuss the newer types of SCSI.

Host adapter

When you install SCSI devices, you first need to install the SCSI host adapter, which is an expansion card that you add to the computer so you can chain SCSI devices off the adapter. In essence, the SCSI host adapter is the brain of the SCSI bus; it acts as the controller for the SCSI bus. Figure 5-12 shows a SCSI adapter being inserted into an expansion slot in the system.

Figure 5-12:
The SCSI host adapter.

The SCSI controller (adapter) is responsible for sending and receiving all information to and from the SCSI bus, just like the IDE controller. When the system has information for one of the devices in the SCSI bus, the system hands the information over to the SCSI controller, which then passes the information to the appropriate device in the chain. Figure 5-13 shows a SCSI bus — made up of the SCSI host adapter (the SCSI controller) — along with two internal SCSI devices and two external SCSI devices.

The beauty of the entire setup is that the SCSI adapter in the computer is assigned resources, such as an IRQ and an I/O address. Each device in the SCSI chain is not assigned these resources because all processor information passes to the SCSI controller, and the controller passes the information to the devices. This means that the system never talks to the devices directly, so each device does not require an IRQ and an I/O address.

Internal device 2

Internal device 1 SCSI controller

Figure 5-13:
Looking at a
SCSI daisy
chain.

External device 1

External device 2

Working with Storage

When you purchase a SCSI adapter, first look inside your system to figure out what type of expansion slots are free. You will typically have some PCI slots, but you might have an ISA or EISA slot as well. The difference between these expansion slots is performance — PCI runs at 33 MHz, and ISA and EISA run at only 8 MHz. Also, PCI and EISA are 32-bit technologies, and ISA is only 16-bit. The bottom line is that if you have free PCI slots, you will probably end up purchasing a PCI SCSI adapter.

So the next big question is when the SCSI controller receives information for a particular device in the chain, how does it send the information to that device?

Addressing

Each device is assigned an internal address — a *SCSI ID* — in the SCSI bus. The SCSI controller knows the address of each device. When the SCSI controller receives information for a particular device, the controller references that device by its ID in the SCSI bus. This way, there's no confusion as to whom the data is destined for.

You are responsible for assigning the SCSI IDs when you connect each device to the SCSI chain. You assign an ID either by jumpers or DIP (dual inline package) switches if the device is an internal device, or by a spinner if the device is external. A *spinner* is an indicator on the back of the external SCSI device whose value you can change by pressing the button to increase or decrease the SCSI ID. Figure 5-14 shows the back of an external SCSI tape drive and how to change the SCSI ID using the spinner.

Figure 5-14:
Assigning a
SCSI ID to
an external
device.

In Figure 5-14, you can also see the type of connector used for external SCSI devices. This is a Centronics 50-pin connector.

If you are installing an internal SCSI device, you will most likely need to assign the SCSI ID by using jumpers. Internal SCSI devices have a jumper set with three pairs of jumper pins. The numeric values associated with these jumpers, although probably not shown on the drive, are 4, 2, and 1 (from left to right). Table 5-5 shows this jumper setup.

Table 5-5	Jumper Block Settings		
	J2	J1	J0
Numeric Value	4	2	1
SCSI ID 0	0	0	0
SCSI ID 3	0	1	1
SCSI ID 6	1	1	0

To assign the device a SCSI ID of 0, you would not jumper any of the pins. This is shown in Table 5-5 by having the off state (represented by 0) at each jumper location. Another example of setting a jumper ID is assigning the device a SCSI ID of 3: Jumper the J0 pins and the J1 pins, but not the J2

pins. This enables decimal values of 1 + 2. Table 5-5 also shows what would happen if you want to set the SCSI ID to 6: Enable jumpers J1 and J2, which enables the decimal values of 2 + 4, while the jumper J0 has an off state.

The IDs you assign to each device are completely up to you, but note that the higher the number, the more important the device is to the SCSI bus. For example, if two devices need to send information through the bus at the same time, the device with the higher SCSI ID is always given priority. This is why the SCSI host adapter is usually assigned the highest number in the chain (usually 7 if the bus supports eight devices — the ID numbers start with 0).

So the host adapter is assigned an ID of 7, and a SCSI bootable hard drive is assigned a SCSI ID of 0, which is the SCSI ID that the controller automatically looks to in order to boot off a SCSI hard drive. Outside of that, you decide what the ID numbers are for each device. As a rule, give slower devices higher ID numbers so that they receive a higher priority in the SCSI bus. Devices with higher priority get access to the bus before lower priority devices.

SCSI cabling

Different types of cabling are used to chain SCSI devices to the SCSI adapter. Internal devices use a 50-wire ribbon cable; external devices require a thick Centronics cable to connect to the Centronics 50 (typically used by SCSI-1) or the Centronics 68 (typically used by wide SCSI-2 technologies or Ultra SCSI-3) connector on the back of the device.

The different versions of SCSI use a large number of different cable types. Figure 5-15 shows some internal SCSI connectors, and Figure 5-16 displays a handful of external SCSI connectors. Be sure to be familiar with these cable types for the exam.

Termination

Both ends of the SCSI bus must be terminated so that when a signal is sent down the SCSI bus, it is absorbed at the end of the bus by the terminator. If the signal was not absorbed, or removed from the bus with a termina-tor, the signal would bounce back and collide with other data on the bus. A collision would destroy the signal. The first device in the chain must be terminated along with the last device in the chain, the first device usually being the host adapter. If the device is an internal device, terminating might involve modifying jumper settings. If the device is external, a terminator will be added to the back of the device. Figure 5-17 shows a terminator for exter-nal devices.

50-pin IDC female

50-pin IDC male

68-pin high density - male

Figure 5-15:
Looking
at internal
SCSI
connectors.

80-pin SCSI SCA connector

If your SCSI chain has a combination of internal and external SCSI devices, the card shouldn't be terminated because it is no longer the end of the SCSI chain. Instead, you should terminate the devices at either end of the SCSI chain.

Most SCSI cards today are self-terminating, so you typically will not need to terminate them manually.

Types of SCSI

Over the past 12 years or so, SCSI technology has increased in performance to stay competitive with advances in IDE and EIDE. Newer versions of SCSI have amazing transfer rates, which is one of the reasons why you find network servers using SCSI hard drives instead of EIDE devices. The following list outlines the key points about the different versions of SCSI:

✦ **SCSI-1:** The original version of SCSI (SCSI-1) was an 8-bit technology with a transfer rate of 5 MBps. One of the major benefits of SCSI was that you were not limited to two devices in a chain like you are with IDE. SCSI-1 allowed you to have eight devices in the chain, with the controller counting as one.

✦ **Fast SCSI-2:** Fast SCSI-2 increased the performance of SCSI by doubling the transfer rate. Fast SCSI-2 devices transfer information at 10 MBps. Fast SCSI-2 is still an 8-bit technology and supports eight devices in the chain.

DB-25 female

DB-25 male

50-pin centronics

50-pin high density

68-pin high density

Figure 5-16:
Looking at
external
SCSI
connectors.

68-pin very high density

Figure 5-17:
A SCSI
terminator.

✦ **Wide SCSI-2:** Wide SCSI-2 doubled the 8-bit data path of SCSI to 16 bits. Doubling the width of the data path raised the transfer rate to 10 MBps, like Fast SCSI-2, but Wide SCSI-2 can support 16 devices in a chain.

When trying to remember the difference between SCSI-1, Fast SCSI-2, and Wide SCSI-2, think of it this way. *Fast* implies speed, so the transfer rate is increased. *Wide* implies "wider" or bigger, which is the data path that has been increased; as a result, you also get a higher transfer rate.

✦ **Fast Wide SCSI-2:** Fast Wide SCSI-2 is the combination of Fast SCSI-2 and Wide SCSI-2. The data path of Fast Wide SCSI-2 is 16 bits, the transfer rate is 20 MBps, and it supports 16 devices in a chain.

✦ **Ultra SCSI:** Ultra SCSI takes the transfer rate of 10 MBps and doubles it again to 20 MBps! With Ultra SCSI, the bus width is only eight bits, and the number of devices that exist in the chain is eight.

✦ **Ultra Wide SCSI:** Ultra Wide SCSI is Ultra SCSI with the bus width increased to 16 bits, and the number of devices in the chain is increased to 16. The transfer rate of Ultra Wide SCSI increased to 40 MBps.

✦ **LVD (Ultra2 SCSI):** *Low Voltage Differential (LVD),* also known as *Ultra2 SCSI,* has a bus width of 16 bits and supports up to 16 devices. LVD is a popular SCSI version due to having a high transfer rate of 80 MBps. Figure 5-18 shows an LVD adapter (or card) with a cable and hard drive.

Figure 5-18:
An LVD SCSI card with hard drive and internal cable.

Be prepared to answer questions on the A+ exam about the different types of SCSI. I suggest memorizing the transfer rates of each type.

Installing SCSI devices

If you understand the issues with SCSI, installing a SCSI bus is fairly simple. First, assign a unique ID number to each device. I usually perform this step at the beginning so that when everything is connected, I won't have to play around figuring out how to change the ID of the devices. For more on assigning the IDs, see the section, "Addressing," earlier in this chapter.

When assigning the ID numbers, remember that you want to assign the bootable drive the ID of 0 because the SCSI host adapter automatically looks to SCSI ID 0 for a bootable device. You also want to enable the SCSI BIOS on the SCSI controller if you are booting off a SCSI hard disk. When you enable the SCSI BIOS, you won't need to install a driver for the card because the PC will recognize the device on startup. If you are booting off an IDE drive and using the SCSI disk as an additional drive, disable the SCSI BIOS and install a driver in the OS.

After you assign the ID numbers to each device, insert the SCSI host adapter into the expansion slot of the PC. After inserting the SCSI card, chain all devices.

When preparing for the A+ exam, know the different terms used for a particular technology. Another term for a *SCSI chain* is a *daisy chain*. When you chain devices, you create a daisy chain.

When you have the devices chained, make sure that each end on the SCSI bus is terminated. If the last device is an external device, put the terminator on the end of the device. If you are installing internal devices, check the documentation on the internal devices to find out what jumpers to set.

At this point, the IDs are configured for each device, the SCSI card is inserted into the PC, and the devices are connected to the card to create a SCSI bus. The SCSI bus is also terminated at either end. Before installing the driver for the SCSI card in the operating system, review the steps to install a SCSI device one last time. To install a SCSI bus

1. Assign unique IDs to each device.

2. Install the SCSI host adapter into the expansion slots.

3. Chain devices to the SCSI host adapter.

4. Terminate the SCSI bus at both ends of the chain.

5. Install the driver for the SCSI card if you are not booting off the first hard disk.

After you connect the hardware for the SCSI chain, you need to load a driver in the OS for the SCSI host adapter. After inserting the SCSI card and powering-on the Windows OS, Plug and Play should kick in, asking for the driver of

the new hardware. If Plug and Play does not kick in, you can run the Add Hardware Wizard found in the Control Panel or My Computer properties of the system. To install a SCSI adapter in Windows if it is not detected automatically, follow these steps:

1. **Choose Start⇨Settings⇨Control Panel in Windows 2000 or right-click My Computer and choose Properties in Windows XP and Windows Server 2003.**

2. **Double-click the Add Hardware icon in Windows 2000. In Windows XP, go to the Hardware tab and click the Add Hardware Wizard button.**

 For both methods, the Add Hardware Wizard now displays a welcome screen.

3. **Click Next.**

4. **Select Add or Troubleshoot a Device and then click Next.**

5. **In the Choose Hardware Device dialog box, select Add a New Device and then click Next.**

6. **Choose the adapter to install, so select No, I Want to Select the Hardware from a List. Click Next.**

 - *If you know the host adapter you are installing:* Select No, I Want to Select the Hardware from a List.

 - *If you are unsure of the host adapter you are installing:* Select Yes, Search for New Hardware.

 The next screen asks you what type of device you are installing.

7. **Choose SCSI and RAID controllers and then click Next.**

8. **In the list of devices, select the manufacturer on the left side and the adapter to install on the right side; then click Next.**

9. **Click Finish.**

10. **Restart the computer.**

The steps to install a driver manually in Windows Vista are similar to Windows XP. To launch the Add Hardware Wizard in Windows Vista, if Plug and Play has not loaded your device driver, you simply choose **Start⇨Control Panel⇨Hardware and Sound⇨Device Manager.** Once in the device manager, right click on your computer at the top of the screen and choose Add Legacy Hardware — the Add Hardware Wizard will launch.

To practice installing SCSI devices in Windows perform Lab 5-2. Lab 5-2 can be found the `Labs.pdf` file in the Author directory of the CD-ROM.

The Serial ATA Hype!

IDE technology has been around for many, many years, and there has been a big need for a change in hard drive technology. That change came as a new hard drive interface called serial ATA (SATA). IDE is a parallel technology (PATA), and although SATA is a serial technology, it offers great speed and other benefits. SATA is also a lot faster than IDE — approximately 30 times faster, with current speeds of 150 Mbps and future speeds of 600 Mbps.

One of the first benefits of SATA is that it is a *hot-swappable* technology, meaning that you can add or remove drives from the system without shutting down the system. This is a huge benefit when you look for RAID solutions for servers that you don't want to spend a lot of money on — like a server for a small company. (For more on RAID, see the section "Securing Data with RAID," later in this chapter.)

Another benefit of SATA is in the cabling. Because SATA is a serial technology, the cables can be longer than your typical IDE ribbon cables. I don't known how many times with IDE I had to switch the CD-ROM and my second hard drive around just so the ribbon cable could reach. SATA cables can be 39 inches long, but the maximum distance for IDE is 18 inches.

The other benefit of the cabling with SATA is that it uses only 7 wires, as opposed to the 80 wires used in newer IDE drives. The benefit here is that it allows for better airflow in the system, which results in a cooler system. Figure 5-19 shows a SATA drive and cable.

If you do not have a motherboard with SATA connectors, you can get a PCI card that does have the connectors. Also, for backward compatibility, you can get a SATA bridge that allows IDE drives to be connected to a SATA system.

With IDE, you have to master and slave the drives when you want multiple IDE devices. Yet another benefit to SATA is that there is no mastering and slaving of devices because you can only connect one SATA device to a single connector, or channel. The reason this is a benefit is because when installing a drive, you don't need to have knowledge of mastering and slaving devices — you simply connect the SATA device to the system!

If you want two SATA drives, you need two SATA connectors — and don't forget that you can get cards to give you more connectors, allowing you to install additional SATA devices.

Figure 5-19:
A SATA cable and power connector connecting to a SATA drive.

SATA power connector

SATA data connector

eSATA Drives

eSATA — *external SATA* — and allows for external hard drives to connect to a system over a SATA port instead of the typical USB or FireWire port. In the past, external drives were enclosures that held SATA drives, but the interface to connect the enclosure to the computer used USB or FireWire. This created overhead as the SATA interface is translated to USB or FireWire, which is slower than SATA. With eSATA connections on the motherboard, you can connect to the external drive using eSATA, thus leveraging SATA speeds with no translation drawbacks!

An eSATA device requires its own power source (it is an external device) and can have an external SATA cable length of 2 meters. eSATA cable is specially designed to help prevent electromagnetic interference (EMI). eSATA cable has also been designed to handle more than 5,000 times of adding and removing of the drive; the current internal SATA cable is suited for only 50 insertions and removals. Figure 5-20 shows an eSATA connector on a 1TB (terabyte) external hard drive.

Figure 5-20:
An eSATA
connector
on an
external
hard drive.

Using Removable Storage

Not all data storage is hard-wired to the system. *Removable storage* is the
term used for storage media that you take away from the system with you.

Floppy disks

The floppy disk was very popular for storing data and being able to carry
the data with you. Floppy disks are not as popular today because they typi-
cally can store only up to 1.44MB of data. Today, one picture from a digital
camera will use that much space.

A floppy disk has a hard plastic casing with a sliding metal shutter that allows the drive to access the silicon disk inside. The floppy drive comes in different sizes, or formats:

+ **5¼-inch:** The 5¼-inch floppy disk came in two formats: 360KB and 1.2MB. The 5¼-inch floppy disk had a soft, flexible shell that did not protect the disk very much. You might not encounter a 5¼-inch floppy because they have been obsolete for years.

+ **3½-inch:** A 3½-inch floppy disk is the floppy disk that you will most likely encounter, if you encounter one at all. Like with the 5¼-inch floppy disk, there is a protective shell, but the shell of this format is hard plastic. The 3½-inch floppy comes in two formats: 720KB and 1.44MB. The 1.44MB format is more common.

Zip drives

A Zip drive is similar to a floppy drive but a little bit larger physically and stores more information. A Zip drive can store 100MB or 250MB of data, depending on what type of drive it is. These drives were popular solutions for backing up data before CD-ROMs and external drives became popular.

CD-ROM/CDRW

A *compact disc–read-only memory (CD-ROM)* is an optical storage technology that uses a laser to read and write data. Originally, as the name implies, one could only read from CD-ROMs. CD-ROMs are the preferred media to distribute software and fairly large amounts of data.

Originally, CD-ROMs stored 650MB of data and could store 74 minutes of music, but today's CD-ROMs store 700MB of data or 80 minutes of music. CD-ROMs are written to from the inside out. If you look at the bottom of the CD-ROM, you see the lines indicating where data was written, which is very useful information if you ever pick up a CD and wonder whether it has been written to.

The speed (transfer rate) of the CD-ROM, measured in multiples of 150 KBps, is indicated with an *X*. For example, an old 1X (pronounced "one times") CD-ROM had a transfer rate of 150 KBps, and an 8X has a transfer rate of 1200 KBps ($150 \times 8 = 1200$), and a much faster 48X has a transfer rate of 7200 KBps.

For many years now, CD drives are writeable: If you want to *burn* your own CD you can. (Writing to a CD is often called *burning a CD*.) This makes CD drives much more popular than the older floppy drives because of the

amount of information you can store on the CD — a great solution for backing up your data!

The two types of writeable CDs are *CD Recordable (CDR)* and *CD ReWritable (CDRW)*. The difference between them is that you can write to CDR only once, but you can reuse a CDRW many times by reformatting the CD and starting again.

CDR speeds are shown in a format like 4x24: The first value is the record speed, and the second value is the read speed. Each value is multiplied by the 150 KBps to calculate the record and read speed. CDRW displays three values to indicate the speed of the device: write speed, rewrite speed, and read speed — for example, 4x4x24.

A CDR is an example of a *write once read many (WORM)* disc. Remember for the exam that the CDR speed is displayed with the record speed showing first and then the read speed (4x24). CDRW displays the speed as the write speed, rewrite speed, and read speed (4x4x24).

You can write to a CDR multiple times, but you cannot overwrite areas of the disc that have already been written to. With a CDR, writing to it many times appends the additional write operations information to the end of the CDR. Each burn operation that you perform is a *session,* and most writeable CD drives today support multiple sessions. For example, say you back up your pictures to CD and use only 350MB of space on the CDR. You can write more data to the CD with the remaining space at a later time. With the cost of CDRs being so low nowadays, I typically don't bother. I burn a CD, label it, and then file it.

When writing to a CD, the process is not done magnetically like it is with hard drives. As I mention earlier, the write operation is performed with a laser. The CD has a chemical-dye layer mixed with a thin reflective layer. When you write to the CD, the chemical layer is heated with the laser to create a solid state at that location. These locations reflect less light, and the different patterns of reflection create the data on the disk.

DVD/DVDRW

Digital versatile discs (DVDs) are similar to CDs in the sense that they are another type of optical storage, but DVDs store a lot more data. The typical DVD stores 4.7GB of data. Some DVDs (unlike CDs) can store data on both sides of the disk, and newer DVDs even store data on different layers on the DVD. This allows the DVD to store more than the 4.7GB, depending upon the DVD standard. Table 5-6 describes the different DVD standards.

Table 5-6	DVD Standards	
Standard	*Specifications*	*Total Storage Space*
DVD-5	Single-sided, single layer	4.7GB
DVD-9	Single-sided, double layer	8.5GB
DVD-10	Double-sided, single layer	9.4GB
DVD-18	Double-sided, double layer	17GB

The transfer rates of DVDs are measured in a similar fashion to CD-ROMs but the transfer rate is 1.35 MBps for each times (x). For example, if you have a 2x DVD-ROM, it has a transfer rate of 2.70 MBps. An 8x DVD-ROM has a transfer rate of 10.80 MBps.

Blu-ray Discs

Blu-ray discs are popular items today in the video world because they offer the capabilities of high-definition (HD) video. Blu-ray has much better quality than DVD.

Blu-ray, created by Sony, was named after the fact that a blue laser is used to read and write to the Blu-ray disc. (DVDs use a red laser.) Not only does Blu-ray offer HD video, but it also stores more information than a DVD. Blu-ray discs can store up to 25GB of data for a single-layer disc, but can store up to 50GB of data for a double-layer disc!

Blu-ray discs also have a faster transfer rate than DVDs. DVD speeds could be calculated by taking the speed indicated and multiplying it by 1.35 MBps, but a Blu-ray disc has a multiplier of 4.5 MBps!

To compare, an 8x DVD has a transfer rate of 10.80 MBps, but an 8x Blu-ray disc has a transfer rate of 36 MBps!

Flash drives/thumb drives

Flash drives, also known as *thumb drives* or *memory sticks,* are the popular method for carrying data from computer to computer. Flash drives, which can store anywhere from 64MB to multiple gigabytes of information, are relatively inexpensive.

Flash drives are USB devices that you simply plug into the USB port on the computer. Plug and Play kicks in, detects the device, and assigns the drive a letter in the My Computer icon. To access the flash drive, you simply double-click the drive in My Computer and open, copy, and move files as you wish. Figure 5-21 shows a flash drive.

Figure 5-21: A flash drive uses a USB connection to interface with the computer.

SD cards

Multimedia devices, such as MP3 players and digital cameras, support adding memory to the device by using *compact flash cards* or *Secure Digital* (SD) cards (as shown in Figure 5-22).

CompactFlash (CF) cards have been very popular but have been replaced by SD cards. SD cards are used by a number of types of devices such as digital cameras, laptops, printers, MP3 players, and PDAs to name a few types of devices. SD cards are a great way to carry your data from one device to another.

SD cards store data up to 4GB, but a newer SD format — Secure Digital High Capacity (SDHC) — can store information up to 32GB or more. The problem is that SDHC cards cannot be read by SD devices, such as a camera. For a device to be able to read an SDHC card, the device must be compatible with SDHC. This is important to remember when you purchase an SD card for your camera. The SD and SDHC cards are the same physical size and appear the same; look for the label indicating SDHC on the SDHC card.

External hard drives

External drives are just as popular as flash drives today. Like flash drives, an external drive uses a USB connection, but could also allow you to connect the drive through FireWire or eSATA. External drives allow you to store hundreds of gigabytes, even a terabyte, of data. These are great solutions to add more space to a laptop computer or desktop PC.

Tape

A popular type of media for data is *tape,* which is typically used to store backup copies of data. This copy of the data stored on tape is used to bring the data back if the hard drive fails. Different types of tape drives are popular today:

Figure 5-22:
A Compact-
Flash, SD
card, and
SD card
carry case.

✦ **Quarter-inch cartridge (QIC):** QIC — one of the oldest and most popular tape standards — supports many different tape sizes. The QIC size depends on the standard, and each standard is labeled similar to QIC-80 — the QIC tape that supports 80MB of data. Other examples are QIC-40 (40MB tapes) and QIC-5210 (25GB tapes).

✦ **Travan:** Travan is a tape drive standard based on the QIC standard but supports compression. Travan is typically more expensive and can store from 400MB to 8GB of data or more. Examples of tape sizes in this standard are labeled as TR-1 (stores 400MB of data) and TR-4 (stores 8GB of data).

✦ **Digital Audio Tape (DAT):** DAT drives store data in a digital format and use two heads: one for reading data and the other for writing data. DAT drives use a standard called *Digital Data Storage (DDS)* to store data. Examples of DDS tapes are DDS-1 (stores 2GB of data), DDS-2 (stores 8GB of data), and DDS-4 (stores 40GB of data).

Understanding File Systems

The file system dictates how information is organized on the disk. For example, the file system determines how large the *allocation unit,* or *storage unit,* of a file is. If you create a 12K file, how much space is that file really using — 12K, 16K, or 32K? Such organizational issues are what the file system deals with.

The following sections introduce the different file systems available and the OSes that support them. You also find out what features the file systems do and do not support.

The FAT file system

The *File Allocation Table (FAT)* file system has been the most popular file system up until the last few years. Although the FAT file system is the most common (it can be used by all OSes), it is losing the popularity contest to its successor — FAT32 — because of its age and limitations.

The FAT file system was the file system used by DOS, Windows 3.1, and Windows 9x; and is supported in all current versions of Windows including Windows Vista. FAT's biggest strength is that it is the file system most widely understood by different OSes — but it has many shortcomings. One of the major shortcomings is that it cannot create a partition larger than 2GB. (A discussion of partitions is coming up in the "Managing Partitions and Volumes" section; for now, consider a *partition* simply as a discrete portion of space on the disk.) The 2GB size limit was not a major limitation until hard drive sizes exceeded a few gigabytes. For example, a problem with the FAT file system is that a 20GB drive would need to be divided into ten partitions to use all the space — an impractical and inappropriate use of space. Can you imagine being required to divide your home up into ten different rooms whether you wanted to or not? Instead of five spacious rooms, you would get ten cramped rooms! Not practical!

Earlier in this chapter, in the section "Disk geometry," you can discover the characteristics of a disk, including *clusters* (groups of sectors; each sector taking up 512 bytes on the disk). To refresh your memory, a cluster is what a file is written to, and only one file can occupy a cluster at a time. The cluster size is determined by the partition size and the file system being used. For example, you might have a 2GB FAT partition with a 32K cluster size. The issue with clusters is that if you have a 32K cluster size and you save a 12K file, you waste 20K of hard disk space because only one file can occupy a cluster. Over time, as more files are saved, this could add up to a lot of wasted space! The solution is to use smaller partition sizes, which create smaller cluster sizes, or to use a different file system that uses smaller cluster sizes.

Bottom line, the FAT file system uses clusters inefficiently. Table 5-7 lists the cluster sizes used with different partition sizes on FAT file systems.

Reasons to dual boot

There are a number of reasons you might want to have a dual-boot system:

✔ Software doesn't run smoothly on one OS, so you install an additional OS and boot to that OS to run your software.

✔ You are part of the help desk team in an organization that runs two different OSes, and you will need to boot to the appropriate OS to find solutions to problems.

✔ You are studying for the A+ exam and need to run Windows 2000 and Windows XP but don't have two different computers.

Understand that in this day and age, instead of dual-booting, IT professionals are using software such as Microsoft's Virtual PC which allows you to run each operating system in a separate window. The benefit is that you can have both OSes running at the same time and network them together.

Table 5-7	FAT Partitions and Their Cluster Sizes
Partition Size	*Cluster Size*
0–127MB	2K
128–255MB	4K
256–511MB	8K
512–1023MB	16K
1024–2048MB	32K

One other limitation of the FAT file system is its lack of built-in security. For example, you might want to set permissions on a folder so that only Bob can create files in that folder. Unfortunately, you can't set permissions on a FAT file system. In fact, if you are using a FAT file system with current versions of Windows such as Windows XP (which are well respected for their security), you will lose the capability of securing the file system even though you are told you are running a much more secure system than a Windows *9x* system. The file system dictates the feature set you get when dealing with files and folders, so no matter what OS you are running, if you are using the FAT file system, you can't secure the files.

So, besides being a file system that all OSes can run on, what is the FAT file system good for? Well, the versatility of FAT might be its only major benefit — most OSes can run on it, which makes it a great file system for configuring a dual-boot system. A *dual-boot system* has multiple OSes installed and has the capability to boot to either OS at any point in time. For example, if you were supporting an organization that was dual-booting its systems with Windows *9x* and Windows XP, you would need to use a file

system common to both OSes. In this day and age, the chances of this happening are very slim so there really isn't a need to use FAT if you are using current versions of Windows.

The FAT32 file system

After the retail release of Windows 95, an update to the OS was created, known as Windows 95 OSR2 (OEM Service Release 2). Windows 95 OSR2 introduced an updated FAT file system called *FAT32*. One of the apparent benefits of FAT32 was that the maximum partition size was increased from 2GB to 2TB. Now, when you go out and buy that 20GB drive, you don't have to divide it into ten partitions; you can keep one 20GB partition.

Although FAT32 has the capability to have partitions of 2TB in size, Microsoft has limited the size of FAT32 partitions in Windows 2000/XP OSes to 32GB when creating partitions. The reasoning for this is that you should be using NTFS as a file system. Windows has no problem recognizing a larger FAT32 partition that was created with some other utility, such as the case when you purchase a new external hard drive that is hundreds of GB.

The other major benefit to FAT32 is that it dramatically decreases the cluster size to make better use of disk space. Table 5-8 compares the default cluster sizes of FAT partitions with the default cluster sizes of FAT32 partitions. Note that FAT32 doesn't support partitions smaller than 512MB.

Book II
Chapter 5

Working with Storage

Table 5-8	Comparing Cluster Sizes	
Partition Size	*FAT Cluster Size*	*FAT32 Cluster Size*
0MB–127MB	2K	Not Supported
128MB–255MB	4K	Not Supported
256MB–511MB	8K	Not Supported
512MB–1023MB	16K	4K
1GB–2GB	32K	4K
2GB–8GB	Not Supported	4K
8GB–16GB	Not Supported	8K
16GB–32GB	Not Supported	16K
Over 32GB	Not Supported	32K

Looking at Table 5-8, if you have a 2GB partition on FAT32, you have a cluster size of 4K. However, if you had created the partition and used the FAT file system, the cluster size would be 32K. If you save a 12K file on the FAT partition, you lose 20K of disk space, while the same 12K file would waste no space on a FAT32 partition because it will span three clusters of 4K each!

One of the shortfalls of FAT32 is that even with today's OSes, no security features are built into FAT32. If you wish to leverage security features in the OS — such as file permissions, auditing file access, and Encrypting File System (EFS) — you need to use NTFS.

NTFS

Starting with Windows NT, Microsoft implemented a new file system: New Technology File System (NTFS). NTFS makes better use of the space available on a particular disk by using 512 bytes as the cluster size (the same size as a sector). This means that you waste even less space on an NTFS file system than on a FAT32 file system.

The original version of NTFS supported a number of features that made it more attractive than the FAT versions of the file systems. With NTFS, you could configure permissions that controlled who could access what files. You could also take advantage of features such as compression and auditing.

One of the biggest complaints with the original version of NTFS is that it had no way to limit how much disk space a user could use. As a result, users could waste gigabytes of hard disk space on the server, and the administrator could not stop the user unless a third-party program was purchased. Limiting disk space usage is one of the improvements that Microsoft made on the next version of NTFS — NTFS version 5.0 — which was implemented with Windows 2000 and every Windows OS after that.

NTFS 5.0

This newer version of NTFS has a few extra features over original implementations of NTFS, one of which has been long overdue — disk quotas. *Disk quotas* allow the system's administrator to choose the amount of disk space that each user is allowed to use by placing a limit on the disk. For example, when managing the home directories, you can ensure that Bob is not allowed to use more than 500MB of disk space.

Another feature of NTFS 5.0 is the Encrypting File System (EFS). EFS uses public key/private key technology to encrypt a file stored on the hard drive. When a file or folder is encrypted with EFS, only the person who created the file or the *recovery agent* (by default, the administrator is the recovery agent) can open the file. When using EFS, even if another user has permission to view the file, he or she will be unable to do so because the file is encrypted. The encrypting file system is a big selling point for organizations with mobile users who need to protect the privacy of the data that sits on their laptops.

To summarize, the NTFS file system offers the following features over FAT and FAT32:

+ Securing the resource through permissions
+ Securing files through encryption
+ Enabling auditing to monitor who accesses the files and folders
+ Compressing file or folder contents

NTFS is the preferred file system for all current versions of Windows, including Windows Vista, because NTFS has benefits such as permissions, auditing, encryption, and compression.

HPFS

Years ago, the High Performance File System (HPFS), which gained its popularity with the OS/2 operating system, was a major improvement over the FAT file system. Some of the benefits of OS/2 are that it supports long filenames, up to 254 characters (including the path). HPFS also supports partition sizes up to 2000GB and uses a cluster size of 512 bytes! When looking at the benefits of HPFS, you might wonder, "What's the big deal? I get that with FAT32." The big deal is that HPFS was released well before FAT32, or even before Windows 9*x* was designed.

The disadvantage of HPFS is that it is not widely supported. OSes such as DOS and Windows cannot access HPFS volumes.

Managing Partitions and Volumes

For the A+ exams, you are required to know the steps to install a hard disk. After you physically connect the drive and configure the jumper settings, you need to be aware of the steps to configure the partitions on the disk. The following is the order in which you configure the partitions on the disk:

1. Create a primary partition.

2. Create an extended partition.

3. Create a logical drive in the extended partition.

4. Format the drives to create a file system.

Understanding the order of the steps for partitioning and formatting a disk is important for the A+ Certification exams. Be sure to memorize the above list to correctly answer exam questions about preparing the hard disk.

A *partition* is a segment of the hard disk, created by dividing the disk logically into discrete units. You create partitions for a number of reasons: say, to organize your applications and operating system on drive C while storing your data on drive D. You might also partition a disk for more technical reasons, such as to run multiple OSes on the same machine.

Whatever the reason for creating a partition, how you create and manage partitions is important for the A+ exam. This section examines different types of partitions and provides steps for creating, deleting, and formatting them.

Frequently, a partition is a means of providing better access to the information stored on a disk. For example, telling the kids that their games are on the D: drive is usually easier than describing a complex path to the folder that holds the games.

You are limited to four partitions per disk, so be sure to plan them carefully.

Operating systems such as DOS; Windows 9*x*; and current versions of Windows, such as XP and Vista, that use basic disks (more on that in the later section "Creating partitions and volumes in Windows") can create two types of partitions: primary partitions and extended partitions.

Primary partition

The *primary partition* is the partition that the computer boots from; the OS's boot files are loaded from here. You are allowed to have four primary partitions per disk. Because you may have multiple primary partitions (say, if you are running several OSes on the same computer), you must designate one primary partition as the *active partition* — the partition from which your normal operating system loads.

Extended partition

An extended partition allows you to extend beyond the four-partition barrier by being a partition that contains one or more *logical drives,* which are blocks of disk space assigned a drive letter. As an example on how you could use extended partitions, you could set up three primary partitions and then decide that you would like to divide the last chunk of free space into three additional parts (for a total of six partitions). If you create another primary partition from some of the free space, you will have four parts — and that is your limit, four partitions per disk. What you can do instead is create an extended partition from the remaining space after the three primary partitions have been created and then create three logical drives inside the extended partition. Logical drives are not partitions, so you are not limited to four. This will give you your six desired parts.

An *extended partition* is, in effect, the space that remains after the primary partitions are defined. The extended partition does not have an actual drive letter assigned to it; it's simply a container that holds all the logical drives that you build. A *logical drive* is a logical division of the hard disk that the computer treats as if it were a separate disk drive; it is the actual area of the extended partition to which documents are saved.

As an example, suppose you are partitioning a 6GB hard drive using the FAT file system. FAT cannot define partitions larger than 2GB, so you have to divide this drive into at least three different partitions: The first partition you define is the primary partition — a 2GB partition that also becomes the active partition (drive C). What's left is a 4GB extended partition that can store two logical drives (D and E), each of which can be no larger than 2GB. Figure 5-23 shows this partition configuration.

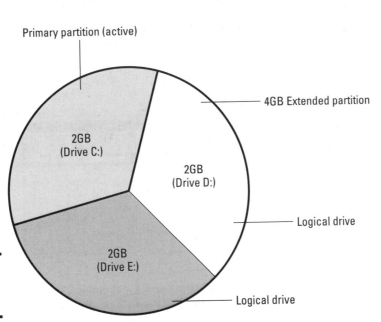

Figure 5-23:
Partitioning
a hard disk.

Note that the extended partition itself has no drive letter assigned to it. The extended partition is just a container to hold the logical drives — and they take the drive letters. Users of the system will be able to store data on drive C, drive D, or drive E.

A hard disk can contain no more than four partitions, only one of which can be the extended partition. This means you could have three primary partitions and one extended partition to hold any logical drives. Having three primary partitions also shows why you have to set the active partition. A primary partition is a bootable partition. But if you have three primary partitions, which one do

you boot from? The answer is simple — the one defined as the *active partition*. Note that when you create the partition during the installation of Windows, the partition is automatically marked as being the active partition.

Creating partitions and volumes in Windows

To create partitions in Windows, you use a partitioning tool known as the *Disk Management snap-in*. You can open the Disk Management snap-in in Windows XP by choosing Start⇨Control Panel, clicking Performance and Maintenance, clicking Administrative Tools, and double-clicking Computer Management. Then, in the Computer Management window, select Disk Management. Figure 5-24 shows the Disk Management snap-in in Windows.

Figure 5-24: Disk Management snap-in found within Windows.

The Disk Management tool is the same for Windows Vista, but to launch it, click the Start button, right-click Computer, and then choose Manage. From the Computer Management console, choose Disk Management in the Storage category.

When managing a disk in Windows, be aware that there are two types of disks: basic and dynamic.

Basic disks

Basic disk is the term Microsoft uses to describe a disk that supports partitions and all the limitations of partitions. If you can create partitions on a disk in Disk Management, you are working with a basic disk. A basic disk has the following characteristics:

✦ The disk is divided into partitions.

✦ You are limited to four partitions per disk.

✦ You are limited to one extended partition per disk.

✦ You create primary partitions, extended partitions, and logical drives.

✦ A basic disk is the default disk type in Windows.

IT professionals have become accustomed to these characteristics when preparing disks for a system. With Windows 2000 and above, you still have these limitations when working with a basic disk, but you may convert the basic disk into a dynamic disk. The benefit of converting to a dynamic disk in newer versions of Windows is that you no longer work with partitions, so there are no partition limitations. I talk more about dynamic disks in the next section, but first you need to see how to create partitions on basic disks.

 The following steps demonstrate how to create a partition on a basic disk within Windows XP. The steps are similar in Windows 2000, Windows Server 2003, and Windows Vista.

1. **Click Start, right-click My Computer, and choose Manage.**

2. **From the Computer Management console, select Disk Management from the left of the screen.**

On the right side, on the bottom half of the screen, notice that the disk type for Disk 1 is Basic Disk.

3. **Right-click the unallocated space and choose New Partition, as shown in Figure 5-25.**

Book II
Chapter 5

Working with Storage

Figure 5-25:
Creating
a partition
within
Windows.

The New Partition Wizard starts and displays a welcome screen.

4. **Click Next.**

The wizard asks what type of partition you will be creating, as shown in Figure 5-26.

5. **Select Primary Partition and then click Next.**

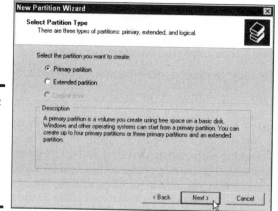

Figure 5-26:
Choose a
partition
type within
the New
Partition
Wizard.

6. **Type the desired size of the primary partition (MB) and then click Next.**

7. **Choose the drive letter you want to associate with this partition and then click Next.**

8. **Choose the file system you want to format the partition as (shown in Figure 5-27) and then click Next.**

Figure 5-27:
Choose the
file system
within
the New
Partition
Wizard.

9. **Click Finish.**

 The drive starts to format in the background, and it indicates the percent complete in the Disk Management utility.

10. **When Disk Management is finished formatting the drive, close the Computer Management utility.**

Dynamic disks

A *dynamic disk* doesn't use partitions but rather volumes as discrete units of space. Because you are creating volumes instead of partitions, you do not have the four-partition limitation of basic disks. With dynamic disks, you can create as many volumes as you wish.

When creating a volume on a dynamic disk, you can create a number of different volume types:

+ **Simple volume:** A block of space that is similar in concept to a partition.

+ **Striped volume:** A volume made up of equal space across multiple hard disks. With striped volumes, when you save a file to the volume, the file is saved across both disks at the same time. The benefit of a striped volume is a performance benefit because multiple disks are working at the same time to save the file.

+ **Spanned volume:** A volume made up of unequal amounts of space that span multiple disks. The benefit of spanned volumes is that you can join multiple areas of free space to create a single volume that users can access through a single drive letter.

+ **Mirrored volume:** A volume made up of two disks. Data that is written to the volume is stored on both disks, each with a full copy of the data. If one disk fails, the other disk has a copy of the data.

Mirrored volumes are supported only on server versions of Windows OSes.

+ **RAID 5 Volume:** A RAID 5 volume uses between 3 and 32 disks. Data saved to the volume is spread across all disks in the volume, along with parity data. The *parity data* is used to calculate data that is unreadable due to a failed disk in the volume.

RAID 5 volumes are also available only on server versions of the Windows operating system, so you won't be able to create one on Windows XP. Read more about RAID in the later section, "Securing Data with RAID." Creating a volume on a dynamic disk in Windows requires you to first upgrade the basic disk to a dynamic disk. After you upgrade the disk to a dynamic disk, note that the `create partition` command changes to a `create volume` command in the Disk Management console. To upgrade the basic disk to a dynamic disk, follow these steps:

1. **Click Start, right-click My Computer, and choose Manage.**

2. **From the Computer Management console, select Disk Management on the left of the screen.**

 On the right side, in the bottom half of the screen, notice that the disk type for Disk 1 is Basic Disk.

3. **Right-click the disk and choose Convert to Dynamic Disk, as shown in Figure 5-28.**

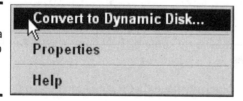

4. **In the Convert to Dynamic Disk dialog box that appears, ensure that the disk number you wish to convert is selected; click OK.**

5. **Click the Convert button on the Disks to Convert screen, as shown in Figure 5-29.**

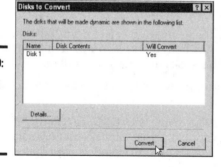

You get a warning message that you will be unable to start older OSes from the disk after it is converted.

6. **Click Yes in the Warning dialog box.**

7. **Click Yes to dismount any file systems being converted.**

After the drive is converted, note that the legend changes to include a simple volume. You will also notice that the disk is now a dynamic disk.

After you convert a basic disk to a dynamic disk, you are ready to create a volume. Creating a volume is similar to creating a partition. To create a volume, follow these steps:

1. **In the Disk Management console, right-click Unallocated Space and then choose New Volume, as shown in Figure 5-30.**

Figure 5-30:
Create
a new
volume on
a dynamic
disk.

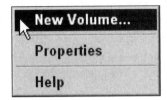

New Volume...

Properties

Help

2. **In the New Volume Wizard that appears, click Next.**

 You see a list of volume types you can create (see Figure 5-31).

3. **Choose the volume type you wish to create and then click Next.**

Figure 5-31:
Select a
volume
type when
creating a
new volume.

4. **Type the amount of space (MB) to use for the volume and then click Next.**

5. **Select a drive letter for the volume and then click Next.**

6. **Specify a file system to use and choose to perform a quick format. Then click Next.**

7. **Click Finish to create the volume.**

Formatting partitions and volumes

After you create the partitions or volumes, your next step is to format these partitions or volumes so that you may start storing data on them. When you format the partitions or volumes, which now show as drive letters in the My Computer (Computer; Vista) icon, you choose which file system to format

them with. Before you format the partitions, you should review the different types of file systems and the advantages and disadvantages of each (see the section "Understanding File Systems," earlier in this chapter).

Formatting a drive prepares the drive for storing information. The `format` command creates a root directory on the disk as well as two tables used to store file information and to aid in file retrieval.

The first table is the Directory Entry Table (DET), which lists all the files stored on the drive, along with the date that each file was last modified. It also stores the starting cluster for each file stored on the drive. The DET is used when the system goes to open a file; the system looks in the DET for the file. When an entry is found for the file being opened, the starting cluster for the file is determined and then the system goes to that cluster to retrieve the file contents.

The second table is the File Allocation Table (FAT), which lists each cluster, showing you which clusters are used and which are free. The FAT also indicates any clusters marked as bad clusters, which are unusable. When a file spans multiple clusters, the FAT shows that the first cluster is linked to the next cluster by indicating the next cluster value as part of the FAT entry. The last cluster that is used to store the data for the file is marked with an end of file (EOF) marker — and this is how the system knows it has reached the last cluster for the file. Figure 5-32 shows a formatted drive along with the DET and FAT.

Figure 5-32: The Directory Entry Table (DET) and the File Allocation Table (FAT).

In Figure 5-32, a file named `first.txt` is listed in the DET with the beginning cluster location of 5. When a user requests the file, the OS looks for the file in the DET. In this example, the DET states that the first cluster containing data

for the file is cluster number 5. Then the system looks at cluster 5 in the FAT and sees that cluster 5 is being used and that it continues on to cluster 6 and on to cluster 8. The system knows that cluster 8 is the last cluster containing data for the file because of the EOF marker.

To format a partition or volume in Windows, open My Computer (Computer; Vista), right-click the drive letter that is assigned to the partition or volume, and then choose Format.

With Windows, you may also format the partition or volume from within the Disk Management snap-in, which is where you created the partition or volume to begin with. To format a partition/volume in Windows using Disk Management, perform the following steps:

Book II
Chapter 5

Working with Storage

1. ***In Windows XP:*** **Click Start, right-click My Computer, and choose Manage.**

 In Windows Vista: **Click Start, right-click Computer, and choose Manage.**

2. **From the Computer Management console, select Disk Management from the left of the screen.**

3. **From the bottom-right side of the screen, right-click the partition you want to format and choose Format, as shown in Figure 5-33.**

Figure 5-33: Choosing the Format command in Disk Management.

Open
Explore

Extend Volume...
Add Mirror...

Change Drive Letter and Paths...
Format...

Reactivate Volume

Delete Volume...

Properties

Help

4. **When the Format dialog box appears, you may choose from a number of settings (shown in Figure 5-34) on how you wish to perform the format.**

 - *Volume Label:* Specify a label for the partition. For example, I usually have a drive labeled Data where I store all my data. This label is just a friendly name used to identify what you might be using the drive for.

 - *File System:* Specify whether you want to use FAT, FAT32, or NTFS as the file system.

 - *Allocation Unit Size:* Select the cluster size for the partition or drive.

- *Perform a Quick Format check box:* The benefit of a *quick format* is that it does not perform a surface scan on the disk to check for errors so the format occurs a lot quicker — recommended if you are pressed for time and do not have any hard drive problems.

- *Enable File and Folder Compression check box:* Implement compression on the drive, which allows you to save disk space by using less space on the disk for the data stored there. The compression feature shrinks the file upon saving and decompresses it upon file opening.

Figure 5-34: Windows format options when formatting a drive.

5. Click OK.

You may also use the command line version of the `format` command by going to a command prompt and typing **format**. For example, to perform a quick format of drive D and then apply a volume label of `Pictures`, the command is

```
format d: /q /v:Pictures
```

Labs 5-3, 5-4, and 5-5 give you the opportunity to practice creating partitions and volumes in Windows XP. You can find these labs in the `Labs.pdf` file in the Author directory of the CD-ROM.

Creating mount points

The disk management tool in Windows allows you to create a mount point, which is an empty folder on one partition that points to another partition. The purpose of the mount point is to make it easy for the user to navigate from one drive to another and access files — and this is transparent to the user. For example, you could have an empty folder on the C: drive called Data that references your second drive, the D: drive. This allows someone on the C: drive to double-click the data folder and see the contents of the D: drive.

To configure mount points in Windows, follow these steps:

1. **Create an empty folder on the C: drive called Data.**

2. **Click Start, right-click My Computer, choose Manage, and then choose the Disk Management snap-in.**

3. **Right-click the D: drive and choose Change Drive Letters and Paths, as shown in Figure 5-35.**

Figure 5-35:
To create a mount point, you must add a drive path to the partition.

**Book II
Chapter 5**

**Working with
Storage**

4. **Click Add to add a drive path as the mount point.**

5. **Click the Browse button and choose the c:\data folder as the mount point for this drive; then choose OK (see Figure 5-36).**

Figure 5-36:
Adding a mount point path.

6. **Close Computer Management.**

7. **Go to drive C: through My Computer (or Computer in Vista) and double-click the c:\data folder.**

 You are redirected to the D: drive.

Understanding drive status

When you install a drive in the system and then navigate to the Disk Management snap-in (in the Computer Management console), you can see that each drive has a status (usually Online) and that each partition or volume has a status (hopefully, all Healthy). This section defines for you what the different statuses mean.

The following are statuses assigned to the physical disk in Disk Management:

✦ **Foreign:** The disk that was added to the system is not originally from this system. To access the disk, you must import the disk into the system by right-clicking the disk and choosing Import Foreign Disk.

✦ **Online:** The disk is available, with no issues.

✦ **Online (errors):** The disk is available but has I/O problems with areas on the disk. If the issue is temporary, use the Reactivate command by right-clicking on the disk to put the disk back online.

✦ **Offline:** The disk is unavailable.

✦ **Audio CD:** This shows the status on a CD-ROM drive when it has an audio CD.

✦ **Basic:** You are using a basic disk and can create partitions on the disk.

✦ **Dynamic:** You are using a dynamic disk and can create volumes on the disk.

The following outlines the status of partitions or volumes in Disk Management:

✦ **Healthy:** The volume is online and accessible.

✦ **Formatting:** You are in the process of formatting the partition or volume.

✦ **Active:** The partition is active.

 (An active partition is the primary partition that you will boot off of.)

✦ **Unallocated:** This status shows for areas of the disk that have not been partitioned and is unusable until you create a partition or volume from the unallocated space.

✦ **Failed:** The partition or volume cannot be accessed because the disk is unavailable or damaged, or the file system has become corrupt.

Securing Data with RAID

Windows servers have a built-in software implementation of RAID (Redundant Array of Inexpensive Disks) that you can take advantage of. *RAID* is a method of implementing redundancy — duplicated information — on your hard drives. If one disk fails, the other disk(s) can provide the missing information. RAID is a method to implement fault tolerance: the idea that in case of a hardware failure in the system (say, a hard drive fails), the system can continue to operate as normal. There are many different levels of RAID, but the only RAID levels that provide redundancy in Windows Servers are RAID 1 and RAID 5.

Windows servers also support RAID 0, called *disk striping* or *striped volumes.* No redundant information is stored on striped volumes, which is why striped volumes are classified as RAID 0. (Think of it as a zero level of redundancy.)

Mirroring/duplexing (RAID 1)

The type of hard drives typically found in servers are SCSI drives, which means that a SCSI adapter (controller) connects the drives to the systems. *Disk mirroring* is the use of two disks on a single controller to create *full redundancy* — whatever is placed on one disk is copied to the second disk. When creating a disk mirror, you must use two disks so that if one disk fails, you can rely on the copy of the data stored on the other disk.

When the mirror is established, you have a new drive letter accessible from the My Computer (Computer; Vista) icon. This drive actually shows the data stored on *both* disks; if you save a file to this drive, it is written to both disks that make up the mirror; you don't see two representations within the My Computer icon. But if you use the Disk Management console, you see that the two disks are part of the mirrored volume.

Disk duplexing is the same idea as disk mirroring but requires the installation of an additional SCSI controller. Disk mirroring is fault tolerant if a drive fails (because the other drive is available), but there is no fault tolerance if the controller fails (because there is only one). If you add an additional controller and place one drive on one controller and the other drive on the other controller, you have a more fault-tolerant solution. If one drive fails, you have the other; if a controller fails, you have the other drive running off the other controller. Figure 5-37 shows the difference between a mirror and a duplex.

To create a mirrored volume on Windows Server, you first need to ensure that you converted both disks that you want to use as mirrors to dynamic disks. See the previous section, "Dynamic disks," to find out how to do this.

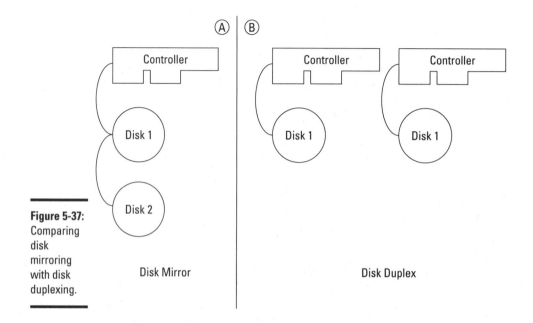

Figure 5-37:
Comparing disk mirroring with disk duplexing.

After you converted both of the disks to dynamic disks, you can create a mirrored volume by following these steps:

1. **Click Start, right-click My Computer, and choose Manage.**

2. **In the Disk Management console, right-click the unallocated space and choose New Volume.**

3. **When the welcome screen to the New Volume Wizard appears, click Next.**

4. **When asked what type of volume you wish to create, choose Mirrored and then click Next (as shown in Figure 5-38).**

5. **From the available disks on the left side of the next wizard page, choose the disk you wish to have the mirrored content stored on and then click Add.**

 The original disk that you right-clicked to create the volume is already selected on the right side. In Figure 5-39, I selected Disk 1 and Disk 2 to participate in the Mirrored Volume.

6. **Specify how much space to use for the volume in the Select the Amount of Space in MB text box; then click Next.**

 In Figure 5-40, I use 1000MB but you can use any value up to the amount of unallocated space on the drive.

Figure 5-38:
Selecting
a mirrored
volume
type when
creating a
new volume.

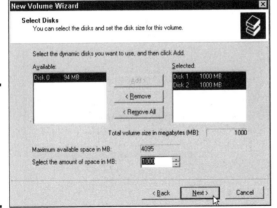

Figure 5-39:
Selecting
the disks for
the mirrored
volume and
setting the
volume size.

7. **Choose a drive letter for the volume and then click Next.**

8. **Select NTFS as the file system and type the volume label**
 MirroredData. **Also select to perform a quick format (as shown in**
 Figure 5-40) and then click Next.

9. **Click Finish.**

 You created a mirrored volume, so anything that is stored on the drive
 will get stored on both disks. If one disk fails, you have a copy of the
 data on the other disk. Notice in Figure 5-41 that the mirrored volume
 takes the same drive letter (E: in this case) for both disks. Therefore, if
 you store something on that drive, it is written to both disks.

Figure 5-40:
Assigning
a volume
label to the
mirrored
volume.

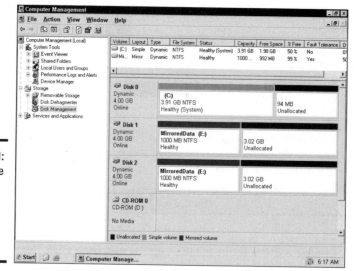

Figure 5-41:
Viewing the
mirrored
volume
in disk
manage-
ment.

RAID 5 Volume (RAID 5)

The problem with RAID 1 is that you essentially waste half the money you spend on hard drives because under normal conditions, you use only one disk. A RAID solution where you get more disk space for your dollar is RAID 5, or a RAID 5 volume.

Microsoft's implementation of RAID 5 volume uses a minimum of 3 disks and can use up to 32 disks. When data is saved to the RAID 5 volume, the information is written across all disks in the array.

A RAID 5 volume also stores parity information on a different disk for each write operation. This parity information is an "answer" that is generated after the data being written is run through an algorithm. The answer is then stored on one of the disks for that write operation. If a disk fails and a piece of data cannot be retrieved, the data is recalculated based on the answer (parity data) stored in the array.

Sound confusing? Here's a simple example: What is the value of x in the following formula?

$$4 + x = 9$$

You probably had no problem coming up the answer of $x = 5$. You simply subtracted the known data from the given answer to calculate what is missing. RAID 5 volumes do the same thing with the parity data (the "answer") when there is a disk failure. When one disk fails, the fault-tolerant disk driver simply subtracts the known data (from the existing disks) from the parity data to generate the missing data on the fly.

A popular question I get is this: "Will RAID 5 volumes be able to recover from multiple disk failures?" To answer that, look at a simple algebra equation. What is the value of x in the following formula?

$$y + x = 9$$

You cannot say for sure what the value of x is because two variables are involved. The software implementation of RAID that is built into the OS can calculate the missing data only when there is but one failed drive.

Now take a look at how to create a RAID 5 volume in Windows Server. Remember that a RAID 5 volume must use at least three disks — so be sure to have three disks with unallocated space. Then follow these directions:

1. **In the Disk Management console, right-click Unallocated Space and choose New Volume.**

2. **On the welcome screen of the New Volume Wizard, click Next.**

 You are asked what type of volume you wish to create.

3. **When asked what type of volume you wish to create, select RAID 5 (as shown in Figure 5-42) and then click Next.**

4. **Choose at least two additional disks to be members of the RAID 5 volume by highlighting each disk on the left side of the screen and clicking Add.**

 In my example, I chose Disk 0, Disk 1, and Disk 2.

Book II
Chapter 5

Working with
Storage

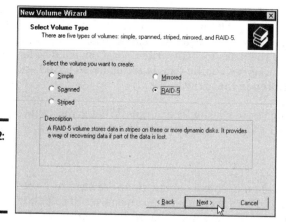

Figure 5-42:
Choosing
to create
a RAID 5
volume.

5. **Specify how much space to use on each disk in the Select the Amount of Space in MB text box; then click Next.**

I used 90MB on each disk, and my total space for the volume is 180MB (see Figure 5-43). But wait a second . . . that doesn't make sense. There are three disks in the RAID 5 volume, and if each disk uses 90MB, the volume size should be 270MB, shouldn't it? No, the volume size is only 180MB because one-third of the space is used for parity data.

Figure 5-43:
Select the
disks to be
members of
the RAID 5
volume and
specify the
size of the
volume.

6. **Choose a drive letter for the volume and then click Next.**

7. **Select NTFS as the file system and type a volume label of** RAID5Data. **Select to perform a quick format and then click Next.**

8. **Click Finish.**

 Figure 5-44 displays the volume as it appears in Disk Management.

Figure 5-44:
Viewing
the RAID
5 volume
in disk
manage-
ment.

Understanding Management Tools

After partitioning the disk and formatting the drive, some maintenance still needs to be done on a regular basis. Drive maintenance helps you address two areas of concern that have an impact on a user's data:

✦ **File system optimization:** Getting the best performance from your file system. If opening files takes much longer than it did two months ago, your system needs optimizing.

✦ **Data integrity:** Having files that are uncorrupted so the data is intact and accessible. Sometimes a file cannot be opened because the file system has lost parts of the file or portions of the disk are bad — in which case you are not concerned with performance but with being able to open the file.

The following sections describe some OS tools that can help you accomplish these two goals as you maintain your system.

Defragmentation utility

After a drive is formatted and you start storing information on it, the information is written to one cluster at a time. This means that on a freshly formatted drive, the contents of a file are written to clusters on the disk

that are side by side. This ensures optimal performance when opening a file because the read/write heads don't have to jump from one end of the disk to another to open a single file. Unfortunately, the disk won't stay in this state because as you add to and delete files, the contents of these files are scattered throughout the disk. The minitable in Figure 5-45 shows a fragmented disk.

1	2	3	4
5	6	7	8

In this example, you can see that blocks 2, 5, and 7 belong to the same file but are scattered throughout the disk. This causes a performance decrease when accessing the file because the read/write heads need to locate the contents of the file that are spread throughout the disk. Disk defragmenting applications clean this up by taking all the data of a single file and placing it in clusters that reside side by side. You can see in Figure 5-46 what the disk would look like after a Windows defragmentation.

1	2	3	4
5	6	7	8

Windows has a Disk Defragmenter utility in the Computer Management console. This great little tool has an analyzer that you can run first to check the selected disk and then report where the used and free space is. This assessment tells you whether you need to defragment. Figure 5-47 shows the Disk Defragmenter utility in Windows after analyzing drive C:.

After the hard drive is analyzed, you can also view a report that shows you detailed information about the analysis. Launch the defrag by clicking the Defragment button. Figure 5-48 shows the report generated by the analysis of drive C:.

Figure 5-47:
Defrag-
menting
a disk in
Windows.

Figure 5-48:
The
analyzer's
report in
Windows.

Check Disk utility

When a drive is formatted, two FAT tables are created — the DET and the
FAT table. (Read about DET earler in this chapter.) The FAT table links all the
clusters that make up a file. What if that link is lost, or points to the wrong
location? If the file system loses the link that joins two clusters together, the
file becomes unreadable and has lost its data integrity. *ScanDisk* is a Windows
utility in older Microsoft OSes that has been replaced by the Check Disk
option in newer Windows OSes (Windows XP and Vista). The Check Disk

option not only looks for lost links but also scans the disk surface for bad blocks (clusters that cannot be written to), marking them as bad so they are not used. To perform an integrity check on a drive in Windows, follow these steps:

1. **Open the My Computer (Computer in Vista) icon and select the drive you want to check.**

2. **Right-click the drive and choose Properties.**

3. **On the Tools tab, click the Check Now button.**

 Figure 5-49 shows the dialog box that appears.

Figure 5-49:
The Check Now option in Windows.

You may automatically fix any file system errors and also specify whether you want Windows to scan the surface of the disk and attempt to fix any problems with sectors.

4. **Select the options you want and then click Start.**

 The scan may take a few minutes, and when completed, will display summary information.

Disk Cleanup

Another important tool in Windows XP and Vista is Disk Cleanup, which scans a disk for files that can be safely removed from your system to free disk space. The Disk Cleanup utility can remove a number of different file types to help free disk space: temporary Internet files, Windows temporary files, and applications no longer used.

To perform a disk cleanup, follow these steps:

1. **Choose Start➪All Programs➪Accessories➪System Tools➪Disk Cleanup.**

2. **Select the drive you wish to clean up, as shown in Figure 5-50.**

Figure 5-50:
Select the
disk to
clean up.

3. **Click OK.**

4. **Select which files should be deleted to reclaim disk space, as shown in Figure 5-51.**

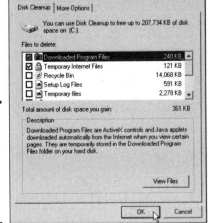

Figure 5-51:
Choose
which types
of files to
remove
with Disk
Cleanup.

5. **Click OK and then click Yes in the confirmation window.**

The unneeded files are removed from your system to reclaim the space.

Using diskpart

Before leaving the topic of hard drives, I just wanted to mention that you can manage your hard drives through the `diskpart` command line utility. `diskpart` is supported by Windows XP, Server 2003/2008, and Windows Vista.

With `diskpart`, you can perform most disk management functions, such as

✦ Create and delete partitions or volumes

✦ View details on disks, volumes, and partitions

✦ Make a partition active

You can pretty much perform all your disk administration from a command line with `diskpart`. From the `diskpart` prompt, you can type as many `diskpart` commands as you need (see Figure 5-52).

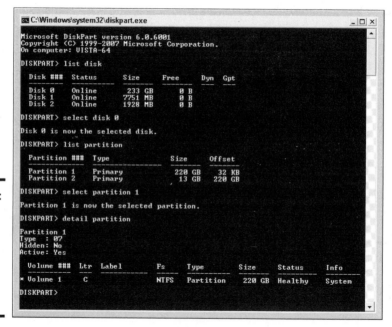

Figure 5-52: Using diskpart to manage partitions from a command line.

Getting an A+

This chapter illustrates the importance of hard disk management and the utilities used to perform that management. The following are some key points to remember when managing hard disks:

✦ A *cluster* is the allocation unit for a file.

✦ The cluster size for a partition is based on the file system used and the size of the partition.

✦ The FAT file system is limited to a maximum partition size of 2GB. FAT32 increased the maximum allowable partition size to 2000GB.

✦ Windows NT implemented its own file system, called NTFS. NTFS has a number of benefits, some of which are security, auditing, and compression. Windows 2000/XP/2003 use NTFS 5.0, where the Encrypting File System and quotas have been added to the list of reasons you should be using NTFS.

✦ To optimize your drive, run the defragmentation tool often.

✦ To verify the integrity of the drive, run Check Disk in Windows XP or Vista often.

✦ A primary partition is the bootable partition for the system and must be set active. An extended partition holds logical drives for storing information.

✦ You can remove temporary files with the Disk Cleanup utility in Windows XP or Vista.

✦ SCSI devices need to have a host adapter and unique IDs, and the SCSI bus must be terminated at both ends.

✦ SATA drives are much faster than IDE and support hot-swapping.

✦ RAID 1 is disk mirroring/duplexing.

✦ RAID 5 stores the data along with parity information.

**Book II
Chapter 5**

**Working with
Storage**

Prep Test

1 **What is the size of a sector on a hard disk?**

A ○ 512 bytes

B ○ 1K

C ○ 4K

D ○ 512K

2 **How many devices can exist in an IDE chain?**

A ○ 1

B ○ 2

C ○ 3

D ○ 4

3 **What physical component of the disk is responsible for reading and writing data on the disk?**

A ○ Platter

B ○ Sector

C ○ Cluster

D ○ Read/write head

4 **How many wires can be found in an IDE ribbon cable for a hard disk?**

A ○ 34

B ○ 40

C ○ 50

D ○ 66

5 **In a SCSI chain, what devices are required to be terminated?**

A ○ The first device in the chain

B ○ The last device in the chain

C ○ Devices at either end of the SCSI chain

D ○ Any hard disk in the SCSI chain

6 **In a SCSI chain, what device should take a SCSI ID of 0?**

A ○ CD-ROM

B ○ The bootable (first) hard disk

C ○ The SCSI host adapter

D ○ Printer

7 In an IDE chain, CD-ROM devices are usually what?

A ○ Masters
B ○ Terminated devices
C ○ Devices assigned ID 0
D ○ Slaves

8 Which of the following describes the cabling for internal SCSI?

A ○ 40-wire ribbon cable
B ○ 34-wire ribbon cable
C ○ 50-wire ribbon cable
D ○ None of the above

9 Which of the following best describes where the Master Boot Record is located?

A ○ Last track on the disk
B ○ First track on the disk
C ○ First sector on the first track of the first side of the first platter
D ○ First sector on the last side of the last platter

10 How many devices can exist in an EIDE chain?

A ○ 1
B ○ 2
C ○ 3
D ○ 4

11 Which of the following tools will help optimize the file system?

A ○ Backup
B ○ Defragment
C ○ ScanDisk
D ○ Format

12 What is the maximum capacity for a partition using the FAT file system?

A ○ 2MB
B ○ 2GB
C ○ 16GB
D ○ 2000GB

13 What type of partition is used to boot the computer?

A ○ Extended

B ○ Primary

C ○ Mirror

D ○ Stripe set with parity

14 What is the allocation unit for the storage of a file?

A ○ Sector

B ○ Track

C ○ Partition

D ○ Cluster

15 Which file system includes the encrypting file system?

A ○ HPFS

B ○ FAT

C ○ NTFS 5.0

D ○ FAT32

16 What utility manages partitions in Windows XP?

A ○ Disk Administrator

B ○ Disk Management

C ○ Backup

D ○ fdisk

17 What type of partition must be flagged as being active?

A ○ Extended

B ○ Logical

C ○ Primary

D ○ All partitions

18 What types of volumes are available on a dynamic disk? (Select all that apply.)

A ❑ Primary

B ❑ Simple

C ❑ Extended

D ❑ Spanned

19 You don't seem to be able to create a simple volume on Windows XP; why not?

A ○ You are not using NTFS as the file system.

B ○ You need to format the drive.

C ○ You must have an extended partition before you can create a simple volume.

D ○ You need to convert the basic disk to a dynamic disk.

Answers

1. **A.** A single sector on the disk is 512 bytes. A group of these sectors makes up a cluster, which typically could be 4K, 16K, or 32K. *See "Sectors."*

2. **B.** IDE supports only two devices in an IDE chain. EIDE improves on this limit by allowing four devices. *Review "IDE/ATA standard."*

3. **D.** The read/write heads are responsible for moving over the disk surface and writing data to the disk. A platter is one of the disk plates, a sector is where the data is written, and a cluster is a group of sectors. *Check out "Read/write process."*

4. **B.** The hard disk is connected to the motherboard with a 40-wire ribbon cable. A 34-wire ribbon cable is used to connect floppy drives, and a 50-wire ribbon cable is used for internal SCSI devices. *Peruse "IDE cabling."*

5. **C.** Devices at each end of the SCSI bus must be terminated. This is usually the SCSI host adapter plus the last device in the chain. *Take a look at "Termination."*

6. **B.** A bootable hard disk should take SCSI ID 0, and the host adapter usually takes an ID of 7. The other devices can be assigned any number in the chain as long as it is a unique number. *Peek at "Addressing."*

7. **D.** IDE CD-ROMs are slaves in an IDE chain. IDE devices do not get assigned IDs and do not have to be terminated. *Look over "Master/slave configuration."*

8. **C.** An internal SCSI connector uses a 50-wire ribbon cable, an IDE device uses a 40-wire ribbon cable, and a floppy drive uses a 34-wire ribbon cable. *Study "SCSI cabling."*

9. **C.** The master boot record is the first sector on the first track of the first side of the first platter. *Refer to "Sectors."*

10. **D.** An EIDE chain can have up to four devices. IDE only supports two devices, and the original SCSI supports eight devices in the chain. *Examine "EIDE/ATA-2 standard."*

11. **B.** A defragmentation will optimize the file system. It will reorganize the clusters on the disk so that all the data that makes up a file is in the same area so the read/write heads will not have to jump around from one end of the disk to the other. *See "Defragmentation utility."*

12. **B.** FAT file systems can access only 2GB partitions. This has seen a big improvement with FAT32, which can access 2000GB partitions. *Review "The FAT file system."*

13. **B.** A primary partition is the type of partition that is bootable. Extended partitions are used to hold logical drives. Stripe set with parity is used as a RAID solution on servers. *Check out "Managing Partitions and Volumes."*

14 **D.** Files are written to clusters on the disk. Only one file can occupy a cluster, regardless of whether the file fills the entire cluster. *Peruse "Clusters."*

15 **C.** Windows 2000's version of NTFS, called NTFS 5.0, implemented the Encrypting File System. *Take a look at "NTFS 5.0."*

16 **B.** The Disk Management utility in Windows 2000 allows you to manage partitions. *Peek at "Managing Partitions and Volumes."*

17 **C.** Primary partitions are the type of partitions that are flagged as being active. If you have two or three primary partitions on your drive, the primary partition that is flagged as being active will be the partition the system boots from. *Look over "Managing Partitions and Volumes."*

18 **B, D.** Of the choices provided, Simple and Spanned are the only volume types available on a dynamic disk. Primary and Extended are partition types and are only available on basic disks. *Study "Dynamic disks."*

19 **D.** To create a volume, you must ensure that you have converted the basic disk to a dynamic disk. After you have converted to a dynamic disk, you can create any of the different types of volumes. *Refer to "Dynamic disks."*

Chapter 6: Working with Power

Exam Objectives

✓ Understanding the features, functions, and installation of ATX power supplies

✓ Identifying features and functions of AC adapters

This chapter takes a look at two main items, power supply units (PSU) and uninterruptible power supplies (UPS). Power supplies should actually be called power converters because the largest single function they perform is a conversion of power from 120 volt (V) or 240V to something that can be used by the computer system.

As a CompTIA A+ Certified Professional, you will at least have to add a component to a computer that requires power from the power supply (such as a hard drive), and you will also probably be required to troubleshoot and replace a power supply in the computer system. The information in this chapter gives you all the technical specifications and connector types you will need to know about a power supply. Together with the troubleshooting chapter (Book IV, Chapter 2), you will have all the information that you need to know about power supplies.

Knowing the Basics of Power Terminology

You should learn four terms that deal with power in computer systems: volts, amps, ohms, and watts. If you have a firm grasp on how they relate to each other, you can understand how power is measured and used within computer systems. Electrical current flows with the same principles that are used when water flows, so water is often used as an analogy for electrical current.

Volt

A technical definition of a *volt* is a unit of electrical potential difference or the potential difference across a conductor when a current of one ampere dissipates one watt of power. In water terminology, voltage is represented by the pressure that is the water supply tank. This is a potential because unless you provide an exit path for water to leave the tank, this potential is not realized. If you increase the pressure in the tank, you increase the potential to supply water or power.

Ohm

An *ohm* is a measure of resistance or electrical impedance. When comparing electricity with water, resistance is determined by the size or diameter of the hose or pipe that is used to supply water, where a smaller hose produces more resistance.

Amp

An *ampere* (amp) is a unit of electric current or the measure of electrical flow. When referring to water, it is also the rate of water flow. There is a direct relationship between volts, resistance, and current: If you reduce resistance or increase voltage, you increase the current. This relationship — Ohm's Law — is represented by this formula:

```
I = V / R
```

where I is current (amps), V is voltage (volts), and R is resistance (ohms).

Watt

The technical definition of a watt is that it is a unit of power, equal to one joule per second. If you equate this to water again, watts have you use flowing water do something. If this water runs over a waterwheel, watts are the measure of how fast the wheel can be turned by the water. If you increase the current, the wheel is able to turn faster. The formula to calculate watts is

```
P = V * I
```

where P is power (watts), V is voltage (volts), and I is current (amps).

In general, when you are working with computer systems, you will be concerned with the voltage supplied by the outlet that you connect your equipment to, the current that your equipment draws from the outlet, and the power that is used by devices that are connected to the computer power supply.

Identifying the Purpose of Power Supply Units

Remember the tasks and specifications listed in this section.

A computer's power supply is responsible for several tasks. The following list contains typical tasks and specifications related to power supplies:

+ **Conversion of voltage** from the building-supplied AC voltage to various DC voltages used by components inside the computer.

✦ **DC voltage regulation** to provide a very small tolerance of error to the devices receiving the power. Typically, a +/–5% voltage differential is allowed through the specification for 12VDC, 5VDC, and 3.3VDC connections.

✦ **Over-current protection** specifies that the power supply should handle some level of abnormally high current to prevent fuses in the power supply from blowing unnecessarily.

✦ **Input-under voltage** specifies that if the voltage being supplied by the building drops below the normal operating level, it should not cause damage to the power supply itself. It will, however, likely cause your computer to turn off. For a 120V power supply, this low voltage level is usually 100V; so, at voltages below that level, the power supply will simply turn off.

✦ **Energy Star** is a specification that defines how much power the power supply should provide to the computer components during reduced power states, such as when the computer is put to sleep or on standby.

✦ The **PS_ON#** feature allows the motherboard to control the power supply though a soft power switch. Power supplies for ATX motherboards do not use a physical switch like your light switch, which allows a circuit to be open or closed (a hard power switch). Rather, your computer's power button is connected to the motherboard; when you press the button, the motherboard determines what action will be taken (a soft power switch). The power supply allows the motherboard to control the power state through the PS_ON# feature. The previous generation of power supplies — AT power supplies — used a hard power switch.

✦ The **power supply specification** might recommend or require the use of cooling fans, depending on the form factor of the power supply.

✦ **Input supply voltage** (120V or 240V) might be static or configured via manual switching or automatic switching. Many laptops have automatic switching, and most desktop power supplies have manual switching.

If you do not see a manual switch on your power supply, read the input voltage range displayed on a label on the power supply. For desktop power supplies, this label is usually found in an inconvenient location on the power supply, and you will likely need to remove the power supply from the case to read the label. In the case of laptop power supplies, even though it might have a switch, you must read the label to ensure that it does support both 120V and 240V.

Automatic switching just means that the power supply will detect and use the voltage setting for the power that is supplied. As I discuss at the start of this chapter, if you increase the voltage, you increase the current. Thus, the power supply not only increases the voltage but also reduces the current inside the power supply, which allows internal devices to have a consistent power level.

Identifying Power Supplies

The most common type of motherboard that you will have to provide power to will be some form factor of the ATX family (see Book II, Chapter 1) — and, because of that, some form of power supply compatible with an ATX motherboard will be required. In the following sections, I discuss the things that are common to all power supplies that are compatible with ATX motherboards. I also take a look at the different form factors for power supplies so that the many sizes and shapes of computer cases can be supported, from tower, to small form factor (SFF), to slim line cases, and all sizes in between.

When the name ATX power supply is used properly, it refers to a power supply that provides power to an ATX motherboard, and it has very specific size characteristics. Many other power supplies (such as CFX, LFX, SFX, and TFX) have different size characteristics, but all provide power to the ATX family of motherboards. Each size and shape of power supply has its own specification. In this chapter, I talk only about power supplies that provide power to ATX motherboards, regardless of their size and shape. All these power supplies use the ATX-compatible power main power connector, which makes them different from the older AT power supply used with older generations of motherboards.

To find out more about the specifications for power supplies for ATX motherboards, look at the Intel Power Supply Design Guide for Desktop Platform Form Factors document at `www.formfactors.org`. This Intel-operated site has specifications for many of the standard form factors used for computers and components.

The ATX power supply has undergone some basic changes in power that is supplied and in the format of the connectors. The current version of the ATX specification is 2.2. The biggest difference between the version 1.3 ATX specification and the 2.x ATX specifications is the use of a 24-pin main power connector used in the 2.x ATX specification, rather than a 20-pin connector under the 1.3 ATX specification.

With ATX power supplies having the same types of power connectors, one big difference between the power supplies you could purchase is how much power they provide to connected devices. The power supply rating refers to the total wattage that the power supply can provide to devices within your computer. Although ATX specification allows for power supplies to have ratings from 250 watts (W) up to large ones at 1200+W, most are typically around 500W to 800W. Lower wattages are available, too, but these usually follow the SFX specifications (sometimes called microATX power supplies), and these have power output down to 160W.

The power supply rating required for any computer depends on the devices within the computer that need power. In most cases, bigger is better

because systems that don't have enough power for devices can experience strange, intermittent problems (see Book IV, Chapter 2). Table 6-1 provides a listing of some basic systems devices and power usage estimates as a guide to sizing up a power supply, but remember to always leave yourself some extra room.

Table 6-1	Power Consumption by Product
Device	*Power*
PCIe video card	30–225W
AGP video card	30–75W
PCI video card	30–35W
AMD Athlon XP 1.5 MHz–2.5 GHz	66–77W
AMD Athlon 64 3.0 GHz–3.4 GHz	89W
AMD Athlon 64 Dual-Core 3.0 GHz–2.4 GHz	125W
Intel Pentium 4 2.2 GHz–2.4 GHz	80W–90W
Intel Pentium 4 2.4 GHz–3.0 GHz	90W–105W
Intel Celeron Socket 478	45W–65W
ATX motherboard	40W–65W
PC133 RAM	12W
PC2100+ DDR RAM	10W
PC3200+ DDR2 RAM	7.5W
CD-ROM drive	20W
CD-RW drive	30W
DVD-ROM drive	25W
5,400rpm IDE hard drive	15W
7,200rpm IDE hard drive	25W
Floppy drive	5W
Network card or modem	5W
Sound card	7–18W
SCSI controller card	25W
FireWire or USB 2.0 controller card	40W
USB device	5W
FireWire device	8W
CPU or case fan	2W

If you are replacing a power supply in a system that experienced a failure, you can get a replacement that provides the same amount of power or more. However, if you expect that your system has more devices than the power supply can support — or if you are building a custom system — you can follow these steps:

1. **Locate on Table 6-1 any devices that your system is going to contain; then record the power usage.**

2. **Add up all the wattages and divide your total by 80 percent (0.8) to give your system some extra room to grow and to accommodate any items you might have missed.**

3. **If you did not get a number that matches an available power supply rating, choose a power supply with the next highest power rating.**

Power Connectors

A computer uses many different types of power connectors. They include the main power, floppy, peripheral, 12 volt (+12V2DC), and serial ATA (SATA) connectors.

The ATX main power connector

On new power supplies, the ATX main power connector is a 24-pin Molex 39-01-2240 connector. In many cases, it is a 20+4-pin connector for backward compatibility with older version 1.3 motherboards. This is a keyed connector, so you cannot connect it the wrong way without a lot of effort. You can see this and other connectors in Figure 6-1.

Table 6-2 provides you with the pin configuration and voltage supply for the 24-pin Molex main power connector. When troubleshooting faulty power supplies, you need to know what power is supposed to be supplied by each pin in the power connector so that you can identify that the issue you are troubleshooting is related to a problem of power supply.

The main power supply connector provides power at 3.3VDC, 5VDC, and 12VDC.

The floppy drive connector

Although floppy drives are nearly obsolete, the floppy connector is an AMP 171822-4 four-pin connector; see its pin configuration in Table 6-3. This connector provides power to a floppy drive at 5V but can supply power at either 5V or 12V to support devices from manufacturers that decide to use this connector.

Figure 6-1:
Power
connectors
that may
be used
on power
supplies.

Peripheral

Serial ATA

Main Power

Floppy Drive

+12V2DC

Table 6-2	Pin Configuration for the Main Power Connector	
Pin	*Signal*	*Color*
1	+3.3VDC	Orange
2	+3.3VDC	Orange
3	COM	Black
4	+5VDC	Red
5	COM	Black
6	+5VDC	Red
7	COM	Black
8	PWR_OK	Gray
9	+5VSB	Purple
10	+12V1DC	Yellow
11	+12V1DC	Yellow
12	+3.3VDC	Orange

(continued)

Table 6-2 *(continued)*

Pin	Signal	Color
13	+3.3VDC	Orange
14	−12VDC	Blue
15	COM	Black
16	PS_ON#	Green
17	COM	Black
18	COM	Black
19	COM	Black
20	Reserved	Varies
21	+5VDC	Red
22	+5VDC	Red
23	+5VDC	Red
24	COM	Black

Table 6-3	Pin Configuration for the Floppy Power Connector	
Pin	Signal	Color
1	+5VDC	Red
2	COM	Black
3	COM	Black
4	+12V1DC	Yellow

The peripheral connector

Until SATA drives rule the world, the four-pin peripheral connector is likely the most used power connector on most computers because it is used for hard drives and optical drives. This connector is an AMP 1-480424-0 or Molex 8981-04P, and its pin configuration is shown in Table 6-4. Like the floppy connector, it provides power at both 5V and 12V, but hard drives draw their power at 12V rather than the 5V sufficient for floppy drives. Hard drives require more power to get their heavier disk spinning.

The 12-volt power connector

The 12-volt power connector (+12V2DC) — also called a P4 connector — is used to supply additional power directly to the processor. It uses a Molex 39-01-2040 connector; its pin configuration is listed in Table 6-5.

Table 6-4	Pin Configuration for the Peripheral Power Connector	
Pin	*Signal*	*Color*
1	+12VDC	Yellow
2	COM	Black
3	COM	Black
4	+5VDC	Red

Table 6-5	Pin Configuration for the +12V2DC Power Connector	
Pin	*Signal*	*Color*
1	COM	Black
2	COM	Black
3	+12V2DC	Yellow
4	+12V2DC	Yellow

The Serial ATA connector

The Serial ATA (SATA) drive offers two more connectors to the long list that are used by computers. One connector is used for data, and the other is used for power. The data connector is discussed in Book III, Chapter 1. The power connector uses a Molex 88751 connector, and an additional wire (5) supplies 3.3V to devices that require it. (Most functions of the SATA drive run on 12V.) The SATA connector has its five wires connected to 15 pins on the connector. The SATA connector pin configuration is listed in Table 6-6.

Table 6-6	Pin Configuration for the Serial ATA Power Connector	
Wire	*Signal*	*Color*
1	+12VDC	Yellow
2	COM	Black
3	+5VDC	Red
4	COM	Black
5	+3.3VDC	Orange

The 6-pin PCIe connector and 8-pin PCIe connector

The 6-pin PCI Express (PCIe) connector and 8-in PCIe connectors are used to supply additional power to energy-hungry PCIe video cards. Many cards on the market contain either a 6-pin or 8-pin connector for this purpose.

The only real difference between these connectors is the amount of power they can supply. The 6-pin connector supplies an additional 75W, and the 8-pin connector supplies an additional 150W. The 6-pin connector is listed in Table 6-7, and the 8-pin connector is listed in Table 6-8.

Table 6-7	6-Pin Configuration for the Serial ATA Power Connector	
Wire	**Signal**	**Color**
1	+12VDC	Yellow
2	+12VDC	Yellow
3	+12VDC	Yellow
4	COM	Black
5	COM	Black
6	COM	Black

Table 6-8	8-Pin Configuration for the Serial ATA Power Connector	
Wire	**Signal**	**Color**
1	+12VDC	Yellow
2	+12VDC	Yellow
3	+12VDC	Yellow
4	COM	Black
5	COM	Black
6	COM	Black
7	COM	Black
8	COM	Black

Power Supply Form Factors

Other form factors also provide power for ATX motherboards. They exist mainly to fit in different sizes and styles of cases. These power supplies typically have the same types of power connectors that were detailed in the previous sections. The specifications for the power supplies usually define mounting points and the maximum footprint (space) that the power supply can occupy. In addition, the specifications also state whether cooling fans are required. In addition to the most common form factor — ATX v2.2 — form factors for the power supplies include the following:

- ✦ **CFX v1.3** is the *Compact Form Factor,* typically supplying power in the range of 220W to 300W.

- ✦ **LFX v1.1** is the *Low Profile Form Factor,* typically supplying power in the range of 180W to 260W.

- ✦ **SFX v3.1** is the *Small Form Factor,* typically supplying power in the range of 160W to 300W.

- ✦ **TFX v2.2** is the *Thin Form Factor,* typically supplying power in the range of 180W to 300W.

The size specifications for these, as well as the ATX power supply, are shown in Figure 6-2. This figure also shows the mounting holes for each type of power supply. Computer power supplies are held in by three or four screws and are usually positioned in the top-rear portion of the computer. After removing the power connector from the internal devices, you can remove the screws and remove the power supply.

Take care when removing the screws. Some cases have rails that support the power supply; with others, the power supply could drop onto the computer components in the case when the last screw is removed.

Figure 6-2:
Power
supply
unit form
factors.

Using AC Adapters

Desktops have large internal power supplies to get AC building power converted to 3.3V, 5V, and 12V for internal use, but laptops typically do not have the internal space to support such a large power supply. Most laptop AC adapters are external and have the job of converting the building power to a voltage that is required by the laptop. Laptops typically require between 12V and 20VDC. The laptop then has internal components that

divide this incoming voltage into segments that are appropriated for the internal devices, such as 12V, 5V, and 3.3V. This allows for part of the power management components to exist outside the laptop.

In some cases, the power supply can use generic output voltages and connectors; in other cases, the voltage or connectors might be customized by a manufacturer, meaning that replacement power supplies are tied specifically to that manufacturer. The AC adapter in Figure 6-3 has a fairly standard connector. If you look closely, you can see that the output voltage is 15V.

AC adapters are used with a wide variety of devices that you deal with every day, converting AC power to DC power for cell phones, cordless phones, PDAs, and a host of other devices. Always take care to match the correct power adapter to the power requirements for the devices to ensure that you don't damage the device — or worse.

When working with your AC adapter, always keep your eye out for possible damage along the length of the cord from wear or perhaps pets. Neat people actually tend to be harder on adapter cables than disorganized ones because neatniks tie up the cables every time they pack their laptops, consolidating the weight of the cable mass right next to the brick of the adapter, causing the cable to wear quickly in the section nearest the adapter. To avoid this problem, the cable should be coiled loosely and placed in your carrying case.

Working with UPS and Suppressors

Some people have such good and stable power that they take it for granted. This is not the reality for many of us, though, and we live with a variety of power issues such as these:

✦ **Spikes:** *Spikes* are sharp increases in line voltage caused by a problem with the power utility equipment, which may be traced back to faulty transformers or lightning strikes.

✦ **Power surges:** Similar to spikes, *power surges* are increases in line voltage that usually last longer than a spike.

✦ **Noise:** *Noise* is interference caused by items not directly connected to the power system. Power lines running near fluorescent lights or microwaves can have their AC sine waves altered or chopped, which affects devices receiving their power.

Figure 6-3:
An AC
power
adapter for
a Toshiba
laptop.

What about DC adapters?

DC adapters allow you to convert DC voltages to different DC voltages, changing the power characteristics, such as current, to allow 12V power from a vehicle to be used for computers and other equipment that do not use 12V power directly. You may use these from time to time to power other devices. However, because the power requirements for most laptops are high, you might not be able to use a 12VDC adapter to provide it power.

✦ **Blackout:** A *blackout* is a total interruption in the line power. The ATX power supply specification has a minimum voltage hold-up time of 17 milliseconds (ms), or about one-sixtieth of a second. This is how long the power supply can sustain computer operation during a power interruption. In other words, if your lights flick off and on because of a very short power outage, your computer might continue to run over that outage, but it would have to be a very brief power outage.

✦ **Brownout:** A *brownout* is the opposite of a power surge in that the line power is below normal for a period of time ranging from seconds to minutes. If the brownout exceeds the Input-Under Voltage limits of the power supply, the power supply will shut off.

Three basic devices help you deal with these power situations:

✦ **Surge suppressors** protect your equipment against spikes and surges by quickly terminating the power connection before your equipment is damaged.

✦ **Line conditioners** take that a step further by cleaning the noise on the line and dealing with some under- and over-voltage situations, as well as generating alarms to notify you of any situations.

In most cases, line conditions deal with surges and spikes while letting your equipment continue to function.

✦ **Uninterruptible power supplies (UPS)** take power protection beyond line conditioners by keeping your equipment working even after total power failures.

The two main types of UPSes are

• *Standby:* Also called *offline,* a standby UPS does not protect you from surges or spikes but takes over quickly in the event of voltage drops or failures. UPS units that are marketed toward home users are usually standby units.

- *Inline:* Also called *online,* an inline UPS always operates between the line and your equipment. In addition to providing power, when the UPS battery power is below a specific level, an inline UPS can initiate a graceful shutdown of the devices connected to it.

Most UPSes include scales or lights to indicate the current load on the UPS as a percentage of its maximum capacity, as well the battery charge condition. Check these indicators regularly or install software that monitors the UPS for you. UPS indicators indicate capacity levels as well as error conditions.

UPSes often have a variety options for receptacle types to supply devices with power. A standard server UPS is shown in Figure 6-4. Notice the six 15-amp (NEMA 5-15R) receptacles as well as the single, 20-amp twist-lock (NEMA L6-20R) receptacle. The 200-amp connector would be used to supply power to a Power Distribution Unit (PDU), which would likely have a series of standard 15-amp (NEMA 5-15R) receptacles.

UPS front view

Figure 6-4:
Front and
rear of a
standard
server UPS.

UPS rear view

Most UPS are rated in volt-amps (VA), which indicates how much power they can supply. VA ranges for UPS start around 200VA and go up to tens of thousands of VA for corporate data centers.

In a perfect world, watts and VA would be identical. Early power supplies were capacitor input power supplies that used capacitors to even out the power supplied by a building's AC power. The method of converting power creates a variance between watts and VA of 55 percent to 75 percent, which is called the Power Factor (PF). This is represented by the formula

```
watts = VA * PF
```

Capacitor input power supplies are still in use on most inexpensive power supplies. The solution is the Power Factor Corrected (PFC) power supply, which uses watt and VA ratings that are the same. Most high-end equipment manufactured since 1996 should include a PFC power supply.

Before buying a UPS, total the power requirements for all the devices you want to plug into it, as well as the amount of time for which you need protection. The protection time is usually between 10 and 20 minutes; longer protection periods are possible if you want to pay the additional cost. Use the information to make sure you get a UPS that is powerful enough to protect all your expensive gear.

Getting an A+

This chapter sheds light on power and how it interacts with your computer. The following points are covered:

✦ The current specification of power supplies is ATX, and the ATX power supply will be found in one form factor or another on most current computers.

✦ The main power connector has 20 or 24 pins. Four-pin floppy and peripheral connectors supply 5V and 12V, and five-pin SATA connectors supply 3.3V, 5V, and 12V.

✦ Power supplies convert 120VAC or 240VAC power into DC power for the computer.

✦ Power supplies come in a variety of power sizes, from 160W up to and beyond 1200W.

✦ AC adapters are used on laptops to convert power from AC to DC, and usually automatically switch between 120V and 240V.

✦ Surge suppressors, line conditioners, and UPS deal with various power-supply problems, including surges and brownouts.

Prep Test

1 What are the main power voltages that are provided by standard computer power supplies? (Select all that apply.)

A ❑ 2.1V

B ❑ 3.3V

C ❑ 5V

D ❑ 12V

2 What is the name given to the main type of power supply used in modern computers?

A ○ AT

B ○ NLX

C ○ ATX

D ○ WPA

3 What components influence the purchase decision of a power supply? (Select all that apply.)

A ❑ Hard drive

B ❑ Monitor

C ❑ RAM

D ❑ Parallel port scanner

4 What are the standard input voltages for power supplies? (Select all that apply.)

A ❑ 110VDC

B ❑ 120VAC

C ❑ 240VDC

D ❑ 240VAC

5 What is the main function of an AC adapter for a laptop or other device?

A ○ Reduce heat involved in converting power between systems.

B ○ Supply 3.3VDC, 5VDC, and 12VDC power to your computer through a 20- or 24-pin connector.

C ○ Provide power availability during brownout and blackout conditions.

D ○ Convert AC power into DC power.

6 Which of the following power conditions does a line conditioner not offer protection against?

A ○ Blackout

B ○ Brownout

C ○ Spike

D ○ Surge

7 Which of the following power conditions does a UPS not offer protection against?

A ○ Surge

B ○ Blackout

C ○ Line noise

D ○ Rapid cutover

Answers

1 **B, C, D.** ATX-based power supplies provide power to devices at 3.3VDC, 5VDC, and 12VDC. *See "Identifying the Purpose of Power Supply Units."*

2 **C.** Most current computers get power from an ATX power supply. *Review "Identifying Power Supplies."*

3 **A, C.** Both of these devices, as well as most other internal devices, affect the total power required by a power supply. Monitors have their own internal power supplies, and most parallel port scanners come with their own AC adapters. *Check out "Identifying Power Supplies."*

4 **B, D.** 120VAC and 240VAC are the two power input voltages that are handled by power supplies. *Peruse "Identifying the Purpose of Power Supply Units."*

5 **D.** The main function of an AC adapter is to convert AC power into DC power for use in a laptop. Power is provided to the laptop through a connector of some type, but it will be a single voltage and will not be a 20- or 24-pin connector. A UPS would be required to provide power during a blackout. *Take a look at "Using AC adapters."*

6 **A.** Line conditioners can deal with some reduced voltage situations, depending on their severity, but cannot deal with complete blackouts. *Peek at "Working with UPS and Suppressors."*

7 **D.** Rapid cutover is a manner of switching to UPS power when using a standby UPS, and the other items are all power line problems that a UPS provides solutions for. *Look over "Working with UPS and Suppressors."*

Book III

Outside the Box

The 5th Wave By Rich Tennant

"Here's a little tip on disassembly that you won't find on the A+ Certification test."

Contents at a Glance

Chapter 1: Describing Ports, Cables, and Connectors

Exam Objectives

✓ Understanding fundamental principles of using a personal computer

✓ Identifying ports and cables

*I*n this chapter, you examine the ports on the back of the computer as well as the cables and connectors used to attach devices. In other chapters of this book, you examine different devices, but this chapter looks at getting them all connected. The other devices and chapters include

+ **Printers:** Book III, Chapter 5

+ **Internal drives:** Book II, Chapter 5

+ **Monitors:** Book III, Chapter 3

+ **USB devices:** Book II, Chapter 1

+ **FireWire devices:** Book II, Chapter 1

+ **Modems:** Book III, Chapter 2

A CompTIA A+ Certified Professional must be able to identify various types of cables and connectors. This chapter introduces you to the most common cables and connectors that you will encounter when using computer systems.

Identifying Common Computer Ports

Start by looking at the different types of ports on the back of your computer. *Ports* are connection points on your computer that allow for devices to be connected to your computer. The connection point has a connector that accepts a cable with a matching connector. Knowing what the ports are used for is important when connecting devices to your computer. You might already be familiar with some of the common ports, such as serial, parallel, and USB. In this section, I discuss these ports as well as IEEE 1394 ports, which are often called FireWire.

Serial and parallel ports

Two of the most common computer ports are serial ports and parallel ports. Most computers have one parallel port and two serial ports. These ports are used to connect devices, such as modems and printers, to your computer.

There has been a trend in the industry to create legacy-free computers: that is, computers without COM ports, LPT ports, or ISA expansion slots, as well as number of other functional changes. Many new laptops on the market already fit into this category.

Parallel ports send data over multiple wires simultaneously; *serial ports* send data over only one wire at a time. Because parallel communication allows for multiple streams of data, which in the early days, when serial controllers were slow, allowed it to provide higher data transfer rates than serial communication. This is no longer true today.

Parallel ports were implemented on the personal computer when it was introduced by IBM in 1981. IBM used nine-wire cables to connect two devices. This enables the cables, at any given time, to deliver 8 bits of data, with the extra wire being used as a ground. However, because there is no way to accurately control the flow of the signal along each wire in the cable, it is recommended that the length of the cable be less than 6 feet (about 2 meters).

Controlling the flow of data became more of a factor when *bidirectional communication* (sending and receiving data with the device) was implemented over the parallel port. The standard for bidirectional communication was delivered in 1994 in the IEEE 1284 specification, which allows for high-speed, two-way communication over the parallel port. This also opened two new specifications for the port: the Enhanced Parallel Port (EPP) and the Extended Capabilities Port (ECP). The maximum cable length for an IEEE 1284 cable is about 30 feet (10 meters).

An EPP-type parallel port is used primarily for nonprinter peripherals, and an ECP-type parallel port is designed to accommodate high-speed printers and scanners. To better handle high-speed data communication, the ECP-type parallel port also implements a dynamic memory access (DMA) channel; this grants the port direct access to a section of RAM.

Serial ports, on the other hand, deliver data sequentially down a single wire. Eight bits of digital data are converted into an analog signal by using a system called baud. *Baud rate* refers to the number of state changes (tones) made on the wire in any given second. If you have heard a fax machine or modem making a connection, you have heard the state changes as a series of squeals. Baud rate is very different from bits per second (bps), which measures the amount of data that is transferred. At one point, 300 bps modems communicated at 300 baud, but compression

standards adopted by the communications industry allowed more data to be delivered at the same baud rate. Today, 56 Kbps (57,344 bps) modems communicate at 9,600 baud.

Depending on the baud rate used to transfer data, the length of the cable can range up to 3,000 feet (just over 900 meters). For data transfer rates at 9,600 baud, the maximum cabling length is 250 feet (just over 75 meters). The RS-232C standard (usually simply referred to as RS-232), which is used as a basis of serial communication, recommends a maximum cable length of 50 feet (about 15 meters).

Find out how to troubleshoot serial and parallel port problems by reading Book IV, Chapter 2.

Universal Serial Bus (USB)

USB is a more modern method of communicating using serial communication methodologies. The standards for USB 1.0 were released in 1996, USB 1.1 in 1998, and USB 2.0 in 2000. The goal of USB was to revolutionize how serial communication was conducted. To fulfill this goal, USB uses a cabling system that allows up to 127 devices to be connected. It also delivers power to the devices connected on this bus.

To go along with this new cabling, the specification for USB dictates that all devices should support Plug and Play. With these two pieces of the puzzle put together, USB enables you to plug in devices and have them work without having to worry about power cables or drivers. Some USB devices that require a large amount of power may use a supplemental power supply, but the USB bus will power most devices.

USB 2.0 increased the fastest transfer rate for USB 1.0 from 12 Mbps to 480 Mbps. This has allowed it to be used for devices that require faster transfer rates, such as hard drives and CD-ROMs. The standards for USB 3.0 have been completed, allowing for device communication up to 5.0 Gbps; however, do not expect to see these devices on the market until 2010 or 2011. For more information about USB, see Book III, Chapter 3.

USB has had a performance boost up to 480 Mbps with the introduction of version 2 of the USB standard. For the exam, you need to pay attention to the version of USB covered in the question. If it is USB 1.0, you are still limited to the 12 Mbps transfer rate.

FireWire (IEEE 1394)

FireWire is an Apple trademark for the IEEE 1394 standard. The 1394 standard implements a version of serial communication across a wiring network that is similar to USB. IEEE 1394 enables connecting 63 external devices on

a bus that supports between 50 and 400 Mbps. With the release of FireWire 800, transfer rates have approached 800 Mbps. One of the goals of the IEEE 1394 standard was to replace SCSI, which is covered in Book II, Chapter 5.

Don't confuse IEEE 1394 (FireWire) with IEEE 1284 (mentioned in the "Serial and parallel ports" section, earlier in the chapter), which deals with bidirectional communication over the parallel port.

Although some disk drives have been implemented through the IEEE 1394 standard, it has seen the most growth in the area of data, voice, and video. Although many PCs have been shipping for the past few years with USB ports, IEEE 1394 has not seen the same level of adoption by the PC manufacturing industry. However, many device manufacturers support IEEE 1394 in their devices, and interface cards are readily available to be added to your PC.

FireWire is covered in Book II, Chapter 1.

Keyboard and mouse

Because you will certainly want to enter data into your computer, the keyboard connector on the back of your computer plays an important role. The two traditional types of keyboard connectors are P/S2 (or mini-DIN 6) and DIN 5. The mini-DIN connector has been the standard keyboard and mouse connector on computers for many years, but it faces being supplanted by USB. You should not be surprised if a new computer you purchase does not have a P/S2 connector for either the keyboard or mouse.

For details on connecting keyboards to your computer, review Book III, Chapter 2.

Monitor

You also need to see what you're doing, so the monitor connector also plays an important role. With the demise of the MDA (Monochrome Display Adapter), HGC (Hercules Graphics Card), CGA (Color Graphics Adapter), and EGA (Enhanced Graphics Adapter) monitor types as well as the release of VGA (Video Graphics Array) and SVGA (Super Video Graphics Array) monitors, the monitor connector on the back of your computer changed from a DB-9 female connector to an HD (high density) DB-15 female connector. With the high adoption rate of LCD monitors, a new port is showing up on computers and video cards, supporting the higher throughput and digital signals that LCD monitors require. This new port is a DVI (digital visual interface) port and accepts a monitor connector that has as many as 24 digital pins and optionally 5 analog pins (for backward compatibility).

You can read more about connecting monitors to your computer in Book III, Chapter 3.

Comparing Cable Types

In this section, you examine several different types of cables and discover the uses of each type. Some of the cables are used inside your computer, and others are external. After you complete this section, you should be able to identify the basic types of cables and where they are used.

Ribbon

Ribbon cables are often used to connect components inside a computer, such as hard disk drives and floppy disk drives. They are made up of several wires laid out parallel to each other in such a way that they resemble a ribbon, as shown in Figure 1-1. These cables usually have keyed connectors on them that prevent them from being incorrectly connected to devices. Note the small tab halfway down the edge of the black connector: This tab matches a groove on the device that it is attached to.

Figure 1-1:
Ribbon cables are usually found inside your computer.

Small tabs

You can read more about ribbon cables when connecting storage devices inside your computer, which is covered in Book II, Chapter 5.

Twisted pair

Twisted pair cables consist of three or four pairs of wires. The grading level is based on how the wires are arranged inside the cable, rather than the number of wires. In Figure 1-2, you can see how each pair of wires is twisted together at a specific rate, and then how all the pairs are twisted together. This procedure reduces the effect of *cross talk* (interference) between the

pairs of wires and interference from external sources. The differences between the different grades of cable include the quality of production material and the overall number of twists per pair of wires per foot of cable. Most networking is done with unshielded twisted pair (UTP) cable, which is more susceptible to interference but is more flexible — and, therefore, easier to work with than shielded twisted pair (STP) cable, which has a metal shielding over each pair of wires.

Figure 1-2:
How wires
are twisted
is one
difference
between
cable
categories.

Table 1-1 provides a brief listing of the different types of twisted pair cables and their uses.

Table 1-1	Twisted Pair Cabling Types
Type	Usage
Category 1 (CAT1)	UTP cable designed for audio signal transmission. This wiring is intended to be used for transferring signals to speakers and other devices.
Category 2 (CAT2)	UTP cable used for low-speed transmissions. This wiring was designed for analog telephone applications. CAT2 cables can also carry lower-speed networking data, as in the case of 4 Mbps token ring networking.
Category 3 (CAT3)	UTP cable designed with data networking in mind. This category is similar in design to all the newer categories, but some electrical characteristics are unique to each. CAT3 cables carry 10 Mbps Ethernet data.
Category 4 (CAT4)	UTP cable was designed to carry 16 Mbps token ring data.

Type	Usage
Category 5 (CAT5)	UTP cable designed to carry 100 Mbps Ethernet data. It also meets the requirements for 1000Base-T. CAT5e is an enhanced version of the cable that better meets the standards of 1000Base-T by reducing crosstalk.
Category 6 (CAT6)	A standard for UTP cable that supports frequencies of 250 MHz Ethernet data. CAT6a increases the frequencies that the cable supports and allows for data transfer rates up to 10 Gbps.
Category 7 (CAT7)	A standard for unshielded twisted pair cable that supports frequencies of up to 600 MHz. CAT7a increases the frequencies that the cable supports and allows for data transfer rates up to 100 Gbps.

You can read more about networking cables in Book VIII, Chapter 1.

Pay close attention to the uses of CAT3, CAT4, and CAT5 cable types because these map directly to network specifications. You will be tested on the minimum required cable type for 10 Mbps Ethernet and 100 Mbps Ethernet.

Thick and thin coax

Thick coax is rigid, half-inch coaxial cable capable of carrying 10 Mbps Ethernet data a distance of 500 meters. Thick coax is also referred to as *Thicknet* or *10Base5*.

Thin coax is a more flexible, quarter-inch coaxial cable capable of carrying 10 Mbps Ethernet data a distance of 185 meters. Thin coax is also referred to as *Thinnet* or *10Base2*.

Coax is not used in many computer networks these days. If you see coax in a network these days, it is typically used to provide Internet service.

For more information about thick and thin coax use in computer networking, flip to Book VIII, Chapter 1.

Fiber

Fiber optic cable is so thin that it is measured in microns or micrometers (µm), or millionths of a meter (or, put another way, thousandths of a millimeter). Fiber optic cable for data networks comes in two core diameter thicknesses 50µm and 62.5µm. There are also cables that support a single communication mode or multiple communication modes, which refers to

how light traverses the cable. Multimode cables can support distances as long as 1 kilometer (km), and single-mode cable can support distances as long as 140 km.

Fiber optic cable is also covered in Book VIII, Chapter 1.

Cable Orientation

Cable orientation refers to how two connectors fit together, so it could actually be referred to as *connector* orientation. More to the point, cable orientation defines how a cable connector attaches to another connector, which is usually on a computer or motherboard. Just about every time the term *cable orientation* is used, it refers to the internal ribbon cables used to connect serial ports, parallel ports, floppy drives, hard drives, and CD-ROM drives to a motherboard. Cable orientation is not usually used when discussing external connectors, which are used on the outside of your computer and tend to be able to connect only one way. The pins or holes on a connector are numbered, and hole 1 on a cable connector needs to match pin 1 on the computer's connector.

The connector with the pins is the *male* connector, and the connector with the holes is the *female* connector. And even though the female connector does not have pins, the holes on the female connector are typically referred to as pins.

Internal cables (of course) are used on the inside of the computer. Some devices use unique cables, such as your sound card and CD-ROM drive. In many cases, these unique cables have Molex connectors (molded plastic connectors) that are usually keyed to prevent mistakes on connecting. A keyed connector is designed to connect only one way. You also see Molex connectors on the power leads that connect your power supply to devices, such as hard drives and the motherboard.

Remembering one simple rule can prevent most connection errors. On a ribbon cable, wire 1 connected to pin 1 has the colored (usually red or blue) stripe on it. This makes it easy to spot. On most devices that you are connecting the cable to, pin 1 is the pin closest to the power connector.

Figure 1-3 shows two IDE connectors on the motherboard. Note that these are keyed and also have a small arrow pointing to pin 1. Most male connectors on the motherboard have a wall around the pins that has a slot, or key opening, that prevent errors — that is, as long as the cable you are using is also keyed. Keyed connectors on your cards or motherboard have a small notch cut from the side of the connector (in the middle of the long side of the connector in Figure 1-3), whereas keyed cables have a small lump or tab on them, which can be seen on the long edge of the connector (refer to Figure 1-1). The only way for the cable to be plugged into the connector is if the tab matches the notch, and there is only one way for that to happen — to line up pin 1 on your connectors.

Figure 1-3:
Pin 1 is
usually
identified
by some
marking.

Arrows indicating pin 1

Connector Types

Many, many types of cables exist on the market these days: video cables, modem cables, printer cables, and extension cables, to name a few. Despite the many types of cables, there are very few types of connectors. The following sections look at the most common types of connectors that you will encounter.

IBM Type 1 connector

The IBM Type 1 connector is commonly used with IBM token ring networks, and will either connect the workstation to a hub or connect multiple hubs. Unlike typical connectors that are either male (with pins) or female (with holes) and must be paired with a connector of the opposite gender to allow them to be connected, the Type 1 connector can be connected to any other connector. IBM calls the connector a "hermaphrodite," being composed of both genders of connectors. Figure 1-4 shows a Type 1 connector, with two connectors joined at the top of the figure.

Figure 1-4:
The IBM
Type 1 data
connector.

DB-9

The DB-9 connector is a D-shell–type connector, so named because of their D shape. The DB-9 has nine connection points arranged in two rows. This connector used to be found on the back of a computer in its female form, to be used with a CGA or EGA monitor. Now, you'll find a male DB-9 connector on the back of a computer as one of the two types of serial connections for COM ports. Figure 1-5 shows male and female DB-9 connectors.

Figure 1-5:
The DB-9
connector.

DB-15

DB-15, also known as HD DB-15, has the familiar shape of the D-shell connector but contains a higher density (HD) pin arrangement, with three rows of five connection points rather than the traditional two rows. Typically used for VGA and SVGA monitor connections, look for this connector in its female form. Figure 1-6 shows the DB-15 connector.

Figure 1-6:
The HD
DB-15.

DB-25

Once again, you see the familiar shape of the D-shell connector on a DB-25, but this connector sports 25 connections arranged in two rows. This connector is found on your computer in its male form in the role of a serial port and in its female form as a parallel port. You can also find the 25-pin male connector on the back of most modems. Figure 1-7 shows a parallel cable and a serial 9-25 pin converter; the latter is used to convert a 25-pin serial connector on the back of a computer down to a 9-pin port to be compatible with a 9-pin serial cable.

**Book III
Chapter 1**

**Describing Ports,
Cables, and
Connectors**

Figure 1-7:
The DB-25
connector.

Serial 9-25 pin converter Parallel cable

Centronics 36 and 50

A parallel cable has a DB-25 connector at one end and a 36-pin male Centronics connector at the other. You will find the female Centronics receptacle on your printer. Also, you will often see 50-pin Centronics connectors used with SCSI equipment, such as external disk or tape drives. Figure 1-8 shows 36-pin and 50-pin Centronics connectors.

Figure 1-8: Centronics 36 and 50 connectors.

50-pin 36-pin

RJ-11

RJ — short for *registered jack* — has small modular connectors that clip into matching holes. The RJ-11 connector is a standard modular connector used for telephones. It accepts four wires, usually in the form of a flat cable, rather than twisted pair cable. Analog telephone service is usually carried only on the two middle wires. You should see a female portion of this connector on your modem.

RJ-45

The RJ-45 connector — the larger cousin of the RJ-11 connector — usually accepts eight wires (four pair). This connector is used for 10BaseT, 10BaseTX, and token ring networking. (Basically, the RJ-45 is used anywhere

UTP cables are used.) Officially, the RJ-45 connector was designed for voice-grade circuits, and what is now referred to as the RJ-45 is officially known as an *8-pin connector.*

Do not confuse RJ-11 connectors with RJ-45 connectors. Figure 1-9 shows a RJ-11 connector on the left and a RJ-45 on the right.

Figure 1-9: RJ-11 connectors are smaller than RJ-45 connectors.

RJ-11 RJ-45

BNC

The *BNC* (Bayonet Neill-Concelman) connector is used for Thinnet networking. (See "Thick and thin coax," earlier in this chapter.) BNC connectors join with a male BNC that has a protruding point that fits into the female connector, and then a ring is turned on the outside edge to lock the connectors together much the same way that a bayonet attaches to a rifle (hence, the name). Figure 1-10 shows a BNC T-connector and a network card with a BNC connector.

BNC is also sometimes referred to as *British Naval Connector* — and a number of other names — but the actual name is a moot point for the exam.

BNC T-connectors are used to attach two Thinnet cables to a network card on the back of your computer. The T-connector has a male connector to attach to your network card and then two female connectors to accept the two Thinnet cables. A Thinnet network segment makes one long chain from all the computers that are on the segment by using T-connectors.

Network card

Figure 1-10:
Thinnet
Ethernet
uses BNC
connectors.

BNC-T connector BNC connector

PS/2, or mini-DIN 6

The PS/2 (also known as the mini-DIN 6) connector is usually used for key-boards and mice for AT and ATX computers. This connector is now favored over the larger DIN 5 connector. Figure 1-11 provides a sample of the mini-DIN connector.

Figure 1-11:
PS/2 (mini-DIN 6)
connectors
are used for
keyboards
and mice.

Universal Serial Bus (USB) connectors

USB 1.0 and USB 2.0 both use proprietary connectors (shown in Figure 1-12) to connect as many as 127 devices. All these devices must be *hot swappable* (capable of being added or removed without turning off the computer off), thanks to the specification for the standard. The two main types of connectors in USB are Type A for hosts and Type B for devices.

With the advent of smaller and smaller USB devices, the device end of the cable has many smaller cousins, such as the mini-A, mini-B, micro-A, and micro-B connectors. Both mini and micro connectors have similar form factors that make getting your cables confused very easy. These connectors are found on many MP3 players, digital cameras, and cell phones.

Figure 1-12:
The USB connector is unique to the USB system.

Type A Type B

IEEE 1394 (FireWire) connectors

FireWire is an Apple Computer trademark for devices that match the IEEE 1394 specification. This specification allows 63 devices (without hubs) to be connected in a single bus. It also uses a proprietary connector, similar in size to the USB connector but with a different shape, as seen in Figure 1-13.

Figure 1-13:
The FireWire connector is unique to the FireWire system.

Standard External Cables

External cables are used on the outside of the computer to connect peripheral devices. The most commonly used connector on external cables is the D-shell connector (named for its shape), which is usually called *DB*. Looking at the connector with the D pointing toward the ground, pin numbering on male connectors starts with the top-left connector. With the connector in this orientation, the upper-left pin is pin 1, and the order goes across the connector and left to right for all subsequent rows. For a female receptor, hole 1 or pin 1 is in the top-right of the connector if the D is pointing down; other pins are numbered right to left. This allows pin 1 on a male connector to match pin 1 on a female connector. This section covers the three most common cables.

Parallel cable

A parallel cable has a male DB-25 connector on the end that connects to your computer, and a male Centronics 36 connector on the end that connects to the printer. This style of cable is a standard parallel cable or an IEEE 1284 bidirectional cable. If the cable is the latter, you should expect to see IEEE 1284 labeled on the cable or connector.

In addition to this cable, you might also see a parallel extension cable, which will have a male BD-25 connector to attach to your computer and a female DB-25 connector to attach to a parallel printer cable. This cable can easily be confused with a serial cable for a computer with a 25-pin serial connector. The only way to positively identify this cable is to use a multimeter or a continuity tester to see what pins on one end of the cable match which holes on the other end. For a parallel extension cable, this is a straight-though cable; and, each pin, 1 though 25, matches with the appropriate hole on the other end of the cable.

Serial cable

Numbering the pins on the connectors makes it easier to describe what the cable looks like at the connector level. This might make more sense when you look at the pin configuration for a standard 9-pin to 25-pin serial modem cable, and the 9-pin to 9-pin null modem cable in the next section. Modem cables are designed for a computer with either a male 9-pin connector or a male 25-pin connector, so the cable has either a female 9-pin or a female 25-pin connector on the end that connects to the computer, and a 25-pin male connector on the end that connects to the modem. Most modern computers have a 9-pin serial connector, if they have a serial port at all. The pin configuration and function for a 9-pin to 25-pin serial cable are summarized in Table 1-2.

Table 1-2		Serial Cable Pin Connections	
Computer (9-pin)	*Data Direction*	*Modem (25-pin)*	*Role*
3	→	2	Transmitted Data (TD)
2	←	3	Received Data (RD)
7	→	4	Ready To Send (RTS)
8	←	5	Clear To Send (CTS)
6	→	6	Data Set Ready (DSR)
1	→	8	Data Carrier Detected, or tone from a modem (DCD)
4	→	20	Data Terminal Ready (DTR)
5	N/A	7	Signal Ground (SG)
9	←	22	Ring Indicator, or ringing tone detected (RI)

Null modem cable

If you need to transfer data via serial ports between two computers that are close, use the same communications programs as if you were actually using modems and telephone lines to connect the computers. Such serial communication (that bypasses a modem) uses a *null modem cable,* which nullifies or eliminates the need for a modem by directly connecting the send and receive ports of the devices on either side of the cable. Table 1-3 shows how the pin connections are made between devices. If you look at the roles of the pins on each side of the connection, you can see that each pin that sends data is connected to the receive pin for that data on the other side of the cable, with the result that a transmit data pin is connected to a receive data pin.

Table 1-3		Null Modem Cable Pin Connections		
Role	*Computer (9-pin)*	*Data Direction*	*Computer (9-pin)*	*Role*
RD	2	→	3	TD
TD	3	←	2	RD
RTS	7	→	8	CTS
CTS	8	←	7	RTS
DCD and DSR	1 and 6	←	4	DTR
DTR	4	→	1 and 6	DCD and DSR
SG	5	N/A	5	SG

Null modem cables are also used to configure many network devices, such as switches and routers, using a console port on the network device and a terminal communication program.

Viewing Cable Adapters

Many types of adapters can join different types of cables and devices. The following sections give a brief description of some of the major types.

Barrel connectors

The term *barrel connectors* comes from Thinnet networking, where cables could be extended by means of an adapter, resembling a small barrel, that accepted a male connector on either end. This term is now often applied to any connector that extends the length of a cable by joining two cables but that does not change the pin configuration. Figure 1-14 shows a barrel or cable connector for an RJ-45 cable.

Figure 1-14: Use barrel connectors to extend the length of cables.

Barrel connector

Gender changers

Gender changers are a bit of a strange beast. They are straight-through connectors that don't change the order or connection of the pins; they only change the sex of the connector that they are attached to. They look like a connector that has either two male or two female ends (as shown Figure 1-15); when attached to a cable of one sex, the connector becomes the other. These are used only in rare cases where your cables have the wrong

sex connector, which is a situation that I often encounter with video connectors when working with KVM (Keyboard, Video, and Mouse) switches and cables made by different manufacturers.

Figure 1-15: Gender changers change the sex of a connector.

Gender changer

Null modem

Null modem cables act as a replacement for two modems communicating with each other. If you have two computers that you want to connect directly, attach two modems and have one dial the other and transfer the files. Or, you can use a null modem cable. The *null modem* removes the modems from the equation and connects the send pins on one serial port to the receive pins on the other, and vice versa. If you don't have a null modem cable, you can use a regular modem cable and a null modem adapter. The null modem adapter looks like a gender changer (see the preceding section) except that it changes the pin configuration as well as the sex of the connection. To tell whether you have a null modem adapter or a gender changer, look for a label, or check the pin configuration on either end of the adapter by using a continuity tester or multimeter.

Multimedia Connectors

Multimedia is one of the new hot areas of computers and how people are using them. Several standard types of connections are used for multimedia purposes. Table 1-4 provides some standard multimedia connectors and their uses.

Table 1-4	Types of Multimedia Connectors
Role	*Connectors Used*
Analog audio	The main analog audio connector used in your computer is the one-eighth-inch connector, which is the standard headphone, speaker, and microphone jack for most sound cards. This form of connector has been around for years as an audio connector.
MIDI	The Musical Instrument Digital Interface (MIDI) connector has been in use since the 1980s, but the standard for it was finalized only in the early 1990s. Most electronic keyboards and many other instruments have MIDI connections on them, which are usually 5-pin DIN connectors; the connector on a computer is a DB-15 connector. MIDI connections allow for time synchronization, sequencing, recording, editing, and playback of MIDI-formatted data. The MIDI file format is extremely efficient.
Analog video and cable	Computers make use of the same video transfer cables used in the home AV market. These include coaxial cable that can carry audio and video signals; RCA cables that can carry either an audio or video signal (but, if you have an RCA connector on your computer, it is likely a yellow video connector); and S-Video, which is used for higher quality video signals and uses a mini-DIN 4 connector. These cables are used to connect your computer to a variety of video devices to either capture or display data.
Digital audio	The main digital audio connection for your computer is a S/PDIF (Sony/Philips Digital Interface Format) connection. Many motherboards and soundcards support this interface for multimedia applications. The S/PDIF connection is often made using coaxial, RCA, or optical connectors and cables.

Getting an A+

In this chapter, you examine the role of different types of connectors. In the process, you discover the differences between serial and parallel communication, as well as the differences between USB and IEEE 1394 (FireWire). You find out about the different types of cables and connectors that are used in different areas of a computer system. You should now have a general understanding about where and why different cables and connectors are used in your system.

Prep Test

1 Which of the following ports offers the fastest throughput or transfer speed?

A ○ Serial

B ○ Parallel

C ○ USB

D ○ IEEE 1284

2 What type of connector on the back of your computer accepts a parallel cable?

A ○ DIN-8 female

B ○ DB-25 female

C ○ DB-9 female

D ○ DB-25 male

3 What type of port uses a three-row DB-15 connector?

A ○ Serial

B ○ SVGA

C ○ Parallel

D ○ Game

4 RS-232 is a term associated with which type of port?

A ○ Serial

B ○ Parallel

C ○ SCSI

D ○ Game

5 Ethernet network cards typically use what type of connector?

A ○ RJ-32

B ○ DB-9

C ○ DB-25

D ○ RJ-45

6 BNC connectors are usually used on your computer to provide which of the following?

A ○ Serial connections

B ○ Parallel connections

C ○ Networking

D ○ Never used

7 How is serial data moved?

A ○ Across multiple cables at the same time

B ○ As a sequential stream of data

C ○ Using a bidirectional information algorithm

D ○ Using multi-clock sequencing

8 Data transfer speed for the IEEE 1394 standard is

A ○ 10 Mbps

B ○ 100 Mbps

C ○ 400 Mbps

D ○ 12 Gbps

9 Most keyboards connect to computers by using which type of connector?

A ○ DB-9

B ○ DIN 6

C ○ mini-DIN 6

D ○ RJ-45

10 Monitors usually connect to a computer through what type of connector?

A ○ DB-15

B ○ DB-25

C ○ USB

D ○ RS-232

11 CAT5 cables are defined by which of the following?

A ○ Number of pairs of wires

B ○ Length of the cable segment

C ○ Type of shielding that is used

D ○ Number of twists per foot in each pair of wires

12 Thin coaxial cable usually implements which type of connectors?

A ○ BNC

B ○ RJ-45

C ○ RS-232

D ○ IEEE 488

13 Pin 1 on a ribbon cable is usually identified by what?

A ○ The number 1 inscribed on the connector

B ○ A colored line on the wire leading to it

C ○ A keyed connector

D ○ Pin 1 is always on the left side of the connectors

Answers

1 **C.** USB offers the highest transfer rates. USB 1.1 has transfer rates of 12 Mbps, and USB 2.0 offers transfer rates of 480 Mbps. This question might have been disputable if IEEE-1394 (FireWire) had been in the question because it has transfer rates of 400 Mbps. *See "Universal Serial Bus (USB)."*

2 **B.** On the back of your computer, the parallel port has a DB-25 female connector. *Review "DB-25."*

3 **B.** VGA and SVGA use HD DB-15 connectors that have three rows of five pins. *Take a look at "DB-15."*

4 **A.** RS-232 is one of the standards associated with the serial port. *Peek at "Serial and parallel ports."*

5 **D.** RJ-45 is typically used for networking. *Look over "RJ-45."*

6 **C.** BNC connectors are used for Thinnet or 10Base2 networking. *Study "BNC."*

7 **B.** Serial cables move data sequentially, one bit at a time, and parallel cables allow for all 8 bits to be sent at one time. *Refer to "Serial and parallel ports."*

8 **C.** FireWire, or IEEE 1394, allows for transfer rates up to 400 Mbps. *Examine "FireWire (IEEE 1394)."*

9 **C.** Older PCs use DIN 5 connectors, and newer ones use the mini-DIN 6 or PS/2 connector. *See "PS/2 or mini-DIN 6."*

10 **A.** VGA and SVGA monitors usually connect to your computer via a high-density DB-15 connector. *Review "DB-15."*

11 **D.** CAT5 cables are defined by the type of copper wire that is used and the number of twists per foot by each pair of wires. *Check out "Twisted pair."*

12 **A.** BNC connectors are used with Thinnet Ethernet networking. *Peruse "BNC."*

13 **B.** Pin 1 is identified by a colored line on the side of the cable that contains Pin 1. Keyed connectors prevent you from putting the cable in the wrong way but do not specifically identify pin 1. *Take a look at "Ribbon."*

Chapter 2: Installing and Configuring Input Devices

Exam Objectives

✓ Understanding keyboards

✓ Working with the mouse

✓ Modems and network cards

✓ Other input devices

A computer's job is to processes information, but only after someone inputs that information into the system. In this chapter, I discuss different types of devices used to input data into the computer.

At anyone's disposal are many forms of input devices with which you can communicate with the computer, such as modems, network cards, touch pads, and biometric devices. A keyboard and a mouse, though, are the most popular.

Minding Your Keys and Qs

The keyboard is the main device you use to interact with a computer system. Keystrokes are converted into the characters that you see onscreen, and maybe eventually print. Most keyboards have five major key parts, or groups, that contain keys grouped by specific purpose. These areas (standard desktop keyboard) are shown in Figure 2-1.

Figure 2-1:
The five major keyboard key groupings.

The five major groupings on a keyboard are

+ **Alphanumeric:** The *alphanumeric* keys are the keys on the keyboard that contain the letters of the alphabet, numerals, and punctuation.

+ **Function:** The 12 function keys on a keyboard offer special features. For example, in Windows, pressing F2 renames a file or icon.

+ **Cursor:** Use the cursor keys to move the cursor or insertion point.

+ **Numeric:** The numeric keypad has the mathematical operators and numbers for quick, single-handed access for inputting numeric information.

+ **LEDs:** The LEDs indicate whether features such as Caps Lock, Num Lock, and Scroll Lock are turned on or off.

Each key on the keyboard has a *keyswitch* that closes an electrical circuit on a grid when a key is pressed. When the key contacts the grid, the keyboard controller detects the keystroke and generates a *keycode*. The keycode is then converted into an ASCII code that is used to display the character onscreen.

Each location on the grid corresponds to a specific keycode. This is why you can't simply move a keycap and expect to move the character as well. For example, the letter *A* is on the left side of the keyboard. Simply moving the A keycap to the right side of the keyboard will not allow you to press that key to type the letter *A* because the location on the grid that generates a keycode for letter *A* is on the left side of the keyboard.

Different keyboards work in different ways when you press a key. Each manufacturer decides what type of keyboard to manufacture and how the keystrokes will be interpreted by the system. The two most popular techniques used to identify what keys are being pressed are

+ **Switch-based:** Uses micro-switches for each key. The keys deteriorate with time and tend to get dirty, but these keyboards are inexpensive.

+ **Capacitive:** Also known as *membrane keyboards* and are more expensive than switch-based keyboards. Despite their higher cost, though, capacitive keyboards are more reliable. Each key pushes a spring, which pushes a paddle to create an impression on the capacitive surface located under the keyboard. The impression on the capacitive surface sends a signal that is interpreted by the keyboard controller. This is the most common type of keyboard in laptops and netbooks.

For a keyboard to work with a system, software must be employed that drives the keyboard actions. Two types of software routines are used to allow the keyboard to work with the system:

+ **Keyboard device driver:** Like any piece of hardware, a driver in Windows is responsible for allowing the device to work in Windows — including the keyboard.

+ **Firmware:** The keyboard firmware is typically stored in ROM in the actual keyboard (as in the case of an XT keyboard) or in a chip on the motherboard. The firmware contains low-level code to communicate with the hardware.

Identifying keyboard types

A number of different types of keyboards have been used over time. The following list identifies the different types of keyboards you need to know for the A+ Certification exam:

+ **XT keyboard:** The older XT keyboard has 83 alphanumeric keys, including 10 function keys. This keyboard has the keyboard processor located on the keyboard itself. In addition to the alphanumeric keys, it has a numeric keypad and cursor control keys on the right side of the keyboard.

+ **AT keyboard:** The older AT keyboard has 84 regular keys (an extra System Request key was added), and also features 10 function keys. The AT keyboard has a bigger Enter key than the XT keyboard, and the keyboard processor moved from the keyboard itself to the computer's motherboard. The AT keyboard uses an AT keyboard connector, which is also known as a DIN-5 connector.

+ **Enhanced keyboard:** The enhanced keyboard is the popular keyboard used today, with 101 keys and 12 function keys. The enhanced keyboard has a numeric keypad along with cursor control keys located on the right side. The enhanced keyboard typically uses the PS/2 connection (also known as a mini-DIN 6 connector) or a USB connection.

+ **Windows keyboard:** A Windows keyboard is similar to an enhanced keyboard containing 101 keys, but the Windows keyboard contains buttons, or keys, that control features of Windows. For example, a Windows keyboard features a button to bring up the Start menu and also a key to bring up the shortcut menu (as if you had right-clicked with the mouse).

+ **Natural, or ergonomic, keyboards:** Natural, or ergonomic, keyboards are a modification of the enhanced keyboards. A natural keyboard separates the alphanumeric keys into two parts: one part for the left hand and the other for the right hand. The keyboard is bowed and might even come apart to allow for more natural hand placement. These keyboards normally also have a wrist rest to help hands sit in a more natural position. These keyboards are designed to reduce repetitive stress injuries. Figure 2-2 shows a typical natural keyboard.

Figure 2-2:
A natural,
ergonomic-
style
keyboard.

Installing a keyboard

Installing a keyboard is fairly straightforward. You pretty much plug just the keyboard into the system, and Windows uses a keyboard driver to communicate with the device.

For the A+ exam, know the different keyboard connectors, as described in the following list:

✦ **DIN-5 connector:** A DIN connector — also known as an AT connector — is used on older systems to connect the keyboard to the computer. You can always tell the DIN connector because it is large and round.

✦ **PS/2 connector:** A PS/2 connector — also known as a mini-DIN 6 connector — has been the most popular keyboard connector found on computers in the past but has been replaced by the USB connector. It is identical to what is found on a typical mouse.

Figure 2-3 compares a DIN-5 connector beside a PS/2 connector.

Figure 2-3:
A DIN-5
connector
(left) beside
a PS/2
keyboard
connector
(right).

✦ **USB connector:** Keyboards that connect to the system via a USB connector have become very popular. A number of systems today are getting away from the PS/2 connections for keyboards and mice and using USB. Figure 2-4 shows a keyboard being connected to a USB port.

Figure 2-4:
A USB keyboard connects to a USB port on the system.

Configuring keyboards and setting accessibility options

Configuring a keyboard in Windows doesn't involve a lot of options. Typically, you just plug it in, and it works. Windows does allow you to configure the blink rate of the cursor and also change the *repeat rate,* which dictates how quickly a letter will repeat if you hold down a key on your keyboard.

To configure the keyboard options, follow these steps:

1. *XP:* **Choose Start⇨Control Panel⇨Printer and Other Hardware⇨ Keyboard.**

 Vista: **Choose Start⇨Control Panel⇨Hardware and Sound⇨Keyboard.**

 The Keyboard Properties dialog box appears, as shown in Figure 2-5.

2. **Adjust the settings to suit your needs.**

 Here, you can configure the character repeat options and the cursor blink rate. The following options are available:

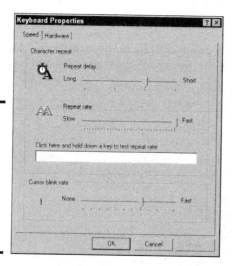

Figure 2-5:
Change
keyboard
properties
through
the Control
Panel in
Windows
XP.

- *Repeat Delay:* Repeat delay controls the length of time between when you first hold down a key and when the character begins to repeat onscreen.

- *Repeat Rate:* Repeat rate controls how quickly additional characters are displayed when the key is held down.

- *Cursor Blink Rate:* Cursor blink rate controls how fast the cursor blinks.

3. Click OK to apply your settings and close the dialog box.

A number of accessibility features are available in Windows that are controlled via the keyboard. Accessibility features in Windows are designed for users who have disabilities. To configure the keyboard accessibility options, follow these steps:

1. XP: Choose Start⇨Control Panel⇨Accessibility Options.

The Accessibility Options dialog box appears, as shown in Figure 2-6.

Vista: Choose Start⇨Control Panel⇨Ease of Access⇨Ease of Access Center⇨Make the Keyboard Easier to Use.

2. Ensure that the Keyboard tab is selected and then configure the following options as needed:

- *StickyKeys:* This feature aids folks with an issue pressing two keys at the same time, such as Ctrl+C. Here is how it works (with StickyKeys enabled). When you press the Shift, Ctrl, or Alt key — or, if you have a Windows keyboard, the Windows key — that key remains active, as if you were holding it down, while you choose the next keystroke. If you press a key, such as the Shift key, twice then the key stays on until you press it again. Because pressing the key keeps the key held

after you let go, if you wanted to perform a keystroke operation such as Ctrl-Alt-Delete with sticky keys you would simply press Ctrl, then press Alt and finally press the Delete key on its own.

- *FilterKeys:* Use FilterKeys to tell Windows to ignore repeated keystrokes. For example, if you hold down a key too long with FilterKeys enabled, the repeat rate of the keystroke is reduced. This prevents a character from appearing many times at a quick rate.

- *ToggleKeys:* Enabling the ToggleKeys option triggers audible tones when the Caps Lock, Num Lock, or Scroll Lock keys are pressed.

3. Click OK.

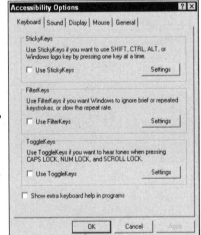

Figure 2-6: Change the keyboard accessibility options in Windows XP.

Catching the Mouse

The other popular input device found on computer systems today is the mouse. The mouse is one of the primary input devices because of the graphical user interface (GUI) features of today's operating systems. The following sections identify the different types of mice and how to install them.

Types of mice

You can find three types of mice on today's desktop computer systems: mechanical mice, opto-mechanical mice, and optical mice.

✦ **Mechanical:** A mechanical mouse was the only type of mouse used with computers for many years. The mechanical mouse uses a rubber ball that moves a pair of wheels inside the mouse. The internal wheels

capture the horizontal and vertical movements of the mouse and then send that information to the computer. The movement is then displayed onscreen.

✦ **Opto-mechanical:** The opto-mechanical mouse is a very popular mouse today. It uses a rubber ball that moves rollers that control the movement of a disc — the encoding disc — which has holes along the side of it.

The prefix "opto" comes into play because LEDs and sensors use an infrared light beam to determine the movement of the mouse. See Figure 2-7. When the rubber ball moves the encoding disc, the infrared beam passes through the holes on the encoding disc, indicating that the mouse has moved and in which direction.

Figure 2-7: As the mouse moves, the holes and solid areas of the encoding disc help determine movement.

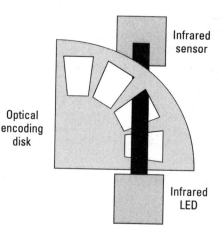

Infrared sensor

Optical encoding disk

Infrared LED

✦ **Optical:** An optical mouse differs from an opto-mechanical mouse because an optical mouse has no moving parts. The rubber ball and wheels are replaced with an optical scanning system that works on pretty much any surface.

The optical scanning system is made up of optical sensors and a Digital Signal Processor (DSP). An optical mouse captures images of the surface at a rate of 1,500 images per second. The DSP then analyzes and compares the images to detect the mouse movement.

Installing a mouse

Installing a mouse is very similar and just as easy as installing a keyboard. You pretty much just plug in the mouse, and the Windows mouse driver controls the device. The following is a list of the different types of interfaces you may use to connect a mouse to the system:

✦ **Serial:** A serial mouse connects to the serial port on the computer. The serial port is the male 9-pin or 25-pin port on the back of the computer that sends data one bit at a time. Serial mice are not as popular as they once were.

✦ **PS/2:** One of the most popular interfaces for a mouse on desktop computers is a PS/2 connection. A PS/2 connection is also known as a mini-DIN 6 connector.

✦ **USB:** The most popular type of connection for mice today is the USB connector. Simply plug the mouse into the USB port and click away! As you find out in many chapters of this book, USB is *hot-swappable* — meaning that you can plug and unplug a USB device without shutting down the system. USB can transfer data at 12 Mbps (USB 1.1) or 480 Mbps (USB 2.0).

More and more, today's systems are using wireless keyboards and mice, which use a USB wireless adapter that connects to the computer that is responsible for receiving the signals from the wireless keyboard or mouse. The wireless signal is sent through radio frequency or via infrared depending on the keyboard or mouse. For more information on wireless, check out Book IX, Chapter 2.

Communicating with Modems and Network Adapters

In this section, you find out about installing modems and network cards that allow computer systems to communicate with other systems on the network.

Working with modems

A *modem* is a communication device that modulates, or converts, the digital signal from the computer into an analog signal so that it can travel over an analog line, such as telephone wire. The signal is then demodulated back into a digital signal at the modem on the receiving system. The process of *modu*lating and *dem*odulating is where the amalgam word *modem* comes from.

A modem allows a computer to send data over an analog line and is useful when you want to dial up another computer over a phone line or access the Internet.

Modem characteristics

A modem is either internal or external:

✦ **An internal modem** is installed in an expansion slot within the computer housing as either an older ISA card or, more popular today, a PCI card.

✦ **An external modem** sits on the desk beside the computer and plugs into the computer's serial port.

Both internal and external modems plug into a telephone jack via a standard telephone cable.

Another very important characteristic of the modem is its speed. The speed of the modem is measured in bits per second (bps) — and like anything else, the more bits the better! When it comes to modem speed, you're looking at 56 Kbps (56,000 bps) as the standard. This is known as a 56K modem.

AT commands

For the A+ exam, you need to be familiar with what an AT command is. AT is short for *ATtention,* and AT commands are the modem commands that are called by software to perform communication. You typically don't need to use these commands unless you're troubleshooting why a computer cannot dial up. Your first question is always, "Is it the modem or the application I am using?" By using these low-level AT commands, you can determine whether the modem is working.

The AT commands that you should be comfortable with for the A+ exam are listed in Table 2-1.

Table 2-1	AT Modem Commands
Command	*Description*
ATDT <number>	Dial a number using touch-tone dialing.
ATDP <number>	Dial a number using pulse or rotary dialing.
ATA	Instruct the modem to answer.
ATH	Instruct the modem to hang up.
ATL	Set the speaker loudness.
ATZ	Reset the modem to the default settings.

Here are sequential-hint tricks to remembering these commands for the A+ exam.

1. Each command starts with the AT prefix

2. Then you have a character, such as D for dial, A for answer, or H for hang-up. The "L" stands for loadness and the "Z" is used for default settings.

3. Because there are two types of dial tones, the dial command has another character representing the type of dial tone to use and requires the telephone number to dial.

For example, to call my friend Ed's house with touch-tone dialing, the AT command would be

```
ATDT 555-5555
```

Okay, this isn't Ed's phone number. He wouldn't like it too much if I put his personal phone number in the book. But you get the idea of how the command works. There are more AT commands than just what I show here, but these are the ones you need to be familiar with for the exam.

Installing a modem

Most modems today ship as PCI cards and are inserted into a PCI slot in the computer: the very definition of an internal modem. You can install an internal modem by following these steps:

1. **Power-off the computer and be sure to ground yourself.**

2. **Remove the cover from the computer.**

3. **If necessary, remove the blanking plate that allows access to the modem from the back of the PC.**

 This allows the modem card to fit in the slot.

4. **Place the modem card into the appropriate expansion slot.**

 For example, you will most likely have a PCI card, so place the PCI modem card into an available PCI slot.

5. **Screw the modem card into place and put the cover back on the PC.**

6. **The modem has two ports on it that both take RJ-11 connections. Connect the incoming phone line to the appropriate port and then connect the phone to the modem's second port.**

7. **Power-on the PC.**

Configuring a modem

After you install the modem and Windows starts up, Plug and Play should kick in and detect the new device. If a driver is not present in Windows for the device, you will be asked for the driver. If you do not have the driver, you can choose to cancel adding the driver at this time and go to Device Manager at a later time to update the driver after you have it. See Book VI, Chapter 1, to find out how to load and configure drivers via Device Manager.

When the driver is loaded, you can go to the properties of the device in Device Manager and query the modem to verify that the modem is functioning properly. In short, *querying the modem* describes sending AT commands to the modem and verifying that the modem responds to the commands. The nice thing is you don't need to type each command listed earlier in

Table 2-1; use the Query button in the properties of the modem to do this for you. To verify that the modem is working, follow these troubleshooting steps:

1. **In Windows XP, click Start and right-click My Computer.**

 In Windows Vista, click Start and right-click Computer.

2. **Choose Properties from the pop-up menu.**

3. **In Windows XP, in the System Properties window, click the Hardware tab and then click the Device Manager button.**

 In Windows Vista, in the System Properties window, click the Device Manager link from the Tasks list on the left side.

4. **In Device Manager, expand the modems node, right-click your modem, and then choose Properties.**

5. **In the Properties window of the modem, click the Diagnostics tab (shown in Figure 2-8) and then click the Query Modem button to perform a diagnostic on your modem using the AT commands.**

 You should notice a list of AT commands that have been issued against the modem as a diagnostic test and whether the test was successful.

6. **Close all windows.**

Figure 2-8: Perform troubleshooting diagnostics on the modem in Windows XP.

Working with network adapters

The most popular communication device found in computers today is a network card. A *network card* is a device that allows you to connect your computer to a network or the Internet, and is responsible for sending and

receiving data on the network. Not only are network cards popular in systems found in the corporate world, but because of the popularity of high-speed Internet, you can also find them in a lot of home computers as well.

Network cards are categorized by their transfer rates. For example, a network card that can transfer 100 million bits of data per second is a 100 Mbps network card, and a network card that can transfer 1000 million bits per second is a 1000 Mbps network card.

The card will run at the highest common speed available between the two communicating devices. For example, if you connect your system to a 100 Mbps network switch but your system has a 1000 Mbps network card, your card will run at only 100 Mbps. This is why most systems have what is called a *100/1000 network card* — the card can talk at either 100 Mbps or 1000 Mbps.

Installing a network adapter (card)

When installing a network card, you first need to determine what type of interface you wish to use. There are a number of types of network cards that could be installed into the system. For example, you could install a USB network card, an old ISA card for older computers, or the more popular PCI network card (shown in Figure 2-9) that is inserted into a PCI slot.

Figure 2-9:
Installing a
PCI network
card into the
PCI slot of a
computer.

To install a network adapter, follow these steps:

1. **Power-off the computer and be sure to ground yourself.**
2. **Remove the cover from the computer.**
3. **If necessary, remove the blanking plate that allows access to the modem from the back of the PC.**

 This allows the network card to fit in the slot.
4. **Place the network card into the appropriate expansion slot.**

 For example, you will most likely have a PCI card, so place the PCI network card into an available PCI slot.
5. **Screw the network card into place and put the cover back on the PC.**
6. **Connect the network cable to the back of the network card.**
7. **Power-on the PC.**

Configuring a network card

After you install the network card, Plug and Play should kick in and either load the driver for you or prompt you for the driver. When the driver is loaded, you can specify settings for the network card in Windows. For example, if you want to force your network card to run at a particular speed, you can do that through the properties of the network card.

To configure your network card in XP, follow these steps:

1. **Click Start and right-click My Computer.**
2. **Choose Properties from the pop-up menu.**
3. **In the System Properties window, click the Hardware tab and then click the Device Manager button.**
4. **In Device Manager, expand the Network Adapters category on the left, right-click your network card, and then choose Properties.**
5. **In the Properties dialog box for the network card, click the Advanced tab to see settings that can be configured for the network card (shown in Figure 2-10).**

 The advanced settings are different for each make and model of network card because the settings are particular to the driver that is loaded. A very popular setting is the link speed, which specifies what speed you wish to run the card at. Most network cards are set to Auto, which means the card will detect the best speed. When troubleshooting, though, you can force a particular speed.

Typically, you may also choose which type of connector on the network card will be used — if it has multiple connector styles. For example, a number of network cards ship with both an RJ-45 port and a BNC (bayonet-type) port — this is called a *combo card.* If you want to ensure that the system is using the RJ-45 port, you set that in the device properties.

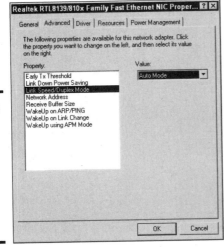

Figure 2-10:
Configuring network card settings through Windows Device Manager.

**Book III
Chapter 2**

Installing and
Configuring Input
Devices

To configure the network card in Windows Vista, you perform the same steps with the exception of how you start Device Manager. To start Device Manager in Windows Vista

1. **Click the Start button.**

2. **Right-click the Computer menu item and choose Properties.**

3. **In System properties, click the Device Manager link in the tasks list on the left side of the screen.**

After Device Manager launches, you can change the settings the same way as mentioned earlier in Windows XP by going to the network card properties.

Other Input Devices

As technology moves on, new input devices appear. For example, laptops use a touch pad as an input device, whereas hand-held devices use a pen-like stylus. The following is a list of input devices you might encounter:

✦ **Touch pad:** A number of laptop systems today use a touch pad as an alternative way to control the mouse pointer in Windows. The *touch pad* — that rectangular area found below the keyboard that you move your finger(s) across to move the mouse pointer — also usually bears two buttons below the square to perform left- and right-click operations. A touch pad is displayed in Figure 2-11.

Figure 2-11: A touch pad is a popular input device to control the mouse pointer on a laptop computer.

✦ **Touch screens:** You see touch screens used a lot at public terminals for things like information booths and bank machines. *Touch screens* require that you actually touch the screen to choose different options.

✦ **Bar code reader:** A *bar code reader* is a type of scanner that reads bar codes and then converts the bar code into data stored on a computer and used in applications. An inventory application is an example of an application that uses a bar code reader as an input device.

✦ **Biometric devices:** *Biometric devices* are used to authenticate, or log, people onto a system by using biological characteristics of that person, such as a fingerprint or a retinal scan. Biometric devices are very popular in high-security environments because of how difficult it is to impersonate someone when dealing with authentication methods such as a fingerprint scan. Some laptop makers are even starting to include fingerprint scanners in consumer-level laptops as security devices and theft deterrents.

Getting an A+

In this chapter, you find out about different types of input devices. The following list outlines some of the key points to remember for the exam:

✦ Keyboards usually connect to the system with a PS/2 connection or a USB connection with today's systems.

✦ Older keyboards use a DIN-5 to connect to the motherboard.

✦ Most mice today connect to the system via a USB port or a PS/2 port.

✦ A serial mouse connects to the serial port, but this type of mouse isn't very common anymore.

✦ Modems are used to convert digital signals to analog and vice versa so that digital data can be delivered over an analog line.

✦ Network cards are the most popular type of communication device in today's systems. Be sure to review the networking chapters to fully understand how to network a system.

Prep Test

1 Which two formats do serial ports come in?

A ❑ 9-pin

B ❑ 15-pin

C ❑ 20-pin

D ❑ 25-pin

2 At what speed does USB 1.1 transfer information?

A ○ 10 Mbps

B ○ 12 Mbps

C ○ 100 Mbps

D ○ 480 Mbps

3 Which type of keyboard is designed to reduce repetitive stress injuries?

A ○ AT keyboard

B ○ Natural keyboard

C ○ Windows keyboard

D ○ Enhanced keyboard

4 Which type of mouse uses a rubber ball and sensors connected to two wheels to determine mouse movement?

A ○ Mechanical

B ○ Opto-mechanical

C ○ Optical

D ○ Wheel

5 What is the AT command to hang up the connection?

A ○ ATDT

B ○ ATA

C ○ ATH

D ○ ATDP

6 At what speed does USB 2.0 transfer information?

A ○ 10 Mbps

B ○ 12 Mbps

C ○ 100 Mbps

D ○ 480 Mbps

7 Which two popular connector types are used with a mouse?

A ❑ USB

B ❑ Parallel

C ❑ PS/2

D ❑ OS/2

8 Which two types of interfaces are typically used to connect a network card to the system?

A ❑ Parallel

B ❑ USB

C ❑ PCI

D ❑ Serial

9 What is the AT command to call 555-5555?

A ○ ATDT 555-5555

B ○ ATA 555-5555

C ○ ATH 555-5555

D ○ ATZ 555-5555

10 What type of input device is used by a warehousing application to take inventory of all the products?

A ○ Touch pad

B ○ Touch screen

C ○ Touch mouse

D ○ Bar code reader

Answers

1 **A, D.** Serial ports, which are used by serial mice, come in two formats: 9-pin and 25-pin. *See "Installing a mouse."*

2 **B.** USB 1.1 devices run at 12 Mbps, and USB 2.0 devices run at 480 Mbps. *Review "Installing a mouse."*

3 **B.** Natural keyboards are a form of ergonomic keyboard that reduces repetitive stress injuries. *Check out "Identifying keyboard types."*

4 **A.** A mechanical mouse uses all moving parts, such as a rubber ball that moves wheels that are picked up by sensors to detect mouse movements. *Peruse "Types of mice."*

5 **C.** The AT command used by modems to hang up a connection is ATH — the H stands for *hang up*. *Take a look at "AT commands."*

6 **D.** USB 2.0 runs at 480 Mbps, and USB 1.1 runs at a lower speed of 12 Mbps. *Peek at "Installing a mouse."*

7 **A, C.** Popular connections used by the mouse today are the USB connector and the PS/2 connector. *Look over "Installing a mouse."*

8 **B, C.** Network cards connect to the system as either a USB or PCI device. *Study "Installing a network adapter (card)."*

9 **A.** The ATDT command is used to dial a number. *Refer to "AT commands."*

10 **D.** A bar code reader is a type of device that reads bar codes and converts the code into data to be used on the computer. *Examine "Other Input Devices."*

Chapter 3: Installing and Configuring Output Devices

Exam Objectives

✔ Understanding video adapters and monitors

✔ Working with sound cards

✔ Other output devices

An *output device* sends data from the computer and creates a tangible output. Examples of output for a system are displaying information on the monitor, printing a report, or even listening to the sound that the sound card puts through the speakers when playing your favorite computer games.

This chapter also looks at the video hardware that is responsible for creating the images on the screen and discusses how a sound card works. These topics are essential to passing your A+ certification exams, so be sure to study them well!

Understanding Video Adapters

A *video adapter* (video card) — the interface between the monitor and the computer — is responsible for converting the digital data from the computer into analog information. The data is converted to an analog signal before being delivered to a monitor because monitors use analog data to create the image.

Because display functions are very time- and memory-consuming, most video adapters these days have their own processing chip and memory to alleviate the processing workload from the CPU. Today's video adapters are typically PCIe or AGP cards, but you might run into some older systems that require a PCI video card because these systems don't have an AGP or a PCIe slot. For more information on PCIe and AGP, check out Book II, Chapter 1.

The following outlines the basic role of what the video adapter does when it comes to displaying data on the computer screen:

1. Data is sent to the video card via the expansion bus that the video card resides in.

2. The video chipset on the video card writes the data to memory located on the card.

3. After being stored in memory, the data is passed to the *digital-to-analog converter (DAC),* where it is converted from digital signals to analog signals that the monitor can understand.

4. The data is passed to the monitor, which then displays the data on the screen.

The video adapter is identifiable by its unique 15-pin female connector, comprising 5 pins in 3 rows. On most systems today, the port on the video card is typically blue and has a monitor symbol beside it. Figure 3-1 shows a video port.

Figure 3-1:
Looking at the back of a video card and the port style.

Looking at the video standards

A number of video standards have been developed over the years, with each standard increasing the quality of the display from the previous standards. The quality of display is measured by the resolution and color support.

The following list outlines some of the popular video standards, which you need to know for the A+ Certification exam:

✦ **Monochrome Display Adapter (MDA):** Displays data in a text format with a single color — white text on the black screen. This standard is pretty much obsolete, but you might encounter an old server that still uses it.

✦ **Color Graphics Adapter (CGA):** The next step above MDA; supports four colors in a 320 x 200 resolution but supports only two colors with a resolution of 640 x 200. CGA video adapters were the first adapters to support color.

✦ **Enhanced Graphics Adapter (EGA):** The next step after CGA; much improved over the CGA graphics standard. EGA supports 16 colors at 640 x 350 resolution.

✦ **Video Graphics Array (VGA):** Video graphics standard that allows for a resolution of 640 x 480 with 16 colors, but also supports 256 colors at lower resolutions.

✦ **Extended Graphics Array (XGA):** Graphics standard that supports resolution of 800 x 600 with 65,536 colors, or a resolution of 1024 x 768 with 256 colors. There are many different spin-offs of the XGA video standard, including Wide XGA (1366 x 768), XGA+ (1152 x 864), and Wide XGA+ (1440 x 900).

✦ **Super VGA (SVGA):** Supports 16 million colors at resolutions as high as 1280 x 1024; a popular graphics standard for many years.

✦ **Super XGA+:** A popular video standard for LCD displays on laptop computers supporting a resolution of 1400 x 1050. The widescreen version (WSXGA+) supports a resolution of 1680 x 1050.

✦ **Ultra XGA:** Supports resolution of 1600 x 1200; the video standard for 20-inch or 21-inch LCD displays on laptop computers.

✦ **WUXGA:** *Widescreen Ultra Extended Graphics Array* (WUXGA) supports a resolution of 1920 x 1200 and is the widescreen version of the UXGA standard. This video standard is popular with widescreen LCD televisions and computer monitors.

Video board features

Although a number of video standards are available as well as a wealth of video cards, some features are common to every video card. This section outlines some important characteristics of video cards, such as resolution, colors, and video memory.

Special connectors

Most video cards come with the typical 15-pin video port (3 rows of 5 pins) that is usually blue in color. Today's video cards, though, typically have a number of additional connectors that can be used to connect your system to a video display.

The following is a listing of high-quality video connectors used by computers, video game consoles, or even projectors:

✦ **S-Video:** The *Separate-Video* (S-Video) connector is designed to carry an analog video signal, using a 4-pin mini-DIN connector or a 7-pin mini-DIN connector. The S-Video standard is just designed to carry the video signal and not the audio signal.

✦ **DVI:** The *digital video interface* (DVI) is a video interface standard (see Figure 3-2) designed to carry the video signal, in high-quality, uncompressed format, from a source (such as computer) to a digital display (such as an LCD monitor or a digital projector).

Figure 3-2:
Looking at a DVI-D connector on a DVI cable.

✦ **HDMI:** The *High-Definition Multimedia Interface* (HDMI) is an audio and video interface designed to carry a digital signal from a source (such as a Blu-ray disc player, video game console, or computer) to a display output (such as an LCD monitor, a digital TV, or a digital audio device).

Built-in coprocessors

A number of new video cards have a built-in coprocessor that processes most display functions on behalf of the CPU. This allows the CPU to service other requests on the system and not have to worry about processing any video commands. These advanced video cards are also known as *accelerated video cards* or *graphics accelerator cards*.

Resolution

Resolution is a term that techies use to describe how functional a video card is. For example, I might brag about my video card being able to run at 1024 x 768, and you could turn around and say, "Is that all? My video card supports 1280 x 768."

Resolution describes how many pixels are supported by both the video adapter and the monitor. A *pixel* is a small dot conjoined with other small dots to help create the image onscreen. The more pixels that are supported on your screen, the closer the dots must be — which gives you a finer display.

As an example, a video card that supports 1280 pixels going across the screen and 768 pixels going down the screen (1280 x 768) will create a much finer image than a video card that supports only 800 pixels going across the screen and 600 pixels going down the screen (800 x 600).

Supported colors

The picture on your monitor will look much better if the video card supports a lot of colors, so one of the other often-touted video card characteristics is how many colors the video card supports. Bottom line, the more colors the better. If you're curious to see what the big deal is about the number of colors supported, here's a quick way to get a look at the difference in Windows XP:

1. **Right-click your desktop and choose Properties from the contextual menu.**

2. **On the Desktop tab, choose Bliss from the Background list.**

 Bliss is the default background that XP uses — the one with the clouds that looks like Teletubby land.

3. **Click Apply to change to the Bliss background.**

4. **Click the Settings tab.**

5. **From the Color Quality drop-down list, choose 256 colors.**

 You might not be able to choose 256 colors because the driver might not let you change your color settings that low.

6. **Click Apply.**

 You should notice that the wallpaper doesn't look good anymore because Windows cannot display all the colors that appear in the image.

7. **Change your Color Quality back to its original value.**

8. **Click OK.**

The steps to change your resolution in Windows Vista are similar — right-click on your desktop and choose Personalize. In the Personalization dialog box, click the Display Settings link at the bottom of the dialog box.

Video memory

Because a video card has to process such a large amount of data, the video card comes with its own memory — *video memory*. Video memory is available in many different sizes, and popular amounts are 64MB, 128MB,

and 256MB. Some video cards simply use DRAM, but because the demands of video display are so high and DRAM was so slow in the past, other memory types were developed for video:

✦ **Video RAM (VRAM):** VRAM has the benefit of being *dual ported* — it can be read from and written to simultaneously — which adds to the performance of the memory.

✦ **Multibank DRAM (MDRAM):** MDRAM is a type of video RAM that uses the full width of the video bus (the expansion bus where the video card resides) with fewer memory chips.

✦ **Window RAM (WRAM):** WRAM stores its data in chunks, which makes the data transfer faster than the more-expensive VRAM. Like VRAM, WRAM is dual ported.

✦ **Synchronous Graphics RAM (SGRAM):** SGRAM is a type of video memory that is *single ported,* which means that you can only read from or only write to the memory at one time. SGRAM is four times faster than other types of DRAM memory and is synchronized with the CPU clock.

Being able to change some of the video card's characteristics, such as color support or resolution, is a characteristic of the video driver that is installed. You might find that you cannot set your video card to 24-bit color because the driver does not support it. Of course, the driver does not support it because the card does not support it. Before I show you how to change your resolution, you need to know how to install a video card, which is covered in the next section.

Installing a video card

Installing a video card is like installing any other card, such as a network card or modem. You simply need to place the card into a supported bus architecture — typically either PCI or AGP — and then load the driver.

The following steps outline how to install a video card:

1. **Power-off and unplug the computer.**

2. **Open the case or side panel of the computer to access the expansion slots.**

3. **If you are replacing a video card, take out the old one.**

 If the old video card is integrated into the motherboard, you will not be able to remove it, but you might be able to disable it in CMOS. (For more information on CMOS, check out Book II, Chapter 4.)

4. **If you are adding the first video card to the system, remove the blanking plate for the AGP or PCIe slot you wish to use.**

5. **Insert the card into the slot until it fits firmly.**

6. **Screw the video card's plate into place to secure the card.**

7. **Place the cover back on the computer, plug it back in, and power it on.**

 When you power-up the system, Plug and Play should kick in and detect the newly added device and either load a driver or prompt you for the driver. After the driver is loaded, you can configure the display settings discussed in the following sections.

Using Your Monitor

After you install the video adapter (see the previous section), you then need to connect the monitor to the video adapter. The following sections identify the different types of displays used with computers today and then discuss how to configure your display through Windows.

Types of displays

You might find a few different types of displays connected to a system: a CRT monitor, an LCD monitor, or even a projector. In this chapter, I focus on CRTs because LCDs are discussed in Book III, Chapter 7, and you are not likely to get any questions on the A+ exam about projectors. I do define each type of display, though.

Cathode ray tube (CRT)

CRT monitors were popular for computing for many years (and were also popular as television screens) and are typically curved screens but there are flat screen versions. After receiving a signal from the video card, a CRT monitor displays the image by using an electron gun that shoots electrons at the phosphors covering the back of the screen, causing those areas of the screen to glow.

The electron gun located in the CRT continues to fire at the back of the screen from left to right and from top to bottom. This causes a glow of three phosphors colored red, green, and blue to create a single pixel on the screen. The combination of all the lit pixels creates the image that you see, and the speed at which the pixels change gives the illusion of moving objects onscreen.

Refresh rate and *dot pitch* are two very important terms used to describe a monitor. A monitor's *refresh rate* refers to how often the electron gun can redraw the entire screen. The faster it can redraw the screen, the smoother any moving objects appear.

A monitor's *dot pitch* is simply the distance (in millimeters; mm) between two pixels of the same color on a monitor. For example, an average monitor has a dot pitch of 0.28 millimeters, and a better monitor has a dot pitch as tight as 0.24mm.

LCD

Liquid crystal display (LCD) — a popular flat-display type found on laptops for many years — is now a popular choice for display with desktop computers and TVs.

An LCD has two sheets of material surrounding a liquid that contains crystals that act as pixels for the display. Each crystal has a red, green, and blue cell illuminated by an electrical charge hitting the crystal, which then creates the onscreen image. You can find out more information about LCDs, such as active and passive matrix, in Book III, Chapter 7.

Plasma

Plasma displays are flat displays like LCDs but use a different approach to creating the image onscreen. Plasma displays create the image by having small cells of gas sitting between two plates of glass. An electrical charge is applied to the cells of gas, which then causes the cells to light.

Plasma displays are popular display types for TVs 32 inches or larger because the plasma panels cannot be created smaller than 32 inches.

Projector

I can't really talk about display types without talking about using a projector to display the image. Screen projectors are becoming popular both for home theater systems and in boardrooms.

When using a computer or laptop with a projector, the projector connects to the video adapter via a 15-pin video port. If you are using a laptop, you might notice that the output does not emanate from the projector right away. Most laptops allow you to choose whether to display the image on the LCD, projector, or both by holding down the function (Fn) key and then pressing either F4 or F5. Look for the key that has a monitor on it to get your projection going.

Configuring your display settings

You can change the characteristics of your display — such as color support or resolution — after the driver is loaded for your video adapter. Whatever settings you choose must be supported by both the video card and the

monitor. For example, choosing too high of a resolution can distort the display. In this example, the resolution is supported by the video card but not the monitor. Mismatched resolution was such a problem in the past that Windows OSes now ask you whether the display is okay when you change the resolution. If you choose Yes, the settings are applied. If you choose No or don't choose anything for a few seconds, the settings are reverted to their previous state.

To configure your display settings in Windows XP, follow these steps:

1. **Choose Start⇨Control Panel⇨Appearance and Themes⇨Display.**

2. **Click the Settings tab (shown in Figure 3-3).**

Figure 3-3:
Configuring the display settings in Windows XP.

3. **From the Color Quality drop-down list, choose how many colors you want your display to support.**

- *16-bit* supports 65,536 colors.

- *24-bit* supports 16 million colors.

- *32-bit* supports over 16 million colors.

4. **In the Screen Resolution section, move the slider to set the resolution of your monitor to the desired setting.**

5. **Click OK.**

6. **When asked whether the display looks okay, click Yes.**

The steps are very similar in Windows Vista to configure your display settings:

1. **Right-click your desktop and choose Personalize.**
2. **Click the Display Settings link.**
3. **In the Screen Resolution section, move the slider to set the resolution of your monitor to the desired setting.**
4. **Choose your color from the Color drop-down list.**
5. **Click OK.**
6. **When asked whether the display looks okay, click Yes.**

Configuring multidisplay support

Windows OSes support a feature called multidisplay support, which allows you to insert multiple video cards into the system and have a monitor connected to each video card. Then, you can extend your Windows desktop to include the second monitor, allowing you to use the screen space from both monitors at the same time.

With multidisplay support, you can move one program to one of the monitors and then use another program on the second monitor. For example, I place my e-mail program on my right-hand monitor and surf the Internet on my left-hand monitor. When an e-mail comes in, I already have the e-mail program open, so I can simply read the e-mail.

To configure multidisplay support in Windows XP, follow these steps:

1. **With your computer off, open your computer case and install an additional video adapter.**

 You can find instructions for installing a video card in the "Installing a video card" section.
2. **Put the computer case back on and power-on the system.**
3. **Plug a separate monitor into each of the two video cards.**
4. **Ensure that a driver is loaded for each video card and for each monitor.**
5. **To enable multidisplay support, right-click the desktop and choose Properties.**
6. **In the Desktop Properties window, click the Advanced tab and select the second monitor (contains the number two in the icon).**
7. **With the second monitor highlighted, select Extend My Windows Desktop to This Monitor.**

8. **Click OK.**

9. **Start Internet Explorer, type www.gleneclarke.com in the address bar (or any viable URL), and press Enter.**

10. **When the Web site appears, restore down the window and move it to the second monitor.**

11. **Start your e-mail program and ensure that it displays on the first monitor.**

To configure multidisplay support in Windows Vista, first ensure that you have installed the second video card and then turn on the computer. To enable the second display in Windows Vista, right-click the desktop and choose Personalize. From the Personalization window, choose the Display Settings link, highlight the second monitor, and choose Extend the Desktop Onto This Monitor. You may also set your color support and resolution for the second monitor.

Lab 3-1 demonstrates how to configure Windows XP for multidisplay support after installing two video cards in the system. Lab 3-1 can be found in the Labs.pdf file in the Author directory of the CD-ROM.

The Sound of Computers

<div style="float:right">**Book III
Chapter 3**

Installing and
Configuring Output
Devices</div>

Another very popular output device is the sound card. As an output device, the *sound card* is responsible for sending sound data to the speakers, but can also be used as an input device by lining-in an external source to the card. For example, you could line-in a stereo system through your sound card and convert some old audio tapes to MP3 files.

The sound card contains a DAC that converts the digital data from the computer into analog signals that create the sound. The sound card has a number of ports on the back that allow you to connect both output devices and input devices:

✦ **Line-in:** The Line-in port is used to connect your CD player or stereo system and use it as a source for what the sound card plays. A great idea to get your old tapes to MP3 format!

✦ **Mic:** Connect a microphone, which acts as a source for information being recorded.

✦ **Headphones:** Connect your headphones.

✦ **Line-out:** Just like you can connect your stereo to the computer via the Line-in port, you can also take sound on the computer and "line it out" to the stereo.

Types of sound cards

You can find a number of different types of sound cards. The most popular interfaces for a sound card are as follows:

✦ **Industry Standard Architecture (ISA):** ISA cards were a popular choice on older systems and in the early Pentium days, so you still might encounter one from time to time. An ISA card runs at 8 MHz and is only 16-bit.

✦ **Peripheral Component Interconnect (PCI):** Today's systems use PCI sound cards that are Plug and Play and are inserted into the PCI slots (those white slots on the motherboard). PCI devices, which are 32-bit cards, outperform ISA by running at 33 MHz.

✦ **Integrated:** Some motherboards also have *integrated* sound cards, meaning that the motherboard has the sound card built in and you don't need to purchase an additional card to install in the computer.

A classic A+ Certification exam question asks what the default IRQ (interrupt request) is for sound cards. The answer is IRQ 5. You can find more information about IRQs and their roles in Book III, Chapter 4.

Installing a sound card

Installing a sound card is no different than installing any other type of card. You first need to decide what type of card you want to use in your system (and then go buy one). With sound cards, you are most likely using a PCI card, but you may use a new PCIe slot.

Here's how to install a sound card:

1. **Power-off and unplug the computer.**

2. **Open the case or side panel of the computer to access the expansion slots.**

3. **If you're replacing a sound card, take out the old one.**

 If the old sound card is integrated into the motherboard, you will not be able to remove it, and you might have to disable it in CMOS.

4. **If this is the first sound card for the system, remove the blanking plate for the PCI or PCIe slot you wish to use.**

5. **Insert the card into the slot until it fits firmly.**

6. **Screw the sound card's plate into place to secure the card.**

7. **Place the cover back on the computer and power-up the computer.**

Plug and Play should detect the device. After Plug and Play detects the sound card, it might prompt you for the driver. If so, supply the CD that came with the card. If you are not prompted for the driver and Windows did not load a driver, you might need to run the driver setup program from the CD that came with the card.

Configuring a sound card

After the driver is loaded for your sound card, you can configure the sound card by going to the Sound applet in the Windows Control Panel. To configure the sound card, choose Start⇨Control Panel⇨Sound, Speech, and Audio Devices, and then choose Sounds and Audio Devices to bring up the Sound and Audio Devices Properties dialog box, as shown in Figure 3-4.

Figure 3-4: Configuring sound settings in Windows XP.

The following list summarizes each tab and the types of settings to configure in the Sound and Audio Devices Properties dialog box:

✦ **Volume:** Set the master volume for the sound card and choose options, such as muting the sound card. You may also choose to have an icon display in the taskbar for quick access to the sound card properties.

✦ **Sounds:** Specify your sound theme, which will set different sounds for different events in Windows, such as when Windows starts or shuts down.

✦ **Audio:** Specify what sound device to use for playback or recording.

✦ **Voice:** Specify which device to use when capturing or playing back voice recordings.

✦ **Hardware:** Find quick access to the sound drivers loaded on the system.

The steps to configure sound on your Windows Vista system are similar, but to navigate to the sound settings you will choose Start➪Control Panel➪Hardware and Sound➪Sound.

Other Output Devices

Video cards and sound cards are two of the most popular types of output devices found in systems today, but they are not the only types of output devices. This section overviews some of the other types of output devices found in computer systems:

✦ **Multimedia cards:** Not really an output device, but when it comes to multimedia, video and sound files have to be stored somewhere. A number of devices today use *multimedia cards (MMC),* which are sticks of memory (the size of a stamp) used with a multimedia device, such as a music player or digital camera.

✦ **I/O devices:** Any number of input/output (I/O) devices may be connected to your system. These devices (such as printers, scanners, and fax devices) can connect to your system in any form, such as SCSI, serial, or even parallel. Here is a summary of some of the technologies used with I/O devices:

• *SCSI:* SCSI technology supports *daisy chaining* (having one device connect to the next). To connect a SCSI device to your system, you need a SCSI card, and you also need to ensure that you assign unique IDs to each device and terminate both ends of the SCSI bus. Typically, storage devices such as drives, CD-ROMs, and tapes appear as SCSI devices.

• *Serial:* Some I/O devices are serial devices that connect to the serial port of the computer. An example of an I/O device that may connect to the serial port is a modem.

The serial connection is defined in the RS-232 standard and sends data one bit at a time.

• *Parallel:* Parallel devices get their name by receiving 8 bits of data at a time, as compared with the 1 bit of data at a time that is supplied by serial connections. Parallel is defined in the IEEE 1284 standard and has different parallel modes, such as SPP, ECP, and EPP. SPP (Standard Parallel Port) is unidirectional and transfers data at 150 Kbps. ECP (Extended Capabilities Port) is bidirectional with a transfer rate of 2 Mbps. EPP (Enhanced Parallel Port) is bidirectional and can transfer information at 2 Mbps — but also supports daisy chaining!

- *USB:* USB is the most popular way to connect devices to your system today. USB 1.1 can transfer information at 12 Mbps, and USB 2.0 can transfer information at 480 Mbps. USB supports 127 devices in a single USB chain and is also *hot-swappable* (meaning that devices can be added and removed from the system without shutting down the system first).

Getting an A+

In this chapter, you find out about the two major types of output devices found on systems today: the video card and the sound card. The following summarizes some key points about video and sound cards:

✦ The video card converts digital data from the computer into analog data that is used by the monitor to create the display.

✦ VGA supports 16 colors at a resolution of 640 x 480.

✦ Super VGA supports 16 million colors at a resolution of 1280 x 1024.

✦ AGP cards are the popular form for video cards today, and sound cards are implemented as PCI cards.

✦ CRT monitors use an electron gun to stimulate the phosphor-covered screen and make it glow.

Prep Test

1 Sound cards are connected to the system using which of the following? (Select two.)

A ❑ AGP

B ❑ ISA

C ❑ PCI

D ❑ USB

2 You wish to enable multidisplay support in Windows XP. How do you do this?

A ○ Select the monitor and choose the Add Monitor option from the video card properties.

B ○ Select the monitor and choose the Add Monitor option from the display properties.

C ○ Select the monitor and choose the Extend My Windows Desktop to This Monitor option from the video card properties.

D ○ Select the monitor and choose the Extend My Windows Desktop to This Monitor option from the display properties.

3 Which video standard supports 16 colors at 640 x 480 resolution?

A ○ EGA

B ○ VGA

C ○ SVGA

D ○ CGA

4 What IRQ is typically assigned to ISA sound cards?

A ○ 1

B ○ 4

C ○ 5

D ○ 7

5 What type of display is found on laptops?

A ○ CRT

B ○ LCD

C ○ RCT

D ○ USB

6 Which video standard supports only four colors?

A ○ EGA
B ○ VGA
C ○ SVGA
D ○ CGA

7 Which type of display uses an electron gun?

A ○ CRT
B ○ LCD
C ○ RCT
D ○ AGP

8 Which video standard supports 16 million colors at 640 x 480 resolution?

A ○ EGA
B ○ VGA
C ○ SVGA
D ○ CGA

Answers

1 **B, C.** Older sound cards were implemented as ISA cards, and newer sound cards are PCI cards. *See "Installing a sound card."*

2 **D.** To enable multidisplay support in Windows XP, open display properties in the Control Panel and choose the Extend My Windows Desktop to This Monitor option, located on the Settings tab. *Review "Configuring multidisplay support."*

3 **B.** VGA supports 16 colors at 640 x 480 resolution. *Check out "Looking at the video standards."*

4 **C.** Sounds cards defaulted to IRQ 5 before Plug and Play became a standard. *Peruse "Types of sound cards."*

5 **B.** LCDs are found on laptops but are also used with desktop computers today. *Take a look at "LCD."*

6 **D.** CGA supports only four colors. *Peek at "Looking at the video standards."*

7 **A.** A CRT monitor uses an electron gun to light phosphors on the screen. *Look over "Cathode ray tube (CRT)."*

8 **C.** SVGA is the video standard used today, and it supports 16 million colors. *Study "Looking at the video standards."*

Chapter 4: Examining System Resources

A part of the A+ exam is all about troubleshooting and configuring a device during installation. In the past, a big part of troubleshooting computer systems was understanding how to configure resources such as IRQs, I/O addresses, and DMA channels on a device — which is what you find out how to do in this chapter. However, because of Plug and Play operating systems (such as Windows XP and Vista) and Plug and Play devices (such as USB and PCI), you most likely won't find yourself configuring an IRQ or I/O address with today's systems. When troubleshooting Windows systems and using tools such as Device Manager, you will notice these resources being displayed in the properties of the devices. And this chapter ensures that you understand what the resources are.

Suppose that one of your best friends, Bob, calls you up one day to borrow your perfectly functional sound card, and you tell him to come over and pick it up. Bob comes over to your house to pick up the sound card, and you show him that the card works perfectly in your computer. You then remove it carefully from the system and hand it over to him. Bob takes the sound card home, inserts it into his system, and powers-on his system. Windows boots up and installs the driver for the card, but after the driver is loaded, Bob notices that no sound is coming from the computer! Viewing the status of the sound card in the Windows Device Manager reveals that the device is not functioning properly. So Bob thinks to himself, "Gee, the sound card worked perfectly on the other system. What gives?"

Or worse still, say you purchase a sound card from your local computer store, insert it into your computer, properly install the driver — and it does not work.

Problems like these were among the most common types of problems that A+ professionals would encounter when supporting older non–Plug and Play devices, such as an old ISA card. In the past, you had to be aware that a

device that works in one computer doesn't initially work in another computer — even when the operating systems on both computers are identical — because you needed to configure the device with the appropriate resources of that specific system.

This chapter helps you understand why many devices don't automatically work in a system and then identify what you can do to make them work. You also discover the different types of resources that you will be required to troubleshoot and how to identify the default resources for any system.

Understanding System Resources

In this chapter, when you see the term *system resource,* think of it as a setting assigned to a device that allows it to function within the computer. A *device* is any piece of hardware that you can install on the computer: for example, a network card, modem, or sound card.

The three major system resources that can be assigned to devices are I/O addresses, IRQ addresses, and DMA addresses. A fourth system resource — a memory address — can sometimes be assigned to devices as well. In the following sections, I discuss each of these system resources.

I/O addresses

It is extremely important to remember that the CPU (processor) is the traffic cop of the entire system. If something is going to happen on the system, the CPU usually enables the action. All devices in the computer need to communicate with the processor from time to time, and the processor needs a method of separating and prioritizing all these communications.

Because the processor needs to send information to a number of different devices, and because those devices need to know which messages coming from the CPU are for them, each device is assigned an I/O (input/output) address. The *I/O address* is a special port address that represents a pathway between the CPU and the device. So, for example, if the processor needs to send information to LPT1, it can send the information to pathway 0378–037F, which is the pathway address that leads to LPT1. (For more on the standard I/O address assignments, see Table 4-1, later in this chapter.) Think of these pathways as tunnels; each device has its own tunnel that extends from the device to the processor and is used for communication between the device and the processor.

Figure 4-1 shows a number of devices that are configured with I/O addresses. (Note that the addresses in the figure are not necessarily the actual addresses that are used by those devices. I made up these addresses

simply to get the point across.) In this example, if the processor needs to send information to the sound card, it knows that if it sends the information down I/O port address 220, the sound card will receive the information. Conversely, when the processor receives information from I/O port address 220, it knows that the information came from the sound card because the address of 220 is assigned to only one device — the sound card!

Figure 4-1:
Each device uses a unique I/O address to send and receive information to and from the processor.

There are 65,536 different I/O port addresses available on a system. (There are actually fewer *usable* addresses than that because when you assign an I/O address to a device, you are really assigning a range of addresses.) The trick to troubleshooting system resources is to make sure that you do not assign the same I/O port address to two different devices. If you do, you get a *resource conflict* — two devices using the same resource, such as an I/O address, an IRQ, or a DMA channel.

The I/O address assigned to a device is really a range of values, such as 0378– 037F. Most people refer to the address block by the first value in the range: in this example, 0378.

To prevent resource conflicts, each device should have a unique I/O address. But how do you know which I/O addresses are already being used by existing devices? One way is to use Device Manager to view I/O addresses being used on the system.

When troubleshooting Windows XP, you can use Device Manager to obtain a list of resources in use. To view I/O addresses in use with these operating systems, follow the steps below:

1. **Click Start.**

2. **Right-click My Computer and choose Properties.**

3. **Click the Hardware tab.**

4. **Click the Device Manager button.**

5. **Choose View⇨Resources By Type.**

The screen should look similar to the one shown in Figure 4-2.

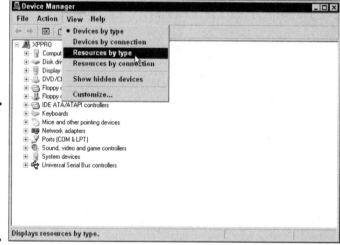

Figure 4-2:
Configuring
Device
Manager
to view
resources
in Windows
XP.

6. **Expand Input/Output (I/O) and view the list of I/O addresses being used (shown in Figure 4-3).**

To navigate to the Device Manager program in Windows Vista, follow similar steps:

1. **Click Start.**

2. **Right-click Computer and choose Properties.**

3. **Click the Device Manager link on the left in the task list.**

4. **Choose Continue from the User Account Control dialog box.**

5. **In Device Manager, choose View⇨Resources by Type.**

Figure 4-3:
Viewing I/O
Addresses
in use with
Windows
XP Device
Manager.

Book III
Chapter 4

Examining System
Resources

The A+ certification exams used to test heavily on the different I/O
addresses, but you are no longer required to know them for the exam. Table
4-1 lists the I/O addresses for general knowledge and your reference.

Table 4-1	Standard I/O Address Assignments
Device	*I/O Address Range*
COM1	03F8–03FF
COM2	02F8–002FF
COM3	03E8–003EF
COM4	02E8–002EF
LPT1	0378–0037F
LPT2	0278–0027F
Math co-processor	00F8–000FF
Primary hard disk controller	01F0–001F7
Secondary hard disk controller	0170–00177
Sound cards	0220–0022F
Floppy disk	03F0–003F7

Interrupt request (IRQ)

Each device has its own tunnel for sending and receiving information to and from the processor, which is the function of the I/O port address discussed in the previous section. But the processor is busy doing something important nearly all the time. How does the processor know when a device has information to communicate to the processor? Too much overhead would be created if the processor had to continuously poll each device to see whether it had data to send to the processor; instead, each device is responsible for notifying the processor if it has information to send. Because devices are responsible for notifying the processor that they have information, the devices need a way to interrupt the processor from its current work to ask it to service their requests. The method that is used to interrupt the processor is an interrupt request (IRQ) line.

If you were standing beside someone involved in a conversation and you really wanted to talk to that person, what would you do? Most people would tap the person on the shoulder and say something like, "Excuse me, sir, can I send you data?" Okay, maybe you wouldn't say that, but you get the idea. Tapping the person on the shoulder is similar to what a device does with the processor when it wants to send the processor some information. The device sends a signal down the IRQ line, which virtually taps the processor on the shoulder. As a result, the device grabs the processor's attention, and the processor is ready to receive information via the I/O address.

When a device taps the processor on the shoulder, the processor needs to know which device needs attention. This is why each device is assigned a unique IRQ line number. When a device sends a signal down the IRQ line to interrupt the processor, the processor checks which line the signal originated from and then attends to that device. For example, in Figure 4-4 (remember that the values shown in the figure are for discussion purposes only — use Tables 4-2 and 4-3, later in this section, to find out which IRQs are used by devices to prepare for the exam), if the network card wants to send information to the processor, the network card must first get the processor's attention by sending a signal down IRQ 10.

When information is sent to the processor, it is sent through the I/O address (the tunnel), not the IRQ line. The IRQ just grabs the processor's attention, but the I/O address is used for the actual delivery of the information.

Cascading IRQs

Originally only 8 IRQs were available on XT (before 286) systems, but now 16 IRQs are available on AT (after 286) systems. To get 16 IRQs, another IRQ controller was added to the system. Having two sets of IRQs managed by two different controllers presented some technical problems, so to help the two IRQ controllers act as one unit, they are *cascaded* (linked) together by IRQ 2 and IRQ 9. The second controller goes through the first controller to send requests. Figure 4-5 shows the two controllers linked.

Book III
Chapter 4

Examining System
Resources

Figure 4-4: IRQs are how a device grabs the CPU's attention.

Here's how cascading controllers work. In Figure 4-5, the path that the math co-processor (which uses IRQ 13) takes to send an interrupt request to the processor is shown in three steps:

1. The math co-processor attempts to send a signal to the CPU. However, because the second interrupt controller handles the math co-processor, the signal is passed to IRQ 9, which forwards all signals for the second interrupt controller.

2. IRQ 9 passes the signal to its linked partner, IRQ 2, which is managed by the first interrupt controller.

3. IRQ 2 then passes the signal through the first interrupt controller, which then sends the signal to the CPU.

Because older systems only had one set of eight IRQs, when the additional eight IRQs came along, only the first interrupt controller was allowed to send information to the CPU. This means that when interrupts 8 through 15 send an interrupt request, they must pass it to the first controller, which in turn passes it to the processor on their behalf.

Figure 4-5:
Two IRQ
controllers
are
cascaded
together.

Like I/O addresses, if you assign two devices the same IRQ value, you get a resource conflict that results in at least one (and maybe both) of the devices not working. To prevent assigning two devices the same resource, you need to understand which IRQ values are already being used by your system.

To view a list of IRQs in use on a Windows XP or Windows Server 2003 system, follow these steps:

1. **Right-click My Computer and choose Properties.**

2. **Click the Hardware tab.**

3. **Click the Device Manager button.**

4. **Choose View⇨Resources By Type.**

5. **Expand Interrupt Request (IRQ) and view the list of IRQs being used.**

The screen should look similar to the one shown in Figure 4-6.

I should note that because of the low number of IRQs available on a system, Intel has been incorporating a newer technology in its new processors: Advanced Programmable Interrupt Controller (APIC). Intel currently has APIC supporting up to 24 IRQs.

Figure 4-6:
Viewing
IRQs in
use with
Windows
XP Device
Manager.

Viewing the list of IRQs in Windows Vista is very similar. You need to locate the Device Manager by choosing Start, right-clicking Computer, and then choosing Properties. Once in the System Properties, click the Device Manager link in the Tasks section on the left side. Once in Device Manager, choose View⇨Resources By Type to view the system resources, such as IO Addresses and IRQs.

Table 4-2 shows a listing of the standard IRQs and their use. Remember that you do not need to memorize this table for the A+ certification exams.

Table 4-2	Standard IRQ Assignments
IRQ Value	*Device*
0	System timer
1	Keyboard
2	Link to second IRQ controller
3	COM2, COM4
4	COM1, COM3
5	LPT2
6	Floppy disk drive
7	LPT1
8	Real-time clock
9	Available, but should not be used if IRQ 2 is being used

(continued)

Table 4-2 *(continued)*

IRQ Value	Device
10	Available
11	Available
12	Available if not used by PS/2 mouse
13	Math co-processor
14	Hard disk controller
15	Available

The lower the IRQ value, the higher the priority the device will have with the processor. Here are a few important points about IRQ assignments:

✦ **IRQs 10, 11, 12, and 15 are generally available.** If you are installing a new device into a computer and need to assign an IRQ, try one of these IRQ values first.

✦ **IRQ 3 and IRQ 5 are used by COM2 and LPT2, respectively.** If you are not actually using COM2 or LPT2, you can consider IRQ 3 and IRQ 5 as being available.

Table 4-3 contains a listing of ports and associated addresses you should be familiar with. However, because the new A+ certification exams do not list them as objectives anymore, I would not try to memorize them for the exam.

Table 4-3	Default IRQs and I/O Addresses	
Device	**IRQ**	**I/O Address**
COM1	4	3F8–3FF
COM2	3	2F8– 2FF
COM3	4	3E8– 3EF
COM4	3	2E8– 2EF
LPT1	7	378– 37F
LPT2	5	278– 27F

When discussing IRQs, I like to ask, "What is the IRQ of a modem plugged into a COM port?" Know that an IRQ is not really assigned to a modem when it is plugged into a COM port but rather to the COM port the modem is using is assigned the resource. You will also want to have an idea of where infrared and USB devices will sit as far as IRQs are concerned. Infrared ports attach themselves to virtual COM or LPT ports, which means that your

infrared device will probably end up using IRQ 3 or 4. USB ports use the IRQ associated with the PCI bus, which can be anywhere from IRQ 9 on up.

Direct memory access (DMA)

A number of different devices today require constant access to system memory. Normally, devices must go through the CPU to write information to system memory, but using such a scheme can cause a lot of unnecessary overhead, so why not allow a device to access memory directly?

To increase performance and to offload some of the work from the CPU, you can assign some devices a direct memory access (DMA) channel. A *DMA channel* is a special pathway that allows the device to read and write information directly to system memory without passing the data to the processor.

For example, in Figure 4-7, you can see that the modem has been assigned DMA channel 6 and the printer has been assigned DMA channel 5. (Like I/O addresses, these addresses may be different on each system. Remember that the values I use in the figure are fictitious.) In this example, the modem and the printer can write information to memory directly, whereas the network card and the sound card must pass through the CPU.

Book III
Chapter 4

Examining System
Resources

Figure 4-7:
DMA
channels
are used
to give a
device
direct
access to
memory.

Only eight DMA channels are available on your system, which should not be a huge problem because not all devices use DMA channels. Some examples of the different devices that you might run into that use DMA channels are sound cards, network cards, and occasionally CD-ROM drives. Table 4-4 shows a listing of common DMA channels.

Table 4-4	Common DMA Channel Assignments
DMA Channel	*Device*
0	Available
1	Sound or Available
2	Floppy drive
3	Available
4	Cascade
5	Sound or Available
6	Available
7	Available

Like IRQs, two DMA controllers are linked by a cascading DMA channel: DMA channel 4. DMA channels 0–3 are used for 8-bit boards and cards; DMA channels 5–7 are used for 16- and 32-bit cards.

To view the DMA channels in use on your system, you can use the Windows Device Manager utility. The following steps demonstrate how to view the DMA channels in use within Windows XP and Windows Server 2003 systems:

1. **Right-click My Computer and choose Properties.**

2. **Click the Hardware tab.**

3. **Click the Device Manager button.**

4. **Choose View⇨Resources By Type.**

5. **Expand Direct Memory Access (DMA) and view the list of DMA channels being used (shown in Figure 4-8).**

Viewing the list of DMA channels in Windows Vista is very similar. You need to locate the Device Manager by choosing Start, right-clicking Computer, and then choosing Properties. Once in the System Properties, click the Device Manager link in the Tasks section on the left side. Once in Device Manager, choose View⇨Resources By Type to view the system resources, such as DMA channels, IO Addresses, and IRQs.

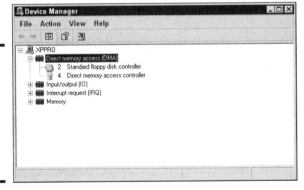

Figure 4-8:
Viewing
DMA
addresses
in use with
Windows
XP Device
Manager.

Memory addresses

A less common resource that might be assigned to devices is a *memory address,* which is an area of memory where the device is allowed to store information.

If multiple devices have been assigned access to the same memory address, a device conflict will occur, and one or both devices might not function. When troubleshooting devices, you need to look out for memory address conflicts. The following steps demonstrate how to view memory addresses in use within XP and Windows Server 2003.

1. **Right-click My Computer and choose Properties.**

2. **Click the Hardware tab.**

3. **Click the Device Manager button.**

4. **Choose View➪Resources By Type.**

5. **Expand Memory and view the list of memory addresses being used (shown in Figure 4-9).**

Viewing the list of DMA channels in Windows Vista is very similar. You need to locate the Device Manager by choosing Start, right-clicking Computer, and then choosing Properties. Once in the System Properties, click the Device Manager link in the Tasks section on the left side. Once in Device Manager, choose View➪Resources By Type to view the system resources, such as memory addresses.

Figure 4-9:
Viewing
memory
addresses
in use with
Windows
XP Device
Manager.

Working with System Resources

In the preceding sections, you can read about system resources and how to view them on a system. In the following sections, I introduce you to methods of viewing and editing system resource settings. One of the biggest issues in troubleshooting device-installation problems is being able to identify and solve resource conflicts.

Identifying resource conflicts

You can use a number of different tools to view system resources (such as I/O addresses, IRQs, and DMA channels) and determine whether a resource conflict exists. Some of the tools are shipped with your operating system, and other tools are third-party products that you need to purchase.

Device Manager is a Windows utility that you can use to view system resources and identify problems with devices. One of the benefits of using Windows Device Manager is that it not only shows you whether a device has a conflict, but also the device that it is in conflict with. To view conflicts with a resource on the device

1. **Right-click the device in Device Manager and choose Properties.**

2. **In the properties window that appears for the device, click the Resource tab.**

When you select a resource, you will see any conflicts at the bottom of the window (shown in Figure 4-10).

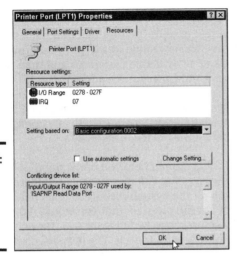

Figure 4-10:
Identify a
conflicting
device via
Device
Manager.

Notice in Figure 4-10 that the LPT port is the device you are troubleshoot-ing. This device has an I/O conflict because you have assigned the LPT port the same I/O address as the ISAPNP Read Data Port. Notice also that the conflicting I/O address is 0278–027F.

With today's systems, this conflict wouldn't happen because most devices are PCI, PCIe, or USB devices and fully support Plug and Play. This means that when the operating system starts up, it dynamically assigns each device a unique resource. However, if you are supporting older devices (such as old ISA cards) and operating systems, you might come across conflicts.

Changing system resources

Although viewing system resources and identifying resource conflicts are important, you also need to be able to make changes that will solve device conflicts.

This section discusses troubleshooting techniques and different ways of changing system resources. You find out different ways to configure resources, such as I/O addresses, IRQs, and DMA channels. You also discover the three typical ways to configure a device for a resource:

✦ Jumper settings

✦ A setup disk

✦ Plug and Play

Book III
Chapter 4

Examining System
Resources

Troubleshooting techniques

Before changing a system resource to solve a device conflict, you need to have a strategy for deciding the new value to assign to the resource. In general, the strategy is to look at all available resources and then reassign them such that each device uses a unique resource address.

With today's Plug and Play systems, you normally don't need to configure I/O addresses or IRQs because the system automatically configures those resources on the device when the device is installed.

The following is a scenario that should help you understand how to troubleshoot resource conflicts. Before Plug and Play became popular, the manufacturer of a device would limit the system resources that could be assigned to the device by providing a setup program that you would run and limit the IRQs that appeared in the setup program. In Figure 4-11, the sound card and network card work with only three IRQs each. The network card gives you the choice of using IRQ 4, 5, or 10; the sound card can function with IRQ 3, 4, or 5.

Network Card	Sound Card
IRQ 4*	IRQ 3*
IRQ 10	IRQ 4
IRQ 5	IRQ 5

Figure 4-11: An example of troubleshooting IRQs, Part 1.

* Assigned IRQ for that device

Suppose that you assign IRQ 4 to the network card and IRQ 3 to the sound card. These resources are normally used by COM1 and COM2, but because you are not using COM1 and COM2, you decide to use those IRQs — makes sense!

A few months later, you decide that you want to install an external modem on the computer. You connect the modem to COM1, which uses IRQ 4, forgetting that you already assigned IRQ 4 to the network card. Connecting the modem to COM1 generates a resource conflict that causes the network card and the modem not to work! Now the fun begins . . .

To fix such a resource conflict, you need to look at the IRQs that can be used for each device and then start juggling resource assignments around until you have all three devices working together on the same system. Figure 4-12 shows a modem being added to the scenario.

Figure 4-12:
An example of trouble-shooting IRQs, Part 2.

Network Card	Sound Card	Modem (COM1)
IRQ 4*	IRQ 3*	IRQ 4*
IRQ 10	IRQ 4	
IRQ 5	IRQ 5	
Reassign	Reassign	

* Assigned IRQ for that device

You can see in Figure 4-12 that when the modem is installed, it will use IRQ 4 and conflict with the network card that is also using IRQ 4. At the same time, you notice that your sound card uses IRQ 3 (normally used by COM2), so to prevent future conflicts, you might be better off reassigning the IRQ for the sound card as well. You decide to assign the network card to IRQ 10 so that the sound card can be assigned IRQ 5. The outcome of these reassignments is shown in Figure 4-13.

Figure 4-13:
An example of trouble-shooting IRQs, Part 3.

Network Card	Sound Card	Modem (COM1)
IRQ 4	IRQ 3	IRQ 4*
IRQ 10*	IRQ 4	
IRQ 5	IRQ 5*	

* Assigned IRQ for that device

The final outcome of your decision on IRQ assignments allows all three devices to function without conflicts, and you are prepared for the day that you decide to use COM2 by having IRQ 3 free.

Changing non–Plug and Play resources

If you are supporting non–Plug and Play devices, such as old ISA devices, you need to manually configure each non–Plug and Play device with system resources. Changing system resources on such a device might take a little more research than managing these resources in a Plug and Play environment. The two popular methods of changing resources in non–Plug and Play devices are

✦ Modify the setting through the use of a jumper.

✦ Use the software setup program that came with the device.

A *jumper* (shown in Figure 4-14) is a set of pins on a card or board that applies a certain setting when a circuit is closed on a certain subset of the pins. Each jumper set on a card has a label associated with it that looks something like *J10,* for *Jumperset 10.* Exactly what this label looks like is, of course, up to the manufacturer of the device.

Jumper

Figure 4-14:
Use jumpers
to configure
resources.

The documentation (finding the documentation is the challenge!) for the card tells you what the jumper set of J10 is actually used for. Suppose that the jumper set of J10 sets the IRQ value, and that the jumper set of J10 has 6 pins. The documentation for the card might tell you, for example, that you need to place the jumper over pins 1 and 2 to assign IRQ 4, across pins 3 and 4 to assign IRQ 5, and across pins 5 and 6 to assign IRQ 10.

Always keep all documentation for your system and any devices you purchase so that any information about the device is available when needed. If you misplace the documentation, though, you can usually find the information on the manufacturer's Web site.

Another method used to change the values of system resources in the past was through software setup, which allows you to change the I/O address,

IRQ, or other settings by running a setup program. The setup program used to come on a floppy disk or CD-ROM and is a much simpler process than messing around with jumper settings. (All you had to worry about was not losing the setup disc!) Again, if you misplace the setup disc, you can normally get the program from the manufacturer's Web site.

Make a backup copy of the setup disc that comes with each device in case something happens to the original disc.

When you run the setup program for the device, you usually have options to view and change the system resources. You change the system resources by saving the setup information (also known as *flashing*) to the EEPROM chip on the card (usually by pressing the F10 key while in the setup program). Figure 4-15 shows an example of a setup (diagnostic) program used to modify the configuration of an old ISA network card.

Figure 4-15:
Changing resources on a non–Plug and Play device using the setup disc.

Changing Plug and Play resources

In a Plug and Play environment, changing settings is a bit easier than in a non–Plug and Play environment. *Plug and Play* systems automatically assign resources to devices dynamically as the operating system starts up. To have a full Plug and Play environment, you must have a Plug and Play operating system (such as Windows), a Plug and Play device, and a Plug and Play BIOS.

In Windows XP, if the operating system wrongly assigned a resource to a Plug and Play device, you can change it through Device Manager:

1. **Right-click My Computer and choose Properties.**

2. **Click the Hardware tab.**

3. **Click the Device Manager button.**

4. **In Device Manager, right-click the device and choose Properties.**

5. **On the properties window for the device, click the Resources tab. If you are allowed to change the resources on the device, clear the Use Automatic Settings check box.**

 Now you can choose a different resource configuration.

6. **Select a new configuration setting from the Settings Based On drop-down list (shown in Figure 4-16).**

 After choosing a different setting, notice the resource change above in the Resource Settings portion of the dialog box.

7. **Click OK and then close Device Manager.**

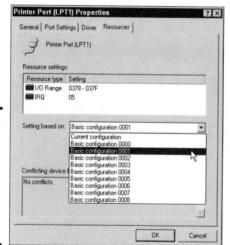

Figure 4-16:
Changing resources through Device Manager in Windows XP.

If you are running Windows Vista you will not need to worry about changing system resources as today's systems and operating systems use plug and play. You can view the resources on the device by choosing Start, right-clicking Computer, and then choosing Properties. Once in the System Properties, locate the device you wish to view the resources of and then right-click and choose Properties. Click the Resources page tab to view the system resources used by that device.

Reserving resources

You might encounter an older system with a mixture of Plug and Play devices and legacy non–Plug and Play devices, which can present problems because the legacy devices have been configured with specific resources, and you want to ensure that the operating system doesn't assign those resources to Plug and Play devices. To prevent the OS from assigning the same resource to a Plug and Play device, you can reserve that resource.

Reserving the resource can be done at two different levels, as the following list details:

✦ **The hardware level:** Reserving a resource at the hardware level means that you enter the CMOS setup program and tell the system what resources it is not allowed to give out. (See "Reserve resources" in Book II, Chapter 4.)

✦ **The software level:** You can also reserve resources at the software level by using Device Manager in older versions of Windows such as Windows 9*x*. If you configure the resource at the software level, the resource is reserved only for the OS you put the reservation in for. So, installing a new OS means that you need to reserve the resource again.

When working with new OSes (such as Windows XP and Vista) and newer devices (such as PCI, PCIe, and USB), the OS does not allow you to reserve a resource because you would not really need to. You should allow the OS to manage the environment through Plug and Play. If you find a reason to reserve the resource when using a newer OS, you can resort to reserving the resource in CMOS.

To practice working with system resources, take a look at Lab 4-1, Lab 4-2, Lab 4-3, and Lab 4-4. These labs can be found in the `Labs.pdf` file in the Author directory of the CD-ROM.

Getting an A+

This chapter introduces you to the concept of system resources. Although you will not find many questions on the exam covering system resources, you need to understand resources and know that today's systems resources are assigned to the hardware automatically by the system. The following is a list of key points to remember about system resources:

✦ An *I/O address* is the pathway used by a device to send and receive information to and from the processor.

✦ An *IRQ* is a signal that a device can send to interrupt the processor from its current task.

✦ A *DMA channel* is a device's direct pathway to memory so that it can read and write information to memory without bothering the processor.

✦ Changing resources on *legacy devices* usually involves changing jumper settings or running the diagnostic program for the device.

✦ Changing resources on *Plug and Play devices* involves going to Device Manager in Plug and Play operating systems and changing the resource for the device.

Prep Test

1 Device A has been configured for IRQ 3. Which of the following devices will device A potentially conflict with?

A ○ COM1

B ○ LPT1

C ○ COM2

D ○ LPT2

2 What is the default I/O address assigned to COM1?

A ○ 02F8

B ○ 0378

C ○ 03F8

D ○ 0278

3 Which of the following best describes DMA?

A ○ DMA stands for *dynamic memory address,* which means that the memory address is dynamically assigned to the device each time the system reboots.

B ○ DMA stands for *direct memory access,* which means that a device can use the operating system's area of protected memory without seeking permission.

C ○ DMA stands for *dynamic memory address,* which means that the device is assigned resources dynamically as the system boots.

D ○ DMA stands for *direct memory access,* which means that the resource is given a special pathway to memory so that it does not have to go through the processor.

4 You assigned your network card to I/O address 0378. Which device will the network card create a conflict with?

A ○ COM1

B ○ COM2

C ○ LPT1

D ○ LPT2

5 What IRQ is assigned to COM1?

A ○ 3

B ○ 5

C ○ 7

D ○ 4

6 What is the default I/O address assigned to COM2?

A ○ 02F8

B ○ 0378

C ○ 03F8

D ○ 0278

7 For a device to interrupt the CPU and request service, the device must be assigned what?

A ○ An IRQ

B ○ An I/O address

C ○ A DMA channel

D ○ A memory address

8 What is the default I/O address assigned to LPT1?

A ○ 02F8

B ○ 0378

C ○ 03F8

D ○ 0278

9 What IRQ is assigned to COM2?

A ○ 3

B ○ 4

C ○ 7

D ○ 5

10 Which two ports use IRQ 4?

A ❏ COM1

B ❏ COM2

C ❏ COM3

D ❏ COM4

11 What is the default I/O address assigned to LPT2?

A ○ 02F8

B ○ 0378

C ○ 03F8

D ○ 0278

12 What IRQ is assigned to LPT1?

A ○ 2

B ○ 4

C ○ 5

D ○ 7

13 What two ports use IRQ 3?

A ❑ COM1

B ❑ COM2

C ❑ COM3

D ❑ COM4

14 What IRQ is assigned to LPT2?

A ○ 2

B ○ 4

C ○ 5

D ○ 7

15 How many I/O port addresses exist?

A ○ 8

B ○ 16

C ○ 16,384

D ○ 65,536

16 What IRQ value is used to cascade the first eight IRQs to the second eight IRQs?

A ○ 0

B ○ 1

C ○ 2

D ○ 7

17 How many DMA channels exist?

A ○ 8

B ○ 16

C ○ 16,384

D ○ 65,536

18 How many IRQs are on an AT system?

 A ○ 2

 B ○ 5

 C ○ 8

 D ○ 16

19 Which Windows utility can you use to view system resources in use?

 A ○ Windows Explorer

 B ○ Device Manager

 C ○ Internet Explorer

 D ○ Regedit

20 How many IRQs are on an XT system?

 A ○ 5

 B ○ 8

 C ○ 16

 D ○ 32

Answers

1 **C.** If device A is assigned IRQ 3, it will conflict with anything connected to COM2 because COM2 (as well as COM4) uses IRQ 3 by default. COM1 and COM3 use IRQ 4 by default, LPT1 uses IRQ 7, and LPT2 uses IRQ 5 by default. *See "Interrupt request (IRQ)."*

2 **C.** The default I/O address of COM1 is 03F8. The default I/O address of COM2 is 02F8, the default I/O address of LPT1 is 0378, and the default I/O address of LPT2 is 0278. *Review "I/O addresses."*

3 **D.** DMA (direct memory access) is a device's unique path to memory so that it can read and write to memory quickly. The benefit of a device receiving a DMA channel is that it will not have to pass through the CPU each time it needs to access a block of memory. *Check out "Direct memory access (DMA)."*

4 **C.** LPT1 uses the default I/O address of 0378, so installing a network card and configuring it for the same address will create an I/O address conflict. The default I/O address of COM1 is 03F8. The default I/O address of COM2 is 02F8, and the default I/O address of LPT2 is 0278. *Peruse "I/O addresses."*

5 **D.** COM1 defaults to IRQ 4. IRQ 3 is used by COM2, IRQ 5 is used by LPT2, and IRQ 7 is used by LPT1. *Take a look at "Interrupt request (IRQ)."*

6 **A.** COM2 uses the default I/O address of 02F8. LPT1 uses the default I/O address of 0378, COM1 uses the I/O address of 03F8, and LPT2 uses 0278. *Peek at "I/O addresses."*

7 **A.** IRQs interrupt the CPU and request service from the CPU. This is where the abbreviation IRQ comes from. An I/O address is a device's communication channel to the CPU so that it can send and receive information to and from the CPU. A DMA channel is a device's direct path to memory so that it can quickly read and write to memory. A memory address is an area of memory used by the device to store information. *Look over "Interrupt request (IRQ)."*

8 **B.** The default I/O address assigned to LPT1 is 0378. The default I/O address assigned to LPT2 is 0278, the default I/O address of COM1 is 03F8, and the default I/O address of COM2 is 02F8. *Study "I/O addresses."*

9 **A.** IRQ 3 is the default IRQ of COM2. IRQ 4 is the default IRQ of COM1, and IRQ 7 is the default IRQ of LPT1. IRQ 5 is the default IRQ of LPT2. *Refer to "Interrupt request (IRQ)."*

10 **A, C.** The two ports that use IRQ 4 are COM1 and COM3. COM2 and COM4 use IRQ 3. *Examine "Interrupt request (IRQ)."*

11 **D.** The default I/O address of LPT2 is 0278. LPT1 uses 0378, COM1 uses 03F8, and COM2 uses 02F8 as the default I/O address. *See "I/O addresses."*

12 **D.** LPT1 has the default IRQ of 7. IRQ 2 is the cascade IRQ that creates a link to the second IRQ controller. IRQ 4 is used by COM1 and COM3, and IRQ 5 is used by LPT2. *Review "Interrupt request (IRQ)."*

13 **B, D.** The two ports that use IRQ 3 are COM2 and COM4. The ports of COM1 and COM3 use IRQ 4. *Check out "Interrupt request (IRQ)."*

14 **C.** The default IRQ of LPT2 is IRQ 5. IRQ 2 is used to create a link to IRQ 9, which is cascaded to the second IRQ controller. IRQ 4 is used by COM1 and COM3, and IRQ 7 is used by LPT1. *Peruse "Interrupt request (IRQ)."*

15 **D.** There are 65,536 I/O address ports available on the system. There are 8 DMA channels available and 16 IRQs available. *Take a look at "I/O addresses."*

16 **C.** The IRQ that creates a cascade link to the second set of IRQs managed by the second IRQ controller is IRQ 2. The system timer uses IRQ 0, and IRQ 1 is used by the keyboard. IRQ 7 is used by LPT1. *Peek at "Interrupt request (IRQ)."*

17 **A.** There are 8 DMA channels on systems today. There are 16 IRQs and 65,536 I/O addresses available. *Look over "Direct memory access (DMA)."*

18 **D.** An AT system uses 16 IRQ channels numbered from 0–15. There were originally only eight IRQ channels on XT systems, but a second set of eight was created for AT systems. *Study "Interrupt request (IRQ)."*

19 **B.** Windows Device Manager is the tool that allows you to view system resources such as IRQs and I/O addresses. You can also use Device Manager to help solve resource conflicts. *Refer to "Identifying resource conflicts."*

20 **B.** Only 8 IRQs were available on XT systems, but an additional set of 8 was created for AT (after 286 processors) systems, creating a total of 16 IRQs for AT systems. *Examine "Interrupt request (IRQ)."*

Chapter 5: Managing Printers

Exam Objectives

✔ **Identifying paper feeder mechanisms**

✔ **Understanding types of printers**

✔ **Identifying printer connections**

✔ **Identifying common printer problems**

✔ **Understanding preventive maintenance and safety precautions**

*I*n today's business world, maintaining a printing environment is one of the most time-consuming parts of managing a network. For a supposedly paperless era, we seem to spend a lot of time troubleshooting why a printer won't print!

This chapter introduces you to the different types of printers and describes how each type of printer works, which is important for the A+ Certification exam. From an exam point of view, be sure you are extremely comfortable with the parts of a laser printer and the six phases of the laser printer's print process — you are guaranteed to get some questions on it!

Be sure to also go over the troubleshooting sections. I think that most people simply skim over this topic area, but you will be presented with some common problems on the exam, and you are responsible for identifying which component of the printer is causing the problem. Be sure to spend some time on this chapter!

Learning about Paper Feeder Mechanisms

A printer is useless without something to print on, so how the paper gets into a printer seems like a perfect place to start the discussion. The paper enters the printer through a *feeder,* technically a *paper feeder mechanism.* The paper feeder mechanism pulls or pushes the paper into the printer. The two types of paper feeder mechanisms are

 ✦ Continuous form feed

 ✦ Friction-feed

The following sections take a close look at both of these types of paper feeders.

Continuous form feeders

Continuous form feed printers use a continuous sheet of 8.5"- or 14"-wide paper. The continuous sheet feeds through the printer, and then the sheets are separated after the print operation. The pages are usually perforated to make this easier and to maintain a consistent size.

The paper has holes along both sides that fit over the sprockets located on the feeder wheel. When the wheel turns, it feeds the paper into the printer. The holes are torn off the paper after the printout is complete.

And, yes, printers still use this type of feeder mechanism. One common use is for printing company paychecks. Blank checks are connected as a continuous sheet of paper and fed into the printer. After a check prints, it moves out of the printer, and the next check is fed in. After all the checks have printed, the accountant then separates each check for distribution to the employees.

Dot matrix printers are an example of a continuous form feed printer.

Friction feeders

The most popular type of printers are friction feed printers, which use two rollers that pick up sheets of paper from a paper tray and feed them through the printer.

With friction feed printers, many different types of rollers are used throughout the print process. The rollers that pick the paper from the tray are "pickup" rollers, but other rollers pass the paper through the different parts of the printer.

Laser printers, photocopiers, and fax machines are friction feed printers.

Understanding Types of Printers

The three different types of printers in today's busy world of computing are laser, inkjet, and dot matrix. You need to be familiar with each type for the A+ exam.

Laser printers

The laser printer — also known as a *page printer* because it prints one page at a time — is the most popular type of printer because it is fast and reliable, and offers the best-quality printout of the three types of printers.

A laser printer gets its name because it uses a laser beam in the printing process. A laser printer, shown in Figure 5-1, is also the most expensive type of printer because of its high-cost components such as the laser.

Figure 5-1:
Looking
at a laser
printer.

Many parts work together to make the laser printer and its printing process run smoothly:

✦ **Paper feeder mechanism:** Laser printers use a set of pickup rollers to grab the paper from the paper tray and feed it into the printer.

✦ **Paper transport path:** Rollers are used throughout the print process so that the paper can continue to move through the printer.

- *Registration rollers* move the paper.

- *Fuser rollers* melt the toner onto the paper.

- *Exit rollers* guide the paper out of the printer.

✦ **Toner cartridge:** The toner cartridge (shown in Figure 5-2) contains the replaceable components of the printing process. It contains three core components:

- *The toner* is electrically charged material made of pigment (to give it its color) and plastic (so it can be melted to the page) that is attracted to the paper to create the printout.

- *The print drum* holds an electromagnetic charge when exposed to the laser. That charge then attracts the toner to the page.

- *The cleaning blade* cleans excess toner off the drum after the print process has completed.

Figure 5-2:
A toner
cartridge
found
in laser
printers.

✦ **Power supply:** The power supply in the printer is responsible for converting AC from the wall outlet into DC that charges the primary corona wire and transfer corona wire as well as with other components of the printer.

✦ **Primary corona wire:** The primary corona wire applies the initial –600V charge to the drum.

✦ **Transfer corona wire:** The transfer corona wire gives the paper a positive electrical charge that is used to attract the toner to the paper.

Each component of the laser printer is used to perform the print operation. The process used to perform the printer operation is the *laser printing process.*

The laser printing process

The laser printing process has six phases, and you are required to know them for the exam. Knowing the process is the basis for effective printer support and is essential for passing the A+ exam. The six phases of the laser printing process are conditioning, writing, developing, transferring, fusing, and cleaning. As you read the following sections, identify where each step occurs in the schematic in Figure 5-3.

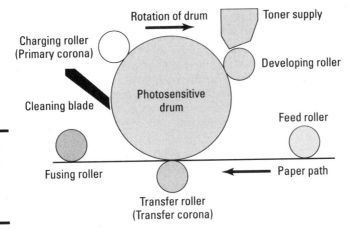

Figure 5-3:
Identifying
the laser
printing
process.

1. Charging the drum (Conditioning)

When the printer receives a command from the computer's operating system to begin the print process, the primary corona wire applies a –600V charge to the photosensitive drum, also known as the *print drum*. This charge is one reason why a printer requires a high-voltage power supply.

2. Exposing the drum (Writing)

After the drum has the –600V charge, a laser beam is used to hit areas on the drum to create the image to be printed. In the areas on the drum that the laser touches, the charge changes from –600V to approximately –100V. Recognize that the areas exposed to the laser beam are more positively charged.

3. Developing the image (Developing)

After the image is created on the photosensitive drum, toner is used to develop the image on the drum. Alongside the print drum is the developing roller. The developing roller has a –600V charge, which attracts the toner from the toner reservoir to the developing roller.

Because the print drum and the developing roller are both charged to –600V (except for the areas of the print drum previously exposed to laser light), the toner from the developing roller is attracted to the –100V charged areas of the print drum. This entire concept is based on the "opposites attract" principle. Although both the drum and the roller are both negatively charged, –100V is more positive than –600V, so the toner on the –600V roller is attracted to –100V areas on the drum. Now that the print drum has toner on only the areas of –100V charge, the image is ready for transfer to paper.

4. Transferring the image (Transferring)

After the toner is on the print drum, the feed rollers (also known as the registration rollers) feed the paper into the printer and over the transfer corona wire. The *transfer corona wire,* also known as the *secondary corona wire,* applies a very strong positive charge of +600V to the paper. The purpose of such a strong charge to the paper is to ensure that the toner will be attracted from the –100V areas of the drum to the paper. This, too, is based on the rule that opposites attract!

The paper continues to move through the assembly, and passes over the drum to attract the toner from the drum to the paper.

5. Fusing the image (Fusing)

After the paper moves past the print drum and holds the toner, the paper then moves through the fusing rollers, which melt the toner to the paper. The fusing rollers are needed because the only thing holding the toner to the paper at this point is a positive electric charge. During the fusing phase, the paper moves between a heated, Teflon-coated roller and a rubber roller, which melt the toner in place. The paper is then ejected from the printer.

6. Cleaning up the mess (Cleaning)

After the printing has completed, any excess toner that remains on the print drum needs to be cleaned off. That's the purpose of this last phase — the cleaning phase. A cleaning blade scrapes any leftover toner off the print drum and into a holding tray to prepare the drum for the next print operation.

The A+ Certification exams focus on laser printers when it comes to asking questions about printers. Be familiar with dot matrix and inkjet printers, but most of all, be sure that you are comfortable with laser printers and the laser printing process.

Lab 5-1 will help you identify parts of the laser printer. You will need a laser printer available to perform this lab. Lab 5-1 can be found in the `Labs.pdf` file in the Author directory of the CD-ROM.

Inkjet printers

Inkjet printers (see Figure 5-4) offer the next highest level of print quality and are relatively cheap compared to laser printers. Inkjet printers are great for home use or small office environments that don't have large print jobs.

Inkjet printers don't use toner like a laser printer; instead, they use ink cartridges. The ink cartridge contains all the working elements needed to get an image from the computer onto a sheet of paper. It contains compartments of ink, each sealed with a metal plate to prevent ink leakage. Each compartment has a tiny pinhole from which the ink is sprayed from the cartridge onto the paper.

Figure 5-4:
An inkjet
printer.

When the printer receives the command from the computer to print an image, the printer starts the print process by applying an electrical charge to the heating elements that are in the ink reservoir. The charge heats the heating elements, which cause the ink to vaporize. The vaporized ink creates pressure and is forced out the pinhole, creating a tiny bubble that hits the paper.

Color inkjet printers are very popular today because of the increased popularity of digital cameras. Color inkjet printers can require two cartridges: one for black ink and one for the colors (cyan, yellow, and magenta). Most inkjet printers today have cartridges that bundle the black ink with the other colors. These cartridges are called *CYMK* (C for cyan, Y for yellow, M for magenta, and K for black).

Some printer manufacturers offer individual cartridges for each color. The benefit of these printers is that if you run out of one color, you simply need to buy only the cartridge that contains that color, not all the colors.

When it is time to replace a spent ink cartridge, take the old cartridge with you to the store so that you know which cartridge type to buy. Some office supply stores can recycle your old cartridges, sometimes even offering a discount when you turn in your old cartridges. If you do not want to take the old cartridge with you to the store, make sure you know the make and model of the printer that you are buying the cartridge for.

Dot matrix printers

Dot matrix printers are considered *impact* printers because they physically strike an inked ribbon with a metal pin to put characters on paper. A dot matrix printer (shown in Figure 5-5) fires off rows of pins that strike the ribbon in patterns to create the image or characters that need to be printed.

Figure 5-5:
A dot matrix
printer.

Each pin — a *solenoid* — is wrapped in a coiled wire held in place with a spring and small magnet. When a solenoid is needed to help create the image by striking the ribbon, an electrical charge is sent down the coil wire that surrounds the solenoid. The electrical charge around the wire causes the magnetic field from the magnet to be lost, resulting in the pin firing against the ribbon.

The solenoids are contained in the *print head,* which moves across the paper printing one line of dots at a time. Originally, dot matrix printers used only nine pins in the print head. The 9-pin dot matrix printers were known as *draft-quality* printers and were later replaced by 17- and even 24-pin dot matrix printers. The quality of the 24-pin dot matrix was much better than that of the 9-pin because the greater number of dots creates a finer image.

Thermal printers

For the A+ exam, you simply need to focus on laser, dot matrix, and inkjet printers. Another type of printer you might encounter, though, is a thermal printer, which creates printouts on special paper by heating a stylus pen located on a print head. The pen then causes a chemical reaction on the special paper that is sensitive to heat.

Thermal printers are popular in restaurants for receipts because of the speed of the printer and how quiet they are.

Viewing Types of Printer Connections and Configurations

In this section, you find out how printers are connected to computer systems in order to communicate. The following are the most popular methods to connect a printer to a computer:

✦ Parallel connections

✦ Network connections

✦ Universal Serial Bus (USB)

✦ Serial

✦ Infrared

Parallel connections

The most popular method for connecting a printer to a computer was, for many years, the parallel port. The end of the parallel cable that connects to the computer is a male DB-25 connector, and the end that connects to the printer is a male 36-pin Centronics connector. Figure 5-6 displays a parallel cable with the DB-25 and Centronics connector.

The maximum length of a parallel cable is 10 feet long. Any longer than that, and the cable runs the risk of *crosstalk* or *data skew:*

✦ *Crosstalk* is electrical interference from other equipment, fluorescent lights, and other cables.

✦ *Data skew* is the concept of the signals that travel down the different wires in the parallel cable not traveling at the same speed and thus arriving at the destination at different times. This results in the data being unreadable at the opposite end.

Figure 5-6:
A parallel
cable uses
a 25-pin/
36-pin
connector
on either
end of the
cable.

Parallel connections deliver data 8 bits at a time at a speed of approximately 150 Kbps. Parallel printers and their cables should conform to the IEEE 1284 standard for parallel cables. This standard addresses parallel communication to and from the device attached to the cable.

Serial cable connections

Serial cables, which aren't very popular for printers, use either a 9-pin or 25-pin connector. Serial connections send data one bit at a time and are not susceptible to data skew. The maximum length of a serial cable is 25 feet long.

Network cable connections

Network-based printers have built-in network cards that allow the printer to connect directly to the network. The printer runs the TCP/IP protocol and is assigned an IP address so that it can participate on the network.

You can assign the IP address to the printer through the menu system of the printer. After the IP address is assigned, you can typically manage the settings on the printer through a Web browser by typing the IP address of the network printer in the address line of the browser.

Advantages of using a network-based printer are

✦ **The network printer is available all the time.** Network-based printers are connected directly to the network, so they don't rely on a computer being powered-on to communicate with the network.

✦ **Dedicated print servers are not required.** A network printer can be accessed from anywhere in the network, and you don't need to have a server to print to it. You may print to the network-based printer from the client computer directly.

Today's network printers also support network connectivity via wireless network cards. This gives the benefit of not needing a network jack close by to connect the printer to the network. You can read more about network cards and wireless networking in Book VIII.

Universal Serial Bus (USB)

Most printers today purchased for home or small offices are USB printers that connect to the computer via a USB port (go figure). Figure 5-7 shows a USB connection.

Figure 5-7: A USB connector is a popular method today to connect printers to computers.

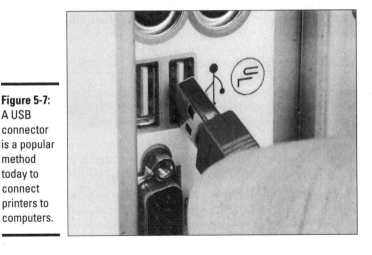

USB has a number of benefits, including the fact that it is a Plug and Play technology (you can plug in the device without shutting down the system). USB 1.1 has a transfer rate of 12 Mbps, and USB 2.0 has a transfer rate of 480 Mbps.

The following are some key points to remember about USB:

✦ It is Plug and Play.

✦ You may connect 127 devices to a USB chain.

✦ You don't need to configure ports, IRQs, or DMA channels for each device.

✦ USB 2.0 has a transfer rate of 480 Mbps.

To find out more about USB ports, check out Book II, Chapter 1.

Lab 5-2 will give you the opportunity to practice connecting a USB print device to your computer. Lab 5-2 can be found in the `Labs.pdf` file in the Author directory of the CD-ROM.

Infrared

Connecting your printer to a system by using infrared technology lets your computer communicate wirelessly with the printer in much the same way you use a TV remote to change channels without getting off the sofa. The infrared signal sent from the computer to the printer is carried as a beam of light, instructing the printer what to print.

To use an infrared printer, you need both an infrared transmitter/receiver connected to your computer and an infrared printer. Today, most computers have an infrared port (transmitter) built-in, especially on laptop systems. Desktop computers normally have a USB device that is installed to give an infrared transmitter.

The three different types of infrared devices are

✦ **Reflective infrared:** Transmitters send the signal to a central unit, which then redirects the commands to the printer. This allows a number of users to print to a single printer at one time.

✦ **Line-of-sight infrared:** With line-of-sight, the printer's receiver must be in a direct line-of-site with the computer's transmitter. If there is a break in the line-of-site, communication is lost.

✦ **Scatter infrared:** Scatter infrared allows the signal to bounce off walls or ceilings (or even people) all the way to the printer's receiver. The benefit is that you don't lose communication like you do with line-of-sight. However, but scatter infrared has limited range and transmission speeds.

FireWire and SCSI

You might also find printers that connect to a system via FireWire or SCSI connections. FireWire has two versions: 400 Mbps and 800 Mbps. FireWire 800, also known as FireWire 1394b, is a fairly recent update to the FireWire technology.

SCSI is another common type of printer device that you might come across with Macintosh systems. Most PC-based systems don't use SCSI printers, although it is possible. For more information on SCSI devices, check out Book II, Chapter 5.

Upgrading Printer Hardware

Printers aren't nearly as upgradeable as computers. There are only a few items that may need upgrading on a printer:

+ Printer memory
+ Disk space on larger printers
+ Firmware updates

I discuss these upgrades in the following sections.

Upgrading memory

A printer uses memory to store the information to be printed, so the more memory a printer has, the larger the print documents it can store. If you ever receive an insufficient memory message when printing a large document, your printer probably doesn't have enough memory. As a workaround, install more memory for the printer.

Adding a disk drive

On larger printers, you can add hard disk space, typically through a PCMCIA slot on the printer. The additional hard drive can store information used by the printer; for example, you might want to install some fonts on the printer, or you could have a print queue stored on the actual print device and use the hard drive to store the queued documents.

Upgrading the firmware

You might also need to update the firmware on the printer. Firmware, which dictates the capabilities of the printer, is similar to the BIOS of a computer. Actually, it is so similar that you upgrade the firmware in a similar way as upgrading a BIOS. Start by downloading the firmware update from the manufacturer's Web site. This update is usually in the form of a self-extracting executable. Then double-click the executable to run the update.

Make sure that the printer is connected and powered-on when the update runs because the update program needs to rewrite the printer firmware within the physical printer.

Installing a Printer in Windows

After you connect the printer to the computer, typically with a parallel or USB connection, you then need to install the "printer" into Windows. Windows uses the term *printer* to describe the software interface (the printer driver) used to communicate with the print device. This software interface is represented as the icon that displays in the Printer folders — the icon that you right-click to change the settings for the corresponding print device. Microsoft refers to the *printer* as the icon found in Windows, and the *print device* as the piece of hardware connected to the computer. I use these terms when discussing how you manage a printer in Windows.

Installing a printer

When you connect a USB print device to a Windows computer, Plug and Play kicks in and detects the hardware. If Windows has a driver for the print device, it loads that driver automatically; if it doesn't, it prompts you for the driver disk. After you supply the driver disk, the printer is installed, and you are off to the races!

For the following example, assume that you have a parallel print device connected to LPT1. You need to install a printer in Windows that connects to that device. To install the printer in Windows XP, follow these steps:

1. **Choose Start➪Printers and Faxes.**

2. **In the Printers and Faxes window that appears, click the Add a Printer link to install a printer driver.**

3. **In the Add Printer Wizard, select whether you are installing a local printer or a network printer, as shown in Figure 5-8.**

- A *local printer* is managed by the system. A local printer is not necessarily physically connected to the system, but it is a resource of the local system — meaning that others will connect to the computer to get to the resource.

- A *network printer* does not exist on your system but lives somewhere else on the network. You still need to install the printer on your computer so you have the driver, but it is not your resource, so it is a network printer.

4. **Also on the screen shown in Figure 5-8, specify whether you want Windows to try to detect the type of printer that is connected to your system.**

You will select the printer you are installing, so turn off that option (make sure the check box is clear) and then click Next.

You are then asked what port the printer is connected to.

Figure 5-8:
Installing a
local printer
in Windows
XP.

5. **Make sure that LPT1 is selected and then click Next.**

6. **Select the type of printer you wish to install (as shown in Figure 5-9) and click then Next.**

 Choose the manufacturer from the left side and then the model of the printer from the right side. If your printer does not appear in the list, click the Have Disk button to provide the driver CD that came with the printer.

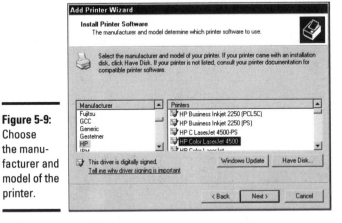

Figure 5-9:
Choose
the manu-
facturer and
model of the
printer.

7. **Click Next to accept the default name of the printer.**

8. **Indicate whether you would like to share the printer and then click Next.**

 Sharing the printer allows other users on the network to connect and print to it from their computers. For now, don't share the printer.

Book III
Chapter 5

Managing Printers

9. **(Optional) Print a test page to verify that the printer you are installing works.**

10. **Click Next to go to the summary screen in the Add Printer wizard.**

 A summary page appears, displaying information about your newly installed printer.

11. **Click Finish to complete the printer installation.**

The steps to install a printer in Windows Vista are very similar, but you must locate the Add Printer Wizard within the Control Panel of Windows Vista. To install a local printer in Windows Vista follow these steps:

1. **Choose Start⇨Control Panel.**

2. **In the Hardware and Sound category, choose the Printers link.**

3. **In the Printers folder that opens, click the Add Printer button in the toolbar of the window (as shown in Figure 5-10).**

The Add a Printer button

Figure 5-10: Installing a local printer in Windows Vista.

4. **Choose Add a Local Printer.**

5. **Choose the port the printer is connected to, such as LTP1. You can also specify to Create a New Port and select Standard TCP/IP port from the drop-down list to reference a print device on the network. Then choose Next.**

6. **Select the manufacturer of the printer and then the model number and then click Next.**

7. **Accept the default name and then make the printer the default printer. Then click Next.**

8. **Click Finish.**

Configuring a printer

After the printer is installed, you might want to configure it. To configure a printer in Windows XP, choose Start⇨Printers and Faxes, right-click the printer, and choose Properties. The printer's Properties dialog box opens. The following is a list of popular printer settings that might need changed, depending on how you want to use the printer:

✦ **Priority:** If a group of users needs a higher priority on a print device on a network, you could install two printers to refer to the same print device. After you have both printers installed, set the priority of one of the printers higher than the other — anyone's print jobs sent to that printer will have a higher priority on the print device. You can set the priority of a printer on the Advanced tab of the printer's Properties dialog box (shown in Figure 5-11).

**Book III
Chapter 5**

Managing Printers

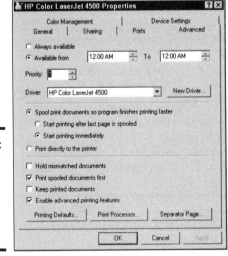

Figure 5-11:
The priority setting and the scheduling option on a printer.

✦ **Schedule:** If you have a group of users that should be printing only at certain hours, you could set the schedule of the printer so that it can print only during those times. The user can send print jobs to the printer, and the printer will queue the job, or store it, until the scheduled time. At the scheduled time, it will then print the job. The schedule option can also be seen in Figure 5-11.

✦ **Spool settings:** In Windows, when a user chooses to print a document, the print job creates a temporary file on the disk for the document being printed. After the file is stored on disk, the user gets control of the application, and the system sends the temporary file to the print device to be printed. While the temporary file is sent to the print device, the user gets to use his or her program again. This is sometimes referred to as *background printing* — where the user thinks the print job has been sent, but the print job is actually being sent while the user continues using the computer. The purpose of this process, called *spooling,* is so that users can continue using the computer instead of waiting for the 20 pages to actually get sent to the print device. Because temporary files are stored on the disk when spooling is enabled (which is the default with all Windows printers), if you don't have the hard disk space on your computer to store the temporary files, you won't be able to print. If you get a spooling error, you may turn off spooling by choosing Print Directly to the Printer on the Advanced tab. Again, you can see this option in Figure 5-11.

✦ **Driver:** If the driver goes corrupt for your printer, you might want to change the driver. Go to the Advanced tab of the printer's Properties dialog box and click the New Driver button. You will then be asked for the make and model of the printer.

✦ **Print Test Page:** If you run into trouble with a printer, you might want to print a test page. On the General tab of the Properties dialog box of a printer, click Print Test Page. Printing a test page will help you determine whether you are having a problem with the printer or a problem with an application. For example, if you cannot print from Microsoft Word but you can print a test page, that indicates a setting in Microsoft Word that is causing the printing problems.

✦ **Sharing:** If you are in a networked environment, you can share the printer so that other users on the network can print to it from their computers. To share the printer, go to the properties of the printer and click the Sharing tab. Select the Share This Printer option and give the printer a share name, as shown in Figure 5-12.

The configuration options to configure the printer in Windows Vista are similar to those found in Windows XP, but it is a little trickier to find the printer properties in Windows Vista. The following steps show how to change your printer properties in Windows Vista:

1. **Choose Start⇨Control Panel.**

2. **In the Hardware and Sound category, choose the Printers link.**

3. **In the Printers folder that opens, select the printer you wish to configure.**

4. **Right-click the printer and choose Properties to display the properties window.**

5. **Change the settings like you would in Windows XP (discussed earlier) and then click OK.**

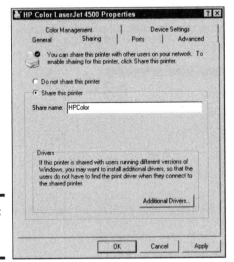

Figure 5-12:
Sharing a
printer.

Connecting to the shared printer

When you have shared a printer, users need to install a printer on their systems that points to the shared printer on the network. Users who install a printer that refers to a shared printer on the network are installing a network printer. A *network printer* refers to a shared printer on the network by what is known as a *universal naming convention (UNC)* path. A UNC path always has the syntax of

```
\\computername\sharename
```

The `computername` parameter is the name of the computer that has the printer shared, and the `sharename` parameter is the name the printer has been shared as. For example, assume you have a system with a computer name of `WORKSTATION1`, which has a printer shared as HP. To connect to this printer, you would type **\\workstation1\hp** from the Run command or when installing the network printer.

To install a network printer and connect to a shared printer in Windows XP, follow these steps:

1. **Choose Start⇨Printers and Faxes.**

2. **Click the Add Printer link.**

3. **In the Add Printer Wizard that opens, click Next on the Welcome screen.**

You are asked if you want to install a local printer or network printer.

4. **When asked whether you want to install a local printer or network printer, select Network Printer and then click Next.**

5. **Select the Connect to This Printer option and then type the UNC path of the shared printer on the network (shown in Figure 5-13).**

Figure 5-13:
Connecting
to a shared
printer.

6. **Click Next.**

7. **Click Finish.**

To install a network printer in Windows Vista, run the Add Printer Wizard and select network printer instead of local printer. The following outlines the steps to install a network printer in Windows Vista:

1. **Choose Start⇨Control Panel.**

2. **In the Hardware and Sound category, choose the Printers link.**

3. **In the Printers folder that opens, click the Add a Printer button in the toolbar of the window.**

4. **When the Add Printer Wizard appears, choose the Add a Network, Wireless, or Bluetooth Printer option.**

 Vista scans for printers on the network.

5. **Choose the The Printer That I Want Isn't Listed option.**

6. **Type the UNC address of the printer (\\computername\sharename) and then click Next.**

7. **Click finish to complete the installation.**

 Lab 5-3 will give you the opportunity to practice installing a printer in Windows XP. Lab 5-3 can be found in the `Labs.pdf` file in the Author directory of the CD-ROM.

Troubleshooting Printer Problems

Printers are wonderful devices that we depend on day in and day out as we prepare, conduct, and report on our business. But one of the major downfalls of a world that depends on printers is that they never seem to work!

You discover a number of general troubleshooting guidelines in the sections that follow to help you troubleshoot printer problems. You also find out about a few specific problems with each type of printer.

Check the simple stuff first

The first thing you want to do when you cannot print is to verify the simple stuff. The following is a list of simple things to check on the printer:

1. **Connection check:** The first thing you want to verify is that the printer is physically connected to the computer or network.

 - *USB:* If you have a USB printer, verify that the USB cable is connected to both the printer and the computer.

 - *Network:* If the printer has a network card, verify that the network cable connects the printer to the network properly. After you verify that the network card is connected, you might want to check that the printer has an IP address by printing out the configuration of the printer.

2. **Visual indicators:** After you checked the physical connection, look at the visual indicators on the printer to verify that it is powered-on. Make sure that you can see the online lamp that indicates that the printer is ready for use.

3. **Error codes:** While looking at the visual indicators on the printer, look at the printer for any error codes that help you identify what the issue is with the printer. Error codes are unique to each printer and are sometimes amber or red lights that turn on in different places to indicate the problem. You will need to research what those lights mean for your printer. Newer printers with an LCD display will typically have text indicating what the error is, and some network printers can even be configured to e-mail the error to the administrator!

4. **Out of paper:** After checking the error codes on the printer, you might as well take out the paper tray while you are at the printer and verify that paper is loaded. Usually, if you are out of paper, the printer will give an out of paper error, but it is worth the time to check.

Paper jams

Another type of problem that occurs often is paper jams. If you experience a number of paper jams over and over again, verify that you are using the correct type of paper for the printer. The best thing to do here is to check the documentation of the printer and verify that you are using the correct size paper. If you are using paper that is too thick for your printer, it may jam up a lot.

Garbage or corrupted output

If you experience *garbage* (text that doesn't make sense) or corrupted output of any type, the driver has gone corrupt or you have the wrong driver installed. Printing a test page is one of the best ways to find out whether you have a bad driver or whether the application you are printing from is causing the problem.

To print a test page in Windows XP, follow these steps:

1. **Choose Start⇨Printers and Faxes.**
2. **Right-click the troublesome printer and choose Properties.**
3. **On the General tab, click the Print Test Page button.**
4. **Click OK if the page printed properly or click the Troubleshoot button if the page did not print correctly.**

 A troubleshooting Web page will appear, giving you a number of tips on how to troubleshoot the problem.

If you print a test page and the printout is still garbage text, the driver has likely gone corrupt, and you need to install a new driver by going to the properties of the printer and choosing the Advanced tab. On the Advanced tab, click the New Driver button to install a new driver.

Spots or smudging on the printout

In general, spots or constant smudging on printouts are good indications that you are using the wrong type of paper for your printer. Again, check the documentation for the printer to find out what type of paper you should be using.

Slow printing

If you notice that printing is overly slow, verify that spooling is enabled. Spooling is enabled by default, but it might have been switched to Print Directly to Printer when you were troubleshooting or configuring the printer. Check the properties of the printer and ensure that spooling is enabled.

Spooling service problems

In Windows, the *print spooler service* is responsible for managing the printing environment. If you notice that a print job is hung in the print queue and will not print or you cannot delete it, you might have a corrupt queue.

When this happens, stop and restart the print spooler service in Windows. Stopping the print spooler service deletes all print jobs and essentially "reboots" your printing environment for you. Figure 5-14 shows the print spooler service being restarted, which you can do from the Services console. The Services console is found in Start⇨Control Panel⇨Performance and Maintenance⇨Administrative Tools.

Figure 5-14: Editing the spooler services properties on a Windows system.

If you have a number of problems printing in Windows and you determined that the problem is not hardware related, you might need to move the print spooler folder. By default, the print job is spooled to the hard drive at the `%systemroot%\system32\spool\printer` directory. The `%systemroot%` variable is typically the Windows folder on drive `C:`.

If you are running out of space on drive `C:`, you might want to change the partition for the spool directory. To change the default spool folder in Windows, follow these steps:

1. **Choose Start⇨Printers and Faxes.**

2. **Choose File⇨Server Properties.**

3. **Click the Advanced tab, as shown in Figure 5-15.**

Figure 5-15:
Changing
the spooling
folder on a
Windows
system.

4. **Enter the path of the new spool folder.**

 If storage or drive speed is your motivation, this should be on a different partition or drive.

Dot matrix problems

This section identifies some problems that occur with dot matrix printers. Be sure to review these problems and the possible causes before taking the A+ exam:

+ **Faint printing:** If you experience faint printing with your dot matrix printer, the print ribbon is simply worn out and needs replaced.

+ **No printing:** If your dot matrix printer simply doesn't print, a print head cable might be disconnected, or the print head might have torn through the ribbon. In these cases, connect the print head cable or replace the ribbon.

+ **Paper jamming:** Again, a lot of paper jams is a great indication that you have the wrong type of paper or the wrong size paper. Check the documentation for your printer.

+ **Line across the page:** If your dot matrix printer prints a line all the way across the page, you might have a pin in the print head that is stuck out. You might be able to loosen the stuck pin, or you might need a new print head.

Inkjet problems

This section identifies common problems that can occur with inkjet printers during day-to-day activity. Again, review these before taking your A+ exam:

+ **Paper jam:** A paper jam indicates that you might have the wrong type or size of paper. If you have the correct size paper, the feeder wheels might be dirty — they are responsible for moving the paper through the printer.

+ **Poor print quality:** Having a poor-quality printout could indicate that the ink needs to be replaced or that you have the wrong type of paper. Change the ink or check the documentation to ensure you are using the correct type of paper.

+ **Fading/Ghosted print:** If the print from your inkjet printer is fading, that could be an indication that you need to change the ink.

Laser printer problems

The following common problems can occur with a laser printer:

+ **Faint or ghosted print:** If the print is getting faint in your laser print-outs, you most likely need to replace the toner.

+ **Paper jam:** If you get a lot of paper jams, verify that you are using paper of the correct size and thickness. If you are sure that you have the right paper, you could also have a problem with misaligned rollers.

+ **White stripes:** If you have white stripes throughout the printout, your transfer corona wire is most likely the problem. There might be a problem getting the charge to the paper, resulting in toner missing on the page in areas.

+ **Blank page:** If you have a blank page for output, you know there is nothing wrong with the feeder mechanisms because the paper is moving through the printer. A blank page indicates a problem getting the toner to the paper, so something is wrong with the corona wires or you have no toner.

+ **Vertical line:** A vertical line on the printout typically indicates a scratch in the print drum. You should replace the toner cartridge because it contains the print drum. If you replace the toner cartridge and the problem still exists, there could be a problem with the laser.

+ **Smeared pages:** If toner smears off after the page has printed, something is wrong with the fuser rollers, which might need replacing. Be cautious when working with the fusing components because they are very hot.

+ **Out of memory:** When sending a large document or a document with a lot of images to the printer, you might get an Out of Memory error if you do not have enough memory installed in the printer. The best solution is to add more memory to the printer so that it can handle the type of print jobs you send. Alternatively, send smaller print jobs to the printer or lower the print quality of the printout through the print settings.

Managing print jobs

When troubleshooting printing problems, it is important to be familiar with how to manage the print jobs of the printer. You can view the print jobs that are stuck in a printer (the print queue) by navigating to the Printers folder and then double-clicking the printer you are troubleshooting.

With the print queue open, you can perform a number of actions to manipulate the queue itself or a single print job. The following are your two major types of tasks that can be performed:

+ **Print jobs tasks:** Manipulate individual print jobs, such as pausing, resuming, or deleting a single print job.

+ **Print queue tasks:** Manipulate the entire queue. Just like a print job, you can pause, resume, and purge the entire queue.

To manipulate a single print job, open the printer (double-click it) and view the list of current print jobs. To pause, resume, or delete a print job, right-click the print job and choose the appropriate command from the contextual menu (see Figure 5-16).

Figure 5-16: Managing a single print job within the print queue.

To manage the entire print queue, open the printer. Double-click the icon in the Printers folder. From the printer's folder, delete all print jobs, pause the queue, or resume the queue from the printer menu; see Figure 5-17.

The following are the popular menu options that deal with managing the print queue:

✦ **Set as Default Printer:** Set the printer as the default printer. The benefit of flagging a printer as the default printer is when you click the Print button in an application, the document automatically prints to the default printer. Also, when you choose File➪Print in an application, the printer is the printer selected by default to print to.

✦ **Pause Printing:** Pause the entire print queue. To resume printing, choose Pause Printing a second time to toggle the option off.

✦ **Cancel All Documents:** Delete all the print jobs sitting in the print queue.

✦ **Properties:** View and change the printer settings that I discuss in the earlier "Configuring a Printer" section of this chapter.

Figure 5-17:
Managing the print queue.

Understanding Safety and Preventative Maintenance

In this section, I show you some common safety and preventative maintenance practices for printers.

For the exam, be sure to review the safety points in Book I, Chapter 3, along with the safety and preventative maintenance points presented here.

Safety precautions

The first point to make about working with printers is to be sure you turn off the printer and unplug it before doing any maintenance on it. Also be sure to give the printer time to cool down because there are many parts in the printer that can get very hot — especially with laser printers.

If you are servicing a laser printer, be sure to give the printer time to cool down because the fuser rollers get very hot. These rollers are hot enough to melt toner to the paper, so they can cause severe burns to your skin. Be careful!

You also want to be cautious when working around toner because it can get very messy. Be sure not to get toner in your eyes or on your skin. If you have spilled toner, get a vendor-approved vacuum to suck it all up. If you have toner on your skin and want to wash it off use cold water instead of hot water — you wouldn't want to fuse it to yourself!

Preventive maintenance

Preventive maintenance for your printer will help reduce downtime. Think of your relationship with your printer like any other relationship — if you treat the printer well, it will stick around; if you don't treat it well, it'll leave you when you least expect it. Care for your printer by cleaning it every once in a while — at least once a year. (Make it an anniversary thing.)

To clean your laser printer, follow these general steps or consult the manufacturer's documentation for exact methods of cleaning your printer make and model. Some general steps to follow to clean the laser printer are:

1. **Turn off and unplug the printer.**

2. **Clean the outside of the printer with a lint-free cloth and a tiny bit of isopropyl alcohol.**

3. **Remove the paper tray and paper. Clean the tray, removing any dust or paper particles. Clean the area inside the printer where the tray resides.**

 Be sure to clean the feeder rollers — they get pretty dirty.

4. **Open the printer and remove the toner.**

5. **Clean the inside of the printer; don't be afraid to clean the rollers.**

6. **Put the toner and the paper tray back in and print a test page.**

Lab 5-4 allows you the opportunity to review the steps to cleaning an ink cartridge on an inkjet printer. Lab 5-4 can be found in the `Labs.pdf` file in the Author directory of the CD-ROM.

Getting an A+

In this chapter, you find out about three types of printers — dot matrix, inkjet, and laser printers. You discover how each printer prints and find out about the six phases of the laser printing process. The following are some key points to remember about printers when preparing for the exam:

+ Laser printers use light, electromagnetism, and heat to create a printout.

+ Inkjet printers use a heating element to vaporize ink and spray it through a pinhole to make characters on a page.

+ Dot matrix printers use solenoids to strike a ribbon, creating characters from patterns of printed dots.

+ You may use a parallel connection, USB, or network connection to send the print job from the computer to the printer. USB is popular for home and small office use, and larger companies typically use a printer with a built-in network card.

+ The six phases to the laser printing process are charging (conditioning), writing, developing, transferring, fusing, and cleaning.

+ You may install a printer in Windows via the Add Printer Wizard. After the printer is installed, you can configure a number of settings, such as spooling, scheduling, and priority.

Book III
Chapter 5

Managing Printers

Prep Test

1 What are the two types of feeder mechanisms used in printers?

A ❑ Continuous tractor feed

B ❑ Continuous form feed

C ❑ Friction feed

D ❑ Injected

2 Which of the following devices use friction feeder mechanisms? (Choose two.)

A ❑ Laser printers

B ❑ Fax machines

C ❑ Dot matrix printers

D ❑ A printer that prints hundreds of payroll checks

3 A positive charge is applied to the paper by which laser printer component?

A ○ The laser

B ○ The print drum

C ○ The registration rollers

D ○ The transfer corona wire

4 What is the purpose of the negative charge on the print drum of a laser printer?

A ○ To attract the toner to every area of the drum

B ○ To attract the toner to the areas of the drum that have a stronger negative charge

C ○ To attract the toner to the areas of the drum that have a weaker negative charge

D ○ To attract the positively charged paper to the print drum

5 Why are both the developer roller and the print drum charged with –600V in a laser printer?

A ○ So the paper is attracted to neither

B ○ So the toner is attracted to neither

C ○ So the toner creates a fusion cloud between the two rollers and the paper

D ○ So the toner is attracted only to weakly charged areas of the print drum

6 The paper is charged with which voltage charge by the secondary corona wire?

A ○ +600V

B ○ –600V

C ○ –100V

D ○ +100V

7 What method does an inkjet printer use to print a page?

A ○ One dot at a time to form a character

B ○ Spray-painting a character

C ○ Striking an inked ribbon

D ○ Dropping ink onto the paper

8 With an inkjet printer, what causes the ink to vaporize?

A ○ Electrical charge

B ○ A heating element within the ink cartridge

C ○ A solenoid in each chamber of the ink cartridge

D ○ Drying of the ink when the cartridge has not been used for some time

9 A vertical line on every page of a printout from a laser printer indicates what?

A ○ Fleck of toner

B ○ Scratch on the print drum

C ○ Light leakage

D ○ Fingerprint

10 What would you do if the print job refused to leave the print queue in Windows 2000/XP?

A ○ Delete the printer and reinstall it

B ○ Restart the computer

C ○ Turn the printer off and then on

D ○ Stop and restart the spooler service

Answers

1 **B, C.** Continuous form feed and friction feed are the two types of paper feeder mechanisms. Dot matrix printers use continuous form feed, and laser printers use friction feed. *See "Learning about Paper Feeder Mechanisms."*

2 **A, B.** Friction feeders use rollers that apply pressure and friction to the top sheet of paper in the paper tray to move it into the print device. Laser printers and fax machines use friction feed. *Review "Friction feeders."*

3 **D.** The transfer corona, also known as the secondary corona wire, charges the paper with a +600V charge. *Check out "The laser printing process."*

4 **C.** The print drum is charged with an initial –600V charge. The laser writes the image onto the print drum by weakening the charge to –100V in areas that create the image. This causes the toner to attract to the –100V areas because the toner is approximately –600V — and opposites attract! *Peruse "The laser printing process."*

5 **D.** The developer roller and the print drum are both equally charged so that they are repelled from one another. The toner on the developer roller will be attracted to neutralized areas of the print drum caused by the laser. *Take a look at "The laser printing process."*

6 **A.** The transfer corona charges the paper to +600V, so the toner on the print drum is strongly attracted to it. *Peek at "The laser printing process."*

7 **B.** An inkjet printer sprays the ink onto the paper. *Look over "Inkjet printers."*

8 **B.** Within the ink cartridge, a heating element vaporizes the ink, forcing it to spray a drop out the pinhole in the nozzle. *Study "Inkjet printers."*

9 **B.** A scratch on the print drum can cause the vertical line to appear in the printout. *Refer to "Laser printer problems."*

10 **D.** You would stop and start the print spooler service, deleting everything from the queue. Stopping and starting the service is a way of rebooting the printing environment. *Examine "Spooling service problems."*

Managing Printers

Chapter 6: Working with Multimedia Devices

Exam Objectives

✔ **Understanding scanners**

✔ **Understanding digital cameras**

✔ **Working with other multimedia devices**

*I*t is amazing to see an old uncle at a birthday party who just a few years back had not even touched a computer but now snaps photos with his digital camera and drones on about how simple it is to upload the pictures to his computer and then burn them to a CD! When I try to think of examples of how computers have entered our daily lives, this is the most promising example I can think of.

In this chapter, you find out about popular multimedia devices used in everyday life. In the following pages, I discuss a number of multimedia devices, starting with digital cameras and scanners — the two most popular types of computer-related multimedia devices. I also introduce a few key points about microphones and MIDI technology, which are very important to the many people who will record music through their computers and are objectives covered by the A+ certification exams.

Understanding Scanners

In this section, you find out about different types of scanners. I also show you how to scan a photo in Windows XP and how to save the photo as a file on the computer.

A few years back, scanners were very popular because they were one of the only ways to get your photos into a digital format. Maybe you wanted to use the computer to alter the photo or to send it to a relative via e-mail. To do any of these actions, you had to use a scanner, which would copy the photo as a digital image that could be saved on your computer.

Many different types of scanners have been manufactured over the years, and you need to be familiar with the different types of scanners for the A+ Certification exam. They are

✦ **Flatbed:** The flatbed scanner is the most popular scanner today. With a flatbed scanner, you lift the cover of the scanner and place the photo on the flat sheet of glass (a *platen*). A scan head then moves beneath the picture, scanning the image by using a piece of technology called a *charge-coupled device* (CCD). Figure 6-1 shows a flatbed scanner.

✦ **Handheld:** A handheld scanner is great where it is impossible to place the object to be scanned on a flatbed scanner. To use a handheld scanner, you move the scanner over the object that you want to scan.

✦ **Sheetfeed:** A sheetfeed scanner acts very much like a fax machine in the sense that the scan head is stationary. You insert the paper object to be scanned, and the feeder passes the paper over the scan head. This scanner type looks very similar to a portable printer and is also the scanner type typically found in multifunctional printers.

✦ **Drum:** A drum scanner uses a technology called a *photomultiplier tube (PMT)*, which involves wrapping the photo around a glass tube. The drum releases light that is converted to electrical data to become the image file.

Figure 6-1: A flatbed scanner uses a scan head that moves under the object being scanned.

You need to be familiar with the different types of scanners for the A+ Certification exam.

Scanning process

Most scanners uses a CCD, which is responsible for capturing the photons created by the light being exposed to the picture and then converting those photons to electrons, which are a form of electrical data. The image is then created from the electrical data.

The scanner has a scan head that contains the CCD along with a number of mirrors and lenses. The mirrors reflect the light from the lamp onto the photo being scanned. That light then passes through the lenses to the CCD to create the image.

Connecting a scanner

You can use a number of different types of ports to connect a scanner to the computer, depending on what type of connection your scanner wants to use. The popular ports used by a scanner are as follows:

✦ **Parallel port:** Older scanners connected to the system by using the parallel port, which might have caused a little problem because the printer was already using the printer port! Do not despair, though. If you look at this type of scanner, you will notice that it has two connectors on it. You can connect the scanner to the computer. Then, with another cable, connect the printer to the scanner, creating a daisy chain. In this scenario, you need to check your CMOS settings to ensure that the parallel port mode is set to EPP (Enhanced Parallel Port), which supports daisy chaining.

 Check out Book II, Chapter 4, if you need to review how to adjust your computer's CMOS settings.

✦ **SCSI:** Another popular form of scanner connection a few years back was the SCSI (Small Computer System Interface) connection. To connect a SCSI scanner to a computer, make sure that you

 • Have an SCSI host adapter.

 • Assign a unique ID to the scanner.

 • Terminate the SCSI bus.

✦ **USB:** The most popular method used to connect a scanner to a computer these days is the USB (Universal Serial Bus). With USB, you simply connect the scanner to the computer, and Plug and Play kicks in and either loads the driver or prompts you for it.

Scanning an image

In this section, I show you how to scan an image in Windows XP. You will most likely not be tested on the actual scanning of a document or picture for the A+ exams, but you may need to scan a document on the job. For this discussion, I assume that you already connected the scanner and loaded the driver for the device.

Follow these steps to scan a picture in Windows XP:

1. **Choose Start⇨Control Panel⇨Printers and Other Hardware⇨Scanners and Cameras.**

 You should see your scanner in the Scanners and Cameras window.

2. **To scan an image, select your scanner and click Get Pictures on the Imaging Tasks pane on the left side of the screen.**

 This launches the Scanners and Cameras Wizard, which copies pictures to your system.

3. **Click Next on the wizard's welcome screen.**

4. **If you want the scan in color then choose color picture and then click Next.**

5. **Type the name for this group of pictures, as shown in Figure 6-2.**

Figure 6-2:
Scanning
a photo in
Windows XP.

 The name you give to the group of pictures will be the name of a folder in My Documents that holds all the photos you scan. It will also be the first part of the name of each image (followed by an incremental number).

6. **Select which graphics file format you would like to save your pictures in.**

 Graphics file formats are beyond the scope of this book, but here is a guideline: As a general rule, if you will use the image only for onscreen viewing, go with JPEG. If you hope to eventually print the image on paper, save it as a TIFF. The TIFF file will be larger, but it will include more detail than a JPEG file.

7. **Click Next.**

 Your scanner starts doing its thing.

8. **When the scanning is complete, click Next and then click Finish.**

 A new folder appears with your newly scanned image(s)!

The steps to scan a document in Windows Vista are similar to Windows XP, but you will navigate to the list of scanners by choosing Start⇨Control Panel⇨Hardware and Sound⇨Scanners and Cameras.

The scanned images are stored in the My Pictures folder in Windows XP and the Pictures folder in Windows Vista by default.

Using Digital and Web Cameras

Just a few years ago, taking pictures involved buying film for your camera, snapping some pictures, and then taking the exposed film to a photo lab to be developed — often only to find out that of the 24 pictures you took, only 4 of them were any good!

Photography has changed dramatically since then. Today, you can use a digital camera, which stores the picture in memory on the camera, not on film. You can also navigate through the pictures by using the built-in viewer on the camera and then delete the ones you do not like — then print only the ones you want developed!

The following sections introduce you to digital cameras, digital video cameras, and Web cameras (Webcams).

Book III
Chapter 6

Working with
Multimedia Devices

Digital cameras

A digital camera is different from a conventional camera because instead of storing the image on film, a digital camera stores the image as a digital file on the camera. This file can then be uploaded to a computer and can be used in any application on the computer, such as e-mail, presentation software, or a photo editor.

The digital camera works the same way that a scanner does — it captures light and uses a CCD to convert the captured light into an electrical charge that is used to create the pixels in the image. The light is captured through the lenses on the digital camera and is then passed through the CCD so the CCD can do its job of converting the light into data.

When shopping for a digital camera, you want to be sure you get the best camera for your dollar. The quality of a digital camera is measured in its resolution and zoom levels.

Camera resolution

Camera resolution is measured in pixels, just like monitor resolution. The more pixels recorded in the photos being taken, the more detail displayed in the picture. The resolution also affects how large the picture can become before becoming grainy. A camera advertises its resolution by indicating how many pixels it supports, which is typically measured in *megapixels* (MP; or millions of pixels). The higher the number of pixels supported, the better quality image you will get from your camera. Here are what some common camera resolutions translate into:

✦ **1MP:** Supports an image resolution of 1216 x 912

✦ **2MP:** Supports an image resolution of 1600 x 1200

✦ **4MP:** Supports an image resolution of 2240 x 1680

✦ **5MP:** Supports an image resolution of 2560 x 1920

✦ **6MP:** Supports an image resolution of 2816 x 2112

✦ **8MP:** Supports an image resolution of 3264 x 2448

✦ **11MP:** Supports an image resolution of 4064 x 2704

By way of comparison, an 11MP camera is professional quality. At the time of this writing, the typical consumer-grade digital camera has a resolution of around 8MP.

Most digital cameras allow you to specify which resolution you would like to take photos in. For example, on my 3MP camera, I can specify that I want to take pictures with a resolution of 2MP, which creates a smaller image file but also creates a lower-resolution image. But if I am happy with the quality of my 2MP images (they are fine for eBay!) because they are smaller files, I can store more of them on the camera.

Zoom

Digital cameras can have two types of zoom, optical and digital, both of which let you zoom in on your subject when taking a photo. In the following list, optical and digital are compared against what is known as *fixed focus:*

✦ **Fixed focus:** A *fixed focus camera* does not support any type of zooming features. What the camera sees is what the camera takes as a picture. To zoom in, you need to physically get closer to the object. This is the zoom type (actually a lack of zoom) used on disposable cameras.

✦ **Optical zoom:** *Optical zoom* is the "good" zoom type that uses lenses on the camera to change the focus and zoom in on the object. This zoom type does not alter the image in any way: It simply zooms in and takes the picture.

✦ **Digital zoom:** Digital zoom is what I like to refer to as a *virtual zoom*. It takes the picture and then goes to the center of the image and magnifies the subject. This is the same as you taking an original photo into a photo editor and magnifying the image and then cutting to the part you like. This typically never turns out right because as you magnify the image, it becomes grainy.

Uploading pictures to the computer

To upload pictures from your digital camera in Windows XP, follow these steps:

1. **With your camera powered-off, plug the camera into the computer's USB port; then turn on the camera. The digital camera uses a dedicated USB cable that has a USB connector on one end to connect to the computer while the connector on the other end is a small connector for that camera.**

 Windows detects the camera, loads the driver for the camera, and then asks which program you want to use to copy your photos to the system.

2. **Choose Microsoft Scanner and Camera Wizard and then click OK.**

3. **When the Camera Wizard displays its introduction screen, click Next.**

 You are presented with a list of photos that can be uploaded.

4. **Make sure that a check mark appears beside each photo you want to upload (as shown in Figure 6-3) and then click Next.**

Book III
Chapter 6

Working with
Multimedia Devices

Figure 6-3: Uploading photos from a digital camera to your computer with Windows XP.

The wizard asks you to name the group of photos you want to upload.

5. **Type a name for this grouping and then click Next.**

 The photos are then copied to your system and placed in the My Documents⇨My Pictures folder.

6. **When all the photos are copied, click Next and then click Finish.**

The steps to upload pictures from your digital camera are similar in Windows Vista — you simply plug the camera into the computer and power it on and the Autoplay window in Vista will appear asking how to upload the pictures. If you choose Import Pictures, the import pictures wizard will launch asking you to tag a name to this group of pictures and then copies the pictures to the system.

Web and digital video cameras

In this section, I introduce you to Web cameras, digital video cameras, and the concept of a codec, all of which are important to understand when supporting video devices or video applications.

Web cameras

Web cameras (also called *Webcams*) can capture video and display it on the computer screen, or they can be used to record a video and store it in a digital format on the computer. Webcams are popular with conferencing applications, which allow you to have a live conversation while seeing the person you are talking to, over the Internet. An example of an application that can use a Webcam is MSN Messenger (see Figure 6-4).

Figure 6-4: MSN Messenger lets you (informally) chat or (formally) video conference.

A Webcam is typically shaped like an eyeball with a lens on the front and connects to the system's USB port. Most Webcams have a stand that holds the camera and allows it to sit on the monitor or desk. There are also laptop versions of Webcams that clip to the frame around the laptop's LCD and also a number of laptops today have a Webcam built-in to the LCD. Figure 6-5 shows a Webcam.

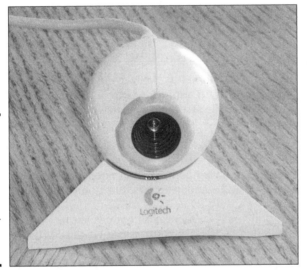

Figure 6-5:
A webcam captures live video and sends it to anyone you are conferencing with.

Digital video cameras

Just like digital cameras have replaced conventional methods of taking snapshots, recording video with a digital video camera has become popular in this day and age. A digital video camera can record directly to the computer and store the video as a file on the computer, or it can store the video to memory on the camera. It can also store the information to a digital video tape that can then be played later and recorded on the computer as a file.

A digital video camera typically connects to the computer via a USB 2.0 or IEEE 1394 (FireWire) connection, which is currently the more popular choice.

Understanding codecs

The problem with digital video is that with all the information that needs to be recorded, the files can quickly become huge. Digital video file sizes are kept to a minimum by compressing the video using special *compression/ de*compression (codec) software. There are a number of different types of video formats and codecs, the most popular of which are

- **DV:** Digital video cameras have their own proprietary format to store the video, known as the DV format. The DV format typically has no loss in quality.

- **DivX:** DivX is one of the most popular codec types today. It supports high-quality video with high compression ratios. A video using the DivX codec uses only about 15 percent of the disk space that other codec types do.

- **MJPEG:** MJPEG is based on the JPEG compression standard used to compress still images. This compression type is optimized for transferring video to and from tape but is not suited for Internet applications because special hardware is required to play the video back.

- **MPEG1:** MPEG1, developed by the Moving Picture Experts Group, has been used heavily for creating videos to be distributed over the Internet because of its small file sizes and because only the codec is needed to play the video back.

- **MPEG2 and MPEG4:** The MPEG1 video compression has been improved again and again to create the MPEG2 and MPEG4 compression standards, which have better compression rates and better resolution. For example, the MPEG2 standard offers four times the resolution of MPEG1.

The important point to remember with codecs is that you must have the same codec installed on your computer that was used to record the video in the first place. Otherwise, the computer will not know how to decompress the video. If you do not have the correct codec, you will not be able to play the video.

Looking at Other Multimedia Devices

Two other multimedia devices that are popular in today's systems are MIDI devices and microphones. Sound cards typically have a microphone port (also known as a *mic port*) and a MIDI port.

Microphones

The microphone port on the computer is indicated with a little pictograph of a microphone. You can use the microphone port to plug a standard microphone into the computer. If you have a microphone whose cable will not connect in the mic port, you need to head to your local electronics store and find an adapter. After you plug in the microphone, you can use it as a recording source as long as you have specified it as a recording source in Windows.

To set the microphone as a recording source in Windows XP, follow these instructions:

1. **Choose Start⇨All Programs⇨Accessories⇨Entertainment⇨Volume Control.**

 Here, you can set the levels for each type of input and output device. For example, when recording, you want to make sure that the level on the microphone is not too high lest the recording will sound distorted.

2. **To ensure that the microphone is set as a recording device, choose Options⇨Properties in the Volume Control dialog box.**

 The Properties dialog box appears. Notice that Playback is selected, which means that you are seeing and can select which devices will play back sound.

3. **Select the Recording radio button and verify that the Microphone is selected, as shown in Figure 6-6.**

4. **Click OK and then close the Volume Control dialog box.**

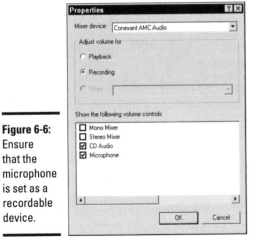

Figure 6-6: Ensure that the microphone is set as a recordable device.

To configure your audio devices in Windows Vista, choose Start⇨Control Panel⇨Hardware and Sound. In the Sound category, click the Manage Audio Devices link to open the Sound dialog box, where you can configure your recording devices and playback devices (shown in Figure 6-7).

MIDI

Musical Instrument Digital Interface (MIDI) is a standard developed to allow musical instruments to communicate with one another or with a computer. MIDI is a common language that all MIDI-capable instruments can speak.

To use MIDI, you must have a MIDI-capable instrument — for example, a keyboard with a MIDI port on it — and a system with a MIDI port. You do not need to worry about the details of MIDI for the A+ Certification exams.

Click this link

Figure 6-7:
Managing recording and playback devices in Windows Vista.

TV tuner and video capture cards

The days of having to sit in front of a big television to watch your favorite TV shows are over. If you are interested in watching TV on your computer, just add a TV tuner card to your system. The TV tuner card has a connector with which you connect the TV cable to the computer to receive the television signal so you can watch TV on the computer.

Most TV tuner cards act as video capture cards and come with software that allows you to record TV shows to video files on the computer that can be played back at a later time. Figure 6-8 shows a TV tuner card. Most TV tuner cards come as PCI, PCIe, or USB devices.

Figure 6-8:
Use a TV
tuner card
to receive a
TV signal on
a computer.

Getting an A+

This chapter introduces you to some of the different devices used when working with multimedia and multimedia applications. Here are some key points to remember about multimedia devices:

◆ A flatbed scanner is the popular type of scanner and uses a technology called a charge-coupled device (CCD). The scan head on the scanner moves under the image, exposing the image to light that is captured and then converted into electrical data by the CCD, which creates the image.

◆ The popular connection used by scanners and digital cameras is USB.

◆ Digital cameras are measured by the quality of image they provide. The measurement unit is megapixels — millions of pixels. The larger the number of megapixels, the higher the resolution and the larger the image.

◆ Codecs compress videos so that they do not use up as much hard disk space. To play a video on the computer, you need the same codec installed on your system that was used to compress the video.

◆ If you are having trouble with your microphone picking up the sound around you, make sure that the microphone is set as a recording device.

Prep Test

1 **What type of scanner is portable and is swiped over the object to be scanned?**

A ○ Flatbed

B ○ Handheld

C ○ Sheetfeed

D ○ Drum

2 **What technology do flatbed scanners and digital cameras use to create an image?**

A ○ OCC

B ○ CCO

C ○ PMT

D ○ CCD

3 **What zoom type on a digital camera simply magnifies the image to emulate the zooming feature?**

A ○ Fixed zoom

B ○ Digital zoom

C ○ Optical zoom

D ○ Pixel zoom

4 **Digital video cameras typically use which type of connection to connect to the computer and upload the video?**

A ○ Serial

B ○ Parallel

C ○ FireWire

D ○ USB 2.0

5 **The standard used by musical equipment to communicate with one another or with a computer is known as what?**

A ○ OCC

B ○ MIDI

C ○ WAV

D ○ Codec

6 Video files are compressed by using what?

A ○ Encryption key

B ○ MIDI

C ○ CCD

D ○ Codec

7 What type of scanner uses a glass tube that emits light?

A ○ Flatbed

B ○ Handheld

C ○ Sheetfeed

D ○ Drum

Answers

1 **B.** A handheld scanner is carried around by the user, and the scanner is moved over the object to scan the object. *See "Understanding Scanners."*

2 **D.** *Charge-coupled device* (CCD) is the technology used by flatbed scanners and digital cameras to create the image. *Review "Understanding Scanners."*

3 **B.** Digital zooming is the zoom type that simply magnifies the image, just like you would do yourself in image editing software. This could make the image appear grainy. *Check out "Digital cameras."*

4 **C.** Digital video cameras typically use IEEE 1394 (FireWire) connections to connect to the computer. *Peruse "Digital video cameras."*

5 **B.** Musical Instrument Digital Interface (MIDI) is the standard that allows musical instruments to communicate with one another or with the computer. *Take a look at "MIDI."*

6 **D.** A codec is used to compress and decompress video files. *Peek at "Understanding codecs."*

7 **D.** A drum scanner uses a glass tube that emits light. *Look over "Understanding Scanners."*

Chapter 7: Dealing with Portable Computers

Exam Objectives

- ✔ Identifying portable computer components
- ✔ Looking at laptop batteries
- ✔ Understanding AC adapters
- ✔ Finding out about LCD panels
- ✔ Upgrading and expanding a laptop
- ✔ Troubleshooting laptop issues

*I*n this chapter, you find out about portable computers and their supporting technologies. On the A+ exam, you're required to identify characteristics of a laptop, such as the types of batteries and displays, and also how to upgrade a laptop's hard drive or memory.

Laptops gained popularity years ago because of their small size and mobility. I suppose you could carry around a standard desktop computer, but that is pretty inconvenient and causes wear and tear on your biceps. And even if you are willing to lug around a big, heavy desktop computer, the other problem with desktop computers is that you will not always have a power outlet to plug it into. A big benefit of laptops is that they use a battery to use as a power source, which is great for when you're on a plane or out on safari and don't have a wall outlet.

Although laptops are the portable computer type to focus on for the A+ Certification exam, you should also be familiar with handheld devices such as *personal digital assistants (PDAs),* which a lot of people use to keep track of their daily schedule and contacts.

This chapter helps you identify, install, configure, and upgrade special portable computer components, such as batteries, hard drives, and memory. Procedures in this chapter guide you through the installation and removal of these components on laptop computers.

Identifying Portable Computer Components

Although a number of different laptop brands are on the market, each make and model of laptop has common components. This section introduces you to some of the common components found in laptop computers. Figure 7-1 displays these components.

Display latch

Display

Keyboard

Figure 7-1:
Identifying
the major
components
of a portable
computer.

Battery bay

Touch pad

Power button

The following is a quick description of some of the major components found on laptop computers. Some of these components are also found on desktop computers and serve the same purpose for the laptop. For example, a video board built into a laptop does the same thing as a video board built into a desktop computer.

✦ **Battery:** The *battery* supplies power to the laptop and its components. The battery is charged or maintains its charge from an AC adapter that plugs the laptop into the wall outlet.

✦ **AC adapters:** The *AC adapter* supplies power to the battery so that the battery can either recharge or pass that power on to the laptop components.

✦ **DC controllers:** The *DC controller* is responsible for protecting devices such as cards, chips, adapters, and circuitry from power surges.

+ **PCMCIA cards:** *Personal Computer Memory Card Industry Association* (PCMCIA) cards are used to add external drives, modems, and LAN adapters to laptop computers that didn't ship with one of these components. PCMCIA cards expand upon the computer's capabilities.

+ **Video adapters:** The *video board* is responsible for converting the digital data from the system into information that the display can use to create the image.

+ **LCD panels:** The primary display type on laptop computers is liquid crystal display (LCD). LCD panel monitors are increasingly replacing CRT (cathode ray tube) monitors for desktop computers as well.

+ **Keyboard:** The keyboard found on laptops works the same way as a keyboard for a desktop computer. However, laptop keyboards are smaller versions of desktop computer keyboards, and some keys (such as the navigations keys) are in different locations than a traditional desktop keyboard.

+ **Hard drives:** Laptops ship with hard drives that are physically much smaller than those in desktop computers, typically use less power, and store less information.

+ **Memory:** RAM is installed in laptop computers in a similar fashion to desktop computers. The only difference is the type of memory modules, known as *small outline dual inline memory modules* (SODIMMs), used on laptop computers today.

Looking at Laptop Batteries

Laptop computers ship with a battery that can be removed or replaced at any time. The battery acts as the primary source of power for the laptop and all its components. The battery maintains its charge, or is recharged, by an AC adapter that plugs the laptop into the wall. The following sections outline everything you need to know about portable-computer batteries for the A+ exam.

Different types of batteries

It is important to understand that a laptop computer has two types of batteries: a main battery and a CMOS battery.

+ **Main battery:** This battery supplies power to the laptop and its components. A laptop is designed to work with one of four types of main batteries:

 • *Alkaline:* Typically found in palmtop computers; the same battery type you find in calculators.

- *NiCad (nickel-cadmium):* Typically found in laptop computers; very heavy. NiCad batteries, which are fairly inexpensive, typically need to be recharged after three or four hours of use.

- *Li-Ion (lithium-ion):* Has a lot more battery charge time than a NiCad battery. A Li-Ion battery is also more expensive than a NiCad battery.

- *NiMH (nickel-metal hydride):* Environmentally friendly because they do not contain toxic materials. They are the same weight as NiCad batteries but are more expensive and don't last as long as a Li-Ion battery.

✦ **CMOS battery:** Just like a desktop computer, a laptop computer has a CMOS battery that is responsible for holding a charge to CMOS RAM so the CMOS configuration can be maintained.

On the exam, if you are asked which battery is the best battery for laptop computers, the answer is a Li-Ion battery because it provides the most durability and performance. It is more expensive than the other types of batteries, though.

Another type of battery that you might hear of from time to time is a smart battery. A *smart battery* has its own power circuitry, which is responsible for monitoring the battery performance, output voltage, and temperature and also communicates the status of the battery back to the system. A smart battery is 15% more efficient than the other battery types and is also the most expensive type.

Handling batteries

Before you handle any batteries, be forewarned that batteries (except NiMH batteries) contain toxic chemicals that can cause harm if the battery explodes. Be sure to follow these guidelines when handling batteries:

✦ **Keep batteries away from fire and water.**

✦ **Never open or dismantle a battery.**

✦ **Try not to drop and never throw a battery.**

✦ **Be sure to follow the manufacturer's guidelines when working with the battery.**

For example, if you're storing the battery, check the documentation on suitable areas for storage.

Maximizing battery performance

One of my major pet peeves with batteries is that over time, the charge time of the battery fades away. For example, when I purchased my new laptop, I could get about three hours of battery life; now, I'm looking at about an hour and a half. To get the best performance from your laptop battery, follow these practices:

✦ **Fully charge and discharge a new battery or a battery that has not been in use for a while.** Completely discharge a battery to allow it to charge to its full potential. To discharge a battery, power on the portable computer without having it plugged in and leave it on overnight (or longer, if necessary) until the battery power is 100% used. You can then recharge the battery by using the AC adapter.

✦ **Regularly charge and discharge batteries completely every two to three weeks to keep them healthy.** Be aware that you need not do this for a Li-Ion battery.

✦ **Keep batteries clean.** Cleaning the contacts with cotton swab and alcohol helps maintain a good connection between the battery and the portable device.

✦ **Don't leave batteries dormant for long periods of time**. Be sure to use the battery every few weeks and you should fully discharge and charge a battery at least once every three weeks.

✦ **Store batteries well.** Be sure to store batteries in a cool, dry, clean place away from dangerous elements, such as heat and other metallic objects.

Changing batteries

A number of laptop users find it useful to purchase an additional battery to keep charged and then switch that one for a battery losing its juice from use. I don't know how many times I've been on a five-hour flight when an hour and a half into the flight, my battery loses its charge. In this example, it would be useful to have another battery that I could switch to.

To change a battery on a laptop, power-down the laptop and turn the laptop over. You will notice a spot on the bottom of the laptop where the battery is placed. It will most likely have a battery symbol beside it, with a lever that you slide to release the battery from its slot. Remove the old battery, lightly place the new battery in the slot, and then clamp it in place by pressing down (as shown in Figure 7-2).

Power-management features

Laptop computers include power-management functions that make the laptop "go to sleep" when there has been no input from the keyboard or mouse for a period of time. When the computer is in sleep mode, it still runs, but power-drawing features like the screen and hard drive are suspended until you "wake" your laptop by pressing a key.

Powering-down the screen and hard drive when you're not using them helps preserve battery life.

Figure 7-2:
Replacing
a battery
on a laptop
system.

APM and ACPI

Two power-management standards that have come out over the years are
Advanced Power Management (APM) and Advanced Configuration and
Power Interface (ACPI). These power-management standards have a set of
features that allows the system to conserve power, again resulting in less
battery usage for laptop systems.

APM and ACPI are designed to accomplish the same goal, but ACPI is
the newer standard of the two and is what most systems support today.
APM was implemented as an application programming interface (API) in
Windows, which allowed developers to call a library of code that controlled
the power management features of the laptop. ACPI was implemented a little
differently; it is a set of BIOS routines that control the power management
features, which means that to configure ACPI, you make changes through
CMOS.

Configuring power management

A number of power management features are available to laptops to help
conserve the life of a battery and to the desktop computer to simply help
conserve power consumption. The following sections list popular power-
management features.

Standby, sleep, and suspend

Placing a system in *standby mode* cuts power from peripheral devices (such as the display or hard drive) but maintains power to critical components (say, memory) so that the current work is not lost. *Standby mode* is the term used in Windows 2000/2003/XP; *sleep* is the term used for this low-power state in Windows Vista. Another term for this power state used by vendors is *suspend.*

Standby mode, sleep, and *suspend* are interchangeable terms for the A+ certification exams.

You can place a system in a standby, or sleep, state automatically or manually. A system can be placed in standby automatically triggered by a certain amount of time when the system has not been used. This is as "idle time" and is configured by using the sleep timers in the Windows Control Panel.

To change the sleep timers in Windows Vista, follow these steps:

1. **Choose Start⇨Control Panel.**

2. **In the Mobile PC category, click the Change Battery Settings link.**

3. **In the Power Options window that opens, click the Change When the Computer Sleeps link on the left side of the window.**

4. **Specify the following settings:**

- When the display is turned off (based on idle time when running on battery or plug into power)
- At what interval the system goes to sleep (see Figure 7-3)

5. **(Optional) Specify the brightness of the display when you are running on battery or plugged in.**

In Figure 7-3, my display has a brightness of 100% when I am plugged in. When I am running on battery, though, the brightness is a little over 50%. This helps conserve battery life.

Windows XP operating systems also have sleep timer intervals as well. To configure the sleep timer intervals in Windows XP, follow these steps:

1. **Choose Start⇨Control Panel.**

2. **Choose Performance and Maintenance.**

3. **Choose Power Options.**

4. **On the Power Schemes page, tab set the values for when to turn off the monitor and when to turn off the hard disk when running on battery or plugged in.**

Book III
Chapter 7

Dealing with Portable Computers

Figure 7-3:
Configuring
sleep timers
in Windows
Vista

You can place a system in standby state manually through a number of
different means. The following outlines some popular ways to place a
system in a standby state manually:

✦ **Start button:** Choose the sleep (Vista) or standby (XP) option from the
Start button in Windows (see Figure 7-4) to place the system in standby
mode.

Figure 7-4:
Choose the
sleep option
from the
Start menu
in Windows
Vista.

✦ **Closing the lid:** Through the Power Options in Windows, you can specify
to place the system in sleep mode when the laptop display is closed.

✦ **Standby button:** Most laptops have a Suspend or a Standby button that
you can choose to place the laptop in standby or sleep.

Hibernate

You can place a system in hibernation if you need to quickly shut down the system. The hibernate feature copies the contents of memory to file on disk so that current work is not lost; then it cuts the power to the system. When you resume the system, the contents of the hibernate file are copied from disk to memory, and your screen appears as it was when you went to hibernate mode.

Wake on LAN

Another term on the A+ certification objective list that you need to be familiar with is Wake on LAN (WoL). *WoL* allows you to bring a system out of a sleep state by sending a special message to the system across the network.

This special message — the Magic Packet — has a target address of the MAC address of the system that you want to wake up on the network. The Magic Packet has the broadcast address of FF FF FF FF FF FF placed in the *payload* section of the packet (the data portion of the packet), followed by the target MAC address of the system you are trying to wake up 16 times. Instead of you figuring out how to craft your own packets to wake a system through WoL packets, a number of tools are available for download such as Depicus tools at www.depicus.com/wake-on-lan/.

To wake your system up via WoL, your system BIOS must support the feature, and you must have the WoL option enabled in the CMOS. For more information on configuring CMOS check out Book II, Chapter 4. After the system has the option enabled, you can then power up the system remotely by using a free WoL utility available on the Web.

Understanding AC Adapters

An AC (alternating current) adapter is nothing new to anyone who has worked with electronic devices. The AC adapter on a laptop, just like on an electric razor or a Game Boy, supplies power to the battery to supply power to the laptop and all its components. An AC adapter also recharges the battery so that you can use it when you are on the road. For example, I am writing this text in a coffee shop and running my laptop off my battery, which was charged up last night by the AC adapter. Figure 7-5 shows an AC adapter.

Be sure to use only the AC adapter that came with your laptop or one approved by the laptop manufacturer. Although other adapters might fit your computer, the voltage and amperage might not match the laptop and could cause damage.

Figure 7-5:
An AC adapter supplies power to the laptop and charges the battery.

AC adapter problems

When it comes to AC adapters, there are not a lot of issues that can arise. Two major problems that you will encounter with AC adapters are

+ **Cable problems:** One major issue that can arise when you travel a lot with a laptop is a break in the cable from wrapping the cables. When you have cable problems, it's best to simply order a replacement adapter.

+ **AC port damage:** Another major AC adapter problem is that the AC port on the back of the laptop can become damaged: for example, when the laptop is not used on a hard, flat surface. A number of people I have talked to with problems with the AC port not holding a connection to the AC adapter use their laptop in bed, resting it on their knees, which bang into the AC connector. In this scenario, it is best to have the laptop serviced by the manufacturer to ensure the correct electrical parts are replaced.

AC adapter troubleshooting and repair

If you find that you have a broken wire or faulty electrical components, you can attempt to repair the problem yourself. However, unless you have an electronics background, you should probably leave that to the experts and simply replace the AC adapter.

Learning about LCD Panels

Liquid crystal display (LCD), a popular display type found in laptops for many years, is now a popular choice for desktop computers and TV display. LCDs also are popular on watches and other electrical devices.

An LCD has two sheets of material, surrounding a liquid that contains crystals that act as pixels for the display. Each crystal has a red, green, and blue cell that is illuminated by an electrical charge hitting the crystal, which then creates the image you see onscreen.

The two major types of LCDs are monochrome and color. The two subtypes of color LCD displays are active matrix and passive matrix.

+ **Monochrome:** The original LCDs were single-color displays that showed blue or dark gray on a light gray background.

+ **Color:** The two forms of color display are active matrix and passive matrix:

 • *Active matrix:* An active matrix display, the most popular type of display today, uses at least one transistor per pixel, or crystal, which allows the electrical charge to be held longer on the crystal. This helps to create very crisp images with high resolution. With active matrix displays, the images are clear and easy to view, even from an angle. Because it uses transistors, an active matrix display uses more power than a passive matrix display. Active matrix displays are also known as thin-film transistor (TFT) displays.

 • *Passive matrix:* A passive matrix display has one transistor for each vertical column of the display and one for each horizontal row of the display. The electrical signal is sent down the appropriate horizontal and vertical row of the display, and where they intersect is the pixel that is illuminated. Passive matrix doesn't have a transistor per pixel, so it does not use as much power as an active matrix, but it is slower to produce images and produces lower-quality images. Another popular term used to describe passive matrix is *dual-scan.*

Handling LCD panels

Because an LCD is so easily damaged, take care when handling it. The following are a number of key points to follow to keep your LCD panel working well:

+ **Keep the temperature and humidity at acceptable levels.** The humidity should be less than 60%, and the temperature should be no more than 40 degrees Celsius (104 degrees Fahrenheit). This means that you should avoid leaving your laptop sealed up in your car on a hot summer day.

**Book III
Chapter 7**

**Dealing with
Portable Computers**

✦ **Use only a manufacturer-approved solution to clean your LCD.** Consult your owner's manual for a description of what fluid you should use to clean the display.

✦ **When cleaning the screen, don't scrub the surface vigorously or touch it with anything that has sharp edges.** To clean the display surface, be sure to wipe the screen gently with a soft cloth and manufacturer-approved cleaning fluid.

Connecting an LCD panel to a computer

The LCD panel is connected to your laptop by small hinges. To replace the old LCD panel with a new one, follow these steps:

1. **For most laptops, press the spring of the hinges gently to detach the old LCD panel.**

 Always check the owner's manual or contact the manufacturer to find out exactly how the LCD panel is replaced on your laptop.

2. **After you remove the old LCD panel, slide the new LCD panel firmly in place.**

3. **With the new LCD panel in place, close the panel and reopen it to verify that you fixed the LCD panel correctly.**

 If it closes and opens easily, you replaced the LCD panel successfully.

Because the LCD panel is the weakest part of the laptop computer, be careful when handling the LCD and even opening and closing the laptop. If you damage the LCD, you need to replace it.

Understanding Laptop Input Devices

After you become familiar with a laptop's major components, such as batteries and displays, take a look at the myriad input devices used to get data into the laptop. The major input devices are the keyboard, touch pad, and rubber mouse ball located on the keyboard of some laptops.

Laptop keyboard

The *keyboard* is the most common input device used on both desktop systems and laptops. The keyboard allows you to communicate with the system by converting the keystrokes into corresponding letters and numbers. For information on the different types of keyboards and how they work, read Book III, Chapter 2.

For the exam, be aware that the enhanced 101-key keyboard is the popular keyboard found on desktop and laptop computers today.

Maintaining keyboards

Over time, a keyboard collects a lot of dust and dirt behind the keys. It is important to clean keyboards periodically, and the following outlines the basic steps for cleaning a keyboard:

1. **Holding the laptop at an angle, use compressed air to blow the dust and dirt from behind the keys.**

2. **Clean the tops of the keys with a soft cloth dipped in a manufacturer-approved cleaner.**

 You can also buy wet cloths with the appropriate cleaning fluid already applied.

3. **Using a lint-free swab, clean any remaining dirt from between the keys.**

Handling keyboard problems

Like most replicable components today, replacing a keyboard is far more efficient than repairing it. The following steps provide a basic guideline you can use to troubleshoot any keyboard-related problems:

1. **If you are having troubles with the keyboard after replacing it, check that the keyboard is seated correctly by making sure it is snug in the molding.**

2. **Reboot the computer.**

 Yes, rebooting does work from time to time! Rebooting the computer reloads the device drivers, which are responsible for controlling the corresponding devices — in this case, the keyboard.

3. **If the keyboard still doesn't work, or if just some keys don't work, you might need to replace the entire keyboard.**

 Personally, I find that the keyboard is the first item to go on laptops.

Function keys

Laptop function keys provide the typical use of a function key, such as pressing Alt+F4 to close the current window. However, function keys on laptops also allow you to control features of the laptop. The following list offers some popular functions you should be able to find on your laptop keyboard:

✦ **Display Brightness:** On a laptop, you can typically adjust the brightness of the display by using the function key (Fn) and then pressing the brightness function button. For example, on my laptop, I use Fn+F8 to increase the brightness and Fn+F7 to decrease the brightness.

✦ **Display Toggle:** If you hook a projector up to your laptop for a presentation, you need to use the display toggle function key to set the laptop to show the output on the projector and on the screen of the laptop. On my laptop, I use Fn+F4 to do this.

✦ **Sleep:** If you don't have a Sleep button on your laptop, you might have a function key allocated for this purpose. To put my laptop to sleep, I can press Fn+F5.

When troubleshooting keyboard issues, make sure that you are not supposed to use a special key — such as Fn or Alt — to go with the keystroke.

Pointing devices

Two other major input devices are the touch pad and the mouse ball, which are both responsible for controlling the mouse pointer on the laptop. Most laptop users use a normal mouse with their laptop by connecting the mouse to either the PS/2 port or a USB port.

If you don't want to use a PS/2 or USB mouse with your laptop, you will typically control the mouse pointer by using a touch pad or a mouse ball.

Touch pad

A touch pad, as shown in Figure 7-6, is a very common component found on laptops. It is a small, rectangular surface at the front of the keyboard. To use the touch pad to control the mouse pointer, drag your finger over the surface; the mouse pointer moves in the same direction.

Below the touch pad are two buttons, which act as traditional left and right mouse buttons. With most laptops, you can tap the touch pad instead of clicking the left button to perform a "click" operation, and you can tap the touch pad twice to double-click. If you find that the touch pad does not react to the tapping, have a look in the driver CD that came with the laptop to see whether a driver needs to be loaded for the touch pad.

Most laptops also have a button that can be used to turn the touch pad on and off. This can be useful if you're going to use a USB mouse and don't want the touch pad to interfere when you accidentally rub over it, which I find I do with my thumb as I type.

Touch pad

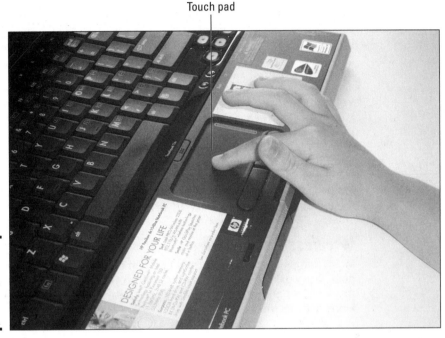

Figure 7-6:
Use a touch
pad to move
the mouse
pointer.

Rubber mouse ball

Instead of a touch pad, some older laptops shipped with a rubber mouse
ball located in the middle of the keyboard. This rubber mouse ball is like a
little joystick that controls the mouse pointer. Along with the rubber mouse
ball are two buttons below the keyboard that perform traditional left- and
right-click mouse actions. Today's laptops usually ship with a touch pad.

Stylus and digitizer

A number of portable devices, such as Tablet PCs, PDAs, or even smart-
phones, use a touch screen with a stylus pen you use to control the device.
(A smartphone gives you features, such as e-mail and Internet access, and
has become a popular solution for mobile users.) The PDA will have a digi-
tizer built in, normally sitting on the display that accepts the input from the
stylus pen, and sends that input to the device.

Laptop Communication Components

Laptops communicate with each other and with networks in a few different
ways. In the following sections, I discuss some of the popular types of
communication components found on a laptop.

Network card and modem

The most obvious communication component on the laptop is its built-in Ethernet network card. You use this network card to plug the laptop into a network via a typical UTP cable. Most laptops today ship with 10/100 Mbps network cards that allow for fast data transfer.

You can identify the integrated network card by looking on the side of the laptop for the RJ-45 jack, which looks similar to a telephone jack, only a tiny bit bigger.

Speaking of telephone jacks, the network port is typically located right beside a telephone port for the built-in modem on the laptop. Most laptops also indicate these ports with little pictures so that you know which port is the modem port and which is the network port.

Wireless network card

Most laptops ship with a wireless network card as well as a wired network port. The wireless network card built into your laptop allows you to connect to a wireless access point to access the network and Internet without using a physical network cable.

Laptops typically allow you to enable or disable the wireless network card quickly by pressing a button on the laptop. The wireless button on my laptop is in the top-right corner, but I have also seen the button on the front panel near the hard drive and power lights. From a troubleshooting point of view, you want to make sure that the wireless network card is enabled if you are trying to connect to a wireless network.

Other communications ports

A few other communication devices are popular in laptops today: infrared, Bluetooth, and WAN-cellular technologies. The following sections give a brief overview of each of these technologies. For more on these technologies, see Book VIII, Chapter 2.

Infrared

Infrared wireless communication uses infrared light signals to send data from one device to another. Infrared is popular with TV and VCR remote controls, but as most of us have found out when using the remotes, infrared requires line of sight. *Line of sight* means that nothing blocks the pathway of the light beam between the two devices. If the pathway is blocked, communication stops. Infrared communication is also limited by its bandwidth; it can deliver information at up to 4 Mbps.

Bluetooth

Bluetooth is a newer form of wireless communication that is often used to connect a portable computer to peripherals, such as a printer on a network. Bluetooth doesn't rely on line of sight because it doesn't send the data as light beams. Instead, it sends the data over a radio frequency and can be used only when the two devices are close together. Bluetooth has a maximum distance of 10 meters (10.93 yards).

Bluetooth is popular in portable devices, such as handheld devices, and sends data at approximately 1 Mbps.

WAN-cellular

WAN-cellular technology allows you to use your cell phone to make a network connection from your portable device to a remote location. The benefit of WAN-cellular technology is that you can connect your portable device to your network from anywhere that you can get a cellular connection. To use WAN-cellular technology, you need a digital cell phone that can connect to your portable devices, such as your handheld device.

Port Replicators and Docking Stations

If you use a laptop at the office a lot, you might want to consider using a port replicator or a docking station to get the functionality of a desktop PC from your laptop. A *port replicator* gives a laptop access to standard computer ports by connecting to an expansion port typically found on the back of the laptop. After you connect the port replicator to the back of the laptop, it provides serial, parallel, keyboard, and mouse connectors, thus allowing you to use those types of devices on the laptop even if the laptop itself does not contain the ports.

A number of companies set up docking stations for their laptop users. A *docking station* acts as a port replicator by having ports exposed from the back of the docking station. The docking station is different than the port replicator, but the docking station also can contain features such as drive bays, network port, and desktop computer-sized expansion slots.

Expanding on a Laptop

Expanding on a laptop's capabilities usually involves upgrading the system memory or hard disk (which I discuss in the "Upgrading Your Laptop" section a bit later) or expanding on the laptop's capabilities by adding an expansion card, such as a PCMCIA card or PCI Express Card.

PCMCIA cards

Personal Computer Memory Card Industry Association (PCMCIA) cards are expansion cards added to the laptop system to provide functionality to the laptop. A PCMCIA card, also known as a *PC card,* is a credit card–sized device inserted into a PCMCIA slot, usually on the side of the laptop. It allows you to expand on the laptop's capabilities, such as a network card, modem, memory, hard disk space, or maybe even a wireless network card (as shown in Figure 7-7).

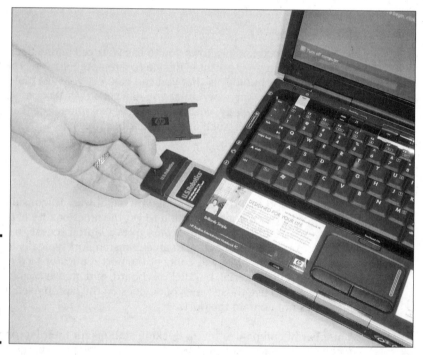

Figure 7-7: Inserting a PCMCIA card into the PCMCIA slot.

Originally, PCMCIA cards were used only to add memory to the laptop, but today, you normally add memory by inserting it into a slot found on the bottom of the laptop. PCMCIA slots are now used for modems, network cards, and wireless network cards.

For the A+ Certification exam, be familiar with the three different types of PCMCIA cards:

✦ **Type I card:** A Type I card is 3.3mm thick, with a single row of sockets that connect into the slot. Type 1 cards were used to add memory to the laptop and are the original reason for the expansion architecture.

✦ **Type II card:** A Type II card is 5.5mm thick, with two rows of sockets that connect into the slot. Type II cards are usually network cards and modems that are added to a laptop.

✦ **Type III card:** A Type III card is 10.5mm thick, with three rows of sockets that connect into the slot. Type III cards are used to add hard disk drives.

Be sure you're familiar with the thickness of each card type and what types of devices are typically delivered in what card type.

Each type of cards has a corresponding PCMCIA socket, and you can mix and match the cards into different sockets as long as the card fits in the socket. For example, a Type I card will go into a Type II socket, but you cannot fit a Type III card into a Type II socket.

For the card to work in your laptop, the laptop has two services used to manage PCMCIA cards:

✦ **Socket services:** BIOS-level routines that detect when a PCMCIA card is inserted into or removed from the system.

✦ **Card services:** Provide the interface between the card and the device driver. Card services also manage the assignment of system resources, such as I/O addresses and IRQs, to the PCMCIA card.

Adding a PC card

One of the most exciting features of PCMCIA is hot swapping. *Hot swapping* allows you to install a device while a computer is still running, and have the device detected and configured by the operating system without rebooting. This is unlike adding a card to a desktop computer, where you typically have to shut down the machine, take the cover off, add the card, put the cover back on the computer, and finally restart the computer. With PCMCIA, you can insert or remove the card from the slot at any time.

Adding or installing a PCMCIA card is easy. Make sure you have the card oriented properly and then slide it into the slot until it fits firmly. If the card is installed correctly, the eject button beside the slot will pop out. When the card is inserted, Plug and Play should kick in and either load the driver or prompt you for the driver.

Removing a PC card

To remove a PCMCIA card from a slot, you simply push the eject button, and the card will pop out. After you remove the card, make sure that the slot is covered to keep dust from getting into the laptop. If the laptop doesn't have its own cover for the slot, you can purchase a *blanking plate*, which acts as an inserted dummy card.

PCI Express cards

Laptop computers can be upgraded today using smaller forms of PCI Express cards and are typically referred to as mini PCI Express (PCIe). These devices typically are fitted into the bottom of the laptop and are placed into a PCI Express (PCIe) x1 slot.

Upgrading Your Laptop

In the following sections, I show you how to upgrade a laptop by adding components such as RAM and hard disk space. Makes and models of laptops vary, but the basic concepts of adding and removing components can be applied to most laptop systems today.

Upgrading memory

To add memory to a laptop, you simply flip the laptop over and find the compartment that holds the RAM. This compartment is normally labeled with a symbol of a memory module, as opposed to the compartment that is labeled with what looks like a hard drive. If you are unsure what compartment to open, check the documentation for the laptop.

Remember to ground yourself before touching any internal computer components! After you ground yourself, you can then remove the old SODIMM module and insert the new memory module. When inserting a SODIMM into a laptop, be sure to gently place the module in the socket at an angle (see Figure 7-8) and then clamp it down in place.

Figure 7-8: Install a SODIMM into the laptop to add more memory to the laptop.

Adding hard disk space

Hard disk space can get eaten up quickly these days when storing media files like videos, MP3s, and pictures from digital cameras. It doesn't take many multimedia files (especially video) to fill up all your laptop's memory.

You can add disk space to the laptop in a number of different ways:

✦ **Add an external USB drive.** One of the most popular methods of adding disk space to the laptop is to connect an external USB hard drive to the laptop. This lets you carry the data to a different PC as well.

✦ **Get a better hard drive.** On most laptops, you can actually replace the original hard drive with a larger, manufacturer-approved hard drive. For example, you could upgrade from a 120GB hard drive to 160GB. Most laptops have a panel on the back that can be removed to replace the hard drive (as shown in Figure 7-9).

Figure 7-9: Replace the hard drive on a laptop for more storage.

✦ **Use portable unique storage.** Portable unique storage devices include a USB external hard disk, or a flash drive that plugs into a USB port (shown in Figure 7-10).

Figure 7-10:
Add storage
space by
using a USB
external
hard disk
(top) or
a USB
flash drive
(bottom).

Understanding Handheld Devices

Handheld devices are another type of portable device that is very popular
today but does not fall into the laptop category. A handheld device — also
known as a personal digital assistant (PDA) — is much smaller than a laptop
and uses touch-screen technology instead of a keyboard. You typically use
a stylus to touch the screen and choose what you want to do with the hand-
held device. Figure 7-11 shows a PDA being used with its stylus.

Most handheld devices are used to keep track of personal information, such
as your contacts or your schedule. PDAs today also have word processors
and spreadsheet programs so that the business user can do some work on
the PDA.

The PDA stores information in memory (RAM) instead of on a disk like a
laptop does. One of the benefits of storing the information in memory is
that the PDA can be activated quickly with no boot-up time. Another benefit
of a PDA is that the batteries typically last longer than the batteries found
in laptop computers. A PDA battery can last anywhere from 12 hours to 2
months without being recharged, depending on the vendor.

Most PDAs allow calendar and contact list synchronization with a desktop
PC by using a docking station. The PDA is placed into the docking station,
and the content on the PDA is synchronized with the desktop computer.

Figure 7-11:
A PDA
controlled
by a stylus.

Of the many different makes of PDAs, some of the popular ones are the Palm Pilot, and Compaq's iPAQ. A number of vendors such as HP and Dell have their own versions of PDAs as well. You can also have smart phones as handheld devices. Smart phones are cell phones that have extra features such as e-mail and calendar support. Examples of smart phones are BlackBerry and the Treo.

Troubleshooting Laptop Issues

When troubleshooting laptop-related issues and when answering A+ certification test questions, you should be familiar with a number of popular troubleshooting best practices:

✦ **Verify power.** When troubleshooting power-related issues, check whether the LEDs are lighting. You can also try swapping AC adapters to see whether the AC adapter is the problem, or the laptop is.

✦ **Remove unneeded peripherals.** Always try to streamline the situation by removing any unneeded peripherals to simplify the situation. After you get the system operating normally, you can then start adding the peripherals back one at a time to see which device is causing the problem.

✦ **Plug in an external monitor.** If you have display issues, try connecting an external monitor and use the display toggle to send the output to the monitor. This allows you to determine whether the video adapter is the problem or the actual LCD of the laptop.

✦ **Toggle Fn keys and hardware switches.** Always check the function keys to see whether you can toggle an option off and then on. Be wary of a Function Lock key on your system, which might cause the alternate features of keystroke to kick in.

✦ **Check the LCD cut-off switch.** If you don't have any display on the laptop, check whether the display is being sent to the LCD by using the display function key. Also check whether there is a cut-off switch on the laptop that is disabling the LCD.

✦ **Verify backlight functionality.** If you have trouble seeing the screen, check that the LCD is toggled on and that the brightness is high enough to see the output. If this checks out, the display backlight could be bad.

✦ **Check the wireless cut-off switch.** I fall for this every time! If you can't connect to a wireless network, the first thing you should check is whether the wireless card has been disabled via the wireless cut-off switch. Most laptops have this switch, and they are designed to give you a quick way to disable the wireless card. Mine is on the front of the laptop, so when I move the laptop on my lap, I end up turning off my wireless. Always check this switch first!

✦ **Numbers print instead of letters for some keys.** This is a popular feature on laptops. Some laptops have a Function Lock key that can be enabled so that the laptop prints numbers when certain keys are pressed. These keys are labeled with numbers on them as well. Another solution to the same problem could be that the Num Lock key has been enabled on the laptop.

Getting an A+

In this chapter, I discuss the different components that make up a laptop. These components include the battery, LCD, and keyboard. Be sure to remember the following facts about portable devices when preparing for the exam:

✦ The battery in a laptop is responsible for supplying power to the laptop and is charged by the AC adapter.

✦ The two types of LCDs used in laptops are active matrix and passive matrix.

+ Most laptops come with built-in ports, such as a network and modem port.

+ To upgrade memory on the laptop, you can add a SODIMM to an empty memory socket located in the laptop.

+ PCMCIA cards are used to expand on the laptop's capabilities.

 - *Type I cards* were used to add memory in the past.

 - *Type II* cards (the most popular these days) are used to add network cards and modems to the laptop.

 - *Type III* cards are used to add removable storage.

Prep Test

Dealing with Portable Computers

1 Bob calls you complaining that he can no longer connect to the wireless network with his laptop. He has using the wireless network for three months now, and nothing has changed on the wireless network. What would you get Bob to check first?

A ○ The WEP settings on his laptop

B ○ That the wireless cut-off switch on his laptop is not enabled or on

C ○ The WPA settings on his laptop

D ○ That SSID broadcasting is enabled on the router

2 Which battery type is the best battery type for laptops?

A ○ Alkaline

B ○ NiCad

C ○ Li-Ion

D ○ NiMH

3 Which of the following components makes the laptop truly portable?

A ○ Battery

B ○ AC adapter

C ○ DC controller

D ○ PC card

4 Which of the following components supports hot swapping?

A ○ Keyboard

B ○ SODIMM

C ○ PCMCIA cards

D ○ None of the above

5 Which type of PCMCIA card is used by network cards and modems?

A ○ Type I

B ○ Type II

C ○ Type III

D ○ Type IV

6 Which of the following statements is true for socket services?

A ○ Socket services is a set of BIOS routines that identifies when the card is inserted into the socket.

B ○ It provides an interface between the card and the device driver when the card is inserted.

C ○ It assigns I/O address and IRQ to the card.

D ○ Both A and C.

7 What does LCD stand for?

A ○ Liquid crystalline display

B ○ Liquid crystal device

C ○ Logical crystal display

D ○ Liquid crystal display

8 Which statements are true for an active-matrix LCD? (Select all that apply.)

A ❑ It is slow.

B ❑ It displays dull images.

C ❑ Each pixel is supported by its own transistor.

D ❑ Images are easy to view from angles.

E ❑ It displays low-quality pictures.

9 What type of memory module is used in laptop systems today?

A ○ SRAM

B ○ DIMM

C ○ SODIMM

D ○ SIMM

10 A user calls complaining that when he presses certain keys on his laptop, numbers print instead of the appropriate letters. What would you do?

A ○ Ask the user to ensure that the Cap Lock key is not enabled.

B ○ Ask the user to ensure that Num Lock key is not enabled.

C ○ Ask the user to not press the Shift key while typing.

D ○ Ask the user to ensure that the Shift Lock key is not enabled.

Answers

1 **B.** Laptop computers have a switch that allows you to temporarily turn off wireless functionality. *See Troubleshooting Laptop Issues.*

2 **C.** Li-Ion batteries are best suited for portable systems because they are lightweight and have a long lifetime. *Review "Different types of batteries."*

3 **A.** The battery is the component that most classifies the laptop as a portable device. *Check out "Identifying Portable Computer Components."*

4 **C.** *Hot swapping* means that the component can be inserted and removed without shutting down the system; this is a characteristic of PCMCIA cards. *Peruse "Adding a PC card."*

5 **B.** Network cards and modems are Type II cards. *Take a look at "Expanding on a Laptop."*

6 **A.** Socket services are the BIOS routines that identify when a PCMCIA card is inserted or removed from the socket. *Peek at "Expanding on a Laptop."*

7 **D.** LCD stands for liquid crystal display. *Look over "Learning about LCD Panels."*

8 **C, D.** Active-matrix LCDs produce high-quality images that are easy to read at angles. *Study "Learning about LCD Panels."*

9 **C.** Small Outline Dual Inline Memory Module (SODIMM) is the memory module type used in laptop systems today. *Refer to "Upgrading memory."*

10 **B.** Most laptops have a Num Lock option that when enabled, different letters will print numbers. These letters usually have a number printed on the key as well to display the functionality. *Examine "Understanding Handheld Devices."*

Dealing with Portable Computers

Book IV

Maintenance and Troubleshooting

Contents at a Glance

Chapter 1: Performing Preventive Maintenance

Exam Objectives

✔ Understanding the purpose and use of preventive maintenance tools and cleaners

✔ Identifying and applying maintenance techniques

*I*f you are the kind of person who takes your car for scheduled mainte-
nance, you probably have very few problems with your vehicle. On the
other hand, if you have repair work performed only when a problem crops
up, you risk always having a major component on your car developing
problems.

My point is this: Long-term, trouble-free use of any device involves practicing
preventive maintenance. You computer is no different. Performing regular
maintenance helps ensure trouble-free use. As a CompTIA A+ Certified
Professional, you need to know what maintenance should be done for your
computer. This chapter takes a look at why you want to perform maintenance,
what tools you can use, and how to prevent problems by controlling the
computer's environment and by maintaining specific computer components.

Preventive Maintenance 101

The goal of preventive maintenance is to prevent problems. Repairs —
remedial or unscheduled maintenance — are the flip side of the coin. The
main reasons to perform preventive maintenance are so that you can

✦ **Save time.** Even though it takes time to perform some maintenance
tasks, many can be automated (saving time). If a computer is well
maintained, you have fewer repairs to make (saving more time), and the
user ends up with less downtime (saving user's time).

✦ **Save money by increasing productivity.** Time is money. Users with less
downtime related to IT activities are more productive. Also, if you're
not spending time repairing computers, your time can be devoted to
other pursuits that can improve the overall IT infrastructure.

✦ **Protect data.** Data is the life of many organizations. A company that experiences a major loss of computerized data has little better than a 40% chance of reopening, better than a 50% chance of going under within two years, and only a 6% chance of recovering and surviving long-term. With these statistics in hand, you can easily see why many companies invest so heavily in backup technologies. In many cases, though, companies do not plan backups, or they forget about the data that resides on desktop computers — even desktop and laptop computers should be protected.

✦ **Improve performance.** All computer systems seem to slow down over time, and some simple steps can eliminate these slowdowns.

Although most businesses can equate everything to saving money, do not forget saving time, protecting data, and improving performance.

One of the biggest things that people do not do when it comes to preventive maintenance is create a schedule. When I bought my car, I got a schedule of maintenance activities and when they should be done.

Schedules are great, but if people do not follow them, what good are they? In addition to the schedule for my car (and so I don't forget), I also get warning lights in the car that remind me to perform maintenance. In the case of the computer environment, the more processes that can be scheduled and automated, the better. If you rely on people to do the task, they will invariable forget to do the task occasionally — or regularly — so automate when possible.

The other important point is to not bite off more than you can chew. That is, keep your maintenance manageable because if it is not, you probably will not do it. Planning to do three things and getting them done is better than planning a dozen and getting nothing done.

Although your schedule for tasks will vary from mine, and might be affected by the industry you are in, having a schedule for your tasks is important. If you do not have a schedule, your tasks will not get done. As I mention, schedules vary from one organization to another, or even within an organization. For instance, a computer on a factory shop floor will likely need its internal components cleaned and its vents checked for obstructions more frequently than a climate-controlled office. A schedule will likely have daily, weekly, monthly, quarterly, and annually scheduled tasks. A list of possible tasks includes

✦ Scanning for file system errors

✦ Scanning for virus and malware

✦ Updating virus and spam definitions and emergency boot disks

✦ Backing up data and CMOS settings

✦ Defragmenting hard drives

✦ Removing unnecessary hard drive files

✦ Cleaning screens, mice, keyboards, floppy and tape drives, and internal and external surfaces

✦ Ensuring that external system fans and vents, internal fans, and heat sinks are functioning properly and are free of dirt and debris

✦ Checking power protection devices as well as internal and external cable connections

Although lists will vary, at a minimum, you should remember these items on your list of preventive maintenance tasks.

Schedules vary depending on the computer's environment and use, but when looking at this list, you likely already have done some classification of daily, monthly, quarterly, and annual tasks.

With scheduled maintenance, you might have most tasks automated and performed remotely, but you should have an interval during which each computer is visited. Visiting the computer allows you to conduct visual and audio checks. This goes to the *see no evil, hear no evil* axiom. When you are near the computer, you might notice environmental issues, such as piles of paper surrounding a computer, blocking intake and output ventilation holes. Or you might hear a noisy fan that is close to failure. (When fans start to fail, they are often unbalanced when they start up, and then they slowly level out.)

Using Preventive Maintenance Tools

Your cache of preventive maintenance tools should include software and hardware devices. A balanced approach to maintenance includes a good number from each category.

Materials and equipment

For you to effectively perform preventive maintenance on your computer equipment, you need the correct tools with you. These tools include the following:

✦ **Compressed air:** Use to remove debris and dust from surfaces you don't want to touch, or to dust small corners.

✦ **Computer vacuum:** These vacuums can be used to remove dust and debris from a variety of surfaces within your computer, such as system fans.

A number of companies produce computer vacuums. One of the largest suppliers is Metropolitan Vacuum Cleaner, which makes the DataVac line (www.metrovacworld.com).

✦ **Cleaning cloths:** Cleaning cloths should be lint-free. If you use synthetic cloths, take care when you're working with cleaning chemicals because some chemicals can decompose the cloth or bleed out the dyes in them, which might leave residue on the surfaces you are trying to clean.

✦ **Cleaners and chemicals:** Most approved cleaners are mild, nonabrasive, and benzene- and ammonia-free. In most cases, using chemicals should be avoided for most surfaces, and either a dry cloth or a cloth moistened with water should be used.

✦ **Cleaning pads:** These soft, lint-free cloths are premoistened with mild cleaners. Cleaning pads are usually more of a convenience item than a necessity.

✦ **Manufacturer-approved cleaning kit:** Such kits are usually designed for components such as floppy disk drives and tape drives.

Never spray cleaners near vents, around keys, or on most surfaces (best to just say "never") of a computer and its peripherals because of liquid damage that can cause malfunctions or electrical arcing.

Software utilities

In addition to the hardware tools listed in the previous section, many software-based preventive maintenance tools are at your disposal, such as

✦ **Automatic update tools** for antivirus, antispam, Windows, and so on

✦ **Firmware updates,** although these should be applied only to respond to a problem because they sometimes create other problems

✦ **Driver updates** can be thought of as firmware updates

If you don't have a reason to update, don't apply updates out of hand.

✦ **OS-level tools,** such as defrag.exe, chkdsk.exe, Task Scheduler (covered in Book VI, Chapter 4), and ntbackup.exe (covered in Book VII, Chapter 3)

✦ **Third-party maintenance tools,** which are often available as packages from large companies (such as Symantec and McAfee) or from smaller, independent companies

✦ **Recovery or rescue boot CD,** which you can use to boot up the computer and repair a damaged OS, or rescue data from a nonbooting hard drive

Many companies provide a disc with prepackaged tools, or you can use a tool like BartPE (www.nu2.nu/pebuilder; covered in Book VII, Chapter 3).

Remember the hardware and software tools used for preventive maintenance.

Maintaining Environmental Controls

In addition to equipment-specific preventive steps, you can take several environmental steps to protect and preserve your computer. This section looks at those factors and elements.

Ventilation and airflow

When discussing equipment ventilation, only two factors come into play: external ventilation and internal ventilation. Poor ventilation can contribute to higher-than-recommended CPU temperatures or other damage. Components that are affected by these internal and external factors include power supplies; processors; hard disk drives; and motherboard components, such as chipsets and capacitors. To see how your system is performing, most modern motherboards and hard drives provide temperature sensors that can be accessed from software within your operating system.

External ventilation

The largest single variable in the area of external ventilation is actually the ambient room temperature. If the room is not cool enough, your computer will never be cool enough because the computer simply brings room air into the case to cool components, which is expected to be cooler than the air that is currently inside of the computer case. Room temperatures should be between 60° and 75° Fahrenheit (15°–25° degrees Celsius), but try to stay at the low end of that scale. Most computer manufacturers provide a recommended operating temperature range for their computers. If the computers are constantly used at higher temperatures, your failure rate will go up.

Just like extreme heat is bad, so is extreme cold, and many systems are exposed to extreme cold when being shipped to final destinations. If the outside temperature is substantially below your room temperature (especially if it is below freezing), you should let your computer acclimatize to its surroundings before plugging it in and powering it up. The length of time depends on the temperature variation and whether this warm-up is done within or outside of the packing material. If the computer is left in the packaging materials, the chance of condensation (which should be avoided) on internal components is reduced. In addition to condensation, thermal stress can damage the computer if it is heated too rapidly. (This is similar to pouring boiling water into a cold glass — do not try this at home! Cold items tend to be more brittle than warm items.)

Most computer cases (with intake vents to bring cool air into the case, and exhaust vents to expel the warm air) are constructed from metal to dissipate additional heat that is not exhausted. Objects placed around the case can block the vents and act as insulation for the case, preventing proper cooling of the computer from occurring. It's obvious enough that exhaust ports should remain open to allow heat to leave the inside of the computer, but if intake ports are blocked, the computer does not get a supply of cool air and will overheat. Without thinking, many people stack papers around and on their computer, blocking intakes.

People also push their computers back to free up desk space, thereby blocking rear exhaust ports. The computer placement and surrounding environment should be checked periodically to ensure that no airflow vents are blocked. In addition, many workstation areas built into desks do not take airflow into consideration, with solid doors on the front and only a small cable routing opening in the rear. Avoid placing computers or monitors in any space that reduces airflow to or from the unit.

Internal ventilation

Besides the environment around the computer, you can do a lot inside the case to aid or hinder ventilation or cooling. The rest of this section looks at factors that affect heat inside the case, and what can be done to reduce heat or increase airflow. To start, I should establish what the typical internal ventilation or cooling process is. As I mention in the previous section, most computer cases are made of metal so that internal heat can be dissipated into the surrounding air. Also part of the case design (and some are better designed than others) are air intake areas and exhaust areas. For tower cases of all form factors, air usually comes in from the front (along the bottom) and is expelled at the top in the back (usually through the power supply). Case form factors are examined back in Book I, Chapter 4.

For power supplies without fans, this exhaust is passive. More often than not, though, the power supply has a fan that provides active exhaust. In either case, this situation takes hot air from the internal components and runs that hot air over the power supply components, adding to the thermal stress that the power supply's components already suffer from. To aid airflow, some power supplies have two fans: one external and one internal. When airflow is increased, the expectation is that each cubic foot of air that passes through the space will be cooler. The internal vents or fan on the power supply open either to the front of the case or to the bottom. When they open to the bottom, they can take more heat away from the CPU.

To keep the airflow going in the correct direction, keep the case cover on and also keep rear expansion slot covers in place. Also make sure that you keep all front ventilation openings clear of obstructions. If you don't do this, the airflow won't go in the direction that the case designer planned.

Many case designers add extra fans and vents to aid airflow. Standard vent locations include an exhaust location on the back of the case below the power supply, which can accommodate a fan that exhausts rising hot air before the power supply has to deal with it. Intake fans are also popular in the lower front of the case, increasing the air intake function. Typical case airflow is illustrated in Figure 1-1, with a power supply having internal vents opening to the front of the case.

Because the fan on a heat sink typically blows air down onto the heat sink (helping with heat dissipation), another common area for vents and fans is on the side of the case, parallel with the heat sink fan, so that cooler air from outside of the case can be drawn directly to the CPU rather than moving the warmer air existing in the case over the CPU. To augment this airflow even more, some cases also include a funnel on the side of the case to directly channel the air to the heat sink fan. You can find out more about heat sinks and cooling in Book I, Chapter 4.

Less popular for most case designs (but sometimes added as an after-market addition) is a *blowhole,* which puts an exhaust port and a fan on the top of the case, drawing all the rising heat directly from the case. If heat is a major problem and this modification makes sense for you, it does give a lot of bang for its buck.

Figure 1-1:
Typical
airflow in a
tower case.
The darker
the arrow,
the warmer
the air.

**Book IV
Chapter 1**

**Performing
Preventive
Maintenance**

Internal airflow can also be improved by using a larger case, which just has more room for air to move around. There is no bigger heat challenge than taking a new multigigahertz processor (which generates more heat than slower processors) and adding it to a small microATX case with 4GB of RAM and a couple of 7200 rpm IDE hard drives. This is a recipe for thermal challenge, especially if noise reduction is also a goal; noise reduction usually means reducing the number or the speed of the system fans. By taking the same components and putting them in a full tower case, the additional air flow from the larger case will reduce the overall system heat.

Reducing the number of ribbon cables used on IDE devices can also improve airflow. These ribbon cables make little walls within the case that air has to go around. Ribbon cables can be replaced by rounded cables; or, the drives can be replaced with SATA drives, which have smaller cables to begin with. Book II, Chapter 5 has more information on hard drives and storage options.

In addition to the items already mentioned, wise placement of internal components can help air flow as well. If you're adding two hard drives to the computer, for example, placing them in adjacent bays might seem to make everything look nice and neat. The reality, though, is that such placement also reduces the airflow between the drives, and heat generated by the bottom drive will rise and increase the overall temperature in the top drive. Leaving the one-bay gap allows the system fans to draw some of that heat away from between the two drives, lowering the temperature of the top drive.

Humidity and liquids

In terms of computer maintenance, humidity is a double-edged sword and should be approached carefully. To reduce the chance of electrostatic discharge (ESD), keep a humidity level of 60%. To reduce corrosion, though, humidity levels should be as low as 35%. Areas that are too damp add to the corrosion of metal components on the motherboard, such as leads for capacitors and the hundreds of metal contact points in the computer. As if corrosion weren't bad enough, condensation is also an issue that can occur if that damp air is also warm when it makes contact with the cooler computer components. Because water is such a good conductor of electricity, condensation is never good and can lead to major electrical problems. Whenever possible, reduce the computer's exposure to overly humid areas, which can sometimes be done by moving the computer to the next room. You can also extend the cables for the monitor, keyboard, and mouse into the damp environment.

Just as how overly damp environments are bad, extremely dry environments increase the risk of static build-up and cause early wear on capacitors, rubber rollers, and some other components.

In addition to damp environments, spills are another source of liquid problems. In general, avoid using liquids around the computer. If keeping liquids away from the computer isn't possible (who am I to deny you your morning caffeine?), perhaps you can remove the computer from the area of the liquid. You can get special computer cases, keyboards, and accessories that have been hardened to protect them from moist environments, but often at the cost of cooling. To moisture-proof a case, most of the unit — including the ventilation openings — is covered with a rubberized material.

ESD

Electrostatic discharge (ESD) is caused when an electrical charge builds up on one surface, and then that surface comes in contact with another surface that has a lower charge. In most cases, your body builds up a charge when any synthetic materials rub against each other, such as your clothing, or your feet moving across a carpet. Then, when you come close to touching the computer (which is plugged into a grounded or bonded source), the electricity naturally attempts to balance itself out, often jumping the remaining gap and producing a surge of electricity and a spark. The discharge is normally absorbed by the device, and the extra electrical power is drained through the grounding device. However, if the gap were formed while you were inserting a piece of RAM or an expansion card, you could damage the slot or the chipset it is connected to.

Because static is more prevalent in dry locations, increase the relative humidity in the area to reduce the chance of static discharge. When servicing a computer, you can also use antistatic work mats and straps to keep you and the device you are working on at the same potential energy. Even though damage rarely results from small ESD, there is no sense in taking needless chances.

Do not forget the relationship between ESD and humidity. Lower ESD risks by increasing humidity.

Dirt and dust

Users are often surprised by how much dust and dirt collect inside a computer even though the room seems dust-free. Computers collect even more dust when they're placed on the floor, where they essentially act as air filters. In most cases, computers should be cleaned annually. If the computer has to be placed in a dirty or dusty location, though (such as on a factory floor), internal cleaning should be scheduled more frequently. Similar to water-hardened cases (read about those earlier in this chapter), special cases are available for dirty and dusty areas — again, usually at the cost of system cooling.

When system components are clear of dust and grime, they last longer and function properly. On several occasions, I have attempted to install a Windows OS only to get errors during the file copy phase. Normally, this would suggest bad media, but it has invariably been caused by a thick layer of dust and dirt very visibly covering all components. After I use compressed air to get rid of the grunge, the file copy problem invariably goes away. In addition to the dust causing various short circuits, it also causes heat to be retained by the components that are covered in the dust and dirt.

EMI

Electromagnetic interference (EMI), also known as *radio frequency interference (RFI)*, is caused by rapidly changing signals in electrical circuits radiating a field around the circuit. This might be caused naturally as part of the circuit's normal operation, or it might indicate a problem with the installation or operation of the circuit. This interference often affects AM frequency bands and other low-frequency devices, such as speakers. If you have been in a boardroom with a speaker phone or radio nearby, you will often hear EMI caused by ring signals being sent to the occupants' cell phones. These signals precede the phone ringing and usually cause a static noise on the speaker or radio. EMI caused by cell phones is why cell phones are banned in certain areas of hospitals — they can disrupt electronic medical devices within about 3 feet.

Solutions to EMI include physical isolation of devices, installation of dedicated circuits, and power conditioning of incoming power.

Power, UPS, and suppressors

Power conditioning comprises cleaning or regulating power that is supplied to devices. In addition to conditioning power and reducing EMI, surge suppressors and a UPS (uninterruptable power supply) can provide protection to your computers and electronic devices. If you are using these power conditioning devices, check the status of these devices periodically. Most major UPS have self-test buttons or automatic tests that can be scheduled and reported to administrators, as well as reporting on load levels and battery health. To help UPS and other power protection devices, using dedicated circuits reduces the chance of other devices on the circuit causing EMI, other line noise, power surges, or circuit overloads.

In addition to keeping the power clean and available, grounding equipment is important. All computer equipment comes with *polarity base* plugs (with one side larger than the other), and most have *ground connectors* (the third connector on the plug).

Some users who need extension cords will cheat and get two-conductor cords, thereby removing the grounding facility for their equipment. This should always be avoided because of the risk of damage to equipment from static discharge.

If power interruptions or blackouts are expected, as happens in some areas of the country regularly, computer equipment should either be protected by a UPS or shut down when not in use. This reduces the chance of data corruption from power loss. If electrical storms are a risk, equipment should be protected by a UPS or unplugged, preventing possible damage from a lightning strike.

Aside from the previous points, many people ask, "Should I usually leave my computer on or shut it off?" There are two schools of thought on that, which should not be a surprise. Some factors that affect this decision are

✦ **The convenience of having the device ready to work:** If you visit your computer regularly, you might want to keep it on.

✦ **Power consumption:** Running your computer 24/7 will consume more power than shutting it down when you aren't using it. Many people shut down systems that won't be used again for 8 or 24 hours. This means either shutting down every night or shutting down just for weekends.

✦ **Thermal stress:** Thermal stress happens every time components heat or cool because they expand and contract. This expansion and contraction causes failures to occur. Leaving equipment on for longer periods reduces this problem.

✦ **Wear-out:** Most equipment has an expected lifespan measured in hours or days. This rating is the Mean Time Before Failure (MTBF). If components are forced to run continuously, they will hit their usage limits more quickly, so this problem is reduced by powering items down or having them enter a low-power mode.

The real answer is that you should find the solution that works better for you and your organization.

Completing Maintenance Tasks

With the principles of preventive maintenance under your belt, take a look at what can be done for specific components. This section looks at each of the major components that make a modern computer, and looks at what tasks should be taken to properly maintain each of them.

Case and components

To keep most components in good health, regularly perform maintenance on your systems. The frequency for these tasks depends on the task, with external tasks being performed daily, weekly, or monthly; and internal tasks being performed monthly, quarterly, or annually. The following tasks should be part of your maintenance routine. Make sure that you

+ **Have good airflow both inside and around the case. This will help prolong the system life.**

+ **Periodically clean the inside with a vacuum or compressed air to ensure that dust and dirt do not built up on the components or fans.**

+ **Verify that all the fans function.**

+ **Check the processor temperature by using internal sensor chips, relative temperature by touch, or a digital infrared thermometer.**

+ **Ensure that the heat sink and fan are clean and free of dirt and debris.**

+ **Check the position of expansion cards and removable chips to verify that they are correctly seated.**

 Newer technology for slots has reduced the chance of chip creep. Still, *chip creep* can occur from thermal expansion and contraction, which happens during the heating and cooling of components. These heat changes can cause components — such as removable chips — to shift position or work their way out of their mounting clips.

+ **Check that external and internal cables are properly seated and connected.**

 Some of these cables can work loose from movement of the case or thermal expansion.

If you have systems that use custom CMOS settings (less of an issue these days), ensure that you have a good backup of the CMOS settings. To learn more about CMOS settings, review Book II, Chapter 4.

Power supplies

Very few maintenance tasks are associated specifically with power supplies. You should

+ Verify that your power protection devices are working properly to ensure system integrity.

+ Ensure that power outputs are correct. This can be verified with the use of a multimeter or power supply–testing tool. Both of these methods are covered in Book IV, Chapter 2.

✦ Verify that the power output is still sufficient if system components have changed.

✦ Make sure that the fans are clean.

Monitors

With their lack of moving parts and low number of failures, monitors are often overlooked during the maintenance process. However, even though they are relatively trouble free, include them in your maintenance routine to ensure that they continue to provide trouble-free operation.

✦ **Ensure that the monitor or OS power-saving feature is turning off the monitor properly.** This not only saves power but also prevents image burn-in of a static image onscreen.

✦ **Make sure the monitor has proper ventilation.** Ensure that the vents on the unit are not covered. With traditional CRT (cathode ray tube) monitors having large, mostly flat, tops, I have often seen users use the top of a monitor for an extra filing area for papers, blocking the upper exhaust openings. Or, users with cluttered desks fill in the area around the base, blocking the lower air intake openings. Even LCD (liquid crystal display) monitors generate heat, so ventilation is still important to get rid of their heat.

✦ Always check the owner's manual for the correct cleaning solutions for your monitor. The screens of many monitors these days have special antiglare coatings that are not supposed to be cleaned with standard glass-cleaning products. When in doubt, use a dry cloth or a cloth moistened with deionized water for troublesome spots.

Always apply cleaners to a cloth — not directly to the monitor. This warning should also be applied to any computer equipment that you are cleaning with liquid cleaners.

Keyboards and mice

For keyboards and mice, preventive maintenance includes checking that cables are not damaged by keyboard trays or other external forces. Verify that they are properly connected and have not been pulled loose.

For keyboards, proper maintenance consists of the following:

✦ **Prevent spills.** Ensure that food and liquids are kept away from the keyboard's spill area, which is usually about 12 inches (30 centimeters).

✦ **Clean carefully.** If a key's surface appears dirty, you can clean key caps with a cloth moistened with a mild cleaner or water.

Hold the keyboard upside down during this process to keep any debris from falling between the keys.

If debris between the keys is causing key motion problems, use compressed air to blow it out.

If there is no issue, you might want to leave the status quo because using compressed air could move debris to a position that does cause an issue.

How you keep your mice clean and happy depends on what type of mice you have:

✦ **Optical mice:** Verify that the optics are clean and that the surface that it is used on is not too glossy. Some tabletops and mouse pads might not be suitable for optical mice, so add or remove a nonglossy mouse pad as needed for mouse problems.

✦ **Mechanical mice:** Check the mouse ball and the mouse pad.

　• *Ball:* Remove the mouse ball's retaining disc and the ball. Then remove any dirt collected on the rollers inside the mouse by using a cotton swab moistened in alcohol.

　• *Pad:* Verify that the mouse pad is clean. If the pad is cloth, replace it regularly. Pads tend to accumulate oils and other little nasties from your hand. That build-up, when paired with dust from the surroundings, accumulates on the mouse rollers.

Drives

Regular preventive maintenance for all types of drives includes verifying that cables are properly connected and that sufficient power is being supplied.

Hard drives

For hard drives specifically, regular preventive maintenance includes

✦ **Running Check Disk scans** of your hard drive for errors

　See Book VI, Chapter 4, to find out more about Check Disk (chkdsk.exe).

✦ **Scanning for viruses with an antivirus program,** which, together with regular backups of important data, reduces the chance of problems that could affect the integrity of your data

✦ **Defragmenting your hard drive** to keep disk access at an optimal level

✦ **Regularly monitoring the temperature and free space** of your hard drives and CPU

You can monitor your hard drives locally with tools like SpeedFan (`www.almico.com/speedfan.php`), or remotely with SNMP (Simple Network Management Protocol — the TCP/IP device management and monitor protocol) tools like MRTG (`www.mrtg.com`) and Cacti (`www.cacti.net`). These tools gather temperature readings from your *S.M.A.R.T. (Self-Monitoring, Analysis and Reporting Technology)* hard drive, which is incorporated into most new drives. In addition, you can gather S.M.A.R.T. messages from your Event Viewer.

Locally, Windows XP and Windows Vista provide warning messages when hard drive space is very low (less than 200MB).

✦ **Avoiding vibration and shock**

 Vibration and shock to the hard drive should be avoided because either can cause substantial data errors.

Floppy and tape drives

Floppy drives can be maintained with the following actions:

✦ **Regular head cleaning** (based on manufacturer recommendations for frequency) with head cleaning kits

✦ **Head alignment verification**

 To verify the drive's head alignment, format a new disk and then try to read it in other floppy drives. If the disk is unreadable, you might suspect an alignment problem in one of the drives.

When dealing with tape drives, you also want to clean the heads with the manufacturer-recommended cleaning tools. This should be done based on the manufacturer's recommended frequency, which is usually based on hours of drive use. Verification on data recovery should also be regularly tested by attempting to read the data from the media.

CD/DVD drives

CD/DVD drives are optical drives, so occasionally the optical components inside the drive might get dirty. However, this is rare when compared with media problems, which is usually where the problems arise. Cleaning kits for the optical components are available, and you should check with your drive manufacturer for recommended use.

Storage media

To have consistent access to data you recorded on storage media, you need to make sure that you protect that media:

✦ **Scratches and pits:** If your optical media is scratched or pitted to a point that it is unreadable, you might be able to repair or polish it by using a commercial repair kit or Brasso metal polish.

✦ **Deep scratches:** For very deep scratches in optical media, check whether your local video store has a repair service.

✦ **Proper labeling:** Optical discs can be damaged by glue found in many types of labels, so a felt-tipped marker is often the safest choice for labeling a CD/DVD, unless you have LightScribe media and burner.

✦ **Body oils:** For all media, avoid physical contact with the media surface. Oil and dirt from your skin can damage the material immediately or over time.

Each type of media has a recommend shelf life, as estimated in Table 1-1; your mileage may vary based on media quality and storage conditions. All media should be kept in a clean, dry, cool, low-light place. If the media is magnetic, keep it away from electromagnetic fields.

Table 1-1	Shelf Life for Recorded and Stored Media	
Media Type	*Examples*	*Shelf Life*
Flexible magnetic media	Floppy disks, magnetic tape, Bernoulli cartridge drives	10 years
Rigid magnetic media	Hard disk drives, removable cartridge drives	15 years
Writable optical media	CD-RW, DVD-RW	5–10 years

Laptops

Laptops have their own maintenance issues, including screen types, battery usage, charging, storage, and theft.

Before cleaning a laptop screen, check the owner's manual for proper cleaning instructions. Many laptop LCD screens have special coatings or mesh filters that can be damaged if you don't know what you're doing.

With each new generation of laptop computers comes a new generation of batteries, each with its recommended care procedures. Nickel-cadmium (NiCad) batteries were replaced by nickel-metal hydride (NiMH) batteries, which were replaced by lithium-ion (Li-Ion) batteries, which were replaced by lithium-ion polymer (Li-Poly) batteries. The latest generations of batteries do not develop charge memories when not fully discharged between charges, cannot be overcharged, and have a better weight-to-power ratio.

One drawback of lithium-based batteries is that at room temperature, they lose 20% of their charge capacity per year, starting at the time of manufacturing. That means that a three-year-old lithium battery will have a maximum charge of about 40%t of what it was when the battery was purchased. This charge loss can be reduced to 6% per year if the battery is stored at 0° Celsius or 32° Fahrenheit, but then the battery needs to be warmed for over 24 hours to return to a usable temperature.

With Li-Ion and Li-Poly batteries, you no longer need to fully discharge batteries. In fact, it is best to keep them topped off; deep discharges can reduce their life.

To keep your battery in tip-top shape, you should let the battery run down (except for Li-Ion and Li-Poly batteries) and perform a charging cycle every few weeks. In general, you can expect to replace your battery every four to five years. If your laptop is going to be used while connected to a power source, some manufacturers recommend removing the battery. See your owner's documentation to find out whether this applies to you.

When moving your laptop between locations, you should use a travel case that is sized and designed appropriately for your computer. This case serves two main purposes: to keep the system free from dust and dirt, and to protect it from shock.

Because laptops are so portable, they are ideal targets for theft, and all come with a lockdown point that you can use with a computer lockdown cable or motion sensor. A *lockdown cable* — a thick, vinyl-coated braided-metal cable, like the cables used for bicycle locks — needs to be attached to an immovable object. A motion sensor sounds a loud alarm when the laptop is moved. You can see samples of each of these at the Targus Web site (`www.targus.com/us/accessories_security.asp`). One of these two types of devices should be used for a laptop when you are traveling, as well as in your office.

Printers and scanners

Dust, dirt, and debris tend to be the three big issues with printers. Much of this can be removed with a vacuum, compressed air, and a cleaning cloth, but here are some other cleanliness issues to take into account to keep your printers running smoothly:

+ **Pickup rollers:** Printer pickup rollers can become dirty and should be cleaned with cotton swaps moistened with alcohol.

+ **Print heads:** The print heads on inkjet printers can become clogged and should be cleaned through built-in cleaning procedures on the printer. (See your owner's manual for the exact procedure for your printer.)

If the printer has its print head as part of the ink cartridge, you can also soak the heads in warm water to clear clogs.

+ **Fans and vents:** Laser printers often have fans and vents that should be checked and cleaned out.

+ **Worn components:** Many laser printers have maintenance kits that should be purchased and installed as necessary. These kits often replace components that wear out, such as pickup rollers.

+ **Calibration text:** Many printers also have a calibration routine and a test or diagnostics page that ensures that multicolor print heads are all in alignment and that all print mechanisms are functioning. As part of your maintenance routine, you should print the diagnostics page.

Scanners, like printers, can suffer from the dust, dirt, and debris issues. Scanners tend to have a sealed body, which keeps the internal optics clean, but they usually need to be opened every year or two to clean the internal components. During regular maintenance, only the deck (the glass *platen*) of the scanner needs to be cleaned; use a glass-grade cleaner unless your scanner has a special coating. As always, never spray the cleaner on the surface, apply it to a cloth and wipe the surface. In addition to this issue, scanners usually have a locking mechanism that should be used when moving the scanner, which will keep the scanner properly calibrated.

Because scanners and printers suffer from a build-up of dust and dirt, try to place them in areas that are clean and dust free. I have seen people save money by not purchasing a printer stand, leaving the printer on a carpeted floor, only to pay more than the cost of a stand in additional cleaning and repair services.

Getting an A+

In this chapter, you should remember

+ Perform preventive maintenance to increase productivity and save time and money.

+ Conduct preventive maintenance tasks at scheduled intervals.

+ Standard tools for preventive maintenance include cleaning materials, vacuums, compressed air, and software tools, such as `defrag.exe` and `chkdsk.exe`.

+ Factors that affect computer lifespan are heat and humidity, ESD, dirt and dust, and incoming power issues.

+ Each major component has specific maintenance that can or should be carried out.

Prep Test

1 Which of the following is *not* an acceptable cleaner for computer components?

- A ○ Alcohol and cotton swabs
- B ○ Dry, lint-free cloth
- C ○ Ammonia-based cleaner
- D ○ Cloth moistened with water

2 Which of the following does *not* help improve computer airflow?

- A ○ Adding exhaust fans
- B ○ Leaving spaces between devices
- C ○ Keeping vents clear of debris and dust
- D ○ Using ribbon cables where possible

3 Which of the following is *not* a reason to implement a preventive maintenance schedule?

- A ○ Reduce office temperature
- B ○ Improve performance
- C ○ Protect data
- D ○ Improve productivity

4 Which two items will help ensure that your preventive maintenance plans are followed?

- A ❑ Filing completed checklists
- B ❑ Keeping the number of tasks limited
- C ❑ Automating tasks
- D ❑ Purchasing colored index tabs for files

5 What tools will help with hard drive maintenance? (Choose two.)

- A ❑ `defrag.exe`
- B ❑ `fdisk.exe`
- C ❑ `chkdsk.exe`
- D ❑ `mem.exe`

6 What is one of the problems caused by low relative humidity?

- A ○ EMI
- B ○ PKI
- C ○ ESD
- D ○ TCP

7 Which of the following can become an issue if you keep your computer running all the time?

A ○ Thermal expansion

B ○ Wear-out

C ○ Chip creep

D ○ EMI

8 What factors affect the storage life of computer media? (Choose two.)

A ❑ Media length

B ❑ Age of facility

C ❑ Temperature

D ❑ Humidity

9 What is usually found in vendor-supplied, laser printer maintenance kits?

A ○ Paper pickup rollers

B ○ Replacement power cable

C ○ Paper

D ○ Toner cartridges

Answers

1 **C.** Ammonia- and benzene-based cleaners are too strong for most computer components. Although alcohol is not used as often as dry or water-moistened cloths, it is still acceptable for many computer-related components. *See "Materials and equipment."*

2 **D.** Ribbon cables create small walls in the path of airflow and can be replaced with rounded cables to improve airflow in most situations. *Review "Internal ventilation."*

3 **A.** Reducing office temperature is something that can help systems as part of a preventive maintenance plan, but it is not a reason to implement the plan. *Check out "Preventive Maintenance 101."*

4 **B, C.** Keeping the number of tasks limited keeps the process from becoming unwieldy. Automating tasks removes the need for action on a user's part, which also promotes having the tasks performed. Filing and indexing physical files will not promote having the tasks completed but can be used to report on what has been completed. *Peruse "Preventive Maintenance 101."*

5 **A, C.** `defrag.exe` and `chkdsk.exe` are both tools that can be used to perform standard maintenance on your hard drives. *Take a look at "Software utilities."*

6 **C.** When relative humidity is too low, there is an increased risk of static build-up and electrostatic discharge (ESD). *Peek at "Humidity and liquids."*

7 **B.** When devices are running all the time, they can wear out. *Look over "Power, UPS, and suppressors."*

8 **C, D.** Media's storage life is greatly influenced by its storage environment, which ideally will be cool, dry, properly lit for archival purposes, and free of EMI sources. *Study "Storage media."*

9 **A.** Most laser printer maintenance kits include replacements for components that wear out, such as pickup rollers, as well as cleaning materials for the inside of the printer. *Refer to "Printers and scanners."*

Chapter 2: Troubleshooting Procedures and Guidelines

Exam Objectives

✔ Identifying uses and purpose for standard troubleshooting tools

✔ Understanding and applying troubleshooting techniques to isolate and resolve problems for major computer system components

In the preceding chapter, I show you preventive maintenance routines for your system's devices. Still, no matter how much preventive maintenance you perform, "something" will eventually go wrong. This chapter continues with the topic of troubleshooting devices — *after* those "somethings" go wrong.

As a CompTIA A+ Certified Professional, you will be required to repair components from many areas of the computer system. This chapter covers the hardware and software tools of the trade that will help you complete troubleshooting tasks quickly. You will also review the major components found in computer systems and address any troubleshooting steps related to those components.

Identifying Troubleshooting Tools

A good troubleshooting arsenal contains many weapons, both hardware and software. After all, not every computer problem is related to the hardware. And even when it is, software tools can sometimes help with the diagnosis. If you are doing field support, create a troubleshooting kit in a handy carrying case with all the tools you use most often.

Hardware tools

To properly troubleshoot equipment-related issues, you want to use the right tool for the job. This section takes a look at the hardware tools you should have, and what jobs you will perform with them.

Multimeter

You could buy a meter to measure voltage (volts; V), a meter to measure resistance (ohms; Ω), and a meter to measure continuity and current (milliamps [mA] and amps [A]). Or you could just buy a *multimeter,* which is a combination of all of these different types of meters.

Make sure that you know what the multimeter is capable of measuring. You will need to identify the proper times to use one, although not details of its operation.

You can find both digital and analog multimeters, and your choice is based solely on personal preference. Many people find digital multimeters easier to read. Also, when testing resistance in circuits, digital meters use only 1.5V rather than 9V, and the lesser voltage is less likely to damage the circuit.

Both digital and analog multimeters are shown in Figure 2-1. The meter usually has a dial that lets you choose what you want to measure and also the scale that you are measuring on, such as 20VDC or 200VDC.

Always use a scale higher than the reading that you are taking to avoid damaging the multimeter. The closer the scale is to the value you are attempting to measure, the more accurate your reading will be.

Make sure you return the dial back to the off position when you are done with the multimeter, or else you find a dead battery when you go to use it the next time.

Some other features to look for in a multimeter are

+ **Size**

 • *Large:* Large meters are usually more feature-rich.

 • *Small:* For computer work, a smaller meter will likely be more convenient to transport with your troubleshooting gear.

+ **Overload protection:** Protects you when voltage or current exceeds what the meter is capable of handling

+ **Auto ranging:** Automatically selects the appropriate scale but usually allows for manual override

+ **Detachable probe leads:** Allows for greater flexibility by substituting different leads for different jobs

+ **Audible continuity test:** Allows you to perform the test without having to look at the meter, as it beeps when there is continuity

+ **Automatic power off:** Conserves battery life in the meter

It's a pain when you discover that the meter was left on and that the battery died.

Figure 2-1:
Analog and digital multimeters can both be used to test many system components.

✦ **Automatic display hold:** Keeps the latest stable reading visible on the display, making it easier to record the value if you cannot see the meter when you are using the probes

✦ **Minimum and maximum trap:** Records the highest and lowest readings in the same manner as the automatic display hold

When measuring resistance, always remove the power from the device you are checking, unlike when you're checking voltage, which is done when the device has power.

In "Power supplies and batteries," later in this chapter, you see how to use a multimeter to verify voltages coming from power supply hard drive connectors.

Antistatic mat and strap

In my discussion of electrostatic discharge (ESD) in the preceding chapter, one of the best solutions to avoid ESD is to use a grounding or bonding strap, as shown in Figure 2-2. In addition to wrist straps, you can get

antistatic mats for your workbench or floor. Both mats and wrist straps are made of nonconductive material and can be grounded to prevent charge build-up.

Taking ESD reduction steps, such as using a wrist strap, is always required when working on computer equipment.

Figure 2-2:
An antistatic wrist strap with a removable clip, allowing the plug to be used with some hardware.

Dealing with screws

This section introduces you to the screws that are common to computer systems, and also talks about problems that you might encounter with screws (such as dropping them).

Many types of pickup tools can be helpful when that screw, jumper, or other component slips from your fingertips. In some cases, you have no other means of retrieving that component where it fell. The two varieties of pickup tools — mechanical and magnetic — and both are inexpensive and have their uses. As long as you have one in your kit, you will be well off.

Some magnetic pickup tools, such as floor sweepers, have extremely high-power magnets that could damage hard drives. And although most small pickup tools use low-power magnets that are safe near hard drives, avoid placing them next to floppy disk media.

To go along with the pickup tool for small bits and pieces, tweezers and needle-nosed pliers are beneficial when it comes to removing and placing small elements, such as jumpers.

And even though a screwdriver is not really a glamorous tool, it will be your most-used tool. In addition to a standard screwdriver, you need a multibit screwdriver as well as a set of *security bits,* which have a small hole in their center, allowing you to easily remove security screws that have small posts in their centers. These screws are another anti-tamper step that some manufacturers have introduced to help corporations reduce theft of expensive computer components, but they can cause a repair to come to a grinding halt as you try to figure out how to get into the case.

Because you will find two common sizes of hex nuts on computers, having both ³⁄₁₆" and ¼" nut drivers handy will make working with them much easier. You use ³⁄₁₆" nuts for *case standoffs* (the small posts that support the motherboard and keep it off the surface of the case) and for the posts that mount most of the ports on the back of the computer, such as monitors and printers. You use ¼" nuts for expansion slots, power supplies, and case panels.

With all the screws on computers, you would think that you would be able to find one when you need it, but that is not always the situation, so having a supply of standard screws on hand (listed in Table 2-1) will be a great help to you. Compaq (and now HP) computers have standardized the two hex screw sizes for optical drives and hard drives, and they use the hard drive screws for everything else. They have also been nice enough to usually provide a few spares for adding extra drives, which you will usually find screwed into the inside of the case somewhere.

Table 2-1	Standard Screws	
Description	*Thread*	*Length*
Hard drive	6-32	5/32" (4mm)
Case	6-32	3/16" (4.8mm)
Optical and floppy drive	M3	1/4" (6.35mm)
Cable plates and ports	4-40	3/16" (4.8mm)
Case fan	Self-tapping	7/16" (11mm)

**Book IV
Chapter 2**

**Troubleshooting
Procedures and
Guidelines**

When disassembling systems — especially laptops — you should keep track where screws and other small parts come from, even going to the point of making a quick diagram.

Miscellaneous tools

You need a variety of other hardware tools in your troubleshooting kit. This list presents a hodge-podge of miscellaneous tools of all sorts.

✦ **Digital infrared thermometers:** Use these devices to find the temperature of CPUs, memory, and other internal devices without having to come into contact with them.

✦ **Mirrors:** It is surprising how many times you need to read information on components that are already mounted inside the computer or need to see exactly where something has fallen. A small mirror can be a big help, and one mounted on an extension arm can be even better. This is useful when you want to see jumper settings or read hidden serial or model numbers. Again, for the cost, mirrors are well worth the investment.

✦ **Flashlight:** The inside of computer cases can be dark, and when you are working on a computer under a desk, the inside of the computer is even darker. Having a small flashlight in your set of tools is often more convenient than moving the computer to a location with more light.

✦ **Case cracker:** Some cases come apart easily after removing all the screws; others do not. The original Macintosh computer was one of those that did not come apart easily — and by design. A *case cracker* helps you separate the pieces of a case that do not easily come apart, without causing the damage that a flathead screwdriver would cause. This device, which comes in a range of sizes and shapes, is inserted in the gap of the case and then used to separate the sections. They were commonly used for Macintosh computers and monitors, which have a groove where the two halves of the case come apart.

✦ **Monitor adjustment tools:** Vertical and horizontal hold isn't an issue with today's monitors. In the past, though, it was not uncommon to make adjustments to this element of the monitor. The adjustment knobs — usually located inside the case to keep users from playing with them — had to be reached with special tools. Monitor adjustment tools are shown amongst the tools in Figure 2-3 (from left to right: multibit screwdriver with case cracker tool, $\frac{3}{16}$" hex nut bit, two monitor adjustment tools, wire cutter/stripper, diagonal cutter, extension pickup magnet, manual pickup tool, and extension mirror).

✦ **Loopback plugs:** *Loopback plugs* serve two purposes: as a diagnostic tool and to eliminate errors messages. When you test parallel and serial ports, it is advantageous to have the system think that there is something connected to the port so that you can test sending and receiving data though the port. Rather than testing a serial port using a modem or null modem cable, and a remote computer to communicate with, you can use a loopback plug to test the port without any outside devices. Many multiport gigabit network adapters ship with loopback plugs, which usually look like a short network cable, an inch or two long, with only one connector on it. This connector makes the network port think

that it is plugged into a switch or hub, thus eliminating error messages from the operating system regarding errors with that port.

Figure 2-3: Keep these tools in your trouble- shooting kit.

✦ **Wire cutters and strippers:** There are always cables and cable ties that need to be cut, or stripped, or connected within the computer. Having a wire cutter, diagonal cutter, or wire stripper handy makes that job much easier. To go along with that, a knife or a box cutter can be useful tools when making detailed cuts.

✦ **Electrical tape:** After your cutting is done, use electrical tape to wrap any exposed wires.

✦ **Slot covers:** All slots should be covered, so you need a few spare slot covers with you for those cases in which you are removing a card from a system.

✦ **Drive faceplates:** Similar to slot covers, drive faceplates should be replaced when you remove a drive from a computer. These tend to not be standard across systems, so having spares that actually fit might be a little more challenging.

✦ **Mounting kit/adapter:** When mounting 3.5" drives in a system, you may choose to mount them in 5.25" bays, although that requires using a mounting kit or adapter. Typically, this kit consists of a couple of side rails to make the drive wider.

**Book IV
Chapter 2**

Troubleshooting
Procedures and
Guidelines

✦ **Extra cables:** Spare internal cables, especially the new 80-wire ATA-100/ATA-133 cables, are useful to have in your kit, as well as other standard internal and network cables. These help you diagnose cable or device issues. If you can replace a questionable cable with a known good cable, you can rule out another element that might be causing the problem.

✦ **Cable testers:** Network and other cable testers can be used to verify not only continuity, but also configuration of cables. In many cases, when people crimp their own network cables, errors can be made with pin configurations.

The "Hardware tools" section should be reviewed to a point where you can identify when you would want to use each type of tool.

Diagnostic software

In addition to various hardware tools that are available to help you troubleshoot a system, various software tools can help you out, too.

Boot/rescue disk

To deal with many hard drive issues, you want a boot disk at your disposal. Just booting your system with a Windows boot disk lets you determine whether you can access your hard drive. But to really be able to accomplish a troubleshooting task, or to recover a system, you need a little more power — which you can find in many third-party boot disks and bootable CDs. Most of these solutions include a variety of testing and troubleshooting tools:

✦ **Knoppix:** www.knoppix.net

✦ **BartPE:** www.nu2.nu/pebuilder

✦ **System Rescue:** www.sysresccd.org/Main_Page

✦ **Microsoft Diagnostics and Recovery Toolkit (DART):** www.microsoft.com/windows/enterprise/products/dart.aspx

Software diagnostic tools

Diagnostic tools are available with which you can test several major components in your computer, including (but not limited to) drives, processors, memory, serial and parallel ports, keyboards and mice, and network adapters. These testing tools typically verify integrity of components or stress components by performing multiple random or sequential reads and writes on the system.

BIOS and hard drive self-test

In addition to other software solutions, many BIOS routines include built-in testing software. These routines usually can test disks, RAM, processors, and other system components. Like the diagnostic software, these tests will usually perform random or sequential reads and writes to verify the integrity of the components that are being tested.

In addition to these tools, all the monitoring-performance tools listed in Book VI, Chapter 3 can also be used for troubleshooting. Make sure you know the appropriate uses for each tool in both of these chapters.

The Art of Troubleshooting

In this section, you take a look at some general factors and then perform an overview of troubleshooting specific components. This chapter covers these components in the same manner as in the preventive maintenance chapter, Book IV, Chapter 1, by touching on each major component one at a time.

Troubleshooting basics

Computer components used to be very expensive. In today's market, though, most components have been turned into commodities and can be purchased very cheaply. Because so many elements are so cheap, replacing components is now more common than repairing them. Because of the reduced cost, you can easily have a small supply of spare components and test components by swapping in new and reliable components.

Most failures in components occur either near installation or around the expected wear-out period; very few components fail during the normal use period. With technology improvements proceeding at their current rates, technology commonly becomes functionally obsolete prior to hitting the wear-out period for that device. This can be illustrated by CD and DVD drives over the last few years, where most CD drives that fail will be replaced with a CD-RW, CD-RW/DVD combo, or DVD-RW drive.

Physical environment

To troubleshoot and repair computer systems, you need a large, clean work surface and enough available power connections to power the equipment you are testing as well as your diagnostic tools. You should use antistatic straps and mats for working on equipment and a place to organize your tools nearby.

When doing remote repairs at a client site, you want your travel tools, an antistatic wrist strap, and a clean space to work, although the latter is sometimes difficult to achieve in a cluttered cube farm.

Audio and visual troubleshooting

After you conduct your interview to get a list of symptoms (as suggested in Book I, Chapter 2), you will often start the first stage of active troubleshooting by looking for audio and visual cues that could be the cause of the described symptoms. This can come in the form of listening to *POST (Power-on Self-Test)* errors or beep codes or an examination of the physical environment.

POST errors

Each BIOS manufacturer has its own diagnostic codes that identify specific errors. You need to consult documentation for the specific beep codes for your BIOS. Many motherboard manufacturers use codes similar to the original IBM POST codes, which are summarized in Table 2-2. If you get only one beep, all is good. In some cases, these beeps are also accompanied by a diagnostic code, which you also have to look up in the BIOS documentation.

Table 2-2	IBM POST Beep Codes
Beep Code	*Description*
One short beep	Normal POST; system is okay
Two short beeps	POST error; error code shown onscreen
No beep	Power supply or system board problem
Continuous beep	Power supply, system board, or keyboard problem
Repeating short beeps	Power supply or system board problem
One long and one short beep	System board problem
One long and two short beeps	Display adapter problem (MDA, CGA)

Connectors and ventilation

As part of the visual troubleshooting, you will also likely check that intake/exhaust ports and vents are free of obstructions and that cables and connectors are securely attached. As part of the audio troubleshooting, you want to verify that you hear typical sounds coming from your computer, such as fans running properly and hard drives spinning. If the computer is too quiet, it may lead you to fan failures or other sources for your problems.

CMOS and BIOS

Modern CMOS settings are numerous and easy to access. If you have a computer that requires specific nondefault settings to operate correctly, you want to verify that default settings have not been loaded back onto the system. This can happen if certain jumpers have been moved on the motherboard, the CMOS battery fails, firmware has been upgraded, or you note a strange failure within the system. Improper changes to the CMOS settings (such as boot order, video memory, power options, disk detection, swapping floppy drive letters, and CPU timing) can render the computer unbootable until the settings are corrected.

In some cases, you will have a problem with a specific BIOS or firmware version, and the motherboard or device vendor documents a fix through a newer version of the BIOS or firmware. If this is the case, refer to the update procedures and follow them. If they give you an option of backing up the current version of the BIOS, perform that step as a recovery option.

Sometimes BIOS and firmware updates can cause more problems than they fix. In some cases, the update is one-way, and you won't be able to revert to older versions. After some upgrades, custom settings need to be reapplied.

Power-saving features in the BIOS may allow you to reduce the speed of the CPU to save power and reduce heat. For some situations, this reduction is used as thermal protection when the heat sink fan has failed. If you're looking at performance issues, this is one area to examine.

Motherboard

Motherboards are made up of many integrated components, and management of these components is done through CMOS settings or by changing jumper settings. You can find specific settings in your motherboard documentation. In addition, you can perform a visual inspection for damage, such as broken connections or capacitor damage, as shown in Figure 2-4. If you are looking for a failure in a component related to the motherboard, you should also verify that all relevant cables are connected to the motherboard correctly.

Processor/memory

Processor failures are rare but not unheard of. In some cases, if failure occurs immediately after installation, the issue may be related to seating of the processor. When the processor is added to the system, a cooling mechanism is added as well, such as a heat sink and a fan. When you install the cooling mechanism, you should use either a thermal pad or thermal gel to improve heat transfer between the processor and the heat sink. If fan or heat sink fan failure occurs, many processors reduce the processor to a lower speed to help reduce heat generation.

Figure 2-4:
This capacitor has sprung a leak. Note the residue on top.

Memory errors are often identified during the POST process, when memory is tested. It should be noted that soft reboots (pressing Ctrl+Alt+Del) usually skip POST tests, so full power cycles (using the power button) should be conducted from time to time. Fan and ventilation problems can also result in memory overheating and generating failures. Other errors occur when technicians unknowingly mix different types of memory, such as ECC and non-ECC memory (covered in Book II, Chapter 3), or memory that runs at different speeds.

Floppy drive

Many issues can affect floppy drives, but the most common is head alignment. Back when these drives cost hundreds of dollars, head misalignment was corrected by having a technician manually realign the heads. These drives are rarely used today — USB flash drives have become much more popular — so replacing faulty floppy drives is typically more cost effective then repairing them.

Other floppy drive errors that can occur include damaged cables and connectors, improperly seated connectors for data or power, dirty heads, and failures in the media. Improper media selection can also be the culprit with some reported errors; there are still some single-density and double-density disks floating around with the high-density disks. Some users with older computers might have used high-density disks in their double-density drives, making them unreadable in high-density drives. Configuration settings in the CMOS (covered in Book II, Chapter 4) could also cause a floppy drive to not function.

Hard drives

When you're troubleshooting hard drives, don't overlook the physical problems. Many people dive straight to the software before checking all the hardware. If the drive is not detected or has data errors, you should check the connectors on the drive and motherboard to verify that the cable doesn't have any signs of damage. Sometimes just replacing the drive cable does the trick.

See whether anything might have recently happened that could have caused a shock to the hard drive, such as dropping the computer. Other causes for errors and drive failure include heat problems, so verify drive placement, airflow, and heat dissipation for the drive. Other issues that can cause detection problems are the jumper settings for the drive. If the drive is set for Master, Slave, or Cable Select operation, you could have problems if the setup is wrong for your situation. In some cases, you might have multiple jumper configurations for each setting (as shown in Figure 2-5), and all should be tried if there is a problem. For complete information about hard drive configuration, read through Book II, Chapter 5.

If you encounter problems with disk size detection, verify LBA (Logical Block Addressing) mode, if available, or the use of drive-overlay programs. Drive-overlay programs are not used very much anymore because they add another layer of code to translate disk locations, which leads to slower access times, but they do let you use drives that are larger than what your system BIOS actually supports. Common disk size limits of some computer BIOS versions are summarized in Table 2-3. When possible, avoid drive-overlay programs because of the added complexity and reduced compatibility when working with that drive. Drive-mounted LEDs can be used to identify disk activity.

Book IV Chapter 2

Troubleshooting Procedures and Guidelines

Figure 2-5: Some drives have multiple jumper configurations for the same setting.

Table 2-3	Common Disk Size Limits
Size	*Limit Reason*
10MB	Early PC/XT limit
16MB	Fat12 limit
32MB	DOS 3.x limit
128MB	DOS 4.x limit
528MB	Limit of CHS (cylinders, heads, sectors) mode, which has a limit of 1,024 cylinders; Fixed by LBA or INT13H translation
2.1GB	Limited by manufacturer-imposed LBA 4,095-cylinder limit or 22-bit LBA translation space
4.2GB	CMOS extended CHS addressing limit of 8,191 cylinders (which was not widely used) or 23-bit LBA translation space
8.4GB	BIOS-imposed INT13H 16,383 cylinder limit or 24-bit LBA translation space
33.8GB	BIOS-imposed 26-bit LBA translation space
136.9GB	Limit of ATA/66/100 BIOS 28-bit translation space
150,994,944GB (144PB)	Limit of UDMA/133, ATA/133 "Big Drives 2001 specification" drives 48-bit translation space.

The ATA/ATAPI-6, or "Big Drives" specification, was passed in 2001 and was incorporated into ATA/133 drives. This system was backward compatible with older drives and involved a change in the basic IDE circuitry. This also involved an introduction of the 80-wire, 40-pin ATA/133 cable. To ensure compatibility, the newer cables can be used for all drives.

On the software side, you can use chkdsk.exe or a similar tool on a rescue disk to test for file system and disk errors if the problem is with unreadable files or an inaccessible disk. If the problem is performance based, checking for disk errors is still a valid step, but you can also check for disk contention on the data bus and possibly move multiple drives to separate IDE/ATA channels or purchase an additional controller. Running Performance Monitor and monitoring disk counters will tell you whether the disk is being overused and is suffering from contention issues, which can be solved by moving some of the data files that are heavily accessed to an additional hard drive. To choose which data files to move to a new hard drive, look at the actual applications running on the drive.

Other issues affecting drive performance include the type of bus that is being used. ATA/66 controllers and drives can be upgraded to ATA/100 or ATA/133 components; SATA 150 to SATA 300; and 5400 rpm drives can be replaced with 7200 rpm drives. When selecting a new drive, rotational speed, onboard cache, access time, and seek time should all be considered.

CD/DVD-ROM

As with hard drives, the connectors, cables, power, and jumper settings affect how the CD/DVD-ROM drives work. In addition, problems with optics and alignment can be a factor with optical drives; and a major shock can knock the drive mechanism out of alignment, requiring that you replace the drive. These drives also support analog audio, which makes an analog connection directly between your CD/DVD player and your sound card, allowing audio CDs to be played without requiring transfer of the data through your ATA data cable. This analog audio cable needs to have its pin configuration verified at both ends of the cables.

Media problems can occur because of media storage or abuse. As I describe in the preceding chapter, some scratches may be repaired to a point that you can recover some or all data from damaged disks. Disk damage from glues, chemicals, or heat may be mostly or entirely unrecoverable.

Keyboard and mouse

Sometimes, keyboard problems are easy to fix. For example, the user enables scroll or number locks, which can be verified by the keyboard's LEDs. Most of the time, though, the problems are a result of damage from abuse or an accident, with the most common accident being spilled liquid.

For the most part, these devices can be considered disposable because they cost so little to replace, but they still might require a few troubleshooting steps to identify where the problem lies.

If the issue involves liquids or debris, such as food stuck under the keys, you might be able recover this device with little effort. For example, food and other debris can be blown out with compressed air. However, if the liquid contaminant contains suspended particles (such as sugar or salt) or is acidic, the keyboard is likely a write-off, especially if the liquid caused a short circuit or corrosion has set in. Cables may be damaged by keyboard trays, and both the cables and connectors should be checked for damage. For wireless devices, the batteries should be checked; failing batteries can cause a variety of usage problems.

If you have an urge to recover a keyboard with liquid or debris damage, you can soak it in *deionized water,* which is free of particles, and is also electrically and acidically neutral.

If you soak the keyboard in deionized water, the keyboard should be hung to dry for 24 to 48 hours. Do not apply heat to it to dry it faster. Adding heat can cause even further damage to the keyboard.

You can disassemble some keyboard models by removing the keycaps and also the case screws on the bottom of the keyboard. When disassembling a keyboard, remember that it contains a lot of little pieces, as shown in Figure 2-6, and they all have to go back in the correct places. Some keyboards also have springs under each keycap. And in addition all the small pieces for all the keys, don't forget the circuit board, which can be cleaned with an isopropyl alcohol–based cleaner and cotton swabs.

If the dirt is just on the keycaps, remove the keycaps with a special removal tool that has two wires that fit under the key and pull the key directly up. After the keycaps are removed, clean them in a mild cleaning solution and replace them.

In general, keyboard repairs are not cost effective because of the time it takes to make repairs.

Tracking problems are the most common ones that occur with mice; optical mice are fussy about the gloss level of the surfaces that they are used on, and internal rollers of mechanical mice can build up a layer of dirt. For an overview of maintenance of mice, see Book IV, Chapter 1.

Figure 2-6:
Keyboards can be taken apart and cleaned, but they do contain a lot of little components.

Sound card/audio

Sound card and audio problems are often related to the connections to the external or internal speakers. Some sound cards and motherboards have additional connections for digital audio using an *S/PDIF (Sony/Philips Digital Interface Format)* connection, and others support 5.1- and 6.1-speaker surround sound. When using these types of connections, you should carefully verify the connections against the manufacturer's guide. When working with external speakers or surround sound systems, note that all of them require power to allow for amplification or separation of audio signals, so make sure that the power is plugged in.

Monitor/video

Some common and easy problems to fix with monitors involve user errors: say, by, adjusting the picture by using the knobs or buttons on the front of the monitor. There's nothing quite as annoying as going to a user's desk to look at a "broken" monitor only to find that the user has reduced the contrast and brightness to zero, leaving the image faint or nonexistent. In addition to contrast and brightness, monitors usually offer horizontal and vertical size and position, curvature, and keystone adjustments.

**Book IV
Chapter 2**

Troubleshooting
Procedures and
Guidelines

When monitor problems are not related to these settings, they might be related to power input or video cable problems (which are easy to correct); or the internal power supply, electron gun, or picture tube. Because of the high-voltage capacitors and charges that are maintained by internal components like the CRT, repairs of the internal components should be left to a good repair shop.

Users have many common monitor symptoms. Here are some of the most common:

✦ **Incorrect colors** may be caused by front panel adjustments, bent or damaged pins on the video cable connectors (which can be easily fixed), or a damaged electron gun (which involves a trip to the repair shop or simply replacing the monitor).

✦ **Burnt or damaged pixels** are irreparable, so after the number is sufficient to affect the person using the monitor, the monitor should be replaced or rotated to a user who is more tolerant of the missing pixels. I have had users extremely bothered by one burnt pixel in the top-left corner of their screen, but other users with a dozen random burnt pixels on their screen hardly even notice the dots are missing. In some cases, the damaged pixel will be visible only when displaying one of the primary colors.

✦ **Blurry images** are usually an issue related to the monitor design and specification (such as dot pitch) or a damaged or misaligned electron gun. In the instance of poor monitor design, do not buy any more of that make or model of monitor. If you suspect a defect with the monitor, contact the manufacturer to see whether the monitor can be replaced or repaired.

✦ **Screen flicker** might be related to the internal power supply but is more often related to trying to run the monitor above specifications for color depth, resolution, and refresh frequency. Or, the refresh frequency is just set too low. These are OS-level settings, so they can easily be resolved in the Display control panel.

✦ **Image skew or discoloration** — although possibly related to electromagnetic interference (EMI) — is often corrected by moving the monitor as little as a few inches. This is often traced back to nearby power cables or other sources of EMI.

Video problems can also be caused by your video card, which might not support settings to correctly communicate with your monitor and use appropriate resolution, color depth, and refresh settings for the monitor. If you have slow screen redraws, which can result in slow screen refresh or screen flicker, the video card might not have enough processing power or video RAM. If your computer has an integrated video card, you might be able to allocate more RAM to be used as video RAM. The final resolution for video card problems is getting your video card replaced.

All video problems that are reported by a user will have to do with the video card or the monitor or both, and will likely have to do with trying to get more out of the system than it is capable of.

Modem

With the proliferation of broadband Internet connections and companies being connected to the Internet, modem use has fallen off, but they are still used for special purposes, such as pager modems. As with keyboards and other components, the cost of low-end modems has made the repair/replace evaluation lean toward replacement. Common modem problems include driver issues, line issues, and speed issues.

For several years, software modems — Win modems — were popular because they had become so inexpensive compared with the old hardware modems. The migration from hardware modems to OS-level software modems meant that if the software drivers were not installed correctly, the modem would not work properly.

Phone line issues occur with your phone company's network and can often be identified by testing the phone line with another device or by using modem or OS diagnostic features (found in the modem's properties). A common line issue is with call-waiting, when the tone interrupts the modem's signal. You can disable call-waiting per call by adding a disable command to the beginning of the number you are dialing. Speed issues are often caused by improper configuration or by using both hardware and software compression (which can greatly reduce transfer speed).

Serial and parallel ports

Serial and parallel port problems can be caused by connectors, OS settings, and CMOS settings. Here are a few troubleshooting tips if you're having a problem with one of these ports:

✦ **Check connectors for pin damage and check cables** for damage at the ends or along the cables themselves. Often cables running along the floor get run over by users' office chairs.

✦ **Watch cable length.** Both serial and parallel specifications have maximum limits to the overall cable length, and exceeding these limits can cause intermittent communication problems with devices. Parallel devices may support a standard Centronics interface (cable length limit of 15 feet [5 meters]), or they may support IEEE 1284 (cable length limit of 30 feet [10 meters]). Serial (RS-232) cables, on the other hand, have a length limit of 50 feet (15 meters) when communicating at 19,200 bps, but that limit increases to 3,000 feet (914 meters) if you communicate at only 2,400 bps.

✦ **Serial and/or parallel ports** might be disabled in the Device Manager. Right-click My Computer, choose Properties, click the Device Manager button on the Hardware tab of the System Properties dialog box, and make sure the ports are enabled. If you are using Windows Vista, then right-click Computer in the Start menu, choose Properties, and click the Device Manager link on the left pane of the System screen. There's nothing worse than spending a few hours trying to install a printer only to find out that the parallel port was disabled.

In addition to being disabled at the OS level, the port may be disabled in the CMOS. Or, in the case of parallel ports, you may be using a standard port when you need to support the bidirectional features of an ECP or EPP port. You can switch between SPP, ECP, and EPP standards for your printer port by changing your system CMOS settings.

✦ **Verify the connection speed and data characteristics** for both serial ports and modems, and verify that match with the device you are communicating with. These are specified by speed, data bits, parity, stop bits, and flow control.

- The *speed* is measured in *bps (bits per second)* and ranges from 110 bps to 115,200 bps.

 Speed used to be measured as *baud rate* (after its creator Jean Maurice Emile Baudot), which is a modulation rate or state change. Baud used to match up with bps (bits per second). With current modulation, encoding, and compression techniques, the bps rate is substantially higher than the phone line's baud rate (2,400 baud). Many people incorrectly use the term *baud* when referring to bps.

- *Data bits* are either 7 bits or 8 bits.

- *Parity* may be set to odd or even and is used to verify the contents of a byte (8 bits) of data. Parity uses the eighth bit of a byte and sets the total value of the byte to either odd or even, depending on the parity setting.

- *Stop bits* are sent after the data to signify that the data byte has finished. Stop bits will be 1 or 2 bits long.

- *Flow control* manages the rate of data transfer between the devices, and it allows for transfer at higher rates. Without flow control, the sender can send data only at a rate that guarantees that the receiver can deal with, or process, the data that it is receiving. When using flow control, if the receiver is about to be overwhelmed or needs a pause to clear a backlog of processing, it can use the agreed system to signal a pause or to request more data.

USB

Some common problems that you can encounter with USB include BIOS support, OS support, driver issues, version incompatibilities, and power requirements for devices. Here are some USB troubleshooting tips:

✦ Like with all the peripherals that I have covered, check all cables and connectors to ensure that they are properly connected and that the cables are not showing signs of damage or exceeding distance limitations for the technology.

✦ Not all system BIOS support or have adequate support for USB, so if you are encountering problems, check with the motherboard manufacturer for a firmware update that addresses your issue.

✦ Just like serial and parallel ports, USB ports can be disabled in the CMOS or through the OS, and this should be checked if the ports don't seem to be working.

✦ If the USB ports are enabled but are not working, the issue could be hardware related. You can look at doing a repair; or, in the case of a desktop computer, adding a separate USB controller via PCI or PCI Express.

✦ If the devices are detected but are not functioning, you might want to ensure that correct drivers are available to the OS.

✦ Although most devices are backward compatible, you might encounter performance or other errors when mixing USB 2.0 and 1.*x* devices and controllers.

USB 2.0 devices plugged into USB 1.x ports will perform slower because of the restrictions of the USB 1.x specification. If devices are not performing at the expected level, check for this situation.

✦ Finally, because most USB devices are powered from the bus, some devices may have power-related problems. Although the USB specification provides up to 500mA of power to a single device, some USB controllers enforce the specification's low-power-mode startup at 100mA and then expect the device to request the necessary amount of power in 100mA increments.

If the device is dumb, such as a USB lamp, it does not have circuitry to communicate with the USB controller. Because it cannot communicate with the controller, it will take whatever power it can get, so it might not get the power that it requires to function properly. Other devices, like some USB hard drives, require up to 1A of power, and this can be

supplied by special double-connector USB cables or cables to draw power from other USB ports. Figure 2-7 shows the back of a USB hard drive, with a thick, silver USB cable and a thin, black power cable to be used for additional power. The connector on the end of the power cable is a *pass-though connector,* which would allow for another device to share the port that is being used to supply power to this drive. This sort of cable is required because some controllers will not allow devices to exceed the USB specified power per port.

All the troubleshooting items for USB devices can also be applied to FireWire devices.

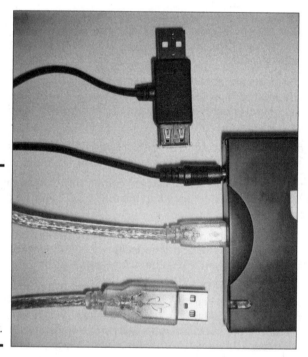

Figure 2-7:
Here is a device powered by two USB ports, using a pass-through connector for the second port.

Power supplies and batteries

When troubleshooting power supplies, you first need to do the following two things:

✦ **Country:** Make sure the power supply is configured for use in the country where the computer operates. Different countries have different standards when it comes to supplying power, and the computer's power source needs to match that.

✦ **Flow:** Make sure the power supply is actually getting power. Checking this is easy enough — just see whether the fan is running.

In addition, ensure that all power supply connectors are correctly attached to devices, including the motherboard. You can test the power coming from the wall receptacle with

✦ **An inexpensive receptacle tester:** Recommended

✦ **A noncontact voltage indicator:** Recommended

✦ **A multimeter:** Not recommended because of the risk involved at the voltage level being tested

Power cords can be tested for continuity by using a continuity tester or a multimeter.

Power supplies can be tested with inexpensive testers, as shown in Figure 2-8. The tester will ensure that the power supply works and provides the proper voltages on each pin of the connectors. The tester in Figure 2-8 supports 20/24 pin power, 12V, peripheral, floppy drive, and SATA connectors. If you suspect a problem with just one of the power connectors or one of the lines leading from the power supply, you can use a multimeter to test the connector, as described later in this section.

Figure 2-8: A power supply tester can save time when testing voltage supplied by power supplies.

In some cases, your power supply might be functioning correctly, but the problem might be that you are attempting to power too many devices, exceeding the total output of the power supply. Power supply testers cannot verify that your total draw does not exceed the amount supplied by the power supply; for that, you need to add up the power usage by hand. For information regarding the draw by devices, see Book II, Chapter 6. If you suspect that you are exceeding the power output of the power supply, you can disconnect or unplug some of the devices and see whether the system returns to normal operation (with the exception of the missing devices).

If the power supply is not functioning or does not have enough juice to power all the components of your system, replace it. Other issues that are often a result of defective power supplies include

✦ Power-up or system startup failures or lockups

✦ Intermittent rebooting or lockups during normal operation

✦ Intermittent memory errors

✦ Hard disk and fan simultaneously failing to run because of a shortage of current

✦ Thermal failures and overheating because of fan failure

✦ Electric shocks received when touching system case or connectors

✦ System operations halted or rebooting from static discharges

Because ATX power supplies use a soft power switch, they need to be connected to a motherboard to be turned on. So, to test the main power connector — the one that connects to a motherboard — you need to

✦ **Have the power-on pin shorted:** Not recommended

✦ **Use a power supply tester:** Recommended and preferred; refer to Figure 2-8

✦ **Back-probe the connector when the computer is running:** Not preferred, but acceptable

Most Molex-type power connectors can be *back-probed,* which is done by having your multimeter's black probe connected to ground and your multimeter's red probe inserted into the back of the connector (which, in most situations, has sufficient space to allow the probe; see Figure 2-9). In this figure, the black probe is grounded, and the red probe is testing the 12V lead on the Molex peripheral connector. This result is valid because it is +/–5%, which is within the specification for power connectors. There is a minimal risk of damaging equipment if this procedure is done correctly, and it allows you to see on the live system what the power issues might be. Read Book II, Chapter 6 to see what the appropriate voltages are for each pin.

Figure 2-9: Back-probing power connectors is a standard method for testing power in systems.

Power supply problems can result in problems with other systems. Check the question for keywords that suggest an issue with the power supply, in addition to the other device(s) mentioned.

Laptops

Many issues with laptops require sending them to an authorized repair depot, but you might be able to fix many problems yourself. As a CompTIA A+ Certified Professional, you should also be able to verify which major component of the system is affected. But because laptops are highly integrated systems, many solutions to problems involve a main board or a motherboard replacement. Laptop manufacturers have also made it difficult to get into places that they do not want you to go.

Some standard issues that affect laptops include

✦ Power-related issues with external power supplies, batteries, or capacitors

✦ External monitors or cutoff switches

✦ All the function (Fn) keys

✦ Pointer recalibration

✦ Tablet PC stylus and word-recognition issues

Power

When troubleshooting laptop power issues, it is best to start with the power supply or power adapter. Verify that either is the correct one for the laptop and that the cables or connectors aren't damaged. You can check the power supply label for the positive lead and use your multimeter red probe on that lead with the black probe on the negative lead to verify the voltage output of the adapter. If the battery is not holding its charge, it is likely just old and should be replaced. If the battery is new, see whether it can be replaced under warranty.

Less detectable is the fact that many laptops have power issues often dealing with overloaded capacitors or circuits. This can be solved by removing the battery, disconnecting the power, and pressing the power button multiple times (as many as 20 times). Replacing the power cable should also fix this problem. If replacing the power cable doesn't work, though, at least you can test the system without the battery in it so that you can rule out a battery issue.

External monitors; cutoff switch

External monitors can also cause issues with laptops. On most laptops, when the external monitor is connected, it is used instead of the laptop screen. When the external monitor is turned off, the lack of a picture on the laptop can trigger a help call, so always check whether an external monitor is plugged into the laptop. If so, you can use a function key to switch from the external monitor to the laptop screen. The specific key combination to switch between the external and laptop screens varies from one laptop model to another, but often it is F4. Hold down the function key while pressing F4 at 2- to 3-second intervals to cycle through the display options.

Most laptops also have an LCD cutoff switch that turns off the display when the lid is closed. This switch is usually either a small button at the top of the keyboard or a hole with a mated post on the lid. Depending on the OS settings, triggering this switch might not only turn off the display but also put the computer into standby mode or hibernation. For some laptop models, this switch is susceptible to either being hit or stuck, thereby making the laptop think that the lid is closed.

Function keys

Most laptops have three options built into a majority of their keys. Two of those functions are the same as on desktop keyboards and are activated with the Shift key. Laptops, though, also have an Fn key and a series of extra functions identified by additional symbols in another color drawn on the

keys. These functions include, but are not limited to, sleep, hibernation, brightness, contrast, battery meter, speaker volume, Print Screen, SysRq, Scroll Lock, Num Lock, Pause, Break, and all number pad functions.

To enable the number pad functions, which are shown in Figure 2-10, do the same thing that you would do on a traditional keyboard: Enable Num Lock. To do this on your laptop, press Fn and Num Lock. This causes several keys on the keyboard to convert from their normal function to act as a number keypad. These keys can be toggled for single keystrokes by using the Fn key as a Shift key. Often, when users accidentally enable the Num Lock, they call you because their keyboard is "broken." This at least should be an easy fix for you. Rather than dealing with this number pad, many users prefer to use a separate USB number pad, some of which do double duty as a standalone calculator.

Figure 2-10: Most laptops have a built-in number pad that you activate with the Fn key.

Pointer recalibration

Your laptop will have one or more pointing devices built into it. In most cases, it will be either

✦ An *Isopoint pointing device,* which is a small post in the middle of the keyboard

✦ A *glidepad* or *trackpad,* which is a flat pad below the keyboard

Regardless of the type of pointing device that your computer has, it sometimes needs to self-calibrate. When the pointing device is performing its self-calibrating, the pointer will drift to one side or corner of the screen. After running a self-calibration, the pointing device will resume normal operation. This process usually catches people off-guard, since the pointer starts moving on its own.

Typically, the need to self-calibrate happens after a certain number of hours, and you might notice it once every few days. If this problem happens more and more often, the pointing device might have an issue, and you might take the laptop to an authorized service depot. Many users will not know what is going on and will fight against the drifting, thinking that something is wrong with the system. However, this is normal operation for these devices — and, thus, a losing battle. As long as recalibration happens only periodically and takes only a few seconds to complete, the computer is working properly. Users should think of it as preventive maintenance.

Tablet PC stylus and word recognition issues

A *Tablet PC* includes a stylus and word recognition software that converts handwriting to text. The stylus works with a special mesh layer on the laptop screen, and its positioning and tracking are controlled by an internal component called a *digitizer*. Problems with the digitizer — evident through stylus problems — will involve a trip to your authorized repair depot. Handwriting recognition — controlled through software — might involve some training of the system (on some systems) to recognize your writing style. If the problem is with recognition, you might need to retrain the system.

Getting an A+

In this chapter, you examine

+ Using a multimeter to test power supplies

+ Using antistatic mats and straps to reduce the chance of ESD damage

+ Third-party disks and tools that are usually helpful when troubleshooting

+ How each major component inside the computer system has unique troubleshooting steps

Prep Test

1 What is *not* typically measured by a multimeter?

- **A** ○ Current
- **B** ○ Capacity
- **C** ○ Voltage
- **D** ○ Continuity

2 What is the purpose of a network card loopback plug?

- **A** ○ To return signals from your network card back to your computer to verify accuracy and pin configuration of network cable
- **B** ○ To allow use of 127.0.0.1 TCP/IP address range
- **C** ○ To eliminate network error messages from the operating system
- **D** ○ To capture network traffic for future analysis

3 Which function is not usually associated with a laptop's Fn key?

- **A** ○ Number pad
- **B** ○ Immediate power-off
- **C** ○ Monitor switching
- **D** ○ Sleep

4 Which issue doesn't indicate a possibly failing power supply?

- **A** ○ CPU thermal speed reduction
- **B** ○ Power-up failure
- **C** ○ System halt
- **D** ○ Internal devices receiving 12V and 5V

5 Why would you use an extension magnet?

- **A** ○ To erase magnetic media in a drive
- **B** ○ To suspend floppy drives inside metal cases
- **C** ○ To pick up dropped metal objects
- **D** ○ To remove Molex filings from inside of the connector

6 What components can be tested by BIOS self-tests? (Select all that apply.)

- **A** ❏ Hard drives
- **B** ❏ CPU temperature deviations
- **C** ❏ Magnetic media
- **D** ❏ Memory

7 **How does the system BIOS report major startup errors or configuration issues?**

A ○ Screen flashes

B ○ Beep errors

C ○ Error message dialog boxes

D ○ Audio interruptions

8 **What can be the cause of reduced CPU performance?**

A ○ Overuse of CPU cycles

B ○ Addition of RAM

C ○ Heat sink fan failure attributable to power supply failure

D ○ Removal of the J7 motherboard jumper as defined by the ATX 1.2 standard

9 **What is the purpose of a security bit?**

A ○ To reduce the chance of users opening system cases

B ○ To secure TCP/IP data packets

C ○ Eight of them create a security byte

D ○ To allow for tracking of sensitive data

Answers

1 **B.** Capacity is not measured by a multimeter. Voltage, current, continuity, and resistance are commonly measured with a multimeter. *See "Multimeter."*

2 **C.** Network loopback plugs are used to reduce error messages related to unplugged network cables. *Review "Miscellaneous tools."*

3 **B.** The Fn key is not usually used to immediately power off the computer; that is usually done with the power button. *Check out "Laptops."*

4 **D.** Power levels for internal devices are supposed to be 12V and 5V. *Peruse "Power supplies and batteries."*

5 **C.** Extension magnets are used to pick up dropped metal items. *Take a look at "Miscellaneous tools."*

6 **A, D.** The system BIOS on some systems allow for testing of IRQs, memory, hard disks, CPU processing ability, and most internal components. *Peek at "CMOS and BIOS."*

7 **B.** Beep errors are the standard way that major system startup failures are reported to the user. *Look over "POST errors."*

8 **C.** Reduced CPU performance is often caused by the temperature of the CPU exceeding limits, and it reduces power to reduce the temperature. Excess temperatures usually occur when the heat sink fan fails. *Study "Processor/memory."*

9 **A.** Security bits are paired with security screws to prevent users from opening system cases. *Refer to "Miscellaneous tools."*

Book V

Operating System Basics

The 5th Wave By Rich Tennant

JERRY CRAMS FOR THE EMOTICON SECTION OF THE A+ CERTIFICATION EXAM.

©RICHTENNANT

Oo-I know this one! It's...uh...

C'mon Jerry. Over 800 more to go.

Contents at a Glance

Chapter 1: Comparison of Major Operating Systems

Exam Objectives

✔ **Identifying the features, functions, and hardware requirements of the Windows OS**

✔ **Identifying the features, functions, and hardware requirements of the Linux OS**

✔ **Identifying the features, functions, and hardware requirements of the Mac OS**

Although it seems like we live in a Windows world, other operating systems (OSes) live and thrive in the world. As a CompTIA A+ Certified Professional, you will encounter these OSes from time to time. You might even find that some OSes are more capable than Windows for specific jobs that you need to do.

Of these other OSes, the ones you will see most are Linux and Mac OS. In this chapter, I briefly introduce you to these, as well as to Windows, and discuss their capabilities.

What Is an Operating System?

All OSes are responsible for managing hardware, resources, and data. Each OS discussed in this chapter can perform these tasks with ease.

The responsibility of the OS regarding user interface (UI) consists of displaying an interface that always reacts the same way and makes it easy for users to perform tasks. A GUI (graphical user interface) attempts to make tasks easy and intuitive for the user. To provide a space for applications to run and for the user to manage his work, most OSes with a GUI use a "desktop" metaphor. That is, the desktop is a work area on which you have a computer, a place to store items, and a waste bin. All these elements also exist in the GUI.

The look and feel of the GUI, such as the look of the windows that are used, also applies to the applications that run on the OS. When applications use the same look and feel as the OS, and by having the OS provide common

routines and dialog boxes for opening and saving files, there is a consistent appearance for the user, which usually reduces the time required to learn new applications.

Although hardware requirements vary and installation procedures are very different, after you get into using the features of the OS, all three OSes I talk about have similar usability features that allow a user to become capable in any other OS with but a short orientation period.

32-bit (x86) versus 64-bit (x64)

Processors have changed from 16-bit to 32-bit, and now the move is on to 64-bit processors. With each change, the internal processing power of the processor greatly increases. To maximize this processing power, you require an OS that can work with data the same way that the processor can work with the data.

In addition to most current Linux distributions and Mac OSX, Windows XP, 2003, 2008, and Vista all support 32-bit and 64-bit processors, depending on the version of the OS installed. For example, if you install the 64-bit version of the OS, you need 64-bit device drivers and applications to achieve performance benefit.

Looking at the Windows OS

I start at the top of the OS hierarchy with the Windows OS. The look and feel of Windows today is very different from the look and feel of Windows 3.0 when I started using it in 1990. Windows XP and Windows Vista streamlined the UI and added features, such as Wireless Zero Configuration, to make it easier to use your computer.

Comparing versions of Windows

MS-DOS was awkward and intimidating for many people to use, as they sat there looking at the command prompt slowly blinking at them. Windows was first developed as a shell, or UI, to go on top of MS-DOS, making MS-DOS easier to user. By the time Windows hit its third iteration, it was a very usable tool. This product — Windows 3.0 — went on to become Windows 95, 95 OSR2, 98, 98 SE, and Me. Windows Me represents the end of this product line, which has always been, because of architectural limitations, a shell on top of some level of MS-DOS.

Looking at the Windows OS **527**

Book V
Chapter 1

Comparison of
Major Operating
Systems

The Windows that we now know and use owes its roots to a Microsoft/IBM venture that built upon the IBM OS/2 family to produce a new, secure server OS. But in the manner of many partnerships, this one fell apart, and both parties took the fruits of their labors and went home. Microsoft took this work and created Windows NT 3.*x*. NT and 3.1 were chosen to be compatible with the version number of the other Windows OS. The Windows NT OS was more stable than earlier versions of Windows because of its architecture (NT; New Technology) and more secure because of its file system (NTFS; New Technology File System). In addition to creating the server OS, Microsoft created a desktop OS in the form of Windows NT 3.*x* Workstation, which had the same core as the Windows NT 3.*x* Server but also had many of the server components removed.

The drawback to the OS was that the architecture was totally different from that of the Windows 9*x* family. Because of this difference, many applications written for the Windows 9*x* family standards did not work with the Windows NT family. This limitation has slowly been overcome with each successive version of the OS albeit sometimes at the cost of some of the stability features. This family went though Windows NT 4.0 to 2000 and then to XP. Windows XP was targeted not only to the existing users of the Windows NT family but also to the users of the Windows 9*x* family; as such, Windows XP took large steps at backward-compatibility with older applications. This focus on security, stability, compatibility, and usability of the Windows NT family continues with Vista, which is the latest addition to the family.

The recent Windows OSes — XP and Vista — are based on Windows NT, and not Windows 3.0 or Windows 9*x*.

Typical system requirements

Although Windows started out with its roots in MS-DOS, current versions of Windows are based on Windows NT. For the most part, you will work with systems running on Windows 2000, XP, or Vista. Starting in 2010, you will also see the next generation of Windows. Table 1-1 lists the system requirements for each version of Windows.

Microsoft started using the term "Built on Windows NT Technology" with the release of Windows 2000 to tie the lineage of these two OSes. That would actually make the statement "Built on Windows *New Technology* Technology."

Table 1-1	System Requirements for Microsoft Windows		
	Windows 2000	*Windows XP*	*Windows Vista*
Processor	133 MHz or higher Pentium-compatible processor	300 MHz or higher Intel- or AMD-compatible processor	800 MHz or higher modern processor
Memory	64MB or better	128MB or better	512MB or better
Hard disk	2GB with 650MB of free space	1.5GB of available disk space	20GB with 15GB of free space
CPU support	Single or dual CPU	Single or dual CPU	Single or dual CPU
Display	VGA or better	SVGA or better	DirectX 9.0 capable

Expect to get a question related to the hardware requirements for these Windows OSes.

The biggest differences between the different Windows OSes are hardware requirements and some advancements in application compatibility. If you have a computer that is lower than or just meets the hardware requirements of an OS, you might want to consider using an older OS for that particular computer.

For instance, although a computer with 512MB of RAM and an 800 MHz processor meets the requirements for Windows Vista, you might compare that with the base model of a car, without all possible options. For any OS, if you choose hardware at the minimum level, you will get minimum performance. Using hardware above that level is like buying an options package for you car. With 512MB of RAM and an 800 MHz processor, you will likely find that Windows XP will offer somewhat better performance than Windows Vista because it has less convenience and less overhead. With the same specs, Windows 2000 would likely offer even more performance. However, in both cases, your cost would be losing Windows Vista features.

As you move backward in the Windows NT family, each version of the OS was designed to work with a lower level of resources. It then becomes a trade-off of features versus speed. There is a minimum level of the OS that you will be able to work with because of minimum requirements, such as security or USB compatibility.

You are the only person who can determine which OS is right for you, and that decision depends on what features you actually feel are important and the hardware that you have available.

Identifying GUI elements

The Windows GUI follows the desktop metaphor I describe earlier, with your files, active applications, and a virtual trash can all within easy reach onscreen. A taskbar at the bottom of the screen allows you to quickly switch between open applications; it also holds a Start menu, from which you can quickly launch applications. See the Windows XP GUI in Figure 1-1.

The Windows interface introduced with Windows 95 "borrowed" (ahem) the features that were working in the other major graphical OS of the time (the Mac OS). Although there have been some functional and cosmetic changes to the GUI, there have not been any major changes to how the GUI functions or operates.

Deletion location

Active
applications

Figure 1-1:
The
Windows
XP desktop.

Taskbar

Start menu

Windows Vista supports three main user interface features or enhancements over Windows XP:

✦ **Sidebar:** The Sidebar interface (see Figure 1-2) is located by default on the right of the Windows Vista screen. The Sidebar supports components called *gadgets,* which are all small Windows apps, typically used to display some sort of data.

✦ **Aero desktop:** This high-performance desktop offers great graphic eye candy (such as glass windows, which appear to be translucent) as well as Windows Flip 3D (which allows you quickly see all open application windows).

✦ **User Access Control (UAC):** UAC adds a layer of authentication or security to the execution of tasks that could damage the OS. In Windows XP, a user needs to be given Administrator rights for certain tasks. Vista, though, allows a user to run most tasks with less privilege, and asks for permissions prior to executing critical tasks.

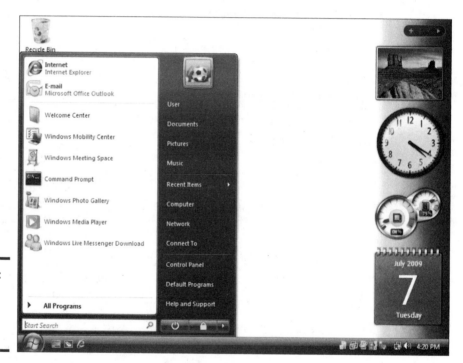

Figure 1-2:
The
Windows
Vista
desktop.

Welcome to the Linux World

The Unix OS was originally designed to control telephone switches for the Bell telephone network. It was designed to be highly stable and configurable. As it grew to maturity, it became popular for its stability and processing power. Over the years, Unix went from solely a command line environment to having a GUI. Its popularity led to a young university student's creation, during the early 1990s, of a Unix-like shell that would work on Intel-based systems. This student was Linus Torvalds, and he created Linus' Unix, or *Linux*.

Comparing versions of Linux

Since the creation of Linux, it has been a worldwide group project, with Linus Torvalds controlling what components go into the Linux *kernel,* or the core components that make up the brains of the Linux OS. Many individuals and groups have contributed programming code to the Linux kernel, usually as completed drivers for hardware. The only thing that is common to all versions of Linux is the OS kernel. Beyond the kernel, there are applications that are used with the kernel to give you a system that you can actually use to accomplish tasks. You can literally download the kernel source from `http://kernel.org`, compile the applications that you want to use, put them together, and have a Linux system. Because it is that easy to make your own Linux system, there are currently just about as many Linux systems as there are tasks you want to accomplish with them.

When a group or company takes the Linux kernel, combines it with a UI (shell), and then bundles in a variety of applications, a *distribution* is created. All Linux distributions are cousins and have been created with the same core components. Where distributions differ are in the mix of tools that are bundled in the distribution, and any customization the creator of the distribution decides to include.

There are a few major distributions of Linux, which have changed over the years. The current major distributions include

+ Debian — GNU/Linux

+ Fedora Core — Red Hat

+ Gentoo

+ Knoppix

+ Slackware

+ SUSE — openSUSE

+ Ubuntu

The main difference among these distributions is packaging. They all run the same kernel (or core), and most applications they run are the same as well because the applications are written to the kernel specifications. The real difference is the wrapping material that ties these elements together. In most cases, this wrapping includes an OS installation tool and a packaging tool, which are used to prepare applications for installation and removal.

All distributions have a command line interface, and most also include a variety of GUIs. Common Linux-based GUIs include XWindows with several Window Managers, such as AfterStep, Black Box, Enlightenment, IceWM,

and Window Maker to name a few. In addition to these standard Window Managers, GNOME and KDE are two complete desktop interfaces that are popular.

Most distributions have packaging tools based on one of two standards — Red Hat Package Manager (RPM) or Advanced Packaging Tool (APT) — both of which offer the ability to install dependent packages and resolve applications that conflict with each other. Both tools can also be configured to work with one or many networks or Internet package sources.

Applications written to Linux standards don't work on Windows-based systems but might work in the Macintosh OS X environment. Some developers write Linux applications to common standards, such as Java or GTK+, which both have components that can be installed on Windows systems.

Each Linux distribution has its own set of revision numbers to identify the distribution version. What matters more than the revision number is the version of the kernel that is used, as well as revision levels on the shared libraries, which are common routines that are used by many applications. Typically, when you install a new application, it has specific requirements for revisions of both the kernel and shared libraries but does not usually care about the distribution revision level.

In addition to the Linux distributions I mention earlier, BSD Unix is making several new inroads into the market. BSD started in the 1970s and has spawned many child distributions, such as FreeBSD, OpenBSD, and PC-BSD.

Typical system requirements

Different Linux distributions have different system requirements. To take a distribution at random, SUSE Linux requires the following:

✦ 500 MHz modern processor or better

✦ 256MB of RAM or better

✦ 800MB of hard drive space

✦ 800 x 600 display

Most distributions have similar installation requirements and can install on substantially less hardware, depending on the purpose of the installation. For instance, some Linux distributions are designed to run routers and firewalls, and these single-purpose distributions require substantially less hardware to function.

Linux runs on all the same hardware on which Windows runs, as well as several hardware platforms on which Windows does not run. If you would like to test Linux, you can find several Live CDs that allow you to boot the distribution directly from the CD without installing any files on your hard drive. These Live CD versions include Ubuntu, Knoppix, and others, which can be seen at www.linux.org/dist.

If you really want to get started with Linux, a great place to begin is *Linux Bible: Boot Up to Ubuntu, Fedora, KNOPPIX, Debian, openSUSE, and 11 Other Distributions, 2008 Edition,* by Christopher Negrus (Wiley Publishing, Inc.). Not only do you get a great *Wiley* book covering most of the major Linux distributions, but the book includes a copy of most of them, such as Ubuntu, SUSE, KNOPPIX, and Gentoo an attached DVD-ROM!

A wide variety of file systems are supported by Linux; some are journal based (such as ext3 and reiser) and others are not (such as ext2). *Journal-based file systems* keep track of writes to the file system, and thereby provide better and faster recoverability in the event of a system crash or power loss. Most Linux distributions will install onto one of these file systems. Like with Windows NT–based systems that support NTFS–based security, most Linux-based file systems support per user or per group security on files and folders.

Identifying GUI elements

Although many people use command line systems exclusively when using Linux, many GUIs can be used as well. The GUI loads as a separate element on top of the core command line OS. Even when you are using a GUI, you will likely find occasions when you need to go back to the command line or a command line window (a *terminal window*) to accomplish your tasks. Figure 1-3 shows the GNOME desktop environment, which is one of the popular GUI environments for Linux. KDE is the other major desktop environment; and then there are several other Window Managers that may be used, such as Window Maker, IceWM, and FVWM95 (which looks like Windows 95), each giving you a different interface for window management on your Linux system.

All GUI environments available for Linux have the same basic features for window management and work in conjunction with a file management application. The major differences between these systems are in the implementation and extra features, such as auto-mounting CDs as they are inserted into the drive. You should note that the GNOME desktop features and layout are similar to those used by Windows XP.

Figure 1-3:
The GNOME desktop environment in action.

Understanding the Macintosh OS

The Macintosh OS has gone through some major changes over the last few years. The original version, Mac OS 1.0, remained essentially unchanged up through version 9.0. The last version of the Classic Mac OS was 9.*x*, which was replaced with a totally different OS, Mac OS X, which was based on the BSD OS.

The first nine revisions of the Mac OS were proprietary, built entirely by Apple. Mac OS X and later are based on a BSD Unix core with Apple proprietary enhancements.

Comparing versions of Mac OS

The Mac OS originally hit the scene in 1984, running on a hardware platform that was very different from the hardware that was used by Windows PCs. It was standardized on the Motorola 68000 processor, and PCs were using Intel processors. The Macintosh also used Small Computer System Interface (SCSI) hard drives, and Windows PCs were using Integrated Drive Electronics (IDE) drives.

Through most of the 1990s, Mac OS 7.*x* was the main Macintosh OS. Shortly after the release of Mac OS 9.1 in 2001, Apple also released Mac OS X, with the goal of allowing capable computers to dual boot these two OSes. Unlike Windows, Apple allowed you to dual boot the old OS to run any applications

that did not work with Mac OS X rather than having to support legacy Mac OS 9 applications in Mac OS X. Mac OS X also offered to run old applications in an emulator called the *Classic* environment, which can be slow and requires that you have a Mac OS 9.1 system folder on your hard drive. Most Mac users were forced to quickly upgrade their applications to new versions or new applications that worked with the new OS.

This change in OSes and the break with the previous OS allowed Apple to create a new, stable OS platform for the Macintosh product line.

Typical system requirements

Unlike Windows, Linux, and Unix — which can run on a wide variety of hardware, as long as it is IBM PC–compatible — Macintosh has always run on proprietary hardware with carefully managed BIOS and system ROMs. Until recently, these systems had always been powered by Motorola and IBM CPUs, starting with the 68000 family and more recently the Power PC G5 chip. Because of the processing requirements, Mac OS X requires at least a G3 processor to function.

Apple switched to using Intel-based 32-bit and 64-bit CPUs in its product line, which is yet another standard component PC hardware platform, blurring the line between the Macintosh and the PC hardware platforms.

Identifying GUI elements

Prior to Mac OS X, the Macintosh desktop environment was referred to as the *Finder* — the place where you would find all the items that you needed to work with. There were no command line interfaces for the OS because unlike other OSes, the Mac OS was developed from the beginning as a graphical OS.

With the adoption of the BSD-like kernel, the system added a powerful command line interface based on Unix to a powerful Apple-developed GUI, which is still referred to as the *Finder*.

As shown in Figure 1-4, the same features present on the Windows and Linux OS user interfaces are present on the Mac OS. One difference (or as a Mac user would think, one thing that is the same) is the Apple menu and the context-sensitive menu bar across the top of the screen. Unlike other OSes, which keep application menus with the application, Macintosh has always had a menu bar across the top of the screen. The Apple menu (the equivalent of the Windows Start menu) is always there, and the remaining menu items change based on which application has the current focus.

Figure 1-4:
The
Macintosh
GUI for
OS X.

Getting an A+

This chapter shows the differences between the major operating systems on the market — Windows, Linux, and Macintosh. Things to remember include

✦ The major operating systems are Windows, Linux, and Mac OS.

✦ Windows and Linux hardware is compatible, but applications are not.

✦ Linux comes in subvarieties called *distributions*.

✦ All three OSes have similar GUI environments.

Prep Test

1 Mary works for a temporary placement agency and uses primarily Windows on her jobs. She is going to be sent to an office that uses Mac OS X. Should Mary expect to have large problems getting used to the new OS?

 A ○ Mary should expect to find the layout of the screen and the method of accessing applications to be completely different.

 B ○ Mary should refuse to visit the client site because the differences are so great.

 C ○ Mary should expect to find the layout of the screen and the method of accessing applications fairly similar to what she is familiar with.

 D ○ This is a moot point because the GUIs on both operating systems are identical.

2 You have been called by a client to give a recommendation on which OS should be installed on several new computers being added to the office. The other computers in the office use Windows-based clients (Windows 2000) and Windows-based servers (Windows NT 4.0). What OS should you suggest?

 A ○ Red Hat Linux

 B ○ FreeBSD Unix

 C ○ Mac OS X

 D ○ Windows Vista

3 Which of the following operating systems are direct ancestors of Windows XP? (Choose all that apply.)

 A ❏ Windows 2000

 B ❏ SUSE Linux

 C ❏ Windows NT

 D ❏ Windows Me

4 What is the variety of packaging of the Linux kernel and applications called?

 A ○ Flavor

 B ○ RPM

 C ○ Revision

 D ○ Distribution

5 You just received a call from a user who is using a Linux workstation and has lost his GUI. What is the likely cause?

A ○ The user has exited the GUI and is now at a command shell.

B ○ The user has deleted the GUI, and it will need to be reinstalled.

C ○ The user has minimized the GUI shell window.

D ○ The user has a disk fragmentation issue that is preventing the GUI from functioning properly.

Answers

1 **C.** Mary should find that the interface is different, but not so different that she cannot accomplish her tasks. If she wants to develop as high a level of competency as she possibly has with the Windows OS, training would be beneficial but not required. *See the "Identifying GUI elements" section of "Understanding the Macintosh OS."*

2 **D.** Because the office is already Windows based and the users likely have a higher degree of proficiency with the new version of the Windows OS, a change to a more different OS should not be implemented unless the client has some specific goal that he wants to achieve by switching the OS. Even though, with the changes that have occurred with Windows Vista, when compared with Windows 2000, the user might be able to pick up any of the suggested OSes with the same level of difficulty. *Review "What Is an Operating System?"*

3 **A, C.** Windows NT and Windows 2000 have a common heritage with Windows XP in that they all use NT technology. Windows 9x operating systems, such as Windows Me, followed a different development path going back to Windows 3.0. *Check out "Comparing versions of Windows."*

4 **D.** A distribution includes packaging of the Linux kernel, and applications. It usually also includes a package of management tools and a system installation program. *Peruse "Comparing versions of Linux."*

5 **A.** Although you will need more information to properly diagnose the problem, when using Linux, it is possible to enter a system mode where the GUI is unloaded and you are left at a command line until you reload the GUI. *Take a look at the "Identifying GUI elements" section in "Welcome to the Linux World."*

Chapter 2: Operating System Functions

Exam Objectives

✔ Identifying the primary operating system components

✔ Describing operating system interface features

✔ Using Remote Desktop Connection and Remote Assistance

*J*ust as the engine is the driving force behind an automobile, the operating system (OS) is the driving force behind your computer. Your choice of engine in your automobile affects the performance of its system, and also affects what you can do with your vehicle. In a similar way, you will find that the performance and functionality of your computer is different if you use MS-DOS, Windows NT Workstation 4.0, Windows 2000, Windows Vista, or some other OS.

The OS is responsible for several major functions on your computer. To manage your computer, the OS relies on its major components. This chapter examines these components and how they interrelate to effectively manage the computer. By the end of this chapter, you will be able to effectively choose from Windows 2000, Windows XP, and Windows Vista for your system. And because the A+ exam focuses on Windows 2000, Windows XP, and Windows Vista, this chapter focuses on these three OSes.

Identifying Major Operating System Functions

As you can read in the preceding chapter, the OS is responsible for two major functions: managing hardware devices and providing an environment in which applications can execute. One of the major applications that needs to execute is the user interface (UI), which lets the user control all other applications and their execution. In the case of Windows-based computers, this UI — the *shell* — is Windows Explorer. So together with hardware, this software that makes up the OS is responsible for getting things done. The hardware and software get tied together in the location where everything happens: memory.

Understanding memory management

Memory is the playing field where hardware and software mix. Memory management is the responsibility of the OS. The OS makes sure that the hardware and software components work within their own confines of memory. As memory resources are requested, the OS releases them either to the hardware device driver or to the application. The OS then takes steps to make sure that only the application accesses the memory areas allocated to that particular application. If an application attempts to access memory not allocated to it, the OS has to decide what to do with the application.

In all cases, attempts to access the memory space of other applications are denied. Usually, the denied application does not know what to do when this happens, so you get an application that "hangs" or terminates through a *General Protection Fault (GPF)*. Most applications really never expect to be denied anything. Hangs and GPFs are annoying because the failed application is flushed from memory, and data may be lost. On the positive side, the other application — the one whose memory was almost accessed — should still be working. The goal is to protect the other application by terminating the application that exceeded its boundaries. For more on GPFs, see Book VII, Chapter 2.

As part of memory management, the OS keeps track of physical memory on the computer as well as hard drive space used as extra memory available to the computer. Access time to physical memory is measured in nanoseconds, and access time to disk drives is measured in milliseconds. These scales are widely different, and so is the access time of information from these memory locations. Both types of memory are lumped together to make up virtual memory. Sometimes the term *virtual memory* is applied to the hard drive space used to simulate memory, but at the OS level, the term is used to refer to all memory available for storage on the system.

As applications launch and get loaded into memory, physical memory is used. When this space becomes limited, the OS moves some data from RAM onto the hard drive. The OS records the change in the actual location so that when the application requests that information again, the information can be moved back into physical memory and accessed.

Checking the OS version

No matter which OS you use, at some point you need to know its exact version number. This is often the case when you install new software, which requires a specific version of the OS. There are many methods for retrieving this information in Windows 2000, XP, and Vista.

The System Control Panel or System Properties lets you know which version and service pack level of the OS you are running (see Figure 2-1). You can get to the System Properties dialog in the following ways:

✦ Choose My Computer⇨Control Panel⇨System.

✦ Choose Start⇨Control Panel⇨System.

✦ Right-click My Computer and choose Properties.

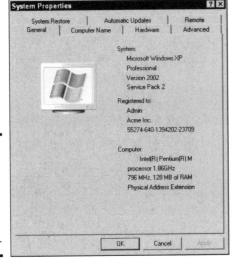

Figure 2-1:
The System
Control
Panel is
available in
all versions
of Windows.

Prior to Windows XP you see the version number (as opposed to the version name, like Windows Vista) of the OS listed in this System Properties dialog box, which we just looked at, but starting with Windows XP you need the System Information tool to locate the version number.

✦ **In Windows 2000:** Choose Start⇨Programs⇨Accessories⇨System Tools⇨System Information.

✦ **In Windows XP and Windows Vista:** Choose Start⇨All Programs⇨ Accessories⇨System Tools⇨System Information.

The System Information tool includes the version number in the main window (see Figure 2-2). The System Information tool can be launched through the Start menu, or you can use the Run command and type **winmsd**. winmsd (short for *Windows NT Microsoft Diagnostics*) is the name of the Windows NT 4.0 tool that can provide the same information, but running it launches the System Information tool.

Figure 2-2:
The System
Information
tool for
Windows
provides a
great deal
of detailed
information.

Some of the version numbers you might see are listed in Table 2-1. Notice that these version numbers are continuations of Windows NT version 4.0 in version and build numbers.

Table 2-1 OS Version Numbers for Modern Versions of Windows

Operating System	Version Number
Windows NT 4.0 Workstation	4.00.1381 Build 1381
Windows 2000 Professional	5.00.2195 Build 2195
Windows XP Professional	5.10.2600 Build 2600
Windows Server 2003 Enterprise	5.2.3790 Build 3790
Windows Vista Enterprise	6.0.6000 Build 6000.16386
Windows Server 2008 Enterprise	6.0.6000 Build 6000.16386

Windows version numbers have three parts: the version number, the build number, and the Service Pack level (although not all tools will show you the Service Pack level). The version number (5.1 for Windows XP) and the build number (2600 for Windows XP) will not change for the lifetime of the product. As patches and upgrades become available for the OS, Microsoft releases hot fixes. *Hot fixes* are listed in the Add or Remove Programs Control Panel. When a sufficient number of fixes have been released, Microsoft releases a Service Pack, which incorporates most hot fixes as well as other unreleased fixes or features. The installation of a Service Pack adds an identifier to the end of a build number. The new version number looks like this:

```
Microsoft Windows XP Professional [5.10.2600 Service Pack 2 Build 2600]
```

Windows Vista changes the build number of the OS as you apply service packs. The two major parts of the build number do change, so they will remain as 6.0; the two minor parts of the build number change, so the minor version number for Service Pack 1 is actually 6001.18000.

After you know which version of the software you are running, you can take a look at what makes up your OS.

Understanding Major Operating System Components

In the following sections, you briefly examine how applications actually run on Windows computers. For a more complete description of how applications are supported, see Book VI, Chapter 2.

Getting into the architecture

Windows 2000 was a complete rewrite of the OS, and, as such, Microsoft was able to do things that it couldn't do with Windows 9*x*. When Windows boots, it immediately enters a 32-bit protected-mode or a 64-bit long-mode state. With a 32-bit processor, the entire OS operates from this 32-bit state, and the kernel is loaded into *Ring 0,* which Microsoft refers to as *kernel mode* (see Figure 2-3). All processes running in kernel mode are protected from any processes running in *Ring 3*, or *user mode.*

The Intel processor design divides operation of the code into four separate execution levels, called *rings.* Ring 0 is at the middle of this arrangement, and Ring 3 is at the outside. These are the only two rings that Microsoft implemented during the development of 32-bit Windows OSes.

The kernel is the core part of the OS that controls everything else that happens on the computer. The kernel is responsible for keeping user-mode processes separated. Each application is started in its own area. One application is not directly allowed to interact with other applications and must pass such requests through *Executive Services,* which operate in kernel mode. This isolation of the applications from each other and from the rest of the OS is one of the keys to the stability of the current Windows system.

Kernel-mode processes are separated from user-mode processes but are vulnerable to corruption by other kernel-mode processes. The processor's architecture is all that protects kernel-mode processes from each other, and it often fails in its job. This means that Stop events (the ones that cause the infamous Blue Screen of Death), which reboot the system, are usually caused by a conflict of the processes running in kernel mode. For more on Stop events, see Book VII, Chapter 3.

Figure 2-3:
The
Windows XP
architectural
overview.

Paging your memory

Windows uses hard drive space to extend the amount of memory available to applications. The total pool of available memory is the *virtual memory page pool,* or just *virtual memory*. Virtual memory, composed of physical RAM and hard drive space, is maintained by the Virtual Memory Manager (VMM). Figure 2-4 shows how these systems relate.

The VMM is responsible for keeping track of where different kinds of information are located in memory. As applications request to have information placed in memory, the VMM places the information in an area of RAM. If RAM is getting full, some information is moved from RAM to an area on the hard drive. The location on the hard drive is a *swap file* (in older version of

Windows) or a *paging* or *page file* (current versions of Windows). As applications request stored data, the VMM moves information so that the data is available in RAM.

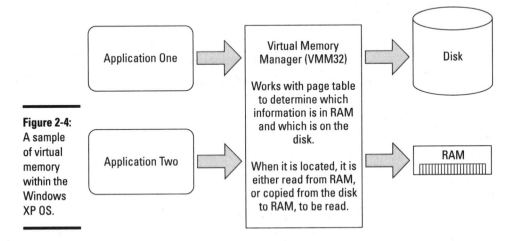

Figure 2-4:
A sample
of virtual
memory
within the
Windows
XP OS.

You configure the paging file in the System Properties. You might want to adjust the virtual memory settings because

✦ **You are running out of space on your boot partition** (the one with the Windows directory).

✦ **You want to improve paging performance by**

• *Reducing disk contention with the OS:* In this case, you can move the paging file to a different physical disk if you have one.

• *Load balancing the page file between different physical drives:* Unlike Windows 9*x*, current Windows systems allow you to have multiple paging files, each on a different disk.

Follow these steps to adjust how much virtual memory your computer uses when using Windows XP:

1. **Open the System Properties dialog box by right-clicking the My Computer icon on the desktop and choosing Properties.**

2. **In the System Properties dialog box, click the Advanced tab.**

3. **Click the Performance Settings button.**

The Performance Options dialog box appears.

4. **On the Advanced tab, click the Virtual Memory Change button (see Figure 2-5).**

In the Virtual Memory dialog box that appears, you can set an initial and a maximum size for the paging file on each logical drive.

Figure 2-5:
Page file settings for Windows XP can be used to improve performance.

5. **Adjust the settings as needed.**

If you reduce the size of the paging file on your boot partition below the size of the physical RAM on your system, you are warned that some of the recovery options will be disabled. The paging file is used as a storage space for the `memory.dmp` file that is generated during a Stop error.

6. **Click OK on three consecutive dialog boxes to close them all.**

Choosing your file systems

Just as many companies have different systems for filing data, with Windows you have several options when choosing a file system. MS-DOS offers the File Allocation Table (FAT), which started out as FAT12 and then became FAT16 in later version of MS-DOS. Windows 95 then added to that base file system with FAT32. In between this time, the different architecture of Windows NT offers New Technology File System (NTFS). The latest versions of Windows — Windows 2000, XP, and Vista — support all three file systems, and you get some control over how to use them.

When using Windows XP or Windows Vista, your choices include FAT, FAT32, and NTFS. Table 2-2 summarizes some of the differences between the file systems.

Table 2-2	Differences between the Major Windows File Systems		
File System	OS Support	Partition Size	Max File Size
NTFS	All versions of Windows NT (including Windows 2000 and Windows XP) support NTFS, but there were major changes to the file system with the release of Windows 2000. Computers running older versions of Windows NT might not be able to access the files.	10MB up to a theoretical limit of 16EB*	Limited only by the size of the volume
FAT32	FAT32 was released with Windows 95 OSR2, and all versions of Windows 9x after that support FAT32. Windows 2000 was the first OS in the Windows NT family to support FAT32.	Up to 2TB,* usually used for FAT volumes larger than 512MB. Windows 2000 and XP will not format partitions larger than 32GB with FAT32.	4GB
FAT	Accessible by all Microsoft OSes since MS-DOS, including Windows, Windows 9x, and Windows NT–based operating systems. It is also widely supported by other OSes.	Up to 4GB. MS-DOS and Windows 9x allow you to create FAT partitions only up to 2GB; Windows NT–based systems can create partitions up to 4GB.	2GB

One terabyte (TB) equals approximately 1,000 gigabytes. One exabyte (EB) equals approximately 1 billion gigabytes, or 1 million terabytes. That's a lot of memory!

In most cases, you want to use NTFS because it

✦ Supports security on folders and files

✦ Is a journaling file system, so it offers better recovery in case of power interruptions

✦ Offers a more stable platform for data storage

Although some older applications might have compatibility issues with NTFS, these issues are rare. For more on file systems, see Book II, Chapter 5.

NTFS should always be chosen as the file system for stability and security. Choose FAT or FAT32 only if you need to dual boot a computer with another OS, such as Windows 9x or Linux.

Registry

Windows uses its Registry to record settings for applications and the OS.

When people first started writing applications for Microsoft-driven computers, they usually needed to record a series of per-use or per-computer settings. In most cases, they wrote these settings to a file stored on that computer. This system worked fine most of the time, but the people who needed to manage those computers and applications found that some of these configuration files were binary files and some were text files, and occasionally they would get corrupted and be unusable. To solve some of this confusion, Microsoft came up with a file standard that appeared when Windows was introduced to the world.

The new solution was the INI ("innie") file, which is a text file that uses sections, settings, and values stored in a standardized format. Because data is written and can be retrieved using a standard format, the OS can use standard procedures to store and retrieve the data rather than relying on each application developer to write their own procedures. Listing 2-1 shows a portion of a sample INI file.

Listing 2-1: A Sample INI File

```
[Options]
WordSel=0
Units=0
Maximized=0
FrameRect=AAAAAAAAAAAAAAAAAAAAAAAAAAAAAAAA
PageMargin=AAAAAAAAAAAAAAAAAAAAAAAAAAAAAAAA
DefaultFormat=5
[Text]
Layout2=CAAAAAAAAAEAAAAAAADAAAAAAAAA
LayoutAux2=CAAAAAAAAAEAAAAAAADAAAAAAAAA
Wrap=0
BarState0=0
BarState1=0
[RTF]
Layout2=CAAAAAAAAAEAAAAAAADAAAAAAAAA
LayoutAux2=CAAAAAAAAAEAAAAAAADAAAAAAAAA
Wrap=0
BarState0=0
BarState1=0
```

Section names are enclosed in square brackets.

Originally, these INI files could be stored in the application directory, in the Windows directory, or anywhere on the file system path. This location variability often led to problems, such as multiple, conflicting INI files and uncertainty as to which file was in use.

With the release of Windows 95 and Windows NT, Microsoft programmers developed a new way to deal with this issue — they created a single location in which to store all configuration information for a computer: the *Registry*.

Like INI files, the Registry uses a standard format, breaking down settings into two basic categories: for computers and for users. Computer settings are stored in a section named HKEY_LOCAL_MACHINE, and user settings are stored in HKEY_CURRENT_USER. Application developers are encouraged to use this new location to store settings for their applications and have even been given a special software key to store their settings. It is up to the software developer to decide whether settings are user- or computer-based and to manage the settings appropriately.

Even though Microsoft provided the Registry as a location to store program settings, not all programmers use it for their programs, and some still use INI files. You should expect to encounter some programs that are still using INI files.

Remember that Registry stores all settings in either HKEY_LOCAL_MACHINE or HKEY_CURRENT_USER, depending on whether the setting is related to the computer or the user.

For detailed information about how to view and manage settings stored in the Registry, read Book VI, Chapter 4.

Navigating Your Computer

Being able to get to the files you need when you need them is crucial. From the command prompt, you can work with cd (change directory) and dir (directory), which I cover at length in Book V, Chapter 5. When you are using Windows, you can choose between Windows Explorer (not Internet Explorer) and My Computer (or Computer in Windows Vista). Either tool can be used for navigation, and your choice is purely preference. This section looks at these tools in a fresh (default) Windows XP installation using the default settings. If you have changed your settings, some windows might not be the same as I describe. When using these tools, Windows XP has a few more options than Windows 2000, and Windows Vista has a slightly different interface as well.

My Computer

My Computer is the most common way people access files on their computers because it's easy to find in the top-left corner of the desktop. When you double-click My Computer, a large window is displayed (as shown in Figure 2-6), listing the drives on your computer. You can then double-click your C: drive to see what files are located on that drive.

Starting with Windows Vista, Microsoft has renamed My Computer to simply Computer.

Figure 2-6:
Use My Computer to navigate file systems at the drive.

The navigation buttons on the toolbar at the top of the My Computer window allow you to go back to the previous folder or up to the parent folder. Cut, Copy, and Paste buttons allow you to move files between folders.

Several tasks are more easily accomplished with an additional open window, such as copying files from one folder to another. To open an additional window, double-click My Computer on the desktop and browse to the correct folder; or, hold down your Ctrl key while you double-click a folder, which leaves the original window in place and opens a new window for the folder that you double-clicked.

If you don't like how the files in the My Computer window are displayed, use the Views button on the toolbar to change the view from Icons to Thumbnails, Tiles, List, or Details. Thumbnails view allows you to see the contents of many files, such as graphics; Details view lists file sizes and modification dates, which is often useful when trying to locate specific files. The choice of viewing style is preference.

In the address line near the top of the My Computer window, you can type the name of the folder that you want to go to and directly switch to it. For example, you could type **C:\Windows** to switch to the Windows folder.

When you select an item in the My Computer window, you see properties for that item in a panel on the left side of the window, as well as common tasks that can be performed on the selected item (dependent upon the window being large enough to display the information).

To explore many of the options for displaying information in the My Computer window, open the Folder Options dialog box from the Tools menu.

Windows Explorer

By the end of this section, you will see that My Computer as an application does not actually exist. To open this application in Windows XP or Vista, choose Start⇨All Programs⇨Accessories⇨Windows Explorer; in Windows 2000, choose Start⇨Programs⇨Accessories⇨Windows Explorer. This opens a window like the one shown in Figure 2-7. This window's right-hand pane resembles My Computer and the left pane hierarchically displays all folders or containers on your computer, starting with Desktop and defaulting to My Documents or Documents in Windows Vista. The left pane — the *Navigation pane* or *Folders Explorer Bar* — is what makes Windows Explorer different from My Computer.

Now, you will see why a My Computer application does not really exist. In the top right of the Navigation pane is a small x, which is the close button for the navigation pane. If you select My Computer in the Navigation pane, close the navigation pane, and change the view to Icons for both Windows, you will see that this window is the same as the My Computer window. To show the Navigation pane, select View⇨Explorer Bar⇨Folders. The Navigation pane allows you to quickly move from one folder to another, or to copy files from one folder to another without opening multiple windows. Many Windows users prefer the Explorer view to the My Computer view of their files.

Figure 2-7:
The hierarchical view of the folder structure makes Windows Explorer a very useful application.

In summary, both views of your files use the same program: Windows Explorer or `explorer.exe`.

`explorer.exe` is not only used for My Computer and Windows Explorer. The first time it is run on your computer, it is launched as the desktop. If you close all open windows and check your Processes tab in Task Manager, you will see one copy of `explorer.exe` still running. If you right-click on `explorer.exe` in the processes list and choose End Process, your desktop will disappear, and you will see only your wallpaper. If `explorer.exe` does not automatically reload, choose Task Manager⇨File⇨New Task (Run) to open the Create New Task dialog box, type **explorer.exe**, and click OK to reload the desktop copy of `explorer.exe`.

To quickly open Windows Explorer, right-click My Computer and choose Explore from the shortcut menu. This Explore option shows up in the contextual menu for any folder.

My Network Places

My Computer is great when you're working with data stored on your computer, but in the connected world that we live in today, more and more of data that you need to work with is stored elsewhere — say, across a computer network. My Network Places (or Network Neighborhood in earlier versions of Windows) is the most convenient way to find those network resources. You can find My Network Places on your desktop and in your Start menu.

Regularly visited network locations can be stored in My Network Places, making them easy to locate when returning to those locations. To add items to this list, click Add a Network Place (in the Network Tasks section of the left pane) to open the Add a Network Place Wizard. Then step through the wizard's instructions.

Microsoft has removed My Network Places starting with Windows Vista.

Command line

The last way to get around on your computer is the oldest of the methods: the command line. Some people refer to this as MS-DOS, but when you're dealing with Windows, you're normally running the 32-bit command line application. This application can execute any command found on the system, but is most often used for commands without a Windows GUI component. Microsoft has command line tools available to perform most system management tasks from the command line, which is useful when troubleshooting or when creating scripts or batch files to perform tasks.

You access the command line in Windows XP by choosing Start➪ All Programs➪Accessories➪Command Prompt. In Windows 2000, choose Start➪Programs➪Accessories➪Command Prompt to open the Command Prompt window. Windows Vista has it in the same location as Windows XP, but if you right-click it, you have the option of running it as the Administrator.

Using Tools and Configuration Utilities

A computer's configuration is very important for both cosmetic and functional reasons. In the following sections, you get a good look at the tools that you use to manage your system configuration.

Control panel applets

Most settings for your computer are stored in the Registry, but the Registry is a place where if you make an error while making changes, it can require that you reinstall your OS. To make your actions less prone to major errors, Microsoft created the Control Panel. The Control Panel contains applets that allow you to change many system settings without requiring you to make direct changes to the Registry. Control panel applets are the recommended method of changing most of your system settings. Table 2-3 provides a summary of each Control Panel applet and identifies on which OS(es) you'll find them.

Table 2-3	Control Panel Applets
Control Panel Applet	*Description*
Accessibility Options	Changes settings for accessibility features for users with physical limitations.
Add/Remove Hardware (2000)	Performs Plug and Play detection, full hardware scan, device configuration, and device removal.
Add Hardware (XP and Vista)	Runs a Plug and Play hardware detection of your computer to detect new hardware devices or allows you to manually select devices to install.
Add or Remove Programs (XP and 2000) Program and Features (Vista)	Allows you to start the installation of programs, displays a list of installed programs that can be removed, and allows you to add or remove optional OS components (such as games).
Administrative Tools	Opens a folder that contains the Administrative Tools for Windows. These tools allow you to configure, manage, and control your Windows computer.

(continued)

Table 2-3 *(continued)*

Control Panel Applet	Description
Automatic Updates	Configures the Automatic Update service on Windows and allows you to choose how and when your updates are installed.
Date and Time	Changes the system date, time, and time zone.
Display (XP and 2000) Personalization (Vista)	Configures display options. This includes video card settings, screen resolution, color depth (number of colors), and color scheme.
Folder Options	Changes default folder options. These options are also available through the Windows Explorer Tools⇨Folder Options command.
Fonts	Displays a list of fonts installed on your computer, allows you to see what the fonts look like, and allows you to delete fonts from or copy fonts into the folder.
Game Controllers	Adds or removes game controllers and joysticks.
Internet Options	Configures Internet options and connection settings; clears your Temporary Internet Files and History folders.
Keyboard	Changes the sensitivity settings for your keyboard and the layout for your keyboard.
Licensing (Server)	Available only on Windows servers; sets or changes the number of client access licenses that you have purchased.
Mail	Configures the mail system for the computer.
Mouse	Configures the orientation, motion, and double-click settings for your mouse.
Network and Dial-up Connections (2000) Network Connections (XP) Network and Sharing Center (Vista)	Configures connections to your network or other networks.
Network Setup Wizard	Sets up your computer to run on a small network; often used for home environments.
Phone and Modem Options	Configures dialing rules and modem settings.
Power Options	Configures power management settings for your computer.
Printers and Faxes (XP) Printers (2000 and Vista)	Adds, removes, or configures printer settings and queues.
Regional Options (2000) Regional and Language Options (XP and Vista)	Configures the OS to support different currency, numeric, date, and time settings for specific countries; inputs and displays languages.
Scanners and Cameras	Configures installed scanners and cameras.

Control Panel Applet	Description
Scheduled Tasks	Adds, modifies or deletes scheduled tasks.
Security Center	Configures and reviews security settings for the computer, including antivirus, Windows Firewall, and automatic updates.
Sounds and Multimedia (2000) Sounds and Audio Devices (XP) Sound (Vista)	Sets sounds for system events, such as "window open" or "new mail"; configures audio or multimedia hardware.
Speech	Changes settings for text-to-speech systems or for voice recognition.
System	Configures advanced system settings for hardware and performance.
Taskbar and Start Menu (XP)	Configures settings for items displayed in the taskbar and the Start menu.
Users and Passwords (2000) User Accounts (XP and Vista)	Configures user profiles and user settings.
Windows Firewall	Contains configuration settings for the Windows Firewall that comes with Windows XP Service Pack 2.
Windows Media Connect	Configures digital media devices.
Wireless Link	Configures infrared ports on system to send and receive files.
Wireless Network Setup Wizard	Wizard for setting up or adding to a wireless network at a small office or home.

Microsoft Management Console

One common complaint about earlier version of Windows was that you had to use a different management tool for every task. For example, Windows NT 4.0 has tools for managing users or computers in a network domain *and* locally on the computer, tools for managing performance, and tools for managing disks and disk partitions. With Windows 2000, Microsoft took steps to consolidate these disparate tools with Microsoft Management Console (MMC).

The MMC is a framework into which other tools — *snap-ins* — can be loaded. All items that you see in your Administrative Tools folder represent MMC sessions configured with preset snap-ins. To see the raw interface, run mmc.exe from the Run command or from the command line.

Taskbar and notification area

To help you keep an eye on programs running on your computer and to allow you to switch quickly between running programs, Microsoft created the taskbar. Its default location is at the bottom of the desktop, but it is movable. The left end holds the Start menu, the other end holds has the system tray, or Systray. The space between holds tiles representing running applications. Starting with Windows XP, Microsoft renamed the system tray to the *notification area*.

Right-click an empty area of the taskbar and choose Properties to modify settings for the taskbar and the notification area, such as auto-hiding the taskbar, displaying the Quick Launch toolbar, grouping buttons, showing the clock, and hiding inactive icons.

Start menu

If all the items on your desktop were missing, you would still be able to accomplish all that you need to do via the Start menu. The Windows 2000 Start menu was always very functional, but Windows XP introduced enhancements that put more resources (such as My Computer, My Documents, and My Network Places) at your fingertips. Windows Vista took that a step further by streamlining the menus; providing an integrated Run/Search command; and removing "Start" from menu name (displaying only the Windows logo).

The Start menu, like its name suggests, can be used to start most applications on your computer. Contrary to its name, you can also use it to shut down your computer.

Remote Desktop Connection

There are a number of tasks that you can perform on a remote computer, such as modifying files, changing printer settings, or editing the registry; but there are times that you want to launch and run applications on that computer, and it is at these times you would use Remote Desktop Connection to connect across a network to another computer and remotely take over the desktop or console. See Figure 2-8. The technology in use is the Remote Desktop Protocol (RDP) from Microsoft, which defines how to send key strokes and mouse movements across a network from one computer to another computer, and how to have what is displayed on the screen of a computer sent to another computer. Using these mechanisms, you can remotely use another computer on your network, just as if you were sitting in front of that computer.

From a computer running Remote Desktop Connection, you can connect to a virtual desktop on a server running Windows 2000 Server, Windows Server 2003, or Windows Server 2008, all of which can support hundreds of remote

users simultaneously. Or, you can connect to the desktop of a Windows XP Professional or Windows Vista (not Home editions) computer. In either case, you can run applications on the remote computer as if you were sitting at the computer. Your computer passes mouse movements and keystrokes up the remote computer, and you see virtual screen shots of what is happening on the remote computer screen. *Note:* These are virtual screen shots because what you are seeing does not appear on the remote computer.

You can find Remote Desktop Connection in the Start menu under All Programs⇨Accessories⇨Communications, or you can launch it from the Run command by typing **mstsc.exe**.

Figure 2-8:
A Remote Desktop Connection to another computer on the network.

Remote Desktop Connection, through RDP, is a great tool for remotely troubleshooting a variety of problems because it can give you control of a computer on a remote network as if you were sitting right in front of it.

Remote Assistance

Remote Assistance allows you to ask for or provide help to another person using a distant computer by watching what that user is doing, or by taking control of that computer and having the user watch you.

Remote Assistance uses RDP just like Remote Desktop Connection, but the implementation is very different. As a CompTIA A+ Certified Professional, you will often be asked to help a remote user perform a series of tasks. Many users just need a bit of extra guidance to complete a task, or have a

question about something onscreen. After being involved in many telephone conversions with remote users, I can honestly say that a picture is worth a thousand words — sometimes even two thousand. Having the user show you exactly what is happening — or being able to show the user exactly what to do — can save a great deal of time.

Here's how Remote Assistance works.

1. A user who needs help goes to Help and Support in the Start menu and opens the Help and Support Center. (The remote help is here as well.)

2. In the Ask for Assistance section is the Invite a Friend to Connect to Your Computer with Remote Assistance option. When the user chooses this and invites you to help, the user has the option of sending an invitation through Windows Messenger or e-mail, or by saving the invitation to a file.

Regardless of the send-message method used, an invitation file is generated, and this invitation is key to the Remote Assistance system.

3. When the tech opens the invitation, he can open the Remote Assistance application and connect to a user's computer via RDP.

Remote Assistance requests are always initiated by the person requesting help.

The Remote Assistance application also provides a chat section as well a section where you can see and/or control the remote system, as shown in Figure 2-9. Unlike Remote Desktop Connection, with Remote Assistance, both the local and remote user can see what is going on with the problem computer.

Figure 2-9:
The Remote Assistance process can be a boon for many help desk personnel.

Location of Major Files

Many types of files are stored on your Windows computer, and most of these files have standard locations where you can expect to find them. This section looks at the major types of files.

User files

Since Windows NT 4.0 was released, all user-related files have been placed in `C:\Documents and Settings`, with each user having a folder in that directory. This location holds all files related to or that are personal to that user. This user-specific folder is called the *user profile,* and it includes the following folders:

✦ Desktop

✦ Application Data

✦ Temporary Files

✦ Documents

✦ Start Menu

Windows Vista has the same basic structure, but it stores all this data in the `C:\Users` folder.

System files

In addition to a number of user useful programs, the Windows OS has certain files required to make the computer operate. The files that are required to make the computer operate are found primarily in the Windows directory. Without these files, the OS would not function. Windows NT and Windows 2000 store these files in a folder named `C:\WinNT`, which differentiated them from the files that were used by the other main family of Windows at the time (Windows 9x), which stored its files in the folder named `C:\Windows`.

Because there is only one official family of Windows, starting with Windows XP, `C:\Windows` is used to hold the OS files. The two main subdirectories of that are `System` and `System32`, which hold critical files for the OS, such as DLLs.

Fonts

Each font or typeface in use in the OS has its information stored in a file in `C:\Windows\Fonts`. There is one file for each version of each typeface. Font files typically have one of two file extensions: `.ttf` or `.fon`.

Temporary files

Temporary files are stored separately for each user within their user profile directory. This allows for security to be placed on each user's temporary files, allowing these temporary files to be kept private and any sensitive data to be kept secure.

Program files

As I mention in the preceding section on System files, some files that ship as part of the OS are critical to the functioning of the OS, but other files that ship as part of the OS are not. For example, `Wordpad.exe` and `MSHearts.exe` are part of the OS (and are useful and fun), but the OS would continue to function without issue if these files were missing. The majority of these noncritical files are stored in the Program files directory, which is `C:\Program Files`, but if you are using a 64-bit version of Windows, you will find these files in either `C:\Program Files` or `C:\Program Files (x86)` depending on whether the application is 32-bit or 64-bit.

Offline files and folders

When accessing files on a shared folder of another computer over a network, Windows can sync these files automatically to your hard drive. When this happens, the files are put into a folder, but you can still refer to them using their original path, such as `\\<Server>\<Share>\<Synced File>`. These files are stored in a cache, which has a finite size. As total storage reaches the limit of the cache, the oldest nonchanging files are flushed to make room for new files.

Getting an A+

This chapter takes a look at the major functions of an OS; to be prepared for the exam, you should remember the following:

✦ The OS is responsible managing the interface between all hardware components that make up your computer.

✦ General Protection Faults (GPFs) and Stop errors are often a result of applications trying to cross memory boundaries.

✦ Virtual memory is composed of physical memory or RAM and space on your hard drive, in the form of a paging file.

✦ NTFS is the most robust and stable of the available file systems but is compatible with the fewest other OSes.

+ System and application settings are stored in the Registry or in INI files.

+ `explorer.exe` makes up most graphical navigation of your computer and is represented as both My Computer and the desktop.

+ Control Panel applets offer interfaces to many system settings for your computer.

+ Remote access to computers is available through both Remote Desktop Connections and Remote Assistance, both of which rely on Remote Desktop Protocol (RDP).

Prep Test

1 Phil is using a Windows XP computer and has run into a problem. He has called you on the phone and has asked for you to open a Remote Assistance connection to his computer to walk him through the solution. What is the first step that you must take?

A ○ Open the Remote Desktop Connections program.

B ○ Ask Phil to choose Help and Support from the Start menu.

C ○ Ask Phil to run `geninvite.exe` from Start⇨Run.

D ○ Open the Remote Assistance program on your computer, File⇨Connect to computer, and choose Phil's computer.

2 Virtual memory is composed of which of the following? (Choose all that apply.)

A ❏ Physical memory

B ❏ Extended memory

C ❏ Hard drive space

D ❏ Compressed memory

3 Bill is looking to see whether he has Service Pack 2 installed for Windows XP. He went to the System Information Tool located at Start⇨All Programs⇨Accessories⇨System Tools. Is there a quicker way he could have found out this information?

A ○ He could have used the Run command to run `systemtool.exe`.

B ○ He could have right-clicked My Computer on the desktop, or from the Start menu, and chosen Properties.

C ○ He could have used the command line tool `ver` from any command prompt.

D ○ There are no other locations in the OS where this information can be displayed.

4 You launched an MS-DOS application on your Windows 2000 computer. When you open Task Manager to see how much processing time the application is taking, you don't see it listed. Why is that?

A ○ The application is running inside an NTVDM.

B ○ MS-DOS applications are not listed on the Processes tab.

C ○ The application is listed, but the Processes tab list is using the name stored in the header of the application rather than the executable name.

D ○ You should check the list again because all running processes are listed, and you must have missed the name.

5 Your computer has just suffered from a Stop event (also known as the Blue Screen of Death). You are trying to decide what has caused the error. What is the most likely possibility?

A ○ A multimedia application

B ○ A background application

C ○ A network error

D ○ A system device driver

6 Bill is setting up a computer that will be used to boot into several different operating systems. He would like to have one partition used for sharing or transferring data between the OSes. What file system should he use?

A ○ FAT

B ○ FAT32

C ○ NTFS

D ○ Reiser FS

7 What tool combines all Windows configuration and management tools into one place?

A ○ Computer Management

B ○ Administrative Tools

C ○ Microsoft Management Console

D ○ Administrative Command Interface

8 What is the main protocol that is used by both Remote Desktop Connection and Remote Assistance?

A ○ Dec/Net

B ○ 802.11g

C ○ SNMP

D ○ RDP

Answers

1 **B.** The Remote Assistance process starts with an invitation being generated by the person requesting help. This invitation is created using the Help and Support Center. *See "Remote Desktop Connection" and "Remote Assistance."*

2 **A, C.** Virtual memory is composed of both physical RAM and a swap or paging file on the hard drive. *Review "Paging your memory."*

3 **B.** You can also launch the System Information tool by typing **winmsd.exe** or **msinfo.exe** at the Run command. In addition to this, you can find the info on the System Properties, which can be opened by accessing the Properties of My Computer. *Check out "Checking the OS version."*

4 **A.** The application is running inside one of the NTVDMs that are listed. *Peruse "Getting into the architecture."*

5 **D.** Most blue-screen errors are the result of conflicts between processes running kernel mode, which would include device drivers. This is not to say that the multimedia application may not have made some unsupported calls to a sound or video card to cause the problem, but this would have been the second choice. *Take a look at "Getting into the architecture."*

6 **A.** Although it has size limitations of 2 to 4GB depending on the OS used, the FAT system is the most compatible with different operating systems. *Peek at "Choosing your file systems."*

7 **C.** Although Computer Management has a lot of management tools in it, it is itself a snap-in for the Microsoft Management Console (MMC). Administrative Tools are also a collection of preset MMC snap-ins. *Look over "Microsoft Management Console."*

8 **D.** The Remote Desktop Protocol (RDP) is used by both of these tools. *Study "Remote Desktop Connection" and "Remote Assistance."*

Chapter 3: Installing and Upgrading Windows

Exam Objectives

✔ Installing Windows

✔ Upgrading Windows

✔ Dual-booting Windows

Although installing an operating system (OS) has gotten easier over the last few years, it is still important to understand some of the issues surrounding installing and upgrading OSes.

This chapter gives you some background on the issues that surround the installation of Windows operating systems such as Windows 2000, Windows XP, and Windows Vista. In this chapter, I walk you through these installations step by step and discuss the different phases of the installation process.

Understanding Installation Methods

You can use a number of different techniques to install an OS. But before I discuss the actual installation procedures, you should understand the overall approach you will take to install the OS.

Boot floppy

Back in the Windows 9x days, you installed the OS by first booting off your Windows 9x boot disk. The boot disk would contain a number of utilities to help prepare the hard drive for installation. For example, with Windows 98, you would boot off a Windows 98 boot disk, which provided you the `fdisk` and `format` commands so that you could partition the hard drive and then format the partitions before starting the installation. In this example, the Windows 98 boot disk also loaded a CD-ROM driver so that you could access the Windows 98 CD and call the `setup.exe` program to perform the installation.

With today's OSes, such as Windows 2000/XP/Server 2003, you can partition and format the hard drive from within the setup program when installing the OS. This is different than the Windows 9x days because back then, you

had to partition the system and format the partitions first. With the newer OSes, you can perform both tasks from within the setup program. So your goal when installing newer OSes is to simply boot from the CD and start the installation.

Today's systems can all boot from CD-ROM or DVD, but in the past, some systems could not. So the folks at Microsoft created a way to produce setup boot disks for Windows 2000. If you have a system that cannot boot from CD because your BIOS does not support it, you can boot off the setup boot disks that are created by `makeboot.bat`. These floppy disks will start the Windows setup, load generic drivers — including a CD-ROM driver — and then continue the setup from the Windows CD-ROM. To create the setup boot disk, you need to run the `makeboot.bat` file located in the support folder on the Windows 2000 CD-ROM from another system.

Just to stress this a little further — you need to create the Windows setup boot disk only when you have a system that does not have the ability to boot off the Windows installation CD-ROM.

Remember that Windows 2000 requires four diskettes when you run `makeboot.bat`. After you create them, Windows boots off the first one and then prompts for the second, third, and fourth — so be sure to label them while you create them!

Bootable CD

With Windows Oses today, the CD that you use to perform the installation is a bootable CD, so you don't need to use a boot floppy. When you boot from the CD with these OSes, the installation is activated automatically, and you instantly begin installing the OS.

The other benefit of the current versions of Windows installations is that Microsoft provides an opportunity to partition and format the disk from within the installation program itself. This is a huge benefit because you don't need to boot from a boot diskette first and use partitioning tools like `fdisk` like you do with Windows 9x. Your goal now is simply to start the installation and take care of all partition and formatting tasks from within the installation.

The folks at Microsoft built an extra security feature into the installation CD-ROMs for Windows. When the CD-ROM boots, you're asked to press a key (any key) before the installation process continues. This feature keeps you from unintentionally reinstalling the OS if you accidentally leave the CD-ROM in the drive.

Network installation

A number of network administrators install OSes and other applications to desktop systems via a network. When performing a network installation, you boot from a bootable floppy disk or CD, which then loads a network card driver and connects to a server on the network.

The server holds the Windows setup files needed to install an OS to the computer. With Windows, these setup files are in the i386 folder located on the Windows CD-ROM. To perform a network installation, the I386 folder is first copied to the network server so that client computers can connect to the folder and perform the installation. After you connect to the server, you run the setup program for the OS, and the installation is run from across the network to your system. You end up installing the OS without even touching the installation CD.

Be aware that this method of installation uses up network bandwidth and can affect the performance of the network! You also need to ensure that you have a valid license for each installation of Windows.

Drive imaging

One of today's most popular techniques for installing an OS is to use imaging software, which creates a snapshot of a system and stores that snapshot in an image file. When you want to configure other systems with the same setup, you apply the image (snapshot) to the other systems. The contents of the image file overwrite the contents of the hard drive of the destination systems.

Here's an example of when drive imaging should be used: Your manager asks you to install Windows XP on 20 new computers. When you receive the systems, you sit down at one system and boot off your Windows XP CD to perform a clean installation on that new computer. After the OS is installed, you install any additional drivers and applications that users will need. For example, most users need Microsoft Office, so you install Office on the computer as well.

After you have the system properly configured, you then create an image of that system by using imaging software, such as Ghost or Drive Image Pro. Typically, you would install the image on an image server so that you can connect to the image from across the network later from the other systems.

When it comes time to configure the other 19 systems, you boot off a network boot disk or CD-ROM and connect to the imaging server and download the image to each of the 19 systems. This takes far less time than performing the installation of the OS, drivers, and applications on each system individually. Most companies today use imaging solutions.

Again, be sure that you have valid licenses for the OS and any applications that you run. You need a license for the OS and any applications for each system that has the image applied.

Preparing for Installation

After talking to many people in the industry about installing different OSes or servers, I have come to realize that one thing that always requires more time is planning. Many people tell me that they can't do any actual work until their head office sends them the server. However, the best time to do your installation and disaster planning might be while the server is being shipped. Planning your installation or deployment of the OS to the desktops can save you time and money in the long run by helping you to anticipate any issues that might arise and to have the solutions ready when the time comes.

This section helps you identify some points you need to consider when installing a new Windows OS. Before jumping into the installation, be sure that you plan a number of installation decisions. Some things you will be asked about during the installation are

+ Hardware requirements

+ Computer name

+ Workgroup/domain

+ Partitions

+ File systems

+ Application support

Hardware requirements

You first prepare to install an OS by finding the OS's hardware requirements and making sure that the computer fits the bill. Table 3-1 shows the minimum hardware requirements for the different Windows OSes

Table 3-1	Windows Hardware Requirements		
Hardware Component	Windows 2000	Windows XP	Windows Vista
Processor	Pentium 133 MHz	Pentium 233 MHz	800 MHz processor
Memory	64MB (128MB is recommended)	64MB (minimum) (128MB is recommended)	512MB (minimum) (1GB is recommended)
Hard disk space	650MB free space	1.5GB free space	15GB free space

Not only should you verify that the computer meets the minimum hardware requirements before installing an OS, but you should also make sure that the hardware components you are using will work with the OS. For example, make sure that the make and the model number of your network card are compatible with the OS you want to install. For years, Microsoft published a list of hardware components — the Hardware Compatibility List (HCL) — that had been tested with each version of their operating systems. You can find the HCL for a given OS on the Windows installation CD in the `hcl.txt` file, or you can find the listing online at the Microsoft Web site.

The HCL is not a list of the only devices that will work with Windows; it is a list of devices that have been tested. If you have a network card that is not on the HCL list, it might still work with the OS, but it hasn't been tested. There is only one way to find out whether it works — install it! Just make sure that you are installing it on a test system and not a production system, just in case it causes the system to crash.

You can view the HCL for current Microsoft operating systems by checking out `http://winqual.microsoft.com/hcl/Default.aspx`. Once on the page, choose the link at the top of the page for either Windows 2000, XP, or Vista.

Computer name

When you install Windows, you must specify a computer name for the machine you are installing. This computer name is a unique name assigned to the system and will be used to identify the system on the network. You want to plan the computer names because you are not allowed to have two Windows systems on the network with the same name. The computer names can be up to 15 characters, and they are not allowed to include spaces. For more information on computer names, check out is Book VIII, Chapter 3.

Workgroup/domain

When installing Windows on a system, you need to specify the workgroup or domain that you want the system to be a part of. A *workgroup* is a logical grouping of computers. For example, you could logically organize all the accounting systems into an accounting workgroup — the benefit being that when users browse the network for resources, they can double-click the accounting workgroup to access all computers in the accounting workgroup.

If you are installing Windows into a Windows domain, you need to specify the domain name instead of the workgroup name during the installation. A *domain* is the term that Microsoft uses for its networking environments. A domain has a central server that stores all the user accounts so that users have to log on to the domain only once to access resources across a network.

If you are not sure whether you are installing your Windows system into a workgroup or a domain, choose a workgroup. You can always join the domain later by going to the properties of My Computer. For more information on changing a computer name, check out Book VIII, Chapter 3.

Partitions

When you install Windows, you need to partition the hard drive or select which partition you want to install Windows to. Plan this ahead of time! *Partitions* are logical divisions of the hard drive that you can use to help separate the different types of information stored on the system. For more information on partitioning a hard drive, check out Book II, Chapter 5.

When installing Windows, you can manage the partitions from within the Windows setup program instead of having to boot from a startup disk first and then create the partitions before installing the operating system, like you had to do in the old Windows 9*x* days. You can build all of your partitions from within the setup program.

Within the Windows 2000/XP setup program, you can build the partitions by choosing an area of free space and then pressing C (for create). The setup program then asks you the size of the new partition. You want to be sure that you create a partition that is large enough to hold the operating system and any future patches or updates to that operating system. For example, the laptop I am using to write this book has a 100GB hard drive. I have created a partition to hold the operating system which is 35GB in size. By the time I have installed the operating system, patched it, and installed my applications, I only have 50 percent of that space available for future updates. Windows Vista now allows you to create partitions using a graphical screen within the setup program.

The Windows setup program also offers a delete command, which lets you delete any existing partitions. After creating the partitions and choosing a partition in which to install the Windows OS, you are asked what file system you want to use.

When you install Windows, you don't have any control over the types of partitions that are created during the setup. For this reason, it is best to only create one partition (to install the OS on) during the installation. Then, after the OS has been installed, use Disk Management to create the remaining partitions. You will get more options and flexibility from the Disk Management console than from the Windows installation program.

File systems

Windows supports three file systems: FAT, FAT32, and NTFS. The primary advantage of using the FAT file system is that it is common to all Windows

OSes. The FAT file system has its limitations, however, in that it can handle only up to 2GB partitions. The FAT32 file system, however, supports up to 2000GB partitions (although the Windows setup program cannot create a partition larger that 32GB with FAT32).

Neither version of FAT supports security features, so beware of these file systems!

NTFS (New Technology File System) is a file system supported by Windows 2000/XP/2003 that offers a richer set of features than FAT or FAT32. For example, NTFS supports setting permissions on folders and files so that you can control who can access what files. NTFS also supports auditing, compression, encryption, and quotas — a feature that allows you to limit how much hard drive space a single user can use. None of these features are available with FAT or FAT32. If you need any of the features provided by NTFS, you need to use an NTFS file system on each partition.

For the exam, be sure to be familiar with the different file systems that Windows supports. Also note that NTFS is the only file system that gives you features such as permissions, auditing, and quotas. For more information on NTFS, check out Book II, Chapter 5.

Other preparation steps

Before you install Windows to your production systems, you also want to make sure that you prepare for the installation by checking that the applications that are going to run on the systems work and that your CMOS is prepared to boot from CD-ROM. This section outlines these two additional preparation steps.

Application support

Make sure you test each application that will be running on the OS completely to verify that it functions correctly. Back in the Windows 9*x* days, OSes were very compatible with most types of applications (there were a lot fewer software companies back then), and Windows NT was very picky about which applications could run on it. Today, you will find that as long as you are installing a 32-bit Windows application on Windows 2000 and Windows XP, the applications will function fine. If you're installing an older application, such as an old DOS program or 16-bit Windows application, make sure that the program functions correctly before installing it on a production system. The bottom line: Test everything before putting it into production! For more information on application support in Windows, check out Book VI, Chapter 2.

CMOS

When you install the Windows OS, you will boot from the Windows 2000 or Windows XP CD, and the setup program will start. Because you are booting from CD, you need to prepare for the installation by verifying in the CMOS settings that the CD-ROM device is the first device in the startup order. This ensures that you can boot off the Windows setup CD. For more information on configuring CMOS, check out Book II, Chapter 4.

Performing Attended Installations of Windows

This section begins with an overview of the installation process for Windows 2000 and Windows XP and then Windows Vista. The attended installation processes for these two OSes are very similar, so if you know how to install one OS, you will be able to install the other with no problem.

I begin with attended installation of the OS. That is, installations that you attend, or sit through, and answer all the questions that the setup program asks.

The Windows attended installation is broken down into three major phases:

✦ **Setup loader:** The setup loader phase is initiated by calling `winnt.exe` or `winnt32.exe` or by booting from the Windows 2000/XP CD-ROM. This phase copies `setupldr`, which is a mini version of `ntldr` used by the setup program, and copies to the hard drive any files that the Windows setup utility needs.

✦ **Text-mode phase:** The text-mode portion of the Windows installation is typically identified by the text-based environment that has a blue background. You will recognize the text mode phase by the lack of a graphical interface. The text-mode portion of the install is controlled by a mini kernel that is started by `usetup.exe`, which is located in the i386 folder and called automatically.

The text-mode phase of setup is responsible for detecting basic hardware components such as CPU, motherboard, and hard drives. This phase also creates the Registry, partitions and formats the drives, creates the file systems, and verifies that you have enough hard disk space to complete the installation. After the setup verifies that you have enough hard disk space, it copies files that are needed by the setup program to the hard disk.

✦ **GUI-mode phase:** After the text-mode portion of the install, the system restarts and moves into the GUI-mode phase. This phase of the setup can be quickly identified by the use of a wizard and its Windows-like shell. The wizard asks questions; you answer each question and click Next to progress to the next question.

This phase of the setup detects additional devices, installs drivers for those devices, and copies additional necessary setup files that weren't copied during the text-mode phase. During this phase, you are asked for information, such as your name, your organization, and your product key for the Windows OS, and you are asked to agree to the end-user licensing agreement (EULA).

Performing a Windows 2000 attended installation

Before I go through how to boot from the Windows CD to start the setup program, I talk about how you can launch the Windows setup program. The installation program for Windows can be launched by booting from a CD-ROM or by calling the setup executables manually — winnt.exe or winnt32.exe. You execute winnt.exe if you are installing the OS from a 16-bit client, such as a DOS-formatted system. If you are installing Windows 2000 on a system that has a 32-bit operating system already installed, you will run the upgrade program, which is winnt32.exe. Table 3-2 and Table 3-3 show popular setup switches (with placeholders) with these programs.

Table 3-2	winnt.exe Setup Switches
Switch	*Description*
/u:<filename>	Tells the installation program the name of a file that has all the answers to the questions asked during the installation. This is used to automate the setup; also known as an unattended installation.
/udf:<id>, <filename>	Points to a database file (really a text file) with a list of unique settings for each computer in the network. This is another file used in automating setup.
/s:<path>	Specifies the source path to the Windows NT/2000 installation files.
/t:<drive>	Tells the setup program to store the temporary files used during the installation process on a different drive.
/r:<folderpath>	Specifies an additional folder that will be copied to the system during setup. This folder remains on the system after the installation is complete.
/rx:<folderpath>	Specifies an additional folder to be copied to the system during setup but deleted after the setup program is completed. Using this switch is a great way to place some additional files needed by the setup program but have them removed after setup.
/e:<command>	Specifies a command that executes after the graphical portion of the setup is complete.

Table 3-3	winnt32.exe Setup Switches
Switch	*Description*
/unattend: <filename>	Tells the installation program the name of a file that has all the answers to the questions asked during the installation. This is used to automate the setup; also known as an unattended installation.
/udf:<id>, <filename>	Points to a database file (really a text file) with a list of unique settings for computers on the network. This is another file used in automating setup.
/s:<path>	Specifies the source path to the Windows NT/2000 installation files.
/tempdrive:<drive>	Tells the setup program to store the temporary files used during the installation process on a different drive.
/copydir:<folder>	Specifies an additional folder to be copied to the system during setup. This folder remains on the system after the installation is complete.
/cmd:<command>	Specifies a command that executes before the final phase of the setup program.
/cmdcons	Installs the Recovery Console on the system. The Recovery Console is used to help recover a system that cannot be booted. You can install the Recovery Console after Windows has been installed.
/checkupgradeonly	Verifies that your existing hardware and software are compatible with the Windows 2000/XP operating system. You would use this command before you upgrade your Windows 9x system to Windows 2000 or XP.

For the A+ exam, be familiar with the setup program switches that are listed in Table 3-2 and Table 3-3.

To launch the setup program by booting from CD-ROM, simply place the Windows CD in the system and power-on the system. Windows prompts you whether to Press Any Key to Set Up Windows. When you boot from the Windows 2000 CD, the setup program runs automatically (after you press a key), and you are installing Windows! Booting from the CD is the approach most people take when installing a single copy of Windows.

Remember that with Windows 2000/XP/2003, you don't necessarily need to call the winnt.exe or winnt32.exe program yourself — you can boot off the CD.

If you have a bootable CD-ROM, the installation will be fairly easy. All you need to do is follow these steps:

1. **Place the CD in the CD-ROM tray and boot up the system.**

The setup program is invoked automatically, as shown in Figure 3-1.

```
Windows 2000 Professional Setup

Welcome to Setup.

This portion of the Setup program prepares Microsoft(R)
Windows 2000(TM) to run on your computer.

    • To set up Windows 2000 now, press ENTER.

    • To repair a Windows 2000 installation, press R.

    • To quit Setup without installing Windows 2000, press F3.

ENTER=Continue   R=Repair   F3=Quit
```

Figure 3-1:
The start
of the
Windows
2000
installation
program.

When the setup program starts for Windows 2000, you are asked whether you want to install Windows 2000 or repair an installation of Windows 2000. You repair an installation of Windows 2000 when your existing installation has failed and you would like to fix it. In this example, though, you just want to install Windows 2000.

2. **Press Enter to continue with installation.**

If you are installing Windows 2000 on a system without defined partitions, Windows 2000 displays a screen that warns you that there is an empty disk or a disk running an OS that Windows 2000 does not understand, as shown in Figure 3-2.

3. **To continue with setup, press C.**

4. **Read the license agreement (see Figure 3-3) and press F8 to agree to the terms.**

You can scroll down through the agreement with the Page Down key.

Figure 3-2:
Partition
warning in
Windows
2000.

Figure 3-3:
Agree to the
terms of the
license.

Windows 2000 shows a screen where you choose the partition you want to install the OS to, as shown in Figure 3-4.

5. **To change your partition information by creating or deleting partitions, press C (for create) or D (for delete).**

6. **Select the partition where you want to install Windows 2000 and then press Enter.**

 You are asked what file system you want to use for that partition, as shown in Figure 3-5.

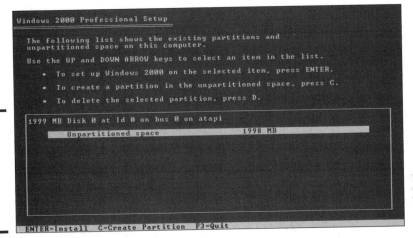

Figure 3-4:
Choose a
partition
where
to install
Windows
2000.

Figure 3-5:
Choose a
file system
during the
Windows
2000
installation.

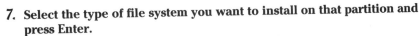

7. Select the type of file system you want to install on that partition and press Enter.

See the earlier section, "File Systems" for the pros and cons of FAT, FAT32, and NTFS file systems.

Setup begins copying the files required for the installation to your hard disk.

After the files are copied to your system, Windows 2000 loads the GUI phase of the installation before the rest of the setup will continue. The GUI phase uses wizard style prompts to ask you the remaining

questions. During this time, the Windows 2000 setup program detects the hardware installed on your system. This part of the installation can take anywhere from three to five minutes, depending on your system, as shown in Figure 3-6.

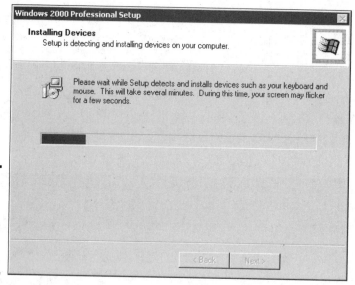

Figure 3-6:
Windows 2000 setup detects your computer hardware.

Windows 2000 continues with the installation and asks for your local settings and your keyboard layout settings.

8. **(Optional) To change the local settings or the keyboard layout settings, click the corresponding Customize button, as shown in Figure 3-7, and tweak the settings as you desire.**

Setup asks you to personalize your software. Specifically, it asks for your name and the organization name, as shown in Figure 3-8.

9. **Enter a name and organization name in the appropriate spaces and then click Next.**

I recommend using a generic name — such as IT Support — instead of your real name in the Name field because any new software installed will display this information.

Setup prompts you for the product key of the OS. You can find the product key on the CD case of Windows 2000.

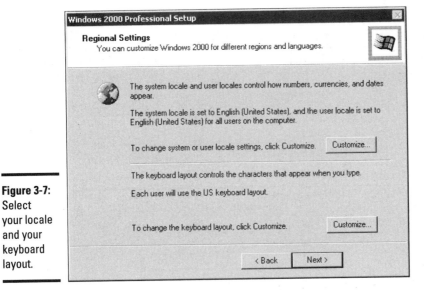

Figure 3-7:
Select
your locale
and your
keyboard
layout.

Figure 3-8:
Entering
personalized
information
during
Windows
installation.

10. **Enter the product key and then click Next.**

You are now required to enter a computer name and a password for the administrator account, as shown in Figure 3-9.

11. **Enter a computer name in the first text box and an administrator password in the next two boxes; then click Next.**

The administrator account has full access to the system. You want to create a password that is unique and difficult for someone to guess. Use a mixture of numbers and letters and also include capitalized characters at different points in the password. *Note:* Passwords are case sensitive.

You will not be asked for the administrator's name. Each Windows installation has an administrative account with full access to the system. When you install the OS, that administrative account automatically has an account name Administrator. You are responsible only for assigning a password to that account during installation.

The next screen asks you to verify the date and time. You can also choose whether you would like the OS to adjust the time automatically to accommodate daylight savings, as shown in Figure 3-10.

12. **Select the correct date, time, and time zone; also select the check box if you want the OS to automatically adjust for daylight savings time. Then click Next.**

Ihe Installation Wizard informs you that it is configuring the networking components of the operating system. Setup then asks whether you would like to install typical network settings or to customize your network settings, as shown in Figure 3-11.

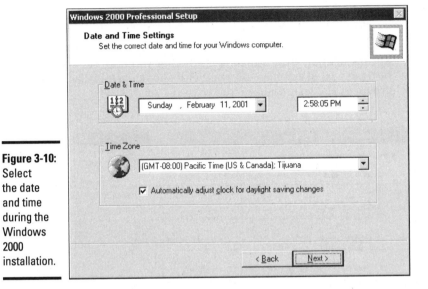

Figure 3-10:
Select
the date
and time
during the
Windows
2000
installation.

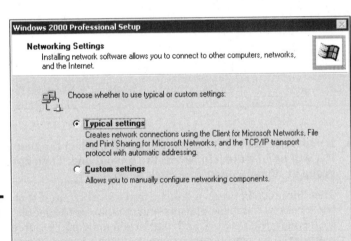

Figure 3-11:
Choosing
a network
installation
type.

13. **Select whether you want the typical networking settings or would like
to customize the settings; then click Next.**

- *Typical Settings:* Setup installs Client for Microsoft Networks, File
and Printer Sharing for Microsoft Networks, and the TCP/IP protocol
configured for DHCP.

- *Custom Settings:* You can modify your networking components, such as assign yourself a static IP address. For more information on networking Windows, check out Book VIII, Chapter 3.

The Installation Wizard then asks whether you want the computer to become part of a domain or whether it should be installed into a workgroup, as shown in Figure 3-12.

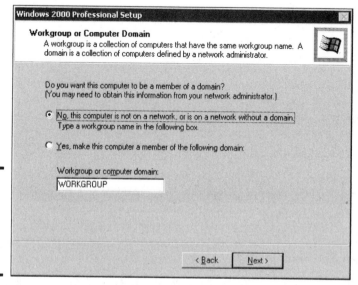

Workgroup or Computer Domain
A workgroup is a collection of computers that have the same workgroup name. A domain is a collection of computers defined by a network administrator.

Do you want this computer to be a member of a domain?
(You may need to obtain this information from your network administrator.)

☉ No, this computer is not on a network, or is on a network without a domain.
Type a workgroup name in the following box.

○ Yes, make this computer a member of the following domain:

Workgroup or computer domain:
WORKGROUP

Figure 3-12:
Select your workgroup or domain during installation.

14. **If your computer will be in a workgroup, select the first radio button; if it will be in a domain, select the second one. Then enter the workgroup or domain name and click Next.**

The difference between a domain and a workgroup is that the domain has a central database of users and computers for people who wish to log on to the network and use certain network resources, such as a printer. A workgroup environment doesn't have a server with a central list of user accounts — each workstation manages its own user accounts in the local SAM database.

If you are not sure whether your computer is in a domain environment, choose workgroup. You can always join the domain later.

Windows continues by installing all the Windows components required by the OS for day-to-day use. It then sets up the Start menu, registers components on the machine, and finally cleans out any temporary files by the installation program, as shown in Figure 3-13.

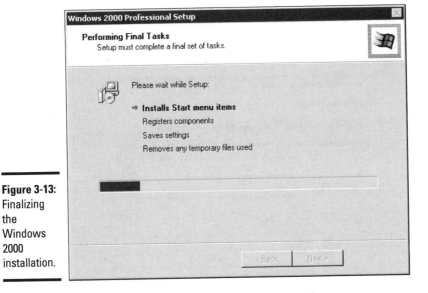

Figure 3-13:
Finalizing
the
Windows
2000
installation.

15. **After the final stage completes, click Finish to restart the computer.**

Upon restart, Windows 2000 takes you into the Network Identification Wizard, where you tell Windows 2000 whether you will be using the same username and password to log on each time or whether each user should provide a unique username and password.

16. **Select the appropriate logon option and then click Next.**

If you tell Windows to log on with the same account each time, Windows will automatically log on — meaning that whoever sits at the computer and turns it on isn't prompted for a username and password. If you would rather the system require you to log on manually each time, select the Users Must Enter a User Name and Password to Use This Computer option, shown in Figure 3-14.

After you finish the Network Identification Wizard, the installation of Windows 2000 is complete. Congratulations!

To practice installing Windows 2000, check out Lab 3-1 of the `Labs.pdf` file in the Author directory of this book's companion CD-ROM.

Figure 3-14: Configuring Windows 2000 for logon type.

Performing a Windows XP attended installation

Installing Windows XP is similar to installing Windows 2000 because both OSes systems are based on the old Windows NT technologies. This means that you will see a lot of similarities between the two OSes — starting with the installation.

To perform a Windows XP attended installation, follow these steps:

1. **Put the Windows XP installation CD in the CD-ROM drive and restart the computer.**

2. **When the screen says, "Press any key to boot from CD," press a key.**

 After you boot from CD, the text-mode portion of the installation begins. You can always tell when you're in the text-mode portion of the installation because of the blue background and the lack of the "Windows-ish" look.

 After booting from the CD-ROM, setup copies temporary files to the hard disk and then asks you whether you want to install Windows or to recover Windows, as shown in Figure 3-15.

3. **Press Enter to start the Windows XP installation process.**

4. **Read the licensing agreement (shown in Figure 3-16) and then press F8 to agree to the terms.**

Figure 3-15:
Just press
Enter to
start the
installation.

Figure 3-16:
Agree to the
licensing
terms.

You are asked to partition the disk. Like with the Windows 2000 installation, you can manage partitions here and perform actions such as deleting and creating partitions.

5. **To create a partition, press C, type** 8000 **(MB) as the partition size (as shown in Figure 3-17), and then press Enter.**

Figure 3-17:
Creating
an 8000MB
partition
to install
Windows
XP.

6. **Select the newly created partition to install Windows XP to and then press Enter.**

 You are asked what file system you would like to format the partition with. You may format the partition with the FAT file system or NTFS, as shown in Figure 3-18.

Figure 3-18:
Performing a quick format and applying NTFS to the partition.

7. **Choose to format for NTFS (Quick) and press Enter.**

 With a quick format, Windows does not scan for bad sectors; with a regular format, Windows does scan for bad sectors. Scanning for bad sectors can be time consuming, so I chose a quick format.

 Setup formats the partition and then copies files to the Windows folder on the hard disk. After the files are copied to the hard disk, setup reboots and the GUI-mode portion of the installation starts, as shown in Figure 3-19.

 Setup installs devices that are detected during installation, and then asks you to choose your Regional options, such as language settings.

8. **Click Next to accept the default regional settings.**

 For this example, I accept the default settings. However, you may change your regional settings at any time through the Windows Control Panel.

9. **Fill in your name (I suggest something generic, like IT Support) type your organization name (see Figure 3-20), and then click Next.**

10. **Type the product key (found on the CD case that the installation CD came in) and then click Next.**

11. **Enter a computer name and type (twice) an Administrator password; then click Next.**

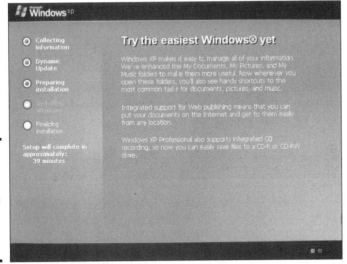

Figure 3-19:
The GUI-
mode setup
phase of the
Windows
XP
installation.

Figure 3-20:
Supply your
name and
organization
to the
Windows
XP setup
program.

The administrator account has full access to the system, so you want to
supply a strong password that incorporates letters (uppercase and low-
ercase) and numbers.

12. **Choose your time zone and then click Next.**

You are asked about network settings.

13. **Click Next to accept the typical network settings.**

If you install the typical network settings, you will have File and Printer Sharing, TCP/IP, and the Client for Microsoft network installed.

14. **Click Next to accept the default workgroup for Windows XP.**

Windows continues with installation and finally reboots. After the reboot, Windows finalizes the setup by walking you through a configuration wizard, as shown in Figure 3-21.

Figure 3-21: Finalizing the Windows configuration after Windows has been installed.

The wizard first asks whether you want to connect to the Internet through the LAN setup.

15. **If your computer will connect to the Internet through the network, select this option and then click Next.**

You may then choose whether you wish to register Windows with Microsoft.

16. **Choose your registration preference and then click Next.**

17. **Type the name of a username to use as your own user account and then press Next to finalize the setup.**

Because you have not been given the opportunity to assign a password for this user account, you will log on without a password for this account until you assign the password through the User Accounts applet in the Control Panel.

When you install Windows XP, you are also asked to prove the validity of your Windows installation by activating Windows. When you activate your installation of Windows, no other installation of Windows can be activated with that copy of Windows. You may activate Windows via the Internet, or via telephone by calling the phone number provided in the wizard.

Performing a Windows Vista attended installation

The steps to perform an attended installation of Windows Vista are very similar to other versions of Windows, but the architecture of the installation program has changed. Windows Vista no longer uses the text-mode installation phase that was part of all other Windows installations. Instead, it uses the Windows Preinstallation Environment (PE), which is a scaled-down version of Windows that runs when you boot from a CD or DVD. The installation sports a GUI interface right off the bat, as compared with Windows 2000 and XP and their text-mode phase where the screen was very DOS-looking.

Because of the size of the newer versions of Windows Vista, Microsoft ships it on DVD instead of CD-ROM: something you will notice more for future software releases as well. To install Vista, follow these steps:

1. **Place the Windows Vista installation DVD in system and restart the computer.**

The computer boots off the DVD and then starts the Vista installation by loading files into memory.

2. **After Vista loads the GUI installation shell, you are asked to set your preferred language, and also time and currency format; see Figure 3-22. Then click Next.**

Figure 3-22:
Select Vista
installation
settings.

3. (Optional) Like previous versions of Windows, you can perform a repair of a system from the Windows installation media.

4. Because I assume this is a clean install, click Install Now. (See Figure 3-23.)

Figure 3-23: Choosing to install Windows Vista.

5. Read the licensing terms, choose the I Accept the License Terms option, and then click Next.

You then asked whether you want to upgrade your current version of Windows to Vista or perform a clean installation by choosing Custom (see Figure 3-24).

6. In this example, I choose Custom.

7. When next presented with a list of hard drives where you can install Windows Vista, choose the drive you wish and then click Next.

If you don't want to use the entire drive to host the OS and you are interested in partitioning the disk, click the Advanced link to access options for creating, deleting, and formatting partitions shown in Figure 3-25.

Windows copies the files it needs, expands them, and then continues installation. The screen shows the progression; see Figure 3-26. This step might take the good part of 30 minutes.

After Windows Vista installs, you are then walked through some final steps.

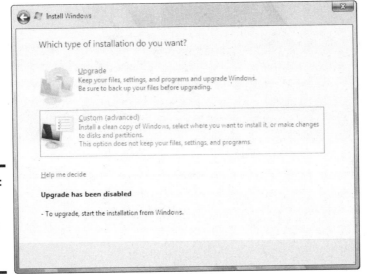

Figure 3-24: Choose a clean installation or to upgrade.

Figure 3-25: Use advanced options to manage partitions during Vista installation.

8. **Create a user account (for yourself), which will have administrator capabilities (Figure 3-27). Type a username and a password; then click Next.**

9. **When asked the name of the computer, enter a name of less than 15 characters. Also choose your desktop background. Then click Next.**

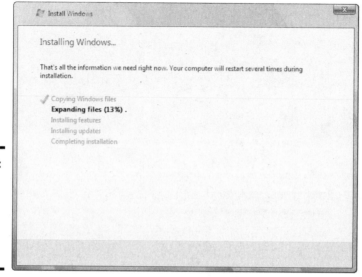

Figure 3-26:
Windows
Vista
installation
copies
files to the
system.

Figure 3-27:
Create
an admin
account
during
installation.

10. **When asked whether you want Windows to automatically protect your system (enabling automatic updates), choose Use Recommended Settings.**

11. **Choose your time zone, verify that the date and time are correct (see Figure 3-28), and then click Next.**

12. **Set your computer location; see Figure 3-29. Because I am using this system for a home network, I opt for Home.**

REMEMBER

The location is important. For example, say you chose Public Location here. Vista security settings are tighter — a good thing — if you let it know that you are in a public site, such as an Internet cafe.

Figure 3-28: Choose date and time settings.

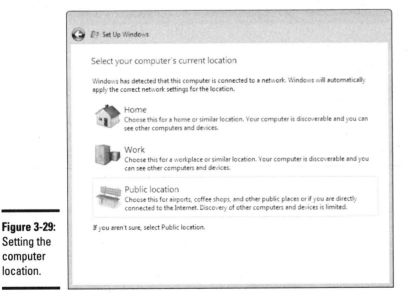

Figure 3-29: Setting the computer location.

13. **With installation now complete, click Start.**

After Vista reboots, you can log on with the account you created during installation.

After you installed Vista, you need to activate it to prove you have a licensed installation of Windows Vista. You will need your software key, which is usually located on the side of the computer or inside the CD case. With key in hand, configure your install to use that key and then choose the Activate feature in Vista. That prompts Vista to connect to the Microsoft site to verify that the software key has not been used.

To activate Vista, follow these steps:

1. **Click Start. Right-click Computer and choose Properties.**

2. **In the System Properties window, click Change Product Key (bottom of Figure 3-30).**

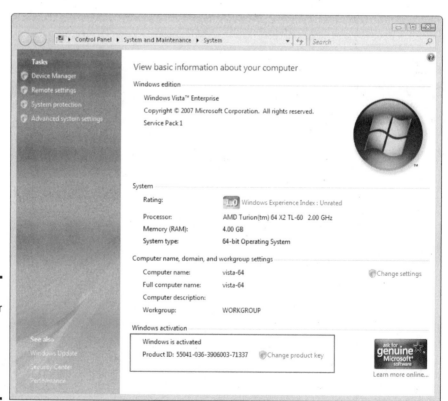

Figure 3-30: Change your product key to activate your copy of Windows Vista.

3. **Type your product key into the product key window that opens; then click OK.**

4. **Back in System Properties, click the Active Windows Now link.**

Performing Unattended Installations of Windows

An unattended installation (compared with an attended installation) frees you from having to be present when the installation is run. Before installation, you place all the answers to the installation questions in a text file, and the setup program reads the text file.

Windows 2000/XP/2003

When you need to install an OS on many computers, you can do an automated, unattended installation. You start this process by creating an answer file (also known as an *unattend file*) that holds all the answers to questions asked during the installation. The Windows 2000/XP/2003 setup program then uses the answers in this file instead of prompting you for each answer during installation. A typical answer file is shown in Figure 3-31.

Figure 3-31:
The structure of an answer file.

The answer file is divided into different sections, indicated by square brackets. For example, see the section in Figure 3-31 labeled [UserData]. Here, you can set what you want the setup program to use for your name and organization, and the computer name of the system being installed.

```
[UserData]
  ComputerName=WORKSTATION1
  FullName="Glen E. Clarke"
  OrgName="CompanyABC"
```

In the preceding sample, ComputerName is a setting that corresponds to a question asked during the installation, and the WORKSTATION1 is the value you are assigning to that entry.

To get a list of settings that can be assigned in the answer file, look at the help file located in the deploy.cab file, which you can find on the Windows CD-ROM in the Support\Tools folder.

To make it easier to create the answer file, Microsoft offers Setup Manager (setupmgr.exe), a wizard that you can run. You can find Setup Manager in the deploy.cab file on the Windows CD as well.

After extracting the Setup Manager from the CAB file, you can run it by double-clicking setupmgr.exe. The wizard launches, asks all the questions you would be asked during a typical installation, and then creates the answer file. Figure 3-32 shows Setup Manager asking for your name and organization. Notice that after you answer a question, you click the Next button to get the next question in typical wizard format.

Figure 3-32:
Running
Setup
Manager
simplifies
creating
answer
files.

After you create the answer file, you pass it to the Windows setup program by calling the winnt.exe or winnt32.exe program and supplying the switch that tells the program what answer file you would like to use. Pop quiz time: Do you remember what switch to use to specify an unattended file for winnt.exe? If you answered /u, you are correct!

Setup Manager is a Windows program used to create answer files. You can then pass the answer file to the Windows setup program by using `winnt.exe /u: <filename>` or `winnt32.exe /unattend: <filename>`.

Assume that you copied the CD contents to a folder on the server and created a network drive (`J:` in this example) to point to that folder. To perform an automated installation of Windows, connect to the `J:\i386` directory and upload your newly created answer file (`companyabc.txt` for the sake of this example).

To start the installation process from a DOS-formatted system that needs Windows 2000 installed, type the following at the command prompt:

```
J:\i386\winnt.exe /s:j:\i386 /u:companyabc.txt
```

The preceding example code runs the `winnt.exe` file and supplies `J:\i386` as the source directory (where the Windows files are located) to the setup program. The `/u` switch tells the `winnt.exe` program to use the `companyabc.txt` file as the answer file — pretty cool technology!

To install Windows to a system running a 32-bit OS, run the `winnt32.exe` program. *Note:* The switches are a little bit different. For example, use the `/unattend` switch instead of the `/u` switch.

If you don't have a network and you want to automate a Windows installation from CD, you can do that! You simply create an answer file (on a computer already running), name it `winnt.sif`, and copy that file to a floppy disk. When you boot from CD to install Windows, quickly pop in the floppy disk. The setup program will automatically read the `winnt.sif` file, and you are off to the races with an automated, unattended installation! With Windows XP, the `winnt.sif` file can be placed in the i386 folder and burned to a bootable installation CD so you do not need to use a floppy disk.

To practice automating a Windows XP installation, check out Lab 3-2. Lab 3-2 can be found in the `Labs.pdf` file in the Author directory of the CD-ROM.

Windows Vista

To automate installing Vista, you use different tools than with the previous OSes mentioned. The concept is pretty much this: You still need to build an answer file, but the tools you use are a little different.

The first change that Microsoft made with automating Vista is that the answer file is no longer a TXT file. It is now an XML file! (An XML file is a plain text file supported by a number of different products.)

To create an answer file for Windows Vista installations, download the Windows Automated Installation Kit (AIK) from the Microsoft Web site. In the Windows AIK is the Windows System Image Manager (SIM) tool, which you use to create an answer file to automate Vista installations.

Verifying and Troubleshooting the Installation

In the previous two sections, I showed you how to perform attended and unattended installations of Windows. In this section, you look at some tips for verifying and troubleshooting a Windows installation.

First things first. After Windows is installed, ensure that all device drivers have been installed. In Device Manager (choose Start⇨Control Panel⇨System and then click the Device Manager button on the Hardware tab in Windows XP; or click Start, right-click Computer, and then choose Manage⇨Select Device Manager in the Computer Management Console for Vista), verify that all drivers are present. If you are missing drivers for some devices, Device Manager will have a category called Unknown Devices, which are indicated by a yellow question mark.

Check out Book VI, Chapter 1 to find out more about updating drivers.

Windows creates a number of log files during installation. If installation does not go as you planned, peruse these logs for more information about an error. These log files report information only for events that happen during the installation, so if you're troubleshooting something like booting Windows or networking, these files won't help.

The log files created during installation are

+ Setupact.log records information about the files that are copied during installation.

+ Setuperr.log records information about errors that happen during installation.

+ Setupapi.log records information about device driver files that are copied during installation.

+ Setuplog.txt records additional information about the device drivers.

Be sure to remember the log files that are created when you install Windows. These files can be used to help troubleshoot problems with the installation of Windows.

A number of problems may arise during Windows installation. The following list outlines a few common ones:

✦ **Bad CD-ROM:** If you experience failure to copy files during the setup process, you might have a bad CD-ROM device, or maybe the CD itself is bad. Try booting from another Windows CD to find out whether the problem is with the media or the CD-ROM device.

✦ **Can't boot after install:** If you have trouble rebooting after you complete an installation, be sure that you did not leave a floppy diskette in the floppy drive. Also check CMOS to ensure that the hard drive appears as a boot device. (See Book II, Chapter 4, to find out how to tweak CMOS settings.)

✦ **Can't start Windows install:** If you can't start the Windows setup by booting off the CD-ROM, make sure that the CD-ROM device is listed as a startup device in CMOS. Also, ensure that the CD-ROM is listed before the hard disk.

✦ **Not enough disk space:** The Windows setup program checks available hard disk space. If your computer doesn't have enough space, Windows indicates this with an error, and the Windows installation stops. You will need to restart the installation again after cleaning up disk space.

Overall, Windows installations have become more reliable with each successive version, so you are less likely to have installation problems with the current version than you would have back in the Windows 9x days.

Upgrading Windows

You will be responsible for understanding how to upgrade from previous versions of Windows to Windows 2000, XP, and Windows Vista. The following sections introduce you to the theory of upgrading an OS.

Preparing to upgrade

Many businesses run Windows, so understanding how to upgrade is important. Whether installing the OS from scratch or performing an upgrade, the process is pretty much the same. *Note:* With an upgrade, though, you will find many installation decisions already made for you during the installation of the previous OS. For example, when you upgrade a Windows NT 4.0 computer to Windows 2000, you will not be asked the name of the computer to be installed — this information is inherited from the previous OS.

Before you upgrade any OS, backup *the system and any important data.* You never know when an upgrade is going to go bad, so make sure you can at least put the system back to its previous state.

Upgrading to Windows 2000 Professional

To upgrade to Windows 2000 Pro, run the Windows 2000 upgrade program (`winnt32.exe`). To check the current OS for known problems with the installed software and hardware, run the upgrade program with the `/checkupgradeonly` switch to launch the Windows 2000 Readiness Analyzer, which reports any hardware or software compatibility problems Windows 2000 might have with your current system. Save the Readiness Analyzer report to file so that you can print it when dealing with any installation issues.

Generally, you will have no problem upgrading Windows 95 or Windows 98 to Windows 2000. Because of security changes in the Windows 2000 OS, though, some software that ran fine on Windows 95 and Windows 98 won't run on Windows 2000. If you encounter this, try to find an equivalent application that will run on Windows 2000 and then install it after you upgrade the OS.

For the A+ exams, know the upgrade path from each OS to the Windows 2000 operating system, as shown in Table 3-4. Windows 95/98/NT can be upgraded directly to Windows 2000. Windows 3.1 needs to be first upgraded to Windows 95 or Windows 98 and then upgraded to Windows 2000 Professional. Because Windows Me came out after Windows 2000, there is no upgrade path from Windows Me to Windows 2000.

Table 3-4	Client Upgrade Paths to Windows 2000 Professional
Current Operating System	*Upgrade To*
Windows 3.1	Windows 95/98 and then to Windows 2000 Professional
Windows 95	Windows 2000 Professional
Windows 98	Windows 2000 Professional
Windows NT Workstation 4.0	Windows 2000 Professional
Windows Me	Cannot be upgraded to Windows 2000

To find any incompatible software or hardware before upgrading to Windows 2000, you can run the setup in the check-upgrade mode by typing `winnt32.exe /checkupgradeonly`.

When you upgrade from Windows NT 4.0 to Windows 2000, you likely won't run into any major upgrade issues because these versions have a similar structure. The similarities between Windows NT 4.0 and Windows 2000 include the following:

✦ Registry structure

✦ File systems

✦ Security

To upgrade from Windows NT 4.0 to Windows 2000, run `winnt32.exe`, which is the upgrade program designed to run from a 32-bit operating system for the purpose of upgrading to Windows 2000. When you run `winnt32.exe`, many of the OS's settings are carried into the installation program from Windows NT 4.0 — this means that you have fewer questions to answer during the installation.

Be sure to review the hardware requirements of Windows 2000 before you upgrade and make sure to set up a test environment in which all applications and existing hardware have been thoroughly tested.

Upgrading to Windows XP

A number of OSes can be upgraded to Windows XP, including Windows 98, 98 SE, Me, NT 4.0 (SP5 or higher), and 2000. You cannot upgrade Windows 95 or Windows NT 3.51 to Windows XP directly, though: You must first upgrade those OSes to Windows 98 (for existing Window 95 systems) or to Windows NT 4.0 SP5 (for Windows NT 3.51). Table 3-5 gives a summary of the OSes that can be upgraded to Windows XP.

Table 3-5	Client Upgrade Paths to Windows XP
Current Operating System	*Upgrade Directly to Windows XP?*
Windows 3.1	No
Windows 95	No
Windows 98	Yes
Windows NT Workstation 4.0	Yes (Windows NT 4.0 with Service Pack 5)
Windows Me	Yes
Windows 2000	Yes

Before you upgrade to Windows XP, check the existing system for known compatibility issues with Windows XP by using the Upgrade Advisor. The Upgrade Advisor identifies compatibility issues and gives details on resolution for these issues.

To run the Upgrade Advisor, execute `winnt32.exe` with the `/checkupgrad only` switch, or you can launch it from the splash page that appears after inserting the Windows XP CD. Select the Check System Compatibility option and then choose to Check My System Automatically. The Upgrade Advisor runs and displays any compatibility problems, as shown in Figure 3-33.

Figure 3-33:
The
Upgrade
Advisor
identifies
known
hardware
and
software
issues when
upgrading
to Windows
XP.

In Figure 3-33, the Upgrade Advisor has identified an issue upgrading the system because the existing system has CD Creator installed. You can save the report to a file by pressing the Save As button, or you can view the details in an HTML page by clicking the Details button, as shown in Figure 3-34.

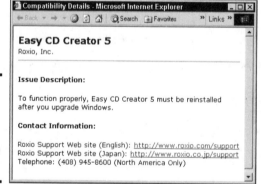

Figure 3-34:
Save a
report
created by
the Upgrade
Advisor.

Upgrading to Windows Vista

You can perform an in-place upgrade of an OS to Windows Vista, but you must prepare for the upgrade. Start by verifying that your existing hardware and software are supported by Windows Vista. To do so, check with each manufacturer's Web site, or run the Windows Vista Upgrade Advisor (downloadable from Microsoft online). The Upgrade Advisor will run on your system and report any installation issues that could arise if you tried to install Vista.

The goal here is to prevent you from installing Vista and then finding out none of your applications run or hardware is supported.

If you wish to upgrade to Vista, you must have one of these three prerequisite OSes: Windows 2000, XP, or another edition of Vista. Yup, you read that right: You can upgrade from Vista to Vista if you upgrade a lower-end edition (such as the Home edition) to a higher-end edition (say, Enterprise).

The other issue to watch for when upgrading to Vista is that the edition of Windows you are upgrading is upgradeable to the edition of Vista. For example, you cannot upgrade Windows XP Professional to Windows Vista Home edition because XP Professional supports features not supported in Vista Home Edition (such as domain environments). Really, when you think about it, if you were successful in that action, you are downgrading — not upgrading!

Installing or Removing Additional Windows Components

After installing Windows, you can add or remove components (or portions of the Windows OS) by going through Add/Remove Windows Components. For example, if you would like to create a Web site, you will most likely want a Web server installed on your system. Windows does not come with Web server software installed by default, so you would need to add one after you install the OS.

To install additional Windows components after the installation of the operating system, follow these steps:

1. **Choose Start⇨Settings⇨Control Panel (in Windows 2000) or Start⇨ Control Panel (in Windows XP).**

2. **In the Control Panel, click Add or Remove Programs.**

In the Add or Remove Programs dialog box is the Add/Remove Windows Components option (left). Use this option to add software that comes with Windows but was not installed by default, such as accessories (including games) and Internet Information Services (IIS; Microsoft Web server software).

3. **Click Add/Remove Windows Components.**

The Windows Components Wizard appears as shown in Figure 3-35.

4. **Select each component to install and then click Next.**

The files are copied to your system from the Windows CD, so be sure to have the Windows CD close by in case you are prompted to insert the CD.

5. **After the files are copied, click Finish.**

6. **Close the Add or Remove Programs dialog box.**

Figure 3-35:
Installing
additional
Windows
components.

To add or remove Windows components from Windows Vista, navigate to
the Control Panel applet.

1. **Click Start; click Control Panel and then click the Programs link.**

2. **Under the Programs and Features heading, click the Turn Windows
 Features On or Off link.**

3. **From the Windows Features window that opens, choose which
 Windows features you wish to install (see Figure 3-36).**

Figure 3-36:
Adding/
removing
Windows
Vista
components.

Understanding How to Dual-Boot Windows

Dual-booting — running multiple OSes on the same computer — is different than performing an upgrade. With an upgrade, all applications and their settings carry forward into the new OS. When you dual-boot, you install each OS into a different folder, which means that the applications do not carry forward into your new OS. With a dual-boot scenario, you need to install the applications with each OS installed.

One reason why you might want to dual-boot multiple OSes is to test or support applications in the different OSes. You might also want to dual-boot if your company uses an application that won't function on your primary OS (for example, Windows 2000) but works great in an older OS (for example, Windows 98). You can install both OSes on the computer and then install the application that doesn't work in Windows 2000 on the Windows 98 system; any time you want to use that application, you just boot to Windows 98.

To dual-boot multiple OSes, the following criteria must be met:

+ The bootable drive (usually drive C:) must have a file system supported by all OSes on the computer.

+ You must install each OS into its own folder.

Here's an example: If you would like to dual-boot Windows 98 and Windows 2000 on the same computer, the first thing you need to do is make sure that your bootable partition (drive C:) is using the file system common to all OSes (in this example, FAT32). After you ensure that you are using a common file system, you may then install each OS. Remember to install each OS into a different directory. For this example, assume you have installed Windows 98 in C:\windows. You can then install Windows 2000 to, for instance, C:\win2k.

You now have a system that dual-boots between Windows 98 and Windows 2000. So how do you select which OS you want to boot to? The Windows 2000 boot menu displays the different OSes; when it appears, you select one.

 In dual-boot scenarios, any application you want to use in both environments must be installed on both OSes. For example, to use Microsoft Word in both Windows 98 and Windows 2000, you need to install it in both OSes.

Updating Installation Files

A number of organizations copy the contents of a Windows CD to a folder on a server and then install Windows from that folder by calling the winnt. exe or the winnt32.exe setup programs. This folder is called a *distribution point* because it is used to distribute the OS to the client systems.

Eventually, Microsoft will release Service Packs that you will apply to the OS on each computer, but you will also want to update the distribution point so that it contains the Service Pack updates for any new systems that install from the folder. The benefit is that after the folder has been updated with the Service Pack, when new systems install the OS over the network, it will already include the updated Service Packs. Updating the source files of an OS at a distribution point to include Service Pack files is *slipstreaming*.

Slipstreaming is the term used when you update your Windows source files with Service Pack files. The benefit is that any new installation of Windows from the updated source files will already have the Service Pack installed.

To slipstream a distribution point, follow these steps:

1. **Create a distribution point on a server by creating a folder.**

 For example, assume that the K: drive is the network drive that will contain the Windows 2000 source files. You might create a folder called K:\win2000\i386.

2. **Copy the contents of the i386 folder from the Windows 2000 CD to K:\win2000\i386.**

3. **Download the proper Service Pack.**

 Assume that you want to update the i386 folder with the Windows 2000 Service Pack 4 files. You would download the executable for Service Pack 4 (w2ksp4.exe).

4. **Run the Service Pack's executable and pass it the /s switch to indicate the source folder to update, like this:**

   ```
   w2ksp4.exe /s:K:\win2000\i386
   ```

After the source files on your distribution server have been updated, anyone who installs Windows from that folder by calling the winnt.exe or winnt32.exe command will automatically have Service Pack 4 installed with the operating system!

Restoring User Data Files

You can move a user's computer's state from one system to another. The *state* of a user's computer comprises the information and settings important to that user. This includes files in the My Documents folder, e-mail settings, Internet Explorer favorites, and the desktop wallpaper, just to name a few.

Saving a computer's state

If you are going to replace a user's computer, you should know how to save the computer's state. You will replace a system for a number of reasons.

Maybe the system is running Windows 98, and you feel that to run Windows XP, the user should have up-to-date hardware. Or maybe the user is running Windows XP on a system, and your manager has a new laptop for the user that will run Windows XP. Bottom line: You have to move the settings from one computer to another.

Windows XP offers the User State Migration Tool (USMT) feature, which is a set of features that can simplify your life when you need to move computer settings from one system to another. The USMT is made up of the Files and Settings Transfer (FAST) Wizard and the command line tools. Just a note that Windows Vista has a similar feature called the Windows Easy Transfer!

To save a computer's state, follow these instructions:

1. **Activate the Files and Settings Transfer Wizard by choosing Start⇨ All Programs⇨Accessories⇨System Tools⇨Files and Settings Transfer Wizard.**

When you run the wizard, it asks you whether you are on the old computer or on the new computer (see Figure 3-37).

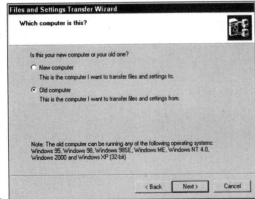

Figure 3-37: Use the FAST Wizard to copy a user's settings from one computer to another.

2. **Select the Old Computer option and click Next.**

The wizard asks how you want to transfer the settings.

3. **Specify where the wizard should save the computer's files and settings and then click Next.**

You can specify a floppy disk or a folder in which to store the settings. If you choose a folder, you can specify to write to a folder on either a removable drive or a network drive.

4. **Select the appropriate option for saving only the user's settings, only the user's files, or both; then click Next.**

See Figure 3-38. Normally, you opt for Both Files and Settings.

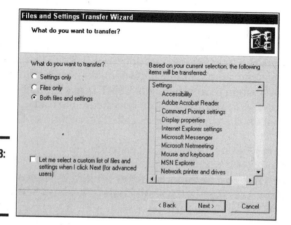

Figure 3-38:
Save
files and
settings.

The FAST Wizard copies all the user state information that you specified on that computer. If you selected the Both Files and Settings option, the FAST Wizard saves these items by default to the location you specified:

- Contents of My Documents
- Contents of My Pictures
- Contents of Desktop
- Contents of Favorites
- Internet Explorer Favorites
- Browser and mail settings
- Accessibility options
- Display properties
- Folder and Taskbar settings
- Mouse and Keyboard settings
- Regional settings
- Microsoft Office applications settings

5. **Click Finish to exit the wizard.**

The FAST Wizard allows you to migrate only one user's settings at a time. To migrate a number of user's settings simultaneously, use these executables:

✦ scanstate captures a user's settings from a source computer and dumps the settings to an intermediate folder.

✦ `loadstate` loads those settings from the intermediate folder to the destination system.

Restoring a computer's state

When time to restore the settings to the destination system (assuming that the destination system is running Windows XP), simply invoke the FAST Wizard (Start⇨All Programs⇨Accessories⇨System Tools⇨Files and Settings Transfer Wizard) and select the New Computer option. Provide the location of the user's state, and the state will be restored.

When replacing an older system (such as a Windows 98 system) with Windows XP, backup the user settings and files with the Windows XP Files and Settings Transfer Wizard. Take the Windows XP CD-ROM to the Windows 98 system and place it in the CD-ROM tray. After loading the Windows XP CD, autorun should kick in and display a list of options on a splash page that you can perform with the CD. To run the FAST wizard, choose Perform Additional Tasks and then choose Transfer Files and Settings from the splash screen.

The Windows Vista feature for transferring files from one system to another, or off a computer before it is upgraded, is Windows Easy Transfer and is very similar to the USMT in Windows XP. To launch the Windows Easy Transfer tool, Start⇨All Programs ⇨Accessories⇨System Tools⇨Windows Easy Transfer.

Getting an A+

This chapter introduces you to some of the guidelines for installing the different Windows OSes. Some key points to remember are

✦ When planning your installation, be sure to plan the partition size, file system, and the computer name that you will use when installing Windows.

✦ You can boot off the Windows 2000/XP CD-ROM to invoke an installation.

✦ Launch the `winnt.exe` setup program from a DOS system; launch `winnt32.exe` from an existing 32-bit Windows interface, such as Windows 9*x*.

✦ To dual-boot multiple operating systems, make sure that drive C: uses a file system that is understood by each OS, and then install each OS into a different folder.

✦ Slipstream your distribution folder so that new installations will deploy with the current Service Packs already installed.

✦ The user state migration tools are used to copy a user's settings and files from one computer to another. A great feature to make your life easier if you need to do this some day!

Prep Test

1 **What command starts a Windows 2000 installation from a DOS prompt?**

A ○ `server.exe`

B ○ `winnt.exe`

C ○ `workstation.exe`

D ○ `setup.exe`

2 **What term describes updating the Windows source files on a server to contain Service Pack updates?**

A ○ service packing

B ○ Windows Update

C ○ slipstreaming

D ○ patching

3 **What setup switch verifies that existing hardware and software will work with Windows 2000/XP?**

A ○ `/checkcompatibility`

B ○ `/verifyhardware`

C ○ `/verifycompatibility`

D ○ `/checkupgradeonly`

4 **What setup switch points the Windows installation to an answer file?**

A ○ `/U: <file>`

B ○ `/UDF:<file>`

C ○ `/UDF:number,<file>`

D ○ `/A:<file>`

5 **What is the minimum processor speed for Windows 2000?**

A ○ 233 MHz

B ○ 133 MHz

C ○ 266 MHz

D ○ 100 MHz

6 Where would you go to install additional operating system components after the installation is complete?

A ○ Add/Remove Hardware

B ○ System icon

C ○ Add/Remove Programs

D ○ You can't install additional operating system components after the OS is installed.

7 What are the minimum RAM requirements for Windows XP?

A ○ 32MB

B ○ 64MB

C ○ 128MB

D ○ 168MB

8 What switch on the Windows setup program allows you to pass a file that contains unique settings per computer?

A ○ /u

B ○ /upgradeonly

C ○ /udf

D ○ /a

9 After installing Windows XP, what will you need to do to prove you have a valid copy of XP?

A ○ Register it.

B ○ Restart it.

C ○ Activate it.

D ○ Shut it down.

10 What is the minimum RAM requirements for Windows Vista?

A ○ 64MB

B ○ 128MB

C ○ 512MB

D ○ 1GB

Answers

1 **B.** The command to start a Windows 2000 installation is `winnt.exe`. *See "Performing a Windows 2000 attended installation."*

2 **C.** When you want to update the source files on the server, you can run the service pack executable with a `/s` switch. This is known as *slipstreaming. Review "Updating Installation Files."*

3 **D.** The `/checkupgradeonly` switch is used by the `winnt32.exe` program to verify compatibility with existing hardware and software. *Check out "Upgrading Windows."*

4 **A.** To point Windows to an answer file, run `winnt.exe` with a `/U:` switch followed by the path to the file that has the answers to use for the installation. *Peruse "Performing Unattended Installations of Windows."*

5 **B.** The minimum processor requirement to install Windows 2000 is a Pentium 133 MHz processor. *Take a look at "Performing Attended Installations of Windows."*

6 **C.** To install additional Windows components, go to Add/Remove Programs in the Control Panel. *Peek at "Installing or Removing Additional Windows Components."*

7 **B.** Although 128MB of RAM is the recommended minimum, Windows XP needs at least 64MB of RAM. *Look over "Hardware requirements."*

8 **C.** The `/udf:<id>,<file>` switch allows you to provide unique information on a per-computer basis. *Study "Performing Unattended Installations of Windows."*

9 **C.** The first time you log on after installing Windows, it prompts you for product activation. Each copy of Windows is validated through activation with Microsoft. *Refer to "Performing a Windows XP attended installation."*

10 **C.** The *minimum* RAM requirement for Windows Vista is 512MB of RAM. *Examine "Hardware requirements."*

Chapter 4: Managing Files and Directories

Exam Objectives

✔ Working with files and directory structures

✔ Understanding file-naming conventions

✔ Comprehending file attributes

*M*ost people agree that money management is important: When you put your money somewhere, it's good to have an organized system so you can remember where the money is and retrieve it as needed. Similarly, file management is an important part of any operating system. You need a way to organize the data on your drive so that it is easily retrievable, as well as a way to identify files that are used for certain purposes.

With the changes that the Microsoft-supported file systems have undergone over the years, an A+ Certified Professional needs an understanding of all the file systems because it is highly likely that the computers a professional is called to work on will not all be running the most current OS. In many cases, the computers that require recovery will be running the oldest OS or will have users on the bleeding edge, trying to make use of the newest features of the latest version of Windows.

In this chapter, you get a brief history of file-naming conventions and how they have changed (and, in some cases, stayed the same) over the years. I also tell you what you need to know about file identification and file management and give you an overview of the file attributes associated with the various Microsoft file systems that have come and gone since the days of MS-DOS 1.0.

Identifying File-Naming Conventions

File-naming conventions have undergone several changes over the years. In this section, you get a look at where they have been and where they are now. You also take a look at the differences between filenames and directory entries.

When MS-DOS was the premier OS on the market, it set the standard of the eight-dot-three (8.3)–character filename. This file system was created by using 32 character fields (bytes) for the filenames. If you work out the math,

you're probably wondering where the extra characters are. Well, 8 plus 3 is 11, and that leaves 21 outstanding characters (bytes). Table 4-1 summarizes how each byte is used.

The File Allocation Table (FAT) is an index on your file system that holds a pointer to where each file is stored on your hard drive. On an NTFS (NT file system), this is called the Master File Table (MFT). To move a file on a file system, you only need to change its reference in the table, and not its location in the file system.

Table 4-1	Directory Entry Format
Use	*Size*
Filename	8 bytes
Extension	3 bytes
Attribute	1 byte
Reserved	10 bytes FAT 32 uses two of these bytes.
Time	2 bytes
Date	2 bytes
First cluster	2 bytes
Size	4 bytes

With every system or component used in a computer, there is a limit; sometimes it is a very large limit, but a limit, nonetheless. That limit is always based on a binary number. Computer systems have RAM limits of 2, 4, 8, or 16GB — never 7.5GB because that is not a binary number. The binary number system is also referred to as Base 2, as compared with our traditional number system, which is Base 10.

Common Base 2 numbers are determined by their digits. For instance, a four-digit Base 2 number has a maximum value of 1111. The following equations figure the value of each digit, from left to right:

$$1 \times 2^3 = 1 \times 8 = 8$$
$$1 \times 2^2 = 1 \times 4 = 4$$
$$1 \times 2^1 = 1 \times 2 = 2$$
$$1 \times 2^0 = 1 \times 1 = 1$$

Then, when you sum value of each digit (8 + 4 + 2 + 1), you get 15. Considering that you could have 0000 as a possible value, there are 16 possible values:

0 through 15. When you count the number of possible values for 1-digit to 12-digit Base 2 numbers, the value limits you end up with are 2, 4, 8, 16, 32, 64, 128, 256, 512, 1024, 2048, and 4096.

In cases where the limit is not based on a binary number, some overhead is usually involved. NetBIOS (Network Basic Input/Output System) computer names are 15 characters long, but they fit into the binary system because there is a 16th character used to identify the type of name, and 16 is a common binary limit. As I mention earlier, filenames are 8 plus 3 characters long, which is only 11 characters or bytes in length. However, the name is only part of a directory entry, and the entire entry is 32 bytes long.

When dealing with file attributes, one byte (8 bits) stores all attribute settings. (For more information on file attributes, see the section "Understanding File Attributes," later in this chapter.) There are not, however, eight attributes.

The 8.3-character naming convention quickly proved to be very limiting. Extensions were often used to allow for longer names and were not directly associated with individual applications. When Windows came onto the market, people began using file extensions properly. Within Windows, the extension was used to identify the application that created a particular document.

Other OSes placed different limits on the length of filenames. For example, Macintosh (before OS/2) limited the length of filenames to 31 characters, and OS/2 limited them to 254 characters. Although 8.3 was very limiting, 254 characters seems excessive, but you likely won't be limited in your choice of filenames.

Long and short filenames

Windows 9*x* and Windows Vista–based OSes both allow for long filenames on a FAT16 partition (to learn more about FAT16, FAT32, and NTFS file systems, go back and read Book II, Chapter 5). These filenames are limited to 255 characters, but different applications like Windows 2000 Explorer (199 characters, including the period separator for the file extension), Windows XP Explorer (220 characters), Windows 98 Explorer (235 characters), and Windows Vista Explorer (255 characters) cannot display all the characters of the filename. If you want to use names longer than Windows Explorer can display, you have to use a different application.

On a FAT16 or FAT32 partition, you are still limited to the 8.3 naming convention. Windows OSes get around this problem by cheating the file system. When you save a file, it is saved by using one directory entry and a short 8.3-character filename. The short filename is created by using the first six characters of the filename followed by a tilde (~) and an incremental number. After creating four files with the same six starting characters, the formula for creating short names is changed. The first two characters are

used, which are then followed by either a randomly or sequentially generated four-digit hexadecimal number (depending on your OS), followed by a tilde (~) and the number 1.

Table 4-2 lists the names of six files and their short filenames that were created in the same directory on a Windows Vista system. To get a listing of the short filenames, you can use `dir /x` — or open the properties window for each file (by right-clicking the file and choosing Properties).

Table 4-2	Short Filenames in Windows Vista
Long Filename Entry	*Short Filename Entry*
ShortFileTest1.txt	SHORTF~1.TXT
ShortFileTest2.txt	SHORTF~2.TXT
ShortFileTest3.txt	SHORTF~3.TXT
ShortFileTest4.txt	SHORTF~4.TXT
ShortFileTest5.txt	SH 04DD~1.TXT
ShortFileTest6.txt	SH 08DD~1.TXT

You have now seen how short filenames are generated, but the question about where the long filenames are stored still exists. The long filenames are stored in additional empty directory entries. The characters for the long filename are stored using 11 characters per additional directory entry. So, a file with a name of

```
My financial report for 2000.txt
```

takes one directory entry of the short filename (possibly `myfina~1.txt`) and one additional entry for each of the 11 characters in the filename, or an additional three entries. That means that this one file would actually occupy four directory entries on your drive. These long filename directory entries have a nonstandard attribute combination of Read-only, Hidden, System, and Volume Label. Although many files on your disk might have a combination of Read-only, Hidden, and System, Volume Label is usually used alone and only on one directory entry that stores the Volume Label for the disk. By using all four attributes, they are a nonstandard combination — and if MS-DOS systems see these entries, they ignore them rather than generating an error.

One of the problems with long filenames occurs when the long filename entries disappear. This can happen if you use older MS-DOS–based disk utilities on your disk. Some of these utilities will tell you that you have a problem with your directory entries and offer to fix them. "Fixing," unfortunately, means deleting all the "invalid" entries, which means you lose all your long filenames. This is not a good thing.

There may come a time when you attempt to copy files to a destination that does not support long filenames. This used to happen with NetWare 3.x servers that had not enabled long filename support (OS/2 namespace). If this happens, you see a Rename File dialog box, similar to the one in Figure 4-1, for each file that has a long filename.

Figure 4-1:
When copying files, you might be prompted to rename files if the destination does not support long filenames.

Creating file associations

Generally speaking, an *association* is a link between two separate things. *File associations* link the file extensions of filenames to the programs that can be used to open the files. When dealing with Windows, file associations let the OS know what program should be used to open a specific type of file. This information is stored in the Registry but can be accessed from a number of locations. The *Registry* is a central location that stores configuration and settings for Windows. Any files not associated with an application will have a generic Windows icon (see Figure 4-2).

Unassociated file

Figure 4-2:
Each file has an icon that represents its file association.

Before OS X, Macintosh systems did not use file extensions for associations. Instead, each file was saved with both a data and a resource portion. The resource portion contained the file type and associated application information. Windows-based files are saved only with a data portion. In OS X, files no longer contain a resource portion, and use file extensions to define types of files.

There are a number of different ways in Windows to associate file types with applications:

+ **Double-click unassociated files and assign an application in the dialog boxes that follow.**

+ **Press Shift while right-clicking associated files and choosing an Open With option.**

+ **Use the Folder Options dialog box.**

+ **Edit the Registry.**

When working with Windows 2000 or newer systems, you will usually not need to hold down the Shift key to reach the Open With options. Windows XP and Windows Vista also display a nested menu with recently chosen options for that file type, making it easier to switch between applications for that file type.

Microsoft does not recommend editing the Registry with the Registry editor to associate file types with applications since there are other methods available for this task. Using the Registry editor is required to change some Registry information. *If you make a mistake with the Registry, you might have to reinstall the operating system.* For more information about editing the Registry with `regedit.exe` and `regedt32.exe`, consult Book VI, Chapter 4.

For any files not currently associated with an application, you can double-click the file. Windows checks its list of associations; if it cannot locate one, it prompts you for the name of the application that should be used, as shown in Figure 4-3. This dialog box gives you the option to Always Use the Selected Program to Open This Kind of File, which, when selected, places an association with the file extension in the Registry. This is by far one of the easiest ways to create file associations.

This process is easier when using Windows XP and Windows Vista, which also offers to check with Microsoft to see what program can be used with that file extension, in addition to letting you choose it manually, as shown in Figure 4-4.

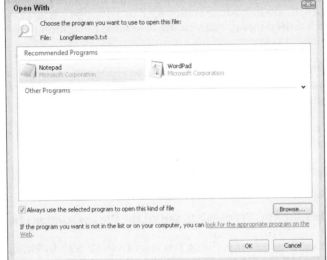

Figure 4-3:
You can
create file
associations
in the Open
With dialog
box.

Figure 4-4:
Windows
XP offers to
locate the
application
required
to work
with a file
based on its
extension.

If you are not sure which program you should use, clear the Always Use the
Selected Program to Open This Kind of File check box (from the Open With
dialog box; refer to Figure 4-3) prior to choosing the application you want to
use with the file. The file will be opened by the application you chose, but the
association will not be recorded in the Registry. So, if you chose the wrong
application, you can just double-click the file and choose another application.

If you make a mistake or need to change the application that opens a file,
you can easily do this through the shortcut menu.

1. **Select the file.**

If you don't do this, the Open With option might be missing.

2. **Right-click the icon.**

In the shortcut menu that appears, you should see an option for Open With. If you are using Windows XP or Windows Vista, Open With will be a nested menu, and you will also have the option to select Choose Default Program.

When you select Always Use the Selected Program to Open This Kind of File, you can associate the file extension with the application you select this time through the dialog box.

If you're looking for a few more options, check out the Folder Options dialog in Windows XP. To get to Folder Options, follow these steps:

1. **Open any directory window, such as My Computer.**

2. **Choose Tools⇨Folder Options.**

3. **Click the File Types tab to see all the file associations in the Registry.**

Windows XP makes this dialog box easy to work with by listing all the file extensions in the top pane, as shown in Figure 4-5. To change the program associated with an application, click the Change button. This opens the Open With dialog box shown in Figure 4-3. From there, you choose a new application for that extension. The dialog layout and use is a little more confusing with earlier versions of Windows.

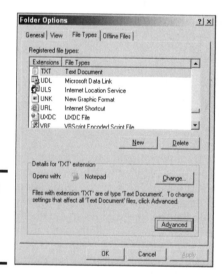

Figure 4-5: Folder Options in Windows XP.

If you select a file type and click the Advanced button (shown in Figure 4-5), you invoke the Edit File Type dialog box (see Figure 4-6). From this dialog box, you can set additional options for this type of file. These options are located under the Actions section of the dialog box and include

✦ **Confirm Open After Download:** This option causes a dialog box to appear after using Internet Explorer (IE) to download files with this extension. The dialog will confirm that you want to open the file.

✦ **Always Show Extension:** Even when Windows Explorer is set up to hide extensions, if this option is selected, the extension will still appear for files of this type.

✦ **Browse in Same Window:** When loading these files into IE, this lets IE know whether to open a new window to show the file or whether to show the document in the current default window.

Figure 4-6:
Use
Advanced
Options
to always
display
certain file
extensions.

When you select one of the listed actions, you can modify how the action is performed on the selected file by clicking the Edit button and then modifying the dialog box shown in Figure 4-7. There, you can specify the full path to the program to open this file type along with any switches (or command options, which are discussed in Book V, Chapter 5) that should be used for that particular program. For example, if the extension has open, print, and printto actions, as shown in Figure 4-7, the Application Used to Perform Action field for the open action might look like this:

```
C:\WINNT\system32\NOTEPAD.EXE %1
```

In this example, %1 is used by Windows to represent the name of the file that you are working with. When working with the print action, the line might look like this:

```
C:\WINNT\system32\NOTEPAD.EXE /p %1
```

Finally, for the printto action, you line might look like this:

```
C:\WINNT\system32\NOTEPAD.EXE /pt %1
```

Most applications will support opening files from a similar command, but fewer will support printing, or printing to a specific device.

Figure 4-7:
Notepad.
exe files can
be opened,
printed, or
printed to
(a device)
through
Windows
Explorer.

Not all applications support printing for the Windows Explorer shell, but for those that do, you can either right-click the file and choose Print or drag them to a printer icon. Dragging the icon to the printer will make use of the document's `printto` action.

These same settings or options that we examined here can be used in Windows Vista by making changes directly to the Registry.

Understanding file extensions

In this section, I show you some of the major types of file extensions you can expect to see within your OS. By default, file extensions for registered file types are hidden. Registered files types are files that have extensions which already have applications associated with them. To display file extensions within Windows Vista, follow these steps:

1. **Open any directory window, such as Computer.**
2. **Choose Organize⇨Folder and Search Options.**
3. **Click the View tab (shown in Figure 4-8).**
4. **Clear the Hide Extensions for Known File Types check box.**
5. **Click OK.**

In the sections that follow, I discuss common file extensions and how they are used on your computer.

Figure 4-8:
You can
tweak your
Folder
Options to
display file
extensions
on your
files.

Executables

Executable files can perform tasks on the system. Table 4-3 summarizes some of the file extensions common to executable files.

Table 4-3		Executable File Extensions
Extension	*Type*	*Description*
.bat	Batch file	A series of commands sequentially typed into a text file
.cmd	OS/2 command file	Usually execute with only a command shell interface
.com	MS-DOS command file	Like the OS/2 command files; usually execute with only a command shell interface
.exe	Command line or graphical program	The most common extension for executable files
.vbs	Visual Basic Script file	Not executable themselves but require either wscript.exe or cscript.exe to be executed; a cross between Visual Basic applications and batch files

Major Office applications

You need to be familiar with the file extensions associated with a few of the most popular office applications on the market. Some of these extensions are listed in Table 4-4.

Table 4-4		Application File Extensions
Extension	*Type*	*Description*
`.doc` `.docx`	Document files	Usually associated with Microsoft Word; `.doc` is sometimes used by installations of WordPerfect. Files extensions with an x at the end are used by Microsoft Office 2007.
`.dot` `.dotx`	Document templates	Document templates for Microsoft Word. `normal.dot` is the default template for new documents.
`.ppt` `.pptx` `.pps` `.ppsx`	Microsoft PowerPoint documents	`.ppt` files open in the PowerPoint interface and are immediately editable. `.pps` files, when you double-click them, open directly in PowerPoint Slide Show mode and close as soon as the slide show finishes.
`.wks` `.wk4`	Lotus 1-2-3 worksheet files	The number at the end denotes that a specific version of Lotus 1-2-3 was used.
`.wpd`	WordPerfect document	This and `.doc` are common extensions for documents.
`.wpg`	WordPerfect graphic	WordPerfect's proprietary graphic format.
`.xls` `.xlsx`	Microsoft Excel document	Spreadsheets associated with Microsoft Excel.

Compression utilities

Over the years, and across operating systems, file compression has always been an issue, leading to the creation of numerous different compression formats. Table 4-5 lists some of the common extensions for compressed files and where they are used. Although some utilities are based in one OS or another, today you can find compression and decompression tools for most formats in most operating systems.

Table 4-5		Compression File Extensions
Extension	*Type*	*Description*
`.ace`	Ace or WinAce	A high-compression format
`.arc`	Arc or Archive	Traditional Linux and Unix utility
`.arj`	Archiver Robert Jung (the creator of the format)	Traditional archive utility for MS-DOS
`.bhx` `.hqx`	BinHex files	Macintosh encoding format

Extension	Type	Description
.cab	Cabinet file	Microsoft format for distributing software
.rar	Roshal Archive (created by Eugene Roshal)	High-compression format used on most operating systems
.sit	StuffIt	Most popular Macintosh compression format
.tar	Tape archive files	Traditional, highly used archive format for Linux and Unix that can back up directory structures into a single file rather than compress them; often used in conjunction with gzip
.tgz	tar-gzip	Traditional, highly used compression format for Linux and Unix; actually a gzip-ed TAR file
.uu .uue	UUencode	One of the most popular encoding algorithms for Linux and Unix
.zip	PKZIP	The grandfather of PC compression formats; still the most used format for the MS-DOS and Windows worlds

System files

Several types of files drive your computer's operating system. Some of the extensions you should expect to see on system files are listed in Table 4-6.

Table 4-6		System File Extensions
Extension	Type	Description
.ani	Animated cursor files	Contains animated mouse pointers
.bak	Backup files	Used as a default extension by a number of applications
.bin	Binary drivers	Used for a few system drivers, such as drvspace.bin
.cpl	Control Panel files	Contains interface to adjust Windows settings
.cur	Cursor files	Holds the graphical information to display your mouse cursor
.dat	Data files	Used with the Registry files, such as ntuser.dat

(continued)

Table 4-6 *(continued)*

Extension	Type	Description
.dll	Dynamic Link Library	Contains common and reusable code that can be called by any application to reduce the amount of code that has to be placed within specific applications
.drv	MS-DOS or real-mode driver files	Contains MS-DOS–formatted binary drivers
.ini	Initialization files	Text files that contain settings for applications; phased out in favor of the Registry
.msc	Microsoft Console settings files	Seen often with Windows 2000 or above and a bit with Windows NT 4.0
.msg	Error message files	Contains messages to be displayed in the event of an error; were used with the MS-DOS network client, and were only required if you wanted to see a text description of error codes
.msi	Microsoft Installer files	A file format used to distribute software to computers running the Windows Installer service
.scr	Windows screen-saver files	Holds binary code to display Windows-based screen saver
.sys	System driver files	Used with MS-DOS and Windows for backward compatibility
.ttf	True Type font definition files	Contains formula description used to display scalable fonts
.vxd	Virtual device drivers	Holds binary code for Windows-based device drivers

Graphic files

Graphics have been an important part of computers since computers were invented and were able to print. Early graphics were generated using the standard ASCII character set and used to create simple graphs or rudimentary graphics. A number of different formats have become popular; with the popularity of the Internet, the number of major graphic formats has greatly increased. For a listing of graphics formats, see Table 4-7.

Table 4-7 **Graphic File Extensions**

Extension	Type	Description
.bmp	Bitmap	Used by MS Paint
.eps	(Adobe) Encapsulated PostScript	Used by several major graphics applications

Extension	Type	Description
.gif	Graphic Interchange Format	Owned by AOL (originally owned by CompuServe); designed to minimize download times
.jpg .jpeg	Joint Photographic Experts Group	A compression format that discards data ("lossy") thought to be invisible to the human eye
.pcd	Kodak Photo CD	A special format of image to be displayed on devices that support Kodak Photo CD
.pcx	PC Paintbrush	An early Windows graphic format
.pdf	(Adobe) Portable Document Format	Readable by Adobe Acrobat and Adobe Reader
.png	Portable Network Graphics	A free photo standard planned as a replacement for .gif and .jpeg because it supports all the benefits of both formats and uses a Zip type algorithm for compression
.tif .tiff	(Aldus) Tagged Image File Format	Used as a common interchange format between most graphics applications; very popular with photographic manipulators; supports LZW* compression format to reduce file sizes and is not lossy

*LZW: Lempel-Ziv-Welch

Other file extensions

Table 4-8 has some other extensions that are worth noting.

Table 4-8	Miscellaneous File Extensions	
Extension	Type	Description
.asp .aspx	Active Server Page Active Server page Extended	Server-side scripted HTML files
.cda	CD Audio	Stores audio data on audio CDs
.css	Cascading Style Sheet	Stores HTML-style data
.htm, .html	HyperText Markup Language	Stores data displayed on Web sites.
.tmp	Temporary file	A short-term storage file
.txt	Text file	ASCII text files that are readable on every operating system
.wav	Windows Audio files	Audio files designed specifically for use with Windows

Web servers use HTTP (HyperText Transfer Protocol) to send the information to your Web browser. HTML is popular for displaying information locally as well. Many vendors send Help files in this format so that they can be used on both their Web sites and as offline files.

You should be familiar with all these extensions and the categories to which they belong. Pay additional attention to executable, application, and system files.

Lab 4-1 provides some practice working with file associations. You will require a computer with Windows 2000 or XP. Lab 4-1 can be found in the `Labs.pdf` file in the Author directory of the CD-ROM.

Understanding File Attributes

Since the first versions of MS-DOS and the FAT file system (see Book II, Chapter 5), files have had some basic attributes. The following sections deal with only the attributes that a computer user will manage: namely, Read-only, Hidden, System, and Archive. The discussion focuses on the basic attributes, the extended attributes offered by Windows NTFS, and how to change the file attributes.

How attributes are stored

Attributes are stored as a single, 8-bit binary number. Because each bit can hold either a 0 or a 1, this yields 256 possible combinations of attributes — from eight 0s (no attributes applied; equal to 0 in decimal notation) to eight 1s (all attributes applied; equal to 255 in decimal notation).

Because each attribute holds a specific bit position, if several attributes are applied to a file, you can add the values (either binary or decimal) together to get a unique number that is 255 (11111111 in binary) or less for each unique combination of attributes. For example, if the file had the attributes of Read-only (1), System (4), and Archive (32), the value of the attribute byte would be 1 + 4 + 32, or 37. Only 37 (00100101 in binary) could represent a file with these attributes. The full list of attributes is listed in Table 4-9.

Table 4-9		File Attributes	
Bit Position	Decimal Value	Binary Value	Attribute
1	1	00000001	Read-only
2	2	00000010	Hidden
3	4	00000100	System

Bit Position	Decimal Value	Binary Value	Attribute
4	8	00001000	Volume Label
5	16	00010000	Subdirectory
6	32	00100000	Archive
7	64	01000000	Unused
8	128	10000000	Unused

For the exam, you will be asked only about the Read-only, Hidden, System, and Archive attributes. Still, you should be aware of the Volume Label and Subdirectory attributes for real-world applications. You do not need to know the bit values of any of the attributes; just know what the four basic attributes are used for.

The basic attributes

All files on your computer, regardless of your Microsoft OS or file system, have these four basic attributes:

✦ Read-only

✦ Hidden

✦ System

✦ Archive

Descriptions of the four common attributes are listed in Table 4-10.

Table 4-10	Basic File Attributes
Attribute	**Description**
Read-only	Cannot be deleted from the command line and cannot be written to or saved over.
Hidden	Invisible to users unless those users have changed their viewing options to display hidden files. Hidden files cannot have their attributes changed by the `attrib.exe` command.
System	Flagged as being required by the operating system. They cannot have their attributes changed by the `attrib.exe` command.
Archive	Ready for archiving or backing up. This attribute is used by some backup programs so that they can perform incremental backups. Currently, the `xcopy` command supports the `/a` switch, indicating that only files that have the Archive attribute set should be copied. When the file is modified, the Archive attribute will automatically be reset on it.

Working with the Volume Label

In addition to these four basic attributes, one more attribute — Volume — is usually set on your hard drive. The Volume attribute is usually applied to only one directory entry per drive (excluding the directory entries that are used for long filename entries) and stores the volume label for the drive. The directory entry that contains the label can be modified through one of the following methods:

✔ Enter the `label` command at a command prompt.

✔ Edit the Label field in the Properties window of your drive (see the figure here).

✔ Use the `Rename` command in the My Computer (or Computer for Vista users) window.

Any time files are modified, the Archive attribute is automatically set. Thus, after Windows is installed, all files have the Archive attribute enabled. Windows also sets Read-only, Hidden, and System attributes on many required system files to prevent accidental modification or deletion by the user. Other than these files, though, the only attribute automatically set is Archive. You can see how to manually set these attributes later in the upcoming section, "Setting basic attributes."

Windows NTFS extended attributes

Windows 2000 and other newer Microsoft OSes have three other file attributes that are used on NTFS partitions. These three attributes are often referred to as *extended attributes:*

✦ **Compress:** Used to enable on-the-fly file level compression of data

✦ **Encrypt:** Used to enables on-the-fly file level encryption of data

✦ **Index:** Used to allow files to be indexed by the OS Indexing Service

The sections that follow take a closer look at each of these attributes.

Compress

The Compress attribute allows and restricts file compression. To compress a file or folder, follow these steps:

1. **Right-click the file or folder and choose Properties.**

2. **In the Properties dialog box that appears, click the Advanced button.**

3. **From the Advanced Attributes dialog box, you can compress the file or folder by selecting the Compress Contents to Save Disk Space check box, as shown in Figure 4-9.**

Figure 4-9:
The Compress attribute is set on a file-by-file or folder basis.

If you are asked about extended attributes on your exam, look at the OS mentioned in the question. If the question deals with Windows NT 4.0 rather than Windows 2000 or newer OSes, remember that Windows NT 4.0 supports the Compress attribute but not the Encrypt or Index attributes.

To compress a file, the file needs to be read in to memory, where compression takes place, and then rewritten to the disk is its compressed form. When you change the Compress file attribute, the OS saves the change to attribute prior to actually going to steps of compression the file. This is done in two steps because the attributes are stored in the MFT and not in the actual file itself. After the attribute change is recorded, file compression for that file is performed. Because of the small chance that something could go wrong during the compression phase, some of the files on your hard drive might have the Compress attribute set yet not actually be compressed. One situation that might cause this inconsistent Compress attribute is a power interruption during the compression process, resulting in the attribute change being made but a compressed version of the file not saved. To ensure that this has not happened, you could use the `compact.exe` command line utility.

You can use `compact.exe` to compress or decompress files from the command line. It supports switches that allow it to process subdirectories as

well. If you suspect inconsistent compression states for your files, you can use the /F (force switch), which goes through the process of compressing all files, even if they already have the Compress attribute. This does not double-compress files, but rather ensures that all files that are supposed to be compressed actually are compressed. See Table 4-11 for a complete list of the switches that compact.exe makes use of. If you run compact.exe without any switches, it will display compression information for the files in your current directory.

Table 4-11	compact.exe Command Switches
Switch	*Description*
/A	Displays files with the hidden or system attributes. These files are omitted by default.
/C	Compresses the specified files. Directories will be marked so that files added afterward will be compressed.
/F	Forces the compress operation on all specified files, even those which are already compressed. Already-compressed files are skipped by default.
/I	Continues performing the specified operation even after errors have occurred. By default, compact.exe stops when an error is encountered.
/Q	Reports only the most essential information.
/S	Performs the specified operation on files in the given directory and all subdirectories. Default directory is the current directory.
/U	Uncompresses the specified files. Directories will be marked so that files added afterward will not be compressed.

If you move a compressed file within a partition, the file will retain its Compression attribute. However, if you copy a compressed file to a folder, it inherits the Compression attribute that is set for the destination folder.

Encrypt

An *encrypted* file is protected only against being read. This means that the file can be moved to another location on the same partition or renamed; these actions require modifying the directory table and do not constitute reading the file. The file may also be deleted if the appropriate NTFS permissions have not been applied to it.

To encrypt a file or folder, follow these steps:

1. **Right-click the file or folder and choose Properties.**

2. **In the Properties dialog box that appears, click the Advanced button.**

3. **From the Advanced Attributes dialog box, you can encrypt the file or folder by selecting the Encrypt Contents to Secure Data check box.**

If the user who encrypted the file then moves or copies a file between NTFS partitions (even between computers), the file will remain encrypted. This is different from Compression or NTFS permissions. If the file is copied to a non-NTFS partition, the file is automatically decrypted. If you cannot decrypt the file, you will receive an Access Denied message when you attempt to move the files to a location which is on a different partition.

Public Key Infrastructure (PKI) is a system that allows for authentication users and encryption of data. PKI works with key pairs that are used to encrypt or decrypt data. The pair of keys is defined as *private* (known only to the user) or *public* (known to all other users of the infrastructure). Public keys are usually stored in certificates. When data is encrypted by using a public key, it can be decrypted only by using the related private key from the key pair. Encrypting File System (EFS) makes use of PKI. If you do not have an infrastructure, the local workstation will auto-generate keys on the local computer to support EFS. If you are using EFS within an organization, you should make use of an enterprise-wide PKI, which can be implemented by using the Microsoft Windows Server Certificate Authority.

Windows does not allow you to both encrypt and compress a file. This is because compression requires that the file be rewritten, and encryption does not allow the file to be rewritten. The reason why encryption does not allow the file to be rewritten is because the file header contains the file's encryption keys. These keys are protected by the public key of the user who encrypted the file as well as the public key of the EFS Recovery Agents. The EFS Recovery Agent is specified in the local public key policies of the computer or in Active Directory. By default on a workstation or an Active Directory domain, the EFS Recovery Agent will be set to the Administrator account. When a file is encrypted, the only people who can read the file are the user who enabled encryption, the EFS Recovery Agent, and any other users who specifically had their public keys used to encrypt the file's encryption keys.

To allow other people to access your encrypted files, follow these steps for a file that has been encrypted:

1. **Right-click the file or folder and choose Properties.**

2. **In the Properties dialog box, click the Advanced button.**

3. **In the Advanced Attributes dialog box, click the Details button.**

 The Encryption Details for the file dialog box opens, listing all users who can transparently access the file.

4. **Click the Add button.**

 The Select User dialog box opens.

5. **If the user you want to grant access to is not on the list, click the Find User button to access the standard OS Select User dialog box; otherwise, select the user you want to add and then click OK.**

6. **Click OK on each of the other dialogs that opened.**

If you do not have an enterprise PKI, you cannot access certificates for other users, so you will not be able to easily grant other users access to encrypted files.

Similar to compress.exe for compressing files, you can use the command line utility cipher.exe to encrypt files from the command line or in batch files.

In the same way that you could use compress.exe for compressed files, you can use cipher.exe for encrypted files. Table 4-12 reviews the switches that can be used with the cipher.exe command.

Table 4-12	cipher.exe Command Switches
Switch	*Description*
/A	Operates on files as well as directories. The encrypted file could become decrypted when it is modified if the parent directory is not encrypted. It is recommended that you encrypt the file and the parent directory.
/D	Decrypts the specified directories. Directories will be marked so that files added afterward will not be encrypted.
/E	Encrypts the specified directories. Directories will be marked so that files added afterward will be encrypted.
/F	Forces the encryption operation on all specified objects, even those which are already encrypted. Already-encrypted objects are skipped by default.
/H	Displays files with the hidden or system attributes. These files are omitted by default.
/I	Continues performing the specified operation even after errors have occurred. By default, ciphere.exe stops when an error is encountered.
/K	Creates new file encryption key for the user running ciphere.exe. If this option is chosen, all the other options will be ignored.
/N	This option works only with /U. This will prevent keys being updated. This is used to find all the encrypted files on the local drives.
/Q	Reports only the most essential information.

Switch	Description
/R	Generates an EFS recovery agent key and certificate, then writes them to a PFX file (containing certificate and private key) and a CER file (containing only the certificate). An administrator may add the contents of the CER to the EFS recovery policy to create the recovery agent for users, and import the PFX to recover individual files.
/S	Performs the specified operation on directories in the given directory and all subdirectories.
/U	Tries to touch all the encrypted files on local drives. This will update user's file encryption key or recovery agent's key to the current ones if they are changed. This option does not work with other options except /N.
/W	Removes data from available unused disk space on the entire volume. If this option is chosen, all other options are ignored. The directory specified can be anywhere in a local volume. If it is a mount point or points to a directory in another volume, the data on that volume will be removed.
/X	Backup EFS certificate and keys into file filename. If `efsfile` is provided, the current user's certificate(s) used to encrypt the file will be backed up. Otherwise, the user's current EFS certificate and keys will be backed up.

Index

Indexing the file system will greatly improve the time it takes to search your hard drive. On the downside, though, indexing demands space on your drive. Indexing not only records the filenames and locations, but will also record words found in your files. The indexing service has a set of "noise words" that it ignores, such as *it, that, is, not,* and *the.* As files are indexed, the results are stored in a catalog; when searching for files, you can specify the catalog you want to use. By default, a catalog — a system — is configured to index your local files on your hard drives. Find this default catalog in the System Volume Information directory of your boot drive or `C:` drive.

To enable basic indexing of your drive, follow these steps:

1. **Right-click your drive in My Computer (or Computer for Vista users) and choose Properties.**

2. **Select the Index this Drive for Faster Searching check box (see Figure 4-10).**

 This enables indexing, provided that the Indexing Service is running.

You can verify that the Indexing Service is running by using the Services Administrative Tool (Start⇨Control Panel⇨Administrative Tools⇨Services) and verifying that the Indexing Service is started. For Windows Vista users, you will find the Services Administrative Tool in Start⇨Control Panel⇨System and Maintenance⇨Administrative Tools⇨Services.

Figure 4-10:
Indexing
can be
enabled for
your whole
drive or for
just a folder.

To ensure that the Indexing Service is running on Windows XP, do the following:

1. **Choose Start⇨Search.**

2. **In the Search companion pane on the left, click Change Preferences.**

3. **In the results that appear, click With Indexing Service (For Faster Local Searches).**

 If the results show an option for Without Indexing Service, you are already set to use them. By following either of these links, the left pane of the search window allows you to change the Indexing Service setting (see Figure 4-11).

The Indexing Service in Windows Vista is always enabled, so this option will not show up in the Search dialog box.

Setting basic attributes

Like so many other areas of an operating system, where there are many different ways to achieve your goal, there are many different ways to change the attributes of files. The first method — using the command line — is the only way common to all Microsoft OSes, but keep reading to see how to set attributes via the Windows GUI.

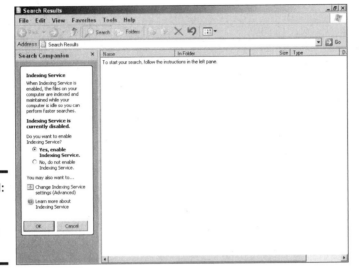

Figure 4-11:
Indexing
must be
enabled to
work.

Command line

To change file attributes from the command line, start at the Command Prompt window (choose Start⇨All Programs⇨Accessories⇨Command Prompt). In the Command Prompt window, you can set attributes by using the attrib.exe command. The basic syntax for the command is this:

```
attrib <attribute to set (H, S, R, A)> <files to modify>
```

Setting an attributes also includes a plus sign (+; enabled) or minus sign (–; disabled), followed by a one-letter code for each attribute. For example, to set the read-only attribute and remove the archive attribute from the C:\boot.ini file, use the following:

```
attrib.exe +R –A C:\boot.ini
```

The one-letter codes are as follows:

✦ A: Archive

✦ H: Hidden

✦ R: Read-only

✦ S: System

If you use the attrib command without any options, it displays a list of current attributes of all files in the current directory. Here is a sample of what that would look like:

```
C:\>attrib.exe
A      C:\7flen.crt
A SHR   C:\arcldr.exe
A SHR   C:\arcsetup.exe
A      C:\AUTOEXEC.BAT
A SH    C:\boot.ini
A      C:\CONFIG.SYS
A SHR   C:\IO.SYS
A SHR   C:\MSDOS.SYS
A SHR   C:\NTBOOTDD.SYS
A SHR   C:\NTDETECT.COM
A SHR   C:\ntldr
A      C:\uninst.log
```

If you use the `attrib.exe` command with options but without specifying a filename, you set the attribute(s) for all the files in the current directory. Here is an example of the command and the attributes that would be set:

```
C:\>attrib.exe -A -S -H -R

      C:\7flen.crt
      C:\arcldr.exe
      C:\arcsetup.exe
      C:\AUTOEXEC.BAT
      C:\boot.ini
      C:\CONFIG.SYS
      C:\IO.SYS
      C:\MSDOS.SYS
      C:\NTBOOTDD.SYS
      C:\NTDETECT.COM
      C:\ntldr
      C:\uninst.log
```

You can specify a file after the `attrib` command to see the current attributes of that file, or you can include the one-letter codes to set the attribute(s), like this:

```
C:\>attrib.exe C:\boot.ini
A      C:\BOOT.INI
C:\>attrib.exe +h +r C:\boot.ini
C:\>attrib.exe C:\boot.ini
A HR   C:\BOOT.INI
```

Another option you can include with the `attrib.exe` command is `/s`, which instructs `attrib.exe` to process the files in all subdirectories. This does not change the attribute on the subdirectories, just the files in the subdirectories. If you are using Windows 2000 or a newer Windows OS, using `/d` will change the attributes of the directories as well.

There are some restrictions on changing attributes with the attrib.exe command. Hidden and System files will not have their attributes changed unless the current Hidden or System attribute is also specified in a single command. Examine the following command sequence, which shows an example of dealing with Hidden or System files:

```
C:\>attrib.exe C:\boot.ini
A  SH   C:\boot.ini

C:\>attrib.exe -S -H -A -R C:\boot.ini

C:\>attrib.exe C:\boot.ini
     C:\boot.ini

C:\>attrib.exe +S C:\boot.ini

C:\>attrib.exe +R C:\boot.ini
Not resetting system file - C:\boot.ini

C:\>attrib.exe C:\boot.ini
  S    C:\boot.ini

C:\>attrib.exe +R +S C:\boot.ini

C:\>attrib.exe C:\boot.ini
  S R   C:\boot.ini

C:\>attrib.exe +H C:\boot.ini
Not resetting system file - C:\boot.ini

C:\>attrib.exe +H +S C:\boot.ini

C:\>attrib.exe C:\boot.ini
  SHR    C:\boot.ini

C:\>attrib.exe +S +H -R C:\boot.ini

C:\>attrib.exe C:\boot.ini
     C:\boot.ini
```

Windows GUI

In addition to the command line interface for changing attributes, Windows offers a GUI interface. When you right-click a file, you only see the options for Read-only, Hidden, and Archive when working with FAT partitions. If you are working with NTFS partitions, the Archive check box is replaced with an Advanced button, as shown in Figure 4-12.

Figure 4-12:
On NTFS
partitions,
you see
only the
Read-only
and Hidden
attributes.

Clicking the Advanced button allows you to set the Archive attribute as well as the Windows NTFS advanced attributes of Index, Compress, and Encrypt. See Figure 4-13.

Figure 4-13:
The
Advanced
Attribute
window is
available
only on
NTFS
partitions.

Lab 4-2 provides some practice working with attributes via the command line. For this exercise, you need a computer running Windows. Lab 4-2 can be found in the Labs.pdf file in the Author directory of the CD-ROM.

Getting an A+

This chapter discusses file and directory management from the point of view of file naming and file attributes. The following major points are covered:

✦ Windows is not limited to the 8.3 naming convention.

✦ Windows supports simulated 8.3 naming for backward compatibility.

✦ The four basic file attributes are Read-only, Hidden, System, and Archive.

✦ Windows 2000 and newer Windows OSes support additional file attributes for compression, encryption, and indexing. These attributes are available only on the Windows NT File System (NTFS).

✦ The Archive attribute is still used by many backup programs to locate files that have changed since the last backup.

Prep Test

(sidebar) **Managing Files and Directories**

1 What is the maximum character length of a filename under Windows XP?

- A ○ 64
- B ○ 128
- C ○ 254
- D ○ 255
- E ○ 256

2 You get a call from Billy. You find out that he has a problem with several of the files on his hard drive. He claims that Windows Vista has renamed many of his files and directories. After questioning him, you find out that he just defragmented his hard drive with an MS-DOS 6.0 boot disk and the MS-DOS version of `defrag.exe`. What is likely the cause of the problem, and is there a solution to correct it?

- A ○ The MS-DOS version of `defrag.exe` was unaware of the long filename directory entries and overwrote the directory entries. There is no easy fix for this problem.
- B ○ The long filename entries have just become unassociated from the files. Run `assoc c: /repair` to reestablish the associations.
- C ○ The filename entries are fine; they were automatically backed up, and Billy just needs to run `lfnbk` from the root of each drive.
- D ○ Everything is fine; Billy just needs to reboot.

3 Which of the following can be used to associate file extensions with an application? Choose all that apply.

- A ○ `attrib.exe`
- B ○ `assoc.exe`
- C ○ Shift+right-click and choose Open With.
- D ○ Choose Tools⇨Folder Options⇨Associate tab.

4 Which of the following are extensions of executable files? Choose all that apply.

- A ❑ `.ini`
- B ❑ `.prg`
- C ❑ `.exe`
- D ❑ `.cmd`

5 Which of the following file extensions are associated with compression programs? Choose all that apply.

A ❑ .com
B ❑ .zip
C ❑ .cmp
D ❑ .cab

6 Which of the following attributes are associated with files on your hard drive? Choose all that apply.

A ❑ Restrict-Modify
B ❑ Archive
C ❑ Visible
D ❑ Hidden

7 When you copy an NTFS compressed file to a FAT32 partition, what happens to the file?

A ○ The copy action is denied.
B ○ The file is copied but remains compressed, so it is unreadable.
C ○ The file is copied but becomes uncompressed.
D ○ The file can be copied only if the FAT32 partition has been compressed with DriveSpace compression.

8 You are moving several of Bob's files from a directory to another directory on the same partition. What message should you receive when you encounter an encrypted file?

A ○ You should not receive a message; the file will just be moved.
B ○ You should get an Access Denied message.
C ○ You should get a message stating that you could not read the file, and that it may be corrupted.
D ○ You should get a message stating that the file cannot be moved because it is encrypted.

9 You are moving several of Bob's files from a directory on an NTFS partition to a directory on a FAT32 partition. What message should you receive when you encounter an encrypted file?

A ○ You should not receive a message; the file will just be moved.
B ○ You should get an Access Denied message.
C ○ You should get a message stating that you could not read the file, and that it may be corrupted.
D ○ You should get a message stating that the file cannot be moved because it is encrypted.

Answers

1 **D.** The maximum length of a filename is 255 characters. *See "Long and short filenames."*

2 **A.** You should only use Windows 2000 or newer utilities to maintain your disks. *Review "Long and short filenames."*

3 **C.** `attrib.exe` is used to change file attributes and not file associations. `assoc.exe` does not exist, and the correct path on a Windows XP computer is Tools⇨Folder Options⇨*File Types. Peruse "Creating file associations."*

4 **C, D.** `.exe` files are executable program files and `.cmd` files are text files similar to batch files but are treated as executable. *Take a look at "Understanding file extensions."*

5 **B, D.** PKZIP files use the `.zip` extension, and `.cab` files are a proprietary, Microsoft compression format. *Peek at "Understanding file extensions."*

6 **B, D.** The four basic attributes are Read-only, Hidden, System, and Archive. The advanced NTFS attributes are Compress, Encrypt, and Index. *Look over "Understanding File Attributes."*

7 **C.** Compressed files copied from NTFS volumes to any other type of disk will become uncompressed. If they are copied to other NTFS volumes, they will inherit the compression attribute from the destination folder. *Study "Windows NTFS extended attributes."*

8 **A.** As long as the move is within one partition, the files will just be moved. If the directories are on different drives, you would receive an Access Denied message. *Refer to "Windows NTFS extended attributes."*

9 **B.** Because the files are being moved to a different drive and you are not the person who encrypted the files, you will be denied access. If you had owned the files, the files would have been decrypted as they were copied. *Examine "Windows NTFS extended attributes."*

Chapter 5: Command Prompt Procedures

Exam Objectives

✔ Identifying the fundamentals of using command line utilities to manage Windows

✔ Using edit.com to create and edit a text file

✔ Using command line tools to manage directories and files

*I*n this chapter, you take a look at several command prompt utilities and a few graphical utilities. Even in the age of Windows, statements that can be issued from command prompt are still required knowledge for support professionals. This knowledge will help you automate processes — such as batch files — and solve problems when the graphical operating system is not functioning. After reading this chapter, you should have a good understanding of many of the basic commands that are available from the command prompt.

As an added benefit, you find out how to build a basic batch file with some controls in it. I put this information at the end of the chapter because you won't be tested directly on that knowledge, but it will sure come in handy on the job.

As an A+ Certified Professional, you will want to use the full range of tools available to you. This chapter introduces you to many of the command line tools that allow you to quickly diagnose and repair problems with operating systems.

The exam objectives call for testing on command line tools, which might not be limited to just the common tools listed in this book. To review new command line tools, choose Start⇨Help and Support and search for *New Command-line Tools*. To review all possible command line tools, choose Start⇨Help and Support and search for *Command-line reference A-Z*.

Using command.com and cmd.exe

Many of the really useful utilities in Windows are command line–based. Windows Vista and earlier OSes give you two options for running command line utilities: command.com and cmd.exe.

When working with MS-DOS and Windows 9*x,* the file `command.com` is the command line interpreter, and it serves as the basic method of executing programs in the OS. Some programs that were executed were programs internal to `command.com`, but others were external and could be found on the hard drive.

Windows NT–based OSes, such as Windows XP and Windows Vista, use `cmd.exe` as the basic command line interpreter for issuing commands. When using `cmd.exe`, you are using a Windows 32-bit application from the point of view of memory management and application stability. `command.com` still exists on these OSes, but it exists for backward compatibility for older applications.

Typically, when you want to use a command prompt within Windows, you should run `cmd.exe` by choosing Start⇨Run, typing **cmd.exe**, and clicking OK. `cmd.exe` can also be found from the Start menu under All Programs⇨Accessories⇨Command Prompt. This runs as a 32-bit Windows application and thereby can spawn other applications or support standard memory management. Each copy of `cmd.exe` that you execute appears on the process list in Task Manager. If you run `cmd.exe`, the first two lines tell you what executed. Here is an example of what Windows Vista shows:

```
Microsoft Windows [Version 6.0.6001]
Copyright (c) 2006 Microsoft Corporation.  All rights reserved.
```

`command.com` on the other hand, is a 16-bit MS-DOS application. It loads a simulated 16-bit environment in the form of `ntvdm.exe` (NT Virtual DOS Machine; NTVDM). You will see `ntvdm.exe` listed on the Process tab of Task Manager. The first two lines listed in this window are

```
Microsoft(R) Windows DOS
(C)Copyright Microsoft Corp 1990-2001.
```

You will notice that, in this case, you are running DOS and Windows Vista (Windows Version 6.0). You will also notice that your long filenames are no longer supported (prior to Windows Vista). If you use the command prompt to launch other 16-bit Windows applications, they will be launched within the NTVDM that is executing. The *NTVDM* is the environment that all 16-bit MS-DOS applications and 16-bit Windows applications run in. For more information about supporting these applications, refer to Book VI, Chapter 2.

`cmd.exe` is used when running all other applications. As I mention earlier, it is a 32-bit command prompt with a number of enhancements, including

✦ The ability to run 16-bit and 32-bit command line utilities

✦ The ability to run POSIX (Portable Operating System Interface for Unix) and OS applications

✦ Built-in DOSKey support for saving and executing commands

Windows XP and Windows Vista use cmd.exe as the main command line interface and provide command.com for backward compatibility.

Managing Directories

All files that are saved to disk are stored in a hierarchical directory structure. All the files could be placed at the top of this structure, but it would be disorganized, and therefore poorly managed. Also, most top-level directories, or *root directories,* can hold a limited number of files. This directory structure can hold as many nested subdirectories as you want. The commands discussed in the following sections allow you to get listings of files as well as create and delete directories on your disk.

All command line tools in this section have not changed substantially since MS-DOS.

dir

The first command that you will see is the directory command (dir). This command is used to get a listing of the files that are in a directory on your disk. Using dir by itself gives you the listing of your current directory. The current directory is usually listed in the command prompt, like this:

```
C:\WINDOWS>_
```

The dir command is very useful and has several options discussed later in this section. First, though, you need a firm grasp of wildcards, relative paths, and absolute paths.

Wildcards

Two wildcards can be used to modify what results you receive: * and ?.These can be used multiple times in different combinations in the same command to filter the results.

The * wildcard represents one or more characters. Here is an example of using the * wildcard to retrieve a list of files that match a certain pattern. The command

```
dir WIN*.*XE
```

returns the following:

```
WINMINE.EXE
WINHELP.EXE
WINHLP32.EXE
WININIT.EXE
WINVER.EXE
WINFILE.EXE
WINPOPUP.EXE
WINIPCFG.EXE
WINREP.EXE
```

The results include all files that start with win and end with xe, with any number of characters in between — even zero. These wildcards are also useful when used in conjunction with copy commands, which I discuss later in the chapter.

The ? wildcard character works a little different than * because ? represents one or zero characters. Here is an example of ? in action, as it looks for all files that were created on the fifth of any month after Jan 01, 2000, given that all the filenames match their dates. The command

```
dir ??052???.TXT
```

would return the following list of files:

```
01052000.TXT
05052000.TXT
10052000.TXT
11052000.TXT
12052000.TXT
04052002.TXT
12052003.TXT
06052008.TXT
```

The ? in the command doesn't return any files that have more than two characters before the 05 and doesn't return any more than three characters after the 2 in the dir statement. This is often helpful when files in a directory are named with six- or eight-character numeric dates with the pattern of mmddyyyy.txt, and you are looking for all files named for the fifth of any month.

Relative paths and absolute paths

When you use dir, you are given a directory listing for your current directory. To see the listing for a different directory, Table 5-1 provides several options for choosing a different directory. All the command examples in the table use this directory structure:

```
c:\parent_dir\child_dir\grandchild_dir
```

with the current directory set to `c:\parent_dir\child_dir`.

Table 5-1	Ways to Specify Directory Paths
Command	*Directory Result*
`dir`	Returns the listing for the current directory `c:\parent_dir\child_dir`
`dir c:`	Returns the listing for the current directory on the C drive `c:\parent_dir\child_dir`
`dir c:\ parent_dir`	Returns the listing for `c:\parent_dir`
`dir \`	Returns the listing for the root of the current drive `c:\`
`dir ..`	Returns the listing for the parent directory of the current directory `c:\parent_dir`
`dir ..\..`	Returns the listing of the parent directory of the parent directory of the current directory `c:\`
`dir ..\ child_dir`	Returns the listing of a directory named `child_dir`, which is a child of the parent directory `c:\parent_dir\child_dir`
`dir grand-child_dir`	Returns the listing of a child directory named `grandchild_dir` `c:\parent_dir\child_dir\grandchild_dir`

Whenever a full path is specified, starting with the drive letter, it is referred to as an *absolute path*. If you do not specify the full path, you are using a *relative path*. Care should always be taken when using relative paths with commands. Look, for example, at the following code sample:

```
dir sub_dir
del *.*
```

In this example, a directory (`dir`) listing is taken of a subdirectory (`sub_dir`), and the following delete (`del`) command was working on the entire contents of the current directory. This is an easy mistake to make. When working with relative paths, double period (`..`) notation refers to a parent directory, and single period (`.`) notation refers to the current directory.

Most programs and commands can have their actions modified by providing options on the command line. These options are usually represented by one or more letters and are introduced to the command with either / or –. The – character is usually used with commands that come from (converted from) the Unix OS, but most MS-DOS programs have implemented /. These options are referred to as *switches*. `dir /on /s` is an example of the `dir` command using switches.

Why does one command have different names?

Many commands used with MS-DOS originated in other operating systems; in some cases, new short forms were created to make them easier to use. To provide backward compatibility, support for the older spelling of the command was also kept.

Table 5-2 summarizes some of the most important switches for the `dir` command.

Table 5-2	Switches for dir	
Switch	*Description*	
/ax	The /a switch is short for "attributes." This switch provides a listing of files that have matching attributes. This switch must be used in conjunction with an additional letter to provide results. Five letters may be used: (d)irectory, (a)rchive, (h)idden, (s)ystem, and (r)ead-only. Use a minus sign with one of these five letters reverses the listing: For example, /a-d shows you things that are not directories.	
/b	The /b command displays a bare listing. A *bare listing* does not include a separate section in the output that tells you the directory that you are working with, but rather displays a single-line listing, like this: `c:\windows\hosts.txt` `c:\windows\lmhosts.txt`	
/ox	The /o switch is short for "order by." This switch is similar to /a in that /o also requires an additional letter to tell it how to order or sort. The options available for sorting are (n)ame, (s)ize, (e)xtension, (a)ccessed date (earliest first), and (d)ate modified (earliest first). Using a minus sign (for example, /o-d) reverses the order. If you use the letter g after the o (for example, /ogd), directories will be grouped at the top of the list rather than mixed in.	
/p	This switch pauses the screen after each full screen of text and waits for a key to be pressed. If you do not use this option, you can use the pipe-more command, which looks like this `dir c:\windows\*.exe	more`
/s	This switch includes listings for each subdirectory under the directory listing.	
/w	This switch displays text in a wide listing. It enables more text to be displayed onscreen by using multiple columns.	
/x	This switch is used on Windows 2000 and Windows XP computers to display short and long filenames.	

If you want to use the same set of switches each time you execute the `dir` command, use the `dircmd` environment variable. This variable can be set in the `autoexec.bat` file or at a command prompt, like this:

```
set dircmd=/on /w
```

Now, every time you use `dir`, you will get output that looks like this:

```
Volume in drive D is DRIVE_D
 Volume Serial Number is FFFF-FFFF

 Directory of D:\DOS

[.]            [..]           CHOICE.COM     DELTREE.EXE    DOSHELP.HLP
DOSKEY.COM     EXPAND.EXE     FC.EXE         FDISK.EXE      HELP.COM
HELP.HLP       HIMEM.SYS      INTERLNK.EXE   INTERSVR.EXE   LOADFIX.COM
SMARTDRV.EXE   TREE.COM
              15 File(s)         525,943 bytes
               2 Dir(s)      446,431,232 bytes free
```

Note that the list is presented in wide format and sorted by name.

If you are using Windows and you want the setting of the `dircmd` variable to be saved, add the variable by using the Environment Variables settings in the System Control Panel, which you can get to choosing Properties when you right-click on My Computer (or Computer for Vista users) to open the System Properties dialog box; then click the Advanced tab (or Advanced systems settings link for Vista users) and the Environment Variables button.

mkdir

`mkdir`, or `md`, is used to create directories; there is no difference between the two commands other than their spelling.

The directory created will be in the current directory unless you provide an alternative path to the command, like this:

```
mkdir "c:\temp\my new directory"
```

chdir

`chdir`, or `cd`, is used to change the current directory for a drive to another directory. The drive need not be your current drive; this command can set a current directory on another drive. For example, if your current drive is `C:`, you could still use `cd d:\my_dir_on_d` to change the current directory for the `D:` drive. You will not see a difference onscreen, but if you change to the `D:` drive by using `d:`, you will see that the current directory is set to `d:\my_dir_on_d`. The current directory is important when you want to use other file operation commands, such as `copy`. If you only specify the drive that you want to work with, you will be working with the current directory on that drive. Take a look at this example:

```
D:\somedirectory\>c:
C:\Documents and Settings\ed\>cd \
C:\>mkdir d:\old_configs
C:\>cd d:\old_configs
C:\>copy a*.bat d:
C:\>copy c:\c*.sys d:\old_configs
```

The first line changes your current drive to `C:`. The second changes to the root directory of the current drive (`c:\`). The third creates a new directory on the `D:` drive, and the fourth line sets `old_configs` as the current directory on the `D:` drive. You will see the `copy` command in the upcoming section "copy," but the fifth line copies all files in the current directory that start with a and end with `.bat` to the current directory on the `D:` drive (currently `old_configs`). The last line copies all files from `c:\` that start with c and end with `.sys` to `d:\old_configs`. Lines 5 and 6 copy files from the same directory (`c:\`); the relative path is used in line 5, and the absolute path is used in line 6. The destination directory in line 6 is also absolute, and the relative path or current directory is used in line 5. In both statements (lines 5 and 6), the same directories are used as the source and destination directories.

Relative paths can save on typing, but they can also cause errors if you are not careful.

rmdir

`rmdir`, or `rd`, is used to remove or delete directories from your drive. Two rules are imposed on you: Before you delete a directory

✦ The directory must be empty.

✦ It cannot be the current directory.

You can *empty* a directory by using the `del` command to delete the files. To remove a directory, though, just specify its location after the `rmdir` command:

```
rmdir c:\remove_me
```

If you are using Windows 2000 or a newer Windows OS, you can use an optional switch — `/s` — that will automatically delete subdirectories and files.

Copying and Moving Files

Doesn't it seem like when you finally get things organized, it's time to start all over again? When organizing and backing up files, you will often be

required to copy or move files to new locations, either in another directory or on another disk. The following sections provide an overview of the commands that help you with these tasks.

All the command line tools in this section have not changed substantially since MS-DOS.

copy

The `copy` command expects you to give at least the name of the file you would like to copy. If you provide only one filename, the selected file is copied into the current directory. If you provide a source filename and a destination directory by using a command like

```
copy c:\source\myfile.txt c:\destination
```

the file will be copied into the destination directory. You can also rename files while you are copying them by using a command like this:

```
copy c:\source\*.bat c:\destination\*.old
```

The preceding command would copy all files with an extension of `.bat` from the source directory and rename them with an `.old` extension in the destination directory.

If you are about to overwrite an existing file, you will be prompted to confirm the operation. This can be suppressed if you use `/Y` at the end of your `copy` command. `/Y` answers "yes" to the `copy` command's "confirm overwrite?" question. If you want to consistently overwrite destination files, you can set the `copycmd` environment variable to `/Y` in the same manner that you set the `dircmd` variable in the "dir" section, earlier in this chapter.

xcopy

Many times, you have to copy entire directory structures from one location to another. If you were to do this with the `copy` command, you would first have to create all the destination directories by using the `md` command. When using the `xcopy` command, though, you can perform this task in a minimal amount of time. To copy an existing directory named `source` to a new directory named `destination`, you would issue the following command:

```
xcopy c:\source\*.* c:\destination\*.*
```

To copy all the subdirectories as well, use

```
xcopy c:\source\*.* c:\destination\*.* /s
```

To also include empty directories, add the /e (empty) switch to the end of the command. To include just files with the archive attribute set, add the /a (archive) switch.

Like the copy command, adding /Y will overwrite files without asking for confirmation. The /Y tells the command to answer "yes" to all overwrite prompts.

move

The move command moves files from one directory to another. It is also used to rename directories. To use the move command, you have to specify the name of the files you want to move and then specify the destination directory, like this:

```
move c:\source\source_file.txt c:\destination\
```

This example moves the file source_file.txt into the directory c:\ destination\. If the destination directory does not exist, you will see an error message.

To rename the directory c:\source, you need to use

```
move c:\source destination
```

del

To delete or remove files or directories, you can use del or erase. Like earlier examples, these two commands are synonymous. If you want to delete multiple files, you have to use the * and ? wildcards. (Read about wildcards earlier in the chapter.) MS-DOS and Windows 9x allow you to delete only files with this command, but Windows 2000 and newer OSes also allow you to delete directories.

It is very easy to unintentionally delete files (or delete the wrong files) when working with relative paths. When possible, use full pathnames to avoid mistakes.

ren

The ren command is used to rename files and directories. Similar to many of the commands that you have looked at, you specify the source name and a new name for the file or directory.

Making Comparisons

Of the many special function commands, this section looks at a few commands that can be used to compare files: diskcopy.com, diskcomp.com, and fc.exe.

All the command line tools in this section have not changed substantially since MS-DOS.

diskcopy.com and diskcomp.com

These two tools do not get very much use these days because they were designed to be used with floppy disks. Both commands take two parameters: the drive letter of the source disk, and the destination disk. Both parameters can be the same drive letter, such as `diskcopy a: a:`. The preceding command will copy the contents of drive `a:` to a temporary location and then ask for the target disk to be inserted in the `a:` drive. `diskcopy.com` will copy the contents of the disk to a new disk, and `diskcomp.com` will compare the contents of the two disks to ensure that there are no errors during or after the copy.

fc.exe

`fc.exe` — still a valid and useful tool — is used to compare the contents of two files and indicate the differences between the two files. This command is very useful when attempting to compare two very long configuration files for differences.

A variety of switches with this command allow you to modify how the output looks or how the comparisons are made. The basic format of the command requires that you specify the two files that you want to compare, using a format like this:

```
fc.exe c:\boot.ini c:\old-boot.ini
```

Listing 5-1 shows a sample of the `fc.exe` command in action.

Listing 5-1: fc.exe Command Example

```
C:\>fc.exe boot.ini old-boot.ini
Comparing files boot.ini and OLD-BOOT.INI
***** boot.ini
[boot loader]
timeout=30
default=multi(0)disk(0)rdisk(0)partition(1)\WINDOWS
***** OLD-BOOT.INI
[boot loader]
timeout=20
default=multi(0)disk(0)rdisk(0)partition(1)\WINDOWS
*****
```

In this example, there is one difference between the two files, in the `timeout=` line. By default, `fc.exe` shows the line before and after the difference in the files, and also shows you which lines came from which file.

Performing Diagnostics and Tuning Performance

At the command prompt, a few commands can be used to optimize and diagnose your computer. defrag.exe can be used to optimize your hard drive, and chkdsk.exe can be used to check your disk for errors. When creating an MS-DOS boot disk, you would have used mem.exe to view memory used when trying to optimize your memory usage.

The MS-DOS or command prompt versions of the defrag.exe and chkdsk.exe utilities have now been replaced by Windows versions.

defrag.exe

The purpose of the defrag.exe utility is to fix speed and performance problems with hard drives. As files are written to and then deleted from a disk, they leave holes or blank areas scattered around your drive. When you write files to a disk, they always write to the largest open spaces that are available to them. There will be times when the largest area is not large enough for the entire file, and the file will have to be split into pieces. These *fragmented* files are slower to access because the disk head has to keep moving to a new location on the drive. To defragment the files on your hard drive, use Computer Management in Windows, or defrag in Windows XP or Windows Vista. To provide command line access to all Windows-based utilities, Microsoft provides command line access to the graphical defragmenter utility.

In either case, you are using the defragmentation utility from Executive Software, and you have the option to analyze only or to force defragmentation when disk space is low.

For more information about using Computer Management in Windows, see Book VI, Chapter 4.

defrag.exe does not exist for Windows 2000. It is available only on Windows XP and newer Windows operating systems.

chkdsk.exe

chkdsk.exe serves an important purpose within the Windows operating system. Its job is to check

✦ The directory structure and directory entries for corruption

✦ The disk for worn-out areas

Its purpose is to reduce the chance of data loss by catching corruption early and by fixing small problems before they become larger.

For more information about `chkdsk.exe`, read Book VI, Chapter 4.

mem.exe

The mem command displays usage information about your computer's memory. This information is often useful when trying to optimize the boot process or when trying to maximize the amount of memory available to MS-DOS-based applications. mem runs from within MS-DOS.

Running the command by itself displays basic information about how much memory is available to the MS-DOS environment. Two main switches are available to the mem command:

+ `/c` (classify) tells you how much space applications are using in upper memory and conventional memory.

+ `/d` (debug) gives you a detailed breakdown of what is stored in the first 1MB of RAM.

Working with Other Useful Commands

The rest of the utilities in this chapter defy easy classification. Although they serve a wide range of functions, they are all important in your computer's usage.

attrib.exe

All files have four basic attributes:

+ a: Archive. Files that have been modified.

+ h: Hidden. Are not usually visible.

+ r: Read-only. Cannot normally be deleted, nor can they be modified.

+ s: System. Have special file protection so that you may not delete or modify them.

The archive attribute is used by some backup utilities to identify changed files for incremental backups.

The attrib command allows you to change these attributes. The attributes are added or removed from files by specifying the attribute with a + or – character in front of the filename, as in the following statement:

```
attrib -s -h +a +r c:\*.sys
```

The preceding statement removes the system (s) and hidden (h) attributes while adding the archive (a) and read-only (r) attributes. Adding /s to the

end of the line would apply the same attributes to all the files in the subdirectories as well.

diskpart.exe

To manage disk partitioning, if the need ever arises, Windows 2000 and newer Windows OSes use the Disk Management graphical disk partitioning tool. Windows XP and newer Windows OSes also use another command line tool: diskpart.exe. Although this tool is capable of all disk partitioning tasks, you need to use this tool only to perform rare disk partition changes that Disk Management cannot perform, such as expanding a partition on a basic disk.

The reason for not using diskpart.exe is that its user interface is awkward. To illustrate the interface, Listing 5-2 holds the steps required to create a partition on a disk and format the drive (extra blank lines have been removed):

Listing 5-2: Creating a Partition on a Disk and Formatting the Drive

```
C:\>diskpart.exe
DISKPART>list disk
  Disk ###  Status      Size      Free      Dyn  Gpt
  --------  ----------  -------   -------   ---  ---
  Disk 0    Online      6142 MB      0 B
  Disk 1    Online       510 MB      0 B
  Disk 2    Online      6142 MB   6142 MB

DISKPART> select disk 2
Disk 2 is now the selected disk.

DISKPART> create partition primary size=1000
DiskPart succeeded in creating the specified partition.

DISKPART> list partition
  Partition ###  Type             Size      Offset
  -------------  ---------------   -------   -------
  Partition 1    Primary          1004 MB    32 KB

DISKPART> select partition 1
Partition 1 is now the selected partition.

DISKPART> assign letter=f
DiskPart successfully assigned the drive letter or mount point.

DISKPART> exit
Leaving DiskPart...

C:\>format f: /fs:ntfs
The type of the file system is RAW.
The new file system is NTFS.
WARNING, ALL DATA ON NON-REMOVABLE DISK
DRIVE F: WILL BE LOST!
Proceed with Format (Y/N)? y
Verifying 1004M
```

```
Volume label (ENTER for none)? More Data
Creating file system structures.
Format complete.
    1028128 KB total disk space.
    1020600 KB are available.
```

This process could have been completed through a single wizard in Disk Management, with less effort.

format.com

Using the `format.com` command prepares a disk to be used by your computer. The purposes of this command are to

✦ Check whether all clusters on the partition are in working order

✦ Create the directory table

On FAT partitions, the directory table is referred to as the *File Allocation Table*. The directory table maintains a list of where each file starts on the disk.

The `format` command requires a drive letter and supports additional switches. The proper syntax to format your `A:` drive is

```
format a:
```

You could modify the command by adding `/q` to the end of the line to perform a quick format of the drive.

The quick format doesn't check the integrity of the sectors on the drive but only deletes and re-creates the directory table.

If you are using Windows 2000 or newer Windows OS, you can use `/FS:`*filesystem* to specify the format of the partition as either FAT, FAT32, or NTFS.

ver

The `ver` command indicates what version of the command prompt you are running. This varies between copies of Windows, as shown in Table 5-3. For example, using `ver` with Windows 9*x* OSes lets you see that they are all sub-versions of Windows 4.0, and all copies of Windows 2000 and XP are sub-versions of Windows NT 5.0. Major and minor version numbers from software manufacturers let you know how much they think the software has changed, so architecturally, each of these OSes has not changed significantly since their initial releases.

Table 5-3	Windows ver Output
Version	*Output of ver Command*
Windows 95 Retail	Windows 95. [Version 4.00.0095]
Windows 95 OSR2	Windows 95. [Version 4.00.1111]
Windows 98	Windows 98. [Version 4.10.1998]
Windows 98 SE	Windows 98. [Version 4.10.2154]
Windows 2000 Professional	Microsoft Windows 2000 [Version 5.00.2195]
Windows XP Professional	Microsoft Windows XP [Version 5.1.2600]
Windows Server 2003	Microsoft Windows [Version 5.2.3790]
Windows Vista	Microsoft Windows [Version 6.0.6001]

help

If you need to know how to do something with the command line, you have two main options. All commands support /? as a switch to get additional information on how to use the command. Additionally, Windows XP and newer versions of Windows also have a `help` command.

Use `help` followed by the command that you would like to get help on: for example

```
help help
```

If you use `help` by itself, you get a list of commands that you can request help for.

Working with the edit Command

Most configuration files on your computer can be edited with any text editor. If you have the Windows interface loaded, you will probably prefer to use a graphical program like Notepad or WordPad. If you don't have a computer that is currently running Windows, you can always use the `edit.com` command.

Opening files

To open files, first launch the text editor. Simply use the `edit` command in any command window. And if you know the name and path of the file that you want to edit, you can specify it after the `edit` command, like this:

```
edit a:\config.sys
```

To open a file in the editor, press Alt to access to the menu, press F to access the File menu, and then press O to open. This brings up the Open dialog box, as shown in Figure 5-1. By default, you will be in the File Name position, with the current name of * . * selected. If you type in the full path and filename of a file, you can open the file. If you choose to browse for your file, it gets a little more complicated.

Figure 5-1:
At first glance, navigating the MS-DOS-based dialog boxes can be confusing.

There are two ways to navigate the Open dialog box. First, you can use the Alt key on the keyboard. Notice the white letters in several places in the dialog box. By pressing a keyboard combo of Alt+a white letter, you can move to a section of the dialog box. For example, pressing Alt+D moves the cursor to the Directories pane, and pressing Alt+F moves it to the Files pane. Use the arrow keys on your keyboard to scroll through either of these lists, and press Enter to select choices. The first entry in the Directories pane is . . to navigate to the parent directory, and the last entries in that pane are all your drive letters (to switch to different drives).

The second way to navigate from pane to pane in the Open dialog box is to use the Tab key. When you press Tab in succession, you move through the panes, fields, and buttons from left to right, top to bottom. The exact order for the Open dialog box is File Name, Files, Directories, Open Read-only, Open Binary, OK, Cancel, Help. If you hold the Shift key while tabbing, you move in reverse order. To select a check box, press the spacebar when the option is highlighted.

When the correct file has been selected, press Enter or select the OK button to open the file.

Saving files

Saving files also requires that you first get access to the menu bar by pressing Alt. Pressing Alt+F opens the File menu, Alt+S saves, and Alt+A opens the Save As dialog box. If the file has already been saved, saving updates

the original; however, if the file has never been saved, either saving option opens the Save As dialog box, as shown in Figure 5-2. This dialog box is similar to the Open dialog box with regard to navigation. After you select a directory and provide a name, select the OK button.

Figure 5-2: When saving, choose a location and then a filename.

Searching and replacing

One of the more powerful features of `edit` is its ability to search and replace text in your file. To perform a search and replace, press Alt to access the menu, and then press S to access the Search menu. The Replace dialog box (shown in Figure 5-3) can be opened by pressing R. You can then type the string that you are looking for, as well as the string that you would like to replace it with.

Figure 5-3: Search and replace is a powerful feature.

To narrow a search, you can also tell the editor to search only whole words and to match the case. Searching for whole words means that when you search for *cat*, for example, you will not find it as part of the words *cats* or

categories. Matching case means that *cat* would not be found if you were searching for *Cat.*

Closing the editor

To close the editor, press Alt; then press F for File and X for Exit. If you have unsaved changes, you are prompted to save your changes, as shown in Figure 5-4.

Figure 5-4:
If there are unsaved changes, you are prompted to save them.

Batch File Basics

The first part of this chapter shows you several basic commands that make the command prompt easier to use — as well as a powerful ally. In the following sections, you find out how to write a batch file, which makes the command prompt an even more powerful tool. A *batch file* is simply a string of commands, which could have been typed at a command prompt, chained together to automate a process.

Starting your file

To start, you need a place to put the commands that you want to execute. To do this, open the text editor of your choice, make a new text file, and save it with a .bat extension.

If you're using a Windows-based editor (such as Notepad) and the operating system option of Hide File Extensions for Known File Types is enabled, you must enclose your filename in quotation marks when saving it.

If you want file extensions to show, use the following steps:

1. **Open My Computer or Computer for Vista users.**

2. **Choose Tools⇨Folder Options.**

3. **Click the View tab.**

4. **Clear (to show) the Hide File Extensions for Known File Types check box.**

5. **Click OK.**

With your batch file open in the text editor, you can now type any commands you want, but remember to put only one command per line in your file. You can use this file to create, copy, or delete files, or anything else that you could do from the command prompt.

After you create a batch file, you can execute or run it by typing the path to file and the filename at the Start⇨Run command or at a command prompt.

I strongly recommend doing testing with the batch file on a test computer. I have seen people create batch files with improperly formatted `rmdir` commands, which then deleted many more files and directories than expected. If you use commands that format partitions, remove files, or delete disk partitions, note that poorly structured commands might result in you being required to reinstall the operating system on your computer. The commands suggested in this section are not dangerous.

Getting your directions

Many people want to be able save the output of their commands — or, more rarely, answer questions or provide input for a command. There are a few ways to do this, and Table 5-4 summarizes the differences among the options. All these options require that your program is generating output going to `stdout` (standard output) or accepting input from `stdin` (standard input).

`stdout` and `stdin` are interfaces or objects that C programmers use almost exclusively when requiring data input and output for command line programs. As a programmer, I can write an application that sends its output to an interface called `stdout`, and then I let the operating system deal with where that actually is: It might be a teletype terminal, printer, monitor, or text file. For all versions of Windows, data sent to `stdout` will be displayed in a command prompt window.

Table 5-4	Redirection Symbols
Symbol	**Function**
<	Sends the contents of a file listed on the right into the command on the left. This is useful when you want to provide an answer to a question that a command will prompt for (for example, when the `format` command prompts for confirmation). By creating a one-character text file with just Y and a return or enter, you can pass a yes into the `format` command.

Symbol	Function
>	By specifying a command on the left and a text file or nul on the right, you can prevent output of a command from going to the screen. Instead, output is passed to the file listed on the right side. If the file exists, it will be overwritten. This is extremely useful if you want to log the results of certain statements.
>>	Similar to the > symbol except that the output is appended to the destination file if it already exists. If the file does not exist, it will be created.
\|	The pipe "pipes," or directs, the output of the file that is listed on the right side into (as input) the command listed on the left. This may allow you to bypass the creation of a text file.

Working with parameters or starting arguments

You can get a lot more mileage from your batch files if you pass and use arguments with them. An *argument* is a piece of data passed to the batch file or command when typing the command, such as

```
copy C:\this.txt C:\that.txt
```

which has two arguments: `C:\this.txt` and `C:\that.txt`. You can use ten arguments with a batch file. This really drops off to nine because the first argument is `%0`, and that represents the name of the running batch file. `%1` through `%9` can be used as arguments for your batch file. If you have a batch file that copies files from one directory to another, you can make your batch file more reusable by working with arguments. Here is an example of this concept:

Old batch file — `StaticCopy.bat`:

```
xcopy c:\dos\*.* c:\dosback
```

This file could be made more generic with these modifications:

New batch file — `DynamicCopy.bat`:

```
xcopy %1 %2
```

This new batch file would be run by using

```
dynamiccopy c:\dos\*.* c:\dosback
```

It's true that you are typing more to achieve the same result. But you have to consider that this line could be in a much larger batch file, which could use the two parameters (`%1` and `%2`) in many different ways. This could

actually save you a lot of typing when creating and editing your batch file because the parameters can be used rather than hard-coding the paths or parameters.

This system works fine until you find yourself in a position in which you need more than nine parameters passed to your batch file. However, if you plan the order in which you use your parameters, you can actually support many more than nine. This is done with the shift command. Each time you use shift in your batch file, all parameters that are passed to your batch file are shifted over one position. For example, %2 becomes %1, %3 becomes %2, and so on.

Making batch files make decisions

So far, you have seen some ways to make your batch file more generic. Now, I'll show you how to make it think for itself — or at least think for you. There are two ways to get your batch file to make some decisions although after you read this section, you might argue that there is only one way, seeing as how both ways make use of batch file labels.

First, the if and :label statements introduce simple program flow logic. For example, if you know that you need two parameters passed to your batch file for it to work properly, you can use something like Listing 5-3 in your batch file:

Listing 5-3: Passing Two Parameters to a Batch File

```
if not !%2==! goto correct

:Instructions
echo.
echo Please provided two parameters. The first is the
echo source directory, and the second is the destination.
echo.
goto end

:correct
xcopy %1 %2
goto end

:end
```

When working with the if statement, you evaluate whether two options are the same or whether a condition is true. In this case, you are testing for two items being equal. To do this, you need two items because you cannot test equality with only one item. In this example, you want to see whether

the second parameter is blank, so you use %2, which represents the second parameter. However, you cannot use if not %2== because that would evaluate %2 to nothing, and you need something on the other side of the equation. This gets worse if the second parameter was not passed to the batch file because %2 will not exist, and you are then asking whether nothing equates to nothing. The if statement cannot handle evaluating nothing in an equation.

To make sure there is something to evaluate on both sides of the equation — and not change the results — you need to add a character to both sides of the equation. In this example, I chose to use the exclamation mark. You should also take note of the use of the word not to reverse the results of the test.

Some other items that the if statement can test for include OS environment variables and whether files and directories exist. To test an environment variable for a specific value, you use a command like this one that checks the name of the computer that is running the batch file:

```
if !%COMPUTERNAME%==EDSPC goto instructions
```

To test whether a file exists, you use something like

```
if exist c:\autoexec.bat goto Instructions
```

If you want to know whether a directory exists, you can test for nul, which only exists for your test if a directory is there:

```
if exist c:\windows\nul goto Instructions
```

The full example also shows you how to work with labels and the goto statement. The goto statement uses only the first eight characters of the label, so try to keep label names unique. The goto statement requires a destination in the batch file to be sent to, and that is where the labels come in. Although end is a label that is meaningful to you, it is just another label to the batch file.

If you use a goto in your batch, you must have a matching label, or you will get errors, and your batch file will not work.

The last method of controlling the flow of your batch file is using the choice or set statement. The choice statement allows you to pause your MS-DOS or Windows batch file to wait for input. Input to the choice statement is a single character. Listing 5-4 shows an example of how to use the choice statement:

Listing 5-4: Using a choice Statement

```
@echo off
choice /c:ynm You choose
if errorlevel == 3 goto m
if errorlevel == 2 goto n
if errorlevel == 1 goto y
goto end

:y
echo You chose Yes.
goto end

:n
echo You chose No.
goto end

:m
echo You chose Maybe.
goto end

:end
```

The choice statement uses the list of parameters after the /c: to listen to input. One of those choices must be provided. The choice statement will actually ignore any other input and wait for one of those choices.

Also, take note of how to handle the input afterward. Each choice is assigned a number, based on its order: Y = 1, N = 2, and M = 3. The if statement should actually be read as, "If the error level is greater than or equal to x, go to label."

Because of how the computer handles if statements, always test the errorlevel from the highest to the lowest. If you test the values in the wrong order and start your evaluation with if errorlevel = 1 goto y, everything will satisfy this test because all possible values are greater than or equal to 1.

If you are using Windows 2000 or Windows XP, you can do the same type of thing in your batch file by using the set command, but I find set to be an inferior tool for this type of test. I suggest getting choice.exe from either a Windows 98 or Windows Vista computer.

Starting with Windows Server 2003, Microsoft has included choice.exe, and it supports slightly different options than the MS-DOS version. This version of choice.exe is also compatible with Windows XP. Listing 5-5 holds a copy of the same batch file using the Windows Server 2003 choice command. Notice the /M and the quotes around the message text:

Listing 5-5: **Batch File Using Windows Server 2003 choice Command**

```
@echo off
choice /c:ynm /M "You choose"
if errorlevel == 3 goto m
if errorlevel == 2 goto n
if errorlevel == 1 goto y
goto end

:y
echo You chose Yes.
goto end

:n
echo You chose No.
goto end

:m
echo You chose Maybe.
goto end

:end
```

The if, choice, and set statements add many options to the design of
your batch files; they can help you make batch files that are flexible and
comprehensive.

Looping

I hate having to repeat myself, and if you feel the same way, loops are
for you. Loops can be used inside or outside batch files with only a small
modification. The loop is a for loop and requires a list of values that are
assigned to a variable and a statement that uses that variable. The variable
is assigned with a preceding % character outside a batch file, and two %
characters when used within a batch file. Here is an example of a loop at the
command prompt:

```
echo off
for %x in (hello world) do echo %x
```

The output of the previous loop would be

```
hello
world
```

If done in a batch file, the loop would look like this:

```
echo off
for %%x in (hello world) do echo %%x
```

Loops may cut down your work when you have several repetitive lines in your batch file.

Locating a command

When you type a command at a command prompt, in a batch file, or at the Run command, your computer follows a set of steps to locate the command:

1. The computer checks the current directory for the command.

2. If the command is not found in the current directory, the computer checks all directories listed in the Path environment variable.

If the command is not located — possibly because you misspelled it — you see the following message:

```
Bad command or file name
```

If you see this message, check the spelling of the command and try again.

The path variable can be set in the `autoexec.bat` file for all Microsoft OSes. It is the only environment variable that can be set without using the `set` command. To set the path variable, you can use either

```
set path = c:\windows;c:\windows\system
```

or

```
path = c:\windows;c:\windows\system
```

The only advantage to the latter is that it uses four fewer keystrokes. If both `c:\windows` and `c:\windows\system` are in the path, they will be checked when a command that is typed is not in the current directory.

Windows 2000 and newer Windows computers provide an additional location for setting the path environment variable. To change the path on a Windows 2000 computer, open the system Control Panel, click the Advanced tab (or the Advanced system settings for Windows Vista users), and click the Environment Variables button. You can use the Environment Variables dialog box to modify the path for the computer.

Putting it together

Listing 5-6 is a short batch file that has been documented with `rem` (remark) statements throughout the file. It shows a completed file that uses many of the techniques discussed in this section. This batch file was designed to

gather the TCP/IP configuration from a computer and place it in a text file on the C: drive; but it could place the information on a drive on a server so that it could be collected by an administrator. The text file that the batch file creates is named for the computer information from which the information was gathered. This data is collected only once. The networking troubleshooting commands used in this file can be found in Book VIII, Chapter 3.

Listing 5-6: Batch File Documented with `rem` Statements

```
rem Check for existing file, and if it exists, exit the batch file,
rem and make the directory if it does not exist.
if not exist C:\IPSettings\nul mkdir C:\IPSettings
if exist C:\IPSettings\%computername%.txt goto end
rem Check to see if the computer is running Windows 9x
rem or Windows NT style OS.
if not !%OS%==!Windows_NT goto Win9x
:WinNT
rem Create a new file containing the output of ipconfig.exe
rem which is the current TCP/IP Configuration.
ipconfig /all > C:\IPSettings\%computername%.txt
rem Add to this file the current routing table using netstat.exe
netstat.exe -R >> C:\IPSettings\%computername%.txt
rem Skip the Windows 9x section and goto the end of the file.
goto end
:Win9x
rem Use Windows 9x compatible versions of the Windows NT commands
rem networking commands.
winipcfg /all /batch C:\IPSettings\%computername%.txt
netstat.exe -R >> C:\IPSettings\%computername%.txt
:end
```

If this file is saved to C:\Windows\GetIPSettings.bat, it can be executed by specifying the name of the file GetIPSettings in a command window or by typing it after choosing Start⇨Run. By specifying the name, the entire path on your computer will be searched for the file with .com, .exe, .cmd, or .bat as the file extension.

Getting an A+

The most important things to remember from this chapter are what the different commands are used for and the major differences between similar commands. Here is a quick review:

✦ attrib changes file attributes, such as read-only, hidden, system, and archive.

✦ copy copies one or multiple files from one directory to another.

✦ defrag defragments your hard drive to increase performance.

- ✦ dir displays a list of files in a directory or directories.
- ✦ edit modifies text or ASCII files.
- ✦ format prepares a disk for accepting data or to erase a disk.
- ✦ mem displays information about memory usage.
- ✦ chkdsk checks a disk for errors that could cause data loss.
- ✦ ver displays the version of Windows that is in use.
- ✦ xcopy is like copy but can be used to copy entire directory structures.

Prep Test

1 You are working on the help desk, and you receive a call from Mary. She is looking for a file that is saved on her hard drive. She has forgotten the name she gave it, but she knows that the title contains the word "budget" and that it is a Microsoft Excel spreadsheet. What command will best help her locate her document?

A ○ `dir *budget.xls`

B ○ `dir *budget*.xls /b`

C ○ `dir *.budget*.xls /s`

D ○ `dir *budget*.xls /b /s`

2 Sitting at your computer one day, you attempt to open a file with the `edit` command, but you see in the title bar that the file is opened as read-only. How can you open the file for editing?

A ○ Open the file using `edit <filename> /modify`.

B ○ Before opening the file, use `attrib -r <filename>`.

C ○ After the file is open, use `attrib -r <filename>`.

D ○ When you attempt to save the file, check off the Overwrite Existing File option.

3 You need to regularly back up files in a directory, but you want to back up only files that have changed. What commands can you use to accomplish this in the easiest way possible?

A ○ `fc` and `xcopy`

B ○ `attrib` and `copy`

C ○ `fc`, `changes`, and `xcopy`

D ○ `xcopy` and `attrib`

4 You want to copy a directory structure (complete with subdirectories), so you use `copy c:\dir1\*.* c:\newdir /s /e`. What will you find in the `newdir` directory?

A ○ All files that were in `dir1`

B ○ All files and subdirectories that were in `dir1`

C ○ Nothing — the command is improperly constructed and will generate an error

D ○ None of the above

5 You receive a call from a user on your network complaining that his computer is slow. You ask a few more questions and find out that he feels that the speed of his hard drive is much slower than when he got his computer. What command would you suggest running?

A ○ diskfix

B ○ quikdisk

C ○ scanfix

D ○ defrag

6 You created a new partition on your hard disk and assigned it a drive letter of F:. The new partition needs to be formatted as NTFS. Which of the following commands will perform the required action?

A ○ format.exe F: /FS:NTFS

B ○ filesystem F: /FS:NTFS

C ○ format.com F: /FS:NTFS

D ○ This can only be performed when creating a partition using Disk Management.

7 You have just been told that an MS-DOS application that you are supposed to run requires 550K of conventional memory. How can you check to see whether you have that much memory available?

A ○ convchck

B ○ memchck

C ○ mem

D ○ freemem

8 You need to copy an entire directory structure from floppy disk over to your hard drive. Which command should you use?

A ○ xcopy.exe

B ○ pathcopy.exe

C ○ copy.exe

D ○ dircopy.exe

9 You are using a Windows XP computer and want to remove the c:\files directory. This directory is not empty. What command do you use?

A ○ deltree

B ○ rmdir

C ○ deldir

D ○ nukedir

Answers

1 **D.** Although C looks like a good choice as well, using the subdirectory switch, it has an additional period in the search string, so will not return as many files and will work only if Mary's document has a period in front of the word *budget. See "dir."*

2 **B.** The `attrib.exe` command allows you to change only the attribute before the file is opened. *Review "attrib.exe."*

3 **D.** The `attrib.exe` command can be used to remove the archive attribute from all files in a directory structure. Then, as files are modified, you can use `xcopy *.* c:\backuplocation /s /a` to copy all the files to a new location. If you want your next copy to copy the files that were modified since the last copy, you have to use the `attrib` command to remove the archive attribute again. *Check out "xcopy."*

4 **C.** The suggested command will cause a syntax error, and nothing will be copied. The `copy` command does not support either `/s` or `/e`; to use these options, you have to use the `xcopy.exe` command. *Peruse "xcopy."*

5 **D.** `defrag` is used to reorganize files, which speeds up access to the disk. Check out *"defrag.exe."*

6 **C.** To assign a specific file system to a drive during formatting, use the `/FS:` option. *Look over "format.com."*

7 **C.** `mem` tells you how much conventional memory is available to your applications. *See "mem.exe."*

8 **A.** `xcopy.exe` can copy entire directory structures. *Examine "xcopy."*

9 **B.** `rmdir` removes directories on a Windows XP computer even if they contain files. *Review "rmdir."*

Chapter 6: Working with System Files and the Boot Process

Exam Objectives

✔ Identify the names and purposes of each file required to boot up a Windows XP and Windows Vista computer

✔ Identify the locations of Windows XP and Windows Vista boot files

*S*tarting a computer has long been referred to as *booting*. Before you can use your computer, you need to be able to boot it to a point where the operating system (OS) is functional. Otherwise, your computer is like a safe without a known combination. This chapter will help you get that "safe" open by examining the boot process, which encompasses a series of steps, from powering-on to loading the OS shell. This chapter reviews the hardware *POST (Power-on Self-Test)* process and will concentrate on the OS portion of the overall process. This chapter also introduces you to the standard Windows boot process and the files that are required, and also how to correct or deal with boot problems related to the boot files. A solid understanding of the Windows boot files will prepare you for the exam, and a general knowledge of the other files will prepare you for working with these systems in the field.

If, as an A+ Certified Professional, you are faced with troubleshooting the boot process on a computer for a user, it is required that you understand the boot sequence. If you do not know what the normal boot process is, you will be at a deficit attempting to troubleshoot issues with it. As a CompTIA A+ Certified Professional, you will often have to bring your knowledge of the core operating system files to bear on your user's computer conundrums.

If you are unfamiliar with boot processes in general, focus on the entire chapter. The exam, though, focuses on the Windows boot process.

Power-on Self-Test (POST) process

The *Power-on Self-Test (POST)* process starts when power is applied to the system. Electrical current makes its way from the power lead on the motherboard to the ROM-BIOS chips; when the current is received by the BIOS chips, they immediately begin executing their programs. One of the first checks is the memory (both a count and integrity test). After the memory check, the POST process moves on to find out what ports or I/O devices

exist on the system. If the system is equipped with a PnP BIOS (Plug and Play BIOS), as most new systems are, the BIOS-level PnP configuration takes place. The next thing that happens is a search for bootable disk devices. The order of this search is defined by the settings stored in CMOS memory, but is often `a:` (floppy drive), `c:` (first partition on the first bootable hard drive), and then CD-ROM.

For each device in the list of potential bootable devices, the partition table is checked for the active partition. Floppy disks and the CD-ROM check only the first partition. For this partition, the first sector is read and checked for a boot loader. For Windows 2000 and Windows XP, the boot loader is `ntldr`; the boot loader for Windows Vista is `bootmgr`. When this file is located, it is executed. If it was not found on the first potential bootable device, the second and third devices are checked before reporting a boot failure.

Standard Boot Process for Windows 2000 and XP

Windows XP—based OSes (from Windows NT3.1 to Windows XP) have their roots in IBM's OS/2. It is partly because of this history that their boot process is very different from older OSes, such as Windows 9x or MS-DOS. Unlike Windows 9x, there is no real-mode boot component to the OS; Windows XP is a pure 32-bit or 64-bit OS. So the boot processes are similar only until the boot loader is located at the end of the POST process.

The *boot sector* is created when the disk is formatted, and it contains a small program that has a mini file-system driver to read FAT, FAT32, and NTFS partitions. This program then looks for the real boot loader, which is `ntldr`.

Because of ARC naming conventions, Microsoft refers to the drive that has the boot sector on it as the *system partition,* and to the partition that has the `windows` directory on it as the *boot partition.* (You can read about ARC in a bit.) To help keep these terms straight, remember that the OS does not really "boot" until `ntoskrnl.exe` is launched from the `windows` directory. The `windows` directory for a Windows 2000 computer is `winnt`.

Windows 2000 and newer OSes use many of the same files as MS-DOS and Windows 9x. However, many files are specific to Windows 2000 and newer OSes. The following sections provide an overview of the Windows 2000 or Windows XP–specific files.

ntldr

The job of `ntldr` — the boot loader for Windows XP—based OSes — is to coordinate the loading of the rest of the OS. `ntldr` is located on the root of your system partition, and if it is corrupted, it can easily be replaced from

any other working copy of a Windows XP—based OS. `ntldr` switches the memory model used on the system to a *flat memory model:* that is, treating all memory on the system as one contiguous block. If your computer requires the `ntbootdd.sys` file, which is a SCSI controller driver, it is loaded by `ntldr` so that the rest of the boot process can access the boot drive. `ntldr` then reads the `boot.ini` file, if it exists, and displays the list of possible OSes that can be booted. If you want to know what happens when the `boot.ini` file is missing, read through Book VII, Chapter 1.

After choosing any version of a Windows XP—based OS, `ntdetect.com` is called. `ntdetect.com` performs a hardware detection, scanning all hardware ports, processor make, model, and description, and the amount of RAM on the system. After this information has been collected, it is returned to `ntldr` and will eventually make up the HKEY_LOCAL_MACHINE\ HARDWARE key of the Registry.

The last step performed by `ntldr` is to launch `ntoskrnl.exe`. To launch `ntoskrnl.exe`, `ntldr` goes to the `system32` subdirectory of the directory listed in the `boot.ini` file.

When formatting a floppy disk using a Windows XP—based OS, the boot sector is set to look for `ntldr`. If you leave a disk in your computer when it is being rebooted, you will see this message:

```
NTLDR is Missing
Press any key to restart.
```

For disks formatted with Windows 9*x*, this message will appear:

```
Invalid system disk
Replace the disk, and then press any key
```

ntbootdd.sys

If you boot your computer from an IDE/ATA drive or a SCSI drive from a SCSI controller that supports its own BIOS, you won't see the `ntbootdd.sys` file on your computer. However, if you are loading Windows XP from a SCSI drive on a controller that does not have its own BIOS, `ntbootdd.sys` appears on the root of the drive that has `ntldr` on it. `ntbootdd.sys` is the SCSI driver for your SCSI controller, but it has been renamed from the driver's actual name to `ntbootdd.sys`.

boot.ini

The `boot.ini` file is a text file on the root of your system partition that lists the OSes that are available to boot. It contains two things: the default timeout value for the boot menu to be displayed, and where `ntldr` can find each

copy of the OS. Upon looking at the `boot.ini` for the first time, you might be confused by the strange notation used to denote locations. This notation is called an ARC pathname, which I discuss in the next section.

Listing 6-1 shows a sample `boot.ini` file.

Listing 6-1: A Sample boot.ini File

```
[boot loader]
timeout=10
default= multi(0)disk(0)rdisk(0)partition(3)\WINDOWS
[operating systems]
C:\="Microsoft Windows 98"
multi(0)disk(0)rdisk(0)partition(3)\WINDOWS="Windows XP"
multi(0)disk(0)rdisk(0)partition(4)\WINNT="Windows 2000"
multi(0)disk(0)rdisk(0)partition(4)\WINNT="Win 2K Error"/SOS
multi(0)disk(0)rdisk(0)partition(2)\WINNT="Windows NT 4.0"
```

The first section in the `boot.ini` file is the `[boot loader]` section. It lists the timeout value, the number of seconds to display the boot menu, and the default OS to boot. The default OS is located in the OS listing in the file. The first OS in the list with a matching path is loaded by `ntldr`.

In this code listing, the `[operating systems]` section lists all OSes that `boot.ini` knows about on the system. This section would be built and added to while you install multiple copies of Windows XP—based OSes on a system. (For example, you might have multiple versions of an OS installed if this is a testing or development system.) The sample `boot.ini` file in the preceding listing also has two entries that refer to the same path (`partition 4`). The difference between them is the application of the `SOS` switch at the end of the second line. The description strings that are used in this section are the display text for the boot menu, but they have no effect on the boot process of the OS.

If you have only one copy of Windows installed, you won't see the boot menu at all because there is only one choice of OS to load.

ARC pathnames

Advanced RISC Computing Specification (ARC) is a rigid set of standards presented by the ACE (Advanced Computing Environment) initiative. This initiative has been sponsored by major vendors in the industry, and one of the standards that arose was a naming convention to refer to disk partitions. To understand the parts of this name, see Table 6-1.

```
multi(0)disk(0)rdisk(0)partition(4)\WINNT="Windows 2000"
```

Table 6-1		ARC Path Components
Type	*Class*	*Description*
SCSI	Adapter	The ordinal number of the SCSI controller located in the system. The ordinal number refers to the order in which the controller was located. The hardware is scanned according to the buses on the motherboard, and each bus is scanned starting with slot 1. If controllers were located in slots 1 and 3, the controller in slot 1 would be SCSI(0), and the controller in slot 3 would be SCSI(1). SCSI is only used in cases where the SCSI controller either does not have an onboard BIOS or is disabled.
multi	Adapter	The ordinal number of the Multifunction controller in the system. Multifunction is used for all devices that do not use the previous listing for SCSI. This includes IDE, SATA, and SCSI controllers with the BIOS enabled.
Signature	Non-Classed	Notation that can be used in place of SCSI or multi to help conform to Plug and Play specifications. Each drive identified by the Windows XP OS has a Signature written to it. The notation looks like Signature(8765bfa4) and tells ntldr to look for a drive that has that signature and load the OS from there, regardless of which controller it is found on.
disk	Controller	The SCSI ID number assigned to the SCSI drive on the system. This is set to 0 when using the multi (multifunction) adapter.
rdisk	Peripheral	The rigid disk number, referring to the physical location on the controller rather than the logical ID. The SCSI ID number refers to a logical ID.
partition	Block Device	The partition number for the partition that the OS will be found on. Partition(0) refers to a drive with no partitions. Because Windows XP requires a partitioned drive to store files, the partition number will always be 1 or greater.

The previous line is from Listing 6-1 in the previous section, multi(0) refers to the first non-SCSI controller on the system; disk(0) does not refer to anything because it would be a SCSI ID of a disk; rdisk(0) refers to the first disk on the controller; and partition(4) is the fourth partition on the disk. Windows XP—based OSes use this specification because the assignment of drive letters to partitions is flexible, but partition locations are very rigid, thus preventing errors.

ntdetect.com

The next step after choosing a Windows XP—based OS from the `boot.ini` menu is to have `ntdetect.com` run. The only job for `ntdetect.com` is to find out what hardware is on the system. This detection process is similar to what happens during the POST process at the hardware level. `ntdetect.com` checks for the following components:

✦ Bus/adapter type

✦ Communication ports

✦ Computer ID

✦ Floating-point coprocessor

✦ Floppy disks

✦ Keyboard

✦ Mouse/pointing device

✦ Parallel ports

✦ SCSI adapters

✦ Video adapters

This information creates a hardware tree that is passed back to `ntldr` and eventually given to `ntoskrnl.exe`, which places it in the Registry.

ntoskrnl.exe

The main goal of the boot process is to get the OS kernel loaded and functioning. The computer has already given you a choice of OSes, inventoried the hardware, and is now ready to actually start loading the OS into memory. `ntoskrnl.exe` represents the first and most important step in this process. The OS kernel for Windows XP—based OSes is responsible for all thread level scheduling on the system. It plays a major control role, managing all other components on the system. Without it, there would be anarchy in the OS.

`ntldr` proceeds to the path specified in `boot.ini` to locate `ntoskrnl.exe` in the `system32` folder. If `ntldr` locates the kernel, it proceeds to execute it. `ntldr` will generate a missing kernel error message if it fails to locate the kernel. Startup error messages are covered in Book VII, Chapter 1. After the kernel is running, `ntldr` passes control of the system to it. There are several steps to the kernel load, starting with loading devices, and then moving on to loading any system services. After the services are running, it loads the default shell application and user profile.

The default user profile is used to run the user logon process. At this point, the logon screen will tell you to `Press Ctrl+Alt+Delete to begin`.

After providing logon credentials, that user session is discarded, and a new one is started for the new user.

The device load process

All the devices to be loaded during the system startup are listed in the Registry. The Registry includes information about each device here:

```
HKEY_LOCAL_MACHINE\SYSTEM\CurrentControlSet\Services\<device>
```

In this location, you can find several values that describe how the device will start up. These values are listed in Table 6-2.

Table 6-2	Device and Service Settings in the Registr
Value	*Description*
Display Name	This string is used to display the name in areas of Windows XP, such as Device Manager or the Services administrative tool.
Error Control	This value configures how errors will be reported back to the OS. A value of 0 does not report any errors with the device back to the OS. A value of 1 reports errors normally. A value of 2 makes errors severe and will cause an automatic reboot of the computer to the "Last Known Good Configuration." A value of 3 makes errors critical and will also cause an automatic reboot of the computer to the Last Known Good Configuration. If the Last Known Good Configuration is already used, severe errors will enable the computer to continue to boot, but critical errors will start the bug-check routine.
Group	Devices can be grouped. This is done mostly for dependencies. If any device in a group fails, dependent devices will not start.
Image Path	This is the path and name of the actual driver file that is used for the device or service.
Start	This identifies when the device will start up. The five start types are boot (0), system (1), automatic (2), manual (3), and disabled (4). Most devices have boot or system for a start value, but you might find a few set to automatic. Most services are set for either automatic or manual.
Tag	A Tag ID is assigned to the service when it is installed, but is not actually used by the OS.
Type	Identifies that type of service or device. All devices should have a value of 1. Service types should be 1 for kernel device drivers, 2 for file system drivers, 4 for arguments for an adapter, 10 for single process Win32 applications that follow the Service Control Protocol, and 20 for Win32 Services that can share their process with other Win32 Services.

The service load process

All services that are to be loaded during the system startup are listed in the Registry. The Registry includes information about each device in the following location:

```
HKEY_LOCAL_MACHINE\SYSTEM\CurrentControlSet\Services\<service>
```

This is the same location used for devices. The biggest difference between devices and services is that devices map out to a physical piece of hardware, but services are only software. The values for services are listed in Table 6-2 in the previous section.

Loading the shell

After processing all the device drivers, the user's shell loads. The application that makes up the shell is actually defined by a `shell  =` line in `system.ini`, the default being `explorer.exe`. If the current shell ever crashes and is removed from RAM, `explorer.exe` will be loaded. Explorer checks the Registry to see what desktop components are supposed to be displayed and then checks the `HKEY_LOCAL_MACHINE\Software\Microsoft\Windows\CurrentVersion\RunServices` key in the Registry to auto-start other applications. One of the services started at this point is the network service. When the network service is started up, you will be presented with a logon screen.

After loading the requested services, Explorer then executes any entries that it finds in the Registry in the `HKEY_LOCAL_MACHINE\Software\Microsoft\Windows\CurrentVersion\RunOnce` key. Each entry under `runonce` is executed sequentially, waiting for each to finish before moving on to the next. When these are completed, Explorer then moves on to the run and load entries in `win.ini` to launch additional applications, followed by the run entries in the Registry, found in `HKEY_LOCAL_MACHINE\Software\Microsoft\Windows\CurrentVersion\Run`, and finally the Startup group from the Start menu, Start⇨Programs⇨Startup.

This process is almost identical for all versions of Windows that are based on Windows NT.

For information on editing the Registry, see the `regedit.exe` section in Book VI, Chapter 4.

Standard Boot Process for Windows Vista

Like with so many areas of the OS, Windows Vista changes the core boot process for Windows. The first change that you will see with the boot process is the boot loader application, as well as where the configuration data

is stored. In the case of Windows Vista, the boot loader is bootmgr. This process is used by Windows OSes that have been released after Windows Vista, so it is the same process that is used by Windows 2008 Server.

bootmgr

The boot manager (bootmgr) now takes over the role previously performed by ntldr. It is responsible for reading the boot configuration data stored in the boot configuration database and displaying the boot menu.

Boot Configuration Database

Rather than relying on boot configuration being stored in a single file, such as boot.ini, Microsoft now uses a Boot Configuration Database (BCD). This database stores more comprehensive information about the boot settings. If you are using a computer that supports EFI (Extensible Firmware Interface), the BCD is stored in the EFI System Partition; but if you are using a computer that supports an IBM-style BIOS, the information is stored on System Volume in the \Boot\BCD file. If you need to make changes to this configuration, you can use the System Properties, msconfig.exe, bootrec.exe, or bcdedit.exe.

winload.exe

If you choose to boot to Windows Vista, the boot manager will transfer control over to \windows\system32\winload.exe. winload.exe — the OS boot loader — has one main job, and that is to load the Windows Vista OS Kernel (ntoskrnl.exe).

Examining Other Boot Process Files

This section takes at a look at some additional files related to the boot process. These include config.sys, autoexec.bat, win.ini, and system.ini, which store configuration information for Windows (primarily Windows 9*x*) but are also used by newer versions of Windows. Finally, you will see the sysedit.exe utility.

config.sys

The config.sys file has been around since early versions of MS-DOS. It stores modifications to the default settings that are set through msdos.sys. config.sys usually contains environment settings and device driver load lines for devices such as CD-ROM drives. If the file does not exist, io.sys will apply system default settings to the environment in addition to the settings that are found in msdos.sys. If the config.sys file does exist, io.sys ensures that after processing the config.sys file, the settings are

equal to or higher than the default settings. If `config.sys` settings do not meet the default settings, `io.sys` will apply the default settings. (Your settings might have been changed from the default settings in order to support an application; the file's value is often increased for application support.)

In Chapter 1 of this minibook, I mention that Windows NT can be traced back to a joint venture with IBM, and originally ran on IBM's OS/2 (Operating System 2). Since that time, Microsoft has provided some support for OS/2 applications in the Windows NT OS. This support was removed with the release of Windows XP. Windows 2000 and newer versions of Windows do not generally use the `config.sys` file. If the file is edited and saved as an OS/2 text file, Windows 2000 will extract any OS/2 configuration information. This information will be written to the Registry and used for running OS/2 applications from within the Windows 2000 OS. This process happens only with Windows NT and Windows 2000 but not with MS-DOS or Windows 9*x*.

autoexec.bat

This file has been around since the first versions of MS-DOS. As the shell loads Windows, it is configured to look for and process `autoexec.bat`. `autoexec.bat` is a batch file. *Batch files* simply store a list of commands that are executed in order, and `autoexec.bat` is configured to be executed at boot. In addition to executing programs, `autoexec.bat` is used to set environment variables and load TSR (Terminate Stay Resident) programs.

TSRs are applications that load and run but do not normally occupy space in the user interface. A good example is `doskey.com`. When you run `doskey.com` from a command prompt, it doesn't appear to do anything, but it actually does: It runs, loads itself into memory, and then returns the command prompt back to you. This return of control is different from a command such as `xcopy.exe`, which controls the command prompt while it runs. It then completes its task and exits (terminates). When it terminates, it removes itself from memory and is no longer running.

`autoexec.bat` is used to set environment variables, such as the location of the temporary directory and the search path.

Post-Windows 2000 OSes will read the `autoexec.bat` file, but they ignore lines that execute programs or load TSRs. The only items or lines that are used out of the `autoexec.bat` file are statements that set environment variables, such as the system path.

system.ini

Before Windows 95, all configuration settings for applications were stored in INI files. All INI files have a similar structure, as shown in the following code:

```
[section one]
setting one = "my mystery word"
setting two = 42

[section two]
setting one = "another mystery word"
setting two = 75
```

The `system.ini` file contains settings used specifically by Windows. The type of information found in this file includes device settings and settings used when loading the Windows kernel. The `system.ini` file isn't used much these days (compared with its importance in Windows 3.*x*), but it still finds use when you need to load 16-bit, MS-DOS real-mode drivers. If you check your `system.ini` file, you should see settings for your mouse and video. Listing 6-2 holds a sample of what to expect:

Listing 6-2: Sample system.ini File

```
[386Enh]
device=*vshare
device=*dynapage
device=*vcd
device=*vpd
device=*int13
mouse=*vmouse, msmouse.vxd
woafont=dosapp.fon
COM1Fifo=0
keyboard=*vkd
display=*vdd,*vflatd

[boot]
system.drv=system.drv
drivers=mmsystem.dll power.drv
user.exe=user.exe
gdi.exe=gdi.exe
sound.drv=mmsound.drv
dibeng.drv=dibeng.dll
comm.drv=comm.drv
shell=Explorer.exe
keyboard.drv=keyboard.drv
fonts.fon=vgasys.fon
fixedfon.fon=vgafix.fon
oemfonts.fon=vgaoem.fon
386Grabber=vgafull.3gr
display.drv=pnpdrvr.drv
mouse.drv=mouse.drv
*DisplayFallback=0
SCRNSAVE.EXE=
```

In the `system.ini` file of Listing 6-2, you can see these settings:

✦ In the [386Enh] section

- File and printer sharing is initialized with *vshare.
- Real-mode support for the mouse and video display is loaded with *vmouse, msmouse.vxd, *vdd, and *vflatd.

✦ In the [boot] section

- Power management support is loaded with power.drv.
- The sound card is initialized with mmsound.drv.
- Serial communication is initialized with comm.drv.
- The system shell application is set with shell=Explorer.exe.

If the system.ini file is lost or corrupted, you will likely have problems with all the devices that rely on it. Because Windows 9x stores some video configuration in this file, you tend to see problems quickly. If the system.ini file is missing, all versions of Windows create a new one and start reloading the settings. This file is not used by the MS-DOS boot process.

win.ini

Like system.ini, win.ini was heavily used by both Windows 3.x and its applications. Today, it is used primarily for backward compatibility with older applications, although it still stores some settings. Listing 6-3 holds a sample of some of the information found in a win.ini file:

Listing 6-3: Sample win.ini File

```
[windows]
run=Qtstub.exe
NullPort=None
ScreenSaveActive=1
UninstallPath=C:\
device=EPSON Stylus COLOR 600,EPS600,LPT1:

[Desktop]
Wallpaper=C:\WINDOWS\APPLIC~1\MICROS~1\INTERN~1\INTERN~1.BMP
TileWallpaper=0
WallpaperStyle=0
Pattern=(None)

[Extensions]
txt=notepad.exe ^.txt
bmp=C:\Progra~1\Access~1\mspaint.exe ^.bmp
vdo=VDOLIV32.EXE ^.vdo
gra=C:\PROGRA~1\COMMON~1\MICROS~1\MSGRAPH5\GRAPH5.EXE ^.gra
Q98=C:\APPS\QUICKTAX\QTAX98.EXE ^.Q98
Q97=C:\QCKTAX97\QTAX97.EXE ^.Q97
Q99=C:\QUICKTAX\Qtax99.exe ^.Q99
```

Listing 6-3 illustrates common items that you will find in your `win.ini` file. `run` lines automatically load applications when the shell loads. `device` lines in the `win.ini` file make hardware devices available for older applications that need to use them. Wallpaper and desktop settings are here as well. Finally, for more backward compatibility, `wini.ini` contains a mapping of some registered file extensions.

Corruption or deletion of the `win.ini` file tends to be less noticeable than that of the `system.ini` file, but it will still cause problems with older applications that refer to the information that is found in the file. If you have a problem with an older application, you should be able to fix the problem by reinstalling the application.

sysedit.exe

The *System Configuration Editor* (shown in Figure 6-1), which you open by typing **sysedit.exe** at a command prompt, gives you quick access to your main configuration files — `win.ini`, `system.ini`, `protocol.ini`, `config.sys` — as well as `autoexec.bat`. It is capable of editing and saving these files. This task could have been accomplished with any text editor, but it is far easier to just use `sysedit`.

Figure 6-1:
sysedit.
exe makes
getting at
configu-
ration files
easier.

Managing Memory and Virtual Memory

If you are lucky enough never to have created a boot disk for your computer, you have never had to get into the down-and-dirty world of memory management. When attempting to load device drivers and applications in the MS-DOS environment, you have a very limited amount of the memory

to work with — 640KB — and if you are not careful, you can quickly run out of space, so you need to manage what and how device drivers and applications get loaded into memory. If you have to support MS-DOS–based applications within the Windows environment, or if you need to create custom boot disks that load your network drivers, you need to pay attention to this section. Memory management skills are becoming a lost art in the world of Windows.

With the adoption of Windows-NT based OSes, like Windows XP and Windows Vista, you no longer need to worry about boot-time memory management because after the OS kernel loads, the memory structure switches to a flat memory model and implements a virtual memory structure.

As improvements were made in the field of RAM, and as computers with more and more memory continued to ship, software developers created applications that used the new memory. To make the entire process of managing memory easier, Microsoft decided to implement virtual memory for the Windows OSes. Virtual memory allows Windows to present a virtual machine (VM) that contains 4GB of memory to applications running in the Windows environment. It then used a Virtual Memory Manager (VMM) to control or manage the mapping of data between the virtual addresses used by the application and where the data was stored in physical memory. The VMM was also able to move data that was not being actively used in RAM to a file on the disk. The swapping of memory data pages to and from the disk file lead to the file being named "swap file:" in Windows 9*x* and "paging file" in Windows NT-based OSes (like Windows XP and Vista). The drawback in the system of swapping data shows up when an application wants to use data that is in the swap file because it then has to wait for the data to be retrieved back into RAM before it can be accessed.

Access speeds of hard disks are measured in milliseconds (10^{-3}), and memory access is measured in nanoseconds (10^{-9}). It should not be hard to guess that this means that when data has to be retrieved from the swap file on a hard drive, the process is extremely slow relative to retrieving it directly from RAM.

The VMM manages virtual memory addresses up to 4GB and the mapping of those addresses to a physical location, either in RAM or on a hard drive. You should rely on using the paging file only when applications need a small amount of additional memory. Most OSes implement virtual memory and allow it to use swap space on a hard drive to allow applications with high memory requirements to function, but greater performance will be achieved by adding more physical RAM to the system.

When an application needs to store information to memory, it passes the request to the VMM. VMM stores the information in RAM but might move the information to the swap file on the drive later. The process for retrieving application data is illustrated in Figure 6-2; the process looks like this:

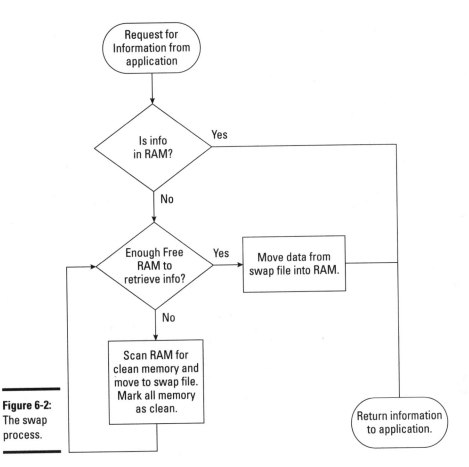

Figure 6-2:
The swap
process.

1. When the application requests information, the VMM checks whether the information is in RAM.

2. If the information is in RAM, the information is simply returned to the application, and the process is complete.

3. If the information isn't in RAM, VMM checks whether there is enough space in RAM to retrieve the information from the swap file.

4. If there is enough space to retrieve the information, the information is retrieved from the drive, stored into RAM, and passed on to the application; and the process is complete.

5. If there isn't enough space to retrieve the information, VMM checks for memory locations that have not been accessed recently and passes them from RAM down to the swap file.

6. When enough information is moved to the swap file to make room for the requested information, that information is moved into RAM and then returned to the application.

A *clean* memory location in RAM is a location that has not been accessed since the last time the VMM marked it clean. If the memory location has been accessed with a read or write request, this location is marked as *dirty*. When looking for memory data to move to the swap file, each location is checked; if it is clean, it is moved to the hard drive, and if it is dirty, it is marked as dirty and left. If the first scan did not free enough RAM, an immediate second search for movable memory data is required, at which time any memory data that is now dirty is data that was accessed since the first scan, mere milliseconds ago. This algorithm is the Least Recently Used (LRU) algorithm, and it ensures that data that is actively used in RAM will stay in RAM.

Getting an A+

This chapter examines the process undertaken by the software on your computer during the boot process. The basic boot process for both Windows XP and Windows Vista computers is discussed, as well as the differences between them.

Key points that you should remember about this chapter are

+ Virtual memory is managed by the Virtual Memory Manager, which presents a 4GB address space to applications on the system.

+ Virtual memory is made up of physical RAM and hard drive space in the form of a swap file or paging file.

+ The Windows XP and Windows Vista boot process uses the `ntldr`, `ntbootdd.sys`, `ntdetect.com`, `bootmgr`, `BCD`, `winload.exe`, and `boot.ini` files.

Prep Test

1 **A user has a program that automatically starts when he logs into his computer. He would like to disable it. Where should he look for possible settings?**

 A ○ `load =` lines in `win.ini`

 B ○ The Startup group in the Start menu

 C ○ The RUN key in the Registry

 D ○ All the above

 E ○ None of the above

2 **A user has attempted to boot his computer, but instead of seeing the Windows XP boot menu, he sees a message stating, "NTLDR is missing. Press any key to restart." What should he do first?**

 A ○ Set the CD-ROM as bootable in the system CMOS and insert the Windows XP CD. This will allow him to complete an emergency repair.

 B ○ Reinstall Windows XP.

 C ○ Reboot the computer and enter Safe Mode; then choose `RebuildBootSect.exe` from the `\windows\system32` directory.

 D ○ Remove the floppy disk from the `A:` drive.

3 **The search order for bootable drives is stored in which location?**

 A ○ System BIOS

 B ○ PNP Configuration

 C ○ `io.sys`

 D ○ CMOS Memory

4 **What driver is used to access virtual memory?**

 A ○ `ramdrive.sys`

 B ○ `himem.sys`

 C ○ `emm386.exe`

 D ○ None of the above

5 **If you need to quickly edit `win.ini`, `autoexec.bat`, and `config.sys`, what command(s) could you use? (Select all that apply.)**

 A ❑ `sysedit.exe`

 B ❑ `cfgedit.exe`

 C ❑ `msconfig.exe`

 D ❑ `notepad.exe win.ini autoexec.bat config.sys`

6 **What is the first file that is loaded as part of the Windows XP boot process?**

A ○ `io.sys`

B ○ `ntbootdd.sys`

C ○ `ntbooter`

D ○ `ntldr`

7 **How large is the memory address space that is presented in applications running on a Windows XP computer?**

A ○ 640KB

B ○ 1MB

C ○ 1GB

D ○ 4GB

8 **What file is a copy of the SCSI drivers for the SCSI controller in your Windows XP computer?**

A ○ `ntbootdd.sys`

B ○ `boot.ini`

C ○ `ntldr`

D ○ `ntdetect.com`

9 **What is name of the file that Windows XP uses to store memory data for the virtual memory system?**

A ○ Memory file

B ○ Swap file

C ○ Storage file

D ○ Paging file

Answers

1 **D.** Automatic commands can be found in any of the listed locations (`win.ini`, Startup group, or the Registry). *Review "Standard Boot Process for Windows 2000 and XP."*

2 **D.** `ntldr` is missing in the error message that you will see if you attempt to boot from a Windows XP formatted disk that does not contain `ntldr`. *Check out "Standard Boot Process for Windows 2000 and XP."*

3 **D.** CMOS memory contains the boot device order. *Take a look at "Power-on Self-Test (POST) process."*

4 **D.** Virtual memory reserves space on the hard drive to be used as RAM. It is managed by VMM32 and is loaded by Windows. *Peek at "Managing Memory and Virtual Memory."*

5 **A, C.** `sysedit.exe` and `msconfig.exe` provide quick means of editing the listed configuration files. *Refer to "Examining Other Boot Process Files."*

6 **D.** `ntldr` is the first file that loads as part of the Windows 2000 boot process. *Examine "Standard Boot Process for Windows 2000 and XP."*

7 **D.** The memory address that is present to each application or VM is 4GB in size. *Examine "Managing Memory and Virtual Memory."*

8 **A.** The `ntbootdd.sys` file is a copy of the SCSI driver that has been renamed and is used during the boot process. *Refer to "Standard Boot Process for Windows 2000 and XP."*

9 **D.** Windows XP refers to the file used by virtual memory as a paging file or the page file. *Look over "Memory and Virtual Memory."*

Book VI

Managing the Operating System

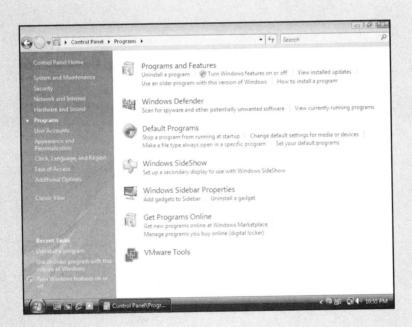

Contents at a Glance

Chapter 1: Loading and Configuring Device Drivers

Exam Objectives

✔ Device driver requirements and installation

✔ Identification and use of signed drivers

✔ Working with drivers and diagnosing driver errors

The United Nations' goal is for the nations of the world to work together and achieve common goals. They achieve this end by communicating with each other, but they first have to overcome the language barrier, which is done by employing hundreds of translators. *Device drivers* serve a similar role for computers that translators serve for the UN, converting information between the operating system and various pieces of hardware. Device drivers are responsible for establishing and maintaining communication links between an operating system and the various hardware devices on a computer. Each hardware device has its own language. The job of the device driver is to translate data from the device into something that the OS can understand, and then translate the OS data into something that the device can understand.

Even with the advent of Plug and Play, an A+ Certified Professional still needs to understand how drivers work and how to diagnose driver-related problems. Even though Plug and Play may allow for default drivers to be automatically selected and loaded, the entire process of managing drivers is not a hands-off process, and intervention will be required on many occasions.

Loading Device Drivers

Because device drivers are so important, you should consider how device drivers are loaded onto your system. In the following sections, you take a look at loading device drivers for Windows. In Book III, you see how to configure the hardware to be added to a system; in this chapter, you focus on the software side of configuring these devices.

Because so many devices and drivers are floating around out there, the steps in this chapter for working with and managing drivers are necessarily broad and generic.

Drivers and their installation are tied to INF files, which contain installation instructions. There are several ways to install drivers with INF files:

✦ Use Add/Remove Hardware in Windows 2000 or Add Hardware in Windows XP and newer Windows OSes.

✦ You might be able to use the INF files themselves.

✦ You might have to load the drivers manually.

✦ You might be able to install drivers directly through a setup program from the manufacturer, which can be used to install other software as well.

Before attempting device detection, ensure that the device is properly plugged in and powered; if not, the device will never be detected. And if the device is not detected, you have to manually load the drivers and configure the device. Loading drivers manually is discussed later in this section.

Some hardware vendors recommend that you copy their drivers onto your system before connecting the hardware to updates the INF files to acknowledge that this hardware exists. This then allows the device to be properly detected when Windows finds it, allowing Windows to automatically load the drivers. This information is usually included with the vendor's Quick Install or Quick Start guide. In most cases, it does not really matter when the drivers are copied; if the drivers are not on your system, Windows will ask you where to find them.

By default, Windows Vista uses Windows Update to locate and install drivers for devices that are installed into or connected to the system, which take a lot of the work out of installing drivers. The settings for this behavior are found in the System Properties, as shown in Figure 1-1. To locate these settings

1. **Click Start.**

2. **Right-click Computer and choose Properties from the shortcut menu to open the System Properties dialog box.**

3. **Click the Hardware tab and then click the Windows Update Driver Settings button.**

4. **In the Windows Update Driver Settings dialog box that opens (see Figure 1-1), select a radio button for how you do/do not want Vista to check for driver updates for new hardware. You can**

 • Have Vista automatically attempt to locate all drivers via Windows Update.

 • Have Vista prompt you for a driver each time you connect a new device.

 • Deny Windows Update.

If you choose not to use Windows Update and if the drivers are not built into Windows or if they have not been installed, Windows will not be able to locate appropriate drivers for the device.

5. **Click OK to close the Windows Update choices and then OK again to close System Properties.**

Book VI
Chapter 1

Loading and Configuring Device Drivers

Figure 1-1:
Windows
Update
driver
behavior
can make it
extremely
easy to deal
with new
hardware.

To install a device driver on Windows XP, follow these steps:

1. **Open the Add Hardware applet by choosing Start⇨Control Panel⇨ Printers and Other Hardware⇨Add Hardware.**

 The Add Hardware Wizard starts.

2. **When the Add Hardware Wizard starts, click Next.**

3. **Indicate whether you already added the hardware to your system; then click Next.**

 If you are adding a device, Windows performs a search of Plug and Play devices. The results of this search are displayed for you and include any unknown devices.

 Because adding a device also includes a troubleshooting option, this is your opportunity to select a device already installed on the system that you would like troubleshoot. If you select to troubleshoot a device, the next screen in the wizard informs you that when you finish the wizard, you will start the troubleshooter. The troubleshooter lets you set resource settings, such as IRQ and I/O addresses.

4. **If the device that you need to load the drivers for is not listed, choose the option to Add a New Hardware Device at the bottom of the list; then click Next.**

5. **You have the option of letting Windows search for new hardware (shown in Figure 1-2), or you can select the hardware from a list.**

 If your computer appears to not be responding, give it some time to finish its detection process.

Figure 1-2:
Plug
and Play
detection
is used
to initially
locate all
devices
on your
computer.

6. **If no devices are found, click Next to manually choose a driver.**

7. **To install a device manually, first choose the hardware type (shown in Figure 1-3). After you make your selection, click Next.**

Figure 1-3:
Choose
the type
of device
you are
installing so
that you can
look at a
filtered list.

8. **A screen listing manufacturers and models appears. Choose the manufacturer and then choose a model from that manufacturer. Click Next after making your selection.**

 If the device cannot be matched to known devices, you can click the Have Disk button to browse for or type the location of the device's INF file, as shown in Figure 1-4.

Figure 1-4:
Device lists
are listed
by manu-
facturer
to make
locating
devices
easier.

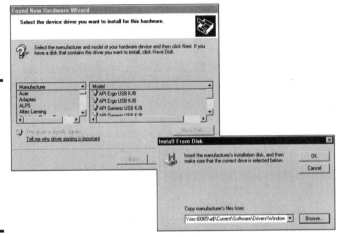

 If Windows cannot detect the device settings for your device, it asks you to manually enter the settings for some of or all the hardware resources, which are I/O addresses, Memory, DMA, and IRQs.

 You might be prompted for special device-related settings. If not, you should have a hardware installation dialog box on your screen.

9. **Click Next to start installing your hardware.**

 If Windows cannot locate some of the required files, it might ask you to insert a disk with the drivers on it or to locate the files that it needs.

10. **Click Finish when the installation is complete.**

 If you need to manually adjust the hardware resource settings, you can change the settings for the device by using either the device's control panel (if one exists) or Device Manager.

 Because control panels for each device are different, I look only at the Device Manager in this section.

To access the resource settings on Windows though Device Manager, use these steps:

1. **Choose Start⇨Control Panel, open the System applet, click the Hardware tab, and then click the Device Manager button. If you are using Windows Vista, Choose Start⇨Control Panel, choose Hardware and Sound, and then click the Device Manager link.**

The Device Manager opens, and you can expand the device tree and select the device that you want to work with.

2. **When you find the device, right-click it and choose Properties.**

From the Properties window for the device, you can troubleshoot the device, examine driver details, change resource settings, and choose which hardware profiles will use the device.

3. **Click the Resources tab to change the resource settings that are used by the device, as shown in Figure 1-5. After adjusting the settings, click OK to close the device properties dialog.**

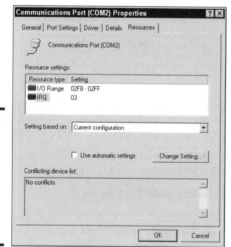

Figure 1-5:
You might have to tell Windows what resources your device requires.

Device Manager is the main tool used for configuring and removing installed device drivers.

Changing Device Settings

Regardless of how you install the drivers for the device, if Windows can't detect the settings for the device, you are prompted to specify IRQ, I/O, DMA, and memory resource settings. The prompt should only be necessary

for non–Plug and Play devices. If you are not sure of the current settings for the device, confirm the settings by examining the hardware or by using the configuration utility that came with the device. A configuration utility should be included on the driver disk of any devices that support software configuration. If the device is configured for Plug and Play, you shouldn't have to worry about this.

For many devices, you can add drivers from the device's Control Panel applet, if there is one. This ability is not available for all devices but is available for modems and several other devices.

If you want to change the settings for a device that is installed on your system, you can use either the Control Panel applet for the device (such as Phone and Modem Options, Display, or Network) or Device Manager. Because each Control Panel applet is different, I do not go through each of them here, but rather show you Device Manager.

To access Device Manager in Windows XP, choose Start➪Control Panel, double-click the System applet (opening the System Properties dialog box), and then click the Device Manager button on the Hardware tab. You can also open the System Properties dialog box by right-clicking My Computer and choosing Properties. With Device Manager open, expand the appropriate device tree until you see the device that you want to work with; then right-click the device and choose Properties. You can use the Properties window to disable the device in the current hardware profile or all hardware profiles, change the driver, and set resources for the device (see Figure 1-6).

Windows Vista does have hardware profiles. Based on how the driver was designed, you might not have a Driver or Resources tab and will not be able to configure the settings on those tabs.

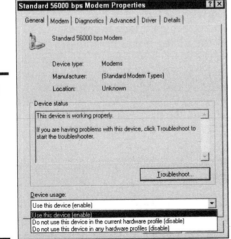

Figure 1-6: Device Manager is a very powerful tool when it comes to device management.

Lab 1-1 will guide you through examining the resources that are in use by your network card. In this exercise, you can use Windows 2000, Windows XP, or Windows Vista. Lab 1-1 can be found in the `Labs.pdf` file in the Author directory of the CD-ROM.

Updating Drivers

From time to time, software vendors update their drivers, and you can choose to not update them, manually update them, or use Windows Update. When these drivers make it to the Windows Update Web site or Microsoft Update Web site, if you have upgraded, you can add them to your updates by choosing the optional hardware components. If you choose to update the drivers manually, right-click the device in Device Manager and choose Update Driver or click the Update Driver button on the Driver tab. Because some drivers do make it to the Windows Update Web site, the first question you will be asked when you choose to update your driver is whether you want to check Windows Update for copies of the drivers. If you choose not to use Windows Update or if there are no updated drivers on the site, you can still update them manually.

The next step in the update process is either allowing Windows to automatically locate the drivers (Recommended) or having you manually specify a location for the drivers (Advanced). If you use the automatic method, Windows checks your currently installed INF files and the root directories of your removable media. If no matching drivers are found, you need to come back and choose Advanced, which allows you to recheck the same paths as well as specify a directory in which to look for drivers. If all else fails, you can select "Don't search. I will choose the drives I want to install." This option gives you a list of all drivers as well as a Have Disk button to load other drivers into the system. In most cases, you won't have to use this screen. Just telling Windows to search a specific directory is usually enough for it to locate the correct driver for you.

Windows Vista streamlines the dialog boxes for this process, and will always check the Windows Update site as part of its automatic driver update process, unless you have changed the default Windows Update Driver Settings, on the Hardware tab of System properties.

Most of the Windows drivers will be updated when you apply an OS service pack. Microsoft often includes new drivers with the OS service packs.

Removing Device Drivers

At some point, you might want to remove a device. The proper and clean removal of devices represents a large step forward in device management for the Windows OS. You can use Device Manager with all versions of

Windows to provide you the ability to cleanly remove devices and drivers. Device Manager allows you to select any installed device on your system and delete it. In addition to Device Manager, you may be able to use the individual device's Control Panel applet, such as the Network Control Panel applet.

To use Device Manager to remove a device from Windows, follow these steps:

1. **Choose Start⇨Control Panel, click Hardware and Sound, and then click the Device Manager link. If you are using older versions of Windows choose Start⇨Control Panel, open the System applet, click the Hardware tab, and then click the Device Manager button.**

2. **Expand the hardware tree to locate your device, right-click the device, and choose Uninstall.**

You are presented with a confirmation dialog box.

3. **Click OK.**

The device will be uninstalled.

Book VI
Chapter 1

Loading and
Configuring
Device Drivers

Like with the Uninstall/Unplug options in Windows 2000, Windows will (by default) unplug devices that you have removed, leaving drives and settings behind for you in case you want to reinstall the device. To see devices with Device Manager that have only been unplugged, choose View⇨Show Hidden Devices in Device Manager. This now shows all devices that have been installed on your computer, even if they are currently unplugged, and you can choose to remove them here and delete their drivers.

Signed and Unsigned Drivers

Driver signing was incorporated into Windows starting with Windows 2000 to prevent installing untested drivers on a system. Hardware vendors have an option to send their completed drivers to Microsoft for testing. After testing the driver and confirming that it doesn't have any apparent problems within the OS, Microsoft returns the driver to the vendor with a signature file. This signature file has a `.cat` extension and contains information about the original driver file to ensure that the driver was not modified since it was sent to Microsoft. When loading drivers, Windows checks for the existence of the signature file. If the signature is not available, you can configure what you want to have happen on the system. Your choices are

✦ Ignore the missing signature and install the drivers.

✦ Warn the user of the missing signature, but still give the option of installing (see Figure 1-7).

✦ Block the installation of the driver.

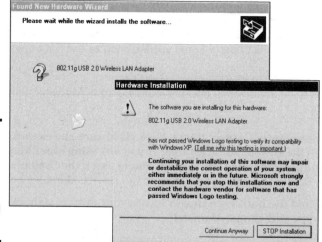

Figure 1-7:
Driver
signing
prevents
installation
of unwanted
drivers.

Prior to Windows Vista, these settings are configured in the System control panel, using the Driver Signing button on the Hardware tab. If you are logged in as an administrator, you can save these settings to affect all users. Typically, the option to block unsigned drivers is enforced on high-availability workstations or servers. To modify these settings for Windows Vista, you can

✦ Choose on a per-boot basis.

 a. *Press F8 at the start of the boot process.*

 b. *Choose Disable Driver Signature Enforcement.*

✦ Use `bcpedit.exe` to permanently disable driver signing by using the following command:

```
bcdedit.exe /set loadoptions DDISABLE_INTEGRITY_CHECKS
```

Any individual user can make his or her individual driver signing policy stronger than the administrator's defined system default.

Driver signing is designed to increase system stability by requiring hardware manufacturers to validate their drivers with Microsoft.

Working with Plug and Play

Thanks to Plug and Play, you have to do less work to add a device because device identification, driver selection, and hardware configuration are handled by Plug and Play (at least after the device has been added to the driver database). The Plug and Play specification says that a device should do the following:

+ Be uniquely identified

+ State the services that it provides and the resources that it requires

+ Identify the driver that supports it

+ Allow software to configure it

The Plug and Play standard also requires that Plug and Play devices be backward compatible with non–Plug and Play systems — at least, that's the recommendation. All Plug and Play hardware should also be independent of operating systems that are installed on the system.

The Plug and Play process starts with the computer BIOS that supports Plug and Play. In addition, you also need an operating system that supports Plug and Play and Plug and Play devices. Current Windows OSs are Plug and Play–aware operating systems. The Plug and Play process contains three major components:

+ Bus Enumerator

+ Configuration Manager

+ Resource Arbitrator

Figure 1-8 shows how these components fit together, and I discuss the whole Plug and Play process in the following paragraphs.

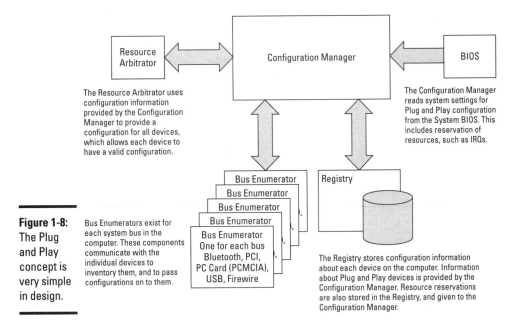

Figure 1-8:
The Plug and Play concept is very simple in design.

Resource Arbitrator

Configuration Manager

BIOS

The Resource Arbitrator uses configuration information provided by the Configuration Manager to provide a configuration for all devices, which allows each device to have a valid configuration.

The Configuration Manager reads system settings for Plug and Play configuration from the System BIOS. This includes reservation of resources, such as IRQs.

Bus Enumerator
Bus Enumerator
Bus Enumerator
Bus Enumerator
Bus Enumerator
One for each bus
Bluetooth, PCI,
PC Card (PCMCIA),
USB, Firewire

Registry

Bus Enumerators exist for each system bus in the computer. These components communicate with the individual devices to inventory them, and to pass configurations on to them.

The Registry stores configuration information about each device on the computer. Information about Plug and Play devices is provided by the Configuration Manager. Resource reservations are also stored in the Registry, and given to the Configuration Manager.

At the lowest level in the Plug and Play process is the *Bus Enumerator,* whose job is to deal directly with individual devices. Each bus architecture in your computer has a Bus Enumerator, and the major bus architectures include PCI, ISA, EISA, PCMCIA (PC Card), SCSI, and USB. When a device is added to the system, especially in the case of PCMCIA devices, it announces its presence to the Bus Enumerator. The Bus Enumerator assigns an ID to the device, interrogates the device IRQ and I/O preferences, and possibly reconfigures the device based on requests from Configuration Manager.

The Bus Enumerator is called into action when a Plug and Play computer boots, and it has work to do whenever a device is added or removed from a particular bus. When the Bus Enumerator (and the rest of the Plug and Play system) is given a notification of device removal, it can prepare for it. For example, if you want to remove a PCMCIA Ethernet adapter, you can notify the Plug and Play system by stopping the device by clicking the PC Card icon in the system tray (XP) or notification area (Vista) and choosing the Ethernet adapter.

Devices that can be removed or added to a running system are *hot swappable. Cold swapping* takes place when the machine is powered down, which is the case for most devices. PCMCIA or PC Cards support hot swapping, and some of the newer computers support hot swapping on the PCI bus. Some manufacturers also use the term *warm swappable* to refer to components that can be replaced when the computer is in a sleep, standby, or other lower-power state.

The Bus Enumerator does *not* decide what resources the new device is going to use — that is the job of Configuration Manager. The Bus Enumerator passes all information about the device to Configuration Manager, which takes a look at all the resources required by all devices on the system. If multiple devices require the same resources, the Configuration Manager calls on the *Resource Arbitrator,* which evaluates which devices can operate at which settings and provides a solution in which all devices are able to use compatible settings.

After the Resource Arbitrator works its magic, a new resource configuration is passed to Configuration Manager. Configuration Manager accepts the new configuration; it contacts each Bus Enumerator and has the Bus Enumerator reconfigure any devices that require reconfiguration. So, although the Bus Enumerator doesn't decide how to reconfigure devices, it does actually carry out the reconfiguration of the devices.

All information about devices on your computer is written into the *Registry,* which maintains the hardware tree. Configuration Manager is responsible for writing the information into the Registry. In a computer that supports the Plug and Play BIOS, the basic Plug and Play configuration is actually performed at the BIOS level. When the OS loads, it goes through the Plug and Play process and modifies any configurations that require modification.

If legacy devices (non–Plug and Play devices) exist on your system, resources are assigned to them first. This makes perfect sense because these devices cannot be reconfigured through the Plug and Play process. To ensure that the proper resources are allocated to legacy devices, you can reserve those resources in the system BIOS.

In most BIOS configurations, you have the option of reserving resources for non–Plug and Play devices. The settings in the BIOS tell you whether you are reserving resources for non–Plug and Play devices, reserving resources for legacy devices, or disabling resources. Those resources are not actually disabled, but their use by Plug and Play devices is disabled; legacy devices are still able to use these resources. The BIOS represents the best place to reserve legacy resources for this reason: It represents the first area where Plug and Play resources are actually assigned to devices.

WARNING!

Before changing any BIOS settings, consult your motherboard documentation. Incorrect modification of your BIOS can result in your computer not functioning.

Because legacy devices cannot be reconfigured through the Plug and Play process, they should always be allowed to use the resources that they require. In a perfect world, that would be all you need. Because we don't live in a perfect world, though, you must reserve resources. Reserving the resources for legacy devices at the BIOS level is more consistent for achieving a working configuration than allowing them to be reserved at the OS level.

When Plug and Play systems first entered the market, they were plagued with difficulty. Much of this difficulty came from devices that were not fully Plug and Play@ndcompliant or from non–Plug and Play–aware system BIOS, not to mention mixing Plug and Play and non–Plug and Play devices together in a computer, which always causes additional problems and was often the case in early systems. Over the years, hardware and software manufactures have learned a lot about how Plug and Play should and can work, and today Plug and Play is much closer to its ideal.

Permissions to Install Drivers

To install drivers on a Windows computer, by default, you need to be a member of the Administrators group. In most cases, you do not want just anybody adding hardware devices to a computer and causing no end of problems for the people responsible for maintaining the computer. This ability to install the software for the device is controlled in the same way all rights on the computer are controlled, through the Security Policy. The computer policy can be changed locally. However, if the computer is part of Active Directory (AD), conflicting AD settings would override the local Security Policy. To view the active security settings on your computer and

to see whether they are being overridden, you only have to look as far as the Administrative Tools folder, located in the Control Panel on your computer.

In Administrative Tools, you will find the Local Security Policy application, which lets you see all security settings on your computer. To see the right to load and unload device drivers, expand the tree on the left to see Local Policies➪User Rights Assignments. After selecting User Rights Assignments, you can browse the list on the right for Load and Unload Device Drivers. The Security Setting column tells you who has the permission, as shown in Figure 1-9. To change the permission, double-click the security setting, and use the Load and Unload Device Drivers Properties dialog box to change the list of people who have permissions.

Figure 1-9:
The Local Security Policy allows you to install device drivers.

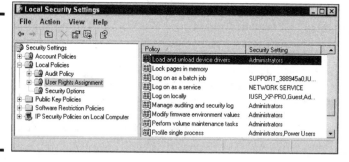

Verifying Driver Installation

To ensure that the drivers for a device are working properly, you should check three things:

✦ **The device is listed in Device Manager, and it displays a "working properly" message.** If you see the Question mark category, you have some devices installed that do not have drivers.

✦ **Make sure that the device available to its own management or control software.** For instance, if a scanner does not show up in the scanning software application, that could be due to a faulty driver.

✦ **Make sure that the device is yielding predictable results when used.** If not, the issue could be driver-related.

In most cases, if the drive is listed as working in Device Manager, the device driver is loaded properly for the device. So, the issues might actually be settings for the device or a hardware failure.

Device Driver Failure

What do you do if a device driver does not work? This is a question heard many times by users with driver problems. The answer is, as always with computers, "It depends." Some actions that you can take to deal with a malfunctioning driver include

+ Upgrading to a newer driver version

+ Removing the device

+ Rolling back drivers

+ Booting to the last known good configuration

+ Using restore points

If the driver is not working or if it has compromised the stability of the computer, you do have the preceding options. Issues with drivers could range from the driver just not working to the computer having a Stop event (blue screen error) during the boot process. In most cases, if the driver is just not working, look at how the device is connected to the computer and also examine any related components. For example, if the problem is with a USB device, are the rest of the USB components (such as the USB hubs and controllers) on the computer working?

After you verify this, and that the device is properly attached and powered, examine the driver version and its settings. Check for a newer (usually) driver or an older (rarely) driver that could fix your problem. Discussion boards often help diagnose driver-related issues, be they a version issue to settings related. In most cases, you should initially load the component with the latest driver available, which means ignoring the CD that came with the device and going directly to the manufacturer's Web site. If the device doesn't work because of a hardware conflict, simply remove the device and replace it with a different manufacturer's version. These hardware conflicts are very rare, but when they happen, you may have no choice but to replace with a different product.

Rather than just not working, the problem with the driver failure might be more prominent, such as a blue screen error during system boot. If that is the issue, your resolution is somewhat more critical. The first step is deciding what your immediate resolution needs to be. If it is to allow the computer to be usable and that the device was considered an extra feature, remove the device and look at adding and troubleshooting the device installation later. If it is to get the device working, you need to troubleshoot the device installation immediately. Your steps might vary some, but usually you want to do the following:

✦ **Boot into Safe Mode to verify that base system files are still operational.** From there, you can remove or disable the device to allow the computer to boot. This can be done while leaving the device in the computer.

✦ **If the error occurred as part of a driver update, choose the driver rollback option on the Drive tab of the device's Device Manager properties.**

✦ **Download a newer version of the driver; you might be trying to load an older version of the driver with known problems.** The vendor's Web site will let you know whether newer versions of both drivers and firmware are available — and, often, what issues they corrected.

✦ **Risking the loss of configuration settings or files, the last two options are last-chance efforts to restore system stability in the form of booting to the Last Known Good Configuration or using a past system restore point.** Because these two items return to a past point in time, you do run the risk of losing additional settings that you were not aware of. For more information about these two procedures, see Book VII, Chapter 3.

In a perfect world, one of these fixes will work for you, and you won't lose any data or settings.

Getting an A+

In this chapter, you look at general processes to load and configure device drivers. Specifically, you find out the following:

✦ The driver installation procedures are found in INF files.

✦ Drivers verified and signed by Microsoft include a CAT file, which contains the signature.

✦ Plug and Play takes care of device resource settings for most devices.

✦ Device Manager is the basic management tool for driver management.

✦ Driver errors can be recovered by updating drivers, using Safe Mode, loading the Last Known Good Configuration, or restoring to a system restore point.

Prep Test

1 Device drivers are used to do what?

 A ○ Provide power to the device while it is operating

 B ○ Act as a software interface between the operating system and the device

 C ○ Provide advanced configuration options for the device

 D ○ Steer the device to a new location on the computer

2 What is the risk of using an unsigned driver?

 A ○ Unsigned drivers are only reliable when using Windows NT 4.0.

 B ○ Unsigned drivers are missing their SIG files.

 C ○ Unsigned drivers are not backward compatible with older hardware versions.

 D ○ Unsigned drivers have not been tested by Microsoft.

3 Which of the following is *not* part of the Plug and Play procedure?

 A ○ Resource Arbitrator

 B ○ Dynamic Reconfigurator

 C ○ Configuration Manager

 D ○ Bus Enumerator

4 Which users on a Windows XP or Vista computer have the right to load device drivers?

 A ○ Guests

 B ○ All Users

 C ○ Administrators

 D ○ Power Users

5 Device settings, such as IRQs, can be modified through which tools? (Choose all that apply.)

 A ❑ Device Manager

 B ❑ Resource Manager

 C ❑ Device's Control Panel, such as Network Control Panel

 D ❑ Device Arbitrator

6 Which tool can be used to examine the status of a device?

 A ○ Device Manager

 B ○ Resource Explorer

 C ○ Device Explorer

 D ○ Status Examiner

Answers

1 **B.** Device drivers act as an intermediary between the operating system and physical devices. *See "Loading and Removing Device Drivers."*

2 **D.** Unsigned drivers have not been tested by Microsoft's hardware qualification labs and, as such, are missing their CAT files. These drivers might work, but they are not verified by Microsoft. *Review "Signed and Unsigned Drivers."*

3 **B.** The Dynamic Reconfigurator is not part of the Plug and Play procedure. *Check out "Working with Plug and Play."*

4 **C.** Only members of the Administrators group have been granted the right to load and unload device drivers, by default. *Peruse "Permissions to Install Drivers."*

5 **A, C.** Most device settings can be modified through either Device Manager or the device's Control Panel. Resource Manager and Device Arbitrator are made-up terms. *Take a look at "Changing Device Settings."*

6 **A.** Device Manager can be used to examine the status of the device. *Peruse "Verifying Driver Installation."*

Chapter 2: Working with Applications

Exam Objectives

▶ **Identify how MS-DOS, 16-bit Windows, and 32-bit Windows applications operate in Windows 2000, Windows XP, and Windows Vista**

▶ **Diagnose applications install, start, or load failures with Windows XP**

When MS-DOS was first created, very few applications were available for it. Many people chose to use the BASIC programming language to write their own applications. But in short order, people developed faster applications by first using Assembler and then higher-level languages, such as C. These applications served users well for several years. When Windows debuted, Microsoft built in as much backward compatibility for these older applications as it could. Microsoft knew that if the Windows operating system (OS) did not allow older applications to work with it, current MS-DOS users might not want to adopt it. To this day, Microsoft attempts to provide the most backward compatibility possible in its OSes.

When the 16-bit Windows environment, such as Windows 3.0, needed applications, they were developed and worked well. In later generations, these applications were superseded by 32-bit versions for the newer OSes, and now 64-bit versions for the newest OSes. The newer applications work with data in larger chunks and run faster. In this chapter, you take a look at how all these applications run on your computer.

To properly maintain and diagnose applications, an A+ Certified Professional must be able to manage the installation and removal of applications. In addition to these skills, this chapter also reveals the operating architecture in which applications run. Understanding this architecture allows the professional to diagnose problems quickly. You also examine the level of backward compatibility that is built into the modern Windows OSes, and you explore multitasking.

Installing and Removing Applications

Before you can work with applications on your computer, you need to install them. With the rate at which the computer industry changes, you cannot avoid the need to upgrade or remove applications on your computer as they become obsolete.

The terms *application* and *program* are synonymous; they are both programming code that performs a function. In this chapter, though, I use the two terms to mean slightly different things. I use the term *application* to describe the programming code that represents the functions you want installed on your computer — like a word processing application or a game. I use the term *program* to describe the programming code that allows you to install the application.

Installing an application

Most applications come with an installation program that must be run to install the application. Some applications (say, Kaufman Mail Warrior) are actually standalone applications that do not require extra files and settings to be created on your computer, but these are rare. Most applications require several files to be installed and often require Registry entries to be created to hold the settings for the application. Because of the complexity involved in copying the files and creating the settings, you use the installation program to ensure that the application is installed properly. The application's developer decides the name of the setup program, which in many cases is `setup.exe` or `install.exe`.

Working with MSI files

Starting with Windows 2000, Microsoft created a new setup installation file. MSI files are associated with `msiexec.exe`, or the Windows Installer service. `msiexec.exe` is a generic application installer, and the Windows Installer service can be used to push applications out to computers on your network through Active Directory (AD).

The MSI file contains the installation script and in most cases also has a compressed copy of the files that need to be installed. If they are not stored in the MSI file, you will also have a CAB file.

Windows Installer or MSI installations have these benefits:

- Consistent user interface and command line interface

- Standard and easy way of customizing applications

- Diagnose and repair configuration problems at application run-time

- On-demand installation

- System-wide management of shared resources

- Restore the preinstallation state of a computer in the event of installation failure

- Elevated installation privileges

To install an MSI file, simply double-click it and follow any installation instructions.

Very few installation programs work in exactly the same way. In general, though, you are asked for the location where you want the application installed. Other options, such as whether you want to create a desktop shortcut to the application or whether you want a specific option to be enabled, are application specific.

The Add/Remove Programs Control Panel applet was created to allow you to manage your installed applications from an easy to use standard interface. When Windows XP was released, the name was changed to Add or Remove Programs. Windows Vista calls this feature Programs and Features. In all cases, it operates basically the same way. Installing a new program on a Windows XP computer is slightly different from earlier versions of the Windows OS and Windows Vista. Your course of action for Windows XP looks like this:

Book VI Chapter 2

Working with Applications

1. **Choose Start➪Control Panel.**

2. **Double-click Add or Remove Programs.**

Depending on how your interface is set up, Add or Remove Programs might appear in a drop-down list attached to the Control Panel, in which case you just single-click Add or Remove Programs in the drop-down list.

The Add/Remove window appears, as shown in Figure 2-1. Notice the toolbar along the left edge of the window.

3. **Click the Add New Programs button on the left toolbar.**

The window adjusts itself to your installation needs.

4. **Click the CD or Floppy button at the top of the window.**

This opens the same Install Program from Floppy Disk or CD-ROM Wizard, which prompts you to insert the floppy disk or CD-ROM that has your installation program.

5. **Click Next.**

Windows XP scans your floppy disk and CD-ROM drives for a program named `install.exe` or `setup.exe`. If either program is present, it is executed. Otherwise, you are asked to provide the path to the setup program for the application you want to install.

6. **If necessary, provide the path to the setup program and then click Finish.**

Figure 2-1:
Add or
remove
programs
in Windows
XP here.

If your computer is part of an AD domain, you might also see applications listed in the section of the Add/Remove Programs Control Panel applet called Add Programs from Your Network. You can filter the list by using the Category drop-down list, and install these by selecting an application and then choosing the Add button. This launches the installation program. If you are using Windows Vista, you see an option to Install a Program from the Network in the Programs Control Panel applet.

Windows Vista allows you to do most of your program management through the Programs Control Panel applet, which allows you to do all the same functions, with a different layout, as shown in Figure 2-2.

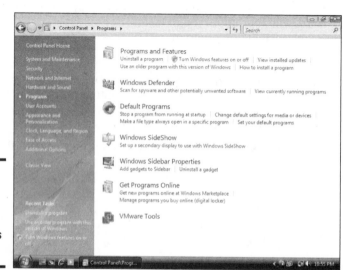

Figure 2-2:
Add or
remove
programs
in Windows
Vista here.

Many applications today are distributed on CD-ROM. When you insert a CD-ROM into your CD-ROM drive, Windows searches for an `autorun.inf` file and launches the program specified by the `autorun.inf` file. In most cases, the specified program is the application setup program if the application is not already installed. This AutoPlay feature of Windows makes installing applications even easier.

Removing an application

Most applications also provide a program to uninstall the application when you no longer want it on your hard drive. The path to the program and any switches that are required for it to function are usually stored in the Registry during the installation of the application.

Always use care when working in the Registry; improper changes can leave you in a position where you will be required to reinstall the OS.

The procedure to uninstall or remove a program from a Windows computer is very easy. After opening the Add/Remove Programs Control Panel applet, select an installed application from the list. You are then provided more details about that application, like its size and how often you use it. You will also see one or more buttons beside the application: Change, Remove, or Change/Remove. To change the installed components of an application, click the Change button; to remove the application, click the Remove button. Some applications will have a Change/Remove button, which will then allow you to make changes to the list of installed components, or to remove the application; it uses the same program to accomplish both tasks. Windows looks up the name of the uninstallation program to run in the Registry and executes it. In Windows Vista, you will use the Programs Control Panel applet and the Uninstall a program option, which provides the same type of information if additional columns are enabled, as shown in Figure 2-3.

Book VI Chapter 2

Working with Applications

UnInstall key and the Registry

If an application uninstalls incorrectly or you would like to know what program is used to uninstall an application, the settings are stored in the Registry under the UnInstall key, which is found at:

```
HKLM\Software\Microsoft\Windows\CurrentVersion\Uninstall\
        <Application_Key>\UninstallString
```

If the application was uninstalled but still shows up in the Add/Remove Programs Control Panel applet, you can delete the entire `<Application_Key>` from the Registry.

With Windows XP or Windows Vista, when you attempt to uninstall an application that is missing the uninstaller, it will ask whether you want to remove the entry from your Add/Remove Programs Control Panel applet.

Figure 2-3:
The
Uninstall
options in
Windows
Vista
stream-
line the
information
displayed.

Like the installation procedure, there is no set uninstall procedure, and it is left up to the software developer to design the uninstall routine. Some developers do an excellent job, and others do not. In the case of applications that do not uninstall properly, you might find the icons, files, or Registry entries still present after the uninstall program has completed. If that is the case, manually remove the leftover components.

Make sure that you are familiar with the standard method of adding and removing applications from your system through the Add/Remove Control Panel.

In many cases, applications are removed by using special options with the setup program that originally installed them. One nice feature of using the setup program is that many developers allow you to not only remove the application, but also to change the components that are installed.

Getting the Most out of Multitasking

Multitasking is a computer's ability to balance the processing time given to multiple applications that are running at the same time. Multitasking comes in handy when running multiple applications at the same time.

The two basic types of multitasking are cooperative and preemptive. In this section, I discuss differences between the two types of multitasking; by the end, you should have a clear picture of which one is better.

Cooperative multitasking

Cooperative multitasking means sharing time on the processor by cooperation. By its name, you would think cooperative multitasking is the better

form of multitasking. This is probably because cooperation has always been thought of as a good thing. If you needed to get a job done (like building a house) and you had five people to help you, you could get the house raised quickly through teamwork and cooperation. This is a good illustration of when cooperation works. However, if a couple of those people do not work with the rest of the team (they go to get more nails and never come back), their lack of cooperation slows down the process.

Likewise, with cooperative multitasking in the computer environment, a few programs that do not cooperate well with others can slow down the process. If you launch Microsoft Excel, for example, and start a large recalculation of the entire spreadsheet, Excel occupies 100 percent of the processor's time. At periodic intervals, Excel checks whether any other programs require processing time, at which time Excel turns control of the processor over to the other applications. Each application follows the same process that Excel does; they occupy 100 percent of the processor's time if needed, and give up control only when they reach their periodic interval for checking with the rest of the OS. If a program doesn't check with the other applications often enough, it is thought of as a *noncooperative program.* The big problem with noncooperative programs is that they can hog 100 percent of the processor time for as long as they want.

Cooperative multitasking was implemented to allow multitasking in a 16-bit Windows environment. Most of that environment was *single threaded,* meaning that only a single element (or thread) in the OS gives the processor instructions. As such, all applications have to work while sharing a single thread of execution. It might seem that cooperative multitasking is inefficient, but cooperative multitasking is better than no multitasking.

Preemptive multitasking

Preemptive multitasking takes a different approach to multitasking in the Windows environment. With *preemptive multitasking,* the OS decides which applications get execution time. Preemptive multitasking is designed to work in a 32-bit *multithreaded* environment, in which applications have multiple execution threads, and the OS can manage multiple threads issuing instructions to the processor or processors. Each thread of operation can run on any available processor in the computer.

Each application is given a certain percentage of execution time to use during each second. The OS then manages each process that accesses the processor. With the OS acting as the conductor, sharing the processor is more equal, with fewer conflicts. This does not mean that certain tasks do not attempt to run away with all the processor's computing time; it is just less likely to happen. Preemptive multitasking entered the Windows OS with the development of Windows 95 and Windows NT, and has been improving ever since.

Running 32-Bit and 64-Bit Windows Applications

The 32-bit Windows applications are the ideal type of applications to run under a Windows 32-bit environment, and 64-bit applications are the ideal type of applications to run under a Windows 64-bit environment. As of Windows 95 and Windows NT, all versions of Windows are 32-bit environments. Starting with Windows XP, all Windows OSes have a 64-bit option when running on 64-bit processors. Because all these OSes are 32-bit or 64-bit in nature, it only makes sense that the applications that are run in these environments are also 32-bit or 64-bit. With that said, you should understand the benefits of running 32-bit and 64-bit applications and how those applications are executed in Windows environments.

Benefiting from 32-bit applications

There are several benefits to running Windows 32-bit applications instead of 16-bit applications, such as

✦ Multithreading

✦ 32-bit data transfers

✦ Process isolation

One of the greatest benefits of 32-bit Windows applications is the ability to be multithreaded. *Multithreaded* applications run several threads of code concurrently. Each thread usually is assigned to a specific task. In the case of Microsoft Word, different threads can process typed characters, check spelling, or check grammar in your document all at the same time. If your computer has only one processor, only one task is actually performed at any given instance even though scheduling of all these different tasks is optimized. If you are lucky enough to have a multiprocessor computer, each thread can be assigned to execute on a different processor. This not only optimizes the execution of the program but also evenly uses the processors.

The 32-bit Windows applications work with data in 32-bit blocks, just as 16-bit applications work with data in 16-bit blocks. In any given clock cycle, a 32-bit application should be able to process more information than a similarly written 16-bit Windows application. In a perfect world, the speed factor of a 32-bit application would be twice that of a 16-bit application. Because we do not live in a perfect world, though, this multiplier is not actually realized. Other factors that affect the performance of the application include how the logic in the code was optimized to allow these 32-bit blocks to provide better performance.

The 32-bit Windows applications also run with some level of isolation from other applications that are running on the system. This provides better stability for the applications that are executing.

Ensure that you can recall the benefits of using 32-bit Windows applications on your system, rather than 16-bit Windows applications.

When running 32-bit applications on a 64-bit version of Windows, the application runs in a 32-bit emulated environment called Windows on Windows 64, or WoW64. This allows the applications to run without any modifications.

Benefiting from 64-bit applications

Microsoft now offers a 64-bit version of all current Windows OSes to run on computers with new 64-bit processors. Like with 16-bit versus 32-bit applications, applications need to be rewritten and compiled to take advantage of this faster 64-bit architecture.

The 64-bit applications offer all the same benefits of 32-bit applications, such as multithreading. They have the additional benefit of 64-bit data transfers and processing units, which theoretically would provide a huge speed improvement over 32-bit processing.

Executing in the Windows environments

The architectural diagram of Windows XP is shown in Figure 2-4, and all newer versions of Windows use a similar architecture. Note that 32-bit Windows applications (or 64-bit Windows applications) are executed as separate processes in the user mode portion of the OS. This architecture is identical to that of Windows XP.

In Windows, 32-bit and 64-bit Windows applications are executed in an area that is completely separate from where the OS executes. This provides the best stability for both the OS and the applications that are running in it, but does hinder some of the backward compatibility of the product. This does not mean that Windows is not backward compatible, but rather that it is *less* backward compatible than the Windows 9x generation. There have been attempts to increase the backward compatibility of the Windows product line, so applications that may not have worked with earlier versions of Windows (such as Windows NT 4.0) may work under Windows XP, and applications that might not have worked under Windows XP may work under Windows Vista.

Figure 2-4:
32-bit
applications
run in
their own
execution
area in
Windows.

Each 32-bit and 64-bit Windows application is given

✦ **Its own address space to work with:** If an application hangs or crashes, the separate memory address space makes it easy to destroy or flush the entire memory that deals with that application.

✦ **A separate message queue:** By having a separate message queue, if an application hangs or crashes, that halted application doesn't block the messages that are destined for other applications.

✦ **The ability to own several threads that are preemptively multitasked by the OS:** Multiple threads per application allow the application to perform multiple operations at the same time.

Address space in the Windows OS

The address space that the OS works with is 4GB of address space. This does not mean that you need 4GB of memory on the system to run the OS; you need only as much physical memory as your applications actual use to store items. Physical memory is used only when an application stores something into a block of address space.

Picture each block of address space as a label, and physical memory as a wall of mailboxes. If I store something in a mailbox, I attach a label to that mailbox, representing what is stored there. When the application wants to store information, it might say, "Put this information in my address block 2045." The OS takes that information and puts it into any free memory block, and it then keeps track of mapping between those two locations for the application. When the application wants that information back, it says, "Give me the information in address block 2045," and the OS retrieves the information from where it was actually stored.

Running 16-Bit Windows Applications

The 16-bit Windows applications were originally designed to run under Windows 3.*x*. Some of these applications look for specific components in the OS to function properly. To support 16-bit Windows application, Windows emulates the 16-bit Windows environment called *Windows on Windows*. (You can read about WoW earlier in this chapter.) The way in which this emulation is performed represents one of the big differences between versions of Windows.

The 16-bit Windows applications are single-threaded applications that actually share a single unit of execution with the 16-bit Windows environment. This is what I referred to earlier in the chapter as *cooperative multitasking*. The entire 16-bit Windows environment executes via a single processor thread. This thread is then shared among all 16-bit Windows applications running in the 16-bit Windows environment.

The 16-bit Windows programming code is *nonreentrant,* which means that each section of code can be executed only once (or by one application) at any given time. When one application starts executing a section of code, it sets a flag — the *Win16Mutex* — on that code. While the flag sets on the code, no other application can execute or enter that code. This is done to prevent multiple applications from executing the same section of code, thereby causing system-wide problems. One of the problems caused by the Win16Mutex flag is that any other program that wants to execute that section of code must wait until the current program finishes and the flag is removed. If the current application freezes, hangs, or crashes, it never removes its flag; thus, the code is not released until the system is rebooted.

All 16-bit Windows applications suffer from these problems. Whenever possible, 16-bit applications should be replaced with equivalent 32-bit or 64-bit Windows applications to create an environment that is more stable and offers greater performance.

Executing in the Windows environments

Running 16-bit Windows applications under Windows 2000 or newer version of Windows is very similar to running them under a 16-bit version of Windows — but, *very similar* does not mean *exactly the same*. The areas of similarity include the following:

+ 16-bit Windows applications run in a common memory space.

+ 16-bit Windows applications share a common message queue.

+ 16-bit Windows applications cooperatively multitask.

Even with these similarities, note a number of differences between Windows 2000 or newer versions of Windows and the 16-bit versions of Windows. These differences start with where the application code is actually run. Within Windows, all 16-bit Windows applications are executed from within a 32-bit or 64-bit Windows *NTVDM (Virtual DOS Machine)*. This NTVDM is a complete, emulated DOS environment onto which a complete emulated 16-bit Windows environment is loaded. It is within this environment that 16-bit Windows applications are executed. Although this seems like a small point, it means that the entire 16-bit Windows environment that is implemented is contained within a newer Windows a 32-bit or 64-bit environment. That makes the entire environment as safe and stable as any other Windows application running on the system.

Within the emulated 16-bit Windows environment, all normal rules that apply to 16-bit Windows still apply, but they can affect only the other applications within the running NTVDM. Applications are still cooperatively multitasked. There is still a Win16Mutex flag, and code is still nonreentrant, but the reentrant code and other processes that can be halted are limited to this one environment. When you consider the separation of 16-bit applications and the fact that current Windows does not contain any 16-bit code at the OS level, this gives post–Windows 2000 OSes a major stability advantage over Windows 9*x* and 16-bit versions of Windows.

Another advantage to using the post–Windows 2000 environments is that 16-bit Windows applications can be run in separate memory spaces. When a 16-bit Windows application runs in a separate memory space, a new NTVDM is loaded along with a new WoW environment, as shown in Figure 2-5. The benefits of running applications in separate memory space are preemptive multitasking between applications and process isolation. Although the application still cooperatively multitasks within this Windows environment, there are no other applications for the clock to share cycles with. Because the

entire 16-bit Windows environment is run within a 32-bit or 64-bit Windows process, the 32-bit or 64-bit Windows process preemptively multitasks other 32-bit or 64-bit Windows processes running on the system. With process isolation, each application can be run within its own 32-bit or 64-bit Windows process.

Figure 2-5:
Task
Manager
shows
that 16-bit
applications
can be
loaded
within
separate
WoW
environ-
ments.

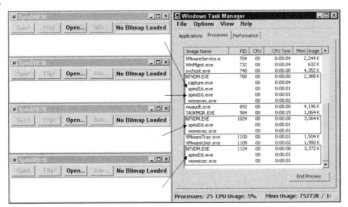

The benefit of separate processes is that when one 16-bit Windows application hangs or crashes, it does not affect any other application running within other processes on the system. Any other 16-bit Windows applications running in the same process as the hung application are halted. Windows uses the default memory space to run all 16-bit Windows applications, with the exception of those run in separate memory spaces. A process running in a separate memory space is the only process that may run in that memory space.

The following is a list of are several ways to start a 16-bit Windows application in a separate memory space:

✦ **At a command prompt:** Use `start /separate <application name>`

✦ **Creation of a shortcut to modify the properties on the Shortcut tab to run in a separate memory space, as shown in Figure 2-6**

✦ **Modifying the Open command for an associated file**

 Check out Book V, Chapter 4 for step-by-step instructions on altering the Open action for a file type.

Any of the preceding methods allow you to launch a 16-bit Windows application in a separate memory space, where it can run in isolation from other 16-bit Windows applications.

Figure 2-6:
Shortcuts
represent
one way to
open 16-bit
applications
in a
separate
memory
space.

Terminating an application running under Windows can be accomplished through Task Manager. Access Task Manager by pressing Ctrl+Alt+Delete and clicking the Task Manager button; or, right-click the taskbar and choose Task Manager. Task Manager has four tabs:

✦ **Applications:** All running foreground applications

✦ **Processes:** All running applications — foreground and background

✦ **Performance:** Performance statistics about your computer

✦ **Networking:** Performance statistics on your network interfaces

You can terminate an application from either the Applications or the Processes tab by selecting the application and clicking the End Task button. To terminate the entire 16-bit Windows environment, select the NTVDM that contains the application and then click the End Task button.

You have seen the benefits of running applications in separate memory spaces, but you should also consider the drawbacks. Here are two drawbacks to running applications in separate memory spaces:

✦ **Applications that communicate with each other through a shared memory address will not be able to communicate because there will not be a shared address.** Microsoft lists this as a minor problem because very few applications that you will run actually perform this type of communication. (This has never been an issue with any of the applications I have worked with.)

✦ **You use additional system resources for every NTVDM and WoW loaded into memory.** The overhead associated with loading these resources is about one-half megabyte for each NTVDM/WoW combination. This might not seem like a lot, but if you are running a large number of applications, it does add up.

You should now feel comfortable about how each OS supports 16-bit Windows applications, and the options which you are able to control, modifying how the 16-bit applications function. As a CompTIA A+ Certified Professional, knowledge of these environments will allow you to address issues with applications and provide compelling reasons for late adopters to upgrade to the current Microsoft Windows OS.

Lab 2-1 gives you some practice examining the resources used by WoW. This lab requires that you obtain copies of specific 16-bit Windows applications from a copy of Windows 9*x*. These applications will be copied into the `c:\labfiles` folder on the lab computer. For this lab, use Windows NT 4.0, Windows 2000, or Windows XP.

Lab 2-2 gives you practice starting applications in their own memory space. This lab assumes that the required lab files have been installed to your disk, using the default installation path of `c:\labfiles`. If you have not completed Lab 2-1, follow the steps at the beginning of that lab exercise to get the proper files in your `labfiles` directory. You can use Windows NT 4.0, Windows 2000, or Windows XP for these lab exercises.

Lab 2-1 and Lab 2-2 can be found in the `Labs.pdf` file in the Author directory of the CD-ROM.

Encountering incompatibilities

When running 16-bit Windows applications within Windows, you might find incompatibilities with your OS. Most developers want to make their applications run as fast as possible. This could mean that they follow nonstandard programming practices under Windows 3.*x*, which can actually cause problems when you attempt to run these applications under newer versions of Windows.

For example, if you developed a fax application, you might use all standard Windows COM driver system calls to communicate with the modem. Upon investigating how the COM calls are actually made, you might decide that you can achieve more speed through the application by making direct hardware calls. Direct hardware calls represent nonstandard communication with that COM device. This will not affect your application when running within the 16-bit Windows environment; but, when running within a *simulated* 16-bit Windows environment, such as Windows 2000, these nonstandard calls might not be properly processed.

Part of the problem arises from the fact that in an attempt to provide better system stability, Windows 9x–based OSes and Windows NT–based OSes restrict direct access to some hardware components:

✦ Windows 9x–based OSes restrict access to COM devices.

✦ Windows NT–based OSes (such as Windows XP and Windows Vista) restrict access to most hardware components.

If an application requires direct hardware access to these components, it simply will not function under these newer versions of Windows, such as Windows XP. Microsoft has taken all possible steps to improve the ability to run older Windows-based applications, but will not take actions that will substantially reduce the stability of the OS.

Running MS-DOS–Based Applications

MS-DOS–based applications represent the oldest type of applications you are likely to run on your computer. MS-DOS applications are supported by Windows XP. MS-DOS–based applications have always been designed to run alone on a computer. They expect to be the only application ever running on that PC, and as such expect to see certain things, like no Windows presence. Microsoft uses virtual machines to provide a unique environment for these applications. These virtual machines simulate all the hardware that would normally be found in a computer, including

✦ Keyboard

✦ Mouse

✦ Monitor

✦ COM ports

✦ RAM

✦ Disk drives

With all these components being virtualized, an MS-DOS–based application believes that it is running alone in a computer. The virtual computer's settings can be modified through a *program information file (PIF)*, which I discuss in the next section.

Program information file (PIF) settings

Every MS-DOS–based application that executes on your computer starts by configuring a working environment from settings found in a PIF. This is the case even if you are not aware that a PFI file is being used because a `_default.pif` file on your hard drive is used if no other PIF exists.

If you want to create a default PIF for a specific application, right-click the application and choose Properties. Even though there is not currently a PIF for the application, you will see all the PIF-related tabs, such as Screen, Memory, Font, and Misc. If you make any changes to the application settings on the tabs and click OK to close the dialog box, a file named `<application>.pif` is created in the same directory as the application executable. This PIF then becomes the default PIF for that application because it is in the same directory as the application and is named `<application.pif>`. Unlike most files, the `.pif` extension stays hidden, even if displaying file extensions is enabled.

You can discern a PIF file by viewing the properties of the file (right-click it and choose Properties). The file type will be Shortcut to MS-DOS Program; and the Font, Memory, Screen, and Misc tabs are specific to PIF files, as shown in Figure 2-7. At any time after closing the dialog box and the default PIF has been created, you can make changes to it by right-clicking either the application or the PIF to bring up Properties; either action allows you to edit the settings. Even though you can access the settings through the properties of the application, you are really editing the PIF.

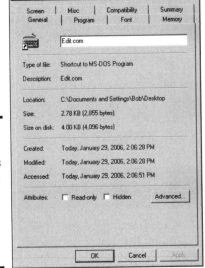

Figure 2-7: PIFs have several tabs that contain settings for a simulated MS-DOS environment.

You might also be confused by the fact that a PIF for an application looks exactly like a shortcut for a LNK file. Figure 2-8 shows a series of PIFs created for four MS-DOS–based applications. Notice that the first four icons in the window are MS-DOS application icons, and the last three icons are the default PIFs for the `fdisk.exe`, `format.com`, and `scandisk.exe` applications. In addition to the default PIF, `edit.com` has three additional PIFs that

have been created for it (the keyboard-looking icons in the middle of the window). Each `edit.com` PIF can have its own unique settings. To access the settings for a PIF, right-click it and choose Properties. The Properties window of a `PIF` contains seven tabs:

✦ General

✦ Program

✦ Font

✦ Memory

✦ Screen

✦ Misc

✦ Summary

Figure 2-8: Each PIF for a common application can contain unique settings.

Each tab is discussed in more detail in the sections that follow.

General tab

The first tab in the PIS Properties window is the General tab, and it is the same as the General tab for any other file on your hard drive. The General tab lists the file type you are viewing the properties for, which is a Shortcut to MS-DOS Application. This tab also lists the location of the file; its size and size on disk; when it was created, modified, and accessed; and its attributes. You should also note the size of the PIF file. PIF files are very small (usually only 1K). You can differentiate a PIF from other shortcuts on your hard drive by its file type because other files with a shortcut arrow are identified only as Shortcut — not as Shortcut to MS-DOS Application.

Program tab

From the Program, you can configure the following settings:

✦ **Cmd Line:** Specifies the path to the executable

✦ **Working:** Specifies the working directory for the program; often used as the default save directory

✦ **Batch File:** Specifies the name of a batch file or program that you would like to execute prior to launching the executable but after establishing the MS-DOS environment

✦ **Shortcut key:** Specifies a keystroke that can be executed at any time to either launch or switch to this program

**Book VI
Chapter 2**

**Working with
Applications**

With much trying, this author very rarely has seen the shortcut key in a PIF work the way it is supposed to. Rather than working, it does nothing.

✦ **Run:** Specifies whether the program is supposed to run in a normal, maximized, or minimized window

✦ **Close on Exit:** Specifies whether the application should close its window when it completes execution

Having the program close on completion sometimes hides error messages that could be useful for troubleshooting.

Note the two buttons at the bottom of the Program tab:

✦ **Change Icon:** Change the icon used by the PIF

✦ **Advanced:** Modify some additional settings

Changing the icon is purely cosmetic, but you can specify an icon from any Windows-based executable or from a few of the system DLLs. Every Windows-based executable contains an icon list (with the first icon in the list having an index number of 0) that includes the executable's icon (icon number 0) and icons for its documents or files. Icons can also be found in several system DLLs, such as `moricons.dll`, `pifmgr.dll`, and `shell32.dll`. `shell32.dll` contains many default system icons that Windows uses.

Clicking the Advanced button brings up the Windows PIF Settings dialog box, from which you can override the default `autoexec.bat` and `config.sys` files. The default files — `autoexec.nt` and `config.nt` — are found in the `%SystemRoot%\system32` directory. These two files are used to create the default MS-DOS environment for Windows NT–based OSes. You can create new files with any names and specify the files here. There is also a check box to enable compatible timer hardware emulation, which reduces the rate at which the computer sends timing signals to the application. In short, it makes the application think that it is running on a slower computer.

If you want to know how to modify your `autoexec.nt` and `config.nt` files, read through the `autoexec.bat` and `config.sys` sections of Book V, Chapter 6.

In Lab 2-3, you create a PIF to launch the MS-DOS `edit` command. You can perform this lab using Windows 9*x*, 2000, XP, or Vista. Lab 2-3 can be found in the `Labs.pdf` file in the Author directory of the CD-ROM.

Font tab

Use settings on the Font tab to specify the type(s) of screen font(s) that can be used by the window that contains the running MS-DOS application. These fonts can be

✦ **TrueType:** TrueType fonts are created on the fly by using a formula, and thereby can be scaled to any size.

✦ **Bitmap:** Bitmap fonts are drawn with pixels or squares to a specific size. Bitmap fonts are faster to draw, but do not scale.

By default, Windows uses both and chooses the best font based on the window size.

Memory tab

The Memory tab enables you to specify limits for application memory. You can configure four types of memory:

✦ Conventional memory

✦ Expanded (EMS) memory

✦ Extended (XMS) memory

✦ MS-DOS protected-mode (DPMI) memory

The default setting for each of these types of memory is either Auto or None. For more information about the different types of memory and how to configure them, consult Book V, Chapter 6.

For MS-DOS applications, *conventional memory* is where the application actually operates. When MS-DOS first hit the market, computers made use of only the first 640K of memory that was installed, with the rest of the 1024K being used to access hardware components and for drivers to load. Windows applications, which came out later, were designed not to use this area, allowing MS-DOS to continue to use the conventional memory space. Because an entire computer is emulated for MS-DOS applications, this first 640K is also emulated. Although the application thinks that it is functioning in the first 640K of memory, Windows could be using any space that the Virtual Memory Manager has available.

On a normal computer, some of the conventional memory is used to load drivers and TSR (Terminate Stay Resident) applications. A TSR would be similar to service in Windows because it runs in the background. When it is time for an application to run, it might not have all the first 640K of memory available. The Total Memory drop-down menu allows you to specify the amount of Conventional Memory available to the application. When the Total Memory drop-down menu is set to Auto, the application is provided with as much conventional memory as it requests.

It seems odd that more conscientious programs actually have problems with this setting. The conscientious programs query the OS before launching to inquire about the amount of free memory available, but rather than returning a value, Windows asks the question, "How much memory do you want?" This merely confuses the application, which then generates an error message stating that an insufficient amount of memory exists to run the program. If that happens to you, adjust the amount of conventional memory available to the application. This drop-down menu is measured in kilobytes.

Book VI
Chapter 2

Working with
Applications

You can allocate up to 640K of conventional memory to the application, but you should allocate only what the application truly requires. If your application requires the entire 640K and you are still having problems, you can allocate up to an additional 4K of memory to hold environment variables. This memory is added by making use of the Initial Environment drop-down menu, which is measured in bytes.

There is also an option to protect the conventional memory, which prevents the memory space from being swapped out to the Windows swap or paging file. (Some applications crash when they are swapped out to the swap or paging file.)

Protecting memory should be avoided unless absolutely necessary because it locks the application into physical RAM, reducing the amount of physical memory available for other Windows-based applications.

When dealing with the virtual memory file that is found on your hard drive, Windows 9*x* refers to this file as the *swap file,* and Windows NT–based OSes refer to it as the *paging file.*

When 640K of memory became too restrictive for developers, hardware vendors developed expansion memory that was able to be added to a computer by using ISA expansion slots, and using a small portion of the memory between 640K and 1024K as a swap area. The application would request certain portions of memory, which would then be swapped from the expanded memory card into conventional memory. This memory was called *expanded (EMS) memory.* To use expanded memory under Windows 9*x*–based OSes, you have to load the Expanded Memory Manager (emm386.exe) in your config.sys file, which allocates the specific memory address blocks that will be used for the swapping process. You will find emm386.exe in your

Windows directory, and you can review Book V, Chapter 6 to learn how to work with your `config.sys` file. After the Expanded Memory Manager is loaded, you can specify as much as 16MB of expanded memory to be available to the application by using the Expanded Memory drop-down menu, which is measured in kilobytes.

As computers started to be produced with more than 1MB of memory, people wanted to make use of this extra memory above the 1MB mark, but MS-DOS natively was able to access only 640K of memory. *Extended (XMS) memory* is the memory above 1MB. Most MS-DOS applications do not use extended memory because it could only be accessed by Protected Mode applications or OSes like Windows.

Extended memory is sometimes also called Protected Mode memory because it is usually accessed by Protected Mode applications.

If you load a driver like `himem.sys`, you can access this extended memory. You can allocate up to 16MB of extended memory for the application via the Extended Memory drop-down menu (measured in kilobytes). The MS-DOS environment can use the high memory area provided by extended memory by specifying an option when loading `himem.sys` in the `config.sys` file. The high memory area is the first 64K of extended memory — and, through a design glitch, can be accessed directly by MS-DOS to load drivers.

Very few applications use DOS protected-mode interface (DPMI) memory these days, and most of those are games like DOOM and Descent. This memory management technique allows MS-DOS-based applications to use extended memory through special MS-DOS and BIOS calls. The big advantage that is provided by DPMI memory use is that it allows an MS-DOS application direct memory access over 1MB, which provides better performance than using extended memory (which uses swapping to move information between extended memory and conventional memory areas). If your application does make use of DPMI, you can specify up to 16MB of DPMI memory. You allocate DPMI memory specifying the amount in the DPMI drop-down menu (measured in kilobytes).

Screen tab

The Screen tab enables you to specify whether the application is to run full-screen or in a window. You can also set the number of lines of text that will appear onscreen. The default is 25 lines, but you can specify as many as 50 lines. The benefit of adjusting the number of lines on the screen is that you can display more data at any given time, but many applications don't accept this setting. If you are running the application within a window, you can specify whether the toolbar is visible and whether Windows should automatically restore your previous settings upon the next startup of the application. These settings and other display settings can be modified on the Screen tab.

Also note the two check boxes that play a big role with video performance:

✦ **Fast ROM Emulation:** Copies the contents of the video ROMs on your system into RAM to optimize performance. Fast ROM emulation is incompatible with some applications.

✦ **Dynamic Memory Allocation:** Allocates only a text mode video buffer for the application. Some applications work in graphics mode from time to time; when they do, if this option is activated, Windows dynamically changes the size of the buffer to support graphics mode. Once again, this may cause some applications to crash.

When troubleshooting problems with an MS-DOS–based application, it is worth checking out these settings. You do not necessarily have to disable the settings, but if you are having video-related problems, there is a good chance that the settings should be disabled.

Misc tab

The Misc (Miscellaneous) tab is a grab bag of settings that affect how the MS-DOS application behaves. The settings affect how the program operates in the foreground or background, how it terminates, the number of clock cycles it receives, and the shortcut keys that it uses.

Foreground settings

The first of these settings, Foreground, lets you choose whether the Windows screen saver is allowed to function when the application is active. If your application is running in full-screen mode, it has to be minimized for the Windows screen saver to be active. If your application does not like running from within a window, or while minimized, using this setting could cause problems. Not allowing the Windows screen saver to be active leaves your screen running 100 percent of the time when the application is active in the foreground. This might not be such a big deal, though, because many monitors now have an energy-saving standby feature.

Background settings

The Background settings specify whether the application is suspended when it is the background task, which means it receives clock cycles only when it is the foreground application. If the application requires clock cycles at all times, having it suspended in the background can cause it to crash. Most applications don't like being suspended when in the background; however, if you have an application that uses a large number of clock cycles, you might want to try this option.

Termination settings

The Termination setting of Warn If Still Active applies to MS-DOS windows that are closed by using the Close box in the top-right corner of the window.

This warning setting has been designed to help prevent data loss when the application is improperly closed by displaying a confirmation dialog box that allows you to cancel the closing of the application. When you try to close normal Windows applications, they usually ask you whether you want to save your changes. Closing an MS-DOS–based application by clicking the Close box, though, bypasses the normal Close functions and promptly terminates the MS-DOS session — and, therefore, the application.

You should always exit your MS-DOS application from within the program, using whatever commands or options are required. Unlike Windows programs that have a standard Exit in the File menu, MS-DOS applications usually have their own special commands for exiting or closing the application, such as key combinations using CTRL or ALT, and Q, X, or W.

Mouse settings

The Mouse settings of Quick Edit and Exclusive Mode affect how the mouse functions for MS-DOS–based application. Quick Edit allows you to use Windows-like mouse movements to select, delete, and insert text. Quick Edit applies only to Windows 9x computers, not to Windows XP or Vista computers. Exclusive Mode may seem a little odd; when enabled, it locks your mouse into the confines of the MS-DOS–based application. This is an option because some MS-DOS–based applications have nonstandard mouse routines.

Typically, when your application is running in a window, you can move your mouse out of the window at any position around the window and bring it back in at any other position. However, in some applications that use nonstandard mouse routines, the application thinks that the mouse is still in the exit location, while Windows thinks the mouse is at the re-entry location — which leaves your application mouse pointer and your Windows mouse pointer in different locations. With most programs that use standard mouse routines, when your mouse is brought back into the application, the location of your pointer is resynchronized. If your mouse is not synchronized in your application, set your mouse in Exclusive Mode. You can still move your mouse outside the window by using any standard Windows shortcut keys, such as Alt+Tab. When you click the application to make it active again, Windows synchronizes the mouse pointers for you.

Fast Pasting option

The Fast Pasting option uses Windows-based routines, rather than standard MS-DOS routines, for inserting text into your application. This works with most MS-DOS–based applications but causes problems for some. You know that you have a problem when pasting operations cause errors or disable the application, so disable Fast Pasting in these cases.

Idle Sensitivity setting

The Idle Sensitivity setting specifies how your application responds to having its clock cycles reduced. When multiple applications are running

on your system, Windows splits clock cycles among all applications that are actively requesting CPU time. When it comes to MS-DOS—based applications, Windows provides clock cycles only to applications that appear to require them. The problem is that some applications that require CPU time do not appear to need it. If an application seems to stall or crash for no apparent reason, you might want to lower its sensitivity to being idle. Selecting this option means that the application receives additional clock cycles even when Windows doesn't perceive that it needs them.

Windows shortcut keys

The last section on the Misc tab provides a list of standard Windows shortcut keys. This is different from the Shortcut Key on the Program tab, which is used to launch the PIF. If your application uses any of the shortcut keys, you must clear the appropriate check boxes here to prevent the standard Windows-based responses to the shortcut keys. For example, if your application uses the Alt+Tab shortcut and you have not cleared the Alt+Tab check box on this tab, every time you press Alt+Tab you will be switched to another application. Unless you clear the check box here, the Windows shortcut keys always take precedence.

Summary tab

The Summary tab contains summary information about the file. This is a standard tab for all files on Windows 2000 and newer OSes. These properties will be used by the Index Service and can help you locate files on your hard drive. The fields on this tab have no effect on how the PIf can be used.

Understanding incompatibilities

When you examined 16-bit Windows-based applications earlier in this chapter, you looked at potential incompatibilities that could arise from direct hardware access. The same incompatibilities apply to MS-DOS–based applications. If your application attempts to make direct hardware calls instead of standard MS-DOS–based system calls, it will not function under modern Windows OSes. Windows XP and newer OSes attempt to be backward compatible, but not at the risk of OS stability. Basically, if you have an application that makes direct hardware calls, it will not work under the newer Windows OSes.

Windows Compatibility Modes

Many applications written for DOS or earlier version of Windows will work with Windows XP and newer Windows OSes with a few minor tweaks. Starting with Windows XP, Microsoft has provided a new set of options to aid with backward compatibility for applications that are not included with the OS. These features are found on the Compatibility tab in the Properties dialog box of the executable, which is shown for an application and a PIF in Figure 2-9.

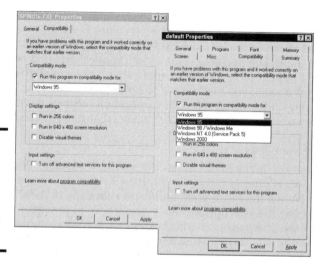

Figure 2-9:
The Comp-
atibility
settings
for an
application
and a PIF.

These options have been designed to be used with locally installed applications. You can use them with applications from CD-ROMs or from a network drive, but the settings will not be saved.

Because many applications have been written to take advantage of specific features found in various versions of the OS, the Compatibility Mode section allows you to emulate the following OSes:

+ Windows 95
+ Windows 98/Windows Me
+ Windows NT 4.0 (Service Pack 5)
+ Windows 2000

This does not emulate the entire OS, but rather disables some newer APIs (application programming interfaces) and emulates some older ones, thereby improving compatibility.

Windows Vista adds the following OSes to the Compatibility Mode section:

+ Windows XP (Service Pack 2)
+ Windows Server 2003 (Service Pack 1)

Another common problem revolves around screen settings. Many times, I have had to change my screen resolution or color depth to run a specific application (and then reset it later). The Display Settings section allows you to automatically change the display settings for the application to one of the following settings:

+ Run in 256 colors

+ Run in 640x 480 screen resolution

+ Disable visual themes

+ Disable desktop composition

+ Disable display scaling on high DPI settings

If you have an application that has problems displaying menus or tool-bar buttons, you can attempt to use the Disable Visual Themes setting. This removes the modern rendering of buttons, with the Windows XP or Windows Vista smoothness, drop shadows, Aero desktop, and so on.

Finally, under Input Settings, you have the option to Turn Off Advanced Text Services for This Program, which disables the features of Windows XP or Windows Vista that do speech-to-text and handwriting recognition. The additional APIs running to support those services can cause unexpected input into your application.

Most of the settings that can be adjusted or disabled on the Compatibility tab can also be changed elsewhere, such as the Performance Options, on the Advanced tab of the System Control Panel, which will change the setting globally for the computer.

If you have an old application that will not run properly on Windows XP or Windows Vista, do not forget about the Application Compatibility Settings.

Application Install, Start, and Load Errors

Many Windows XP or Windows Vista application errors are related to permissions to the file system when using NTFS and the Registry. Starting with Windows XP, the default permissions restrict changes to files, addition of files to specific directories, and changes to portions of the Registry. In addition to these restrictions, many applications that attempt to directly access hardware will fail. If the application is a modern 32-bit or 64-bit Windows application that is supposed to work with Windows XP or Windows Vista, most installation errors can be traced to not meeting either the minimum installation requirements or permissions.

Microsoft has made these permissions changes to prevent most users from being able to install their own applications and make unauthorized changes to the OS. One way to see whether the problem is with a user installing or launching an application is to temporarily add the user to the local Administrators group and see whether the problem is resolved. If that resolves the issue, you know that the problem is related to permissions to one of these locations.

If you can't get permissions information from the application vendor or can't grant the user elevated group membership, the Microsoft's Sysinternals (`http://technet.microsoft.com/en-us/sysinternals/default.aspx`) has utilities (such as RegMon and FileMon) that can help you identify the permissions changes required.

Getting an A+

This chapter examines application management from installation to execution. The following points are covered:

✦ 16-bit, 32-bit, and DOS-based applications function under Windows 9*x* and Windows XP, and 64-bit applications if the OS is 64-bit Windows.

✦ There are core architectural differences between 32-bit and 64-bit Windows. Support for applications differs based on the architectural differences of the OSes.

✦ The new application compatibility features in Windows XP allow it to support a wider range of older Windows applications.

Prep Test

1 Which of the following types of multitasking are supported by Windows XP? Choose all that apply.

A ❑ Share-based multitasking
B ❑ Equality multitasking
C ❑ Cooperative multitasking
D ❑ Preemptive multitasking

2 Which of the following types of multitasking provides better sharing of CPU time between processes?

A ○ Share-based multitasking
B ○ Equality multitasking
C ○ Cooperative multitasking
D ○ Preemptive multitasking

3 Which operating system allows for 16-bit Windows applications to be preemptively multitasked?

A ○ Windows XP
B ○ Windows 98
C ○ Windows 95
D ○ MS-DOS

4 Which of the following are benefits of 32-bit Windows applications? Choose all that apply.

A ❑ They share a common message queue.
B ❑ They run in separate memory spaces.
C ❑ They are preemptively multitasked.
D ❑ They support running multiple applications in one virtual machine.

5 How large is the memory space that each 32-bit Windows application has to work with?

A ○ 16MB
B ○ 1GB
C ○ 2GB
D ○ 4GB

6 **Which of the following operating systems support 16-bit Windows applications? Choose all that apply.**

 A ❑ Windows XP

 B ❑ Windows 98

 C ❑ Windows 3.1

 D ❑ MS-DOS

7 **How can you preemptively multitask 16-bit Windows applications when using Windows XP?**

 A ○ Right-click the application icon and choose Launch in Separate Memory Space.

 B ○ Choose Start⇨Run, use the Browse button to locate the application, and then select the Start in Separate Memory Space check box.

 C ○ Use `start /separate <application>` in a command prompt.

 D ○ This cannot be done.

8 **What effect does a 32-bit Windows application have on the rest of a Windows XP system when it hangs or crashes?**

 A ○ It halts 32-bit Windows applications that are running on the system.

 B ○ It halts 16-bit Windows applications that are running on the system.

 C ○ It halts MS-DOS-based applications running on the system.

 D ○ It has no effect on other applications.

9 **What effect does a 16-bit Windows application have on the rest of a Windows XP system when it hangs or crashes?**

 A ○ It halts 32-bit Windows applications that are running on the system.

 B ○ It halts 16-bit Windows applications that are running on the system.

 C ○ It halts MS-DOS-based applications running on the system.

 D ○ It has no effect on other applications.

10 **How many applications can be assigned to an NTVDM when using separate memory spaces to launch the applications?**

 A ○ 1

 B ○ 2

 C ○ 4

 D ○ 8

Answers

1 **C, D.** Windows XP supports cooperative and preemptive multitasking. *See "Getting the Most out of Multitasking."*

2 **D.** Preemptive multitasking provides more even distribution of CPU time between applications. *Review "Preemptive multitasking."*

3 **A.** A 16-bit application can be preemptively multitasked within Windows XP by running each application in a separate memory space. *Check out "Running 16-Bit Windows Applications."*

4 **B, C.** A 32-bit application uses separate message queues so that when one application hangs, it does not affect the others. Only 16-bit Windows applications may be run in a common VM. Running applications in separate memory spaces and preemptive multitasking are benefits of running 32-bit applications. *Peruse "Benefiting from 32-bit applications."*

5 **D.** Each application or VM runs in a 4GB memory space. *Take a look at "Running 32-Bit and 64-Bit Windows Applications."*

6 **A, B, C.** Only Windows-based OSes can run Windows-based applications. Windows 3.1 could run only 16-bit applications, and Windows XP and Windows 98 support 16-bit applications in an effort to be backward compatible. *Peek at "Running 16-Bit Windows Applications."*

7 **C.** Using the `start` command allows you to run applications in separate memory spaces. *Look over "Executing in the Windows environments."*

8 **D.** When a 32-bit Windows application crashes, it has no effect on other applications running on the system. *Study "Executing in the Windows environments."*

9 **B.** When a 16-bit Windows application crashes, it halts other 16-bit Windows applications in the same memory space. MS-DOS–based applications and 32-bit Windows applications should continue to operate. *Refer to "Executing in the Windows environments."*

10 **A.** When starting applications in separate memory spaces, you can assign only one application to each NTVDM. *Peruse "Executing in the Windows environments."*

Chapter 3: Optimizing the Windows Environment

Exam Objectives

✔ Optimizing operating systems by modifying virtual memory settings

✔ Using utilities to monitor and identify optimization areas

✔ Optimizing hard drives and temporary files

✔ Improve performance by turning off OS features

✔ Managing services and startup of applications to optimize system performance

Few things in life are perfect, and if you put them on a scale from perfect to lousy, most things fall somewhere in the middle. Computers play a part in my life, and I can safely say that they are not perfect, especially when dealing with speed and performance. I regularly work with other people's computers and find the responsiveness of many computers far less — very far less — than perfect. Over time, if left to its own devices, your computer will slow down, sliding down the scale from the perfect end to the lousy end. When I comment on the slow response of a computer that just completed a 15-minute boot and logon, I am often surprised, or absolutely floored, when the owner says that it is acceptable. Although some people find "acceptable" to be, well, acceptable, as the saying goes, "good enough" is never good enough. As a CompTIA A+ Certified Professional, you should be able to identify areas that might cause a slow down — and then resolve those issues.

In this chapter, you look at the major problems responsible for many slowdowns — and how to avoid them.

Identifying Areas of System Bottlenecks

The tapered neck of a bottle, with its substantially smaller diameter than the body of the bottle, restricts the flow of liquid from the bottle. Bottlenecks occur on your computer as well. They happen when most system resources are fine, except for that one subsystem that is heavily overused. To perform

any task, a limited number of resources can be applied to a task; when the task exceeds the available resources, you run into problems. Computers have four critical resources that can be the source of a bottleneck:

+ Processor

+ Memory

+ Disk

+ Network

All system bottlenecks will occur in one of these four resources, which are the main subsystems in a computer.

In addition to resource overuse, hardware errors might also cause problems. This chapter does not examine possible hardware errors that can cause problems or issues that might be specific to a particular type of application or service. Most hardware issues are dealt with in Book IV, Chapter 2, which is devoted to troubleshooting.

Using Monitoring Tools

To effectively diagnose a problem in one of the four critical resources (processor, memory, disk, and network), you need to monitor what is going on with your system. In the following sections, you look at two tools that you can use to diagnose problems in these resource areas.

Task Manager

Task Manager (or `taskman.exe`) is a nice, quick, and simple tool. It is not as full-featured as Performance Monitor (see the following section), but what it lacks in features, it makes up for in simplicity and speed. To open Task Manager, press Ctrl+Alt+Del and click the Task Manager button in the Security dialog box. In Windows XP Home, just pressing Ctrl+Alt+Del opens Task Manager. You can also open Task Manager by right-clicking an empty area of the Taskbar and choosing Task Manager from the contextual menu.

Performance tab

You can use Task Manager to diagnose processor, memory, network (with Windows XP), and service (with Windows Vista) bottlenecks. Figure 3-1 shows the Performance tab of Task Manager, which is typically the tab you will use first to identify a problem.

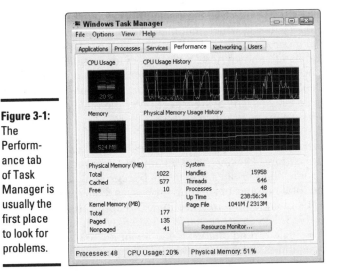

Figure 3-1:
The
Perform-
ance tab
of Task
Manager is
usually the
first place
to look for
problems.

On the Performance tab, you can find critical data about your system's performance. This tab is broken down into two main sections: the graphs and the numeric data. In the graph section is CPU usage and PF (Page File) usage information (or Physical Memory usage in Windows Vista). In the numeric section, you see information on processes and memory usage. At the very bottom of the window, you see summary information in the status bar.

The Task Manager window stays on top of all others, which is normally preferred; however, if you want it to go to the background, choose Options⇨Always on Top to deselect this option.

In the graphs section is the graph for the overall CPU usage, which is the same image shown in the system tray next to the clock. (This image appears automatically when you open Task Manager.) In this context, *CPU usage* is the average of CPU usage over all processors in your computer.

Next to this graph is a line graph showing you historic CPU usage over the past few minutes. If you have multiple processors, processors with hyper-threading, or multicore processors, you will see multiple line graphs, each in its own small window. If the graph is too small, resize Task Manager. And if you have multiple graphs, you can get a single graph showing the averages by choosing View⇨CPU History⇨One Graph, All CPUs. If you choose View⇨Show Kernel Times, you get a red line showing kernel processor utilization to help identify whether the problem is related to kernel processes or user processes. It is not uncommon for processor utilization to jump to 100%, but if it is consistently higher than 80% or 90%, you are likely experiencing a slowdown.

Page file usage (also recorded in the graphs section) is actually application-specific virtual memory usage, which includes paging file usage and a portion of the physical memory that the application is using. Just like CPU utilization, two graphs are shown here: a histogram for instantaneous usage and a line graph showing the historical usage. If you are running low on space in your page file, you are likely running short on memory. Windows Vista shows page file usage in the System section of the dialog, and shows physical memory usage in the graph area.

In the numeric section are totals for handles, threads, and processes. Think of *processes* as applications. However, not all applications run in windows that you can see. Some, like services, run in the background, and these are included in the total number of running processes. Each process is composed of threads of code that are executed. Old applications from the 16-bit Windows and MS-DOS days are *single threaded,* which means that the program runs a single thread of code from beginning to end. Newer multithreaded applications can run several different threads of code, each performing a different task, all working together to perform the task that processor is attempting to accomplish. On a multiprocessor computer, these threads can execute simultaneously, improving the overall speed of the process.

Handles are resources that the processes are using, such as memory locations, files, or Registry keys. Most likely, you will be primarily concerned with how many processes are running, because each running process consumes some of the total processor cycles available.

The other numeric sections all deal with memory — physical memory, kernel memory, and commit charge (prior to Windows Vista). *Physical memory* is the actual RAM that is installed in your computer. In the physical memory section, you can see how much physical memory is on your computer, is free (or available), and is allocated to system cache or disk caching for the disk drives. The cache space dynamically adjusts as demands for memory go up, but the goal is to improve disk access by caching in fast memory.

Kernel memory is memory allotted to the kernel. The kernel memory section shows you how much memory is allocated to the kernel, which is in charge of running all operations in your computer. If a driver has a memory leak, you might see kernel memory increase higher than normal for your computer, which is typically less than 100MB. The short-term solution is to reboot your computer.

Kernel memory is split between paged and nonpaged memory. Paged memory is part of the *page pool,* which is the memory swapped between physical RAM and the page file on the hard drive.

Commit charge is the amount of memory that is in use, or committed. This section shows you current usage, total available (including the page file), and the peak usage since the last reboot. Windows Vista does not have a section for commit charge, as it shows this information, but rather displays the total committed memory in the System section as Page File.

Windows Vista adds a Resource Monitor button to this tab, which opens another performance tool that provides more detailed information related to the four critical resources, as shown in Figure 3-2. One big difference between Resource Monitor and Task Manager is that Resource Monitor shows the resource usage by application or process.

Figure 3-2:
Resource
Monitor
shows
detailed
information
related to
processes.

Networking tab

In most cases, looking at the data on the Performance tab leads you to either the Processes tab or the Networking tab. On the Networking tab (shown in Figure 3-3) is a line graph with lines for each network interface on your computer, representing the percentage of bandwidth being used by each one. To see additional information on your graph, choose an option from the View➪Network Adapter History submenu. This allows you to add Bytes Sent and Bytes Received to the existing Bytes Total line on the graph. This is useful for seeing whether a network-related problem is because of data coming in or going out.

Figure 3-3:
The
Networking
tab of Task
Manager
can help
you identify
network use
problems.

You can also find the same information from the graph presented numerically at the bottom of the window. To see more data, choose View⇨Select Columns. This opens the tool to a lot more troubleshooting capabilities by allowing analysis of many network-related counters, such as the breakdown of bytes sent, bytes received, and traffic type being unicast or nonunicast. *Unicast* network traffic is information that is sent only to your computer; *nonunicast* traffic is simultaneously sent to multiple computers on your network.

Processes tab

If the problems are not network-related, you might be led to look at the Processes tab, which is shown in Figure 3-4. This tab lists all running processes on your system in columns. You can toggle a sort on the columns (ascending or descending) by clicking the column heading. The default columns include Image Name, User Name (the user executing the process), CPU (the percentage utilization of this process), and Memory (the amount of memory this process is using). If you are logged on as an administrator, you can also choose to Show Processes from All Users to see processes other than your own.

In most cases, you will be able to locate the process using up most of the CPU cycles and slowing down your computer. To see additional troubleshooting information, choose View⇨Select Columns to select from many other counters, such as Virtual Memory Size, Page Faults, and Peak Memory Usage, to list just a few.

Figure 3-4:
The
Processes
tab of Task
Manager
helps
identify CPU
utilization
problems.

Page faults occur when information that your computer wants is not in physical memory and must be initially loaded into memory or be read from the page file on the hard drive. If the number of page faults takes a sharp rise, you might also notice that your available memory is low.

Right-clicking any running task on the Processes tab invokes a contextual menu with several options, including ending the process, ending the process tree, changing the application priority or the processor affinity (if you have more than one processor). If you end the process tree, you terminate the process and any other processes that it started. Changing a process' priority changes the percentage of CPU time that an application gets when it is running. If you set the affinity, then you are able to force it to run on a specific processor.

Be careful when using high and real-time priorities; they can cause system instability. If you have a highly active program, such as a counter, setting it to real-time priority can allow it access to all CPU cycles on your computer, which can cause the system to ignore user input from the mouse or keyboard, preventing you from doing anything else with your computer.

Services tab

The Services tab (Vista) shows you the same list of services that you will find in the Services MMC management tool, but in an abridged format. This allows you to stop or start these services, or launch the Services MMC to have full control of the services.

Applications tab

The Applications tab shows what applications are running in the foreground (as shown in Figure 3-5). These applications should list Running in the Status tab. If the application is not listed as running, it may not be responding. At this point, you can either give the application more time to respond (after all, it might just be busy), or you can end a task by selecting the application and clicking the End Task button. To bring an application's window to the foreground, select the application and click the Switch To button. To launch a new application, click the New Task button, which brings up the Run dialog box.

Figure 3-5:
The Applications tab lists running foreground applications and their responsiveness.

Users tab

The Users tab (in Windows Vista and Windows Server OSes) shows what users are logged on, if they are currently active, the remote computer they are connected from, and the session they are logged onto (either remote or console). For any of the users that are connected, you are able to disconnect the user or to log the user off.

Performance

Although Task Manager might be where you first look for solutions to performance problems, it is really a 10,000-foot view of the situation. To get down to ground level, you need a more powerful tool, and that is where the Performance administrative tool comes in, with its two main components: System Monitor and Performance Logs and Alerts.

TIP

Windows Vista calls this tool Reliability and Performance, which can be found in the Windows Vista Administrative Tools. This tool also adds a component called Reliability Monitor, which graphs major failures in the OS and what was happening on the computer at the time, all presented in a timeline.

System Monitor is Task Manager's big brother. It does not allow you to change settings or terminate tasks, but it does allow you to monitor a whole series of available counters. Launch Performance by choosing Start⇨Control Panel⇨Performance and Maintenance⇨Administrative Tools⇨Performance, or by running either `perfmon.exe` or `perfmon.msc`. The Performance screen starts with three default counters loaded into the System Monitor, as shown in Figure 3-6. A counter is a numeric measure of an element of a system component, such as bytes of available memory. The three default counters are

✦ **Pages/sec** from the Memory object to show memory shortage problems

✦ **Avg. Disk Queue Length** from the Physical Disk object to show disk access bottlenecks

✦ **% Processor Time** from the Processor object to show processor utilization problems

View Report button

View Histogram button | Properties button

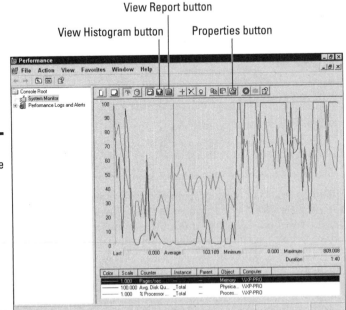

Figure 3-6:
Performance
Monitor's
System
Monitor
shows
graphs for
a variety of
counters
built into
Windows.

On the exam, you might see references to System Monitor as well as Performance. *System Monitor* is the component of Performance that makes the graphs of current and logged activity. Windows Vista has gone back to calling the component that makes that graphs *Performance Monitor*.

For each counter, you will see a graph with just over 90 readings, which by default are taken once per second. To change this frequency, bring up the Properties for the graph by clicking the Properties button on the toolbar or by pressing Ctrl+Q and changing the value of Sample Automatically Every X Seconds.

If you don't like the line graph look, click the View Histogram button (think bar graph) or View Report button (gives only numeric data). These buttons are indicated in Figure 3-6.

Many other counters can be added to the graph. If you click the Add button on the toolbar or press Ctrl+I, you can add counters to your graph, as shown in Figure 3-7.

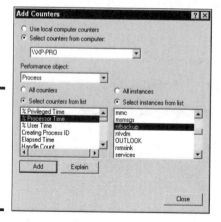

Figure 3-7:
A wide variety of counters may be added to your graph.

By default, you add counters from *your* computer, but you have the option to add counters for any computer that you have admin rights for. If you prefer to view counters from a remote computer, choose it from the Select counters from the Computer drop-down menu to type the computer name into the drop-down menu box. If you choose another computer, your list of Performance objects is updated to include the objects on that computer. Many counters are defaults for the OS, and any software you install has the option of adding custom counter objects, which is the case for many Microsoft programs. If you look at the list of counters, you will see that they can be categorized into the four critical system resources: processor, memory, disk, and network. Table 3-1 lists some of the related objects for the four critical system resources.

Table 3-1	Related Objects for Critical System Resources
Critical System Resource	*Related Object*
Processor	Process Processor System
Memory	Memory Paging File
Disk	Cache Physical Disk
Network	Browser IP Network Interface Redirector Server Server Work Queues

Table 3-1 is just a partial list of all the possible objects available to you. Each object has a series of related counters. For instance, the Process object has counters for % Privileged Time, % Processor Time, and % User Time. Each counter may have a series of *instances*. In the case of the Process object and % Processor Time, there are instances for each running process on the system.

For any counters that you do not know, select that counter and then click the Explain button to access help on that counter.

When you click the Add button to add a counter to your graph, the new counter lines show up immediately. When you have added all the counters you want to view, click Close.

When you have many lines on your graph, click the Highlight button or press Ctrl+H to highlight the line as a white line on your graph for any counter you selected on the bottom part of the screen. To delete any counters that you added, select the counter and click the Delete button on the toolbar or press the Delete key on your keyboard.

So far, you have been taking data from current activity. If the problem is periodic, you want to create logs and alerts to try to catch the problem when it occurs. If you want to create an alert based on your counters, click Performance Logs and Alerts; then right-click Alerts and choose New Alert Settings. You first provide a descriptive name used to identify the alert, and then you can select counters and set the alert-firing threshold for each counter, as shown in Figure 3-8. These values are checked at the Sample interval. When the firing threshold criteria are met, the actions on the Action tab are performed. These include logging the alert in the Event Log,

sending a network message to a NetBIOS name, starting a counter log, or running an external program, which might be a script to perform additional actions. This log will be active during the times listed on the Schedule tab.

Figure 3-8:
Set alerts to
notify you
of problem
conditions.

If you want to create a counter log, click Performance Logs and Alerts; then right-click Counter Logs and choose New Log Settings. This opens the window shown in Figure 3-9. Select the counters or objects that you want to log and the interval at which you want to take readings. Then you can set the type of log to create — if you plan to view the data in the Performance Monitor, you need to use a binary log format. Just like the alerts, you can choose a schedule for this log so that it can run at a specific time. For instance, if you are having problems with a computer regularly between 2 p.m. and 4 p.m., you could schedule the log to run from 1 p.m. to 5 p.m. You can also have the log file stop when the file is full or reaches its configured maximum size. When the logging stops, you can have a program run, which might be used to notify you that the logging has stopped or to copy your new logs to another computer or location.

After a log file is created, you can view it from the Performance Monitor by clicking the View Log Data button or by pressing Ctrl+L. You are asked for the name of the log file that you want to use, and then you can add counters to the graph normally, but you can choose only from the counters included in the log file. The resulting graph charts all readings taken for the counters, not just the default 90 readings.

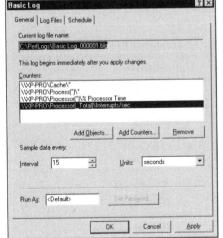

Figure 3-9:
Counter
logs can
be used to
record data
for historical
analysis.

To change the time range displayed on the graph, click the Properties button and the Source tab, from which you can adjust the time range. As you adjust the range, a vertical bar moves through the graph, showing you where that range is. To return to getting graph data from current activity, click the View Current Activity button or press Ctrl+T.

Other tools

Windows Vista has introduced two new tools in an attempt to allow for more functions to be completed from the command line interface: tasklist.exe and taskkill.exe. These tools take the functionality of the Processes and Services tabs of the Vista Task Manager and bring them to the command line. One additional feature of these programs is that they can be run locally on the computer, or they can be used to view processes on another computer on the network.

The tasklist.exe program will show you what processes are running the computer, which can be seen in greater detail using the /v option, which is just one of many options. The basic output from the command looks like Listing 3-1:

Listing 3-1: `tasklist.exe` Output

```
C:\Users\User>tasklist
```

Image Name	PID	Session Name	Session#	Mem Usage
=========================	========	=================	===========	============
System Idle Process	0	Services	0	24 K
System	4	Services	0	2,312 K
smss.exe	416	Services	0	640 K
csrss.exe	504	Services	0	3,932 K
wininit.exe	540	Services	0	3,816 K
csrss.exe	560	Console	1	3,260 K
winlogon.exe	604	Console	1	4,736 K
services.exe	636	Services	0	6,412 K
lsass.exe	656	Services	0	2,464 K
lsm.exe	664	Services	0	5,512 K
svchost.exe	832	Services	0	6,496 K
LogonUI.exe	980	Console	1	15,460 K
audiodg.exe	548	Services	0	12,964 K
SLsvc.exe	884	Services	0	4,328 K
aswUpdSv.exe	1320	Services	0	528 K
ashServ.exe	1348	Services	0	15,944 K
spoolsv.exe	1616	Services	0	8,548 K
svchost.exe	824	Services	0	4,768 K
SearchIndexer.exe	2076	Services	0	14,508 K
ashMaiSv.exe	2372	Services	0	1,688 K
ashWebSv.exe	2436	Services	0	26,124 K
msdtc.exe	3020	Services	0	4,908 K
taskeng.exe	2288	Services	0	5,976 K
csrss.exe	3068	RDP-Tcp#0	2	5,812 K
winlogon.exe	492	RDP-Tcp#0	2	5,184 K
taskeng.exe	2244	RDP-Tcp#0	2	10,004 K
rdpclip.exe	3184	RDP-Tcp#0	2	5,612 K
dwm.exe	3496	RDP-Tcp#0	2	5,288 K
explorer.exe	3516	RDP-Tcp#0	2	51,836 K
MSASCui.exe	3744	RDP-Tcp#0	2	7,620 K
ashDisp.exe	4044	RDP-Tcp#0	2	4,496 K
wmpnscfg.exe	4052	RDP-Tcp#0	2	5,004 K
svchost.exe	2180	Services	0	4,648 K
EasyCapture.EXE	2324	RDP-Tcp#0	2	7,404 K
mmc.exe	3692	RDP-Tcp#0	2	27,344 K
taskmgr.exe	3380	RDP-Tcp#0	2	9,548 K
cmd.exe	3528	RDP-Tcp#0	2	2,464 K
WmiPrvSE.exe	2216	Services	0	9,036 K
tasklist.exe	1892	RDP-Tcp#0	2	5,992 K

The `taskkill.exe` program is used to terminate tasks that you need to stop, in the same manner you would with End Process option in Task Manager. If I were to terminate the `EasyCapture.exe` process in Listing 3-1, I would be able to run the following command:

```
taskkill /PID 2324
```

Optimization Best Practices

There are many simple steps that you take to optimize your system for best performance. Some components that you can make changes to include virtual memory, hard drives, printers, scanners, system services, running processes, and temporary files. After you make changes to the components, you can use Task Manager and System Monitor to see whether your changes had any effect on system performance.

Virtual memory

Virtual memory uses both RAM and hard drive space to create a memory pool. The hard drive space used is called a paging file; in Windows, the filename is `pagefile.sys`. Access to the paging file is much slower than access to RAM, so the paging file is used for information that is accessed less often. The default paging file size is 1.5 times the amount of RAM in your computer. To improve performance, you should not set this any larger than it really needs to be. You can find out what your maximum size should be by running your system for several days of typical or hard use and then checking your peak usage in Task Manager or System Monitor. Set your paging file size between 1.25 times to 1.5 times your peak paging-file usage. To see how to gather your memory usage data using Task Manager or System Monitor, review the "Using Monitoring Tools" section earlier in this chapter; to see how to change the size of your paging file read Book V, Chapter 2; and to get an overview of how virtual memory works, read Book V, Chapter 6.

**Book VI
Chapter 3**

Optimizing
the Windows
Environment

If you find that you are using a lot of virtual memory and accessing the paging file, you need to either reduce the processes using RAM or add more RAM (see Book II, Chapter 3) to improve overall system performance by reducing paging-file usage.

If neither step is an option, move the page file to a drive other than the drive that holds your Windows installation. You should also choose the fastest drive that you have. That is, 7,200 rpm or 10,000 rpm drives over 5,400 RPM drives, ATA 133 drives over ATA 66, and so on. The chosen drive should not have other highly intensive processes using it.

To avoid having your page file fragmented, defragment your drive prior to creating your page file.

To change the location of your paging file, follow these steps:

1. **Choose Start⇨Control Panel and open the System applet.**
2. **Click the Advanced tab and click the Performance Settings button.**

3. **In the Performance Options dialog box, click the Advanced tab and then click the Virtual Memory Change button.**

4. **From the Virtual Memory dialog box, shown in Figure 3-10, select the drive you want the paging file saved on, choose the size, and then click the Set button.**

5. **To finish, press the series of OK buttons to close the dialog boxes.**

 Depending on the changes you made, you may need to reboot your computer.

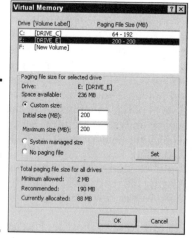

Figure 3-10: Changing the page file settings can improve your overall system perform-ance.

Depending on the Startup and Recovery setting in your System control panel applet, you might require a paging file on the drive that contains your Windows directory that is at least equal to the amount of RAM installed in your computer.

Hard drive

You can do several things to optimize your hard drives. The first thing is to choose the fastest possible drives for your system. If you can choose ATA 133 over ATA 66 or SATA 300 over SATA 150, do so. Keep enough free space on your drives to allow for efficient defragmentation; Disk Defragmenter sug-gests 15% free space. If you have multiple drives in your system and you are suffering from a disk bottleneck, move some applications from one drive to another to better balance drive utilization.

Printers

To optimize printing, here are a few things that you can do.

✦ **Use current drivers for your printers.** Upgraded drivers often implement new features and are better optimized for your hardware.

✦ **Move your spool directory to a different drive.** Prior to sending data to the printer, the data is spooled to the computer's hard disk. In order to improve disk access, you should always try to place the spool directory on a fast disk that does not have competition from other applications or services that are running on the computer. For information about spooling, refer to Book III, Chapter 5.

Book VI
Chapter 3

Optimizing
the Windows
Environment

To change the location of the spool directory, choose Start⇨Printers and Faxes, choose File⇨Server Properties, and then click the Advanced tab, as shown in Figure 3-11. From there, you can change the Spool Folder path.

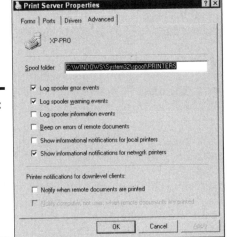

Figure 3-11:
Changing the spool folder path may improve printing performance.

If you are just printing the odd document, optimizing the printing process is not an issue. But if you are using a computer as a print server for an office and interfacing with multiple printers, these steps improve your printing performance.

Scanners

Optimizing the scanning process relies mostly on the hardware being used. Scanners come with a variety of interfaces, with the oldest being SCSI and parallel. To improve scanning performance, choose a scanner that matches

the fastest bus architecture (see Book II, Chapter 1) available on your computer — that usually means USB or FireWire. This increases the transfer rate between the scanner and the computer.

The other factor that affects scanner performance is the dots per inch (DPI) level at which you are scanning. If you scan at a lower rate, your scans run faster, and the output has a smaller file size — but the quality of the image is lower. The lowest acceptable quality level is dictated by how you want to use the image. Photographic reproduction requires a higher quality level than does newsprint.

Temporary files

Many applications create temporary files, which are kind of like a scratch pad that is a working area for data. An application uses a temporary file to store data that it is working with and then deletes the file when the task is completed. For instance, when you open a document in Microsoft Word, Word creates other files in the same directory that start with a ~ character. These other files are temporary files, which hold changes to the original document as well as automatic recovery information. When you close the document, Word deletes these files — or, at least, it is supposed to.

It is the job of each application to delete its temporary files when they are no longer needed. Windows uses the environment variables of %temp% and %tmp% to point applications to the temporary directory. The default location for the temporary directory is in the user's profile, using the path

+ **XP:** %USERPROFILE%\Local Settings\Temp

+ **Vista:** %USERPROFILE%\AppData\Local\Temp

Having the temporary file directory in the user's profile means that a temporary directory exists for every user on the computer. You can modify each user's temporary directory settings to point to a single location and Scheduled Tasks by running a command like C:\Windows\system32\cmd.exe /c del /s /q c:\temp when the computer starts up. Applications are suppose to clean up their files, but after a period of time, you will likely have several files in your temporary directory. You can use the Windows Disk Cleanup utility can delete temporary files, as well as other files not needed on your hard drive.

To get to Disk Cleanup choose Start⇨My Computer; then right-click a hard disk, choose Properties, and click the Disk Cleanup button. A Disk Cleanup dialog box will open, and after scanning your disk the dialog box will change, presenting you a list of items that can be cleaned off your hard disk, such as temporary Internet files, items in the Recycle Bin, and temporary files. Place a check in the box next to any items you want cleaned, click OK, and then click Yes in the confirmation dialog box.

Services

Each *service* represents an application running on your computer. The more applications that are running, the fewer system resources you have available for other applications or processes. To improve overall resource availability and system security, disable any services that are not required. You can see a list of all system services though the Services Administrative Tool. Choose Start⇨Run and type **services.msc**, or locate it in the Administrative Tools folder, which is found in the Control Panels folder. The Services tool lists

+ **Name:** The name of service

+ **Description:** A brief description of what the service does

+ **Status:** Tells you whether the service is currently running

+ **Startup Type:** Tells you whether the service startup is Automatic or Manual, or whether the service is disabled

+ **Log On As:** The user credentials used to start the service

 Most services start as the Local System, which is the computer's own account.

When you select a service, you can read its description on the left of the window. With that information, you might be able to decide whether you need that service running. To test whether you need a service, turn it off, right-click the service name, and choose Stop. You can then tell quickly whether you need that service because something you use will stop working. When you turn off services by choosing Stop, the service restarts when you reboot. To have a service remain stopped after a reboot, right-click the service name and choose Properties; to open the service properties dialog box, choose Manual from the Startup Type drop-down menu, and click then OK to close the dialog box.

Prior to randomly turning off services, you can check whether the service is required by using Internet resources, like the Microsoft Web site, which will provide detailed descriptions of what most services are used for. If you *still* cannot decide whether a service is required, disable the service on a test computer and see what happens. Table 3-2 has a summary of the major services that are part of Windows.

Table 3-2	Windows Services
Name	*Description*
Alerter	Processes and delivers administrative alerts
Computer Browser	Maintains a list of other computers on the network
Error Reporting Service	Allows error reporting to user and to Microsoft

(continued)

Table 3-2 *(continued)*

Name	Description
Event Log	Logs messages issued by Windows-based programs and components into logs viewed with Event Viewer
Fast User Switching Compatibility	Provides management for applications in a multiple user environment
Help and Support	Enables the Help and Support Center to run
IMAPI CD-Burning COM Service	Manages Windows-based CD recording, rather than using third-party tools
Indexing Service	Indexes contents and properties of files
Logical Disk Manager	Detects and monitors new hard disk drives and sends disk volume information to the Logical Disk Manager Administrative Service
Messenger	Transmits and receives net send and Alerter service messages
Network Connections	Manages the Network and Dial-Up Connections folder
Performance Logs and Alerts	Collects performance data from local or remote computers and generates alerts, based on settings found in Performance Logs and Alerts
Print Spooler	Loads files for deferred printing
Secondary Logon	Allows starting of applications using an alternate set of user credentials
Security Center	Monitors system security settings and configuration
Server	Supports file and print sharing over the network
System Restore Service	Performs system restore functions based on System Restore Points
Task Scheduler	Enables configuration and scheduling of automated tasks
Terminal Services	Holds base multiuser components used by Remote Desktop, Fast User Switching, Remote Assistance, and Terminal Server
Themes	Manages XP general desktop themes
Volume Shadow Copy	Allows Volume Shadow Copies used for backup and other purposes
Windows Firewall/ Internet Connection Sharing (ICS)	Provides firewall and Internet gateway services, such as name resolution, network address translation, and intrusion prevention services
Windows Installer	Base Windows component that allows for the installation of MSI files
Wireless Zero Configuration	Provides a standard configuration interface for 802.11 adapters (called WLAN Autoconfig in Windows Vista)
Workstation	Creates and maintains client network connections to remote computers

Properties can be set and managed for services. To change the properties of a service, open the Services Administrative Tool, as previously mentioned; then locate and select the service you want to modify or view settings for and then right-click Properties. This opens the service properties dialog box, which has four tabs: General, Log On, Recovery, and Dependencies.

General tab

On the General tab, you can see basic information for the service, and, most of the time, this is the only tab you need to use. This shows you the display name used in the Services tool, as well as the path to the executable that is run to start the service. A startup type can be set to Automatic, Manual, or Disabled. The Automatic settings start the service on computer reboot; Manual allows it to be started by using the `net start` command or the Services tool; Disabled disallows the service to be run at all.

There are also service control buttons to start, stop, pause, and resume a service. Start and Stop are self-explanatory and are supported by all, but some services support Pause and Resume. Pause typically prevents new requests from being processed by the service, but will allow existing requests to be processed. Resume restores a paused service to normal operation. One case in which you might use this is with the Server service, which allows people to access files on your computer from across the network. Stopping the service disconnects all users. Pausing the service prevents new users from accessing files on your computer, but people who already have that connection open are able to finish their work. After all users have completed their work and have disconnected from your computer, you can complete what you were intending to do, which might be to stop the service, make a configuration change, and restart the service.

Some services accept start-up parameters in the same way that you can pass parameters to other applications. When a service is stopped, you can add or change the Start parameters, and then start the service.

Log On tab

All services are programs, and all programs on a Windows NT-based computer will run using security settings of a user account. Most services run using the OS's account, also called Local System; however, you might want a service to run using a different account so that you can restrict what the service can do or so that the service can interact with other computers on the network.

In addition to account settings, the Log On tab allows you to specify which hardware profile this service should run for. This allows you to use hardware profiles as tools to control which services are loaded during any reboot. Hardware profiles are covered in Book VI, Chapter 1.

Book VI
Chapter 3

Optimizing
the Windows
Environment

Recovery tab

The Recovery tab allows you to deal with what to do when the service stops unexpectedly. Three drop-down menus enable you to specify an action for the First failure, Second failure, and Subsequent failures. For each menu, you can choose Take No Action, Restart the Service, Run a Program, or Restart the Computer. The default is to take no action.

If a service fails for an unknown reason, you can set the service to restart on failure while you are trying to find the root cause, which might be enough to continue to provide the functionality required.

If you specify to run a program, you can use the bottom of the Properties dialog box to specify what program or batch file you want to run and the parameters to pass to the program. The program or batch file may be used to automatically fix a known problem or to send an e-mail or alert to the administrator of the computer.

If you choose to restart the computer, click the Restart Computer Options button at the bottom of the dialog box to set the delay for the reboot, and a message to send to people connected to the computer.

Finally, the Recovery tab enables you to specify the number of days at which you will reset the failure counter and the time to wait before restarting a service.

Dependencies tab

Some services require that other services are running prior to starting up. If you try to start a service that depends on other services not running, the required services will also be started. The Dependencies tab allows you to see both services that the selected service requires as well as what other services need the selected service.

One service that I often disable on systems with limited resources is the Themes service. This service is responsible for drawing windows with rounded corners and most of the Windows XP or Windows Vista graphical enhancements. All these items take processor time and memory to render for the user. By disabling the Theme service, these enhancements are automatically disabled. There may be some cases in which a user might feel that this service is required, and the same can be said of any service. For instance, an anti-spyware service running in real-time mode, checking each file that is accessed on your hard drive is a good service to have running on a computer connected to the Internet and used for Web browsing, but this same service may be of limited use on an isolated computer with no Internet access.

Startup

When your computer starts up, it loads all its services as well as any applications that are referenced in the Run Registry keys and the Startup group in your start menu. The Run Registry keys include:

```
HKEY_LOCAL_MACHINE\SOFTWARE\Microsoft\Windows\CurrentVersion\Run
HKEY_LOCAL_MACHINE\SOFTWARE\Microsoft\Windows\CurrentVersion\RunOnce
HKEY_LOCAL_MACHINE\SOFTWARE\Microsoft\Windows\CurrentVersion\RunOnceEx
HKEY_CURRENT_USER\Software\Microsoft\Windows\CurrentVersion\Run
HKEY_CURRENT_USER\Software\Microsoft\Windows\CurrentVersion\RunOnce
```

These items represent applications running on your computer. Many of these items, as well as some services, are responsible for the ever-growing string of icons next to your clock in the system tray. Each is a running application or process that takes system resources away from other applications or processes.

Many icons in your system tray have preferences or options that allow you to stop the background process from running. If you disable this service, some applications might take longer to load. For instance, Sun's Java or Apple's QuickTime use the startup Registry key to place one of their startup applications in the system tray, and they use the application to prelaunch their main application environments. For example, when you launch a QuickTime movie, QuickTime is already running and only needs to open the media file. If this process were not running, you would have to load QuickTime into memory before running the media file. On systems with limited resources, you want to remove many of these preloaded components to free the critical resources they use. Even though each icon represents a small amount of resource, they all make up the straws on the camel's back, and you never know where the breaking point is.

GUI Enhancements

There are many GUI Enhancements that have been added to the Windows OS over time. These enhancements have made the user interface more attractive, and in some cases more functional; but always at a cost of resource utilization. On computers that are underpowered, turning off these enhancements can provide a significant performance increase. These enhancements include:

✦ Windows Aero in Windows Vista

✦ Advanced Themes

✦ Visual Effects

✦ Windows Vista Sidebar

Each of these enhancements can be disabled to improve the overall performance of the computer, but at a loss of the features provided.

Windows Aero

The Aero desktop experience provides much of Windows Vista's eye candy in features such as Windows Flip, Windows Flip 3D, Glass effects, and the live taskbar thumbnails. All of these features make Windows Vista a little nicer to use, but each feature consumes system resources. To disable the Aero desktop, use the following steps:

1. **Right-click an empty spot on your desktop and click Personalize.**
2. **Click on the Window Color and Appearance link.**
3. **When the Windows Color and Appearance window opens. Click on the "Open classic appearance properties for more color options" link.**
4. **Choose any Desktop theme, other than the Vista Aero theme.**
5. **Choose OK to save your settings.**

Advanced Themes

Both Windows Vista and Windows XP have default desktop themes that present windows and dialogs using windows with rounded corners, and other window dressings. Displaying windows this way consumes more system resources. Microsoft provides a theme called Windows Classic which does not use these appearance features.

To change your theme using Windows Vista, follow these steps:

1. **Right-click an empty spot on your desktop and click Personalize.**
2. **Click on the Theme link.**
3. **When the Theme Settings dialog opens, choose Windows Classic from the Theme menu.**
4. **Choose OK to save your settings.**

To change your theme using Windows XP, follow these steps:

1. **Right-click an empty spot on your desktop and click Properties.**
2. **When the Display Properties dialog opens, choose Windows Classic from the Theme menu.**
3. **Choose OK to save your settings.**

Visual Effects

Visual Effects add basic enhancements to the GUI, which include displaying window contents when moving or resizing windows, animating windows minimize and maximize actions, sliding taskbar buttons, etc. Each of these niceties uses system resources. To turn off all visual effects, use the following process:

1. **Click Start, right-click Computer (My Computer for Windows XP), and then click Properties. The System window will open.**

2. **Click Advanced System Settings (or the Advanced tab for Windows XP). The System Properties window will open.**

3. **Under Performance, click Settings. The Performance Options window will open.**

4. **Click the Visual Effects tab.**

5. **Select Adjust for best performance, and then click Apply.**

This process turns off all GUI Enhancements that have been covered in this section thus far.

Windows Vista Sidebar

The Windows Sidebar in Vista provides an area where Gadgets are loaded. These gadgets provide many functions from displaying a slide show of your pictures to showing CPU utilization; the possibilities are endless. Each gadget that is running, performing some task, will utilize system resources, and to improve system performance, should be closed. To close the entire Sidebar, right-click anywhere in the Sidebar and choose Close Sidebar.

Indexing

Indexing was first introduced in Book V, Chapter 4. This process reviews all data on your hard drive and builds a content index to allow you to search for the data much faster than would otherwise be possible — think of it like the index in this book. The process of building and maintaining the index take some of your system resources. This feature should be carefully evaluated before disabling, as it greatly improves search times.

In Windows Vista, this feature is called Windows Search. It not only indexes files, it also indexes e-mails, and most other content on your computer. If you stop the Windows Search service, then virtual folder views will not be available, and searching for files will use the slower item-by-item searching.

To stop the indexing process from running you can go to the Services applet using the following process:

1. Right-click My Computer (or Computer on Windows Vista)⇨Manage.

The Computer Management window opens.

2. Chose Services and Applications in the navigation pane, and then choose Services.

3. Locate Indexing Service (Windows Search for Windows Vista), and choose the Stop button on the tool bar.

If you want to prevent the service starting up during a restart of the computer, right-click on the service and choose Properties, then change the Startup type to either manual or disabled

4. Click OK to close the Properties window.

Getting an A+

This chapter reviews optimization of the Windows environment. Major points covered in this chapter include

✦ Virtual memory and applications that access the paging file reduce performance.

✦ Performance is increased by using the computer's faster interface available for a device, such as using FireWire rather than serial.

✦ To improve performance, reduce the number of processes and services running.

✦ Printers can be optimized by changing the location of the spool directory.

Prep Test

1 **What tools would you use to monitor disk I/O? (Choose all that apply.)**

A ☐ `replmon`

B ☐ `perfmon`

C ☐ `defrag`

D ☐ `taskman`

2 **Virtual memory contains which item?**

A ○ A special section of memory used for caching data

B ○ An area of a hard drive for caching data

C ○ An expanded memory PCI expansion card

D ○ An extended memory PCI expansion card

3 **What tool manages your virtual memory settings?**

A ○ Memory Control Panel

B ○ `setver` command

C ○ System Control Panel

D ○ `mem` command

4 **What two steps can you take to improve hard disk access? (Choose two.)**

A ☐ Double the number of pins on your drive that are carrying data.

B ☐ Defragment your drive.

C ☐ Add a speed doubler to the drive bus.

D ☐ Change to a faster bus architecture.

5 **Which of the following will *not* help optimize printer performance?**

A ○ Using a newer driver

B ○ Moving the spool directory to a faster drive

C ○ Reducing the number of other applications running on the print server

D ○ Allocating more RAM to the printer cache

6 **Overall system performance can be improved by all of the following except for which item?**

A ○ Defragment drives

B ○ Add more memory

C ○ Reduce the number of processes

D ○ Increase the page file size

Answers

1 **B, D.** Both Task Manager and Performance Monitor can be used to monitor disk input and output. Performance Monitor has more detailed results, while Task Manager provides only a few basic counters. *See "Using Monitoring Tools."*

2 **B.** Virtual memory is created by using a page file, which resides on a hard drive. Disk caching uses memory to cache data from the hard drive. *Review "Virtual memory."*

3 **C.** Virtual memory settings are managed through the System Control Panel. *Check out "Virtual memory."*

4 **B, D.** Two things that can be done to speed up disk access are defragmenting your hard drive and changing to disks that have faster bus architectures. *Peruse "Hard drive."*

5 **D.** There is no specific area of RAM that is used for caching printer data. *Take a look at "Printers."*

6 **D.** Increasing the size of the page file will not provide a performance benefit. *Peek at "Optimization Best Practices."*

Chapter 4: Using Windows-Based Troubleshooting Utilities

Exam Objectives

✔ Managing Registry data with `regedit.exe` and `regedt32.exe`

✔ Working with system and disk management tools

This chapter is all about Windows-based troubleshooting utilities. These utilities fall into categories such as disk maintenance, configuration, diagnostic, and the ever-popular miscellaneous category. One major utility topic covered in this chapter is Registry-editing utilities. I examine this component thoroughly because this topic is often neglected. The content that you examine for Registry editing is more detailed than what you need for the exam; when you finish this book, you'll have a great grasp on the capabilities of the Registry editing tools.

As a CompTIA A+ Certified Professional, you will be called on from time to time to use the tools that are discussed in this chapter. So, in addition to knowing this content for the exam, you need to understand these tools to do your job as a support professional.

Understanding Operating System Utilities for Disk Maintenance

In this section, you examine different utilities that you can use to perform disk maintenance on your system. These utilities include `fdisk` and Disk Management, `defrag`, and `chkdsk`. Each of these utilities serves a specific purpose for your operating system.

diskpart.exe and Disk Management

Before you can store any data on your disk, you need to prepare the disk for use. You can use the `diskpart.exe` utility to prepare your disk to hold data if you are using the Windows Recovery Console, or you can use Disk Management (`diskmgmt.msc`) if you are in Windows.

Data is stored on a disk in a partition, and that partition is assigned a drive letter. Because of decisions made when early computer disks were created, you are allowed to create only four partitions on a disk, and a table was created in the disk's BIOS to hold the partitioning information. The partition table has only four entries in it. The solution to the four-partition limit was to create a special partition, which is always stored in the last partition. This special partition is an *extended partition,* and it is designed to extend the number of drive letters you can associate with a drive. Remember that this is four, the same as the number of partitions. The extended partition does not have a drive letter associated with it, but rather allows you to create any number of logical drives within it, each of which do have drive letters.

Windows allows you to use either tool to manage your drives, either diskpart.exe or Disk Management, which is a *snap-in,* or a tool component for the Microsoft Management Console (MMC). Disk Management is fully covered in Book II, Chapter 5.

Knowing your way around diskpart.exe is still important because you may have to resort to using diskpart.exe to prepare a drive to store data during a Recovery Console session or to perform certain tasks that Disk Management does not support, such as extending a primary partition on a drive. In order to boot, a hard drive requires that one of its primary partitions be made active. Each partition that you create can then be formatted with a file system. Each file system has a maximum partition size, and Windows may have some imposed limits on top of that.

Each primary partition or logical drive that appears on your computer is still limited to the size specified by the file system that you use on it. FAT16 drives are limited to 2GB, and FAT32 drives are limited to 2TB.

You can boot only from an active partition, so if you don't set up an active partition on a new drive, you will not be able to boot from that drive.

If you use Disk Management, you can create up to four primary partitions on each drive. If you want to create an extended partition, you can create only three primary partitions. You also have the option of updating your disk to a *Dynamic Disk,* which eliminates the traditional limits to partition table entries by maintaining its own partitioning information in a separate location on the disk.

Dynamic Disks do not have as many recovery tools as traditional Basic Disks and are compatible only with Windows 2000 and newer Microsoft operating systems (Oses). Because of this recoverability aspect, you should avoid using Dynamic Disks unless they are necessary for your disk configurations.

In the Disk Management utility (see Figure 4-1), the entire contents of the disk partitioning scheme are visible in the display, and you are given control over the drive letters that are assigned.

Book VI
Chapter 4

Using
Windows-Based
Troubleshooting
Utilities

Figure 4-1:
Disk
Manage-
ment is
more user-
friendly
than `disk`
`part.exe`.

defrag.exe and dfrg.msc

In this section, I discuss only the defragmentation options available to you in Windows because you will be tested only on the concepts of defragmentation or on the methods used to defragment disks within Windows.

As you write data to your hard drive, it is always written into the largest area of available free space. When you delete files, though, areas of free space become broken up and scattered around your drive. Sometimes the largest area of free space is not large enough to hold the data being written. When this happens, the file is broken up into pieces — *fragmented* — to the areas of free space.

To "repair" the disk fragmentation, you can use `dfrg.msc` or `defrag.exe`:

 ✦ `dfrg.msc` is the graphical defragmentation tool for Windows.

 ✦ `defrag.exe` is a command line front end for the same tool.

Both tools for Windows XP are shown in Figure 4-2. `dfrg.msc` for Windows Vista offers a simplified user interface. If you want to create a batch file or script to defragment your hard drive, you want to look at `defrag.exe`.

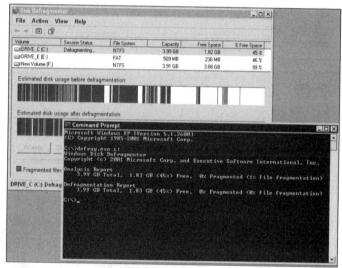

Figure 4-2:
You have two interfaces to choose from to defragment your drives.

Defragmentation requires free space to do its job because it copies the files to new locations before removing them from the old locations. In addition to making all files contiguous, defragmentation attempts to consolidate most free space into a single unit, reducing how often new files are fragmented.

While the defragmentation process takes place, all files on your drive are read, and the system is checked for errors, in the same manner as `chkdsk.exe` (discussed in the next section).

Because the disk fragmentation utility rearranges the data on your drive and can therefore improve performance, it should be run periodically to ensure maximum performance of your computer. How you define "periodically" depends upon your system and how you use it. If your hard drive is extremely full (containing perhaps only a few gigabytes of free space), you should run `defrag.exe` as often as every few days. Comparatively, if you have a large amount of free space on your drive, files will take longer to become fragmented on your disk, and you might need to defragment your drive only once every month or two.

To open the graphical disk defragmenter, choose Start⇨All Programs⇨ Accessories⇨System Tools⇨Disk Defragmenter. When you select a drive and then click the Analyze button, the defragmenter recommends whether you need to defragment your drive. If you have noticed a degradation in

performance, though, go ahead and defragment your drive. (Select a drive and click the Defragment button.) There is no harm in defragmenting your drive even if the computer says you don't need to; you might still increase the computer's performance.

You can use Scheduled Tasks to regularly run disk defragmentation in Windows XP; Windows Vista has scheduling built right into dfrg.msc. I cover scheduling tasks in the "Miscellaneous Utilities" section of this chapter.

Free space and disk performance should be monitored to achieve an optimal level of performance.

Book VI
Chapter 4

Using
Windows-Based
Troubleshooting
Utilities

chkdsk.exe (Check Disk)

The chkdsk.exe utility can identify potential problems with either your file system's allocation table or index, or the physical hard drive. chkdsk.exe can be run from the command line or from the Tools tab of your disk drives' Properties. It has several options, of which the most important are

+ /F: Fixes errors found on the disk, rather than just identifying them

+ /R: Relocates bad sectors and recovers readable information

+ /X: Forces a dismount of the volume, which closes all open files

If you suspect that you have a disk problem, you should run a scan of your disk. However, because fixing errors requires exclusive access to the disk, you want to run chkdsk.exe in scan-only mode, which is the default. If errors are detected, then you would want to specify /F and /X to correct any errors that are identified.

The system volume (C:) cannot be dismounted, so chkdsk.exe offers to schedule the scan during the next reboot of the system. On a system with a large C: drive, and depending on the number of errors, this scan can be very time consuming. The results of a scan can be seen Figure 4-3.

Figure 4-3:
Standard
scans
check the
structure
of the file
tables.

```
C:\>chkdsk.exe C:
The type of the file system is NTFS.
Volume label is DRIVE_C.

WARNING!  F parameter not specified.
Running CHKDSK in read-only mode.

CHKDSK is verifying files (stage 1 of 3)...
File verification completed.
CHKDSK is verifying indexes (stage 2 of 3)...
Index verification completed.
CHKDSK is verifying security descriptors (stage 3 of 3)...
Security descriptor verification completed.
CHKDSK is verifying Usn Journal...
Usn Journal verification completed.
Correcting errors in the Volume Bitmap.
Windows found problems with the file system.
Run CHKDSK with the /F (fix) option to correct these.

  41B4900 KB total disk space.
  2218224 KB in 14670 files.
     3772 KB in 952 indexes.
        0 KB in bad sectors.
    45396 KB in use by the system.
    22976 KB occupied by the log file.
  1917508 KB available on disk.

     4096 bytes in each allocation unit.
  1046225 total allocation units on disk.
   479377 allocation units available on disk.

C:\>
```

In addition to issues with directory index entries and Master File Table (MFT) problems, `chkdsk.exe` looks for cross-linked files and orphaned directory entries or lost file fragments. The File Allocation Table (FAT) contains a pointer to the starting cluster for each file. As the file is read, a pointer at the end of each cluster identifies where the next cluster of the file can be found, with the last cluster of the file not containing a further pointer. From time to time, the pointer at the end of a cluster becomes corrupted and starts pointing to the wrong location for the next bit of data. If the new location already contains file data (which contains a pointer to the next bit of data for a second file), you end up with two files using the same set of clusters.

When two files point to the same cluster (and clusters that follow), the situation is known as a *cross-linked file*. Depending on your outlook, you may choose to make copies of these files or to ignore them altogether. If you are a pessimist, you probably believe that both of these files are corrupt and probably garbage. If you are an optimist, you probably believe that one or both of these files are still readable and usable. There is no harm in having Check Disk create the files because your worst case scenario will be that the files are of no use.

File fragments or lost chains, on the other hand, tend to be the leftover portions of cross-linked files (the portions of a file that would have belonged to a file had its clusters not been corrupted or lost). You have the option of either deleting these file fragments or converting them to files. If you choose to convert them to files, each chain is saved to the root directory with a name following the format `filennnn.chk` with an incremental number in place of the *nnnn*.

Although you have the option to convert lost file fragments to files, I have yet to see useful data recovered from file fragments, so you might as well delete them and free the space.

`chkdsk.exe` serves an important purpose on your system by ensuring data integrity of the files on your disk, and it should be scheduled to run periodically on important volumes because some disk corruption can be prevented if identified early.

Configuration Utilities

This section discusses many of the configuration utilities that ship with the Windows OS. These utilities provide easy ways to modify configuration files and the Registry.

System Configuration utility

The System Configuration utility (see Figure 4-4) is one of the newer utilities for maintaining settings on your Windows computer. To launch System Configuration, run `msconfig.exe`. This utility can change many aspects of your system startup. To use this utility, you need to be a member of the computer's Administrators group.

Figure 4-4: The initial window for System Configuration allows you to modify the basic system files.

**Book VI
Chapter 4**

Using
Windows-Based
Troubleshooting
Utilities

The six tabs in the Windows XP version of this utility allow you to launch the System Restore utility, expand files, perform selective boots, modify the loaded drivers in `system.ini` and `win.ini`, change the boot options in `boot.ini`, and change the services and applications that are loaded at boot time.

Even though the Windows Vista version has only five tabs (General, Boot, Services, Startup, and Tools), it offers similar functionality to the Windows XP version.

Use System Configuration to do the following:

✦ Create custom startup configurations (for troubleshooting)

✦ Perform a selective startup, which processes only some of the system files

✦ Edit `boot.ini`, `system.ini`, and `win.ini` files

✦ Expand operating system files from the OS CD

✦ Disable services or programs that have been added to the Run key of the Registry

All the changes in the preceding bulleted list can be accomplished from within a simple Windows user interface, making System Configuration an easy configuration tool to work with.

If you suspect that a computer problem is related to one of the components loaded at startup, this is the tool you want to use. If you can boot into Safe Mode but not perform a normal boot, you can use this tool to select which components you want to load on reboot. By disabling components, you should be able to narrow down which component is causing the problem, by performing multiple boots with different combinations of the items selected.

regedit.exe

If you have ever talked to anybody about the system Registry, you have probably been given a stern warning that this is not a place for the timid. The reason for this warning is that the Registry stores system-wide configuration information for almost all services on your computer. If you experience major problems with the Registry, you will likely have major problems with your entire computer.

In Windows 3.1, the Registry only held information about file associations. With the creation of Windows 9*x*, Windows NT, and more recent Windows OSes, the Registry now stores key information about all system services.

The Windows Registry has five major subtrees, as shown in Figure 4-5:

+ HKEY_CLASSES_ROOT contains information about all the file associations and registered file types that exist in your computer. This information is actually a copy of the information stored in the HKEY_Local_Machine\software\classes key.

+ HKEY_CURRENT_USER contains a subset of the information that is found in HKEY_USERS key, but contains only the information related to the current user. This key contains configuration information for the currently logged-on user. This information includes items such as Control Panel settings (including mouse acceleration and screensaver preferences) and user-related software settings for installed applications.

+ HKEY_LOCAL_MACHINE contains information about your computer. This information includes configuration information for hardware components and system settings for all software on the computer.

+ HKEY_USERS contains information for the currently logged-on user, as well as information for the default user and all other users who are logged onto the computer.

+ HKEY_CURRENT_CONFIG contains settings that are dynamically rebuilt on every boot of the computer, which is mainly composed of Plug and Play information.

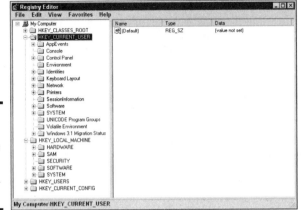

Figure 4-5:
Settings in
the Registry
cover most
aspects of
the system.

**Book VI
Chapter 4**

Using
Windows-Based
Troubleshooting
Utilities

Of these subtrees, you really need to worry about only two: HKEY_CURRENT_
USER and HKEY_LOCAL_MACHINE. The information in the other subtrees is
either duplicated within these two subtrees or the data cannot be modified.

All Registry entries are stored in a hierarchical tree. This tree contains sev-
eral subfolders: *keys.* If you want to create new keys within the Registry,
use the Edit➪New➪Key command. Every key within the Registry can store
values. The Registry Editor contains five different types of values (as shown
in Figure 4-6):

✦ String

✦ Binary

✦ DWORD

✦ Multi-String

✦ Expandable String

Figure 4-6:
There are
five basic
data types
for the
Windows
Registry.

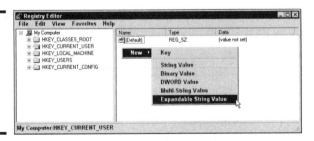

Some hardware components or software components that you can install on
your computer may create entries inside both HKEY_LOCAL_MACHINE and

HKEY_CURRENT_USER. This makes sense if you think about applications like Microsoft Office. Microsoft Office creates entries in HKEY_LOCAL_MACHINE that relate to the location of Office components on the particular computer, such as the spell checker that can be found within C:\Program Files\ Microsoft Office\Tools. At the same time, Microsoft Office installs entries in HKEY_CURRENT_USER that relate to the user configuration on the system. *User-related settings* are items such as the default Save As file type in Microsoft Word.

The Registry is an important part of your computer, and great care should be taken not to corrupt this database. Before you start doing any procedure that involves the Registry, make sure you have a clean backup of the Registry. You can create this backup in a variety of ways, such as by exporting the Registry, by creating a System State backup, or by physically copying the files that make up the Registry.

To copy the files that make up the Registry, you need to know where the files actually are. HKEY_CURRENT_USER, the user portion of the Registry, can be found in your user profile directory. It will be named NTuser. dat. HKEY_LOCAL_MACHINE is actually composed of several files that are found in the Winnt or Windows directory. These files should be backed up and restored by using the Windows backup program. Windows 2000 has a backup utility to create an Emergency Repair Disk, which can restore your Registry; with Windows XP and Windows Vista, you can perform a System State backup or a Full backup.

Rather than backing up the entire Registry, though, you can be more selective and back up and restore individual keys within the Registry by using the Registry Editor.

To back up individual keys, follow these steps:

1. **Choose Start⇨Run.**

2. **Type** regedit **in the Run dialog box that appears.**

3. **Click the key that you want to back up.**

 This highlights the key.

4. **Choose File⇨Export.**

 The Export Registry File dialog box appears, as shown in Figure 4-7. This dialog box looks similar to a standard Save As dialog box, with the addition of the Export Range panel at the bottom. The Export Range panel contains your selected branch within the Registry by default.

5. **Type a name for the file and choose a location for** regedit **to save it.**

6. **Click Save.**

 The file is given the default .reg extension.

**Book VI
Chapter 4**

Using
Windows-Based
Troubleshooting
Utilities

Figure 4-7:
Export
sections of
the Registry
as backup
prior to
editing.

Files that end in the `.reg` extension are Registry export files that you can
edit with a text editor (as shown in Figure 4-8). REG files share the same basic
structure as an INI file, which I introduce in Book V, Chapter 6. To import a
REG file into the Registry, just double-click the file. To help prevent acciden-
tal importing of Registry files, Windows has added a safety feature: Windows
prompts you to confirm that you would like to import the settings into your
Registry, as shown in Figure 4-9. After you import the settings, a dialog box
confirms that a file has been successfully merged into your Registry.

Figure 4-8:
All Registry
export files
share a
structure
that
resembles
INI files.

Figure 4-9:
Heed the
confirmation
to limit
accidental
imports.

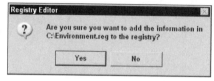

Registry Editor

? Are you sure you want to add the information in
C:\Environment.reg to the registry?

Yes No

On Windows computers, REG files are automatically imported into your Registry if you double-click them. Rather than using the `.reg` extension on your files, you may choose to use TXT files. Files with the `.txt` extension can also be imported into your Registry by using `regedit.exe` *file-name*`.txt` at the command line.

Periodically, REG files become corrupted from being edited with certain text editors, such as Notepad. This corruption occurs because some text editors add extended (invisible) characters into the text file that are not compatible with `regedit.exe`. The only editor that does not exhibit this behavior is `edit.com`. If you have a corrupted file, you can fix it by opening the file through `edit.com`, resaving the file, and closing. Even if the file is corrupt, you still receive a dialog box stating the information has been successfully entered into your Registry, as shown in Figure 4-10.

Figure 4-10:
A successful
Registry
import.

Registry Editor

i Information in C:\Environment.reg has been successfully entered
into the registry.

OK

regedt32.exe

The `regedt32.exe` program is the Registry Editor for Windows NT and Windows 2000 (but not Windows XP or newer Windows OSes). Most of the user interface for `regedt32.exe` is still based on the Windows NT 3.51 user interface. Thus, many of the windows have a Windows 3.0 look and feel to them (see Figure 4-11). The `regedt32.exe` program supports many features not available in `regedit.exe`, including

✦ Viewing and setting permissions on Registry keys

✦ Loading and unloading Registry *hives* (Registry files on your hard drive)

With Windows XP and newer Windows OSes, all features of `regedt32` have been incorporated into `regedit.exe`. If you run `regedt32`, `regedit.exe` will launch, instead.

Book VI
Chapter 4

Using
Windows-Based
Troubleshooting
Utilities

Figure 4-11:
regedt32
sports the
Windows
3.0 user
interface.

When you work with Windows XP and newer Windows OSes, you can use regedit.exe to connect to a remote Registry, which allows you to change the Registry settings on a remote computer without having to leave your own computer. To connect to a remote Registry from across the network, choose Registry⇨Connect Network Registry.

One big advantage of the Registry Editor is that you can load Registry hives. This capability becomes useful when you want to modify the entries for the default ntuser.dat. The default ntuser.dat is used as a template to create new user profiles for users who do not yet have a profile. You can find the ntuser.dat file for this default template account in C:\ Documents and Settings\Default User\NTUSER.DAT or C:\Users\ Default User\NTUSER.DAT, and you can load this subtree or hive into regedit.exe and edit the settings for this default template.

Do not confuse this default user template with the default user in use prior to a user logging on to your computer. The Registry settings for the pre-logon default user are actually found in the Registry under HKEY_USERS\. DEFAULT.

Another thing that you do with the Registry Editor is manage the security on Registry keys. To view or modify the security settings on a Registry key, first select the key and then choose Security⇨Permissions. You can work with permissions on Registry keys only — not on Registry values.

To allow for command line editing of the Registry, Microsoft introduced reg.exe as a standard component of Windows XP and newer Windows OSes. This allows for loading and unloading of Registry hives as well as editing Registry keys and values.

Lab 4-1 will have you export your current desktop settings into a file, and create a Registry file that is used to change wallpaper settings. Lab 4-2 will modify desktop settings for the user environment that is in effect when no users are logged on. This is the wallpaper and color scheme that you see behind the logon screen. Lab 4-1 and Lab 4-2 can be found in the Labs.pdf file in the Author directory of the CD-ROM.

Device Manager

Device Manager is covered in more depth in Book VI, Chapter 1. The primary job of Device Manager is, appropriately enough, managing devices. You can access Device Manager by clicking the Device Manager button on the Hardware tab of the System Properties window. Use Device Manager to remove devices from your system, configure drivers, configure hardware resources, and manage hardware profile settings.

In Device Manager, you can easily pick out the devices with hardware problems because they sport a red X on the icon in the device tree. The red X identifies devices that are in conflict or are disabled. A yellow exclamation mark identifies devices that are not properly configured (as shown in Figure 4-12). You can use Device Manager to identify problems with your hardware; configure the drivers for the devices; and configure hardware resources, such as IRQs and I/O addresses.

Figure 4-12: When looking for malfunctioning devices, look for the warning symbols like the one next to USB Device.

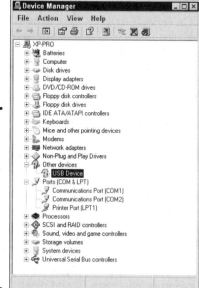

Computer Management

Windows includes the Computer Management utility, shown in Figure 4-13. Computer Management is actually more of a user interface to a number of other utilities than an actual utility. Computer Management is a MMC settings file that contains the following utilities or snap-ins:

✦ **Event Viewer:** Shows the contents of event log files

✦ **Shared Folders:** Shows the status of shared or published folders on the computer

✦ **Local Users and Groups:** Manages the local account database

✦ **Performance Logs and Alerts or Reliability and Performance:** Records system status and health based on measurable counters and generates alerts when the counters exceed threshold values

✦ **Device Manager:** Displays hardware status and configuration information in a format that can be edited, unlike the System Information Tool

See the upcoming section, "The System Information Tool."

✦ **Disk Management:** Manages disk partitions

✦ **Disk Defragmenter:** Optimizes disk performance by defragmenting files

✦ **Removable Storage Management:** Manages and tracks removable media on your computer, such as CD-ROMs and magnetic tapes

✦ **Task Scheduler:** Manages and schedules tasks or applications to run automatically

✦ **Services:** Manages system services (such as the Server and Workstation services) on the local computer

✦ **Other administration utilities:** Other tools are included with this tool, including Telephony, WMI Control, Indexing Service, DNS, Internet Information Services, and Routing and Remote Access

Computer Management is an MMC snap-in that acts as a container for other MMC snap-ins. Its only offering or benefit over the individual tools is that you have to add only one snap-in to the MMC, rather than a whole series.

By putting all these utilities together in one location, system management is made substantially easier for most users.

Figure 4-13: Computer Management is your one-stop shop for system management utilities.

In addition to using Computer Management to view and manage your computer, you can manage a remote computer:

1. **Right-click Computer Management (Local) at the top of the tree in the left-hand pane.**

2. **Choose Connect to Another Computer.**

This opens the Select Computer dialog box, from which you can type the name of another computer on the network.

3. **Click OK.**

After you are connected to that other computer, you can use all the management tools, with the exception of the Disk Defragmenter, which operates only on the local computer.

Lab 4-3 walks you through creating a custom Computer Management MMC. Lab 4-3 can be found in the Labs.pdf file in the Author directory of the CD-ROM.

Getting a Handle on Diagnostic Utilities

To figure out what is wrong with a faulty computer, you need to first find out everything it is doing, both right and wrong. The tools in the following sections are designed to provide you with information on a variety of areas of your computer.

The System Information tool

The System Information tool (msinfo32.exe) is available in Windows 2000 and Windows XP. This tool was designed to provide information about as many components in the OS as possible. Figure 4-14 should give you a good feel for the type of information that is available within this tool. If it's part of the OS, the System Information tool can give you information about it.

To open the System Information tool, choose Start⇨All Programs⇨ Accessories⇨System Tools⇨System Information Tools.

Book VI
Chapter 4

Using
Windows-Based
Troubleshooting
Utilities

Figure 4-14: The System Information Tool provides information about your installation and hardware configuration.

Microsoft used to use a tool called WinMSD.exe, which showed similar information to that displayed in the System Information tool. If you spend a few minutes investigating the data found in this tool, you will get a feel for the very detailed information it can provide. Very few areas of your system's hardware are not covered by this tool. It is well worth your time to get to know this tool to see what information it can gather.

If you want to save the current system information for archiving or to use as a baseline, choose File⇨Save to save the information into an NFO file, which can later be opened and viewed with the System Information tool.

In addition to the information that this tool provides, the Tools menu gives you links to other common tools that you might want to run, such as Net Diagnostics, System Restore, File Signature Verification Utility, DirectX Diagnostics Tool, and Dr. Watson.

Event Viewer

On some computers, you can check log files to look for errors with the system, applications, or hardware. Microsoft created a central logging and reporting tool that many components in the OS and many applications use. Any application can log events to the event logs or even create its own event logs to be viewed with the Event Viewer (the tool you use to view all this logged information) as well as configure log settings or clear the logs.

To view information, choose Start⇨Control Panels⇨Administrative Tools⇨Event Viewer. The interface has the log files on the left of the screen and the log data on the right. There are five different log entry types and three default logs: System, Application, and Security.

The Security log has two event types: either a lock or a key for Failures or Successes. The other two logs have three different entry types — Information, Warning, and Error — identifiable by symbol or color (blue, yellow, and red, respectively). To view log files on another computer, right-click Event Viewer (Local) in the left pane, and choose Connect to Another Computer from the shortcut menu. This opens the Select Computer dialog box, where you can type another computer name and then click OK.

Figure 4-15 shows a typical System log. The Security log has audit information about your system if you have enabled auditing of system events or file system access. The System log records major system events, such as service failures, system startup or shutdown, and Stop events. The Application log records events from applications although you might find that some applications record their events in the System log, and some items thought of as system events are recorded in the Application log.

Figure 4-15: The System log has several types of messages telling you about major system events.

To see detailed information about the log entries, double-click any line item to bring up something that resembles Figure 4-16, listing date and time, source (system area or application), type of event, event ID (the error code returned by the application), user (if related to a user account), computer (if related to a computer account), a text-based description of the error, and data (which might show raw data related to the event as hexadecimal and ASCII data).

Read the Description section carefully because many developers put troubleshooting steps right into their error events.

**Book VI
Chapter 4**

**Using
Windows-Based
Troubleshooting
Utilities**

Figure 4-16:
The detailed information for an event gives you several relevant pieces of information.

To navigate to the next or previous events, use the arrows in the right side of the dialog box; to copy all event information to the Clipboard, use the button with the sheet of paper on it (or the Copy button if you are using Windows Vista). You can then directly paste this information into a document or e-mail when reporting this event to other support people.

If you can't decipher the event message, you can find additional help at www.eventid.net, which allows you to plug in the EventID and the source. Then you are able to view recorded events and descriptions of both the errors and the fixes. This site also contains links to the Microsoft Knowledge Base for articles related to the errors. To follow the links, you need to register on the EventID site, but because the site provides the Q article numbers (Microsoft's knowledge base has all articles number, with a Q as the initial character in the filename), you can go directly to http://support.microsoft.com and locate the articles yourself.

When you right-click a log file, you have the option to save the event log as a text file or an EVT file, which can be loaded back into Event Viewer, or to clear or empty the event log. The View submenu has options to allow you to find specific entries or filter the log file to show certain events. You can filter the log by any of the field values.

To change how long the log files are kept, right-click a log file and choose Properties. The default log file size is 512KB but can be set all the way up to 4194240K (4GB), and settings are available on what to do when the log reaches its maximum size. When it reaches its maximum size, you can over-write events as needed, overwrite events older than a number of days (the default is seven days), or not clear the events at all (in which case, you stop logging new events).

In most cases, you should use Overwrite Events Older Than X Days and choose a number of days for which normal activity will not fill the log file. This system means that you can ignore the logging activity, but you will be notified when the log file fills up, and you can start your investigation into the activity that filled it prematurely. I typically leave this setting between 7 and 14 days, and make the size of the log file larger if necessary.

Network Diagnostics

Use the Network Diagnostics tool to test and report on overall system health, with specific focus on the network. This tool is only part the Windows XP Help and Support Center, but the easiest way to access it is through the System Information tool. Choose Start⇨All Programs⇨Accessories⇨System Tools⇨System Information. When the System Information window opens, choose Tools⇨Net Diagnostics. After you run a scan of your computer, the reported results are broken into three categories:

✦ **Internet Services section:** Reports on Outlook Express and Internet Explorer settings

✦ **Computer Information section:** Reports on the same general information that is reported via the System Information tool

✦ **Modems and Network Adapters section:** Reports on the settings and status of your modems, network adapters, and network clients after a series of tests

To save a copy of the findings, click the Save to File button. The report will be saved to both your desktop and here:

```
C:\Windows\pchealth\helpctr\system\netdiag\Netdiag <Date> <Time>.htm
```

This is just another tool that you can use to gather information to diagnose problems.

Dr. Watson

Dr. Watson is used to gather information about application crashes, which can be used by application developers to help diagnose errors, so you will use this information only when you're working with an application developer. To launch Dr. Watson, choose Start⇨Run and type **drwtsn32.exe**. If you have been using another debugger for your applications, you can make Dr. Watson the default debugger by running `drwtsn32 -i`.

Within Dr. Watson, you can specify the locations for log files and crash dump files. *Crash dump files* are similar to the binary log files that are created during a Stop error, but they capture only the memory data related to the crashed application. The capture configuration for Dr. Watson includes the number of instructions and errors to save that defines the range of data around the error that is captured. Just like Stop errors, you have the option to save full or mini logs, and the choice here depends on which debugging tools the developer is planning to use.

Full logs are larger and contain all the information that the developer could want captured. However, if the developer is using only a small amount of that data, the mini dump might include enough data to resolve the problems with the application. Mini dump files are much smaller in size, which will make them easier to send the developer.

A Dr. Watson error log has information in the following categories:

- ✦ **Application error statement:** Includes the date, application name, and exception number
- ✦ **System information:** Related to the computer that was running the application
- ✦ **Task list:** Includes all running processes, like the Task Manager would list
- ✦ **Module list:** Includes the memory addresses of DLL files and drivers
- ✦ **Memory and state dump information:** In a variety of formats for each referenced thread

System File Checker

The System File Checker (`sfc.exe`) is part of the Windows File Protection interface and must be run by an Administrator. With the proliferation of applications and with software developers replacing stock Microsoft DLL files with custom versions, there is a real need for Windows File Protection and the System File Checker.

Book VI
Chapter 4

Using
Windows-Based
Troubleshooting
Utilities

DLL (Dynamic Link Library) files contain compiled application code that is the same type of code that makes up an application. By saving this code as a DLL, the developer makes the code available to many applications so that it can be reused, reducing application development time. One dialog box found in a system DLL is the common Save As dialog box.

Windows keeps the cached copies of these files for your use when corruption occurs in the original files. To illustrate this feature, you can delete both `c:\windows\system32\freecell.exe` and `c:\windows\system32\cards.dll`. By the time you have the second file deleted, you should see that the first file has already been replaced. The missing copy of the file has been replaced by the copy that was stored in the cache in `%systemroot%\system32\dllcache`. If the file was not in the cache, Windows would have prompted you for the OS CD.

When you run the System File Checker, you have a choice of switches that you can use:

- `/SCANNOW`: Immediately scans all files for incorrect versions and verifies the versions that are stored in the cache
- `/SCANONCE`: Scans all files on the next boot
- `/SCANBOOT`: Scans all files at every boot
- `/REVERT`: Changes `sfc.exe` to its default settings
- `/PURGECACHE`: Purges the file cache to allow it to be rebuilt
- `/CACHESIZE=x`: Sets the size, in megabytes, of the file cache

Miscellaneous Utilities

A number of miscellaneous utilities are also available within Windows. The following sections take a look at some of them.

Task Scheduler

The system Task Scheduler service is responsible for running scheduled tasks. This service (like all services) runs in the background — and in this case, making sure that your tasks are performed at the times you planned.

Your interface to this service is found via Start➪All Programs➪Accessories➪System Tools➪Scheduled Tasks (or Task Scheduler with Vista), which opens the Scheduled Tasks folder.

To schedule a task, follow these steps:

1. **Double-click Add Schedule Task.**

2. **In the Scheduled Task Wizard that opens, click Next to continue.**

You will be presented with a list of applications to chose from and a Browse button to find and to select applications not listed.

3. **Select an application that you want to execute and then click Next.**

4. **Type a name for the task and then select the scheduled interval for the task, which includes**

- Daily

- Weekly

- Monthly

- One Time Only

- When My Computer Starts

- When I Log On

5. **Click Next.**

Depending on your schedule interval, you will be presented with different scheduling times.

6. **Specify the exact times you want the task to run; then click Next.**

7. **Type the user credentials that you want the Task Scheduler to use when running the task — the user credentials will require appropriate rights to perform the actions you want performed — then click Next.**

You are now on the last screen of the wizard. You can choose to view the Advanced properties for the task, which include the settings already discussed for this wizard, as well as these:

- Do not run the task if you have a laptop running on batteries.

- Maximum duration for the task to run.

- Run the task only if the computer is idle, and stop the job when the computer is no longer idle.

8. **If you do not want to view these settings, just click Finish; otherwise, select the Open Advanced Properties for the Task When I Click Finish check box, and then click Finish.**

When you exit the wizard, you will see the new task in the Scheduled Tasks folder. To see the properties for any task, select the task and right-click Properties. From the properties window of the task, you can adjust the command line options for the application scheduled to run and also change the schedule or the advanced options that were mentioned during the wizard.

**Book VI
Chapter 4**

**Using
Windows-Based
Troubleshooting
Utilities**

If you do not want to wait for the schedule but rather have the task run immediately, select the task, right-click it, and choose Run from the shortcut menu. You will see the status of the job change to Running. The other information shown in the Scheduled Tasks folder includes

◆ When the task is scheduled to run next

◆ When the task last ran

◆ The status or what error code was returned the last time the task was run

0x0 is the standard code for a successful execution.

Windows Script Host

Windows Script Host (`wscript.exe` and `cscript.exe`) is a utility that doesn't fit easily into any other categories. Windows Script Host is used to execute Visual Basic Script (VBScript) or JavaScript. The tasks that you are able to accomplish by using VBScript are numerous and almost unlimited. Most Windows-based applications support ActiveX automation and can be controlled through VBScript. You can use Windows Script Host to execute such scripts.

Windows Script Host has two components that can execute script:

◆ `wscript.exe`: Executes VBScript from within the Windows environment

◆ `cscript.exe`: Executes scripts from the command prompt

Both utilities are interpreters for VBScript. If the scripts were converted into true Visual Basic and compiled into executables, you would achieve much better performance.

Windows Script Host was introduced to the OS with Windows 98 and is included with all current versions of Windows. To get code samples or information about using Windows Script Host, visit `http://msdn.microsoft.com/scripting`. You can also get scripting information from the Hey, Scripting Guy! site through `www.microsoft.com/technet/scriptcenter/learnit.mspx` or `www.microsoft.com/technet/scriptcenter/default.mspx`.

Lab 4-4 has you create a few simple scripts using Windows Script Host. Lab 4-4 can be found in the `Labs.pdf` file in the Author directory of the CD-ROM.

edit.com

The `edit.com` program allows you to modify the contents of text files. I cover `edit.com` in detail in Book V, Chapter 5. The version of `edit.com` that ships with Windows XP and newer Windows OSes includes some enhancements over the original version that ships with MS-DOS. The two largest enhancements are the capability to

✦ Open multiple files

✦ Use standard Windows shortcut keys for Cut, Copy, and Paste operations

expand.exe

Book VI
Chapter 4

**Using
Windows-Based
Troubleshooting
Utilities**

You can use the command line `expand.exe` utility to expand individual source files shipped in a compressed format on your OS CD, for all Windows OSes. This utility can be used to replace corrupt files being used by the OS.

Files that have been compressed for expansion with `expand.exe` are found on your OS CD with the last letter of their filenames replaced with an underscore, or they are compressed as CAB files.

Common tasks you might use expand include

✦ **Viewing the names of all files in a CAB file,** such as seeing the names of all GIF files contained in `iis6.cab` file on the Windows XP Installation CD, where `D:` is the drive letter of the CD drive that contains the Windows XP installation CD:

```
expand.exe -D D:\i386\iis6.cab -F:*.gif
```

✦ **Extracting a file from a CAB file,** such as extracting the `IIS_winxp.gif` file from the `iis6.cab` file to the root of the `C:` drive:

```
expand.exe D:\i386\iis6.cab -F:IIS_winxp.gif C:\
```

✦ **Expanding a compressed file** — for example, extracting a fresh copy of the Freecell Help file to the root of the `C:` drive:

```
expand.exe D:\i386\freecell.ch_ c:\freecell.chm
```

Lab 4-5 gives you some practice using this command line. Lab 4-5 can be found in the `Labs.pdf` file in the Author directory of the CD-ROM.

Getting an A+

This chapter examines several Windows-based utilities. You find out about the following:

+ Disk maintenance programs, such as `fdisk`, `defrag`, and `chkdsk`, are used to improve performance and reliability of the disk subsystem.

+ Configuration utilities, such as the System Configuration utility, System Information tool, Registry editors, Registry scanners, Device Manager, and the Computer Management Console are used to view or change Windows configuration settings.

+ `edit.com` can be used to create or modify text files when `notepad.exe` or other editors are not available or appropriate.

+ `expand.exe` can be used to decompress Windows XP source files.

Prep Test

1 `defrag.exe` does what for your computer?

A ○ Rearranges memory so that access to it is improved

B ○ Removes dust and fragments from your computer

C ○ Rearranges data on your disk drive so that access to it is improved

D ○ Recovers files that have been corrupted

2 `chkdsk.exe` can do which of the following?

A ○ Rearrange data on your drive so that disk access is faster

B ○ Consolidate free space on your hard drive

C ○ Correct problems with file storage on your hard drive

D ○ Change the partition table of the drive from FAT16 to FAT32

3 What programs can be used to edit the Registry on a Windows XP computer?

A ○ `registry.exe`

B ○ `cfgedit.exe`

C ○ `regedt32.exe`

D ○ `regedit.exe`

4 What command is used to export a section of your Registry while using `regedit.exe`?

A ○ Registry⇨Export Registry File

B ○ Registry⇨Extract to Recovery File

C ○ Export⇨Set Restore Options

D ○ Registry⇨Backup Key

5 What tool should you use to change an exported Registry file?

A ○ `sysedit.exe`

B ○ `regedit.exe`

C ○ `edit.com`

D ○ Microsoft Word

6 Which files on your hard drive make up the Windows XP Registry?

A ○ `system.dat` and `registry.dat`

B ○ `user.dat` and `system.dat`

C ○ `user.dat` and `hardware.dat`

D ○ `system`, `sam`, `security`, and `ntuser.dat`

7 Which operating system uses `regedt32.exe`?

A ○ MS-DOS

B ○ Windows 95

C ○ Windows 98

D ○ Windows 2000

8 You need to find out which memory addresses are being used by a driver. What tool will tell you what you need to know?

A ○ `memedit.exe`

B ○ System Resource Meter

C ○ Device Manager

D ○ System Driver Checker

9 You need to automate a procedure on your computer. What tools could you use?

A ○ `wscript.exe`

B ○ `ScriptIt.exe`

C ○ `config.sys`

D ○ Local ASP

10 You need to automate the process of copying information from a Microsoft Excel spreadsheet into a Microsoft Word document. What tools could you use?

A ○ `wscript.exe`

B ○ `ScriptIt.exe`

C ○ `config.sys`

D ○ Local ASP

11 What is the name of the command-line version of Windows Script Host?

A ○ `ComScript.exe`

B ○ `wscript.exe`

C ○ `cmscript.exe`

D ○ `cscript.exe`

12 You need to create a new Visual Basic script for Windows Script Host. What tool will you use?

A ○ Script Developer

B ○ Script Editor

C ○ Notepad

D ○ Visual Basic Script IDE

13 You need to replace `notepad.exe`, which was accidentally deleted from your Windows XP computer. What command can you use to retrieve a copy from the original CAB files?

A ○ `extract.exe`

B ○ `expand.exe`

C ○ `filerepl.exe`

D ○ `cabget.exe`

14 What command is used to create or modify text files?

A ○ `textedit.com`

B ○ `notepad.com`

C ○ `edit.com`

D ○ `fileedit.com`

15 What command is used to change the partitioning on your hard drive?

A ○ `format.com`

B ○ `cfdisk.exe`

C ○ `diskpart.exe`

D ○ `repart.exe`

Answers

1 **C.** `defrag.exe` rearranges data on your disk so that access to files is faster. By allowing your disk to perform reads of data in contiguous blocks, it takes less time to read files. *See "diskpart.exe and Disk Management."*

2 **C.** `chkdsk.exe` fixes minor problems with files that are stored on your hard drive and can also test and verify the clusters on your drive. *Review "chkdsk.exe (Check Disk)."*

3 **D.** `regedit.exe` is the editor for Windows XP computers. If you are using Windows 2000, you can use either `regedit.exe` or `regedt32.exe`, but with Windows XP, if you run `regedt32.exe`, you will actually open `regedit.exe`. *Peruse "regedit.exe."*

4 **A.** Export Registry File from the Registry menu will export a section of your Registry. *Take a look at "regedit.exe."*

5 **C.** Registry import files must be straight text. Notepad and many other programs that edit text files add different characters to handle carriage returns and line feeds. This can create files that will not be imported through `regedit.exe`. *Peek at "edit.com."*

6 **D.** `system`, `sam`, `security`, and `ntuser.dat`, in addition to software, are the files that make up the Registry. All of the files are found in `<%systemroot%>\system32\config`, with the exception of `ntuser.dat`, which is found in each user's profile directory. *Look over "regedit.exe."*

7 **D.** Only Windows NT, Windows 2000, and Windows XP use `regedt32.exe`. *Study "regedt32.exe."*

8 **C.** Device Manager will tell you what resources are being used by which devices. *Refer to "Device Manager."*

9 **A.** `wscript.exe`, or Windows Script Host, can be used to automate processes. *Examine "Windows Script Host."*

10 **A.** `wscript.exe` can control applications that support ActiveX automation, such as Microsoft Word and Microsoft Excel. *See "Windows Script Host."*

11 **D.** `cscript.exe` is the command line script interpreter. *Review "Windows Script Host."*

12 **C.** Notepad or another text editor can be used to create or edit your Visual Basic scripts. *Check out "Windows Script Host."*

13 **B.** `expand.exe` is used to extract files from the source CAB files, and `expand.exe` can also be used to uncompress the individual source files for Windows XP. *Peruse "expand.exe."*

14 **C.** `edit.com` can be used to create or modify text files. *Take a look at "edit.com."*

15 **C.** `diskpart.exe` is used to change the partition table on your hard drive. *Peek at "diskpart.exe and Disk Management."*

Book VII

Recovering Systems

The 5th Wave By Rich Tennant

"Drive carefully, remember your lunch, and always make a backup of your directory tree before modifying your hard disk partition file."

Contents at a Glance

Chapter 1: Managing Error Codes and Startup Messages

Exam Objectives

✔ Recognizing and resolving common error codes and startup messages

✔ Identifying steps to correct operational problems

✔ Using diagnostic utilities and tools to resolve operational problems

This chapter examines problems common to the Windows environment. Many of these problems occur during the boot process, but a few can occur at any time. I examine boot or startup errors first and then other errors that occur within the OS. The end of the chapter reviews some tools used to help diagnose the cause of the errors.

As an A+ Certified Professional, you will often need to diagnose problems based on error codes and messages from the OS. This chapter introduces you to many common boot or startup error messages that you might see when using Windows. You will also be introduced to the key files required to allow you to boot a computer running Windows.

Windows Boot Files and Boot Errors

Just like older OSes (say, MS-DOS and Windows 9x) suffer from boot problems, so do newer OSes, such as Windows XP and Vista. This section takes a look at some of the boot problems that affect Windows XP computers. These problems will affect all Windows NT–based computers (such as Windows 2000 and Windows Server 2003), and Windows Vista and Windows 2008 Server are slightly different.

The Windows boot process can suffer from boot sector corruption, boot loader problems, and drive identification problems within boot.ini or the BCD. For most problems, the Emergency Repair Process or Recovery Console are reasonable troubleshooting and repair steps. (I discuss the Emergency Repair Process and the Recovery Console in Chapter 3 of this minibook.)

SCSI issues

The `boot.ini` file on your hard drive identifies the controller bus that contains the hard drives in your computer. This controller bus is identified as either SCSI or multi. If your drives are connected to a SCSI controller with the BIOS disabled, the controller is identified as SCSI. In all other circumstances, the controller is identified as multi. If your system is unable to initiate the boot process, or if you receive an error regarding a missing `ntoskrnl.exe`, the problem could be a misidentified SCSI controller. Book V, Chapter 6, has more information about the `boot.ini` file.

No operating system found

The `No operating system found` error in Windows, just like in MS-DOS, is tied to severe corruption of the boot sector on your hard drive. To restore your drive to working condition, perform the Emergency Repair Process to restore the boot sector on your hard drive. The Emergency Repair Process is covered in Book VII, Chapter 3. Minor corruption of the boot files would report missing files, such as `bootmgr`, `winloader.exe`, `ntldr`, or `ntdetect.com`, and the next section will tell you how to deal with missing files. Like with MS-DOS, the `No operating system found` error could be caused by having left a formatted floppy disk with no boot loader in the floppy drive during boot.

Missing boot files

Windows requires several core files to boot, and an optional file. The required files are

+ `ntldr`
+ `ntdetect.com`
+ `boot.ini`
+ `bootmgr` (Windows Vista)
+ Boot Configuration Database (BCD) (Windows Vista)
+ `winload.exe` (Windows Vista)
+ `ntoskrnl.exe`

The optional file is

+ `ntbootdd.sys`, which is the SCSI adapter driver that Windows XP boots from if the SCSI adapter doesn't have an active BIOS

In the following sections, you get a look at what you can do if any of these files are missing or appear to be missing on your computer. For further information about the Windows XP boot processes, consult Book V, Chapter 6.

ntldr

If `ntldr` is missing, you will receive the following error message when your computer tries to boot:

```
NTLDR is missing
Press any key to restart
```

This message often means that a formatted floppy was left in the disk drive. If this file is actually missing, it can be replaced with a working copy from any Windows NT computer, although try to replace the missing file with a copy from the same or a newer version of Windows to maintain full compatibility. To replace this file, you might have to make a boot disk to get your computer booted. This can be done with the following steps:

1. **Format a disk on a working Windows XP computer.**

2. **Copy the files `ntldr`, `ntdetect.com`, and `boot.ini` from the root of the `C:` drive.**

 These files are hidden, system, and read-only, so you have to modify their attributes to copy them. Check out Book V, Chapter 4 for the low-down on modifying attributes.

3. **Edit the `boot.ini` file to reflect the boot configuration of your target computer (the one that will not boot).**

boot.ini

If the `boot.ini` file is missing and you installed Windows XP in its default location, the system will boot but will not display a boot menu. The default location for Windows XP and newer versions of Windows is `c:\windows`; for Windows 2000 and Windows NT, the default location is `c:\winnt`. If you have not installed Windows in its default location, you will receive a message stating that `ntoskrnl.exe` or `hal.dll` is corrupted or missing and that you should replace the file. The message will look similar to this, from Windows 2000:

```
Windows 2000 could not start because the following file is missing or corrupt:
<Windows 2000 root drive>\system32\ntoskrnl.exe
```

The message might also be similar to this, from Windows XP:

```
Windows could not start because the following file is missing or corrupt:
<Windows root>\system32\hal.dll
Please re-install a copy of the above file.
```

This message is misleading because the problem is really with the `boot.ini` file. The reason for the message is that the boot loader (`ntldr`) has gone to the default location, and `ntoskrnl.exe` or `hal.dll` files were not there. If the `boot.ini` file is replaced and the boot path is correct for your installation, the boot process will continue as normal.

boot.ini is a text file and can be edited with any text editor, such as notepad.exe. To replace the boot.ini file, you might need to create a boot disk like you did to replace the missing ntldr file.

ntdetect.com

If ntdetect.com is missing, you receive the following error message:

NTDETECT failed

This file is generic, like the ntldr file, and can be replaced in the same way that you replace the ntldr file. See the earlier section, "ntldr."

bootmgr

If bootmgr is missing, you receive the following error message when your computer tries to boot:

BOOTMGR is missing
Press Ctrl+Alt+Del to restart

To resolve this type of error, look at using the Vista Startup Repair process or the repair Command Prompt with tools like bootrec.exe /fixboot. For more information about the Vista Startup Repair process as well as repairing errors, see Chapter 3 of this minibook.

Boot Configuration Database (BCD)

If BCD is missing, you receive the following error message when your computer tries to boot:

```
                      Windows Boot Manager

Windows failed to start. A recent hardware or software change might be the
cause. To fix the problem:

    1. Insert your Windows installation disc and restart your computer.
    2. Choose your language settings, and then click "Next."
    3. Click "Repair your computer."

If you do not have this disc, contact your system administrator or computer
manufacturer for assistance.

    File: \Boot\BCD

    Status: 0xc000000f

    Info: An error occurred while attempting to read the boot configuration
          data.

Enter=Continue                                                    ESC=Exit
```

To resolve this type of error, look at using the Vista Startup Repair process or the repair Command Prompt which includes tools like `bootrec.exe /RebuildBCD` or `bcdedit.exe`. `bcdedit.exe` will allow you to manually rebuild the BCD.

winload.exe

If `winload` is missing, you will receive the following error message when your computer tries to boot:

```
                            Windows Boot Manager

Windows failed to start. A recent hardware or software change might be the
cause. To fix the problem:

    1. Insert your Windows installation disc and restart your computer.
    2. Choose your language settings, and then click "Next."
    3. Click "Repair your computer."

If you do not have this disc, contact your system administrator or computer
manufacturer for assistance.

    File: \Windows\system32\winload.exe

    Status: 0xc000000f

    Info: The selected entry could not be loaded because the application is
          missing or corrupt.

Enter=Continue                                                    ESC=Exit
```

To resolve this type of error, look at using the Vista Startup Repair process or the repair Command Prompt which includes tools like `bootrec.exe /RebuildBCD` or `bcdedit.exe`. `bcdedit.exe` will allow you to manually rebuild the BCD.

ntoskrnl.exe or hal.dll

You should be able to find the `ntoskrnl.exe` file in the `<Windows XP root drive>\windows\system32\` directory. If it's missing, you receive a message like this, from Windows 2000:

```
Windows 2000 could not start because the following file is missing or corrupt:
<Windows 2000 root>\system32\ntoskrnl.exe
```

The message might also look like this, from Windows XP:

```
Windows could not start because the following file is missing or corrupt:
<Windows root>\system32\hal.dll
Please re-install a copy of the above file.
```

These messages may look familiar; they are the same messages that you receive if your boot.ini file is misconfigured. After checking the boot.ini file, if the ntoskrnl.exe or hal.dll files are actually missing, you have to do one of the following:

+ **Perform an Emergency Repair Process** for Windows NT 4.0 or Windows 2000 or a Startup Repair in Windows Vista to replace any missing or corrupted files on your system.

 For more information on Emergency Repair Process, see Book VII, Chapter 3.

+ **Attempt to replace the file by using the Recovery Console.**

+ **Reinstall the operating system.**

Ninety-nine out of 100 times, the missing ntoskrnl.exe or hal.dll error message means an error with the boot.ini file or the BCD, and the ntoskrnl.exe or hal.dll file is fine.

ntbootdd.sys

Most systems boot either from ATA/SATA hard drives or from SCSI drives attached to a SCSI controller or an adapter with a working BIOS. In either case, you will not find the ntbootdd.sys file on your drive. If you are booting from a SCSI drive attached to a SCSI controller that has its BIOS disabled, you will find the ntbootdd.sys file on the root of your bootable drive, along with ntldr, ntdetect.com, and boot.ini. This file is computer-specific because it is the SCSI driver for *your* SCSI controller. It can be replaced with a copy of the file found on any other computer that boots from the same SCSI controller. If you do not have another system with the same configuration, you can get a copy of the SCSI driver from either the driver disk for the SCSI controller or possibly from your Windows installation CD-ROM. This driver will have to be renamed to ntbootdd.sys and copied to the boot drive, and you might need to make a boot disk like the one described in the earlier section "ntldr."

Device-Related Errors

It is unfortunate that the devices and their drivers that allow us to accomplish so much of our day-to-day work with computers are also one of the biggest factors in not being able to do work on our computers. Ideally, when all the devices are configured on your computer, you should be able to work with no problems from your drivers. Most people's computers don't remain in a static mode but are in constant flux. Even though devices are working fine, many people feel the need to try to improve performance by changing settings, upgrading drivers, or installing Service Packs. Although upgrading drivers and installing items such as Service Packs are common practice,

they should be done carefully. A Service Pack, for instance, can change how all drivers on your computer function. In the rare case when something does go wrong, you may find that the fix is difficult, but in most cases, it will be related to a file version or configuration setting. This section takes a look at how to address these problems.

A device referenced in system.ini, win.ini, or Registry is not found

From time to time, you will find that one of your startup files still references a device that you thought had been removed from your system. The files that reference devices include `system.ini`, `win.ini`, and the Registry. If this happens, you might have to edit these files manually in order to fix the problem. If an error message tells you that a referenced device does not exist, take note of the device being referenced because you will have to search for it in your startup files. Most devices are found within your `system.ini` file, so this is the first file to check. Both INI files can be opened and edited with `notepad.exe` or `sysedit.exe`. To find out how to use `sysedit.exe`, take a look at Book V, Chapter 6.

If the device is listed in the Registry, it should be listed in Device Manager. Choose Start⇨Control Panel⇨System, click the Hardware tab of the resulting dialog box, and then click the Device Manager button. Locate the device in Device Manager and delete it. If the device is still physically present in the computer, it will be re-added to Device Manager when your computer is rebooted. If you keep removing the device and it keeps coming back, that is because it is still physically present. Physically remove the device first, and then remove it from Device Manager.

In Windows XP or Windows Vista, if you do not see the device that you want to remove in Device Manager, choose Show Hidden Devices from the View menu. If the device is not listed in Windows 2000, you can use the Add/Remove Hardware Wizard. If you can't find the device in the Windows GUI, you can attempt to search the Registry to locate the device and correct the issue. To find out about editing the Registry, see Book VI, Chapter 4.

Registry corruption

The two main ways that the system Registry can become corrupted are updates to the Registry via one of the Registry editing tools or an import of a registry settings file, and by the files that make up the Registry becoming damaged or deleted.

Of the many ways to import data into the Registry, most of them involve storing settings in a file and importing that file into the Registry. If the settings in the file are incorrect, you might be able to just continue computing without any problems, or you could end up with a system that no longer

boots normally. If your system will not boot normally, your only option is to boot the system by using an alternative method, such as the Recovery Console, and replace the base Registry files with an untainted version.

You also need to use an alternative method to boot the system if the Registry files on the drive itself have become corrupted, and then you have to replace the Registry files. The user portion of the Registry — ntuser.dat — is found in your user profile directory. Your user profile directory is in C:\Documents and Settings\<*username*> (C:\Users\<*username*> for Windows Vista). The system portion of the registry is found in %systemroot%\sysetm32\config, in the files SAM, SECURITY, system, and software. For information about editing the Registry, see Book VI, Chapter 4.

Safe Mode

In order to let you repair the OS from within the OS, Microsoft provides Safe Mode. *Safe Mode* is available with most versions of Windows (including Windows XP, Server 2003, and Vista) and is a special boot of Windows that loads a minimal set of drivers. The only drivers that are loaded are the ones that are required to get the OS running. Instead of loading the normal video driver, Safe Mode loads a 16-color VGA graphics driver. The config.sys and autoexec.bat files are skipped completely. If you have issues with drivers or driver configuration, booting into Safe Mode can allow you to bypass these driver-related problems so that they can be fixed.

Enter Safe Mode by pressing the F8 key when the OS is booting. If your computer boots into Safe Mode, the words Safe Mode appear in each corner of your desktop. If Windows XP or Vista fails to boot properly, it will suggest — and attempt — to boot into Safe Mode on the next boot. If your computer boots into Safe Mode automatically, the last boot process was likely interrupted (usually by the user). For more information about Safe Mode and other boot methods, consult Book VII, Chapter 3.

Other Errors

Like with all things in life, some things cannot easily be categorized, so this section discusses errors that do not fit in the other categories in this chapter.

Paging file errors

The Windows *paging file* is a hard drive file that is used as additional RAM memory. Typically with Windows, the file is called the paging file or page file, but some people may still use the Windows 9*x* name for the file: "swap file." The location of the paging file is recorded in the Registry. If the drive

that contains the paging file becomes too full, you might encounter errors informing you of this fact. If this happens, create some additional space for the paging file by deleting some unnecessary files, reducing the size of the paging file, or moving the paging file to a new location. The default location for the paging file is in the same drive as your Windows directory. Windows allows you to move the paging file to an alternate drive. If you have done so and that drive has been removed from your system, you encounter errors telling you that the paging file could not be created. If this happens, configure Windows to use another drive for the paging file as shown in Book VI, Chapter 3.

Failure to start GUI

Sometimes, Windows cannot complete the boot process, but it will not generate an error, either. Instead, it seems to hang at one spot in the boot process without going any further. You can deal with this problem in a number of ways.

First, see whether the OS has loaded the networking components, which you can do using the ping utility discussed in Book VIII, Chapter 3. If the networking services are running, you might be able to connect to the computer using Computer Management or Event Viewer, as described in Book VI, Chapter 4, which will allow you to view information about the OS and read the event logs. The event log might show errors that let you know what the problem is.

If you cannot connect to the computer, your only options are to continue to wait or to cycle the power on the computer. If the computer has locked up hard enough, the soft power button might not work, and you might have to unplug the computer. For a laptop, you have to remove the battery.

This action, like any power interruption, risks causing corruption to the file system, and should be used as a last resort.

On reboot, the system might boot properly, or you might want to use one of the F8 boot options discussed in Book VII, Chapter 3, such as Safe Mode. Safe Mode allows you to view the Event Logs via Event Viewer, and that might give you insight into the problem. The F8 boot options also allow you to create a bootlog, which if your next boot is unsuccessful, will let you know approximately where the failure is occurred. If you are unable to find the solution, disconnect all peripherals (such as USB devices) and attempt to reboot the computer. If the problem is with a peripheral or its driver, you might see a successful boot. In some cases, I have seen errors with peripherals occur after the system has successfully booted for years, and the problem can usually be traced to an OS update, a drive update, or file system corruption of the driver.

If you think you know what is causing the problem, perhaps a driver or service that will not start, you could also use Recovery Console to try to fix those problems. For more information about Recovery Console and its use, consult Book VI, Chapter 2.

Error Diagnostic Tools

The following sections examine the different tools you can use when diagnosing errors.

Dr. Watson

Dr. Watson, first included with Windows 3.*x*, has been designed to help troubleshoot problems on your system. It helps troubleshoot problems after they occur by generating log files and system snapshots.

Figure 1-1 shows Dr. Watson's configuration screen for a Windows XP computer. Configure Dr. Watson in a Windows XP computer by running `drwtsn32.exe` from the Run command. Dr. Watson can take the entire contents of an applications memory space, and write that information to a file on your disk (also called a "crash dump file"). This can be useful for the application developer to troubleshoot the error. Dr. Watson also logs and creates crash dump files for a variety of OS background services, which are really just applications, as shown in Figure 1-2. With Windows XP, Dr. Watson is always ready to generate these logs and crash dump files.

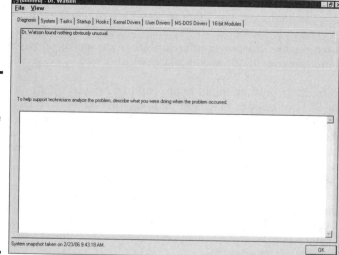

Figure 1-1: Dr. Watson provides the Diagnosis tab for you to describe what you were doing when the error occurred.

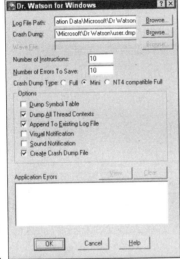

**Book VII
Chapter 1**

**Managing Error
Codes and Startup
Messages**

Figure 1-2:
How Dr.
Watson
deals with
applications
that crash.

Windows Error Reporting

With Windows XP, Microsoft introduced a tool for error reporting that replaced most of the functionality originally covered by Dr. Watson. The Error Reporting tool allows you various levels of reporting. By default, it is configured to report errors in both applications and the OS directly to Microsoft, which allows its programmers the potential to use the information when creating new patches for the operating system. This "call home" functionality can be disabled by going to Error Reporting button on the Advanced tab of the System Control Panel applet. Clicking the Error Reporting button opens the Error Reporting dialog shown in Figure 1-3. From this dialog, you can disable the "call home" functionality but still have Windows report the errors to you; specify that Error Reporting works for both OS components and program; or use the Choose Programs button to specify which programs you want to have Error Reporting work with, or exclude.

When an application crashes, you will see a message similar to the one in Figure 1-3. If Windows has a Stop error, though (described in Book VII, Chapter 2), you see the message after you reboot and log in. Click the link at the bottom of the dialog box to find additional information related to the error. When you see this dialog, you can send a summary of the error data and system state to Microsoft, as shown in Figure 1-4. If you disabled Error Reporting but kept the notify option enabled, you get a smaller dialog box without the option for notifying Microsoft, but only an OK button to acknowledge the error.

Figure 1-3:
Windows Error Reporting helps Microsoft fix problems with the OS.

Figure 1-4:
Even with Error Reporting enabled, you can control what errors go to Microsoft.

Event Viewer

Windows XP offers various logging tools, the greatest of which uses the Event Log service. The Event Log service logs errors and events into several different log files. The Event Viewer is the application you use to view the contents of these log files. Windows always has at least three default logs: Application, Security, and System. These log files have a default size of 512KB each and automatically overwrite events after seven days. These settings can be adjusted for each file by right-clicking the log file in Event Viewer and choosing Properties to open the System Properties dialog box, shown in Figure 1-5.

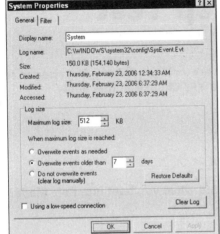

Figure 1-5:
The default settings for the log files should be enough to prevent filling.

In the event that any log fills up, you receive a pop-up message. When this happens, open the Event Viewer by choosing Start⇨Control Panels⇨ Administrative Tools and then Event Viewer. To clear the log, right-click the log and choose Clear All Events. When you clear the log, you have the opportunity to save the events to a file.

Before clearing the filled log, examine the most recent events for an error that might have caused the log to fill quickly.

Getting an A+

This chapter examines a number of common errors that you are likely to encounter with Windows computers. These errors range from configuration settings and files to boot files and driver-related problems. You also see some common resolution methods, such as booting into Safe Mode. Some key elements to remember in this chapter are

✦ `No operating system found` is an MS-DOS error message and might mean that a floppy disk was left in your Windows XP computer.

✦ Most Windows boot sector or boot file errors can be fixed with either the Emergency Repair Process or Recovery Console.

✦ Safe Mode is used to diagnose and resolve driver or startup problems.

✦ Event Viewer should always be checked as part of the troubleshooting process to see what error messages are being reported by Windows.

Prep Test

1 **Which of the following options are valid procedures for trying to resolve corrupted boot files with Windows XP? Choose all that apply.**

A ❑ Recovery Console

B ❑ `sys.com`

C ❑ `fdisk.exe`

D ❑ Emergency Repair Process

2 **Which of the following are loaded when you boot into Safe Mode? Choose all that apply.**

A ❑ Your normal video driver

B ❑ Your mouse driver

C ❑ `config.sys`

D ❑ `autoexec.bat`

3 **What is the purpose of a swap file?**

A ○ To prepare files to be copied to other disks

B ○ To act as additional memory for the system

C ○ To act as an extension to the hard drive

D ○ To prepare files that are saved to disk

4 **Where do you go to read and clear the Windows XP Event Log?**

A ○ Event Log

B ○ Event Viewer

C ○ Log Reader

D ○ Disk Cleanup

5 **You installed Windows 2000 in the default location, `C:\winnt`. What will be the effect of deleting your `boot.ini` file?**

A ○ Your system will boot as normal but will not display a boot menu.

B ○ Your system will not boot and will display a `missing boot.ini` error message.

C ○ Your system will not boot and will display a `missing ntoskrnl32.exe` error message.

D ○ Your system will not boot and will display a `missing ntdetect.com` error message.

6 You are missing your copy of `ntldrm`, and your Windows XP computer will not boot. How can you replace your copy of `ntldrm`?

A ○ Use the `retrieve.exe` command to get a copy from the Windows XP installation CD-ROM.

B ○ The only way you can replace this file is through the Recovery Console.

C ○ This file is not required and does not have to be replaced.

D ○ Copy it from any other computer that is running Windows XP.

7 You just noticed that your `ntbootdd.sys` file is missing from your computer. What is the `ntbootdd.sys` file?

A ○ Text configuration information for your Windows XP system

B ○ The boot loader

C ○ The SCSI driver for your SCSI adapter if the BIOS is disabled on the adapter

D ○ The boot menu configuration file

8 When should you boot into Safe Mode?

A ○ At every boot-up

B ○ When your system will not boot normally

C ○ When your computer is connected to the Internet

D ○ Only to play `freecell.exe`

9 The system Registry for Windows XP is extremely important. What file or files make up the user portion of the Registry?

A ○ `registry.dat`

B ○ `system.ini` and `registry.dat`

C ○ `user.dat`

D ○ `ntuser.dat`

Answers

1 **A, D.** Both Recovery Console and the Emergency Repair Process allow you to repair problems with the boot files. *Check out "Windows Boot Files and Boot Errors."*

2 **B.** Your mouse driver is the only item on the list that loads when you enter Safe Mode. It also loads a VGA-compatible video driver and a minimal set of device drivers. *Peruse "Safe Mode."*

3 **B.** The Windows swap file acts as additional memory, or virtual memory, for the OS. *Take a look at "Paging file errors."*

4 **B.** Event Viewer is used to read, back up, and clear your event logs. *Look over "Event Viewer."*

5 **A.** Your system will boot as normal; when `boot.ini` is missing, Windows 2000 attempts to boot from the default installation location. *Study "Windows Boot Files and Boot Errors."*

6 **D.** `ntldr` is identical across all copies of Windows XP, so it can be copied from any working installation of Windows XP. *Refer to "ntldr."*

7 **C.** The `ntbootdd.sys` file contains the SCSI driver for your SCSI adapter if the BIOS on the adapter has been disabled. *Examine "ntbootdd.sys."*

8 **B.** You should enter Safe Mode to correct problems when your computer won't boot normally. *See "Safe Mode."*

9 **D.** The file that makes up the user portion of the Registry in Windows XP is `ntuser.dat`. *Review "Registry corruption."*

Chapter 2: Managing Common Problems

Exam Objectives

✔ Recognizing and resolving Windows-specific printing problems

✔ Identifying and correcting auto-restart and blue screen errors and system lockup problems

✔ Knowing and fixing device driver failures

✔ Distinguishing and rectifying application install, start, and load failures

*I*n this chapter, you examine some common errors that you will encounter when servicing computers. I show you how to gather the information that you need to properly diagnose and correct the problem. You also look at several common errors and problems that you are likely to encounter when dealing with Windows-based systems.

And because these are some of the most common problems that you will run into at the OS level as a CompTIA A+ Certified Professional, this chapter will prepare you for these problems, and will help you on the exam.

Solving Windows-Specific Printing Problems

If you have read this book to this point, you should be familiar with the process of printing that I cover in Book III, Chapter 5. This section look specifically at a few problems commonly encountered with printing from the OS perspective.

Even though people often say that we are moving toward a paperless society, people still do a substantial amount of printing every day. And because so many people are printing so often, everybody, at some point, has some sort of issue with printing. In the following sections, you examine stalled spoolers as well as incorrect drivers and configuration parameters — and what you can do about them.

Dealing with a stalled print spooler

Change gears slightly for a minute and think about sewing. You use thread that has been wound on a spool for temporary storage. From the spool, a sewing machine draws thread at a rate convenient for the machine, freeing the operator from having to constantly deal with tangled thread. Print spooling works similarly for a printer.

Prior to print spooling being integrated with an OS, the application that was printing had to send each piece of data to the printer, halting the user from doing anything until the printing process was complete. A print spooler is used to quickly accept print data from the application, allowing control of the application to be returned to the user after a very brief spooling process. When the spooler takes the print data from the application, it stores the data in a temporary file, until the spooler has time to send the data out to the printer, or de-spool the data.

From time to time, when dealing with Windows Vista and other Windows versions, you can encounter a stalled print spooler. This seems to be a feature of the print spooler. After a period of printing, and printing well, the print spooler decides to stop responding to further commands. This has been a long-running issue for Microsoft, but seems to happen less frequently with newer versions of the Windows OS.

You can identify a stalled spooler from the following:

+ Users cannot add new jobs to the print queue.

+ Nobody can remove jobs from the print queue.

+ Existing jobs do not print.

+ The print queue appears empty even though it was sent print jobs.

If the print queue exhibits these symptoms, restart the print queue. Use either of the following methods to restart the spooler Service:

+ **The Services MMC snap-in**

 The Administrative Tools folder holds Services console. In Windows XP, choose My Computer➪Control Panel➪Administrative Tools➪Services, or in Windows Vista, choose Computer➪Control Panel➪System and Maintenance➪Administrative Tools➪Services. Locate the spooler service in the list of services, right-click it, and choose Restart (as shown in Figure 2-1). You could also choose to Stop, wait for that action to complete, and then choose Start.

+ **The net command**

Figure 2-1:
Restarting
services is
easy from
the Services
Administra-
tive tool.

From the command prompt, use

```
net stop spooler
net start spooler
```

or

```
net stop "print spooler"
net start "print spooler"
```

If you don't know the name of the service you want to start or stop, use
net start, and Windows lists the registered Services.

If your print spooler is suffering from any problem, restarting the
spooler service is usually the correct answer.

Lab 2-1 provides practice restarting the print spooler via the command
prompt. This lab requires a Windows 2000 Professional, Windows 2000
Server, or Windows XP computer. Lab 2-1 can be found in the Labs.pdf file
in the Author directory of the CD-ROM.

After the spooler restarts, your problems should be gone, assuming you
have configured the clients to use the correct driver.

Incorrect/incompatible driver for printing

Drivers are often a big problem for administrators. You notice that the printer
is being heavily used, spitting out page after page of data, and you are happy
that this printing device is being put to such a good use. These feelings are
then shattered when you examine one of the printed pages. You notice, up

at the top of the page, a small band of text that looks like it was typed over about 100 times. This should not greatly concern you, though, because the problem is not likely a major hardware problem with the printer but rather from a user on the network using the wrong printer driver. Easily fixed.

The *printer driver* for your computer acts as a translation tool between your computer's OS and the printer. If you install the incorrect driver, you have a poor translation taking place, which shows up in the printout. Sometimes an incorrect driver causes some special characters to not print; other times, it causes a much larger problem, such as the one that I just described.

The solution to the problem is easy: Just install the correct driver. This involves checking the printer model, getting the software for it, and installing the correct driver for the OS. If you do not have the driver disks or CD, you can likely download the driver from the printer manufacturer's Web site or other online source.

Incorrect parameters

Several parameters (settings) can be configured for a printer that are specific to that model. Find these settings on the Device Options tab of the printer's Properties dialog box. Because the settings are specific to the device, I can't discuss them all here. Instead, I discuss generic settings that apply to all printers, and those that are most likely to cause problems are the port settings.

To access a printer's Properties dialog box using Windows 2000 or XP, choose Start⇨Printers and Faxes. In the Printers and Faxes window that opens, choose the desired printer and then right-click⇨Properties. In Vista, choose Start⇨Control Panel. In the Control Panel window that opens, choose Printer, choose the printer, and then right-click and choose Properties.

Port settings are found on the Ports tab. When choosing a port, you can pick from a local port (such as LPT1), a network port (such as \\<server>\<printer>), or a file to be redirected to a printer later. If you specify an incorrect network location, you will not be able to print; and if you print to a file, you might not know where the file is. These can cause problems for users when printing, and you should verify that you have expected settings on this tab. For example, if you think you should be printing to LPT1 but you see that your selected port is COM1, this is likely the cause of your printing problem.

Another problem that can be caused by settings on the Ports tab and the Configure Port button are the timeout settings. If these values are set too low, you can have communication problems with your printer. The problem is caused by your computer not waiting long enough for your printer to answer any queries. If you are unsure of the correct port settings, verify the port settings with information found in the printer's documentation.

Solving Boot Errors and Errors Requiring Restarting

With the number of computers in most offices and how the law of averages works, it seems like there is always a problem that requires or causes a reboot. In large offices, it can seem like the Welcome to Windows chime is always playing. In fact, so many support people have used rebooting as the first step in dealing with problems that some users now instinctively reboot even before calling in a support person. This is not always the best course of action because it often removes information that can be used to locate the root of the problem.

Auto-restart errors

In many cases, auto-restart errors are caused by power-related issues, other hardware failures, or software configuration problems. If the computer auto-restarts, something is definitely wrong.

Some common issues that can cause auto-restarts include

✦ **Service configuration:** When configuring Services, you can choose an action to be taken when the Service fails. One action is to restart the computer. If you have a Service that is failing and it is configured to restart the computer when it fails, this causes an auto-restart. This setting can be seen in Figure 2-2. More information on Services can be found in Book VI, Chapter 3.

**Book VII
Chapter 2**

Managing Common
Problems

Figure 2-2:
Auto-
restarting a
service after
a failure is
just one of
the options.

✦ **CPU fan:** Most computers have a default thermal setting for the computer to cause a temporary shutdown. If the CPU fan fails, the CPU's temperature quickly rises to where the motherboard interrupts the power to prevent damage to the CPU. Dust caked in and around the heat sink and fan has the same effect. A visual inspection of the CPU fan will show you whether it is running, or whether dirt or debris are the culprits. Book IV, Chapter 1, talks about ventilation methods as well as problems related to poor ventilation.

✦ **Power supply problem:** Power supplies have limited life spans. When they fail, their demise is often complete and immediate. In some cases, they can supply some power for a period of time, but as they heat up, they cause an interruption in the power, thus restarting the computer. It is easier to diagnose a complete failure of the power supply rather than a power supply that fails when it is hot because for the latter, you need the power supply operating for a period of time — possibly days — before you see the problem. When in doubt, swap it out. Power supplies are not expensive and are easy to replace — and if it fixes the problem, you will know it quickly. For more on power supplies, see Book II, Chapter 6.

✦ **Power source problem:** Some buildings are notorious for power spikes or drops. In some cases, the power can drop to a point that there is insufficient power for the computer, even though other electrical devices do not show any signs. If this problem happens regularly, it will likely affect a number of computers.

 Choose from a variety of tools for testing the quality of the power coming from the wall. Some low-end, single-computer uninterruptible power supply (UPS) systems give you a display of the current voltage and provide line conditioning on a 120V line, down to 89V. The UPS can also supply some power when the voltage drops below that level. For more on power sources, see Book II, Chapter 6.

✦ **Bad memory:** When memory is the problem (the computer's, not yours), you might see the system running fine until the damaged or bad blocks of memory are used. At that time, the system spontaneously reboots itself or generates a Windows Stop error. Testing tools are available to test for bad memory, so this situation should be easy to diagnose after letting the system run with the testing software working through the blocks of memory. Of course, as the size of the system memory increases, so does the length of time that it takes to test it.

✦ **Network attack:** The TCP/IP network stack is very complex, and with Services running over the stack, many software systems can have flaws. Many network attacks performed on Windows systems cause various buffer overflows, which then cause the system to reboot. Worms like

Zotob fall into this category. Tools like TDIMon and TCPView (`http://technet.microsoft.com/en-us/sysinternals/bb897437.aspx`) can be used to view current Transmission Control Protocol (TCP) and User Datagram Protocol (UDP) network activity on a computer, which can in turn be used to identify network attacks or problems. It is beneficial to learn how these tools work when you are not experiencing a problem because it will make it easier to identify nonstandard traffic. In most cases, keeping your system up to date on security patches and virus definitions offers a high level of protection. The only sure protection from network attacks is to not be connected to the network. For more information about network security, read through Book IX.

✦ **Automatic Updates:** If your system is configured for Automatic Updates from the Microsoft Windows Update or Microsoft Update Web site, you might find that your computer reboots while you are not there. If the computer is configured to install updates in the middle of the night, you might see the next morning that it rebooted. Usually, there are warning messages leading up to the reboot although you might not be there to see them. To solve this issue, check the Windows Event Logs and the settings on Automatic Updates in the Control Panel. As part of the Windows Security Center, Windows suggests enabling Automatic Updates. Book IX, Chapter 3, has more information on the Windows Update process.

Unexpected reboots can happen for other reasons, but the preceding list describes the most common.

Automatic reboots of a system can have a variety of causes; make sure to be familiar with the list of the most common reasons.

Blue screen errors

Blue screen errors (shown in Figure 2-3) are almost always related to driver, DLL, or configuration errors. As some people call them, "Blue Screen of Death" errors are officially Stop errors. In many cases, these will be related to a recent driver change prior to the last reboot. If this is the case, try booting to the Last Known Good Configuration, which will restore the system configuration to the state it was in during the previous reboot. For more information about booting to the Last Known Good Configuration, see Book VII, Chapter 3.

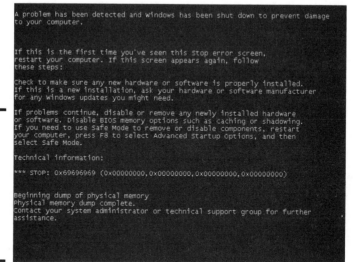

Figure 2-3:
Stop
errors are
"affection-
ately"
known as
the Blue
Screen of
Death.

The most common reasons for Stop errors are

✦ Service, application, or device errors

✦ Compatibility problems

✦ Hardware problems

✦ File system corruption or errors

✦ Compatibility issues with firmware or BIOS

✦ Viruses

Stop errors occur when one driver or application attempts to access the memory used by another driver. Because drivers operate in the unprotected kernel memory space, this is very bad for system stability. When this happens, Windows does the only thing that it can think of to prevent further corruption — it stops everything. Because applications run in protected memory spaces, they cannot write to memory being used by another application. Thus, Stop errors are caused only by access attempts in the kernel memory space.

The image referenced in Figure 2-3 is a Stop error caused by an application, and the format of the text on the screen is not the same as the Stop error you might be more familiar with, which I discuss later in this section. Alternatively, the first two lines of the Stop error message tell you the name of one of the drivers involved, or at least the memory locations involved.

Listing 2-1 shows text that might appear on a standard Stop error:

Listing 2-1: Sample Stop Error Message

```
*** STOP: 0x0000000A (0x802aa502, 0x00000002, 0x00000D00, 0xFA84001C)
IRQL_NOT_LESS_OR_EQUAL*** Address fa84001c has base fa840000 - i804prt.SYS

CPUID: GenuineIntel 5.2.c irql:1f     SYSVER 0xF0000565

Dll Base  Date Stamp - Name          Dll Base  Date Stamp - Name
80100000  2be154c9   - ntoskrnl.exe  80400000  2bc153b0   - hal.dll
80200000  2bd49628   - ncrc710.sys   8025c000  2bd49688   - SCSIPORT.SYS

...

Address  dword dump   Build [1381]                   - Name
fe9cdaec fa84003c fa84003c 00000000 00000000 80149905 - i8042prt.SYS
fe9cdaf8 8025dfe0 8025dfe0 ff8e6b8c 80129c2c ff8e6b94 - SCSIPORT.SYS
fe9cdb10 8013e53a 8013e53a ff8e6b94 ff8e6f60 ff8e6b94 - ntoskrnl.exe

...
```

Hexadecimal (the Base 16 number system) is used to display all error codes and memory addresses on the Stop error. The first line tells you the error type numerically (0x0000000A), then the memory address of the code that was attempted to be accessed (0x802aa502), the type of access attempted or error parameter (0x00000002, 0x00000D00), and the memory address that made the access attempt (0xFA84001C). This is followed by a line providing you with a text-based description of the error and, if possible, the name of the driver that was found at that location. This driver might be the one that caused the error or the target of the error. After these lines is a section that lists the drivers found in the memory spaces near where the error occurred, then a section listing memory information for some of those memory spaces. If the error was a result of a recent change to the system, undo that change or update your drivers.

Some common Stop errors you may encounter are

◆ 0x0000000A IRQL_NOT_LESS_EQUAL

◆ 0x0000001E KMODE_EXCEPTION_NOT_HANDLED

◆ 0x00000024 NTFS_FILE_SYSTEM

◆ 0x0000002E DATA_BUS_ERROR

◆ 0x00000050 PAGE_FAULT_IN_NONPAGED_AREA

◆ 0x0000007B INACCESSIBLE_BOOT_DEVICE

◆ 0x0000007F UNEXPECTED_KERNEL_MODE_TRAP

◆ 0xC000021A STATUS_SYSTEM_PROCESS_TERMINATED

Be familiar with the basic type of information returned in Stop messages.

System lockup

System lockup happens when your computer stops responding to any system functions or user input. If you are using Windows XP or Vista, system lockups should be rare compared with older OSes, such as Windows 9x. More likely, you will have a period of slow responsiveness. If you are using older Windows OSes, you are likely to have complete system lockups. This has to do with how the operating systems work. Read Book VI, Chapter 2 to see how the Windows XP system architecture has been designed to prevent lockups.

If you are using Windows 2000 or newer Windows OS, you might experience a runaway application or Service that can cause the system to become unresponsive. This unresponsiveness might fool you into believing that your computer is locked up, when in fact it just doesn't have enough clock cycles to pay attention to you. Press Ctrl+Alt+Del to open the security dialog box (shown in Figure 2-4), where you can launch Task Manager.

I have seen Windows XP lock completely up very few times, but there have been many other times when I have powered a machine off because it was slow to respond.

Figure 2-4:
Use the Security dialog box in Windows XP to launch Task Manager.

How long you wait for an unresponsive system is typically related to the number of critical unsaved documents that you had open when it became unresponsive. Prior to turning off the computer's power, I have waited an hour to get the dialog boxes to close Microsoft Word and save my documents. Turning off the power (as opposed to performing a graceful shutdown) is usually to be avoided because of the risk of disk corruption. This wait is not typical because in most cases if the system is unresponsive to the point that Task Manager takes more than five minutes to open, I usually hit the power button to kill the power to the computer.

The Processes tab of Task Manager lets you see which application is the runaway. You just have to look for the application with the highest CPU value. This indicates which application is hogging the CPU. You can try to switch to the application and close it normally, but there is a good chance that this will not work. If you cannot shut down the program normally, return to Task Manager, select the task, and click the End Task button. This should return your system to its previous level of responsiveness. In some cases, the application at fault will be a critical system service, like WinLogon, which cannot be stopped, so you will just have to reboot.

If you are using 16-bit Windows applications on Windows XP or Vista, you are in for a different experience. Book VI, Chapter 2 examines how the system architecture lends to a lack of system stability. This is mainly because of OS components running in the same area of the system that 16-bit applications execute. When any 16-bit application crashes, it has the potential to lock the 16-bit OS components as well, which can lock up an entire NTVDM (NT Virtual DOS Machine) but not the entire OS. If this happens, your only choice will be to terminate the NTVDM that has the problem.

Resolving Device Driver Errors

Other than a system Stop error, device drivers might fail to load for a number of reasons:

+ **Version:** The version of the driver might not be compatible with the OS version.

+ **Configuration:** The driver could be misconfigured, and some settings require changing.

+ **Incompatibility:** The driver might not be compatible with some other driver or application running on the system.

In most cases, the startup error for the driver will be listed in the Event Viewer error logs. Open Event Viewer from Start⇨Control Panel⇨ Administrative Tools⇨Event Viewer; then click one of the three log files to view the error logs. After locating the error in Event Viewer, you may use other OS tools, such as Device Manager, to correct the problem. Typically, the fix for these issues involves a visit to the vendor's Web site and down-loading the latest version of the driver or reviewing the vendor knowledge base for a fix to the compatibility problem. In rare cases, it might mean changing to a different version of the device, possibly from a different manufacturer.

Application Install, Start, and Load Failures

From time to time, you will have applications that will not start. A few reasons for this problem include corrupted or damaged shortcuts, damaged program information file (PIF) settings, or corrupted memory space. In the following sections, I take a closer look at these three types of errors as well as application installation errors.

Corrupted shortcuts

When you create a shortcut to a program, the shortcut records information about the target file, such as size and creation date. If something happens to the original file, such as being moved to another directory, the shortcut will attempt to search the hard drive and repair the shortcut. In Windows 2000, you will be prompted to verify that the correct file was found, as shown in Figure 2-5. If you are using Windows XP or newer OSes, automatic link tracking is enabled on shortcuts. What this means to you is that unless the file was deleted — in which case you will be asked to delete the shortcut — your shortcut links will always work, no matter how much you move a target file.

Do not always choose to delete damaged shortcuts because Windows will report that a file is missing if your files are on a network server but you are disconnected from the network. If you reconnect to the network, your shortcut should work again. In the worst case, you have to re-create the shortcut by hand.

Problematic shortcut

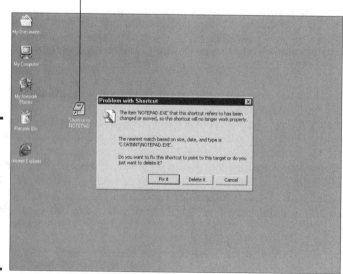

Figure 2-5: Shortcuts in Windows 2000 prompt you to confirm corrections for broken links.

Damaged PIF

In addition to improper locations, MS-DOS PIFs could also have inappropriate information in them. The PIF or shortcut to an MS-DOS application has information about the memory environment and reserved keystrokes. If this information has changed, you have to update the PIF. This can be done by right-clicking the PIF and choosing Properties. Which settings must be changed depends on your application, and Book VI, Chapter 2, deals with what those settings should be.

Corrupted memory space

Corrupted memory space occurs mostly with 16-bit Windows applications. Occasionally, 16-bit Windows applications can crash completely or partially when they are closed. When a 16-bit application crashes, it has a chance to corrupt the 16-bit Windows operating environment. If this happens, you will find that you cannot open or launch 16-bit Windows applications even though 32-bit Windows applications run fine.

If you are using Windows 9*x*, you have to reboot to allow a new 16-bit Windows environment to load. If you are using Windows XP or Vista, you can terminate the 16-bit Windows environment through Task Manager by following these steps:

1. **Press Ctrl+Alt+Del and click the Task Manager button.**

2. **In Task Manager, click the Processes tab.**

3. **Locate the NTVDM that contains only** wow.exe, **which will be indented in the column.**

4. **Right-click it and choose End Task.**

The next time you load a 16-bit Windows application, it will reload the default 16-bit Windows environment.

Applications will not install

In some cases, you will find that applications just do not install. In some cases, this is caused by the application performing a compatibility test, which your computer fails. If this is the case, you should be notified of the compliance failure by the application. If your computer is less powerful than recommended, it should be upgraded to support the application.

In some cases, specifically with Windows Installer applications, you might not be able to perform an installation if there is a previous installation that is still pending a reboot. The older setup applications might not install if they see another copy of setup.exe running. If this copy of setup is not expected to be running, check Task Manager to see whether it is there. Rebooting the system will correct both issues.

In addition to compliance failure, there might be a problem with how the setup program was written. Very often, the setup program itself is a 16-bit Windows-based application. If you recently had a 16-bit Windows application crash on your system and you have not corrected the corruption of the 16-bit memory space by rebooting Windows 9x or by terminating the NTVDM in Windows XP or newer Windows, the setup program might fail.

Solving Other Problems

In addition to the problems already discussed in this chapter, a number of other things may go wrong. In the following sections, I examine some of those problems.

General Protection Faults

General Protection Faults (GPFs) are OS-level errors. When applications are running, Windows prevents applications from interfering with each other by running them in their own memory space. However, some applications (and OS components) share a memory space, and these applications are mostly 16-bit applications. When a component attempts to reference memory that does not belong to it, Windows generates a GPF and attempts to prevent the improper reference by terminating the offending application.

Because this problem can affect some of the 16-bit OS components on the system, reboot after a GPF to ensure system stability. To reduce the occurrence of GPFs, reduce the number of running applications.

Illegal operation

An illegal operation error is similar to the GPF. In most cases, but not necessarily all, the illegal operation is a memory reference problem. When one 32-bit application attempts to reference an area of memory that belongs to another application or that it has somehow corrupted, it generates an illegal operation. When this happens, Windows treats it as a rogue or damaged application and terminates it before it can cause damage outside its own memory space.

The big difference between illegal operations and GPFs is what components are in use and affected at the time. In most cases, you can recover from an illegal operation by relaunching the application. Reducing the number of open applications reduces the chance of illegal operations because less space will be considered "out of bounds."

Invalid working directory

When creating shortcuts of MS-DOS–based applications, you configure a
working directory. This directory is used to create any associated files that
the application requires and to locate subapplications that it requires to be
able to perform its functions. If, after installing and configuring the applica-
tion, this directory is removed or renamed, you will see an error regarding
the working directory (see Figure 2-6). As part of the error message, you are
given a chance to launch the application. If you choose to launch the appli-
cation, realize that some functions might not work.

Figure 2-6:
Notification
for working
directory
that does
not exist.

This error can be resolved by changing the working directory path in the PIF
for the MS-DOS–based application. Right-click the shortcut to the application
(or the application itself) and choose Properties. On the Program tab, change
the Working Directory setting to the correct directory, as shown in Figure 2-7.
If the application requires support files, they might need to be restored. For
more information about configuring PIFs, see Book VI, Chapter 2.

**Book VII
Chapter 2**

**Managing Common
Problems**

Figure 2-7:
The
Working
Directory
setting
appears in
all PIFs.

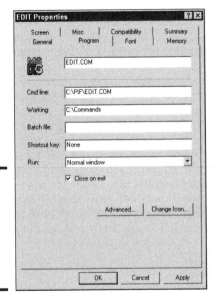

Optional device will not function

Although, in addition to a keyboard, many devices might be attached to your computer from time to time, the three devices that most computers have are a sound card, modem, and mouse. These devices all require an IRQ and an I/O address. You will have other devices that take resources. If all the devices are Plug and Play — and you have a Plug and Play BIOS — this is not an issue. But if you are using legacy devices, you will have to configure IRQ and I/O settings for your devices. Sound cards usually use IRQ 5, and your COM ports (for your modem) are IRQ 3 and IRQ 4. If you are using a serial mouse, you want to make sure that it is not sharing its IRQ with COM 3 or COM 4. To find out more about configuring resources, read Book III, Chapter 4.

In addition to configuring the hardware support for the devices, you also have to load the appropriate driver for the device. This can be done through Add New Hardware in the Control Panel. For more information about installing devices on your computer, see Book VI, Chapter 1.

Terminate Stay Resident (TSR) programs and viruses

Microsoft DOS allows one only program to operate at a time, and this was often very limiting. *Terminate Stay Resident programs* (TSRs) are usually small, useful programs designed to overcome the single application limitation of MS-DOS. When TSRs are launched, they are loaded into memory, and then they tell the OS that they are done, while remaining in memory, performing the task for which they were designed.

Book IX, Chapter 3 discusses viruses and some of the ways they attempt to hide from detection. One way that a virus spreads is by loading into memory as a TSR and then infecting other files on your system.

This is not to say the TSRs are to be avoided, but any program that runs without a user interface may be running when you are not aware. With Windows, you can see which applications are running in the background (as Services) by bringing up the Task Manager by pressing Ctrl+Alt+Del.

Your virus scanner has a list of known viruses that it will not permit to run. There is a chance that it will prevent others from running if they are doing suspicious things. If you are sure that the file is not a virus, you can temporarily disable your virus protection. Many virus programs have an agent that runs all the time as a background Service, looking for suspicious activity. In some cases, malware (which is not actually a virus, but still a program

you don't want on your computer) will be allowed to run. Malware also runs in the background and should show up in your task list. Most malware applications or viruses try to disguise themselves so as to not be obvious about their presence. For more information about viruses, see Book IX, Chapter 3.

Getting an A+

This chapter goes over some problems that computer support personnel typically encounter. The problems include

+ Dealing with stalled print spooler by restarting services
+ Fixing printing issues by replacing drivers or changing settings
+ Identifying root causes for auto-restart and Stop errors
+ Using Event Viewer to diagnose driver problems
+ Dealing with application start problems in the form of shortcuts, PIF, or memory space issues

Prep Test

1 When the print queue is unresponsive, what should you do first?

- **A** ○ Reboot the server.
- **B** ○ Reinstall the printer.
- **C** ○ Restart the spooler service.
- **D** ○ Redirect the printer to a remote print device.

2 What command is used to restart a service from the command prompt?

- **A** ○ service.exe
- **B** ○ services.exe
- **C** ○ cmdrun.exe
- **D** ○ net.exe

3 You get a call from a user who is complaining that his document has bullets in it, but when he prints the document, he gets check boxes instead. What is the problem?

- **A** ○ He is using the incorrect printer driver.
- **B** ○ The application that he is using does not support bullets.
- **C** ○ His computer has a problem with the serial cable connecting his printer.
- **D** ○ He is using the wrong parallel cable.

4 Only 16-bit Windows applications will produce GPFs. True or False?

- **A** ○ True
- **B** ○ False

5 What program can be used to terminate programs running on your computer?

- **A** ○ Device Manager
- **B** ○ Computer Administration Console
- **C** ○ System Information
- **D** ○ Task Manager

6 Your computer has had a Stop error, and the first two lines read

```
*** STOP: 0x0000000A (0x802aa502, 0x00000002, 0x00000D00, 0xFA84001C)
IRQL_NOT_LESS_OR_EQUAL*** Address fa84001c has base fa840000 - i804prt.SYS
```

Which of the following statements are true? (Choose all that apply.)

A ❑ The type of error was `IRQL_NOT_LESS_OR_EQUAL`.

B ❑ The error is due to the BIOS version.

C ❑ The driver `i804prt.sys` was involved in the error.

D ❑ The driver `i804prt.sys` is located at memory address `0x802aa502`.

7 What Windows XP function keeps your shortcut links from breaking?

A ○ Link Tracking

B ○ Shortcut Locator Service (SLS)

C ○ System Information

D ○ Task Manager

8 What tool should you check first when things are not working properly and you suspect an error, but you have not seen an error message?

A ○ System Information

B ○ WinMSD

C ○ Device Manager

D ○ Event Viewer

9 During your computer's boot process, your computer reboots automatically. There is no sign of a blue screen error. What are the most likely issues? (Choose all that apply.)

A ❑ Hardware problem with power supply

B ❑ Driver issue

C ❑ Service configuration

D ❑ Memory error

Answers

1 **C.** Restarting the print spooler service should fix problems with the print queue. If it does not, then you may have to restart the server. *See "Dealing with a stalled print spooler."*

2 **D.** net.exe is the command that can stop and start services from the command prompt. *Review "Dealing with a stalled print spooler."*

3 **A.** He is probably using the incorrect printer driver. The problem should go away when the driver is updated. Most printers are attached by parallel cables. *Check out "Incorrect/incompatible driver for printing."*

4 **B.** This is false. 16-bit applications will GPF more often and are responsible for most GPFs, but not all of them. *Peruse "General Protection Faults."*

5 **D.** Task Manager can terminate running applications or background processes. Device Manager can be used to configure hardware devices. System Information can provide status and configuration information about most areas of your computer. *Take a look at "System lockup."*

6 **A, C.** The error is of type 0x0000000A: IRQL_NOT_LESS_OR_EQUAL. The error involves i804prt.sys, which is found at memory address 0xFA840000, not 0x802aa502. There is no information suggesting that the problem may involve the system BIOS. *Peek at "Blue screen errors."*

7 **A.** Link tracking is the OS function that keeps track of the executables that short-cuts refer to. *Look over "Corrupted shortcuts."*

8 **D.** Event Viewer is one of the first utilities that you should use when trying to find out why your system is not responding correctly. WinMSD is the old term used for the System Information tool. Device Manager would list devices that did not start up correctly but would be unrelated to some errors that your system may experience. *Study "Resolving Device Driver Errors."*

9 **A, C, D.** The only item that it might not be is a driver issue. Most of the time, if there is a driver issue, the driver will either not start up or will trigger a Stop (blue screen) error. *Refer to "Solving Boot Errors and Errors Requiring Restarting."*

Chapter 3: Preparing for Disasters with Disaster Recovery

Exam Objectives

✔ Managing emergency boot disks

✔ Booting Windows into special modes

✔ Understanding the Emergency Repair process

✔ Performing backups and restores

*E*ven with the best planning, things go wrong. And when they do, you need to know your options for dealing with the situation. In this chapter, I show you the available options for recovery that are built into the OS. I also introduce you to the concept of a recovery partition and show you how to use a recovery CD.

Small issues that arise can be dealt with on the fly if you know what tools are available. This chapter reviews the tools that you need to know. When a large issue appears, it is critical to have a backup, and know how to restore files from it. This chapter also shows you how to perform both processes.

Working with Boot Disks

If you find yourself with a computer that will not boot because of an Os problem, you want to use a startup disk or a boot disk to get your system back into a bootable state. A *boot disk* holds system files and can start the OS on your computer.

Windows XP doesn't truly have a boot disk like older OSes have, but a disk can be formatted with Windows XP, and the Windows XP boot files can be copied over to the disk. This disk can then take the place of a corrupted boot sector on a Windows XP system. Book V, Chapter 6, describes the files that are required for booting Windows XP and provides details about each. Book VII, Chapter 2, looks at boot issues related to these files and how to resolve the boot issues. The files required on this disk are

✦ NTLDR

✦ NTDETECT.COM

✦ `BOOT.INI`

✦ `NTBOOTDD.SYS` (if it exists)

Use a Windows XP boot disk only as a replacement for a damaged or corrupted hard drive boot sector.

A similar disk can be created for Windows Vista, but this disk would require the following files on a Windows Vista–formatted disk:

✦ `bootmgr`

✦ `\boot\BCD`

Using F8 Options During Boot-up

In Windows 2000 or XP, a message appears at the bottom of the splash screen at the start of the boot process, telling you to press the F8 key to see the advanced boot options. In Vista, there is no prompt, but you can still access the boot menu to appear by pressing F8 immediately after the POST process. After you open the boot menu, you can choose Safe Mode or Safe Mode with Networking. Windows 2000 and Windows XP also have a Safe Mode with Command Prompt option that loads `cmd.exe` as your shell application.

When you access the F8 boot menu at system startup, you reveal several advanced boot options, depending on your OS:

✦ Safe Mode

✦ Safe Mode with Networking

✦ Save Mode with Command Prompt

✦ Enable Boot Logging

✦ Enable VGA Mode

✦ Enable low-resolution video (640x480)

✦ Last Known Good Configuration

✦ Directory Services Restore Mode

✦ Debugging Mode

✦ Disable Automatic Restart on System Failure

✦ Disable Driver Signature Enforcement

Booting into Safe Mode

If the computer hangs or crashes and reboots during the boot process, you might have a device-related error. If a Windows XP or Vista computer fails to boot properly, and you think that the problem is related to a service or driver that is loading, you might be able to boot the computer into Safe Mode.

Windows NT 4.0 does not have a Safe Mode boot, but it does have Enable VGA (Video Graphics Array) mode that you can select from the main boot menu. This is similar to Windows XP Enable VGA Mode, which loads all system drivers with the exception of the video driver. The idea of this option is that with the exception of having the video settings set wrong, the computer will boot and report that some drivers had failed to load — but, it will boot.

When Vista detects that it failed to boot properly, it automatically attempts to boot into Safe Mode during the next boot.

When booting into Safe Mode, the OS skips `config.sys` and `autoexec.bat` as well as any drivers not considered crucial to the boot process. This means that you get a VGA driver providing video in a daring 640 x 480 resolution (16 colors), a keyboard, and a mouse. Initially, you will be presented with a warning telling you that you are entering Safe Mode, after which, the words `Safe Mode` appear in each corner of your screen, as shown in Figure 3-1. Outside of these devices, you will have very few working devices: no sound cards, scanners, or CD burners. With just the basics running, you should be able to identify the driver that did not load properly and then correct the problem.

Figure 3-1:
Safe Mode should be easy to spot, with the wording in each corner.

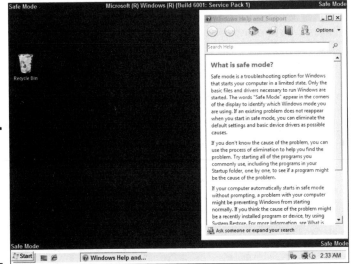

Windows 2000 and newer Windows OSes also support a Safe Mode with Command Prompt. In these versions of Windows, this mode boots the Windows GUI (graphical user interface) but opens cmd.exe as your shell. This allows you to perform many actions to correct your problem (by using utilities such as chkdsk.exe or the Registry Editor). When you are done, exiting the Command Prompt reboots your system.

Both Windows 2000 and newer Windows OSes have a boot option for Safe Mode with Networking. This mode is useful when you need to download new drivers for a failed device or access files that might be stored on your server. With the exception of the loading of the networking drivers, this is a standard Safe Mode boot.

Tracking the boot with a bootlog

When choosing the Enable Boot Logging option from the Windows F8 menu, you create a log file called ntbtlog.txt, which is saved to the winnt or windows directory. This file is appended to when performing logged boots but has a similar structure to the Windows 9x bootlog.txt file.

The ntbtlog.txt file is very useful for troubleshooting boot problems. It logs all drivers, services, and resources while they are loading. This file can then be referenced to locate problems with the boot, especially because the system does not give you much indication of what is happening during the boot.

The structure of a ntbtlog.txt file from Windows Vista is shown in Listing 3-1.

Listing 3-1: A Windows Vista ntbtlog.txt File

```
Service Pack 1 6  1 2009 02:27:51.484
Loaded driver \SystemRoot\system32\ntkrnlpa.exe
Loaded driver \SystemRoot\system32\hal.dll
Loaded driver \SystemRoot\system32\kdcom.dll
Loaded driver \SystemRoot\system32\mcupdate_GenuineIntel.dll
<Lines Deleted>
Did not load driver @hal.inf,%acpiapic.devicedesc%;ACPI x86-based PC
Did not load driver @netrasa.inf,%mp-l2tp-dispname%;WAN Miniport (L2TP)
Did not load driver @netrasa.inf,%mp-ip-dispname%;WAN Miniport (IP)
Did not load driver @netrasa.inf,%mp-ipv6-dispname%;WAN Miniport (IPv6)
Did not load driver @netrasa.inf,%mp-pppoe-dispname%;WAN Miniport (PPPOE)
Did not load driver @netrasa.inf,%mp-pptp-dispname%;WAN Miniport (PPTP)
Did not load driver @netsstpa.inf,%mp-sstp-dispname%;WAN Miniport (SSTP)
Did not load driver @nettun.inf,%isatap.displayname%;Microsoft ISATAP Adapter
Did not load driver @cpu.inf,%intelppm.devicedesc%;Intel Processor
Did not load driver @netrasa.inf,%mp-l2tp-dispname%;WAN Miniport (L2TP)
<Lines Deleted>
Loaded driver \SystemRoot\system32\DRIVERS\i8042prt.sys
Loaded driver \SystemRoot\system32\DRIVERS\kbdclass.sys
Loaded driver \SystemRoot\system32\DRIVERS\vmmouse.sys
```

```
Loaded driver \SystemRoot\system32\DRIVERS\mouclass.sys
Did not load driver @msports.inf,%*pnp0400.devicedesc%;Printer Port
Did not load driver @msports.inf,%*pnp0501.devicedesc%;Communications Port
Did not load driver @msports.inf,%*pnp0501.devicedesc%;Communications Port
<Lines Deleted>
Did not load driver AFD.SYS
 Service Pack 1 6  1 2009 02:15:26.500
Loaded driver \SystemRoot\system32\ntkrnlpa.exe
Loaded driver \SystemRoot\system32\hal.dll
Loaded driver \SystemRoot\system32\kdcom.dll
<Lines Deleted>
Loaded driver \SystemRoot\system32\drivers\peauth.sys
Loaded driver \SystemRoot\System32\Drivers\secdrv.SYS
Loaded driver \SystemRoot\System32\drivers\tcpipreg.sys
```

The ntbtlog.txt file in Listing 3-1 lists the devices that were loaded and the order in which they were loaded. Look through the listing to see what other drivers or devices you can identify. When checking the file, look for items that list LoadFailed or Did not load driver because those are failures related to current problems.

Using the Last Known Good Configuration

If you just updated a driver on your Windows-based computer and your computer will not boot, try booting into Safe Mode to troubleshoot the issue. If the driver update is causing problems with Safe Mode as well, you still have options. Later in this chapter, you can read about the Recovery Console or the Emergency Repair Process, but in some cases, it is quicker to restore the Last Known Good Configuration.

The HKEY_LOCAL_MACHINE\SYSTEM\CurrentControlSet Registry key stores the load or startup settings for all devices and services on your computer, including the path to the driver that is to be used. By choosing to restore the Last Known Good Configuration from the F8 boot menu, you can quickly and automatically restore this section of the Registry with a copy that was used during your last successful boot. If your computer had been running for a long time with many potential changes to this Registry key, those other changes will be lost while you are repairing the boot problem. You will have to decide whether the loss of those other changes is worth the quick restoration of a bootable computer.

Other Windows boot options

There are a few other advanced boot options for Windows XP that you will rarely use, so they are briefly covered here:

✦ **Directory Services Restore Mode (for Windows 2000 or Windows 2003 Domain Controllers):** This boot option will never be used with Windows XP (even though it is in the Options menu) because it is designed to restore the Active Directory database which would be running on a server.

+ **Debugging Mode:** This option is for use with external debuggers, which you might be asked to set up during troubleshooting sessions with Microsoft Professional Services after placing a support call.

+ **Disable Automatic Restart on System Failure:** Some drivers may be configured to cause the system to reboot if they fail to load, but this option prevents the system from rebooting. This option is used to allow the system to complete its boot so that you could perform troubleshooting from within the OS.

Emergency Repair

When things go wrong with the boot of Windows, you can try booting into Safe Mode to repair the error, but sometimes the system will not boot at all. At these times, you can make a final attempt to resurrect the system or start the installation. If you choose to attempt the Emergency Repair Process, you should be prepared by creating an Emergency Repair Disk prior to your computer experiencing problems, and you should be familiar with the repair process.

Emergency Repair Disk (ERD)

Windows 2000 and Windows NT both allow you to create an *Emergency Repair Disk* (ERD), which contains a small replacement version of the system account database and a major portion of the system Registry. This disk can restore the settings and list of the devices or services on the system. It can also replace the account database with a copy of the account database that existed when you created the ERD.

The ERD is not required when performing an Emergency Repair with Windows XP and newer Microsoft OSes.

With Windows NT, the Emergency Repair Disk is created by the `rdisk.exe` utility. You can run `rdisk.exe` from a command window or the `run` command. This utility updates several system files and places copies of them in a special directory, `%winroot%\repair`, which can be copied to a floppy disk after updating. The normal `rdisk` command does not update the SAM and SECURITY files (see Book VI, Chapter 4), but these can be updated by using `rdisk /s`.

For Windows 2000, the Emergency Repair Disk is created with the `backup` utility found at Start⇨Accessories⇨System Tools⇨Backup. When you open this utility, there is an option to create an Emergency Repair Disk on the Welcome tab.

With each new version of the Windows OS, the Registry has become larger. Until Windows XP was released, the registry was able to fit onto a floppy disk. Windows XP and Windows Vista do not use an ERD because it cannot fit the required files onto a disk. The Windows Emergency Repair Process stores its backup copy of the Registry files in the Windows directory, so unless you have hard drive failure, these files will be available when they are needed.

Emergency Repair Process

The Emergency Repair Process begins with booting the system with the Windows OS CD and starting the setup process. After starting the setup process, the first question you are asked is whether you would like to perform an installation of Windows 2000 or Windows XP, or if you would like to perform an Emergency Repair. Windows Vista offers the option to Repair Your Computer on the second screen of the installation process.

After choosing to perform an Emergency Repair, you are asked whether to launch the Recovery Console (discussed in the next section) or perform an Emergency Repair. If you choose an Emergency Repair, you are asked for the Emergency Repair Disk. If you have your ERD, Windows uses the files on the disk; if you do not have your ERD, the Emergency Repair Process searches your drive for a Windows 2000 or Windows XP installation. If it finds one, it uses the repair information found in the `%win-root%\system32\repair` directory. You then have four choices for the Emergency Repair Process:

+ Inspect boot files
+ Inspect startup environment
+ Inspect system files
+ Inspect Registry

If you choose to inspect the boot files or the startup environment, the Emergency Repair Process automatically fixes problems that may exist with either the boot sector or start files, such as `boot.ini`.

If you choose to inspect the system files, the Emergency Repair Process compares every file that makes up the Windows installation with the originals on the Windows CD. If it finds any files that are different, the files might be corrupted, so the Emergency Repair Process asks whether you want to replace the file with the original copy from the Windows CD.

If you choose to inspect the Registry, you then have three choices:

+ Load the `SYSTEM` key.
+ Load the `SOFTWARE` key.
+ Load the `SAM` and `SECURITY` keys.

The Inspect Registry option doesn't so much inspect the sections of the Registry as replace them. The SYSTEM and SOFTWARE sections of the Registry contain settings for services, devices, and applications that are operating on the system. Most services store their settings in the SYSTEM key, but some (for Windows logo requirements) are also stored in the SOFTWARE key. The SOFTWARE key is used primarily for applications.

The SAM and SECURITY keys are replaced as a set. They contain the entire local account database. Replacing the account database on a member server affects only that one computer. If you make the replacement on your Windows NT primary domain controller, you will have replaced your entire domain account database. On Windows Server domain controllers, the local account database is not used.

Rather than choosing to perform the emergency repair process, you could choose to launch the Recovery Console, which contains its own repair and troubleshooting tools. For more on the Recovery Console, proceed to the next section.

If you are using Windows Vista, you will come to System Recovery Options screen, which has the following options:

+ Startup Repair

+ System Restore

+ Windows Complete PC Restore

+ Windows Memory Diagnostic Tool

+ Command Prompt

Windows Vista uses the Command Prompt option rather than the Recovery Console, but it serves the same purpose. This interface allows you to run commands, such as bootrec.exe and bcdedit.exe.

Recovery Console

Recovery Console is a command line–based OS that can be used to help diagnose and repair problems with your installation of Windows 2000 or Windows XP. This command line interface comes with several commands that look familiar to MS-DOS or Windows commands, as well as some that are unique to the Recovery Console. Even the commands that are named the same as MS-DOS commands tend to perform different functions.

Keep in mind that this is not MS-DOS, nor is it Windows XP. Recovery Console is a unique OS used to repair Windows XP.

You can access Recovery Console through the emergency repair process, or you can install it into your boot menu by re-running the Windows XP setup program with the `cmdcons` switch:

```
<winnt_src>\i386\winnt32.exe /cmdcons
```

To initially get into Recovery Console, you have to log into it. Recovery Console checks for copies of Windows XP on your system and lets you log in to one that you choose. To log in, you need the name and password of the local Windows XP administrator account. After providing that information, you will have access only to the files that make up that copy of Windows XP.

By default, you have access only to the `winnt` or `windows` directory. By limiting your access, Microsoft increases security and restricts the amount of damage/harm you can do. If you are booting to Recovery Console, your computer is likely having major problems that you were not able to solve through other means.

Recovery Console offers you several file management tools. Of these, the most notable are `copy`, `del`, and `ren`. All three commands work with only one file at a time and do not support wildcards like their Windows XP equivalents. `format` is the other major file management command at the console. `format` enables you to specify the file system for your partition — FAT, FAT32, or NTFS.

Several commands let you manage the disk and boot sectors on your drive: `chkdsk` for checking your disk for errors; `diskpart` for repartitioning, much like `fdisk` would; and `fixboot` and `fixmbr` for rewriting either the boot sector or the Master Boot Record (MBR) to resolve system startup errors.

In addition to using these commands, you often need to control services and devices during the troubleshooting process. To help with this, you can use the following commands:

+ `listsvc` lists the available services and devices.

+ `disable` disables selected services and devices at boot.

+ `enable` enables selected devices and services at boot.

A couple of unclassified commands include the `logon` and `systemroot` commands. `logon` allows you to log on to another local copy of Windows 2000 for systems that dual boot. `systemroot` switches you to the Windows directory that you are logged onto.

With this assortment of tools, you should be able to get an unbootable copy of Windows XP bootable again. Don't expect to perform much troubleshooting through Recovery Console, but if your server is having Stop errors on boot,

Recovery Console will allow you to get around them. When you are once again running a full copy of Windows XP, you should be able to complete your troubleshooting procedures.

Lab 3-1 gives you some practice working with Recovery Console. For this lab, you need a computer running Windows 2000 Professional or a version of Windows 2000 Server. In addition, you need an installation CD for the operating system and four blank floppy disks. Even though your computer might be able to boot directly from the CD-ROM, this lab makes installation boot disks for Windows 2000 and uses them to initiate the setup routine. If you choose to boot from the CD-ROM, you may have to change the settings in your CMOS, and you can skip down to Step 5 in this lab exercise. Lab 3-1 can be found in the Labs.pdf file in the Author directory of the CD-ROM.

Understanding Backup and Restore

Ensuring data recoverability involves performing a *backup* (normally to another type of medium) in addition to storing the file on the hard drive. This medium could be (for example) a floppy disk, another hard drive, a tape drive, a Zip drive, or CD-ROM.

If you have lost a single file (or all the files) on your hard drive, you will want to perform a restore. You need to have your backup files or tapes available and use the Windows XP backup utility to restore your files.

Backing up your computer

The Windows 2000 and Windows XP backup software is greatly improved over Windows NT 4.0 backup software, and Windows Vista has improved this process even more. Windows 2000 and Windows XP backup software picks up where its predecessor left off, allowing you to schedule regular automatic backups and to back up to nearly any medium you like (including, but not limited to, tape drives). Even though the tool is new, Microsoft has kept the name of ntbackup.exe, and supports all the old command line switches for backward compatibility.

The backup utility allows you to create a backup of all local files on your disk drives, as well as the system state. Open files, such as the Registry and system databases, cannot normally be backed up on your computer, but system state allows you to back up these files by using new file locking methods.

Each organization decides how often it needs to back up each of its computers. This decision is often based on the size and ease of use of the backup media and the value that the organization puts on its files. For example, the loss of a week's worth of invoice records might represent a large amount of revenue to a company, or the loss of a day's worth of rental records at a video store might put a substantial portion of the video store's inventory in jeopardy because they will not have a record of where their movies are. These types of costs are weighed against of the cost of decent backup hardware. Some organizations back up important data once a week, once a day, or several times a day, depending on the perceived cost of data loss.

You start a typical backup by launching the Backup utility, which can be done in one of two ways:

✦ **Run ntbackup.exe.**

All options for the backup utility are available via the command line interface. To get a complete list of the options and their command line switches, type `ntbackup.exe /?` at a command prompt.

✦ **Choose Start➪All Programs➪Accessories➪System Tools➪Backup.**

Either method launches the backup utility. The first time you launch it, it launches in wizard mode, which can be used for backup, and will allow you to back up files using simplified or default settings. This section guides you through the process using advanced mode, which allows you to set detailed options for your file backup or restore.

If you don't want to launch it in wizard mode, clear the Always Start in Wizard Mode check box in the Backup or Restore Wizard dialog box and then click the Cancel button or the Advanced Mode hyperlink. The next time you launch the backup utility, it will launch in advanced mode instead of in wizard mode. When the utility is in advanced mode, you can run the Backup, Restore, or ASR wizards. You can also choose the appropriate tabs to perform a manual backup or restore. The last tab available in the program is the Schedule Jobs tab, which is used to schedule automated backup jobs.

To schedule a basic backup of your system without using the wizard mode, follow these steps:

1. **Choose Start➪All Programs➪Accessories➪System Tools➪Backup.**

The Backup Utility dialog box should open.

2. **If the Backup or Restore Wizard opens, deselect the Always Start in Wizard mode check box and then click the Advanced Mode link.**

3. **Click the Backup tab.**

4. **Select all the drives, folders, or files that you want to back up, as well as the System State, by clicking in the Selection boxes to the left of the names.**

 Backing up the system state backs up core OS files, including files that are open. For Windows 2000 and newer Windows OSes, this option includes

 - COM+ Class Registration database
 - Boot files, including the system files
 - Registry

 If you are backing up a server, the system state may include some or all of the following, depending on what Services are installed on the server:

 - Certificate Services database
 - Active Directory database
 - SYSVOL directory
 - Cluster service information
 - IIS Metadirectory

 System state backups are required to fully restore a computer to its original state and identity on the network. If you are concerned with the data and file system permissions only, you do not need to back up the system state.

5. **Select a location to back up to and then click the Start Backup button.**

 You can back up the files to another local drive or to a tape drive if there is one attached to the computer.

 If you are saving to a file on a drive, the default extension for a backup file is .bkf.

6. **In the Backup Job Information window, click the Advanced button to set the advanced options for the job.**

 The main items to be aware of are

 - *Verify Data after Backup:* This option rewinds the tape or rereads the backup file and compares its contents with each file that was backed up. You can disable this option if you find that some files managed by third-party applications become corrupted during the verification process. This is not normally the case.

- *Disable Volume Shadow Copy:* Volume Shadow Copy is a service that takes a snapshot of all open files on your drive to allow them to be backed up. Some third-party applications might have problems with the Volume Shadow Copy process, so you have the option of disabling this feature, but disabling the Volume Shadow Copy process will prevent some open files from being backed up because the older file lock mechanisms will be attempted.

- *Backup Type:* You have five options, which are summarized in upcoming Table 3-1.

7. Click OK.

8. In the Backup Job Information window that reappears, click the Schedule button.

You are prompted to save your backup selections into a BKS (backup selections) file.

9. Select a location, name the file, and then click Save.

This file can be stored anywhere on your drive, but for organizational purposes, I suggest that you save it in the same location as the BKF file. Saving the backup selections file allows the utility to know what files are to be copied during each scheduled backup time. The BKS file can be loaded into the backup utility any time you want the same selections for a backup.

The Task Scheduler Service prompts you to enter your credentials. The default Windows Task Scheduler Service is used when creating the scheduled automatic backup jobs that appear on the Schedule Jobs tab of the Backup Utility.

10. Provide the credentials of a user with the OS rights to perform a backup of the system.

This includes members of the Administrators or Backup Operators groups. The system uses the credentials you supply when it automatically starts the scheduled backup process.

11. Click OK.

You are presented with the standard options for the Scheduling Service.

OS rights are similar to file system permissions, but they grant a username the ability to perform an action that is not directly related to an object, such as a file. You assign rights using the Local Security Policy or an Active Directory Group Policy Object (GPO). To learn more about rights, read through Book IX, Chapter 2.

12. Select when you would like the backup to run and then click OK.

Table 3-1	Backup Types
Name	*Description*
Normal	Backs up all selected files and clears the Archive attribute so that files can be selected by incremental or differential backups if they are modified. If time and storage capacity permit, normal backups are usually the most desirable.
Copy	Backs up all selected files but does not clear or modify the Archive attribute of the file. This allows you to perform a full backup of your files with the intention of giving the backup to another group, such as the finance department at month's end. Because the Archive attribute isn't touched, your other incremental or differential backups will still be valid and will work as normal.
Incremental	Backs up any selected files that have their Archive attribute set and then clears the Archive attribute. This means that only files that have changed since the last full or incremental backup will be backed up. To restore the files, you need the last normal backup and all incremental backups that have been taken since the normal backup. Even though you need several backups to perform a restore, each backup will be small in comparison with the normal backup.
Differential	Is similar to incremental backups in that it reduces the time it takes to perform the backup, reduces the space required for the backup, and relies on an existing normal backup. The difference with this backup is that the Archive attributes of files are not touched. So with each backup, more and more files are backed up. The benefit of this is that only the most recent normal backup and the most recent differential backup are required to perform the restore.
Daily	Backs up only the files that were changed today and does not touch the Archive attribute. If my normally scheduled backup runs at midnight, and at 4 p.m., I want to run a utility on my drive that might corrupt data, I can run a Daily backup. Because it backs up only the files that were modified during the day, it will be a quick backup; and because it doesn't touch the Archive attributes, if the backup isn't needed, I can continue to use my normal routine for backing up and restoring files. It's like the backup didn't happen — much like the Copy type listed above.

By default, backups create a summary log that lists exceptions or the files that were not backed up. After scheduling and running a backup, you can log onto the computer by logging on as the backup user account that was specified when scheduling the job (Step 10 in the previous instructions).You can then open the backup utility and choose Tools⇨Report. This allows you to read the last ten backup logs.

Windows Vista has modified the backup process even further by integrating scheduling into it, as well as streamlining the file selection process. This has been done to make the entire process more user friendly, as shown in Figure 3-2.

Book VII
Chapter 3

Preparing for
Disasters with
Disaster Recovery

Figure 3-2:
The
Windows
Vista
backup
process.

Restoring files from a backup

You should also become familiar with the steps required to restore those files. To restore files on your system without using the wizard mode in the Backup Utility, follow these steps:

1. **Choose Start⇨All Programs⇨Accessories⇨System Tools⇨Backup.**

 The Backup Utility dialog box should open.

2. **If the Backup or Restore Wizard opens, deselect the Always Start in Wizard ode check box and then click the Advanced Mode link.**

3. **Click the Restore and Manage Media tab.**

 This tab has two panes. The left pane is used to select and catalog backup files you want to restore from and to display the directory tree in a backup file; the right pane allows you to view information about backup files that have been cataloged and to select items that you want to restore. This dialog should already have a backup file cataloged, which will be the one that you created in Step 6 of the backup process.

 If you need to import or catalog a backup file that was created on another computer, or that you have manually deleted from this window, right-click File in the left pane and choose Catalog File, locate and select the backup file that you want to work with, and then click OK.

4. **Double-click the Backup Identification Label of the backup file that you want to work with.**

5. **Using the navigation controls in both panes, navigate through the list of files and folders that are found in the backup and select the files that you want to restore.**

6. **Select one of the three options for the Restore files to drop down menu.**

 - *Original location:* Restores folders and files to the same locations from which they were backed up.

 - *Alternate location:* Restores folders and files to an alternate location, creating a duplicate of the directory structure that was used during the backup, but places the restored files in the directory specified in the Alternate Location text box. This option is useful when you do not want the current copies of the files overwritten.

 - *Single folder:* Restores folders and files to the location specified in the Alternate Location text box. Does not maintain the original directory structure, but rather places all the files restored into the specified directory. This option is useful when you are looking for a few specific files that are buried or lost in a complicated directory structure.

7. **Click Start Restore.**

 This opens the Confirm Restore dialog box, where you can modify advanced options. I will not explore these options in this book.

8. **Click OK to start the restore.**

 The Restore Progress dialog box opens, displaying the status of the file restore. When this process is complete, Close and Report buttons (top-right of the dialog box) appear.

9. **Click Close.**

 The Restore process is now complete, and you can close the Backup Utility.

As with the backup process, the restore process of Windows Vista has been streamlined to make this process more user friendly.

Restore points in Windows

With Windows XP, Microsoft introduced a new system for backing out of driver changes — System Restore. When critical operations (say, updating drivers) are conducted on your system, Windows automatically creates a system restore point. This *restore point* can then be used to revert the system to a previous state in the event of an immediate failure. You can also manually create your own restore points.

If your computer encounters problems related to changes in its system files or settings, you can use a restore point (assuming that you have one saved) to quickly revert your computer to a previous state. It is like having an Undo button for your OS.

Restore points are a replacement for the F8 boot option of Last Known Good Configuration although Microsoft still supports the older and widely known Restore feature.

Manually creating a restore point or reverting your computer to a previous restore point is done via the System Restore Wizard, shown in Figure 3-3. The following sections show you how.

Figure 3-3:
The System
Restore
Wizard.

Manually creating a restore point

You can manually create a restore point from within the System Restore Wizard by following these steps:

1. **Choose Start⇨All Programs⇨Accessories⇨System Tools⇨ System Restore.**

In the System Restore dialog box that opens (refer to Figure 3-3), you can

- Restore My Computer to an Earlier Time
- Create a Restore Point

2. **Select Create a Restore Point and then click Next.**

3. **Provide a description and click Create.**

 A restore point description makes it easier to locate an appropriate restore point during the restore process.

4. **When the creation process is complete, click Close to exit System Restore.**

For the system restore to work, Windows monitors all hard drives on your system. By default, up to 12% of your drive space holds system restore data. This system restore cache setting can be adjusted by choosing Start➪ Control Panel and double-clicking the System applet. Then click the System Restore tab. Figure 3-4 shows the dialog box and the settings for the C: drive which I accessed by selecting the drive and clicking the Settings button. You can adjust the system restore cache by moving the slider and clicking OK.

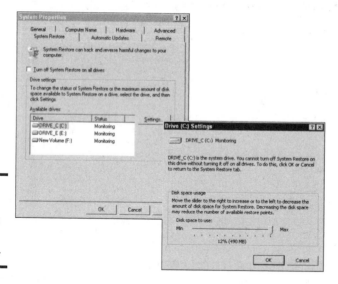

Figure 3-4: Changing the system restore cache size.

Reducing the size of the cache reduces the disk space used by System Restore but also reduces the number of restore points that Windows will keep track of for you, which also reduces the age of your oldest restore.

If you have only one partition or drive on your computer, you can adjust the cache size without going into the settings for the disk.

Restoring your computer to a previous state

Minor and major disasters can require you to access a restore point to return your computer to working condition. The following instructions guide you through restoring your computer to a previous state by accessing a system restore point:

1. **Choose Start⇨All Programs⇨Accessories⇨System Tools⇨System Restore.**

 The System Restore Wizard (refer to Figure 3-3) gives you two options:

 - Restore My Computer to an Earlier Time
 - Create a Restore Point

2. **Select Restore My Computer to an Earlier Time and then click Next.**

 The wizard presents you with a list of restore points, as shown in Figure 3-5.

Figure 3-5: Restoring a system restore point.

3. **Select the appropriate restore point and then click Next.**

 You see a warning you that you will lose recent changes on your system if you choose to restore.

4. **Click Next.**

 Your system reverts to how it was configured at the restore point you chose, and your computer reboots.

ASR in Windows

Before the development of the Automatic System Recovery (ASR) process, restoring a Windows computer via the backup utility required a complete reinstallation of Windows on the system, followed by a restore of the latest backup from backup media, which would be a file or tape. Now, the ASR process integrates a minimal Windows reinstallation with the backup utility's restore process to reduce the total time it takes to get a system up and running.

To use the ASR features in Windows XP, Vista, Windows Server 2003, or Windows Server 2008, you need to first create an ASR backup. Use the ASR Wizard, which can be opened from within the Windows XP backup utility (choose ASR Wizard from the Tools menu). To run the backup, you need backup media and a blank floppy disk (which the backup process will ask for at the end of the ASR backup, as shown in Figure 3-6). The ASR backup does not perform a complete backup of your system; it backs up only the boot partition and system state. Any data on other partitions needs to be backed up and restored separately.

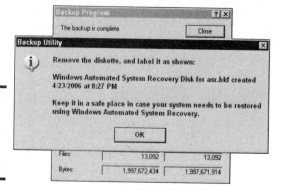

Figure 3-6:
The ASR backup will ask for a floppy disk.

If you lose your ASR floppy disk, you will not be able to restore that ASR backup.

After the backup is completed, you can restore the system by using the following process:

1. **Boot the system from the setup CD.**

2. **Press F2 when prompted to start the ASR process, as shown in Figure 3-7.**

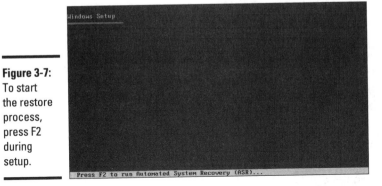

Figure 3-7:
To start
the restore
process,
press F2
during
setup.

3. **Insert your backup disk when prompted, as shown in Figure 3-8.**

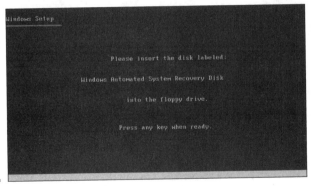

Figure 3-8:
Use the
floppy disk
you created
during the
backup to
complete
the restore.

The Automated System Recovery Wizard appears, as shown in Figure 3-9. The process proceeds automatically, or you can choose to go through it manually. It will perform a base OS installation onto the same partition that was backed up and then attempt to restore the backup that was conducted during the ASR process.

When the process is complete, your system should be in the same state that it was in during the ASR process.

This process was designed to speed up the recovery time for systems that require a restore from backup. With the ASR complete, you can then restore data that is found on other partitions of your system. If the only problems that you encountered were related to your boot partition, your job is complete.

Figure 3-9:
The ASR
restore
process is
automatic.

In Windows Vista, this process was again streamlined. When you choose to create a backup, any backup that is created as a Complete PC Backup can then be restored, similar to the ASR, by booting from the Windows Vista installation CD.

Recovery and Rescue Methods

So far in this chapter, you have seen many different tools that you can use to repair your computer when it is in a nonbooting state. This has included boot disks; Microsoft tools, such as Recovery Console; and the Windows backup utility. This section looks at manufacturer recovery tools, third-party tools, and special Windows installations.

Recovery CDs and recovery partitions

Many large computer companies, such as HP and IBM, provide a quick way to restore your computer to its default factory installation. In the past, this was done by using recovery CDs. When you unboxed your computer, you would get a set of bootable CDs that held some type of image of your computer. If your computer became unusable because of a virus, hard drive failure, or

other issue, you could quickly boot from the CDs and restore your computer to its factory state. One problem with this scenario is that it usually meant that you also lost all of your data if it was not otherwise backed up.

Over the years, with vendors prepackaging applications with their computers, the size of that factory image has gotten larger and larger, so that now it would take multiple CDs, or even multiple DVDs, to store all that data. This change in the preparation of the computers has caused some vendors to use a recovery partition instead. This hidden partition contains the tools needed to restore the image to the rest of the hard drive. If you use partitioning tools and delete the partition, you lose your ability to restore the system to its factory default settings. The vendor will usually, however, give you the ability to back up this partition to CDs or DVDs. Usually, this partition is accessed by pressing one of the computer's function keys during boot-up.

Rescue CDs

A *rescue CD* is a bootable CD that includes tools used to rescue files from a failing hard drive, or to repair problems that occurred with a Windows installation that made it nonbootable. Many third-party rescue CDs are available to the CompTIA A+ Certified Professional. Some rescue CDs are commercially available, but a wide variety of them are available for free. A quick Internet search for *Live CD* will reveal a wide range of these CDs. It seems that there are as many types of custom Live CDs as there are problems that you need to solve. With a little searching and experimenting, you can find one that meets your most common problems to add to your arsenal of tools.

Many rescue CDs run a version of Linux, which has been prepackaged onto a bootable CD or CD image that includes a variety of tools. Knoppix, running a version of Debian Linux, is just one of these Live Linux CDs that many people use as a rescue CD, partly because it has a wide selection of tools and partly because it includes a GUI in the form of the X Window System and KDE. With the variety of applications bundled on the Knoppix CD and the fact that the system runs entirely off of the CD, Knoppix is a great way to try Linux without having to install it. The following offers a brief overview of some of the rescue options that are available to you when using Knoppix, and most of the other Live CDs offer a similar mix of features. Try a few to find one that works for you.

Conveniently enough, Wiley Publishing also publishes *Knoppix For Dummies,* by Paul G. Sery, which includes a complete Knoppix 4.0 distribution on DVD. So you can have your cake and learn how to eat it, too.

The Knoppix boot process starts off with a confirmation of your intention to boot into Knoppix, as shown in Figure 3-10. There are advanced boot options that you can access or get information about by pressing F2 or F3, but in most cases, the system will boot without additional information.

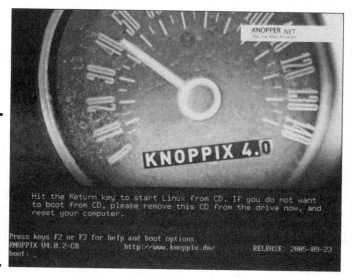

Figure 3-10:
If your computer has unique hardware, you might need to use special boot options.

If you are not familiar with Linux, here's a pointer: Linux identifies hard drives with letters and partitions with numbers, so in a typical IDE/ATA system, your four devices or drives are identified as hda, hdb, hdc, and hdd, with the C: drive usually being hda1 (The 1 means partition 1). In the case of Knoppix, all local disk partitions are automatically mounted for read-only access and will appear on the desktop. You can change the properties of the disk to allow writing to it; otherwise, you can browse and read files on your system. Figure 3-11 shows the properties of a Windows shortcut file that is found on hdb1 in a labfiles directory.

With the tools on this Live CD, you can verify many settings and even modify files that are found on your Windows installation. In Figure 3-12, the boot.ini file on hda1 (the C: drive) is being modified with correct settings for the controller and partition.

Figure 3-11:
Local files can be managed and many settings viewed.

Figure 3-12:
Editing local files to correct configuration problems.

Knoppix has several tools that you will likely find useful, such as `partimage` (partition image; allows you to perform disk imaging tasks on your partitions) and `parted` (a command line, disk partition–editing tool). Figure 3-13 shows the interface of QTParted (a GUI front end for `parted`). This interface is reminiscent of Partition Magic. You can use QTParted to create, resize, delete, and move partitions around your drive.

Figure 3-13: The disk partition management is easy to use after you understand how Linux refers to disks and partitions.

To copy files to or from a Windows server on your network, you can use tools like Samba Network Neighborhood to access shared folders on your servers. You can use this tool to copy network drives to a computer that doesn't have them or to rescue files from a hard drive that is very near failure and can no longer support booting. Figure 3-14 shows the shares that are available on the server `192.168.1.3`.

Figure 3-14:
Files may be
transferred
to and from
file servers.

Another popular option for a rescue CD is BartPE, which can be created
with PE Builder (www.nu2.nu/pebuilder). (PE stands for Preinstalled
Environment, which is a minimally installed copy of Windows XP that runs
off of a bootable CD.) The unique feature of this disk is that you are running
Windows XP, which allows you to run native Windows tools rather than
Linux tools. This greatly increases the number and type of tools available to
help repair your computer system. Some of the types of tools include

+ File management

+ Antivirus

+ Disk management and maintenance

+ Internet and download Tools, such as a Web browser

+ Editors and other Windows applications

Because of licensing and copyright restrictions, PE Builder does not include
OS or application files for most applications; but rather, it copies required
files from your original OS installation disk and from copies of applications
that you already have installed on a working computer. A running copy of
BartPE with many of its applications is shown in Figure 3-15.

Figure 3-15:
BartPE is
a popular
Windows-
based
rescue CD.

Many people have created plug-ins for Bart-PE, which are skeleton directory structures that contain instruction files for setting up the applications in PE-Builder. Because most of these are contributed by the user community, duplication can occur, and sometimes one version of a plug-in is better than one contributed by another user.

This disk has gained a great deal of popularity for disk imaging tools such as Symantec Ghost because it supports a wide variety of network drivers by default. This makes loading images off a network very easy, and you are not required to squeeze network drivers and the application onto a 1.4MB floppy disk.

You will find Lab 3-2, Working with PE Builder, on the CD that walks you through setting up a BartPE disk. You will require a computer running Windows XP as well as your installation CD for Windows XP.

Rescue partitions or rescue installations

Many of the quickest ways to repair a Windows installation are actually built into Windows. To repair a Windows installation from a Windows installation, you need only a small amount of planning. If you leave some free, unpartitioned space on your hard drive, you can create a rescue partition. A *rescue partition,* or *rescue installation,* of Windows is simply another copy of Windows that is installed onto your computer.

This second copy of Windows is not the default for booting, and is used only to repair problems to your normal installation of Windows. So if your default copy of Windows is installed on Drive C:, your rescue install could be installed on Drive D: or Drive E:. The partition should be used only for the Windows installation, and not used to store data for your normal installation. After installing Windows in the second location, it will be automatically set as the default boot. To change the default booting installation of Windows, follow these steps:

1. **Choose Start⇨Control Panel.**

2. **If your Control Panel folder displays in category view, choose Performance and Maintenance⇨System; if your Control Panel folder displays in classic view, double-click System.**

3. **In the System properties dialog box that opens, click the Advanced tab and then on Settings in the Startup and Recovery section.**

4. **In the Startup and Recovery dialog that opens, choose the copy of Windows that you would like to be the default booting installation from the Default Operating System drop-down menu. Then click OK twice to close both open dialog boxes.**

Getting an A+

This chapter helps you prepare for disasters by covering the following topics:

✦ Using the NTBackup.exe utility to protect your data

✦ F8 boot options that can be used to correct startup problems

✦ System restore points and how to use them to repair configuration problems

✦ Recovery CDs and partitions, and rescue CDs and partitions

Prep Test

1 When enabling a logged boot of Windows 2000, what is the name of the log file that is created?

- **A** ○ `ntbtlog.txt`
- **B** ○ `bootlog.txt`
- **C** ○ `btlog.txt`
- **D** ○ `ntlog.txt`

2 What command would you use from Recovery Console to attempt to repair the boot sector?

- **A** ○ `listsvc`
- **B** ○ `disable`
- **C** ○ `systemroot`
- **D** ○ `fixboot`

3 Which of the following files is not required on a Windows XP boot disk?

- **A** ○ `ntldr`
- **B** ○ `ntbtlog.txt`
- **C** ○ `ntdetect.com`
- **D** ○ `boot.ini`

4 A user bought a new video card with 128MB of RAM. He needs it to play the new version of his favorite video game. After installing the video card, he boots up his Windows XP computer and is overjoyed when he sees the Plug and Play Wizard detect the new hardware. When prompted, he provides the driver disk that came with his computer. After loading the driver for his new video card, his computer reboots. During the next boot, his computer halts and will not respond to any controls. What should he do next?

- **A** ○ Reboot his computer by using the power button. His computer will automatically boot to the Last Known Good Configuration.
- **B** ○ Reboot his computer by pressing Ctrl+Alt+Del and then pressing F8 when he sees the message to Press F8. He will then be able to choose Disable Advanced Video Options from the boot menu.
- **C** ○ Reboot his computer by using the power button. His computer will automatically display the boot menu and attempt to boot to Last Known Good Configuration without user intervention.
- **D** ○ Reboot his computer by pressing Ctrl+Alt+Del and then hold down F9 to enable Safe Mode.
- **E** ○ Reboot his computer by using the power button. When he sees the message to Press F8, press it and select either the Last Known Good Configuration or Enable VGA Mode.

5 Where does Windows XP store the boot log file, `ntbtlog.txt`?

A ○ The root directory of the first hard drive, typically `C:\`

B ○ The `C:\Windows` directory

C ○ The `C:\Windows\system32` directory

D ○ The `C:\recoveryerrors` directory

6 What items are required to perform an ASR system restore? Choose all that apply.

A ❑ The ASR floppy disk

B ❑ Your most recent backup

C ❑ Your ASR backup

D ❑ Your ERD floppy disk

E ❑ A Windows XP installation CD

7 When you boot the F8 option of Last Known Good Configuration, what action restores the configuration?

A ○ Deleting the recent drivers that have been installed. All driver locations are stored in `C:\Windows\inf`.

B ○ Restoration of old Registry keys from backup tape.

C ○ Execution of `rollback.com`, to reset the correct configuration.

D ○ Replacing the registry key `HKEY_LOCAL_MACHINE\SYSTEM\CurrentControlSet` with a backup copy.

8 What operating systems can create an ERD for the Emergency Repair Process? Choose two.

A ❑ Windows 2000

B ❑ Windows 98

C ❑ Windows NT

D ❑ Windows XP

9 What tasks are completed by the Windows XP Emergency Repair Process? Select all that apply.

A ❑ Inspect boot files

B ❑ Inspect driver configuration

C ❑ Inspect system files

D ❑ Inspect Registry

10 What type of backup will back up all selected files and clear the archive attribute of all files that are backed up?

A ○ Daily Copy

B ○ Differential

C ○ Copy

D ○ Normal

Answers

1 **A.** The file is named `ntbtlog.txt`. *See "Booting into Safe Mode."*

2 **D.** `fixboot` is the command to repair the boot sector. *Review "Recovery Console."*

3 **B.** The only files that are required on a Windows XP boot disk are `ntldr`, `ntde-tect.com`, and `boot.ini`. *Check out "Working with Boot Disks."*

4 **E.** Either of these two options, Last Known Good Configuration or Enable VGA Mode will allow him to boot his computer. If he chooses to boot the Last Known Good Configuration, any changes that he made to the hardware configuration since the last boot will be lost. If he chooses the Enable VGA Mode, he will be able to select a different driver to be used by the graphics controller or apply other software patches to get the system running. Safe Mode should be his next step on correcting the problem. *Peruse "Using F8 Options During Boot-up."*

5 **B.** The boot log file is stored in the Windows directory. *For more information, see the section titled "Tracking the boot with a bootlog."*

6 **A, C, E.** To complete an ASR restore, you need an ASR floppy disk, your ASR backup, and the Windows XP installation CD. After completing the ASR restore, you might want to restore a more recent backup to update any files on your boot drive that were changed since the ASR backup or to restore files from par-titions other than the boot partition. The ERD is used when performing emer-gency repairs on Windows 2000 computers. *Take a look at "ASR in Windows."*

7 **D.** *Peek at "Using the Last Known Good Configuration."*

8 **A, C.** Only Windows 2000 and Windows NT can create an Emergency Repair Disk (ERD) to be used in the Emergency Repair Process. This disk is not required for Windows XP to complete the Emergency Repair Process. *Examine "Emergency Repair Disk (ERD)."*

9 **A, B, D.** The Emergency Repair Process does not inspect driver configurations. *Check out "Emergency Repair Process."*

10 **D.** The Normal backup will back up all selected files and clear the archive attri-bute on all files that are backed up. *Review "Understanding Backup and Restore."*

Book VIII

Networking

Contents at a Glance

Chapter 1: Down to the Networking Basics

Exam Objectives

✔ Identifying network types

✔ Understanding network topologies

✔ Working with network cables

✔ Becoming familiar with network architectures

✔ Accessing the network

✔ Installing a Small Office/Home Office (SOHO) Network

The A+ Certification exams cover two areas of networking: networking theory/networking hardware and networking at the operating system (OS) level. This chapter focuses on the networking theory and the networking hardware area of the A+ exams. For the exam, you are required to know popular terms and features of networking environments that you will encounter on the exams and in the real world — which is what this chapter will help you with. Networking at the OS level is covered in Chapter 3 of this minibook.

Identifying the Types of Networks

A *network* is a group of connected systems for sharing data or devices. This section provides an overview of the two major types of networks: peer-to-peer and server-based (client-server). I discuss the advantages and disadvantages of each type as well as how to implement them.

Peer-to-peer networks

In a *peer-to-peer* (P2P) network, all systems connected to the network can act as clients or servers. A *client* is a system that makes a request for a resource or service on the network; a *server* is the system providing the resource or service. In this type of networking environment, all systems are considered equal because they can all play the same roles on the network — either as client or server or as both client and server. The recommended number of systems in a P2P network usually involves ten or fewer systems because of the lack of centralized administration. As a network administrator working in a P2P environment, you will constantly run from machine to

machine to perform administrative tasks. Typically, a P2P network involves each system running a desktop operating system, such as Windows XP, to provide network functionality (see Figure 1-1).

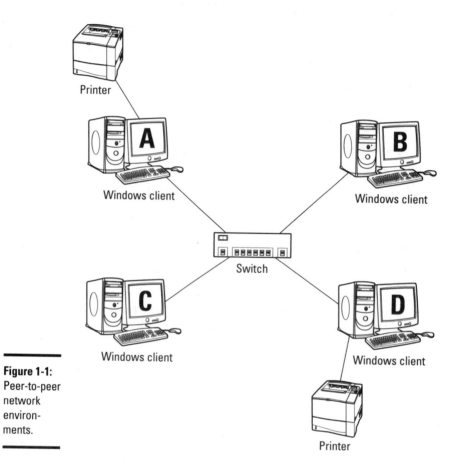

In Figure 1-1, notice that client A provides a network resource — a printer — as does client D. This shows that client A is acting as both a server and a client, which is the purpose of a P2P network.

Because a central machine doesn't store files in a P2P network, your networking environment isn't based on the centralized administration approach. With *centralized administration,* you (as network administrator) could perform network administration tasks for the entire network from one place. Looking back to Figure 1-1, you can see that because all four computers act as *peer servers* (meaning they all act as servers to one another), you need to do the administration on all four computers — a major disadvantage of P2P networking.

Some examples of the administration you must perform on each system are creating user accounts on each computer and managing file and folder sharing from each system. In Figure 1-1, for example, if you want Bob to log on to client A, you would create the Bob account on client A. At the same time, if you want Sue to log on to client B, you would create the Sue account on client B. Because the Bob account doesn't exist on client B, Bob can't log on to that computer even though he might be able to access the files on client B from client A. This leads to a *distributed administration* model because your work is spread across multiple machines.

The major advantage of P2P networking is that you save money by not needing to purchase a central server, which can cost thousands of dollars in hardware and software. Too, with a P2P network, you also don't have to purchase a separate network operating system (NOS). A NOS, required on a server-based network (discussed in the next section), is designed for networking services (such as Dynamic Host Configuration Protocol [DHCP], Web, file, and print services) and allows the server to share its files and printers with clients on the network. The cost of the NOS, and the licenses to have clients connect to the server, is where a number of large companies spend most of their IT budget. Licensing is expensive!

Server-based (client-server) networks

Server-based networking, also known as *client-server* networking, is the networking model that most companies usually choose for ten or more workstations on a network. Unlike a P2P network, server-based networking uses a central machine (the server) that delivers network services to the workstations. Once again, these network services could be services such as file and print sharing, user account authentication, or Web services.

The benefit of a client-server configuration is that you can leverage centralized administration by performing the bulk of your work on the one server. For example, if you need to create user accounts for each of the ten users, you create the ten accounts on the one server. Compare that with a P2P network, where one account is created on each system. As the administrator of this network, you create all shared directories on the server along with user accounts so that the server may verify the credentials of a client who attempts to log on to the network. All users on the network connect to this server to save and retrieve files.

Tighter security is another benefit of using a server-based networking model. Creating a more secure environment is easier with a server-based network because your resources and user accounts are not spread across multiple machines. Looking at Figure 1-2, you can focus on the server because it contains the files, folders, and user accounts. When a user logs on to the network, the logon request is sent to the server, which verifies that the username and password are valid. After a user is logged on, the

server allows the user access to resources, such as files and printers, that the user has permission to use. Figure 1-2 illustrates a server-based networking environment.

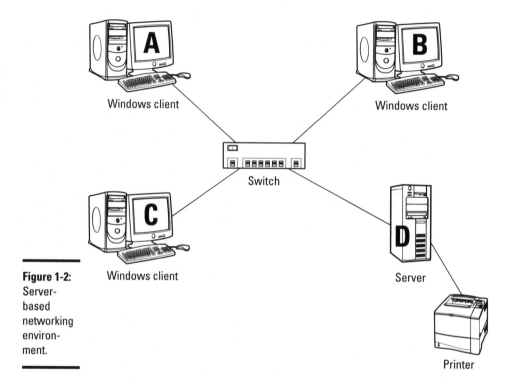

Figure 1-2:
Server-
based
networking
environ-
ment.

Notice in Figure 1-2 that the client systems connect to the server to access the printer. In this environment, all systems have a defined role: They are either a client or a server — but not both.

The disadvantage of using a server-based environment is the cost of purchasing the server hardware and the NOS. When designing your networking model, make sure that you work with someone familiar with software licensing so you get the best bang for your buck!

Additional networking terminology

Another set of terms you will hear when talking with other IT professionals about network concepts is local area network (LAN) and wide area network (WAN).

A *LAN* is a network that typically involves one office building, or maybe even networked systems on one floor. The major point to remember when identifying a LAN is that there isn't a lot of distance between the systems on the network.

Comparatively, a *WAN* is a network environment that involves connecting two or more LANs. Each LAN typically covers its own building or office location. Companies typically link each office location to network with the other office locations. Connecting all office locations creates the WAN.

Understanding Network Topologies

When building a network, be cognizant of some upfront decisions regarding the overall network setup. Building a network is like building a database: You have to understand the theory before you start the hands-on work.

Topology refers in a general sense to layout; similarly, a *network topology* defines the layout of the network. The three basic network topologies are bus, star, and ring. The following sections discuss the different network topologies and their characteristics.

Bus

A *bus topology* uses a main wire (or trunk) to connect all network devices so that they can communicate with one another. The main trunk is fairly cheap to install but expensive to maintain. Figure 1-3 shows a diagram of a bus topology; notice that all systems are connected to a main cable.

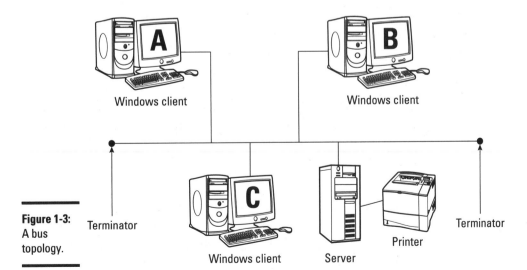

Figure 1-3:
A bus
topology.

Windows client

Windows client

Terminator

Windows client

Server

Printer

Terminator

When a workstation sends data to another workstation in a bus topology, data (in the form of an electrical signal) is delivered across the full length of the trunk. Each workstation looks at all data that runs along the trunk. If the data is destined for a particular workstation, that workstation copies the data to the memory on its network adapter.

For example, Figure 1-3 shows what happens when client A sends information to client B.

1. The information runs along the trunk.

2. When it passes by client C, client C checks whether it is also a destination for the information; if not, client C ignores the data.

3. The information continues down the wire and makes its way to client B.

4. Client B looks at the data to determine whether the data is destined for it; if so, client B copies the data and stores it in the memory on the network card.

Note that because client B has made a *copy* of the data, the data is still on the wire. The data continues on the wire past the server and hits the terminator at the end of the trunk segment.

A *terminator* is a device that absorbs the electrical signal when it reaches the end of the network trunk. If there were no terminator at the end of the cable, the signal would bounce back in the other direction and collide with any new data being placed on the wire. So, to prevent this collision, the terminator grabs any signals that hit it and ensures that it is absorbed off the wire.

In a bus topology, any break in the wire creates a nonterminated end. When there is a nonterminated end on the bus signal bounce occurs and as a result the entire network collapses.

Star

One of the most popular types of network topologies today is the star topology. A *star topology,* shown in Figure 1-4, involves a central component, called a *hub* (older networks) or a *switch* (today's networks), which connects all systems and is used to send the electrical signal to all connected systems.

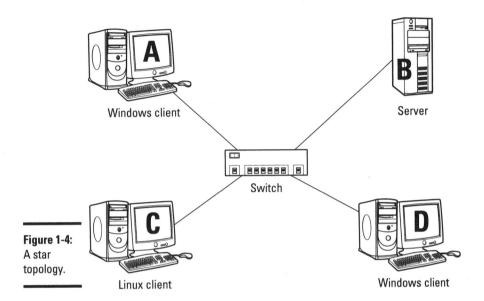

Figure 1-4:
A star
topology.

With the star topology shown in Figure 1-4, if client A sends information to client D, the information first travels from client A to the hub. The hub sends the information through each port on the hub: as a result, reaching each workstation connected to the hub. Each workstation is responsible for determining whether it is the data's intended destination. When client D receives the data, it checks the destination address of the packet, identifies itself as the recipient of the data, and then copies the data to the network adapter's memory. If the data is not destined for the client, the client simply discards the packet.

Today's networks use switches instead of hubs. Here's an example of how a switch works. When client A sends data to client D, the information first travels from client A to the switch and then the switch forwards the information only to the port that client D resides on. The information does not get sent to all the clients connected to the switch, like what a hub does. This data path offers performance benefits and also security benefits. Find more on hubs and switches later in the "Working with Network Devices" section of this chapter.

One of the major benefits of using a star topology is that if a cable breaks, it doesn't take down the entire network like it would with a bus topology; only the workstation connected to the broken cable is affected. If a hub device breaks, however, the entire network fails. In all fairness, though, the cost to implement a star topology might be a little more than a bus topology because of the price of the hub or switch device used.

Ring

In a *ring topology,* each computer is connected to the next computer, creating a physical ring. Although ring topologies are not common today, you still see them in IBM's token ring architecture (see the section "Token ring," later in this chapter). Figure 1-5 shows a ring topology.

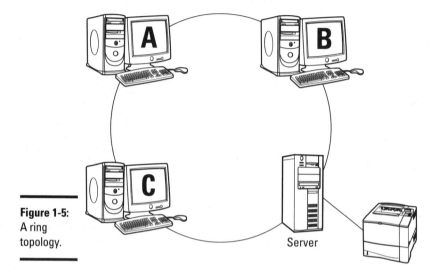

Figure 1-5:
A ring
topology.

In environments that use the ring topology, data is usually passed from workstation to workstation. Because data becomes distorted when it travels great distances, each workstation is responsible for reading the data, regenerating the data, and then passing the information on to the next workstation. Like with a bus topology, any break in the ring causes the entire network to fail.

Hybrid

A *hybrid topology* is a mixture of two or all of the three basic topologies. For example, you could use a bus topology as a main trunk, connect hubs to the main trunk, and then connect the systems to the hubs. Figure 1-6 shows an example of this type of hybrid topology.

To be more accurate, the configuration shown in Figure 1-6 could be called a *star-bus topology* — a star topology mixed with a bus topology. Today, the most popular topology in use is the star topology — or maybe even a hybrid topology using a star-bus layout.

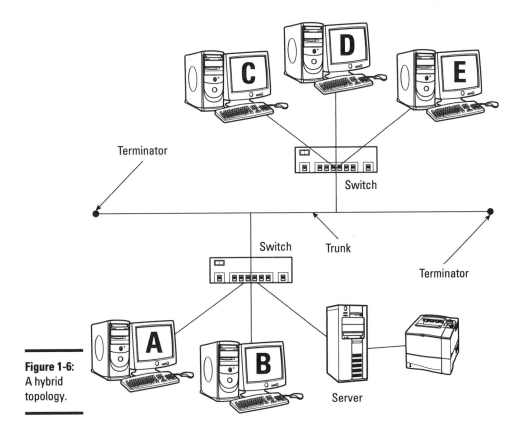

Figure 1-6:
A hybrid
topology.

Wireless

Today's networks allow more mobility for network clients by supporting wireless technologies. To implement a wireless solution, you build a wireless network that uses a wireless topology. A *wireless topology* typically involves a wired network with wireless clients connecting to the wired network through a *wireless access point (WAP)*, which is a device that sends and receives signals to a wireless client via radio waves (shown in Figure 1-7).

Notice in Figure 1-7 that the wireless client sends data to the WAP, which has a connection to the wired network. The WAP sends the wireless data to the destination system by sending the signal through the wired media.

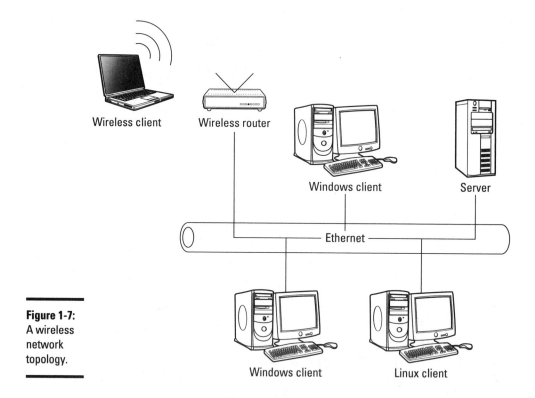

Figure 1-7:
A wireless
network
topology.

Connecting with Network Cabling

After choosing your network topology, it is time to connect all the network devices together, which means deciding the type of cabling to use. The following sections discuss and evaluate the different types of cabling available for standard networks.

Twisted pair

Twisted pair cabling, which is inexpensive and easy to use, is one of the most popular types of cabling used. It gets its name from the fact that it contains four pairs of wires twisted around each other inside the cable's outer *jacket,* the outer covering of the cabling shown in Figures 1-8 and 1-9. Twisted pair cabling comes in two flavors — unshielded twisted pair (UTP) and shielded twisted pair (STP) — shown in Figure 1-8 and Figure 1-9, respectively.

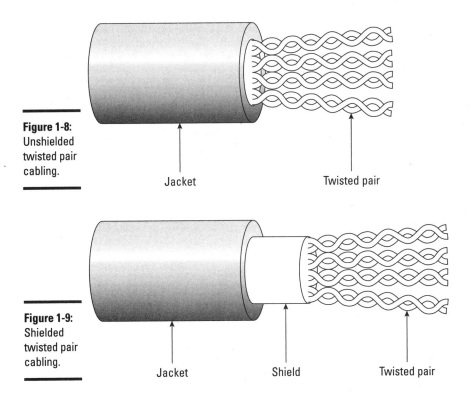

Figure 1-8:
Unshielded
twisted pair
cabling.

Jacket Twisted pair

Figure 1-9:
Shielded
twisted pair
cabling.

Jacket Shield Twisted pair

The only difference between UTP and STP is that STP cabling has an extra layer of insulation, which helps prevent interference from outside devices or cabling. Such interference can distort the data traveling along the cable length.

UTP comes in a number of different flavors, called *grades* or *categories*. Table 1-1 lists the categories of UTP cabling, as well as their purpose and speed.

Table 1-1	UTP Category	
Category	*Purpose*	*Speed*
Category 1 (CAT1)	Voice only	
Category 2 (CAT2)	Data	4 Mbps
Category 3 (CAT3)	Data	10 Mbps
Category 4 (CAT4)	Data	16 Mbps
Category 5 (CAT5)	Data	100 Mbps
Category 5e (CAT5e)	Data	1 Gbps
Category 6 (CAT6)	Data	10 Gbps

**Book VIII
Chapter 1**

**Down to the
Networking Basics**

Because twisted pair cabling does not have the layers of shielding found in other forms of cabling, the data is pretty much unreadable — or the integrity of the data is questionable — after 100 meters. For this reason, twisted pair cabling has a maximum length of 100 meters.

For the exam, you are expected to know the speeds of the different categories of UTP cabling. Also, remember that twisted pair cabling has a maximum distance of 100 meters regardless of whether it is a shielded or unshielded twisted pair.

Twisted pair cabling uses a special type of connector to connect the cable to the system or network devices. This connector is similar to those used to connect a telephone to a telephone jack. Network devices that use twisted pair cabling use the RJ-45 connector, and telephones use the RJ-11 connector. Figure 1-10 shows both.

Figure 1-10:
An RJ-45 connector (left) and an RJ-11 connector (right).

Coaxial

Coaxial (coax) cabling is the type of cable you use for cable television. A copper wire in the center of the cable is responsible for transmitting information. Furthermore, the copper wire is protected by two levels of insulation and an exterior plastic covering, as shown in Figure 1-11.

Like UTP, coaxial cabling used for networking comes in different flavors — two, to be exact. *Thinnet* is only one-quarter-inch thick, and *Thicknet* is one-half-inch thick. Table 1-2 shows the difference between Thinnet and Thicknet.

Figure 1-11:
Looking
at coaxial
cable and a
coax cable
with the
BNC style
connector.

Table 1-2		Types of Coax Cabling		
Type	*Coax Type*	*Maximum Cable Length*	*Diameter*	*Speed*
Thinnet	RG-58	185 meters	¼"	10 Mbps
Thicknet	RG-8	500 meters	½"	10 Mbps

Notice in Table 1-2 that the coaxial cable type is specified by a *radio grade (RG)*. There are a number of grade standards for coaxial cable, and each standard has a specific purpose and connector type that will work with that type of cabling. For example, RG-58–grade cabling (Thinnet) uses BNC connectors (discussed in more detail in the next section), and an RG-8–grade cable uses an AUI connector.

Another popular grade of coaxial cable is RG-6 — the grade of coax used for television cable — which uses the F-type connector to connect the cable to the device. Figure 1-12 displays coaxial cables along with an F connector and a BNC connector.

**Book VIII
Chapter 1**

**Down to the
Networking Basics**

Figure 1-12:
An F-type connector and a BNC connector.

Connecting with Thinnet

When using Thinnet to connect to a workstation, you need to use a *Bayonet Neill-Concelman* (BNC) connector — also known as British Naval Connector (BNC), which comes in a few forms. You will most likely encounter the plain old BNC and the BNC-T.

The BNC connector connects Thinnet cable to a networking device, such as a network card, using the barrel connector on the back of the network card, as shown in Figure 1-13.

Figure 1-13:
A BNC connector connecting to a workstation.

The BNC-T — shaped like the letter T — is used to continue the cable length while "T-ing" off to connect a system to the network, as shown in Figure 1-14.

Figure 1-14:
A BNC-T
connector
used on
Thinnet
coax cable.

Notice in Figure 1-14 that the BNC-T connects to a metal barrel–type port on the back of the network card. If you do not need to continue the cable length and this is your last workstation, you are required to terminate the end with a terminator on the T connector, as shown in Figure 1-15.

Figure 1-15:
A BNC-T
connector
with a
terminator.

Connecting with Thicknet

A system or device connected to a Thicknet network uses an *adapter unit interface (AUI)* port (shown in Figure 1-16), which connects the system to the Thicknet cabling by using a transceiver known as a *vampire tap*.

Figure 1-16:
An AUI port.

The vampire tap gets its name by having small "teeth" that clamp to the cable and cut into the cable's core, allowing the electrical signal to travel from the system to main network cable and beyond.

Fiber optic

Fiber optic cabling — one of the fastest types of network media available — is made of a glass fiber core (optical fiber) surrounded by a layer of glass cladding insulation that is then covered with an outer covering (jacket). There are two fiber channels in fiber optic cable: one for sending information and the other for receiving information. Figure 1-17 illustrates a fiber optic cable.

Figure 1-17:
Fiber optic
cabling.

Outer covering Glass cladding Optical fiber

Fiber optic cabling can reach distances of 2 kilometer (km) or more, carrying a signal for a much greater distance than twisted pair and coaxial cabling. Fiber optic cabling is also fast, transmitting information at speeds of 1 Gigabit per second (Gbps) and higher. And, because fiber carries data in pulses of light instead of electronic signals, data cannot be corrupted by outside electronic interference.

You will be expected to know details regarding fiber optic cabling for the exam. Fiber carries data through pulses of light along its glass core and can reach distances of 2 km. Fiber optic cable transmits information at speeds that range from 100 Mbps to 10 Gbps.

The two implementations of fiber optic cabling are single-mode fiber (SMF) and multimode fiber (MMF):

+ **Single-mode fiber (SMF):** Uses only one ray of light, known as a *mode*, to carry the transmission over great distances.

+ **Multimode fiber (MMF):** Takes advantage of multiple rays of light, or modes, simultaneously. Each ray of light runs at a different reflection angle and is used to transmit data over short distances.

Fiber optic cabling uses a number of different types of connectors. The following list provides a few that you need to be familiar with for the A+ exam:

+ **Straight tip (ST):** The straight tip connector is derived from the BNC-style connector but uses a fiber optic cable instead of the copper cabling used with BNC. Figure 1-18 shows an SC and ST connector.

+ **Subscriber connector (SC):** The subscriber connector is rectangular and is somewhat similar to an RJ-45 connector.

+ **Fiber local connector (LC) and mechanical transfer-registered jack (MT-RJ):** These newer fiber optic connector types resemble the registered jack and fiber SC shape. The MT-RJ is a small connector similar in appearance to an RJ-45 connector. The LC is similar in appearance to the fiber SC connectors and is the preferred connector for transmissions exceeding 1 Gbps because of its small form factor.

Figure 1-18:
Looking at strands in fiber optic cabling along with the SC (bottom) and ST (top) connectors.

The primary disadvantage of using fiber optic cabling is the implementation cost and the expertise required for the wiring.

Troubleshooting Networking Cables

Most network professionals use cable testers to test the cabling and verify that the cable is properly crimped and making contact with the networking devices. For example, cable testers for CAT5 cabling identify whether each of the eight wires is crimped properly and identify other problems, such as wires being crimped in the wrong order.

Another problem you need to be aware of when running cable throughout a building is that twisted pair and coaxial cables are susceptible to outside interference from other electrical components. For example, do not put networking cable alongside the electrical cabling because the electrical cabling could cause interference that could make the data on the network cable unreadable. For more information on cable testers and troubleshooting cabling problems, check out Book IV, Chapter 2.

Here is one last point to make about cabling to help you prepare for the A+ certification exams. *Plenum* — the space between the ceiling tile and the floor above — is a popular place to run cables. If you are going to run cables in this area, make sure that you are use plenum-grade cabling. If you are use nonplenum-grade cabling in this space and a fire happens, nonplenum-grade cabling can give off a toxin that could be spread throughout the building.

Examining Network Access Methods

Network access refers to the different methods that computers use to place data on the network. This section discusses these methods and identifies the advantages and disadvantages of each.

CSMA/CD

One of the most popular types of access methods is CSMA/CD (Carrier Sense Multiple Access/Collision Detection). Understanding this term is easier if you break it down into its individual parts and examine each part in detail:

✦ **Carrier sense:** All computers on the network are watching, or sensing, the network for network traffic. If the network has data already on the wire, a system will wait until the wire is free of traffic.

✦ **Multiple access:** All computers on the network have equal access to the network at any given time. In other words, anyone can place data on the network whenever he or she chooses. Note, however, that workstations on the network will try not to place data on the wire at the same time the wire is transmitting other data because the two pieces of data will collide, destroying the data. That's why it's so important for workstations to "sense" the wire.

To summarize, *carrier sense multiple access* suggests that all workstations have access to the network and are watching the network to make sure it is clear of data before they send out their information.

✦ **Collision detection:** When two workstations send information at the same time, the data will collide and be damaged in transit. When two workstations have data that has been involved in a collision, they resend the information out on the network at variable intervals to prevent the data from colliding again.

The nice thing about CSMA/CD is that the workstations decide when to send data, trying to prevent collisions. However, there is always the possibility that multiple workstations will send data out at the exact same moment the network is clear, resulting in data collision.

CSMA/CA

Carrier Sense Multiple Access/Collision Avoidance (CSMA/CA) is similar to CSMA/CD except for one main difference: When a workstation senses that the wire is free, it sends out dummy data first instead of real data. If the dummy data collides with other information on the wire, the workstation has avoided a collision with the real data; if the dummy data does not collide, then the workstation sends the real data. Like CSMA/CD, if the real data collides and does not reach its destination, it will be resent by the sender.

CSMA/CA is not a popular access method, but it has been used in AppleTalk networks.

Token passing

You might have attended a meeting where a ball was passed around to indicate who had the authority to speak: In order to speak, you had to be holding the ball; if you didn't have the ball, you had to wait your turn. Token passing is based on the same principle. A token — an empty piece of information running around the network from computer to computer — must be in a computer's possession before the computer can put data out on the wire.

When the token reaches a workstation, the workstation puts data out on the wire by filling the token with information and marking the token as being used. The token (with the information) is then released onto the network and travels toward its destination. Each workstation checks whether the token is destined for it when the token passes by. Each workstation regenerates the data and passes it to the next workstation.

When the token reaches the destination, the destination system reads the data and then sends a reply or confirmation message to the sending computer. When the sending computer receives the reply, it places a new, empty token on the wire.

Piecing Together the Network Architectures

A *network architecture* describes a network technology that uses a specific topology, cable type, and access method. This section describes the major types of architectures and their characteristics.

Many people use the term *architecture* to mean *topology,* stating that the three main types of architectures are bus, star, and ring. However, bus, star, and ring are properly defined as topologies, not architectures. Be careful not to confuse the two terms. A *topology* defines the network layout, whereas an *architecture* is made up of a topology, cable type, and access method.

Ethernet

Ethernet is probably the most popular type of network architecture in use. Ethernet is an example of a network architecture that comes in multiple flavors. If someone says to you, "I have an Ethernet network," you are likely to ask, "What type of Ethernet?"

There are a number of types of Ethernet: 10BaseT, 10Base2, 10Base5, 100BaseT, and 1000BaseT being a few popular ones. All Ethernet architectures use CSMA/CD as the access method, but each type of Ethernet uses a different topology or cable type. The following sections outline the differences among them.

10 megabit Ethernet standards

The following outlines some of the popular 10 Mbps network architectures that have been popular in past years. You need to be familiar with these for the A+ Certification exams.

When trying to remember the names of these network architectures, start by looking at the number at the beginning of the name — it indicates the transfer rate. In this case, the transfer rate is 10 Mbps. You can then look at the tail end of the name to tell what type of cable the architecture uses. For example, in 10BaseT, the letter "T" at the end of the name implies "twisted pair." The word "base" in the middle means *baseband transmission,* which means that the signal takes up the entire width of the media when sending and receiving data.

+ **10BaseT:** A network architecture that typically uses a star topology but can, in some cases, use a hybrid star-bus topology. 10BaseT networks primarily use CAT3 UTP cabling, which transfers information at 10 Mbps. 10BaseT uses the CSMA/CD access method for putting information on the network.

✦ **10Base2:** A network architecture that uses a bus topology, but can sometimes use a hybrid star-bus topology. 10Base2 networks typically use Thinnet coaxial cabling, which transfers information at 10 Mbps. 10Base2 uses CSMA/CD as its access method.

✦ **10Base5:** A network architecture that uses a bus topology. 10Base5 networks primarily use Thicknet coaxial cabling, which transfers information at 10 Mbps. Like 10Base2, 10Base5 uses CSMA/CD as its access method.

✦ **10BaseFL:** An old Ethernet architecture that ran at 10 Mbps and used fiber optic cabling. 10BaseFL uses CSMA/CD as the access method.

Remember that 10BaseFL used fiber cables by the *F* in the name.

100 megabit Ethernet standards

You are unlikely to see a 10 Mbps network architecture on today's networks, so it is more important that you have an idea of some of the popular 100 Mbps Ethernet architectures:

✦ **100BaseT:** An improved network architecture over the 10BaseT networks. It uses a star topology, but can also be found using a hybrid star-bus topology. 100BaseT networks primarily use CAT5 UTP cabling, which transfers information at 100 Mbps. 100BaseT also uses CSMA/CD as its access method.

✦ **100BaseFX:** Another Ethernet architecture that runs at 100 Mbps but is different than 100BaseT in that it uses fiber optic cabling instead of UTP cable. 100BaseT and 100BaseFX are referred to as the "Fast Ethernet" standards. 100BaseFX uses CSMA/CD as the access method.

Gigabit Ethernet standards

Today's corporate networks are reaching 1 Gbps (1000 Mbps) and higher, so it is important that you are familiar with the Gigabit Ethernet standards for the A+ certification exams:

✦ **1000BaseT:** Uses UTP cabling; uses CSMA/CD as the access method

✦ **1000BaseSX:** Uses multimode, fiber optic cabling for short distances; uses CSMA/CD as the access method

Remember this architecture by the *S* in the name, meaning *short* distances.

✦ **1000BaseLX:** Uses single-mode fiber optic cabling; uses CSMA/CD as the access method

Because single-mode fiber optic cabling is designed for long distances, it is the type of fiber optics used for 1000BaseLX.

Remember this standard by the *L* in the name, implying *long* distances.

10 Gigabit Ethernet standards

Some of the fastest network standards today fall into the 10 Gbps Ethernet architectures. The 10 Gbps Ethernet architectures use fiber optic cabling, either SMF or MMF, depending upon the architecture. For example, the 10GBaseSR standards uses multimode fiber optic cabling that can reach a short distance of 100 meters, and 10GBaseLR uses single-mode fiber optic cabling that reaches a distance of 10 km.

Nowadays, you will probably purchase network cards that are marketed as 10/100 cards or maybe even 10/100/1000 cards. This means that the network card can be used with networking environments that transfer information at 10 Mbps, 100 Mbps, or 1000 Mbps.

Token ring

Token ring is a unique network architecture because it is completely different in design from Ethernet. As its name implies, *token ring* uses a ring topology with token passing as the access method. Although a token ring network can use almost any type of cabling, it typically uses CAT5 UTP.

Token ring, which comes in two flavors (4 Mbps and 16 Mbps), also has a special name for the hub that connects all the workstations together — multistation access unit (MAU). Because of this MAU, a token ring network appears to use a star topology, but internally, the MAU is connected as a ring, making a complete circle. Figure 1-19 shows a token ring MAU.

Figure 1-19: A token ring MAU.

For the exam, remember that all Ethernet environments use CSMA/CD as an access method, and token ring architectures use token passing as their access method. Also remember that token ring was developed by IBM.

When IBM developed token ring architecture, the company also developed its own cable type and a proprietary connector: the *IBM-type data connector (IDC)* or *universal data connector (UDC)*. Figure 1-20 shows an IBM proprietary cable with an IDC connector.

Figure 1-20:
An IBM-type data connector (IDC) cable with a token ring MAU.

FDDI

The *Fiber Distributed Data Interface (FDDI)* network architecture uses token passing as an access method and fiber optic cabling as a cable type. FDDI also uses a ring topology like token ring does, but the difference is that with FDDI there are two rings: a primary ring and a secondary ring. The secondary ring is used for fault tolerance if the primary ring goes down, meaning that the second ring is only used if the primary ring fails.

Lab 1-1 will help you identify the different network architectures. Lab 1-1 can be found in the Labs.pdf file in the Author directory of the CD-ROM.

Understanding Network Protocols

To ensure that all the networking components work with one another, networking standards have been developed. If a company decides that it wants to develop something like a network card, it will ensure that the network card follows a standard so that it can communicate with all the other networking components. In this section, you find out about the different network standards that help each networking vendor develop networking components that function alongside other networking devices.

IEEE standards

The *Institute of Electrical and Electronics Engineers (IEEE)* has developed a number of LAN standards that define the physical components of networking technologies. In these standards, the IEEE has defined such things as how network cards place data on the wire and the type of cabling used

in different types of LANs. The LAN standards are defined by Project 802, which was launched in February 1980. These 12 standards, shown in Table 1-3, define different networking architectures.

Table 1-3	Project 802 LAN Standards
Project	*Description*
802.1	Internetworking
802.2	Logical Link Control (LLC)
802.3	Ethernet (CSMA/CD)
802.4	Token Bus LAN
802.5	Token Ring LAN
802.6	Metropolitan Area Network
802.7	Broadband Technical Advisory Group
802.8	Fiber Optic Technical Advisory Group
802.9	Integrated Voice/Data Network
802.10	Network Security
802.11	Wireless Networks
802.12	Demand Priority Access LAN

A few of the networking standards that you should be familiar with are 802.3, 802.5, and 802.11:

+ **802.3:** This networking standard defines the Ethernet architecture, also known as CSMA/CD. This standard defines how data is placed on the wire. A system senses the wire to verify that it is free of data and then submits the data.

+ **802.5:** This IEEE standard defines the token ring network architecture. This architecture uses the token passing access method, which is a set of rules that control how a system submits data on the wire.

+ **802.11:** This IEEE standard defines wireless networking. Wireless networking has evolved over the past few years, and as a result, there are a few different types of wireless networks, wireless 802.11b and 802.11g being the two dominant standards:

 • *802.11b:* This wireless standard has a transfer rate of 11 Mbps and runs at the 2.4 GHz frequency range. 802.11b created the Wi-Fi standard.

- *802.11g:* This wireless standard has a transfer rate of 54 Mbps and is backward compatible with 802.11b because it also runs at the 2.4 GHz frequency and is part of the Wi-Fi standard. This means that you can have an 802.11b WAP and have a system with a more current 802.11g wireless network card, and both systems will still be able to communicate. They will use the lower transmission rate of the two, though!

- *802.11n:* This new wireless standard has a transfer rate of up to 300 Mbps and is compatible with 802.11b and 802.11g wireless networking environments because it runs at the 2.4 GHz frequency.

For the exam, you don't need to memorize the entire list of standards. However, know that Ethernet is defined in project 802.3, token ring is defined in project 802.5, and 802.11 defines the wireless standards. You will be tested on them!

For more information on wireless networking, check out the next chapter.

The OSI model

The *Open Systems Interconnect (OSI)* model is a seven-layer model defined by the International Standards Organization (ISO) that provides a framework that manufacturers of networking components can use to develop networking hardware and software components.

Each layer of the OSI model is responsible for specific network functions. For example, the network layer is responsible for logical addressing, so any devices or protocols that provide logical addressing run at this layer — such as the IP protocol. Table 1-4 outlines the seven layers of the OSI model and provides examples of networking components that run at that layer.

Table 1-4	The OSI Mode
Layer	*Description*
7, Application	Responsible for making or receiving a network request and is typically the networking software. For example, a Web server, FTP server, and DNS server run at this layer.
6, Presentation	Responsible for formatting the information so that the information is understood on the receiving system. Examples of formatting are compression and encryption.
5, Session	Responsible for opening, closing, and managing a connection (a *session*) to another system or device.

(continued)

Table 1-4 *(continued)*

Layer	Description
4, Transport	Responsible for breaking the information down into smaller pieces so that it can be sent along the network in parts. This layer is also responsible for ensuring that the information reaches the destination.
3, Network	Responsible for routing of information and logical addressing. A router runs at this layer, and the IP protocol runs at this layer, which provides a logical address (IP address).
2, Data Link	Prepares the information to hit the physical network by placing the data into packets. The data link layer also provides the physical addressing (MAC address), so any device that works with a MAC address runs at this layer (such as a network card, switch, and bridge).
1, Physical	Deals with the network media such as cabling and connectors. The physical layer is also responsible for sending the electrical signal on the wire. Any device that works with the electrical signal runs at this layer such as a hub or repeater.

Although the OSI model is more of a Network+ topic, you might receive a few questions on the OSI model with your A+ Certification exams. Be familiar with what layer of the OSI model a hub, switch, and router run at.

Voice over IP (VoIP)

Voice over IP (VoIP) is a fairly hot topic these days. VoIP deals with allowing subscribers to the VoIP service to have telephone conversations over a TCP/IP network, such as the Internet. The benefit of such a service is no more long-distance charges — just your monthly subscription to the service.

VoIP not only allows for the transmission of voice but also other types of data, such as video. VoIP has become a popular method of communication that supports PC-to-PC communication, essentially using the PC as a phone.

Working with Network Devices

A computer network is a lot more than just a few computers and a tangle of cables. A computer network needs a number of different types of devices to connect the systems or to connect the network to another network. This section identifies the different types of network devices popular in network environments today and covers the devices you will be tested on for the A+ exams.

Be familiar with these devices for the A+ exam and understand their benefits.

Network interface card (NIC)

The network interface card (commonly referred to as a *network card*) is responsible for connecting the computer or device to the network. More importantly, the network card on the sending computer is responsible for converting digital data into an electrical signal for copper or optical signal for fiber that can be placed on the wire. The network card on the receiving computer is responsible for picking up the electrical signal and then converting it back to digital data that can be understood by the computer system.

Each network card has a unique address burned into the ROM chip on the card. This unique address is considered the *hardware address* of the network card because the manufacturer of the card burns it into the card. The address uniquely identifies your system on the network. The hardware address is also known as the *Media Access Control (MAC) address.* An example of a MAC address is 00-20-3F-6B-25-13.

Looking at the example of a MAC address, notice that the MAC address is made up of hexadecimal addresses — not your typical decimal numerals or binary values. Of the six groups of digits, the first three pairs identify the manufacturer of the network card, and the last three pairs are a unique set of digits assigned to a particular card built by the manufacturer. So, 00-20-3F, which appears at the beginning of my example MAC address, represents the manufacturer of the card, and 6B-25-13 identifies the card.

The MAC address of the sending and receiving system is stored in the header of the network packet that travels the network wire. When each system sees the packet traveling by it, it looks at the destination MAC address to decide whether the data is destined for it. If a system finds that it is the intended recipient for the data, it copies the data to its *buffer,* which is memory used to store the information while it waits to be processed. Figure 1-21 shows a network interface card.

<div style="float:right">

**Book VIII
Chapter 1**

Down to the
Networking Basics

</div>

Two lights on the network card act as status indicators — the activity light and the link light. The link light is always lit when you have a connection to the network; the activity light blinks when the network card is sending or receiving information. When troubleshooting network problems, always check that the link light is on, indicating a connection to the network.

Figure 1-21:
A network
interface
card.

Repeater

One major concern with cabling is the maximum usable length of the cable. For example, UTP cabling has a maximum length of 100 meters, and Thinnet has a maximum length of 185 meters. The reason for putting a maximum distance on cable lengths is that the signal traveling along the cable becomes too weak to read at the destination system by the time the maximum length is reached. The receiving computer cannot read the information, and thus does not acknowledge that it received the data. When the sending computer does not receive an acknowledgment, it simply resends the data. This causes the information to be resubmitted, generating more network traffic.

One way to increase the distance of a cable length is to use a *repeater,* which regenerates a signal so it can travel the extra distance. For example, the repeater shown in Figure 1-22 joins two lengths of Thinnet coaxial cable. It joins the two cable lengths so that the signal can travel the distance from computer A to computer B. Note that this distance exceeds 185 meters, which is the maximum distance of Thinnet. When the signal hits the repeater, the repeater rebuilds the signal so that it can travel another 185 meters.

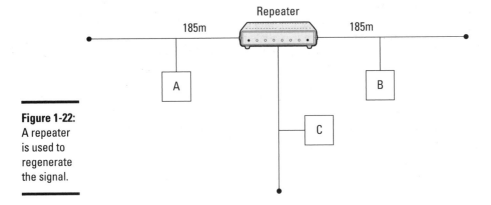

Figure 1-22:
A repeater
is used to
regenerate
the signal.

Bridge

Because all data passing through a repeater is regenerated and sent to all parts of the network, a great deal of network traffic is generated that affects the overall performance of the network.

To prevent this buildup of network traffic, you can use a bridge (as shown in Figure 1-23), which is a device that connects network segments and also regenerates the signal (like a repeater). A bridge also filters the data so that it is sent only to the proper portion of the network, cutting down on network traffic and increasing overall performance.

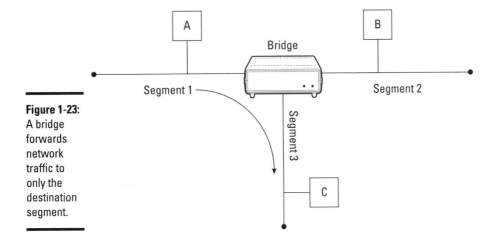

Figure 1-23:
A bridge
forwards
network
traffic to
only the
destination
segment.

Figure 1-23 illustrates that when computer A sends information to computer C, the information travels along segment 1 and eventually reaches the bridge. The bridge looks at its *bridging table* (a list of MAC addresses and

**Book VIII
Chapter 1**

Down to the
Networking Basics

corresponding network segments that runs in memory) to see which network segment computer C exists on. In this example, it lives on segment 3. At this point, the bridge forwards the information only to segment 3, where computer C resides, and not to any other segment, thus filtering traffic and cutting down on network noise.

Bridges increase performance on the network by filtering the network traffic, which gives the network and all its devices and applications more bandwidth to work with. The less network traffic, the less chance of collision and retransmission.

Router

A *router,* which is responsible for sending information from one network to another, is an important network device because most companies are connected to the Internet. When a computer on your network wants to send information to a computer on another network, your computer passes the information to your router. Figure 1-24 shows three different networks, each connected to the Internet by a separate router. All computers on network A know that any information with an outside-network destination must be passed to the router because the router is the only device with a physical connection to the outside world.

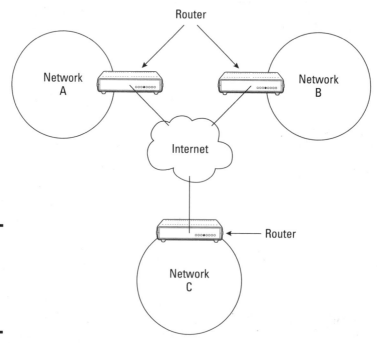

Figure 1-24: Routers send data from one network to another.

Gateway

A *gateway* is a unique network device responsible for converting information from one format to another. Think of a gateway as a translator between two different languages: As information passes from one side to another, the gateway "translates" the information to a format that can be understood on the other side.

You might encounter questions on the exam in which you must identify the device based on a description. For the exam, remember that a *gateway* is a device or piece of software that translates data from one format to another.

Hub

A *hub* is a central device that acts as a connection point for all hosts on the network. A hub is a very basic device that passes all data that hits the hub to every port on the hub. This means that when a computer sends data to another computer, all systems will see the data on the network even though only the destination system for the data will process the data. Figure 1-25 shows a network hub.

Figure 1-25:
A network hub with eight RJ-45 ports and one BNC port.

Book VIII
Chapter 1

Down to the
Networking Basics

As the number of hosts on the network grows, you can "cascade" or connect one hub to another. Any data that reaches a port on a hub will be sent to all ports on all connected hubs, which could congest the network with traffic.

As I mention earlier, today's networks use switches instead of hubs. The term "hub" is used in this chapter only so that you know what a hub is in case you come across it in conversation or readings.

Switch

A network *switch* is a device that looks similar to a network hub but differs in that the switch does not forward the data to all ports like a hub would. Instead, the switch sends the data only to the port that the destination system resides on. Figure 1-26 shows a network switch.

Figure 1-26:
A 24-port network switch.

Switches can dramatically increase network performance because they filter the traffic by sending the data only to the destination port on the switch instead of to all ports on all hubs. Switches also offer security benefits because a system that is not the destination of the information does not receive a copy of the information, thus reducing the opportunity that someone other than the intended recipient can see your information.

Wireless access point (WAP)

A very popular network component today is a wireless access point. A WAP, typically connected to a wired network, is responsible for accepting data from wireless clients and then passing that data to systems on the wired network. The wireless access point can also receive information from the wired systems and then send that information to the wireless systems.

You can find a number of popular brands of wireless access points, such as Linksys, D-Link, and NetGear. Wireless access points that include additional features, such as firewall capabilities, are *wireless routers*. Figure 1-27 shows a wireless router used by home and small office networks.

A wireless router has an antenna that collects the radio waves that carry the data from the wireless client. The wireless router also has a WAN port on it so that you can connect your Internet cable into it and share the Internet connection with all systems on the network. The WAP in Figure 1-27 also has four additional RJ-45 ports to connect four wired systems.

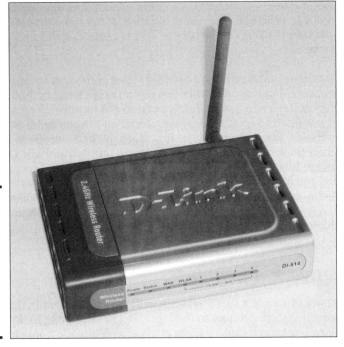

Figure 1-27:
A four-port wireless router also contains a WAN link for the Internet connection.

The WAP is a multifunction device in the sense that it not only allows wireless clients to connect to the network, but it is also a four-port switch, allowing wired clients to connect to the network.

Understanding Communication Methods

Different network devices, such as network cards, support different methods of communication. The three major communication methods in the computer world are simplex, half-duplex, and full-duplex:

✦ **Simplex:** A device that supports simplex communication can deliver information in only one direction. Typically, the device can send information but cannot receive information.

✦ **Half-duplex:** A device that supports half-duplex communication can deliver information in two directions, but not at the same time. A typical example of a half-duplex device is a walkie-talkie or CB radio, which enables you to send and receive information but not at the same time. When you use a CB radio, you say "Over" to let the person on the other end know that you are done talking and that it is the other person's turn to send information.

✦ **Full-duplex:** A device that supports full-duplex communication is one that can send and receive information at the same time. Full-duplex is similar to talking on the phone: You are free to speak and to listen at the same time.

When purchasing networking or other types of devices for your computer, it is important to know whether you are buying a simplex, half-duplex, or full-duplex device to avoid problems later. For example, a musician friend of mine wanted to record his own material on the computer with recording software. After recording the first track, he had a problem recording a second track because his sound card was only a half-duplex device. He wanted to listen to the first track while playing along and recording the second track, which was impossible with his half-duplex sound card. He needed to have the sound card send and receive information at the same time, something that a half-duplex device can't do. The solution: Get a new, full-duplex sound card.

Ways to Network a Computer

If you want to build a small network with four computers in the home and have each system connect to the Internet, the best thing to do is to buy a home router from D-Link or Linksys. After you buy the home router, which is also a four-port switch, connect the four computers to the ports on the router and then plug the Internet connection into the WAN port. All systems are now interconnected and also to the Internet. But what if you need to connect two systems and you cannot connect them by using a hub or switch? You need to be aware of the different and varied methods used to network two computers, including the following:

✦ Installing network cards

✦ Using serial or parallel ports

✦ Using infrared ports

The following sections describe the different computer networking methods.

Network card

The first task when using network cards to network two computers is to find out what type of network card you need for each system. You will have to find out whether the network card will be an ISA, EISA, or PCI device. Open up the system and look at the different expansion slots that exist, or you can look at the documentation for the system.

After you purchase the network card and install it into your system, load the driver for the network card. If you're lucky and the network card is a Plug

and Play device, the driver might load automatically for you, or you might be prompted by the OS to provide a manufacturer diskette with the driver for the device.

After you install the driver, you might have to spend some time troubleshooting the device because of resource conflicts with other existing devices. Once again, if you have a Plug and Play device, this step will probably not happen because the resources will be assigned dynamically by the OS.

Serial and parallel ports

You may also network two computers via the serial or parallel ports of both systems. Using standard parallel or serial ports for networking two devices can be a lot slower than networking two computers via a network card. You will connect the parallel ports with a *laplink cable,* and you will use a *null modem cable* for serial ports (RS-232 ports).

Here are the two networking methods that use serial ports:

✦ Connect a modem to each computer's serial port and have the modems use the phone lines as the cabling.

✦ Connect two computers directly by connecting the serial ports with a null modem cable.

If you try to connect two computers with a normal serial cable, the transmit data (TD) wire on one computer will be connected to the TD wire on the other computer, and the receive data (RD) wire on one computer will be connected to the RD wire on the other computer. No communication will occur in this situation. What you need is the TD wire on one computer connected to the RD wire on the other computer. A null modem cable is designed to do this, crossing the sending and receiving wires.

Infrared port

Many systems today, especially laptop computers, have built-in infrared ports that can connect to other devices on the network. For example, you can print to a printer sans parallel cable by using infrared technology.

Infrared technology uses an infrared light beam to carry data between devices. It typically requires clear line-of-sight — a clear path between the two devices. Infrared is limited in distance to about 100 feet and can transfer information up to 10 Mbps.

Lab 1-2 will give you some practice creating a small office or home network. Lab 1-2 can be found in the `Labs.pdf` file in the Author directory of the CD-ROM.

Installing a Small Office/Home Office (SOHO) Network

When installing a *Small Office/Home Office* (SOHO) network — a home office network or a network to be used by a small office with a few employees — you need a number of network components to get the network up and running. This section introduces you to the network components needed to build a small network.

The first major component that you need is a home router, which is a multifunctional device that provides you with all the network components that are needed for your SOHO. Then decide whether to go wired or wireless. If you opt for wired, you need the appropriate type of cabling. If you go wireless, make sure you get a wireless router. Finally, you might want to think about using a server. After the networking nuts and bolts are in place, think about security.

Functions and benefits of a home router

A home router has a WAN port that you use to connect to your high-speed Internet connection. This could connect to your cable modem or your DSL modem, and will be used to share the Internet connection with any users on the network.

The following is a list of benefits to having the home router in your SOHO network:

✦ **DHCP:** The first feature of the home router that is important is that the home router is a DHCP server, which is responsible for assigning IP addresses to clients on the network so that they can gain network access.

✦ **Internet sharing:** The home router will also share the Internet connection that is plugged into the WAN port to all the users on the network. This functionality is provided through Network Address Translation (NAT) capabilities.

✦ **Wireless capabilities:** Most home routers are also wireless routers, which allows computers or devices with a wireless card to access the network. The wireless client sends data to the router, which will then be forward to the Internet through the WAN port.

✦ **Web site filters:** Through the configuration of the home router, you can limit which Web sites users on your network can view. You can also put schedules in place that control when users can use the Internet. Today, home routers provide a number of filtering capabilities to control the type of content that can be surfed.

✦ **Network switch:** A home router typically has a four-port switch built in to allow any wired clients to connect to the network. These clients will receive an IP address from the DHCP server built into the router as well so that they can use the network.

✦ **Firewall:** A home router has firewall features built in to prevent persons on the Internet from connecting to the systems on your LAN. By default, the firewall is enabled!

To use a home router, simply connect the WAN port of the wireless router to your high-speed Internet connection and then connect your systems to any of the four LAN ports on the router. These systems will get an IP address from the DHCP server built into the router and then will be able to surf the Internet.

Running a server on a SOHO

You might eventually look at installing a server for your SOHO. The server performs many different functions, such as holding files that you want to share with other users on the network. The server could also be used to share a printer to all other users on the network.

This server doesn't have to be a system running the Windows Server OS. It could be a Windows XP or Vista system with sharing enabled, and sharing a folder for everyone else to access or sharing a printer that everyone else on the network can access.

For more information on sharing printers and files, check out Book VIII, Chapter 3.

Wireless networking for a SOHO

A very simple way to allow systems to connect to your network without needing to run cables throughout the entire office or home is to use wireless networking. If you purchase a wireless router, it will allow computers with a wireless network card to connect to the wireless router and any systems connected to it. The wireless client will also be able to surf the Internet because the wireless router will share the Internet connection with not only the wired computers but the wireless systems as well.

To learn more about wireless networking, check out Book VIII, Chapter 2.

SOHO security practices

When building a SOHO network, you have to create a security network structure to protect your business assets. The three chapters in Book IX give you the foundation to network security, so be sure to read over those three chapters and incorporate them into your SOHO network.

**Book VIII
Chapter 1**

**Down to the
Networking Basics**

Here is a summary of popular security best practices when creating a SOHO network and using a wireless router:

✦ **Wireless security:** There are a number of steps to take to secure your wireless network. For more information on wireless networking check out Book VIII, Chapter 2.

- Change the Service Set Identifier (SSID)

- Disable SSID broadcasting

- Implement MAC filtering

- Enable an encryption protocol, such as WPA or WPA2

To learn more about wireless security, read Book VIII, Chapter 2.

✦ **Router security:** Regardless of whether your router is wireless, look at disabling DHCP and statically assign an IP address to each system. The benefit is that if someone else connects to your network (especially if you have not secured the wireless), they will not get an IP address.

✦ **Firewall:** Use a firewall to protect the network and to protect the systems. A home router has firewall features built in, but you might also look at installing personal firewall software on each system.

✦ **Administrator password:** Change the usernames for any administrator accounts on your routers and servers if possible. Be sure to set a strong password on these accounts after they are renamed.

✦ **Update firmware:** To make sure you are dealing with the most up-to-date features on the router, do a firmware update of the router. You can get any updates to the firmware from the manufacturer's Web site.

Again, this section is definitely not designed to give you details on how to set up a SOHO network but rather to expose you to the term and some of the considerations with SOHO networking. You can incorporate all the networking and security features covered in Books VIII and Book IX in your SOHO network, so be sure to read those chapters carefully!

Getting an A+

This chapter introduces you to a number of key concepts in network terminology. Understanding networking and how to troubleshoot the network has become an important skill for an IT professional, and you will be asked a few networking questions on the A+ exam. Remember the following points when preparing for the exam:

♦ The three types of cables used on networks are twisted pair, coax, and fiber optic.

♦ The three basic types of network layouts (topologies) are bus, star, and ring.

♦ An access method determines how a system places data on the wire. Two popular access methods are CSMA/CD and token passing.

♦ Ethernet is the most popular network architecture used today. Other examples of network architectures are token ring and FDDI.

♦ Some of the most popular networking devices are hubs, switches, and routers.

♦ *Switches* filter network traffic by sending the data only to the port used by the destination system. *Routers* are responsible for sending data from one network to another.

Prep Test

1 What category of UTP cabling transmits data at 16 Mbps?

 A ○ Category 2

 B ○ Category 3

 C ○ Category 4

 D ○ Category 5

2 Which of the following defines simplex communication?

 A ○ Allows information to be sent and received, but not at the same time

 B ○ Allows information only to be sent

 C ○ Allows information to be sent and received at the same time

 D ○ Allows information to be sent, but only after dependent information is received

3 What is the transfer rate of Category 3 cabling?

 A ○ 2 Mbps

 B ○ 10 Mbps

 C ○ 16 Mbps

 D ○ 100 Mbps

4 What is the maximum distance of a Thinnet segment?

 A ○ 100 meters

 B ○ 500 meters

 C ○ 250 meters

 D ○ 185 meters

5 What is the recommended number of users for a peer-to-peer network?

 A ○ Fewer than 100

 B ○ More than 100

 C ○ Fewer than 10

 D ○ More than 10

6 What access method is used for Ethernet?

 A ○ Token passing

 B ○ CSMA/CA

 C ○ Twisted pair

 D ○ CSMA/CD

7 Which of the following defines half-duplex communication?

 A ○ Allows information to be both sent and received, but not at the same time

 B ○ Allows information only to be sent

 C ○ Allows information to be sent and received at the same time

 D ○ Allows information to be sent, but only after dependent information is received

8 What category of UTP allows for data transfer at 1 Gbps?

 A ○ Category 3

 B ○ Category 4

 C ○ Category 5

 D ○ Category 5e

9 Which topology must be terminated at both ends to prevent signal bounce?

 A ○ Ring

 B ○ Star

 C ○ Bus

 D ○ Coaxial

10 What access method best describes CSMA/CA?

 A ○ Data is placed out on the wire; the sending workstation detects whether there is an error and retransmits if there is.

 B ○ A token runs around the network; when a computer wishes to send data out on the network, it fills the token with information.

 C ○ Dummy data is placed on the wire; if the dummy data collides with other information, then the real information is not transmitted. If the dummy data does not collide, then the real data is delivered.

 D ○ Dummy data is placed on the wire; if the dummy data collides with other information, then the real information is transmitted. If the dummy data does not collide, then the real data is withheld.

11 Which of the following best describes a client-server environment?

 A ○ All users on the network connect to one another for the purpose of file sharing.

 B ○ All users on the network connect to a central server and access resources on that central server.

 C ○ All users on the network connect to one another for the purpose of printer sharing.

 D ○ Each user accesses only one other user's computer.

12 **What is the maximum distance of UTP cable?**

A ○ 100 meters

B ○ 185 meters

C ○ 250 meters

D ○ 500 meters

13 **Which of the following best describes token passing?**

A ○ Data is placed on the wire; the sending workstation detects whether there is an error and retransmits if there is.

B ○ A token runs around the network; when a computer wishes to send data on the network, it fills the token with information.

C ○ Dummy data is placed on the wire; if the data collides with other information, the real information is not transmitted. If the dummy data does not collide, the real data is delivered.

D ○ Dummy data is placed on the wire; if the data collides with other information, the real information is transmitted. If the dummy data does not collide, the real data is withheld.

14 **Which of the following sends data in the format of pulses of light?**

A ○ Fiber optic

B ○ 100BaseT

C ○ 10BaseT

D ○ Coaxial

15 **What is the maximum length of 10Base5 cabling?**

A ○ 100 meters

B ○ 185 meters

C ○ 250 meters

D ○ 500 meters

16 **Which of the following best describes full duplex communication?**

A ○ Allows information to be both sent and received, but not at the same time

B ○ Allows information only to be sent

C ○ Allows information to be sent and received at the same time

D ○ Allows information to be sent, but only after dependent information is received

17 What Ethernet architecture transfers information at 1 Gbps over short distances and uses fiber optic cabling?

A ○ 1000BaseSX

B ○ 1000BaseLX

C ○ 1000BaseTX

D ○ 100BaseTX

18 What type of connector connects a Category 5e cable to a network card?

A ○ BNC Barrel

B ○ RJ-45

C ○ RJ-11

D ○ BNC

19 What is the maximum distance of fiber optic cabling?

A ○ 100 meters

B ○ 185 meters

C ○ 500 meters

D ○ 2 kilometers

20 What type of connector connects a 10Base2 cable to a network card?

A ○ AUI

B ○ RJ-45

C ○ RJ-11

D ○ BNC

Answers

1 **C.** Category 4 UTP cabling transfers data at 16 Mbps. *See "Twisted pair."*

2 **B.** Simplex devices deliver information in only one direction. *Review "Understanding Communication Methods."*

3 **B.** Category 3 cabling transfers information at 10 Mbps. *Check out "Twisted pair."*

4 **D.** The maximum distance of a Thinnet segment is 185 meters. *Peruse "Coaxial."*

5 **C.** The recommended number of computers in a peer-to-peer network is ten or fewer. *Take a look at "Peer-to-peer networks."*

6 **D.** CSMA/CD is the access method that is used in all Ethernet environments. Token passing is used in token ring architectures, and CSMA/CA has been used in AppleTalk networks. *Peek at "Ethernet."*

7 **A.** Half-duplex devices allow you to send and receive information, but not at the same time. *Look over "Understanding Communication Methods."*

8 **D.** Category 5e UTP cabling transfers data at 1 Gbps. *Study "Twisted pair."*

9 **C.** A bus topology must have all loose ends terminated to prevent signal bounce. *Refer to "Bus."*

10 **C.** With CSMA/CA, your computer avoids a collision with the real data by placing dummy data on the wire first. If the dummy data collides, your computer knows that it isn't safe to send the real information; if it doesn't collide, then the real data is sent. *Examine "CSMA/CA."*

11 **B.** Client-server environments are implemented for the purpose of centralized administration and security. It is much easier for an administrator to control resources if he is sitting at one computer and all users connect to that one computer. *See "Server-based (client-server) networks."*

12 **A.** The maximum distance of UTP cable is 100 meters. *Review "Twisted pair."*

13 **B.** With token passing, an empty token runs around the network, and when your computer wants to submit information on the wire, it fills the token with the information and releases the token onto the network. *Check out "Token passing."*

Down to the Networking Basics

14 **A.** Fiber optic cables send information in pulses of light on cabling with a glass core. *Peruse "Fiber optic."*

15 **D.** 10Base5 is Thicknet that has a maximum distance of 500 meters. UTP cabling has a maximum distance of 100 meters, and Thinnet has a maximum cable distance of 185 meters. *Take a look at "10 megabit Ethernet standards."*

16 **C.** Full-duplex devices can send and receive information at the same time. *Peek at "Understanding Communication Methods."*

17 **D.** The 1000BaseSX Ethernet architecture can transfer information at 1 Gbps over fiber optic cabling using short distances. *Look over "Gigabit Ethernet standards."*

18 **B.** RJ-45 connectors connect UTP cabling to the network card. *Study "Twisted pair."*

19 **D.** Fiber optic cabling has a maximum distance of about 2 km. *Refer to "Fiber optic."*

20 **D.** A BNC connector connects a 10Base2 cable to a network card. *Examine "Connecting with Thinnet."*

Chapter 2: Understanding Common Wireless Communications

Exam Objectives

✔ Identifying infrared, Bluetooth, cellular networks, and 802.11 wireless network characteristics

✔ Optimizing features of 802.11 wireless networks

✔ Identifying security settings for 802.11 access points and wireless networks

✔ Connecting to 802.11 wireless networks

*O*nce the domain of cutting-edge techno-geeks, wireless technology is now for everyone. Wireless technology has entered all aspects of our lives, so as a CompTIA A+ Certified Professional, you need to deal with wireless connectivity. This chapter gives you an overview of the technologies involved.

The main types of wireless devices that you see in this chapter are infrared, Bluetooth, cellular networking, and 802.11 wireless networking.

Understanding Infrared Devices

Of the wireless technologies I cover in this chapter, infrared is the technology that has been around the longest and is likely the most stable in its development. *Infrared* uses light beams in the infrared spectrum, which is beyond the visible light spectrum. You likely use infrared technology daily if you use a remote control for your TV, VCR, or DVD player. This technology, when used with computerized equipment, follows the standards of IrDA (Infrared Data Association). You can find more information about the association and infrared standards at http://www.irda.org.

Infrared is a *line-of-sight* technology; it requires a direct, unobstructed view between the transmitter and the receiver. Because infrared is line-of-sight, it has obvious limitations as to where it can be used. Any objects obstructing the line of sight prevent data transmissions. (Nothing more frustrating than trying to change the TV channel with someone blocking the set.) However, the benefit of line-of-sight is that you do not have interference from or interference with areas outside the line-of-sight, such as devices in the next room.

The goal of infrared networking was for short range (less than a meter), direct line-of-sight (+/–15° cone), and low speed (technologies between 1.6 Kbps and 2.4 Kbps). There are many different specifications, each with a different speed specification. One of those specifications is used for open office–networking, a technology that has been replaced by 802.11b and involved infrared repeaters placed around an office. Currently, infrared is used for printers and personal digital assistants (PDAs).

Most tasks handled by infrared technology have switched to use newer 802.11 networks and Bluetooth technologies, which use radio frequencies (RF).

Working with Wireless Networks

"Why do I need a wireless network?" was a question people used to regularly ask. You will not hear this question much anymore, though. The main reasons why people want wireless networks these days are increased mobility and to avoid cabling issues.

When wireless networks started, they had access speeds of 1–2 Mbps; current standards have network speeds higher than 100 Mbps. At one time, wireless networking equipment was a premium addition to a network, but this equipment has become a commodity and is inexpensive enough that anybody can start up a wireless network.

Wireless networking should not be used for a primary network because of its limitations, such as obstructions and interference. (See "Troubleshooting Issues," later in this chapter.) If the user knows what those limitations are, the network should be considered a best-effort network — and as such, it should not be expected to be available or to function at full speed at all times. As a secondary network, though, wireless networking does offer a great deal of flexibility for getting to your data. Any devices that exist on your normal wired network can be present on your wireless network, including firewalls, servers, and printers.

Components of a wireless network

The two main components of wireless networks are clients and access points. *Clients* are computers with wireless network cards; these cards work just the same as wired network cards, but without the wires. *Access points,* which act as a consolidation point for multiple wireless clients, have a connection to a traditional wired network. Some new access points allow linking multiple access points through wireless links, extending the range and coverage of a wireless network without having all access points connected to a wired network, thereby saving on wiring costs.

Most laptops now include wireless network cards as an integrated feature, and wireless network cards are available for desktop computers, connecting through PCI, PCI Express (PCIe), or USB. It is great that many computers have integrated wireless cards, but be prepared as new technology arrives on the scene since you will likely end up using an expansion option on your computer to add an updated wireless card to your computer.

Wireless networks used to command a premium, but wireless networking components have become a commodity. You now have several choices, all less than $100. The difference in price between the inexpensive units and expensive units is based on the strength of the radios, the features that are available on the unit, and the brand.

If you work with a wireless network that has an access point, the network client runs in *infrastructure mode,* which has access points making up the underlying network infrastructure. If the network is composed only of clients joined to form a network, the network runs in *ad hoc mode,* which is typically used only when people need to exchange files or work together in a location without an access point. This type of work situation often happens when people use a temporary location — say, a conference room — to work on a project for a couple of days. Instead of relying on a 4–8-port mini-switch or hub with which files could be shared, folks can just use an ad hoc wireless network. Both wireless network types are shown in Figure 2-1.

Most wireless networks are composed of access points and wireless clients, so unless the question specifies *ad hoc*, access points should be expected to be on the network.

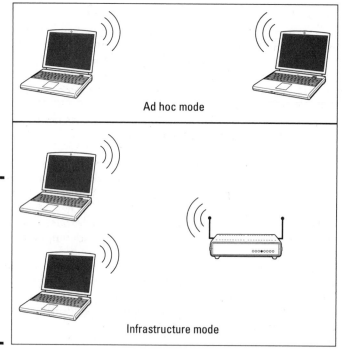

Connecting to a network

Every wireless network is identified by an SSID (Service Set Identifier), which is used by all clients on the network, identifying them as members of the network. The *SSID* is a case-sensitive name of 32 or fewer characters. Every manufacturer sets a default SSID. However, for security and to reduce confusion with neighboring access points, this default should be changed to a unique name. To connect to a wireless network, you need to know the SSID.

Some manufacturers refer to the SSID as a BSSID (Basic Service Set Identifier) or an ESSID (Extended Service Set Identifier). The IEEE 802.11-1999 wireless network standard defines an ESSID as a set of access points using the same SSID and channel, and operating as a single BSSID to their wireless network clients.

After your wireless network card is installed in the computer, determine whether to use Microsoft Wireless Zero Configuration (XP), WLAN AutoConfig (Vista), or the custom software that comes with some wireless network cards.

XP

If you use the default Windows XP software, open the Network Connections folder and double-click your wireless network card to open the Wireless Status dialog box. This gives you information about your current wireless connection, including connection speed, SSID, and signal strength.

If you are not yet connected to the network, click the View Wireless Network button, which shows you all networks in your area that are broadcasting their SSIDs. To configure a connection to one of the networks, simply select the network and click the Connect button. If you need to enter a security key, you are prompted to enter the required information. The Wireless dialog box and the Wireless Status dialog box are shown in Figure 2-2.

Figure 2-2:
Wireless configuration is easy and straightforward with Windows XP.

Vista

If you use the default Windows Vista software, open the Network and Sharing Center and click the View Status link next to your wireless card. This provides you with the same information that you would see with Windows XP, such as connection speed, SSID, and signal strength. If you are not yet connected to the network, click the Manage Wireless Connections link in the Network and Sharing Center. From there, you can choose to add a new wireless network manually or by viewing from the networks in your area that are broadcasting their SSIDs.

To configure a connection to one of the networks, simply select the network and then click the Connect button. Just like with Windows XP, if you need to enter a security key, you are prompted to enter the required information.

Both the Network and Sharing Center and the Wireless Network Connection Status dialog box are shown in Figure 2-3.

Figure 2-3: Windows Vista's wireless settings are accessed via the Network and Sharing Center.

Wireless standards

Wireless networks are defined by several standards, and the performance and security features for wireless networks are constantly improving. What's more, because of constant improvements, new standards continually emerge. Gordon Moore of Intel predicted that the components in a processor's integrated circuit would double every 24 months. This statement has since been named Moore's Law, and has been applied to many areas of the computing industry. As Moore's Law is applied to more sections of the computer industry, wireless is just another section of the industry that falls to those general rules, with speed doubling every two years.

The main wireless standards currently in use are 802.11a, 802.11b, and 802.11g — with some adoption now being made with the draft version of 802.11n (expected to be ratified early in 2010), with other standards on the horizon. Each of these technologies is based upon published standards, and the upcoming ones are usually based upon several draft standards. Some hardware manufacturers have started to supply hardware capable of supporting the upcoming standards and using some of the new features. Typically, if the manufacturer can meet the hardware standards, the software can be updated later via a firmware update.

To go along with the standard features, many vendors choose to implement additional features not in the standard or make propriety enhancements, like many of the vendors who advertise special speed enhancements.

The following sections outline the main features of each of the 802.11 wireless networking standards.

802.11a

Released in 1999 (but not actively shipping until component supply issues were resolved), 802.11a networks operate in the 5 GHz radio spectrum. Other devices, such as newer cordless phones, also run in this unlicensed spectrum. Overall, the 5 GHz space is less occupied by devices compared with the 2.4 GHz space used by most other wireless devices. For 802.11a networks, there are 12 non-overlapping signal channels.

The network rated speed of 802.11a is 54 Mbps, but in most situations you can expect to see about half that speed. The typical range for this type of network is about 100 feet (30 meters).

Although the 5 GHz frequency range is unlicensed, its use for wireless networking has been approved only in the United States, Canada, and Japan; and prior to 2002, only in some European countries. Regulatory changes in 2002 and 2003 opened the 5 GHz frequency range throughout the European Union.

802.11b

Released in 1999, 802.11b technology was able to beat 802.11a technology to the market because it was built on DSSS (Direct-Sequence Spread Spectrum) technology. As such, components required for it were all readily available for production facilities. 802.11b operates in the 2.4 GHz radio spectrum, which is heavily cluttered with cordless phones, Bluetooth (see the "Bluetooth" section, later in this chapter), and spill-over interference from microwave ovens.

The network rated speed of 802.11b is 11 Mbps, but in most situations you can expect to see about 6.5 Mbps because 802.11b is a CSMA/CA (Carrier Sense Multiple Access/Collision Avoidance) network, which sends "I'm going to send data" broadcast messages prior to sending its data, which increases the traffic on the network. (See Book VIII, Chapter 1, for the low-down on CSMA/CA.) The typical range for this type of network is about 100 feet (30 meters).

Wireless networks in the 2.4 GHz range have 14 channels available for use. Eleven channels are acceptable everywhere, the United Kingdom and some European countries allow up to 13 channels, and Japan allows all 14 channels.

Channels are defined by the center frequency that they use. Some vendors use wider channels than others, overlapping their neighboring channels. Typically channels 1, 6, 11, and 14 are thought to be non-overlapping, so in North America there are three channels that are normally non-overlapping and will not interfere with each other. See Figure 2-4 for a channel diagram of the 802.11b/g spectrum.

Figure 2-4: Normal channel frequencies used for 802.11b/g networks.

Channel 1	Channel 6	Channel 11	Channel 14
2.401 – 2.423	2.426 – 2.448	2.451 – 2.473	2.473 – 2.495
Center	Center	Center	Center
2.412	2.437	2.462	2.484

Channel 2	Channel 7	Channel 12
2.404 – 2.428	2.431 – 2.453	2.456 – 2.478
Center	Center	Center
2.417	2.442	2.467

Channel 3	Channel 8	Channel 13
2.411 – 2.433	2.436 – 2.458	2.461 – 2.483
Center	Center	Center
2.422	2.447	2.472

Channel 4	Channel 9
2.416 – 2.438	2.441 – 2.463
Center	Center
2.427	2.452

Channel 5	Channel 10
2.401 – 2.423	2.446 – 2.468
Center	Center
2.412	2.457

802.11g

Released in 2003, 802.11g is an updated version of 802.11b, still running in the 2.4 GHz spectrum but allowing faster data transfer speeds to put it on a performance par with 802.11a. Because it operates in the 2.4 GHz spectrum, it is also backward compatible with 802.11b, making migration to 802.11g an easy step for many organizations because they could update the back-end infrastructure and then update the wireless clients in a manner that fits within the corporate requirements.

The network rated speed for 802.11g is 54 Mbps, but in most situations you can expect about half that speed because the throughput is reduced as distances between the client and access point increase, and the signal suffers

from greater interference. Because wireless networks are a shared medium further reduces throughput as the number of users sharing an access point increases the competition for the wireless signal. The typical range for this type of network is about 100 feet (30 meters).

With all the benefits that are available with 802.11g, many companies began producing products well before the standards were ratified.

802.11n

Draft 2.0 for 802.1n was released in 2007, and Draft 3.0 is expected to be ratified in 2010. 802.11n represents the latest improvements to networking in the 2.4 GHz and 5 GHz spectrums. Originally planned as a replacement for 802.11b/g, the draft standard now allows for radios operating in the 5 GHz spectrum of 802.11a. This slow ratification process has not slowed adoption of 802.11n hardware, which vendors are guaranteeing to be compatible with the released standard. Again, this solution will suffer from an already congested spectrum. The biggest change that you will see with this technology is the implementation of multiple transmitters and receivers and multiplexing of signals. This technology is referred to as MIMO (Multiple-Input Multiple-Output).

The expected ratified network-rated speed is expected to be beyond 200 Mbps (600 Mbps when multiplexed or connected over multiple radios). As with most wireless technology, you should expect typical transfer rates at about half that — in the 300 Mbps area. The typical range for this type of network is about 165 feet (50 meters).

When a proposal request was announced for the 802.11n wireless networking standard, 32 responses were sent in. After voting by the standards committee, four of these proposals were considered further. In 2005, the three groups backing the three remaining proposals announced that they would work on a joint proposal to be accepted as the standard. Because multiple groups are working together to design the final standard, there remains a possibility that the current draft standard could be substantially changed. Many hardware vendors started producing and shipping equipment based on the prerelease draft standards.

Today, hardware shipping that is 802.11n ready is becoming the standard rather than a rarity.

Although there is a lot of talk about cordless phones causing interference with wireless networking, there has been a big boost in 5 GHz phone sales because they do not interfere with 802.11b/g/n networks. New DECT 6.0 phones — which run at 1.9 GHz — are starting to become popular because they do not interfere with any 802.11 wireless networks.

Securing wireless networks

With the proliferation of wireless technology, security has come to the forefront of many conversations, which is odd because it should have been prominent from the very beginning. The main steps you can take to improve wireless security include password management, SSID management, MAC address filtering, WEP, WPA, WPA2, DMZ, DHCP settings, and updating the firmware. Many of these configuration settings can be seen in Figure 2-5. The configuration screens for most access points are accessed using a Web browser and connecting to the IP (Internet protocol) address of the access point, as I did when connecting to the Linksys access point shown in Figure 2-5.

Figure 2-5: Security options for a typical wireless access point.

Passwords

All access points ship with a default Administrator username and password. A quick search of the Internet will give you the default usernames and passwords for most manufacturers and models. Usually, in addition to an owner's manual, a new access point will ship with a Quick Start guide containing an abridged set of steps to follow to apply a basic configuration to the access point. This guide typically includes the default IP address, username, and password used by the access point. When wireless networks started to become widespread, these guides did not suggest changing the default passwords, but most of them now offer the suggestion in the initial setup steps — if not actually forcing you to do it before making any other configuration changes.

Changing the Administrator password should be the first step in the setup procedure. Until you change the password, any person within the range of your access point can make any configuration changes they wish.

SSID broadcasting

Security through obscurity is not the best security measure, but it provides one more layer to your overall network security. The Microsoft Wireless Zero Configuration (XP) or WLAN AutoConfig (Vista) service tries to make it easy for you to connect to wireless networks (as do many hardware vendors that have custom management software), and these configuration tools display all the SSIDs for wireless networks in range of your computer if the access points are broadcasting their SSID. This allows you to select the SSID or wireless network that you want to connect to and quickly configure it. By disabling the broadcasting of your SSID, your network will not show up in the list of detected wireless networks within Windows. If you are not on the list, most people won't even know your network is there — and, therefore, won't connect to it.

Disabling SSID broadcasting is only a mild security setting, as you discover in the section, "Troubleshooting Issues," later in this chapter. If someone wants to gain access to your wireless network, disabling SSID broadcasts won't slow him very much nor prevent that person from knowing that a wireless network exists.

MAC address filtering

Media Access Control (MAC) address filtering is another step that will slow most casual users from gaining access to your network, but it is not considered strong security on its own. Most access points allow you to perform different types of filtering, and most allow you to at least filter traffic by MAC addresses that are hard-coded onto each network adapter on your wireless network.

Implementing this security step means that for each new network card that you want to operate on your network, you need to adjust your access points. Even with the MAC address restriction in place on your access point, an unscrupulous person can use a network sniffer like AirSnort to see some traffic on the wireless network. In this traffic, such a person can see the MAC addresses of clients who are communicating on your wireless network. By taking this information and using a network card or operating system that allows him to manually control the MAC address, the individual can imitate one of the valid MAC addresses that are allowed to be used on your network. The timing on this is important because if two computers on a network have the same MAC address, all sorts of communication errors can happen.

As I mention previously, MAC address filtering keeps the casual user out of your network, but it shouldn't be your sole security measure. If somebody wants to get onto your network, this will not slow him down very much.

WEP

The security measures I've discussed thus far do not deal with encryption. Wired Equivalent Privacy (WEP) was the first attempt to secure wireless networks by using encryption. Early WEP used a 64-bit key, which was a 40-bit encryption key joined with a 24-bit initialization vector (IV). This was easily breakable. Newer WEP uses a 104-bit encryption key joined with the 24-bit IV, providing a higher level of security.

The benefit of WEP is that it's fairly easy to configure on both the access point and the client and again provides security against the casual wireless user. One of the main drawbacks to WEP is that technology has not substantially changed on how security keys are managed, such as IVs being sent over the network in plain text. And, if an intruder captures enough traffic from your network, he can deduce your WEP keys, giving him full access to your network. The answer to this problem is WPA.

WPA

Wi-Fi Protected Access (WPA) and WPA2 (also called 802.11i) are all about improving security on wireless networks. Rather than using a single WEP key, WPA uses per-session keys that are agreed upon by the wireless client and the access point after an initial handshaking process. This technology was created in response to the weaknesses that were found in WEP. No security is unbreakable, and creating a better mousetrap just seems to create smarter mice. Still, the security settings available in WPA2 make wireless networks as secure as they can be. As of this writing, the time needed to break the keys used would render the broken keys mostly useless because they would have already been changed on the network.

WPA allows you to use two initial handshaking methods:

+ An 802.1x authentication (Radius) server

+ A manually typed preshared key (PSK), which is configured on both the access point and the clients

In your list of security methods, you can choose TKIP (Temporal Key Integrity Protocol), which uses a 128-bit encryption key and a 48-bit IV to secure the data. In addition, after every 10,000 packets of data have been sent, new TKIP keys are generated and used. This regular changing of the keys keeps the network more secure.

WPA2 builds upon this security by adding the U.S. government standard AES (Advanced Encryption Standard) to the data encryption methods, which allows for encryption keys of up to 256 bits.

Not all wireless products support WPA and WPA2, but the list grows every day. If compatibility with the widest range of devices is required, WEP might be a requirement for you.

WEP and WPA are the two most common security methods used to secure wireless networks.

VPNs and DMZs

Although it requires more setup, you can treat your wireless network as a hostile remote network. By *hostile,* I mean that the network contains many individuals who would like to gain access to the company's private information stored on its corporate network. Some companies have faith that the security settings that they configured on their wireless access points will keep all unwanted visitors or trespassers off their network. And that is not an unreasonable thought, given the current security settings that are available. However, for those companies that do not trust these security levels available in the current wireless technology, or who are afraid of the smarter mouse arriving on the scene sooner rather than later, other steps can be taken to provide even more secure wireless.

Most companies today have a connection to the Internet coming into their organization, and they treat the Internet as a large hostile remote network. To prevent their private data from being accessed, companies use a firewall where the Internet meets their network, allowing them to inspect and control the data that moves between their network and the Internet. If they have data that they would like some people on the Internet to be able to access (such as data on a Web server or an FTP server), they may implement a second firewall, making another private network. This strategy provides some protection from unwanted visitors gaining access to the Web or FTP server but offers less protection than their normal private network because some people have a right to access the server. In most cases, this more open private net will be placed between the hostile Internet and the private corporate network, creating a less hostile, but still not absolutely safe, Demilitarized Zone (DMZ).

It is also common for companies to have remote workers who need access to the corporate network while they are away from the office. This access is given through a special secure channel: a Virtual Private Network (VPN). A VPN relies upon secure authentication and data encryption methods to create a secure and private connection through a firewall to a corporate network. Most often, this security is handled by SSL (Secure Sockets Layer) or IPSec (IP Security), which are two industry standard methods of encrypting TCP/IP or Internet data.

Book VIII
Chapter 2

Understanding
Common Wireless
Communications

More information about firewalls, VPNs, DMZs, SSL, and IPSec can be found in Book IX, Chapters 1 and 2.

So, by segregating your wireless users into their own DMZ or private segment (protected from the Internet), you can keep any potential wireless intruder away from your private corporate data because users of that wireless network do not have direct access to the corporate network. For your users to access corporate data, they use the same remote access methods, such as a VPN connection, that they would use when on the road. These additional security steps can be layered atop the previously discussed techniques, such as WEP and WPA, forcing users to take more steps to get access to your corporate data, but making the connection more secure.

DHCP server settings

A *DHCP* (Dynamic Host Configuration Protocol) server provides automatic TCP/IP configuration to network clients by changing normal items that DHCP provides, such as a default gateway or DNS settings for name resolution, or by disabling DHCP altogether. By failing to distribute accurate TCP/IP information to unwanted visitors, and using manual TCP/IP configurations to users, you are implementing another rudimentary security step. This security based on DHCP settings might prevent most casual users from getting ready access to information or gaining access to the Internet through your wireless network. Still, any unwanted intruder who wants to gain access will be able to find correct TCP/IP settings by using a standard packet capture utility, such as Wireshark (www.wireshark.org).

Client isolation

This option, available on many network switches, has found its way to wireless networks as well. When this setting is enabled, wireless clients can talk to the rest of the network but cannot communicate with other clients on the same wireless access point.

Firmware

Not to be forgotten when setting up new wireless networks (or periodically after a network is set up) is to check for firmware updates for your wireless network components or driver updates for your network cards. These updates are how new security features are retrofitted into your wireless products.

Take care when doing this because features are occasionally removed, or you might encounter problems with the new code in the firmware.

Many people have opted to stop using the firmware from their hardware manufacturer and instead use a third-party or open source firmware, such as DD-WRT (www.dd-wrt.com). This firmware works on a variety of hardware platforms, which are listed on its Web site.

Other Wireless

Two more products fall into the wireless networking category: Bluetooth and cellular. Bluetooth is used as a communication link between different devices, and cellular is used for remote dialup networking or Internet access. In both cases, using these wireless devices is very different than the 802.11 wireless networking protocols, which are designed to be a short-range extension of a LAN (local area network).

Bluetooth

Bluetooth follows the standards set out in the IEEE 802.15.1 specification. As a personal area network (PAN), Bluetooth is designed primarily for use in very small areas or short ranges, such as on a person's body. You have probably seen cordless cellular phone headsets, which operate over the space between the headset in the ear and a phone carried on the hip or in a purse. Most wireless links for today's cell phones and PDAs use Bluetooth. You might not immediately think of these links as being on a network — after all, you are not surfing the Internet or transferring files — but you are transferring data, in some form, between the devices. There are three classes of devices on Bluetooth networks:

+ **Class 1** devices operate at 100 milliwatt (mW) and have a range of 100 meters.

+ **Class 2** devices operate at 2.5 mW and have a range of 10 meters.

+ **Class 3** devices operate at 1 mW and have a range of about 1 meter.

Most devices are Class 3. Class 3 Bluetooth devices include telephone and computer headsets, PDA-to-PC synchronization, printers, digital cameras, cell phones for synchronizing with PCs, game controllers, remote controls, and instrument collection devices.

Bluetooth has replaced serial or infrared connections that would have been used for many of these functions in the past. Bluetooth is used mainly in low-bandwidth, short-haul situations.

Bluetooth operates in the 2.4 GHz spectrum, specifically around the 2.45 GHz mark. This means that it is open to interference from other devices running in the same spectrum. However, because of its limited range, it tends to cause fewer problems with devices that are outside of its range.

Some Bluetooth devices have a security feature — pairing — that can and should be used when available. There have already been viruses affecting Bluetooth cell phones that were originally set to freely associate with any other Bluetooth device in the area. Most phones now require pairing with devices to communicate.

Pairing registers a pair of devices with each other by using a shared secret key so that they can talk only with other devices that are known. Pairing is used as a means of authentication between devices and can also be used to encrypt data communication between them. Some devices, such as printers, might end up being left open and unsecured to keep a high level of functionality, but this would be a conscious decision to leave pairing turned off, and to leave the device unsecured.

WAN cellular

A wide area network (WAN) — unlike a LAN, which is contained within one or two adjacent buildings — spans a large geographical area and usually involves communication links operated by a Telco. Considering the number of communities and cities planning to set up wide-scale public access wireless networks and the cost of cellular data transfer rates, WAN cellular technology might not become extremely widespread.

In conjunction with your data network provider, you can sometimes get cellular WAN access to your network: wireless wide area network (WWAN). You need a special cellular gateway or a data-enabled phone, which some people might refer to as a modem. Unlike a normal cellular modem that needs to dial another modem to establish a connection, the gateway makes a connection directly to the cellular provider's network. The gateway may be connected to your computer by USB, Bluetooth, or PCMCIA. This gateway connects to your data network provider and sets up a secure tunnel for access to your corporate network's resources. The data rates on these connections are usually faster than traditional dialup connections, and they do provide secure access to your LAN data services, but most service providers charge a substantial fee for the service.

Increasing Wireless Network Performance

Some basic steps that you can take to improve wireless performance include the following:

✦ **Reduce interference from other sources.** This might include changing channels that you are using or changing the spectrum that you are using, such as switching from 2.4 GHz to 5 GHz technologies.

+ **Reduce the number of clients per access point.** Because wireless is a shared medium, the fewer clients the access point has to share bandwidth between, the faster each client will be.

+ **Reduce the range between the clients and the access points.** As the range between the client and access point increases, the signal quality decreases — and, therefore, the data throughput rate decreases.

+ **Use faster technology.** For example, upgrade from 802.11b to 802.11g or 802.11n.

+ **Reduce the material that the signal must travel through.** The distance ratings are usually open-air ratings, and construction materials and other objects in the path of the signal will reduce the signal strength.

Outdoor wireless networks set up during the winter can experience problems in the spring when trees in the path of the signal leaf out. Try to anticipate how annual weather and seasonal changes in your area will affect both your wireless equipment and wireless signal.

+ **Use proprietary or nonstandard technology to improve data transfer speeds.** This might work only when teamed with specific networks cards from the wireless vendor.

Troubleshooting Issues

Any issues that affect wired networks can affect wireless networks as well. Very often, symptoms show up first on the wireless network. The bandwidth on the wireless network is substantially lower, so when a problem on your network consumes bandwidth — like a worm — it will cause connectivity and performance issues on your wireless network before users of your wired network notice the problem.

A number of outside factors, such as microwaves and cordless phones, can affect wireless networks. Because these devices operate throughout and beyond the 2.4 GHz spectrum, and because they do not advertise themselves as wireless networks, they won't show up in the results in Network Stumbler (more on that in a bit) when you are viewing the strength of wireless networks in the area. To locate these rogue signals, you need to perform a physical inspection — or, better yet, run a spectrum analysis tool. These tools used to cost thousands of dollars, but the price of quality tools has dropped to hundreds of dollars, and some tools cost even less. Managing your wireless frequencies is becoming just as important as managing your wired data networks.

To survey wireless networks in your area so that you can choose a clear channel, take a look at Network Stumbler (www.netstumbler.com). Use this tool to view detailed information about the wireless signals in your area. Figure 2-6 shows how Network Stumbler displays information about access points, including the channels on which they are running, what SSIDs are broadcast (AP 0011951FBEBF is not broadcasting its SSID), and whether they have security enabled. Many other applications do the same type of thing, and this feature is even incorporated into the management software that ships with some network card drivers.

If you know that an access point is not broadcasting its SSID, you can find the SSID by using wireless network auditing tools, like BackTrack (formerly Linux Auditor Security), available at www.remote-exploit.org.

Figure 2-6:
Use Network Stumbler and similar tools to see wireless networks in your area.

If you can get a good signal but you don't seem to be able to establish a connection or transfer data with the network, look at the security settings on both the access point and the client computer. If the WEP settings are incorrect or if the network authentication is not set correctly, you might experience either of these problems.

Much the same as WEP keys and settings, if you are using WPA, your problems could be with the shared secret that is configured or the settings for the authentication server, which verify user or access point credentials.

Getting an A+

This chapter goes over some common wireless communications. The following points are covered:

✦ Infrared technology depends on line-of-sight and tends to be used for low-bandwidth solutions.

✦ A number of factors affect wireless signal quality and strength, such as interference, range, and the number of connected clients.

✦ 802.11a/b/g networks all have a range of 100 feet (30 meters), and 802.11n has a range of 165 feet (50 meters). 802.11a networks operate in the 5 GHz spectrum, and 802.11b and 802.11g networks operate in the 2.4 GHz spectrum; while 802.11n networks can operate in both spectrums.

✦ WEP and WPA are the most common methods to secure wireless networks, but other options include disabling SSID broadcasting, MAC filtering, placing wireless APs in a DMZ, and changing default passwords.

✦ Bluetooth is used only for short-range communication.

Prep Test

1 Which of the following is not a technology that can be used to connect to a printer?

A ○ Bluetooth

B ○ WWAN

C ○ 802.11b

D ○ Infrared

2 Typical client Bluetooth implementations have what ranges? (Select all that apply.)

A ❑ 1 meter

B ❑ 5 meters

C ❑ 10 meters

D ❑ 25 meters

3 What is the standard range of 802.11a/b/g wireless networks?

A ○ 10 meters

B ○ 30 meters

C ○ 50 meters

D ○ 100 meters

4 Which of the following does *not* impact the quality of wireless signals?

A ○ Microwave ovens

B ○ Air temperature

C ○ Cordless phones

D ○ Distance between access point and clients

5 802.11g networks are backward compatible with which other 802.11 technology?

A ○ 802.11a

B ○ 802.11b

C ○ 802.11i

D ○ 802.11n

6 Which of the following would be used to provide wireless connectivity across a metropolitan area?

A ○ Bluetooth

B ○ Infrared

C ○ Cellular

D ○ MIMO

7 What frequency ranges are used by 802.11 wireless networks? (Select all that apply.)

A ❏ 900 MHz

B ❏ 1.5 GHz

C ❏ 2.4 GHz

D ❏ 5.0 GHz

8 Which of the following is not a technology used to secure wireless networks?

A ○ WPS

B ○ WEP

C ○ WPA

D ○ 802.11i

Answers

1 **B.** Printers from different manufacturers support some of or all the listed wireless technologies, and WWAN is a technology used to connect to your network while out of the office. *See "Understanding Infrared Devices," "Bluetooth," and "Working with Wireless Networks."*

2 **A, C.** Bluetooth technology has ranges of 1, 10, and 100 meters depending on the class of devices that are being used. *Review "Bluetooth."*

3 **B.** Most 802.11 wireless networks have a range of 30 meters in open air. *Check out "Wireless standards."*

4 **B.** Air temperature has not been documented to have an impact on wireless networks. *Peruse "Troubleshooting Issues."*

5 **B.** 802.11g uses the same 2.4 GHz spectrum and was designed to be backward compatible with 802.11b. 802.11n is expected to be backward compatible with both 802.11g and 802.11b. *Take a look at "802.11g."*

6 **C.** The only technology that will work across a metropolitan area is cellular, which is used for WAN cellular or WWAN connectivity. *Peek at "WAN cellular."*

7 **C, D.** 802.11 networks run at either 2.4 GHz for 802.11b/g/n or 5.0 GHz for 802.11a. *Look over "Wireless standards."*

8 **A.** WPS is not a technology used for wireless security. *Study "Securing wireless networks."*

Chapter 3: Networking the Operating System

Exam Objectives

✔ Understanding networking components

✔ Identifying network protocols

✔ Configuring the TCP/IP protocol

✔ Troubleshooting with TCP/IP utilities

✔ Understanding name resolution

✔ Sharing network resources

✔ Connecting to shared resources

*O*ne of the most important skills IT professionals need to master is troubleshooting networking connectivity: that is, computers establishing a connection with one another. A number of components facilitate this communication, and many times, IT professionals end up troubleshooting issues with these components.

This chapter discusses the software components that allow a computer to network with other computers as well as the troubleshooting issues that could arise while configuring a network. In this chapter, you find out how to connect to networking resources and how to troubleshoot when you cannot make the connection.

Understanding Networking Components

When setting up a network, you must have the appropriate hardware and software in place to allow systems to communicate with one another. Because this chapter focuses on the software components needed to allow Windows to network, you can assume that you have all the necessary hardware in place. You have a hub or switch, at least two computers and network cards to go in the computers, and the appropriate cabling to connect the network cards to the hub/switch is already connected. After all the hardware is in place, consider what you have to do at the operating system level to get these computers talking. Not only do you need the physical hardware

in place but you also need to load software components, such as a network card driver, protocol, service, and client software. These are the four major software components required to network.

When building your network, it is important to identify the four major software components that allow a Windows OS to function in a networking environment:

✦ Network adapter driver

✦ Network client

✦ Protocol

✦ Services

I discuss each component in detail in the sections that follow. Be sure to be comfortable with them for the A+ exams!

Network adapter driver

The *network adapter driver* is the physical network card inserted into one of the computer's expansion bus slots, connected as a USB device, or integrated into the system board. The network card is responsible for sending information onto the network and receiving information from the network.

Before purchasing a network card, you have to figure out what type of card you need. To do this, open up the computer (for more information on safety procedures, refer to Book I, Chapter 3), look at the expansion buses supported in your system, and then identify which has an empty slot. For example, if you have a PCI slot and a PCIe, you can choose between a PCI or a PCIe network adapter. Typically, you would opt for the PCIe network adapter because of the performance benefits of PCIe devices over PCI devices.

A USB network adapter is a popular choice today. If you go with a USB network adapter, you won't need to open the computer — simply plug the USB adapter into an available USB port.

After you install the network card into the empty expansion slot or USB port, you install the driver for that card within the OS. Installing the network card driver is the first major step to networking a system because the driver software allows the OS to communicate with the physical device — in this case, the network card. Figure 3-1 shows how the driver sits between the OS and the physical hardware, controlling communication between the two.

Figure 3-1:
The
relationship
between
the OS and
a hardware
device is
controlled
by the
device
driver.

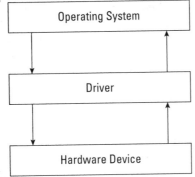

Installing a network adapter in Windows

After you insert the network card into the computer, Plug and Play will kick in when the computer is powered on. If the OS has the device driver for the card, it will load the driver automatically, and you will see the device listed in Device Manager.

If the OS doesn't have the driver, it will either prompt you for the driver (and then you need to supply the manufacturer's CD for the network card), or the device will be listed in Device Manager as an unknown device. To update the driver for the device in Windows, go to Device Manager to update the driver. The following steps demonstrate how to update a driver in Windows XP:

1. **Click Start, right-click My Computer, and choose Properties.**

2. **In the System Properties dialog box, click the Hardware tab.**

3. **On the Hardware tab, click the Device Manager button.**

 The Device Manager appears.

4. **Within Device Manager, right-click your network card and choose Update Driver, as shown in Figure 3-2.**

 If your network card isn't listed in the Network Adapters section of Device Manager, look under the Unknown Devices category. If the device is in the Unknown Devices category, right-click it there and choose Update Driver.

 The Update Driver Wizard starts.

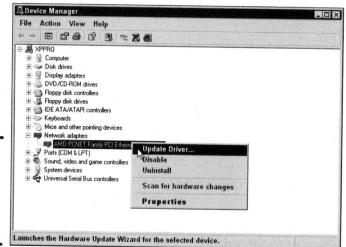

Figure 3-2:
Updating
a network
card driver
in Windows
XP.

5. **Select Install from a List and then click Next.**

6. **Select Don't Search, I Will Choose the Driver to Install; then click Next.**

7. **Select the manufacturer of your network card (on the left) and then choose the model of your network card (on the right). Click Next.**

 If your network card model isn't in the list, click the Have Disk button so that you can supply the location of the driver.

8. **After the driver is copied, click Finish.**

Updating the driver in Windows Vista follows similar steps. Again, you use Device Manager, but locating Device Manager is a little different.

1. **Click Start, right-click My Computer in XP or Computer in Vista, and choose Properties.**

2. **In the System dialog box, click the Device Manager link on the left side.**

3. **Within Device Manager, right-click your network card and choose Update Driver Software.**

4. **Follow the wizard that opens.**

Understanding the local area connection

After you load the network card driver, Windows creates an icon that represents the network card; this icon is called the *local area connection*. If you have multiple network cards installed, you have multiple local area connections — one representing each network card.

The purpose of the local area connection icon is to give you a place to configure any network settings responsible for communication between the network card and the local area network (LAN). For example, if you want to ensure that TCP/IP is used by your network card, right-click the local area connection and choose Properties. In the Properties of the local area connection, you can add or configure networking components, such as TCP/IP.

To view your LAN connections in Windows XP, choose Start⇨Control Panel⇨ Network and Internet Connections⇨Network Connections. You see a window that displays your local area connection icon, as shown in Figure 3-3.

Figure 3-3:
Viewing a local area connection in Windows XP.

To view your LAN connections in Windows Vista, click Start, right-click Network, and choose Properties. Click the Manage Network Connections link on the left.

When you right-click the local area connection icon, its contextual menu gives you a number of tasks. Here are tasks that you might use when you troubleshoot networking issues:

- ✦ **Disable:** Temporarily cut off communication to and from the network. This is a quicker solution than physically removing the network card from the computer.

- ✦ **Enable:** This choice is a toggle of Disable when you disable a card. After you troubleshoot your network (hopefully, you fix the problem) and you need to re-enable the network connection, choose Enable.

- ✦ **Status:** Display a dialog box showing how long the connection has been up and running and also the speed of the connection. On the Support Page tab, you can view your IP (Internet protocol) address information and MAC (Media Access Control) address.

✦ **Repair:** Have Windows perform maintenance on the connection by performing tasks such as renewing your IP address, flushing the ARP (Address Resolution Protocol) cache, and flushing the NetBIOS and domain name system (DNS) resolver cache.

✦ **Rename:** Give the connection a more meaningful name. For example, I renamed the LAN for the network card connected to the Internet to *Internet Connection*. The Rename command is shown in Figure 3-4.

✦ **Properties:** Open the Properties dialog box for your LAN connection. In the Properties dialog box, you can modify the network setup of the network card. For example, you can add or remove network protocols or change their configuration.

Figure 3-4: Rename a local area connection to give it a more meaningful name.

After you make sure that the correct hardware settings are applied to the network adapter, your next step is to connect to a network resource. Unfortunately, you cannot connect to a network resource until you have the appropriate network client running. The following section describes the purpose of the network client.

Network client

In essence, a network client is no different than a client or customer in the real world. A client in the real world visits your company because you provide some sort of service. Say you run a tailor shop. The customer is a *client* of the tailoring service.

Computer networks work the same way. On your computers, you must run a client for the type of service you are requesting on the network. For example, if a company runs Novell NetWare as the server OS, you must load a client that will connect your computer to the Novell server. Or, if you want to connect to a Windows server, you have to load a Microsoft client on your system.

The Windows OSes come with the Client for Microsoft Networks already installed so that you can automatically connect to a Windows network.

If you are running Windows OSes in a Novell environment, you will probably decide *not* to load the Client Service for NetWare, which is the client that Microsoft built in to its OS to connect to Novell networks. Microsoft built that client with limited capabilities, so most networks that run Novell actually load the Novell client on Windows instead.

To return to my tailor shop example, say that your client asked your service to tailor some pants. When the client finally receives the mended pants, that client is pleased — however, the pants have to be dry-cleaned before they are used. Unfortunately, your business doesn't offer dry-cleaning services, so your client has to request that service from a third party. The point is that your client can be a client of tailoring *and* a client of dry cleaning at the same time. There is no rule that says you can be a client of only one particular service at a time.

This applies to the network as well. A lot of companies run Windows servers and Novell servers on the same network and at the same time. Maybe they use the Novell server for file sharing and use the Windows server for e-mail services. In this instance, the desktop computers on the network have to run two clients: Client Service for NetWare; or the Novell client software *and* Client for Microsoft Networks.

To install a network client for Microsoft networks in Windows, follow these steps:

1. **Locate the network connections.**

 - *Windows 2000:* Choose Start⇨Settings⇨Control Panel⇨Network and Dial Up Connections.

 - *Windows XP/2003:* Choose Start⇨Control Panel⇨Network and Internet Connections⇨Network Connections.

 - *Windows Vista:* Click Start. Right-click Network and choose Properties. Click the Manage Network Connections link on the left.

2. **Right-click your local area connection and choose Properties.**

3. **If it isn't already active, click the General tab.**

4. **Verify that Client for Microsoft Networks appears in the list of components and has a check mark beside it, as shown in Figure 3-5.**

 If the check box is not selected, select the Client for Microsoft Networks check box to enable the Microsoft networking client. If the Client for Microsoft Networks is not in the list, install it: Click the Install button and choose Client from the Network Component Type dialog box. Click Add, choose Client For Microsoft Networks, and then click OK.

Book VIII
Chapter 3

Networking the
Operating System

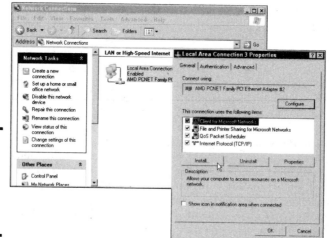

Figure 3-5:
Verify that Client for Microsoft Networks is installed.

The steps are very similar to install Client Service for NetWare and to have a Windows system connect to the Novell server on the network. To install Client Service for NetWare, follow these steps:

1. **Locate the network connections.**

 - *Windows 2000:* Choose Start➪Settings➪Control Panel➪Network and Dial Up Connections.

 - *Windows XP/2003:* Choose Start➪Control Panel➪Network and Internet Connections➪Network Connections.

2. **Right-click your local area connection and choose Properties.**

3. **Click the Install button to install a network component.**

4. **From the Network Component Type dialog box, select Client and then click Add.**

5. **Select Client Service for NetWare and then click OK.**

6. **Click Yes to restart the system.**

When you reboot after installing Client Service for NetWare, you need to configure the client for your NetWare tree and the context within that tree. The Client Service for Netware dialog box, shown in Figure 3-6, appears on reboot or can be configured later through the Client Service for NetWare applet in the Control Panel.

The *tree* setting is the name of the NetWare tree that holds your user accounts, and the *context* setting is the organizational unit (OU) in that tree that holds your user account. *Organizational units* are containers that hold objects in the directory.

Figure 3-6: Configuring Client Service for NetWare to authenticate with a particular NetWare tree and context within that tree.

At this point, you should have your network card and its driver installed, and you should also have installed the appropriate client. Unfortunately, you still cannot communicate with someone on the network because you still have to install the appropriate protocol. In the following section, I talk about the purpose of protocols and what common protocols are running on networks today.

Protocols

Protocols are languages used to hold a conversation on a network. Your system can have a network card installed and have the proper client running, but if it is not speaking the same language (um, protocol) as the remote system, the two systems cannot hold a conversation. Back to the tailor shop example: You are now ready to service your clients, but you have a teeny problem. The first client who walks into your store and requests service speaks French, but you speak only English. To solve this problem, you and your client must speak a common language — and it doesn't matter what that language is, as long as you both can speak it.

There are a few things to look for when choosing which protocol to install, but the bottom line is that all computers on the network must have the same protocol installed — a common denominator to allow all individuals to participate in a conversation. In the following sections, I discuss a few different protocols that you might encounter when working with networks. Be sure to be familiar with these protocols when you take the A+ Certification exams.

**Book VIII
Chapter 3**

**Networking the
Operating System**

NetBEUI

NetBIOS Extended User Interface (NetBEUI) was originally developed by IBM to be used on small networks (fewer than ten computers). Microsoft implemented NetBEUI in the different Windows OSes for the same purpose — small networks — because it is a *nonroutable* protocol, meaning that it cannot leave the network. Because many companies have large networks spanning some form of wide area network (WAN) link and containing routers to connect different networks, this protocol is impractical in those environments and for environments that want to connect to the Internet.

In the past, you would use NetBEUI if you had a small number of computers that needed to be networked in a workgroup-type environment. You wanted to get this network up and running without the hassle of having to configure all kinds of settings. This is the benefit of NetBEUI: There is no configuration — it just works! In today's networking environments, though, seeing NetBEUI on any major network is unlikely.

IPX/SPX

Internetwork Packet Exchange/Sequenced Packet Exchange (IPX/SPX) — the Novell native protocol — has been used on large networks since its design. IPX/SPX is a *routable* protocol, meaning that the data it delivers can move from one network to another. Because the Internet is so popular, though, even Novell networks today don't run IPX/SPX but run TCP/IP instead. (See the following section for information about TCP/IP.)

Microsoft OSes have their own implementation of IPX/SPX — NWLink — which you will want to install if your computers communicate with Novell servers on the network.

Like NetBEUI, there is not a lot of configuration to IPX/SPX, but one very important property of this protocol is the frame type. The *frame type* is the type of "envelope" used to deliver the information from one computer to another computer on the network. Different envelopes have different characteristics, and you need to make sure that everyone uses the same type of envelope on the network. That is, if you are running IPX/SPX, you need to ensure that you are running the same frame type on the client as on the Novell servers.

Windows OSes can autodetect the frame type running on the network, which is usually first set by the Novell server. Although autodetect generally works out fine, you still need to know how to install IPX/SPX and configure the frame type. The big question is, what frame type do you use? The answer is probably whatever is set on the Novell server, but you should ask the network administrator. Popular frame types are 802.2, 802.3, and Ethernet II.

Do not worry about the frame types for the exam, but be aware that the frame type must match that of the Novell server. For example, if the server is using 802.3, the client computers must be configured for 802.3.

The following steps walk you through installing NWLink (IPX/SPX) on Windows 2000 and Windows XP and demonstrate how to set the frame type:

1. **Locate the network connections.**

 • *Windows 2000:* Choose Start⇨Settings⇨Control Panel⇨Network and Dial Up Connections.

 • *Windows XP/2003:* Choose Start⇨Control Panel⇨Network and Internet Connections⇨Network Connections.

2. **Right-click your local area connection and choose Properties.**

3. **Click the Install button.**

4. **Select Protocol from the Network Component list and then click Add.**

5. **Select NWLink and click OK, as shown in Figure 3-7.**

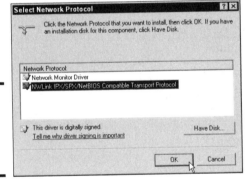

Figure 3-7:
Installing
NWLink on
Windows
XP.

6. **When the NWLink protocol is in the list of network components used by the connection, select the NWLink IPX/SPX protocol — *not* NWLink NetBIOS — and then click Properties to change the frame type.**

7. **Change the frame type setting from Auto to the value used by your IPX network.**

 For example, if you know that your Novell servers use 802.2, select 802.2 from the list. Check with your network administrator to find out what frame type your Novell servers use.

Book VIII
Chapter 3

Networking the
Operating System

If you are running a Novell network today you will most likely be using TCP/IP as the network protocol and not IPX/SPX, which is why Windows Vista no longer lists NWLink (IPX/SPX) as a protocol. Vista also has removed the Client For Netware Networks — if you wish to connect to a Novell Netware network you should install the client software from Novell.

TCP/IP

Transmission Control Protocol/Internet Protocol (TCP/IP) is the hot protocol on the market these days because it is the protocol of the Internet and Internet-based technologies. TCP/IP has become the protocol of choice for Windows, Linux, and Novell networks because of its ability to communicate in heterogeneous environments. The bottom line is this: It doesn't matter what kind of OS you are running — if you're running TCP/IP, you can communicate globally.

TCP/IP is a protocol suite. *Protocol suites* are like application suites in the sense that there is more than one protocol in the group. For example, if you purchase the Microsoft Office suite, you purchase an entire group of applications, or an entire *suite* of applications. TCP/IP is a group of protocols that make up the protocol suite, and some of these protocols are used day in and day out. For example, adding the TCP/IP protocol suite to your computer means that you have a Telnet application for running applications from another computer, and you have an FTP application for downloading files from another computer.

Because configuring TCP/IP is such a big topic, I devote an entire section of this chapter, "The TCP/IP Protocol," to it.

TCP/IP and IPX/SPX are routable protocols, and NetBEUI is a nonroutable protocol.

Services

One of the most forgotten networking components is the *service,* which is a piece of software running on the computer that provides certain functionality. An example of a service that runs on the computer is file and printer sharing, which is the service that provides files, folders, and printers to other systems on the network.

Going back to the tailor shop example: Before you can have clients, you must have first made the decision to offer the service. If you do not offer the service, there is no reason for customers to want to communicate with you.

So, on a network, someone has to offer the service, but not everyone needs to. For example, a small company with five Windows machines might have only the machine with the printer connected to it providing the file and printer sharing service. The other four Windows computers connect to it by installing Client for Microsoft Networks and ensuring that they are using the same protocol. There is no reason for them to have the service installed because they are offering nothing to the network.

Windows and Novell servers usually run at least two services by default:

✦ **File sharing services:** Allow the server to share files with other users on the network.

✦ **Printer sharing services:** Allow a printer to be used by multiple users on the network. You don't need to purchase a separate printer for each user on the network, which is a real cost cutter!

File and printer sharing services were the original purpose in life for servers and networks, but the number of services that can be added to these systems has grown over the years to include mail services, Web services, FTP services, name resolution services, and many more.

Real-world scenario: Planning network components

You are responsible for determining what networking components are required in order to build the following scenario. The answer follows the scenario.

Scenario: You are in charge of implementing the network infrastructure for your organization. There are two Windows Server 2003 servers and three Novell servers servicing 200 Windows XP clients. The word processing department will be sending print jobs to one Windows XP computer in the manager's office. What networking components would you load to allow the clients to access both the Novell servers and the Windows 2003 servers?

Answer: The Windows XP computer in the manager's office will have File and Print Sharing for Microsoft Networks loaded so that the Windows XP client in the word processing department may connect to it.

You will have to load a Novell client so that the Windows XP clients can connect to the Novell servers. If the Novell servers are using IPX/SPX, you also have to make sure that the IPX/SPX protocol is loaded and the proper frame type is configured, but chances are that those servers are using TCP/IP.

To allow the Windows XP clients to connect to the Windows Server 2003 servers, you have to load the Client for Microsoft Networks if it isn't already loaded.

The TCP/IP Protocol

Since the dramatic growth of the Internet, TCP/IP has become the preferred protocol on networks today. TCP/IP is the common protocol on all desktops — including Windows, Linux, and Macintosh systems — allowing all these different OSes to communicate over a common protocol. It doesn't matter what OS you run or what kind of network you have: As long as you are running a common protocol such as TCP/IP, you can access resources across any platform.

TCP/IP is installed by default with every major OS (Windows, Mac OS X, and Linux). When configuring TCP/IP on these systems, three major settings need to be configured to allow the computer to communicate with other computers on different networks or the Internet:

✦ IP address

✦ Subnet mask

✦ Default gateway

To troubleshoot communication across TCP/IP, you need to understand the types of settings that need configuring. In the sections that follow, you look at how to configure TCP/IP and at some utilities to help you troubleshoot the protocol.

IP address

The *IP address* is a 32-bit number that is unique to your computer. No two systems can have the same IP address. An IP address is similar to the address of your home, which is the method by which other people send mail to you. An IP address works the same way on a TCP/IP network: You will assign the number to your computer, and it is the method other computers use to send information to your computer.

An IP address is made up of four sets of numbers separated by periods: dotted decimal notation format. Here's an example

```
131.107.2.200
```

Each of the four sets of numbers an *octet* (because each octet represents 8 bits of data).

The IP address comprises a network ID and a host ID:

✦ **Network ID:** This unique number is used only by your network and is also the same for all computers on the same network.

For example, in the IP address 131.107.2.200, the first two octets (131.107) make up the network ID. So if computer A with an IP address of 131.107.2.200 talks to computer B with an IP address of 131.107.3.5, you can assume that the two computers are on the same network because 131.107.*x*.*y* is the network ID for both computers.

✦ **Host ID:** This portion uniquely identifies a computer on the network.

For example, in the IP address 131.107.2.200, the last two octets (2.200) make up the host ID. Only one computer on the 131.107.*x*.*y* network can have the host ID of 2.200.

The network ID is not always the first two octets of the IP address. So how do you know which octets make up the network ID and which octets make up the host ID portion of the IP address? The *class* of IP address you have dictates which numbers correspond to which IDs.

The three major classes of IP addresses are Class A, Class B, and Class C. The different IP address classes support a different total number of workstations on the network. For example, a Class A network (a network using Class A addresses) supports as many as to 16,777,214 network devices, a Class B network supports 65,534 network devices, and a Class C network supports only 254 network devices.

Class A networks use the first octet as their network ID and the remaining three octets as the host ID. A Class B network uses the first two octets for the network ID and the last two octets as the host ID. A Class C network uses the first three octets as the network ID and the last octet for the host ID.

How do you know what class IP address you have? Look at the first octet. If it has a value between 1 and 126, it's a Class A IP address; if it has a value between 128 and 191, it's a Class B IP address; and if it has a value between 192 and 223, it's a Class C IP address. Table 3-1 summarizes IP address classes.

Table 3-1	IP Address Classes		
Network Class	*Number of Hosts*	*Octet Summary*	*First Octet Value*
Class A	16,777,214	n.h.h.h*	1–126
Class B	65,534	n.n.h.h	128–191
Class C	254	n.n.n.h	192–223

*n = network, h = host

In the Number of Hosts column, two numbers are missing. For example, a class C address *could* have 256 possible addresses, numbered 0 through 255. However, you are not allowed to use 0 because it is reserved for the network ID. Also, you are not allowed to use the 255 because it is the broadcast address, which is how systems send data to every computer on the network. To summarize, with each address class, you lose two addresses because of the network ID and the broadcast address.

Also notice in Table 3-1 that the number 127 is skipped in the First Octet Value column. This is because it is illegal for a system on the network to have an IP address that starts with 127. Any address starting with 127 is illegal because this address is reserved for the *loopback address,* which is an address that always refers to the TCP/IP software stack that initialized on *your* system. Typically, the loopback address is referred to as 127.0.0.1, but you could use any address that starts with 127. For example, you could issue the following command in a command prompt to test that TCP/IP is functioning properly on your system:

```
Ping 127.0.0.1
```

No matter what your IP address is, the loopback address is a constant that you can use to verify that your system is running correctly.

Here's an IP address example: Computer A has an IP address of 194.12.11.10, and it initiates communication with computer B, whose IP address is 194.13.11.9. Are the two workstations on the same network? Looking at the first octet, you can see that the number 194 is a Class C address, which means that the first three octets make up the network ID, and the last octet is the host ID. Because there is a difference in the first three octets (which is the network ID), these two computers are on different networks.

Identifying whether the computer you are trying to communicate with is on your network could be important when troubleshooting communications. If the computer you are trying to communicate with is not on your network, the problem could be with your computer, the remote computer, or the router. This means you have more places to look for the cause of the problem.

Subnet mask

Another way to tell whether your computer is on the same network as the computer you are trying to communicate with is to look at the subnet mask. The *subnet mask* is what your computer uses to determine whether the network device it is trying to communicate with is on the same network. The subnet mask helps the system determine the network ID portion of the IP address by comparing the subnet mask against the IP address. If there is a 255 in the subnet mask, the corresponding octet in the IP address is part of the network ID. After the network ID is known, any systems that have the same network ID are considered to be on the same network; otherwise, they would have a different network ID.

Different classes of IP addresses are associated with different default subnet masks. For example, a Class A address has a default subnet mask of 255.0.0.0, a Class B address has a default subnet mask of 255.255.0.0, and a Class C address has a default subnet mask of 255.255.255.0. Looking at the subnet masks, any octet with the value of 255 means that the corresponding octet in the IP address is part of the network ID.

To put this all together, Table 3-2 shows an example of two computers and their IP address configurations.

Table 3-2	Comparing IP Addresses with Subnet Mask
Item	*Address*
Computer A (IP address)	13.10.12.120
Computer A (subnet mask)	255.0.0.0
Computer B (IP address)	18.23.48.119

Using this example, computer A tries to connect to computer B. The first thing that computer A does is compare its IP address with its own subnet mask to determine what octets make up the network ID. Here it sees that the first octet is the network ID because the subset mask has the number 255 in only the first octet. Then computer A compares its subnet mask with the IP address of computer B (the remote computer it is trying to communicate with) and identifies that the network IDs of computer A and computer B are different — the two computers are on different networks.

When computer A realizes that the remote computer it is trying to communicate with (computer B) is on a different network, it starts to panic because it doesn't have the capability to send the information to the other computer. Computers can pass information directly to other computers only if both systems are on the same network. So what happens? This is where the default gateway fits into the story.

Default gateway

When information has to be forwarded from a computer on one network to a computer on another network, a special network device called a *router* must be used. The router has a table that lists all the networks it knows about and the network ID associated with each of those networks. When the router receives information destined for a particular IP address, it checks its table of network IDs for a match. If a match is found, it delivers the information to the appropriate network.

How does the information get to the router so that it can be forwarded? Looking at the example from Table 3-2 in the previous section, computer A has information for computer B, and computer A realizes that computer B sits on a different network. At this point, computer A looks at its *default gateway,* which is the address of the router that will forward the information on to computer B's network. The default gateway is a TCP/IP option configured on each workstation. Typically, all computers on the same network point to the same router.

When you are comfortable with the concepts of an IP address, subnet mask, and default gateway, you are ready to configure these options on a Windows OS, which I cover in the next section.

Configuring TCP/IP in Windows

To configure TCP/IP on a Windows system, access your local area connection properties and configure the TCP/IP protocol. Be aware that all Microsoft OSes today have TCP/IP installed by default. You simply need to configure the IP address on the system. To configure TCP/IP on a Windows system, follow these steps:

1. **Locate the network connections.**

 - *Windows 2000:* Choose Start⇨Settings⇨Control Panel⇨Network and Dial Up Connections.

 - *Windows XP/2003:* Choose Start⇨Control Panel⇨Network and Internet Connections⇨Network Connections.

 - *Windows Vista:* Click Start. Right-click Network and choose Properties. Click the Manage Network Connections link on the left.

2. **Right-click your local area connection and choose Properties.**

3. **In the list of items used by the connection do one of the following:**

 - **Windows 2000/XP/2003:** Select TCP/IP and then choose Properties.

 - **Windows Vista:** Select Internet Protocol Version 4 (TCP/IPv4) and then click Properties.

4. **To assign a static address, select Use the Following IP Address (as shown in Figure 3-8) and then type your computer's IP address, subnet mask, and default gateway in the corresponding text boxes.**

5. **Type the address of your DNS server in the Preferred DNS Server text box.**

 To know what to enter as the IP address of your DNS server, consult the network administrator or maybe even the network architects. Whoever has designed the network knows the IP address of the DNS server. (DNS is covered in more detail in the section "DNS," later in this chapter.)

Figure 3-8:
Configuring
TCP/IP on
a Windows
XP client.

6. **Click OK and then OK again.**

To communicate with systems off the network, your computer will need an
IP address, a subnet mask, and a default gateway configured. To communi-
cate with systems on the network, you need only an IP address and subnet
mask configured.

Configuring TCP/IP en masse using DHCP

If you are the network administrator of a large network, you do not want to
run around to 400 workstations and configure an IP address, a subnet mask,
and a default gateway on each computer. Not only is this time-consuming
to initially set up, but it also becomes a nightmare to manage because of all
the potential for human error. I have spent my days running around to each
computer on the network, a sheet of paper in my hands, making sure that
each computer is configured properly, and I can tell you that it is *not* fun!

Today's network OSes support Dynamic Host Configuration Protocol
(DHCP), which is a standard that allows the network administrator to tell
the DHCP server a range of IP addresses that it is allowed to give out, along
with the other TCP/IP options such as a subnet mask and default gateway.
When the DHCP server is configured to give out the addresses, the desktop
computers automatically request an IP address from the server when they
start up, and the server hands them all the IP address information. This
means that the network administrator does not have to run around to each
computer individually to configure TCP/IP — which, in the long run, saves
time and money.

The steps to configure a Windows system to obtain an IP address from a DHCP server are very similar to actually assigning the IP address manually.

To configure a Windows client for DHCP, follow these steps:

1. **Locate the network connections.**

- *Windows 2000:* Choose Start⇨Settings⇨Control Panel⇨Network and Dial Up Connections.

- *Windows XP/2003:* Choose Start⇨Control Panel⇨Network and Internet Connections⇨Network Connections.

- *Windows Vista:* Click Start. Right-click Network and choose Properties. Click the Manage Network Connections link on the left.

2. **Right-click your local area connection and choose Properties.**

3. **In the list of items used by the connection do one of the following:**

- **Windows 2000/XP/2003:** Select TCP/IP and then choose Properties.

- **Windows Vista:** Select Internet Protocol Version 4 (TCP/IPv4) and then click Properties.

The Internet Protocol (TCP/IP) Properties dialog box appears.

4. **On the General tab, select the Obtain an IP Address Automatically option, as shown in Figure 3-9, to enable this system to be a DHCP client.**

Figure 3-9:
Configuring
Windows
XP as a
DHCP client.

5. **Click OK and then OK again to close the network connections dialog box.**

Automatic Private IP Addressing (APIPA)

If a DHCP server isn't available and your Windows clients are configured to obtain an IP address automatically, will they receive an IP address? Yes, because Windows operating systems supports the Automatic Private IP Addressing (APIPA) feature. APIPA allows the client to self-assign an IP address if the DHCP server does not respond to the DHCP request. The address that the client self-assigns is within the 169.254.$x.y$ network range. The system will also configure itself with a subnet mask of 255.255.0.0 but will not configure the default gateway entry. This means that if the DHCP server is down and your network clients boot up, they will all have an address in the 169.254.$x.y$ range and will be able to communicate with one another. Because they are not configured for a default gateway entry, they will not be able to communicate with systems off the network or with the Internet.

When troubleshooting networking connectivity, use the `ipconfig` command to view the TCP/IP settings on a client. If the IP address is 169.254.$x.y$, that means the client cannot communicate with the DHCP server. Make sure that the client is connected to the network correctly and then verify that the DHCP server is functioning!

Private IP addresses

Another type of IP addresses you should be familiar with for the A+ certification exams is the concept of a private IP address: an address assigned to a system that cannot have its traffic routed on the Internet. These address types are designed for internal use only.

The three private IP address blocks are

◆ `10.0.0.0` to `10.255.255.255`

◆ `172.16.0.0` to `172.31.255.255`

◆ `192.168.0.0` to `192.168.255.255`

It is interesting to note that the third range of `192.168.0.0` is what most home networks use because the home router is using the `192.168.0.0` network range. The reason why I say this is interesting is because you can surf the Internet at home using this address, but yet I said private addresses cannot be used for Internet access. Huh? This doesn't make sense!

Network Address Translation

Home routers use the Network Address Translation (NAT) technology. The router is a NAT device, and a NAT device has two network cards: one

connected to the Internet and one connected to the inside network. Your client systems use the NAT device (the home router) as their default gateway, so they send all outbound Internet traffic to the NAT device.

The NAT device converts the private address being used as the source IP address of the packet to the public address assigned to the WAN interface on the NAT device. As a result, the packet looks like it is coming from the WAN port of the NAT device, which is actually using a valid public address. When the reply comes back, the NAT device translates the address back to the private address and then sends the packet to the client system inside the network. This is completely transparent to the clients on the network.

One benefit of NAT is that you can share the one public IP address assigned by your ISP to the WAN port on the router, thus allowing you to have multiple computers on your home network surfing at the same time. Another benefit is a security benefit: that is, your internal network structure is hidden from the outside world. From the Internet's point of view, the system surfing the Web is the NAT router. If nefarious folks decide to attack that address, they are attacking the NAT device — and not the IP of a machine on your network.

Understanding Name Resolution

To communicate with another computer across a TCP/IP network, you have to know the IP address of the computer you are trying to communicate with. This is unrealistic, considering that you are probably not too interested in trying to memorize all the IP addresses of the different Web sites you visit every day.

When running a TCP/IP network, you assign a friendly name to each computer and reference each computer by the friendly name instead of using the IP address. This means that instead of using an address like 204.56.78.6 to connect to Bob's computer, you would use a friendly name — say, bob.

The two types of names to understand when troubleshooting TCP/IP networks are

+ Computer names (also known as *NetBIOS names*)
+ Fully qualified domain names (FQDN)

NetBIOS names

In the Windows world, you access resources on a system by connecting to the computer name of the system. As an administrator, you assign a computer name to each computer on the network. The *computer name*

(NetBIOS name) is a friendly name of as many as 15 characters assigned to a computer and used to uniquely identify the computer on the network. Users can then connect to the computer by the computer name *or* by the IP address — and people find it much easier to remember the computer name!

Changing the computer name in Windows

Changing your computer name in Windows is a common task, and is fairly straightforward with today's Windows OSes.

To change your computer name in Windows 2000/2003/XP, follow these steps:

1. **Right-click My Computer and choose Properties from the contextual menu.**

 If you don't see My Computer on the desktop, you can find it in the Start menu.

2. **Click the Computer Name tab.**

3. **Click the Change button.**

 The Computer Name Changes dialog box appears, allowing you to type a new computer name, as shown in Figure 3-10.

 When changing your computer name, notice that you can set the workgroup as well. A *workgroup* is the term given to a logical grouping of computers. When users browse the network, they may choose a workgroup, such as Accounting, and then they will see any systems that are a part of the Accounting workgroup. To place your system in a particular workgroup, simply type the name of the workgroup in the text box.

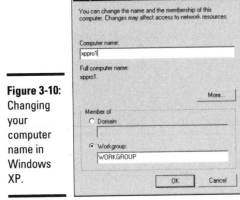

Figure 3-10:
Changing your computer name in Windows XP.

4. **Click OK to close out all the dialog boxes.**

5. **Reboot the system.**

 The computer name does not take effect until you reboot the system.

To change your computer name in Windows Vista, follow these steps:

1. **Click Start, right-click Computer, and choose Properties.**

2. **Click the Advanced System Settings link on the left side of the System Window.**

3. **Click Continue to give Windows permission to perform the requested task.**

4. **Click the Computer Name page tab.**

5. **Click the Change button, type a new computer name, and then reboot.**

WINS

When you network in a Microsoft environment, you connect to other computers by using those computers' names. These computer names must be converted to IP addresses for communication to happen in a TCP/IP network. For example, you may want to connect to Bob's computer, so you connect to \\ bob through the Run command on the Start menu. When you try to connect, \\bob has to be converted to an IP address for the computer to be able to look for it. The process of converting a name from one format to another is *name resolution.* In this example, the computer name is being converted to an IP address, which is known as *NetBIOS name resolution.*

With NetBIOS name resolution, before your computer tries to connect to another system, it sends a query to a Windows Internet Naming System (WINS) server, asking the server this: "Hi there, Mr. WINS server. I am trying to connect to a computer named bob — do you have an IP address for this computer?" The WINS server holds a database of NetBIOS names and matching IP addresses: the WINS database. Think of this database as having two columns: one for the computer name (NetBIOS name) and one for the matching IP address. Upon receiving the question, the WINS server checks the database for the computer named bob and then returns its IP address to the client who asked for it. Then the client can connect by using the IP address for bob.

For a Windows system to send a query to the WINS server, you must ensure that you configure the WINS server setting within the TCP/IP properties of the client system. Configuring the Windows client for a WINS server directs the client to the server that it must register its name and IP address with and also who to send name resolution queries to.

Before configuring your clients for WINS, you must be aware of the IP address used by the WINS server. If you do not know this information, consult the network administrator. After you have the IP address of the WINS

server, you are ready to configure the WINS clients. To configure a Windows system as a WINS client, follow these steps:

1. **Locate the network connections.**

 - *Windows 2000:* Choose Start⇨Settings⇨Control Panel⇨Network and Dial Up Connections.

 - *Windows XP/2003:* Choose Start⇨Control Panel⇨Network and Internet Connections⇨Network Connections.

 - *Windows Vista:* Click Start. Right-click Network and choose Properties. Click the Manage Network Connections links on the left.

2. **Right-click your local area connection and choose Properties.**

3. **In the list of items used by the connection do one of the following:**

 - **Windows 2000/XP/2003:** Select TCP/IP and then choose Properties,

 - **Windows Vista:** Select Internet Protocol Version 4 (TCP/IPv4) and then click Properties.

4. **In the Internet Protocol (TCP/IP) Properties window, click the Advanced button.**

5. **Click the WINS tab.**

6. **Click the Add button to add the IP address of the WINS server.**

7. **Type the IP address of the WINS server and click Add, as shown in Figure 3-11.**

8. **Keep clicking OK until you close all dialog boxes.**

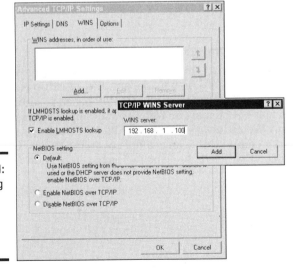

Figure 3-11: Configuring a WINS client in Windows XP.

The LMHOSTS file

If you do not have a WINS server but an application you are running requires the use of a NetBIOS name (computer name), you need to use the LMHOSTS file. The LMHOSTS file resides on each computer and is used to resolve, or convert, computer names to IP addresses. This file exists on each system on the network. You simply need to add an entry for the computer name and the corresponding IP address for each system that you want the file to resolve. Figure 3-12 displays a typical LMHOSTS file.

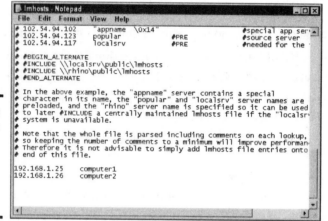

Figure 3-12: An example of an LMHOSTS file in Windows XP.

Windows stores the file in `%systemroot%\system32\drivers\etc`. In Windows, the folder has an existing LMHOSTS file that you can use as a sample, but it has a `.sam` extension that needs to be removed because the true LMHOSTS file has no extension.

Fully qualified domain names (FQDN)

The other type of name that can be assigned to the computer when you are running a TCP/IP network is a host name, or a *fully qualified domain name (FQDN)*. FQDNs are used when you run a TCP/IP-based or Internet-based application, such as FTP, e-mail, or Web browser applications. For example, to navigate to my Web site via your favorite Web browser, you would type **www.gleneclarke.com** — this is an example of an FQDN. An FQDN is an Internet-style name that needs to be converted to an IP address for communication to occur.

The point is that when you use a computer name or an FQDN on a TCP/IP-based network, the names always need to be converted to the actual IP addresses. Again, converting names (either computer names or FQDNs) to IP addresses is *name resolution*.

There are a few techniques for FQDN resolution, and some are more popular than others. The following sections describe the name resolution techniques and their purposes.

DNS

DNS (domain name system) is the desired name resolution technique for resolving (converting) fully qualified domain names to IP addresses. Remember that FQDNs are the names that are used with Internet-based applications, such as e-mail and Web browsers. DNS is like a big database of FQDNs and their matching IP addresses. Think of this database as having two columns — one for the FQDN and the other for the IP address.

When you are running Internet or TCP/IP applications and you type in a FQDN, your computer sends a query to the DNS database asking something like this: "I am trying to connect to `www.gleneclarke.com`. Do you have the IP address that matches this FQDN?" The database looks up the FQDN and returns the IP address to your computer, and your computer then connects to that IP address.

The big question is, where is the database stored? The database is stored on DNS servers. These servers hold the actual records and also where each client computer on your network sends its name queries.

To configure a Windows client to use a DNS server, you add the IP address of the DNS server while configuring TCP/IP. (Refer to the section "Configuring TCP/IP in Windows," earlier in this chapter.) Notice also that in Windows, the DNS server option is on the same screen as where you assign the IP address for a computer, which shows how critical DNS is to today's computing! To configure a Windows client to use DNS, follow these steps:

1. **Locate the network connections.**

- *Windows 2000:* Choose Start➪Settings➪Control Panel➪Network and Dial Up Connections.

- *Windows XP/2003:* Choose Start➪Control Panel➪Network and Internet Connections➪Network Connections.

- *Windows Vista:* Click Start. Right-click Network and choose Properties. Click the Manage Network Connections links on the left.

2. **Right-click your Local Area Connection and choose Properties.**

 The local area connection Properties dialog box appears.

3. **In the list of items used by the connection do one of the following:**

 • **Windows 2000/XP/2003:** Select TCP/IP and then choose Properties.

 • **Windows Vista:** Select Internet Protocol Version 4 (TCP/IPv4) and then click Properties.

4. **In the TCP/IP Properties dialog box, select the Use the Following DNS Server Addresses option and type the IP address of your DNS server, as shown Figure 3-13.**

Figure 3-13: Configuring a Windows XP client for DNS.

5. **Click OK twice to close the dialog boxes.**

The HOSTS file

Very similar to the idea of using an LMHOSTS file for NetBIOS name resolution (see "The LMHOSTS file" section, earlier in the chapter), you can use a text file, called the HOSTS file, for host name resolution. The HOSTS file is located in the %systemroot%\system32\drivers\etc folder on Windows systems.

The configuration of the HOSTS file is similar to the configuration of the LMHOSTS file. You simply create two columns — one for the FQDN and the other for the IP address of the system. Separate these columns with a Tab. Figure 3-14 shows a sample HOSTS file.

Figure 3-14:
An example of a HOSTS file used for FQDN resolution.

ARP

Be aware that another layer of resolution needs to happen after your client has the IP address of the system it wants to communicate with. You know that there is a different database for FQDN resolution and computer name resolution: namely, the DNS database stores FQDNs and their IP addresses, and the WINS database stores computer names and associated IP addresses. After the name is converted to the IP address, the IP address then must be resolved to the hardware address burned into the network card. This hardware address assigned to each network card is the MAC address. This means that there has to be a process that converts the IP address to the MAC address, and this process is Address Resolution Protocol (ARP). ARP is an address resolution protocol that converts the IP address to the physical address assigned to the network card.

ARP is a broadcast, or a yell, out on the wire for a particular address. Look at an example of computer A trying to send information to computer B: After computer A has the IP address of computer B (204.56.78.3), computer A yells at the top of its lungs, "Hey, 204.56.78.3! What is your network card's MAC address?" This yell runs along the network and eventually reaches computer B, which responds with its MAC address. After computer A has the MAC address of computer B, it can then send the data to computer B.

ARP messages are *broadcast messages,* and broadcast messages do not pass through routers. This does not cause a problem because when you want to communicate with a system on a different network, your system sends the data to the default gateway, or router, and then the router sends the data off the network by ARPing the router on the destination network. In this example, your system communicates with the router, so it would ARP the router, not the destination system!

Real-world scenario: Planning TCP/IP settings

Determine what TCP/IP services are required to fit the following scenario. The answer follows the scenario.

Scenario: You are responsible for implementing a TCP/IP-based network across all office locations in your region. What TCP/IP options will you set, and which additional TCP/IP-based services will you implement?

Answer: You might want to set a DNS server to store the FQDN and IP addresses of the different

servers on your network. You might also want to run a WINS server for computer name resolution because it is a WAN environment.

After you set up the DNS and WINS servers, you will install a DHCP for each network segment so that you can hand out IP address, subnet mask, and default gateway information to the clients on the network. You will also hand out the IP address of the DNS server and the WINS server through DHCP so that the clients are fully configured.

DNS and the HOSTS file resolve FQDNs to IP addresses. WINS and the LMHOSTS file resolve computer names to IP addresses.

Troubleshooting with TCP/IP Utilities

After you have TCP/IP installed and configured and you have your TCP/IP network running, you need to be able to troubleshoot the network. When problems arise on a Windows network, you can use some of the following commands to do your troubleshooting:

+ IPCONFIG
+ PING
+ TRACERT
+ NBTSTAT
+ NETSTAT
+ PATHPING
+ NSLOOKUP

The following sections discuss these popular TCP/IP utilities that are used to troubleshoot TCP/IP connectivity.

IPCONFIG

On Windows systems, you can run the ipconfig (IP configuration) utility, which shows you the current TCP/IP configuration of the Windows desktop, such as the IP address, subnet mask, and default gateway. If the computer is

a DHCP client, `ipconfig` identifies the server that has given the IP address and also shows how long the IP address will be used by the client. Table 3-3 shows some of the switches supported by the utility `ipconfig.exe`.

Table 3-3	IPCONFIG Switches
Switch	*Description*
/?	Shows a list of switches supported by `ipconfig.exe` and a brief description of each switch
/all	Shows all TCP/IP information — for example, DHCP lease period and the DNS server
/release	Releases the current IP address information assigned by the DHCP server
/renew	Requests new IP address information from the DHCP server
/display dns	Displays the DNS resolver cache which stores recent results from DNS queries
/flushdns	Clears the DNS resolver cache

For example, to use the `ipconfig` utility and view just the basic TCP/IP settings, you type the following at a command prompt:

```
ipconfig
```

But to view all the TCP/IP settings, such as your MAC address or the IP address of your DNS server, DHCP server, and WINS server, use the `ipconfig/all` command. You might also view when your lease time is up for the address you have been assigned when you use the `/all` switch on `ipconfig`.

Before leaving the topic of viewing your IP address settings, I want to add the point that on a Linux system, you use the `ifconfig` command to view your TCP/IP settings.

Lab 3-1 gives you practice working with the `ipconfig` command. Find Lab 3-1 in the `Labs.pdf` file in the Author directory of the CD-ROM.

PING

One of the most popular TCP/IP utilities is the `ping.exe` utility. *Ping* (Packet Internet Groper) is used to test whether your computer can communicate with a remote network device. If the ping test is successful, you get a ping response from the remote device; if it is not successful, the response

will time out. The general syntax for using the ping utility is `ping <IP address>`, the IP address being the IP address of the network device you are testing.

When troubleshooting TCP/IP communication problems, it is important to understand the steps to find exactly where the problem occurs. Is the problem in the computer you are using, in the computer you are trying to connect to, or in the default gateway?

Table 3-4 lists the order in which to ping each network device when trying to figure out at what stage the TCP/IP communication is failing.

Table 3-4	Troubleshooting Network Connectivity
Address to Ping	*Description*
`127.0.0.1`	This IP address is the *loopback* address. It always tests your own workstation's TCP/IP software to ensure that it has loaded.
IP address of your computer	After you get a response from loopback, ping the IP address that has been physically assigned to your network card. To find out what IP address is assigned to your network card, use `ipconfig.exe`.
IP address of default gateway	If you get a response from your network card's IP address, ping the IP address of the default gateway. If you don't know the IP address of your default gateway, run `ipconfig.exe` to view the address of the default gateway. Remember that the default gateway is the router, which is responsible for passing information on to other networks. If you are having trouble communicating with the router, you can't communicate with any devices off the network.
IP address of remote computer	After verifying that the default gateway is not the problem, if you know the IP address of the computer you wish to talk to (and chances are you don't because you are not the person who assigns the address to that computer), you can try pinging it. If you get a timeout at this step, you know that the computer you are trying to communicate with is the problem.

When you're troubleshooting a system that doesn't have Internet access, use the `ipconfig` utility to view the default gateway of the system; then ping the default gateway.

Lab 3-2 gives you practice changing your TCP/IP settings and working with the ping command. Lab 3-3 allows you to test your TCP/IP communication. Lab 3-2 and Lab 3-3 can be found in the `Labs.pdf` file in the Author directory of the CD-ROM.

TRACERT

The ping utility is probably the most used TCP/IP utility, and rightfully so. The ping utility is a very useful utility for troubleshooting communication problems, but the ping utility tells you only whether your computer has communicated with the remote hosts; it does not tell you what path the information took. This is where the *trace route* (tracert.exe) utility is useful. It is similar to the ping utility in the sense that responses are sent back to you if communication is established. The difference is that tracert.exe sends a response from every network it hits on the way, not just a response from the final destination. So tracert.exe shows you the *path* the information takes and also the number of networks between your computer and the computer you are talking to.

The trace route utility uses the following syntax (note the space after tracert):

```
tracert <IP address or DNS name>
```

NBTSTAT

Another popular network troubleshooting utility is nbtstat, which is used to troubleshoot NetBIOS name resolution. (Remember that discussion? If not, look back to the "NetBIOS names" section.) nbtstat stands for *NetBIOS over TCP/IP Statistics*. When your system resolves a computer name to an IP address, it stores that information in memory (the NetBIOS name cache) so that the next time the name needs to be converted to an IP address the request is resolved from cache instead of broadcasting or querying a WINS server. If you wanted to verify that the entry is in cache, use the nbtstat utility.

There are a number of uses for the NBTSTAT utility, so there are quite a few switches for the command. Some of the most useful switches are listed in Table 3-5.

Table 3-5	NBTSTAT Switches
Switch	**Description**
/?	Shows a list of switches supported by nbtstat and a brief description of each switch.
-c	Displays the contents of the NBTSTAT cache. This cache shows the computer names and matching IP addresses that have been resolved recently.
-A <ip address>	Displays the list of NetBIOS names used by the IP address typed with the —A. The listing also indicates what types of services the system is running. Note that the —A is uppercase and has a space after it and before the IP address.
-n	Displays the NetBIOS names used by the local system.
-r	Lists which addresses have been resolved through WINS.

To use the `nbtstat` command, type something like the following at a command prompt:

```
nbtstat -A 192.168.1.200
```

NETSTAT

The `netstat` command line utility is used to troubleshoot TCP/IP connections. If you use the `netstat` command by itself, it displays a list of connections that your system has with remote systems and the associated ports.

Like `nbtstat`, `netstat` supports a number of switches to help you get the most information possible out of the command. Table 3-6 lists some of the more popular `netstat` switches.

Table 3-6	NETSTAT Switches
Switch	*Description*
`/?`	Shows a list of switches supported by `netstat` and a brief description of each switch.
`-a`	Displays all connections that your system has but also all listening ports. A port is what an application uses as an endpoint of communication. For example, applications such as Internet Explorer use a port, and that port is where a Web server sends the data so that the data reaches Internet Explorer.
`-o`	Displays the process ID of the application that opened the port. You can use this information with the `tasklist` command to track down the application that opened the port. You can then use the `taskkill` command to terminate the program that opened the port.
`-p <protocol>`	Shows the connections for the protocol provided to the switch. For example, you could use `netstat -p TCP` to view all the TCP connections. In this example, you will not see the UDP connections.

An example usage of the `netstat` command is as follows:

```
netstat -a -o
```

PATHPING

`pathping` is a newer command line utility to the Windows world that allows you to ping a destination, and — like the `tracert` command — you get a list of hops (routers) from the source to the destination. After the list of hops is determined, `pathping` sends a number of messages to each hop to calculate statistics on each hop, such as the number of lost packets.

NSLOOKUP

`nslookup` is a TCP/IP utility used to query DNS and to troubleshoot problems associated with DNS. With `nslookup`, you can query for a specific type of record, such as e-mail server records (MX records) if you want to know the mail servers for a particular company. Take a look at a few `nslookup` commands.

```
nslookup www.gleneclarke.com
```

The preceding command queries DNS and reports back to you the IP address for the server at `www.gleneclarke.com`. To find the mail servers for `glen eclarke.com`, you would type the following commands in a command prompt:

```
nslookup
set type=mx
gleneclarke.com
```

In the previous example, Windows will report to you the entries from DNS that have an MX record type, which are the entries in DNS that reference the e-mail servers for `gleneclarke.com`.

net commands

Windows has a number of different networking commands that you can use to perform tasks such as create user account, modify group membership, and map network drives, to name a few.

net user

The `net user` command is used to view or manage user accounts on the system. When you go to a command prompt and type

```
net user
```

this command shows a list of user accounts that exist on the system. To create a user account, you can expand on the command by typing

```
net user aplusguy P@ssw0rd /add
```

This command creates a user named `aplusguy` with a password of `P@ssw0rd`.

net localgroup

The `net localgroup` command is used to manage membership to a specific group. If you want to add a user to the administrators group, you would type the following command:

```
net localgroup administrators aplusguy /add
```

net view

You can also view a list of domains or workgroups on the network by using the net view command. The following shows a listing of domains:

```
net view /domain
```

From this list of domains, you can then view a list of servers in a particular domain by using the net view command as well. The following command is asking to view a list of systems in the glensworld domain:

```
net view /domain:glensworld
```

From the list of servers in the domain, you can then potentially view a list of shared folders on one of those systems by typing

```
net view \\server1
```

net use

Don't confuse the net user command with the net use command. net user is used to manage user accounts, and net use is used to map network drives. For example, if you want to create a J: drive on your system that references the shared folder called data on a server called Server1, you would type

```
net use j: \\server1\data
```

These are just a few examples of popular networking tasks that can be performed by using the net commands in the Windows OS. To read more about what the net command can do in Windows, use the net /? command.

Sharing File System Resources

In this section, I discuss how to set up the Windows OS for sharing network resources. I begin with a discussion of some of the core options that must be set to network within a Windows OS.

Every Windows computer must have a computer name to participate in a Windows network, and each computer name must be unique on the network to properly address a specific computer. To review the steps to change your computer's name, take a look at the section, "Changing the computer name in Windows," earlier in the chapter.

User-level access control

Current versions of Windows operating systems use a type of access control known as user level access control. *User-level access control* means that when you share a resource out onto the network, you actually assign permissions to particular users. If someone wants access to the share, his or her user account has to have been given permissions to the share, and the user must log in with that particular account.

Windows OSes today always use user-level access control while older versions of Windows, such as Windows 9x, supported share-level access control as well. Share level access allowed you to put a password on the share and not based your security on a list of permissions assigned to users. There is not an option to switch to share-level access control in today's versions of Windows. This means that when you share a resource today, you need to choose a list of users or groups who have access to the resource — and this is a good thing!

Enabling file and printer sharing in Windows

Now that you understand the two levels of access control, you are ready to allow your Windows machines to share resources on the network. First, you must ensure that File and Printer Sharing Services are installed and that File and Printer Sharing is enabled. Then you can start sharing folders and printers.

All Windows OSes have File and Printer Sharing enabled by default. To verify that File and Printer Sharing is enabled within these operating systems, perform the following steps:

1. **Locate the network connections.**

- *Windows 2000:* Choose Start⇨Settings⇨Control Panel⇨Network and Dial Up Connections.

- *Windows XP/Server 2003:* Choose Start⇨Control Panel⇨Network and Internet Connections⇨Network Connections.

- *Windows Vista:* Click Start. Right-click Network and choose Properties. Click the Manage Network Connections links on the left.

2. **Right-click your local area connection and choose Properties.**

3. **Select the File and Printer Sharing for Microsoft Networks check box, as shown in Figure 3-15, and then click OK.**

When this check box is selected, File and Printer Sharing is enabled, and you're finished. If File and Printer Sharing for Microsoft Networks wasn't listed, you need to install it first, so keep reading.

Figure 3-15:
Verifying
that File
and Printer
Sharing is
installed on
Windows
XP.

4. **If File and Printer Sharing isn't listed, click the Install button to install the service.**

5. **Choose Service in the Component Type dialog box and then choose File and Printer Sharing for Microsoft Networks. Then click OK to close all the dialog boxes.**

Creating shared folders

When a user on the network wishes to access a file on another system, he must connect to a share on that system. *Shares* are a way to publish the folder on your system for other users on the network so that they can access the files in that folder. If you have not shared any resources, there is no reason for anyone to want to connect to your computer — it would be like giving someone the key to a locked but empty room.

You can share only folders or printers; you cannot actually share a file specifically. To allow users to access a file from across the network, you have to place the file in a folder and then share that folder.

Sharing a folder in Windows 2000

To share a folder on a Windows 2000 network, simply right-click the folder you wish to share and choose the Sharing command. In the Sharing dialog box that appears, select the Share This Folder option to share the folder. Within the Sharing dialog box, you will need to set a number of options (shown in Figure 3-16).

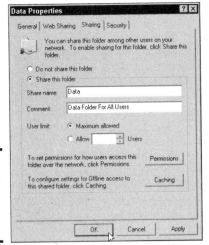

Figure 3-16:
Sharing a
folder in
Windows
2000.

The options are:

+ **Share Name:** You need to give the share a name. This is the name that
 will be referred to by users who want to connect to the share.

+ **Comment:** This is an optional description of the share that displays in
 Windows when the user views the list of shares in Detail view.

+ **User Limit:** You may limit how many users can connect to the share at
 any given time. This could be useful if you notice that the system is slow
 after a certain number of users connect. For example, if you're sharing
 a CD-ROM, you may notice that access to the CD-ROM slows after six
 users connect. In this example, you may want to set the user limit to
 five. Setting the user limit to maximum allowed will configure the user
 limit for ten users connected to the share at once because Windows
 desktop OSes can allow only ten connections at a time.

+ **Permissions:** Set permissions on the share. You set permissions to
 control which users can modify data in the share and which ones can
 simply read information in the share.

+ **Caching:** This feature allows the client to store a local copy of data
 accessed in the share. This could be useful if you wish to allow a laptop
 user to take a copy of the data home and update the data. The modified
 data could then be synchronized with the content on the server when
 the user returns to the office.

Notice in Figure 3-16 that I shared the folder named Data. As mentioned ear-
lier, when sharing a folder, you need to set the share permissions. To set the
share permissions, click the Permissions button. The default permissions in
Windows 2000 are Everyone and Full Control, as shown in Figure 3-17.

Figure 3-17:
Setting
share
permissions
in Windows
2000.

This means that any user can create, delete, and modify files in the share or modify the share permissions. These default permissions are not good! The following steps show you how to adjust these permissions to your liking:

1. **To remove the Everyone group from the permissions list, click the Remove button.**

2. **Add specific users to the permissions list by clicking the Add button.**

The Select Users or Groups dialog box appears.

3. **Select which user or group is allowed to connect to the share by selecting the user.**

You may add multiple users by clicking the first user, holding down the Ctrl key, and clicking additional users.

4. **Click Add to return to the Permissions dialog box.**

5. **To set a user's permissions, select one of the following permissions for that user:**

- *Full Control:* Allows a user to read and change the contents of files on the share, to delete files on the share, and to change the share per-missions. This permission is not normally assigned to users.

- *Change:* Allows a user to read the contents of files in the share, change the contents of files that exist in the share, and delete files. Users cannot change permissions on the share with the Change permission.

- *Read:* Allows a user or group to read but not modify the content in the shared folder.

6. **Click OK and then click OK again to exit the dialog boxes.**

Sharing a folder in Windows XP

The steps to share a folder on a Windows XP system are very similar to sharing a folder in Windows 2000, but Microsoft has tried to simplify managing the security by hiding the security settings by default. To share a folder in Windows XP, follow these steps:

1. **Locate the folder you wish to share on your system.**

2. **Right-click the folder and choose Sharing and Security.**

3. **On the Sharing tab, choose the Share This Folder on the Network option (shown in Figure 3-18).**

 Notice that the share name is the same name as the folder.

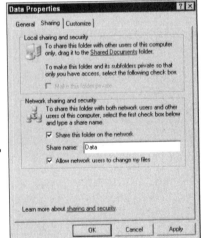

Figure 3-18:
Sharing a folder in Windows XP.

4. **If you would like users to be able to alter the files in the folder, select the Allow Network Users to Change My Files option.**

5. **Click OK.**

 You share a hard drive or CD-ROM in exactly the same way that you share a folder. To share the hard drive or CD-ROM, open My Computer, right-click the drive, and then choose the Sharing command — a great idea to share the CD to a number of users on the network so that all users can access the contents of the CD-ROM at one time!

To modify the permissions on the share in Windows XP like you do with a shared folder in Windows 2000, disable the Simple File Sharing option within Windows XP. Follow these steps:

1. **Open My Computer.**

2. **Choose Tools⇨Folder Options.**

3. **Click the View tab.**

4. **Scroll to the bottom of the Advanced Settings and clear the Use Simple File Sharing (Recommended) option, as shown in Figure 3-19.**

5. **Click OK.**

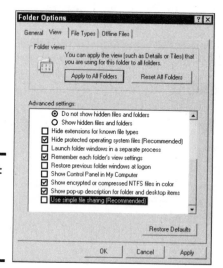

Figure 3-19: Disabling simple file sharing in Windows XP.

After you disabled Simple File Sharing in Windows XP, you can set share permissions by selecting individual users and groups and what permissions you would like to assign by following the instructions in the "Sharing a folder in Windows 2000" section. Also note that Windows XP Home edition only supports Simple File Sharing.

Sharing a folder in Windows Vista

The steps to share a folder on a Windows Vista system are very similar to sharing a folder in other versions of Windows OSes. But like Windows XP, Microsoft has tried to simplify managing the security by creating a wizard style interface to share folders. To share a folder in Windows Vista, follow these steps:

1. **Locate the folder you wish to share on your system.**

2. **Right-click the folder and choose Share.**

3. **In the File Sharing dialog box, choose the user (or group) you wish to share the folder with from the drop-down list; then choose Add.**

4. **Choose the Permission Level for the share (shown in Figure 3-20):**

- *Reader:* Allows the user or group to read files from the share folder but not make changes to the content of the shared folder

- *Contributor:* Allows the user or group to add a file to the share and modify or delete his/her own files

- *Co-owner:* Gives the user full permission to the share including modifying and deleting any files in the share

5. **Click the Share button.**

6. **Click Done.**

Figure 3-20:
Assigning
permissions
levels in
Windows
Vista.

Hidden shares

In the Windows world, you can also create hidden shares, which are like normal shares in the sense that users on the network can connect to them. The difference is that hidden shares are not advertised — you can't find them by browsing through the shared folder list on a server. Users will connect to the hidden share by typing the universal naming convention (UNC) in the Run command or by mapping a drive, which you can read about in the "Connecting to Shares" section.

To create a hidden share, use the steps for creating a normal share (see the section "Creating shared folders," earlier in this chapter). However, when you type a share name in the Share Name text box, you create the hidden share

by appending a dollar sign ($) to the end of the share name. For example, if the share name is `data` and you want it to be a hidden share, you would type **data$** in the Share Name text box. The share is then automatically hidden from Windows and users on the network when they browse the servers.

Multiple shares

In Windows, you have the ability to create multiple shares for the same folder. This gives flexibility to the network administrator so that a user can have different permissions for a single folder, depending on what share that user connects to.

On my office network, I implemented multiple shares per shared folder so that during day-to-day activities, not even an administrator can alter files on the server. If an administrator wants to make changes to a folder, he has to connect to the secondary share for that particular folder to have full-control access. This helps prevent a lot of unfortunate mistakes in modifying or deleting files by accident — even network administrators make mistakes! A big rule I follow is "Protect the network from yourself as well!"

Connecting to shares

After you create the shared resource, you can connect to the shared resource from anywhere on the network. There are a number of ways to connect to shared folders; here are a few of the most common:

✦ Browsing My Network Places

✦ Using a UNC path through the `Run` command

✦ Mapping a drive

The following sections examine each of these methods.

Browsing network resources

To browse network resources in Windows 2000/XP, follow these steps:

1. **Go to My Network Places.**

2. **Click the View Workgroup Computers link on the left in the Network Task list.**

 You see a list of computers.

3. **Double-click a computer to see a list of shares on that computer.**

4. **You can open any share just by double-clicking it.**

You cannot see any hidden shares while browsing network resources. For this reason, it is important to know additional ways to connect to shares, such as through the UNC path.

To browse network resources in Windows Vista, you simply navigate to the network resources by choosing Start⇨Network. To view a list of shared resources on a system, double-click the system.

Using a UNC path

You may also connect to a share by using the universal naming convention path. The UNC path is made up of two backslashes (\\), the computer name you want to connect to, one more backslash, and the share name of the folder you want to connect to. The entire syntax looks like this:

```
\\computername\sharename
```

You would type this into the Run command, found by clicking the Start button.

Using UNC paths means that you have to be aware of the exact names used for resources on the network, including hidden shares. When you get used to the computer names and share names on the network, you'll find that the Run command is quicker than waiting to see the list of computers in Network Neighborhood or My Network Places.

Mapping a network drive

You may also connect to shares by mapping drives. If you find that you are constantly connecting to the same resource, you may want to map a drive for the sake of simplicity. The idea of mapping a drive is that, in the end, you have a new drive letter in your My Computer folder that points to the UNC path of the resource. After the drive is mapped, anytime you wish to access the folder on the network, you go to My Computer and double-click the mapped drive.

To map a drive, right-click My Computer (in XP) or Computer (in Vista) and then choose Map Network Drive. In the Map Network Drive dialog box, select the letter for the drive you want to create and then type the UNC path to the shared resource into the Path text box. You may also choose the option to re-create this drive mapping the next time you log on so that you do not have to do this again. Figure 3-21 shows the Map Network Drive dialog box.

Figure 3-21:
Mapping
a network
drive in
Windows
XP.

Lab 3-4 allows you to practice sharing resources and connecting to
resources. Lab 3-4 can be found in the `Labs.pdf` file in the Author directory
of the CD-ROM.

Sharing Printer Resources

You share printers in much the same way that you share folders on your
system. After you install the printer and configure the settings so that the
printer functions properly, it is time to share it.

Sharing a printer in Windows

To share a printer in Windows 2000, XP, or Server 2003, follow these steps:

1. **Choose Start⇨Printers and Faxes.**

2. **Right-click the printer you want to share and choose Sharing.**

3. **Select Share This Printer and type the name of the share.**

4. **Click OK.**

To share a printer in Windows Vista, the steps are similar but you need to
navigate to the printer's folder a different way:

1. **Choose Start⇨Control Panel.**

2. **In the Control Panel, click the Printer link from the Hardware and
Sound category.**

3. **Right-click the printer you want to share and choose Sharing.**

4. **Click the Change Sharing Options button and then click Continue to
give Windows permissions to perform the task.**

5. **Enable the share by selecting Share This Printer and then give a share name, such as "Canon" or "HP."**

6. **Click OK.**

When sharing printers, all the same rules for sharing folders apply as far as the share name goes and how to create hidden shares.

Installing a network printer in Windows

To print, or connect, to a shared printer out on the network, you have to install a network printer on your Windows client that points to the UNC path of the shared printer. A *network printer* in Windows is a printer installed that refers to a shared printer on the network. When you print to a network printer, the print job is sent to the computer that has the printer installed and prints from the print device connected to that system.

You can install a network printer in a number of ways. The two most popular methods are through the Add Printer Wizard and through the Run command, depending on the network setup. To install a network printer using the wizard, run the wizard from the Printers folder. The wizard starts up and walks you through connecting to a shared printer. The following section shows you how to install a printer that points to a network location.

Installing a network printer is very similar in all Microsoft OSes today. To install a network printer in Windows 2000/XP, follow these steps:

1. **Choose Start⇨Printer and Faxes.**

2. **Click the Add a Printer link.**

3. **Read the welcome message and click Next.**

4. **Select the network printer option and click Next.**

5. **Choose Connect to This Printer and type the UNC path to the printer.**

6. **Click Next.**

7. **Click Finish.**

In Windows Vista, you install a network printer in pretty much the same fashion, but navigating to the Add Printer option is a little different:

1. **Choose Start⇨Control Panel.**

2. **Click the Printers link in the Hardware and Sound category.**

3. **Click the Add a Printer button on the toolbar.**

4. **Select the Add a Network, Wireless, or Bluetooth Printer option.**

5. If the printer appears in the list, choose it. If it does not appear in the list, choose the The Printer That I Want Isn't Listed option.

6. Type the UNC path to the printer and click Next.

7. Click Finish.

Installing a network printer by using Point and Print

One of my favorite ways to install a network printer on a client is by taking advantage of Point and Print within Windows. Point and Print is a feature that copies the printer driver from one system to another as soon as you connect to the printer — no matter how you connect to the printer! What method is quickest to connect to the printer? Using the UNC path in the Run command!

After you type the UNC path of the shared printer you wish to connect to, Windows asks whether you want to install the printer on your system. When you choose Yes, a new printer is created in the Printers folder without you having to run through the wizard. The printer driver is automatically copied from the system sharing the printer to your local system.

To install a printer by using Point and Print, follow these steps:

1. Choose Start⇨Run.

2. Type `\\computername\PrinterShareName`, where *computername* is the name of the system that is sharing the printer, and *PrinterShareName* is the name of the shared printer.

3. When asked if you wish to install the printer, click Yes.

The printer is now installed and ready to print to.

Understanding Windows Services

In this section, I introduce you to the concept of a service within the OS and then give an overview of some of the most popular services found in Windows.

A *service* is a software component within the OS that provides a specific feature. For example, the spooler service provides printing functionality. For you to print, you must have the spooler service running. When you are troubleshooting a system that isn't working properly, make sure that you check that the service that manages that aspect of the OS is running. You might also want to restart the service if it is running, which is essentially rebooting that service.

Restarting a Windows service

To stop, start, or restart a service in Windows XP, follow these steps:

1. **Choose Start⇨Control Panel.**

2. **Choose Performance and Maintenance⇨Administrative Tools.**

3. **In the Administrative Tools window, double-click the Services icon.**

4. **After the Services console opens, you can stop, start, or restart a service by right-clicking the service and then choosing the appropriate command from the contextual menu, as shown in Figure 3-22.**

Figure 3-22: Stopping a service in Windows XP.

After you know how to stop and start a service, the next step is to understand some of the key services that exist within the Windows OS and what the service offers to the system.

To stop, start, or restart a service in Windows Vista follow these steps:

1. **Choose Start⇨Control Panel.**

2. **Click the System and Maintenance link.**

3. **Click the Administrative Tools link to open the Administrative Tools window.**

4. **Double-click the Services icon to launch the Services console.**

5. **From the Services console, stop, start, or restart a service by right-clicking the service and then choosing the appropriate command from the contextual menu.**

Server service

One of the critical services responsible for the networking of the Windows OS is the Server service, which provides file and printer sharing capabilities. So, if you want to print to a printer that is shared on computer A from your system, computer A needs to have the Server service running to allow your system to connect to it.

Workstation service

The Workstation service — the exact opposite of the Server service — is responsible for making the connection to the system running the Server service. Compare this with the example in the preceding section: If you want to print to a printer on computer A, the Workstation service on your computer sends the request to the Server service on computer A.

DHCP Server service

The *DHCP Server service* handles DHCP server functionality: that is, a server that hands out IP addresses to clients on the network. This service must be running if you want the DHCP server to hand out the IP addresses to network clients. *Note:* This service exists only on Windows Servers and not on Windows client OS.

Print Spooler service

As I mention earlier, the *Print Spooler* service is responsible for the printing environment in Windows. If this service is not running, you cannot print.

Messenger service

The *Messenger service* is responsible for sending and receiving messages within the OS. For example, some features of the OS allow an alert to be sent to the network administrator — and the Messenger service is responsible for the message (alert) being sent. You can send a message to another user on the network at any time via the following command at a command prompt:

```
Net send BOB "Hi there"
```

The above command sends a message to a user or computer called BOB, and the message that appears on Bob's screen reads Hi there. For Bob to receive the message, your computer and Bob's computer need to have the Messenger service running.

Browser service

When connecting to network resources, clients need to know what system is out there providing the resources. They can find this out by contacting the computer browser for their workgroup. The *computer browser,* or *browse master,* is a computer that maintains a list of servers with File and Printer Sharing services enabled.

The first computer in the workgroup to start up with File and Printer Sharing enabled becomes the computer browser for that workgroup. All other computers that start up and have File and Printer Sharing enabled advertise themselves to the browse master so that the browse master can update the lists of computers sharing network resources.

When Windows clients browse the network, they contact the browse master and ask for a list of servers on the network. The browse master returns the lists to the client, and then the client connects to the appropriate system to see a list of shares provided by that system.

You can control which system acts as the browse master. The browse master is determined by an election process in which each system submits criteria used to determine which computer should be the browse master. Generally, the system with the newest OS wins. Also note that server OSes will win an election over desktop OSes.

To control which system can be a browse master, change a setting in the Registry in Windows. You need to truly understand how to designate a browse master because certain machines on the network cannot be adequate browse masters. Being the browse master takes up resources on the system, so if you have a low-end computer, you might not want it to ever be a browse master.

To configure whether a computer will be a browse master, go to the Registry Editor (enter **regedit** from the Run command) and then set the following Registry setting:

```
HKEY_LOCAL_MACHINE\SYSTEM\CurrentControlSet\Services\Browser\Parameters
```

Modify the `MaintainServerList` setting to one of the following by double-clicking on the entry:

✦ **Auto:** The computer has the potential to become a browse master, and the decision is made through election. Any computer set to Yes (see the next bullet) takes precedence over this system's Auto setting and becomes the browse master.

✦ **Yes:** This computer should be the browse master for the workgroup. This option takes precedence over any system with an Auto setting.

✦ **No:** This computer will never become the browse master for the workgroup.

 Be very careful any time you venture in to modify the Registry. Making the wrong change can cause the system to become unstable or even prevent it from starting.

Getting an A+

This chapter discusses the different networking components that allow a Windows OS to function in a networking environment.

✦ Four major networking components are required in Windows networks:

- A network client

- A network adapter

- A common protocol

- A service

✦ TCP/IP is the most popular networking protocol used today. When installing TCP/IP, you need to configure the following:

- An IP address

- A subnet mask

- A default gateway

✦ The NetBEUI protocol is a nonroutable protocol used on small networks.

✦ The IPX/SPX protocol is primarily used on older Novell networks.

✦ In Microsoft networking environments, to allow users to connect to your hard drive or printer, you must install the File and Printer Sharing service.

✦ You may use the `ipconfig` command on Windows 2000, XP, and Server 2003 to view your TCP/IP configuration.

✦ The `ping` command is used to send test messages to a remote system to verify that communication can take place on that system.

Prep Test

1 What networking component allows you to connect to a Windows Server?

A ○ File and Printer Sharing service

B ○ Client Service for Netware

C ○ TCP/IP

D ○ Client for Microsoft Networks

2 There is a shared folder named `public` on a computer named `Server1`. What is the syntax to connect to the shared resource via the UNC path?

A ○ `\\server1\public`

B ○ `\\server1\data`

C ○ `\\data\server1`

D ○ `\server1\\data`

3 Which of the following IP addresses has a default subnet mask of `255.255.255.0`?

A ○ `10.45.65.78`

B ○ `132.107.2.34`

C ○ `48.123.45.67`

D ○ `216.83.24.56`

4 You have installed a new Windows XP computer in a Novell environment, and you are having trouble connecting to the Novell server. You have verified that you have the Client Service for Netware installed. What other networking component should you make sure is installed?

A ○ Client for Microsoft Networks

B ○ File and Printer Sharing

C ○ The TCP/IP protocol

D ○ The IPX/SPX protocol

5 You would like other people in the office to be able to access the printer that is attached to your Windows XP computer on your small network. Which networking component must you install?

A ○ Client for Microsoft Networks

B ○ Client Service for Netware

C ○ File and Printer Sharing for Microsoft Networks

D ○ NetBEUI

6 Which of the following is an example of a Class B IP address?

 A ○ 164.34.56.8
 B ○ 12.45.76.2
 C ○ 202.34.65.32
 D ○ 125.67.6.7

7 What two properties of TCP/IP must be configured to communicate with other hosts on a small, local network?

 A ❑ IP address
 B ❑ DNS server
 C ❑ Default gateway
 D ❑ Subnet mask

8 A user tries to connect to a shared resource called `data` on `server1` by using the UNC path `\\server1\data` but is unsuccessful. The user knows the IP address of `server1` and can successfully ping it. What is the problem?

 A ○ The user should use `\\data\server1`.
 B ○ The client computer is not configured to query the WINS server.
 C ○ The client computer is not configured to query the DNS server.
 D ○ The user needs to install TCP/IP.

9 Which utility allows you to see the path that information may take when communicating with a remote system?

 A ○ `ipconfig.exe`
 B ○ `tracert.exe`
 C ○ `winipcfg.exe`
 D ○ `arp.exe`

10 Which of the following TCP/IP settings are required to connect to the Internet? (Choose all that apply.)

 A ❑ IP address
 B ❑ WINS
 C ❑ Subnet mask
 D ❑ Default gateway

11 Which resolution technique is used to resolve the IP address to a MAC address?

 A ○ DNS
 B ○ WINS
 C ○ ARP
 D ○ `ipconfig.exe`

12 Which utility allows you to see the IP address information on a Windows NT computer?

A ○ `winipcfg.exe`

B ○ `ipconfig.exe`

C ○ `tracert.exe`

D ○ `arp.exe`

13 Which service is responsible for automatically assigning IP address information to each computer on the network?

A ○ DNS

B ○ WINS

C ○ `winipcfg.exe`

D ○ DHCP

14 You verified that you have a network adapter installed and an appropriate client, but you cannot connect to computer B across NetBEUI. What could be the problem?

A ○ You have the wrong IP address assigned to the computer.

B ○ Computer B is not running NetBEUI.

C ○ You should check the frame type on your computer.

D ○ You need to install File and Printer Sharing to connect to another computer.

15 When you use `ipconfig.exe`, you do not see the IP address of the DHCP that has given you the IP address. What should you do?

A ○ Use `ipconfig /renew` at the command prompt.

B ○ Use `ipconfig /all` at the command prompt.

C ○ Ping the IP address of the DHCP server.

D ○ Use `ipconfig /release` at the command prompt.

16 You installed a printer and want to share it out to the network. How can you do this?

A ○ Use `net print` at the command prompt.

B ○ Install the Client for Microsoft Networks.

C ○ Install the IPX/SPX protocol.

D ○ Right-click the printer in the Printers folder and choose the Sharing command.

17 Which service is responsible for converting `www.wiley.com` to an IP address?

A ○ DHCP

B ○ DNS

C ○ WINS

D ○ ARP

18 You want to share the data folder as a resource to be used only by network administrators. How should you do this?

A ○ Hide the share by naming it data$ and then set up the permissions so that only administrators have access. Tell the administrators the UNC path.

B ○ Don't share the folder; tell the administrators to go to the local computer to access the resource.

C ○ Set up the share permissions so that only administrators have access to the share.

D ○ Share the resource and don't set any permissions.

19 You need to install software on all five computers on your small network. What should you do?

A ○ Place the software in a CD-ROM on one computer and share the CD-ROM drive to the network.

B ○ You must go to each computer to install the software because CD-ROMs cannot be accessed from across the network.

C ○ Use DHCP to automatically install the software.

D ○ Use net install at a command prompt.

20 Which of the following services is responsible for keeping track of the computers on the network that are sharing resources?

A ○ DNS

B ○ WINS

C ○ Computer Browser

D ○ DHCP

Answers

1 **D.** To connect to a resource, you must have the appropriate client running. In this example, you are logging into a Windows server, so you must load the Client for Microsoft Networks. *See "Network client."*

2 **A.** To connect to a shared resource on the network use the UNC path. The proper syntax for a UNC path is \\servername\sharename. *Review "Using a UNC path."*

3 **D.** 216.83.24.56 is an example of a Class C address, whose default subnet mask is 255.255.255.0. The other addresses are Class A and Class B, which have different default subnet masks. *Check out "Subnet mask."*

4 **D.** After you have Client Service for Netware installed, you have to ensure that IPX/SPX is installed and configured for the same frame type as the server you are trying to communicate with. *Peruse "IPX/SPX."*

5 **C.** File and Printer Sharing must be installed to allow someone to connect to your resources. *Take a look at "Enabling file and printer sharing in Windows."*

6 **A.** The number in Class B addresses' first octet ranges from 128 to 191. The number in Class A addresses' first octet ranges from 1 to 126, and the number in Class C IP addresses' first octet ranges from 192 to 223. *Peek at "IP address."*

7 **A, D.** Because the computer is functioning on a small LAN with no router, all you need to configure the functionality of TCP/IP is the IP address and subnet mask. Because no information leaves the network, you do not have to configure a default gateway. *Look over "The TCP/IP Protocol."*

8 **B.** The computer name, server1, must be converted to an IP address. WINS is the service that maintains a database that holds computer names and matching IP addresses. *Study "WINS."*

9 **B.** tracert.exe is the utility used to see the number of networks between you and the remote host. ipconfig.exe and winipcfg.exe display the TCP/IP configuration. *Refer to "TRACERT."*

10 **A, C, D.** To participate on the Internet, you need an IP address, a subnet mask, and a default gateway. The default gateway is the IP address of the router that sends information off the network. *Examine "Configuring TCP/IP in Windows."*

11 **C.** Address Resolution Protocol (ARP) converts the IP address to the network card address (MAC address). DNS and WINS convert different types of names to an IP address. *See "ARP."*

12 **B.** ipconfig.exe is the utility run on Windows NT products to view TCP/IP configuration. winipcfg.exe is the utility on Windows 95 and Windows 98. *Review "IPCONFIG."*

13 **D.** Dynamic Host Configuration Protocol (DHCP) is a service on a server that automatically assigns IP address information to each computer on the network, saving the network administrator from having to manually configure each computer. *Check out "DHCP Server service."*

14 **B.** If you have a client and a network adapter installed, and they are working correctly, the reason why you cannot connect across NetBEUI is because the person on the other end is using a different protocol. *Peruse "NetBEUI."*

15 **B.** Without switches, `ipconfig.exe` displays only the IP address, subnet mask, and default gateway. Use the `ipconfig /all` switch to view all TCP/IP configurations, including the DHCP server that assigned your computer an IP address. *Take a look at "IPCONFIG."*

16 **D.** After you install File and Printer Sharing, you need to right-click the printer and choose the Sharing command. *Peek at "Sharing Printer Resources."*

17 **B.** DNS is responsible for converting fully qualified domain names to IP addresses. WINS converts the computer name to an IP address, DHCP is responsible for automatic configuration of TCP/IP, and ARP is responsible for converting IP addresses to MAC addresses. *Look over "DNS."*

18 **A.** The best way to be sure that no one except network administrators can access a shared resource is to share the resource and set the proper permissions. When you share the resource, though, it may be best to hide it from the network by making it a hidden share so that no one tries to sneak into it. *Study "Sharing File System Resources."*

19 **A.** One of the most efficient ways of installing software is to share the CD-ROM on one computer and have the other computers connect to the CD-ROM to install. This is one of the purposes of having a networked environment. *Refer to "Sharing a folder in Windows XP."*

20 **C.** The Computer Browser service maintains a browse list, which is a list of computers with File and Printer Sharing enabled. *Examine "Browser service."*

Networking the Operating System

Chapter 4: Configuring Internet Access

Exam Objectives

- Getting connected to the Internet
- Working with TCP/IP technologies on the Internet
- Configuring Internet settings with Internet Explorer
- Working with firewall devices to protect your computer

*I*n this chapter, you examine how to connect to the Internet and discover some of the basics of how it works. This chapter is chock-full of terminology that you need to be familiar with as well as different methods available to access the Internet. Because the Internet now plays such an integral part in many people's lives, as a CompTIA A+ Certified Professional, you should be familiar with where it came from — and how to connect to it.

Understanding the Internet

The Internet was originally created and implemented by DARPA (Defense Advanced Research Projects Agency; often referred to as just *ARPA*) in response to a U.S. Department of Defense (DoD) request. At the time, the DoD was concerned about its centralized communications network. Most communications were relayed through a central computing system or hub, and damage to that system could stop computer communication. To avoid this problem, the DoD gave ARPA the responsibility of devising a new system.

The first thing that ARPA had to do was to create communication protocols that would allow computers to talk to each other in a new and nonstandard, decentralized manner, and ARPA needed a small network on which it could test and develop the new protocols. It eventually interconnected four hosts, which formed the start of the ARPANET.

ARPANET (and the now the Internet) was defined by a series of standards that are currently being put forth by the Internet Architecture Board (IAB), which represents the governing body of the Internet. These Internet standards are defined by IAB but are discussed in RFC (Request for Comments) documents. The first RFC defined how the initial hosts on the ARPANET would send to and receive data from each other.

TIP

All RFCs — currently, more than 5,500 — are available from `www.ietf.org`. Technologies in RFCs sometimes make it into STD (Standards) documents, of which there are currently fewer than 70. An index of the standards can be found at

`http://www.rfc-editor.org/std-index.html`

During the 1970s, protocols were created and evolved, allowing for support of more and more services over ARPANET, and the number of members continued to increase. Most ARPANET members were locations that did research for ARPA — mainly universities and research centers. Terminal connections via Telnet were created, as was the fashion of using the @ character (meaning *at*) as a separator between username and mail server for e-mail addresses. Emoticons were soon to follow, starting with joke markers, such as -) (tongue in cheek) in the late 1970s, and the first Smileys :-) in the early 1980s.

During the 1980s, several major events occurred:

✦ TCP/IP became the standard communication protocol.

✦ The term *Internetwork,* truncated to just *Internet,* became the name of the network.

✦ Many operating systems standardized on TCP/IP.

✦ The National Science Foundation took over management of the Internet.

✦ The IAB was established to manage accepted standards on the Internet.

Also during 1980s, other countries started to join their national networks to the U.S. Internet, making it a true world-wide network. Several new application protocols were created to allow communication, such as NNTP (Network News Transfer Protocol) and IRC (Internet Relay Chat). This was also the decade that saw the first Internet worm released — namely, the Morris Worm, which was named for its creator.

TCP/IP — Transmission Control Protocol/Internet Protocol — is the protocol suite that is used by the Internet, but it comprises many different protocols that function at different levels of the network model. There are network protocols, transport protocols, and application protocols. In fact, the number of protocols is limitless. Many key protocols are discussed in earlier chapters (see Book VIII, Chapter 1, and Book VII, Chapter 3), but this chapter covers some of the others, such as

✦ **SMTP:** Simple Mail Transport Protocol

✦ **POP3:** Post Office Protocol version 3

✦ **HTTP:** HyperText Transfer Protocol

+ **FTP:** File Transfer Protocol

+ **IMAP:** Internet Message Access Protocol

TCP/IP — the communication protocol used on the Internet — is actually a suite of protocols that covers all aspects of the communication process.

In the 1990s, the biggest single change to the Internet was caused by CERN (Conseil Européen pour la Recherche Nucléaire, or the European Council for Nuclear Research) developing a new method of linking documents stored on different servers. CERN modified SGML (Standard Generalized Markup Language), created a new language called HTML (HyperText Markup Language), and named the technology the World Wide Web. This single technology changed the face of the Internet, which went from a method of linking documents for information to a conduit for shopping, personal expression, media production and delivery, and untold other things.

Since 2000, technologies created for and used over the Internet have steadily risen to allow for remote access, collaboration, file sharing, streaming media, and VoIP (Voice over Internet Protocol). Government services and major corporations have all embraced the Internet as a major method of communicating with clients, and people in general have changed how they communicate, using instant messaging and social networking sites. Internet gaming has become popular, with software companies generating steady revenue streams from monthly gaming fees. Today, if the Internet disappeared, many people would be at a loss to figure out how to communicate with one another.

Many countries now offer public access terminals for the Internet in convenient locations, such as libraries. Users can connect to the Internet through these public access terminals, Wi-Fi hot spots, and any number of other methods. Some cities have gone so far as to set up city-wide public wireless access.

The Internet has evolved from something small to become what we now know as the Internet. Even today, the Internet is constantly evolving, with new protocols created daily and new uses for the technology limited only by imagination. I wonder what the Internet will look like by the end of the next decade.

Using an ISP

Essentially, the Internet is a large, routed network, with technology similar to the networks found in a large corporation. The main difference between the Internet and a corporate network, though, is that all the small networks that make up the Internet are conjoined, but corporate networks are kept private. To access the Internet, you must access one of the networks that

are connected to the Internet. These networks are run by Internet service providers (ISPs), which are in place simply to allow you to access the Internet. Figure 4-1 illustrates how a connection to the Internet works. In order to get connected to the Internet, the following would occur:

1. Connect your computer to your ISP's network by using a communication device, such as a modem or router.

2. The ISP connects its network to its provider's network by using a router and a communication link, such as a leased Telco line.

3. Eventually, a connection is made to part of the Internet backbone, which allows connections to every network that is connected to the Internet.

How you get your connection to the Internet

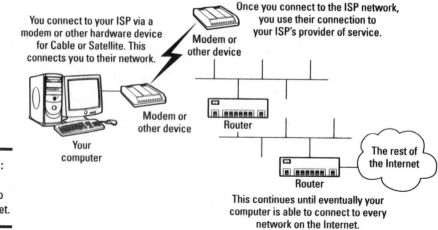

You connect to your ISP via a modem or other hardware device for Cable or Satellite. This connects you to their network.

Modem or other device

Once you connect to the ISP network, you use their connection to your ISP's provider of service.

Your computer

Modem or other device

Router

The rest of the Internet

Router

This continues until eventually your computer is able to connect to every network on the Internet.

Figure 4-1:
How you connect to the Internet.

In addition to connection services, most ISPs provide other services, such as

✦ **E-mail addresses and message space on servers**

✦ **Local news servers that replicate Usenet news groups**

These are discussion groups for various topics in a bulletin board format.

✦ **Web page storage space**

Most Internet access service used to be provided over standard modems or through a dedicated link, such as 56K frame relay. Dialup access to the Internet is giving way to permanent connections, such as cable and ADSL (Asynchronous Digital Subscriber Line), which offer great improvements in access speed.

Active Server Pages

Active Server Pages (ASP) are a form of HTML document that contains Visual Basic script or JavaScript rendered into straight HTML by the server before passing data to the Web client. Active Server Pages are used to limit the amount of work that has to be done by the client and to protect your code by sending only the results to the client.

Working with an ASP

The acronym ASP is used for two different technologies: Active Server Pages and application service providers.

Application service providers host servers for their clients. These servers may be database or mail servers, and may be shared or dedicated to a single customer. In either case, the server's hardware and software are maintained by someone other than the customer. This is a useful setup for smaller organizations because they do not have to invest in large servers or personnel to manage them. Rather, they basically rent space on them.

You will not be tested on ASP for the exam. I include this information, though, because application service providers are sometimes considered to be a type of ISP, although they usually offer only data and content services and not connection services.

Understanding Internet Protocols

When many people think of protocols and computers, network and transport protocols come to mind. These two types of protocols seem to get all the credit. Network and transport protocols are the network communications components that connect your computer to a network, sending and receiving bundles of data between hosts. They include such protocols as TCP/IP, IPX/SPX, and NetBEUI.

Generically, a *protocol* is a set of standards or conventions that are followed when formatting data to be used for electronic communications, and data transfer is just one level in the electronic communications model. This definition of protocol is not limited to data transfer, and a number of protocols work at other layers: most notably, the application layer. *Application layer*

protocols establish a standard or format for data that is to be communicated. These protocols are so-named because they are the first layer to which programs or applications on a computer (as well as the server components) communicate.

TCP/IP

TCP/IP is not a protocol in and of itself; rather, it is a suite of industry-standard protocols. It is a routable wide area network (WAN) protocol that shares many similarities with Novell's IPX/SPX, both of which are covered in Book VIII, Chapter 3. One main difference, however, between IPX/SPX and TCP/IP is that TCP/IP is an open (free) protocol, and IPX/SPX is proprietary. TCP/IP standards are developed, established, and used by the computing community itself. Novell is responsible for the development and standards for the IPX/SPX protocol.

Figure 4-2 shows some protocols used as part of the TCP/IP protocol suite and what each protocol is responsible for. At the lowest level, IP offers best-effort delivery services. That is, IP attempts to deliver all network packets to the best of its ability. It also processes any errors reported back from routers. At the next level, TCP offers guaranteed delivery services, and UDP (User Datagram Protocol) offers best-effort delivery services.

A Breakdown of the TCP/IP Protocol Suite

Figure 4-2:
TCP/IP
uses many
protocols
at different
layers to
accomplish
its task.

Session services for TCP/IP are offered by either NetBIOS over TCP/IP (NetBT) or Windows Sockets (Winsock). The NetBIOS session interface is used by all Microsoft network clients, including Windows 9*x* and Windows NT 4.0, as their method of communicating with Microsoft servers on the network. Windows 2000 and later Microsoft OSes use the NetBIOS interface for backward compatibility, preferring to make connections using the Winsock interface. The Winsock interface is Microsoft's implementation of *BSD sockets,* which is the primary session interface that has been used on all Unix and Unix-based systems. Because most Internet servers originally ran Unix, the application layer protocols (such as HTTP, FTP, SMTP, and POP3) are all designed to communicate through the socket-based session interface.

E-mail

E-mail is one of the applications that made the Internet indispensable to most people. E-mail was an early tool for ARPANET that enabled users to communicate ideas and concepts to colleagues many miles away. E-mail allows for individually addressed text messages to be transferred over the Internet and delivered directly to the targeted recipient(s). Compared with conventional land-based mail (snail-mail), these transfers are instantaneous.

Attachments that accompany e-mail messages are converted into a text stream by means of encoding. MIME (Multipurpose Internet Mail Extensions) is currently one of the most popular encoding methods on the Internet. Other popular encoding formats include BinHex and UUencode. *Encoding,* which converts binary data containing 8 bits per byte to ASCII or text data with 7 bits per byte, enables binary attachments to be sent over the text-based e-mail network. When you receive attachments, they must be decoded by your e-mail program. If your e-mail program cannot do this, however, you have to use a third-party application to decode the files.

When it comes to reading your e-mail, you can choose from a wide variety of applications. In fact, the list of clients is extensive, including command line clients, Windows-based clients, and Web-based clients.

The three basic protocols used with e-mail are POP3, SMTP, and IMAP. Some e-mail clients may support more than one access protocol. SMTP and POP3 are the most commonly used protocols although IMAP is increasing in popularity on private networks. Figure 4-3 shows how these three protocols fit together, and the following sections discuss them in more detail.

Know the main e-mail protocols and their role in the e-mail system.

**Book VIII
Chapter 4**

**Configuring Internet
Access**

SMTP is used to transfer your messages between servers on your network or the Internet. At this level, SMTP is used for bi-directional communication.

Mail server one

Mail server two

SMTP client

POP3 client

IMAP client

Figure 4-3:
Where mail protocols are used.

SMTP is used to transfer your messages from your computer up to a mail server. From the client's perspective, this is a one way conversation.

POP3 is used to transfer your messages from your mail server to your client computer. All messages must be downloaded to your computer. From the clients perspective, this is a one way conversation.

IMAP is used to transfer your messages from your mail server to your client computer. Mail is left on the server, and copied locally for reading. From the client's perspective synchronization is a two way conversation.

SMTP

Simple Mail Transport Protocol (SMTP) is a mail delivery protocol, used to transfer mail messages from your mail client to a mail server. After the mail message is in queue on the server, SMTP is also used to transfer the message to the mail server that is responsible for the target domain, such as @ `mailtarget.loc`. The primary goal of SMTP is to get the mail messages to the targeted server.

POP3

Post Office Protocol version 3 (POP3) is a client access protocol, used to access or retrieve mail from a server. POP3 does not *send* e-mail — that is the responsibility of the SMTP. When you configure your e-mail client, you will configure it with the pair of servers: POP3 for downloading or reading, and SMTP for sending (see the preceding section). POP3 clients usually download all mail messages for their servers and delete the mail from the server. This action then leaves the mail only on the client computer.

IMAP

Internet Message Access Protocol (IMAP) is also a client access protocol for mail. As an IMAP client, you retrieve a list of messages that exist on the mail server and download only messages that you want to read. Any downloaded messages are also left on the server. Changes to your mail files locally can also be replicated to the server. Because you can download all messages,

you can work entirely offline. If you delete messages while working offline, those deletions will be replicated to the server the next time you connect, in turn deleting the messages on the server.

HTTP mail accounts, such as Hotmail and Gmail, have become increasingly popular. These accounts leave their mail messages on the server in a manner similar to IMAP.

HyperText Transport Protocol

Much older than the Internet, the concept of hypertext has been around since 1945 when Vannevar Bush wrote an article titled *As We May Think*. The word *hypertext* was coined in 1965 by Ted Nelson. Hypertext was a means of indexing, or cross-referencing, data found in different documents, allowing users to quickly move to linked documents.

In the early days of the Internet, you could transfer data as files between computers. After being uploaded to the server by the data owner, these files were available for download from those servers, which meant you had to know what files you needed and what servers they came from. Your text files, formatted documents, and graphics could be transferred between computers. After you downloaded the files, they could be opened and viewed, but there was no way to view them in an attractively formatted style in the online environment, especially in a format that was universally accessible. Most formatted documents were created and formatted in proprietary programs like Microsoft Word or Adobe PageMaker — and thus readable only by people who have those programs.

To address the problem of knowing which servers you were accessing data from, Paul Lindner and Mark McCahill (University of Minnesota) came up with an idea that became the Gopher protocol in 1991. Gopher used hypertext concepts and allowed you to place a pointer on your server that would connect people to specific directories on other servers elsewhere on the Internet. This made browsing information scattered across servers very easy because switching between servers became completely transparent. Gopher became the most popular tool for downloading files and data from the Internet.

Hypertext in action: HyperCard

One commercial implementation of hypertext was the Apple Macintosh program HyperCard (released in 1987). HyperCard was a kind of stack of virtual index cards, each holding common GUI items, such as text boxes, graphics, or buttons. These cards could be reviewed in order, or links could be made to allow for hypertext navigation through the stack. This feature allowed the HyperCard to be used for presentations, games, and a variety of other functions.

At the same time Gopher was being developed, the researcher Tim Berners-Lee at CERN was working on a hypertext system he called World Wide Web (choosing that name over The Information Mesh). This system implemented a protocol called HTTP, which allowed for transparent linking of documents between servers. This capability was possible thanks to the new HyperText Markup Language (HTML) that was being used for World Wide Web data.

The tool that accesses HTTP servers and HTML files is, of course, the Web browser. A Web browser retrieves the files from the server, displays the formatted document, and links to other servers as required. Early Web browsers displayed text and images as separate but linked documents, so you could view images if you followed an image link. The Web really took off in 1993 when Marc Andreessen of the National Center for Supercomputing Applications (NCSA) released NCSA Mosaic and offered something the Gopher and other Web browsers lacked — the capability to view text and graphics mixed together in a single frame. Internet users flocked to this new technology that gave their data the same appearance as the paper-bound copies. Figure 4-4 shows a formatted document in a Web browser.

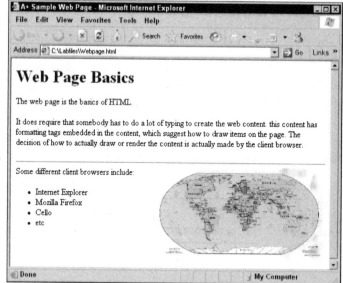

Figure 4-4:
Web browsers let you retrieve data from a server using HTTP.

HyperText Markup Language

HyperText Markup Language (HTML) is a form of SGML that offers a universal way to format documents. Standards for SGML are more complex than for HTML. SGML is actually a method of creating interchangeable, structured documents so that they can be universally accessed from

different types of systems. SGML can take data from a variety of sources (such as word processors and graphics applications) and join them as a single structured document by using Document Type Definitions (DTDs). Different DTDs are identified in a document with the aid of markups or tags, which show or identify the divisions or sections.

HTML is actually just a DTD that is one of the many small parts of SGML. With the simple initial requirements for formatting of documents, Tim Berners-Lee decided that keeping the formatting language simple was the best course of action for the Web, so HTML was adopted in favor of SGML.

HTML files are text or ASCII files, but they contain formatting codes that are embedded in the text. The Web, or HTML, page displayed in Figure 4-4 was generated with the following script (Listing 4-1):

Listing 4-1: Script for Figure 4-4

```
<html>
<head><title>A+ Sample Web Page</title></head>
<body>
<h1>Web Page Basics</h1>
<p>The web page is the basics of HTML.</p>
<p>It does require that somebody has to do a lot of typing
   to create the web content. This content has formatting
   tags embedded in the content, which suggest how to draw
   items on the page. The decision of how to actually draw
   or render the content is actually made by the client
   browser.</p>
<hr>
<img src="photo.jpg" width="320" height="176" align="right">
Some different client browsers include:
<ul>
<li>Internet Explorer
<li>Mozilla Firefox
<li>Cello
<li>etc
</ul>
</body>
</html>
```

Early HTML files were saved with either the .html or .htm extension (for MS-DOS's 8.3 character filename compatibility), but now may have a variety of extensions (such as .php or .asp) because of various scripting languages being used to build dynamic Web pages.

HTML has gone through many revisions; the last revision was version 4. Changes are being made to HTML with the integration of XML (Extensible Markup Language). XML, which adds functionality to support database data

exchange, is designed to transfer not only sections of data from a database but also its structure. XML has become very popular and is a huge Internet buzzword.

As I mention, XML has been rolled into the HTML standard, forming the XHTML (Extensible HyperText Markup Language) standard, so HTML is now XHTML. The current version of XHTML is 1.0, with 2.0 just around the corner with a working draft already in place. For more information about XML, HTML, and XHTML standards, visit the World Wide Web Consortium at www.w3.org.

HTTPS and SSL

HTTPS is a secure version of the HyperText Transport Protocol. When you use HTTP, all communication between you and the server is in cleartext, so anyone can easily read all that communication. HTTPS uses SSL (Secure Sockets Layer) or its successor, TLS (Transport Layer Security), to provide authentication and encryption services.

HTTP communicates with a server on TCP port 80, and HTTPS uses TCP port 443.

To implement SSL, a Web server needs to have a security certificate installed to verify its identity for you. When you are confident that the server is who it says it is, you can then carry out secure and encrypted data transfers with it.

Early SSL used 40-bit encryption keys, which were not secure and were easy to break. Current SSL uses 128-bit or larger keys and is very hard to break, making data protected with SSL very secure.

Do not confuse the flurry of H-based acronyms used for the World Wide Web. HTML is the document formatting; HTTP is the cleartext transfer protocol that uses TCP port 80; and HTTPS is an encrypted transfer protocol — secured by SSL or TLS — which uses TCP port 443.

File Transfer Protocol

The first scientists using the Internet established early during the evolution of the Internet that there would have to be some format to allow for the transfer of data (as opposed to text messages) across the Internet. The solution was File Transfer Protocol (FTP), which allows files to be uploaded and downloaded from servers. FTP requires an accessible directory or folder, a server-side service (or *daemon*), and a client.

TECHNICAL STUFF

Daemons

A *Windows service* is an application that runs without a user interface and without anyone being logged onto the computer. This background application provides functions to the local computer or to remote users. These functions include items such as file- and printer-sharing, messaging, and publishing Web pages. Linux and Unix servers call these background services *daemons*.

There are a large number of FTP clients to choose from, ranging from command line–based to graphical (like Filezilla or WinSCP). Figure 4-5 shows some different FTP clients available on the Windows platform. If you regularly work with FTP, then you will likely want to learn one of these clients, rather than relying on the FTP features that are included with most Web browsers.

Figure 4-5:
Choosing the right client for the job is important.

Because of the method that traditional FTP servers used, they were not Network Address Translation (NAT) friendly when the server was placed behind a NAT gateway or firewall. That led to the creation of passive FTP, which changes the orientation of connections in the FTP process. To make use of a passive FTP server, your FTP client has to support and be configured to use passive FTP.

Because the FTP authentication and data-transfer process is all in cleartext or unencrypted data packets, a new protocol has been created — Secure Copy Protocol (SCP) — which transfers files over ssh (covered later in this chapter) on TCP port 22. SCP has been replaced for most people with Secure File Transfer Protocol (SFTP), which also uses ssh and is a more feature-rich protocol.

Command shells

A *shell* is an interface for users to connect to. When you log onto your Windows computer, your desktop environment is generated by explorer. exe. On Unix and Linux servers, if administrators choose not to load a graphical environment, the shell application would be command line driven, usually with some variant of bash (Bourne-Again Shell). Because most Unix or Linux server administration can be done from the command line, remote shell access to a server is very important, both from the aspect of remote administration and for security. In addition to these servers, many network devices (such as routers, switches, and hardware firewalls) support a remote management command shell. The two most common methods of connecting to these command shells are telnet and ssh.

Windows Server 2008 has an installation method called Server Core Installation that does not install the default GUI (explorer.exe) but rather allows all administration to be performed via a command prompt. This type of installation reduces maintenance, the attack surface, and management; and also uses less disk space.

telnet

telnet, developed in 1969, has been the long-standing standard for remote management, in spite of its long-standing security flaw. The largest single flaw with telnet is that the entire communication process between the client and server takes place in cleartext. For any person in a position to view the raw network traffic, the entire conversation can be viewed, including the logon usernames and passwords. Server administrators moved to newer management technology some time ago, but many hardware manufacturers kept using telnet until fairly recently. Windows includes a default command line telnet application, and you can also get third-party graphical telnet applications that allow you to easily manage multiple sessions or capture log files of sessions.

ssh

ssh, developed in 1995, is short for *secure shell*. Remote access to a shell on a computer is what ssh is designed to secure, just like the name suggests. In addition to allowing remote shell access to servers, ssh allows for opening secure tunnels, allowing secure access to other systems on a remote network through the tunnel. When working with ssh with the lowest security

level, the server uses a certificate to generate initial encryption keys and then encrypt the data stream between the client and server. For stronger security, client certificates can be used for authentication of the client as well as the server using its certificate. Server administrators that dealt with `telnet` cleartext data for years quickly converted to `ssh` when it became available, making it the new standard in remote shell access. Some `telnet` holdouts, like network switch manufacturers, have finally listened to their customers and added support for `ssh`. It is now prevalent on all systems that traditionally supported `telnet`. In order to use `ssh`, you will require a client, such as Putty (`www.chiark.greenend.org.uk/~sgtatham/putty/`).

`ssh` should be considered the minimum connection mechanism for remote devices. `telnet`, with its cleartext data transfers, should no longer be considered.

Installing and Configuring Browsers

Internet Explorer (IE) is the default Web browser for most Windows computers, partly because it comes installed with that OS. With this boost, Microsoft won the browser wars of the 1990s, which saw the main battle between IE and Netscape Navigator (even though both owed their roots to NCSA Mosaic). Although many different browsers were available in the beginning, these two products quickly rose to the top of the pile and battled it out.

Right around the turn of the century, Netscape released the source code for the core Netscape engine — *Mozilla* — to the open source community. This powerful engine quickly formed the core of many open source products, and one product — Mozilla Firefox — gained widespread adoption by the open source market. Firefox offers many features not originally included in Microsoft products, such as pop-up blocking and tabbed browsing, plus the ability to choose from thousands of add-ons (extensions) written by the open source community. This product was released at a time when IE was experiencing several security problems, and many people wanted a product that did not suffer from the same problems.

Like with all browser wars (and all wars), products are continually enhanced, and the next version of IE will include many features that have lured people to Firefox. You can find Firefox at `http://www.mozilla.com/firefox`, and the latest version of IE is at `http://www.microsoft.com/windows/ie`. Both sites have links you can click to download and install the browser, and you have the option each time you start the nondefault browser to set it as your system default browser.

The following sections look at IE version 7.0, although similar settings are available in most Web browsers.

To configure IE settings, open IE and choose Tools➪Internet Options, which opens the Internet Options dialog box shown in Figure 4-6. This dialog box contains seven tabs, and I discuss each in the following sections.

Figure 4-6:
Manage
Web
browser
settings
through
Internet
Options.

Configuring General settings

From the General tab (shown in Figure 4-6), you configure settings for your home page, browsing history (including temporary Internet files), search defaults, and tabbed browsing. The other settings are primarily cosmetic. The settings for temporary Internet files allow you to choose the location of the files, how much space they will take on your hard drive, and your setting for refreshing content from the Web site directly.

Configuring Security settings

From the Security tab, you set security settings for sites in one of four zones. Most sites that you visit will fall into the Internet Zone, and the Local Intranet, Trusted Sites, and Restricted Sites affect only sites that you specifically enter onto those lists. Each zone can have different security settings. And, for each zone, you can choose from one of five security levels or specify your own custom settings. The five built-in levels are High, Medium-High, Medium, Medium-Low, and Low, although for the Internet setting, you can choose from only the three highest settings.

Click the Custom Level button to see exactly what settings are enabled. The settings in the resultant dialog box, also shown in Figure 4-7, allow you to set IE to handle a variety of components that may be embedded in Web pages. For example, you can have IE disable, enable, or prompt you when it encounters certain components on Web sites, such as .NET Framework–reliant components, ActiveX controls and plug-ins, downloads (for files and fonts), scripting (including ActiveX scripting and Java applets), user authentication (often done automatically in the background), and a slew of user interface options.

Figure 4-7:
Security settings in Internet Explorer can make the browser much safer.

Configuring Privacy settings

The IE Privacy tab, which deals with cookies and pop-ups, works in a similar fashion to the Security tab. Here, you can configure settings for cookies on a per-site basis as well as configuring general settings by using either the slider for levels from Allow All Cookies to Block All Cookies (with four levels in between) or by clicking the Advanced button and then customizing your cookie settings.

Cookies — settings that are stored on your computer by your Web browser. When you return to the Web server later, these settings are sent back to a Web server. Web sites use cookies to track users, especially if the site uses a shopping cart–transaction system. Shopping carts allow you to browse a catalog, select items you want, and check out. This mechanism is not only used at shopping sites but also at download sites, where you can select multiple files and download them all in one action at the end of your visit.

In addition to shopping carts, many sites will store a unique ID in a cookie on your computer to track your return to the site. In some cases, the IDs are used to set user preference or to track unique visitors. Cookies are generally safe; no one has yet found a way to implant malware in a cookie, and cookies take up only a small amount of memory. When visiting one Web site, you might see content that comes from another Web server, which is the case with most of the banner ads that appear on Web sites. If this other Web server attempts to have a cookie stored, it is called a third-party cookie. You might want to block third-party cookies or all cookies if you are concerned about having companies track your activity on their Web sites.

If you choose to block pop-ups, click the Settings button to configure settings as well as a list of sites that are allowed to use pop-ups.

Configuring Content settings

From the Content tab, you can enable the Content Advisor, which makes use of voluntary tags that Web content developers can include on Web pages. These tags rate the level of language, nudity, sex, and violence found on the page. With the Content Advisor enabled, you can block content that is above the customized configured level. The Certificates section allows you view and modify SSL certificates that IE uses. The Personal Information section allows you to modify the AutoComplete settings that are used on forms you encounter on Web sites.

Configuring Connections settings

A proxy server acts as a middleman when you request information from the Internet, allowing network administrators to restrict access through the network firewall, as well as audit what Web sites network users are going to. If you need to use a proxy server to browse the Internet, you can use the proxy settings to configure your access to proxy servers.

Proxy settings, found on the Connections tab, can be configured for each of the dialup settings individually or for your LAN connection. Both have similar settings, so I discuss the LAN settings, which you reach by clicking the LAN Settings button. The settings are shown in Figure 4-8 and include automatic proxy detection and configuration, which requires specific configuration settings on your network.

In addition to this setting, you can manually configure a proxy server address and port for your particular network and use that same server for `http`, `https`, `ftp`, `gopher`, and `socks`. The `socks` setting allows you to proxy protocols other than the default ones that are listed. You might use

socks to proxy IRC or POP3. As with most cases, you can also configure a list of servers that are exceptions to using the proxy server, which might be the case when you have servers on your internal network that you don't want to use a proxy server for.

Figure 4-8: If you are using proxy settings, you might need to regularly enable or disable the settings.

Configuring Programs settings

From the Programs tab, you can specify which programs to use for different types of Internet services, such as HTML editing, e-mail, and newsgroups. In addition, you can configure and manage *IE add-ons,* which are third-party components loaded automatically by IE.

Working with Advanced settings

The last tab in Internet Explorer's Internet Options dialog box is the Advanced tab. It has a variety of settings you can modify (by enabling or disabling features and functions) how IE works. These settings are Accessibility, Browsing, HTTP 1.1, Java, Multimedia, Printing, and Security. See Figure 4-9.

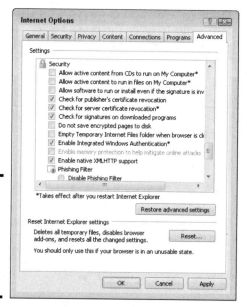

Figure 4-9:
Security
Settings are
just one of
the types of
Advanced
Settings.

Using the Internet

When using the Internet, be aware where you are going when you click links on your Web browser. This section looks at what makes up the parts of a *URL* (Uniform Resource Locator), the string of text that appears on the address line in IE. The standard URL has an access method, a server name, and the path to a file or directory on the server. A typical URL resembles the following:

```
http://www.edtetz.net/sample_files/default.htm
```

In this example, `http:` represents the access method, `//www.edtetz.net` represents the name of the server being contacted, `/sample_files` represents the directory being navigated to, and `/default.htm` represents the file being requested. All URLs follow the same basic structure, but if you leave out one part of it — such as the document name — you will be given the default document for that directory or server.

Access methods

Table 4-1 summarizes some of the access methods for resources on the Internet. These access methods can be specified from the command line or from within a Web browser.

Table 4-1	Access Methods
Access Method	*Description*
`http:`	Used to access Web content on servers
`https:`	Used to secure `http:` access, using SSL to provide authentication and encryption services `https:` requires a certificate to provide verification of the server's identity.
`ftp:`	Used to copy files to and from remote servers
`telnet:`	Used to access remote terminal services with a remote server
`gopher:`	A hyperlink protocol similar to `http:` but with less flexible display options
`mailto:`	Activates the local e-mail client to send a message to the address specified in the server portion of the URL
`news:`	Used to access files on an NNTP server or Usenet newsgroup

Domain names and Web sites

Every computer on the Internet has a unique IP address. This address enables a computer to find and establish communications sessions with any other computer — that is, as long as you know the IP address of the computer you want to connect to.

Every IP address is a 12-digit number. Because every IP address is a 12-digit number — and because most people cannot remember hundreds of 12-digit numbers — the domain name system (DNS) was established in 1984. With DNS, you specify a name, and the DNS resolver or client on your computer will look up the required address for you on a DNS server.

Because each server could never be able to hold the names of all the computers on the Internet, DNS servers split up the job. Each server is responsible for knowing only a small number of computers, but the servers know how to find other servers. Figure 4-10 illustrates how the DNS is structured. At the top of the structure is the root (`.`) domain, which knows about all the servers that manage the top-level domains (TLDs). TLDs include `com` (commercial), `org` (organization), `mil` (military), `edu` (education), `gov` (government), and `net` (network), as well as a two-letter domain for every country in the world, such as `au` (Australia), `us` (United States), `uk` (United Kingdom), and `de` (Germany). The servers at the top level know about the servers that are responsible for the next level down, and so on.

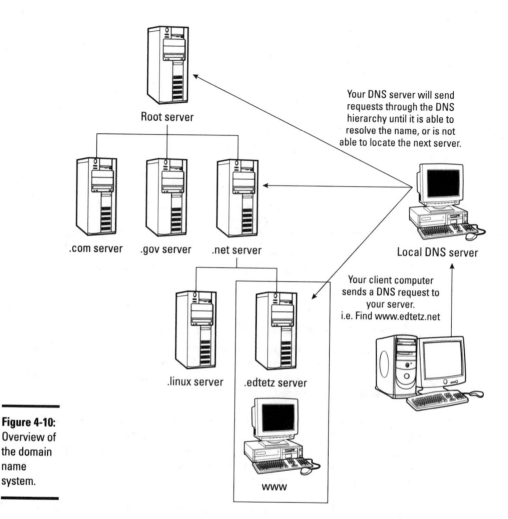

Figure 4-10: Overview of the domain name system.

Restrictions around top-level domains have become more relaxed. As such, the Internet Corporation for Assigned Names and Numbers (ICANN) has registered several new TLDs, such as `travel` (travel industry), `name` (personal names), `museum` (museums), `mobi` (mobile products and services), `jobs` (HR related), `info` (informative Web sites), and `aero` (air transportation and aerospace; maintained by Internet Assigned Numbers Authority [IANA]). There are also misused TLDs, such as `ws` (officially for the country of Western Samoa, but often used for personal Web sites) and `tv` (officially for the country of Tuvalu, but often used for television-related sites).

DNS is a global directory that allows friendly names to be resolved to IP addresses. Without this function being performed, you would have to know every server's IP address.

Here's how it all works in real life. Say you want to connect to a server with a DNS name of www.edtetz.net. Your DNS client checks against your local server to see whether it knows the IP address for that DNS name. Even if your server is not the owner of that DNS name, it may have looked it up before and have the information cached. If the information is not cached on the local server, your server forwards the request to one of the root-level servers, which directs it to the .net server, which directs it to the edtetz server, which then looks up the www record.

This system gives your browser the capability of finding any computer on the Internet with a name registered with DNS. Many people register their servers by the type of service that they offer, such as ftp.edtetz.net, smtp.edtetz.net, pop3.edtetz.net, or mail.edtetz.net. HTTP allows you to place links on any server to any other server on the Internet, which allows you to have a very complex path configured to lead people through the Internet. Because this path is web-like, the interconnection of HTTP servers is referred to as the *World Wide Web* (www). www is the standard name that is given to the HTTP or Web servers on the Internet.

When you connect to a server, the URL might have a path listed beyond the root directory, or it might have the complete path to a file on the server. If no filename is given, the Web server usually displays a default document for that directory, such as default.htm or index.htm. If no default document exists for that directory and the server allows for viewing the directory listing, you will see a list of filenames found in the directory, with each filename being a link to the file. When no other condition is met, the server returns an Object not found or 404 error message.

Ways to Access the Internet

In addition to dialup connections, many other types of connections can connect you to the Internet, and some of these connection types might be available in your area from local Internet service providers (ISPs). Some of these are used for home connections, and others are used primarily for connecting LANs to the Internet:

+ Dialup
+ Cable
+ ADSL
+ ISDN
+ T1/T3
+ Satellite
+ Wireless
+ Cellular

The following sections take a closer look at each of these methods.

Dialup

Good-old reliable dialup has remained a true friend of remote access and access to the Internet for years. For years, dialup was the method available to most users, and dialup access was much better than no access. Dialup is still a standard way to connect to the Internet in many markets in which faster alternatives do not exist. The listed data rate for dialup connections is 56 Kbps.

Cable

Cable connections implement a cable modem in your home or office that takes a digital network signal from your network card and translates (modulates) it into an analog broadband signal. This signal is then passed on to the cable network. Cable companies usually offer transmission speeds between 4 and 10 Mbps to their customers although actual speeds vary. This signal runs over existing cable, using previously unused signal areas of the medium. When using cable, you are on a shared medium with other users until your connection reaches the cable company's office.

ADSL

Asynchronous Digital Subscriber Line (ADSL) implementation works similarly to cable (see the preceding section) except that the device you have in your home or office takes the digital signal from your network card and passes it to a digital phone line. ADSL companies usually offer transmission speeds between 4 and 8 Mbps although actual speeds vary. Cable offers the same transmission speeds going to and from the Internet, but ADSL always has slower upload speeds because the connection is broken into upstream and downstream channels. With ASDL, surfing the Internet and copying large files from Web sites is very fast, but if you want to store a file on a Web site or send e-mails with large attachments, your speeds will be substantially slower. Typical upload speeds for ADSL range between 64 Kbps and 1 Mbps.

The standards for ADSL2 and ADSL2+ have been released, so some vendors may choose to implement these versions of ADSL, allowing for download speeds from 5 to 12 Mbps for ADSL2 and up to 24 Mbps for ADSL2+, although both offer upload speeds only in the 1–3.5 Mbps range. With ADSL, you share the line only until you hit the Telco switching office, which typically must be closer than 3 miles (5 kilometers).

Broadband, high-speed Internet connections through cable, and DSL (of which ADSL is a subtype) have replaced dialup in many regions.

ISDN

Integrated Services Digital Network (ISDN) service comes in two basic forms: basic rate and primary rate.

✦ **Basic-rate ISDN:** Uses three channels: two 64 Kbps lines for data (128 Kbps) and one 16 Kbps line as a control channel which is used for establishing and maintaining connections. The data channels are referred to as B channels, and the control channel is referred to as a D channel.

✦ **Primary-rate ISDN:** Uses twenty-three 64 Kbps B channels (1.44 Mbps) and one 64 Kbps D channel.

T1/T3

T1 connections offer transmission speeds of 1.544 Mbps over 24 pairs of wires. Each pair of wires can carry a 64 Kbps signal, called a *channel*. T1 connections can be implemented over copper wire.

T3 connections, on the other hand, require a better medium than copper, such as microwave or fiber optic. They are capable of speeds ranging from 6 Mbps to 45 Mbps.

T1 and T3 are North American standards, and E1 and E3 are similar standards for the European community.

Satellite

Satellite Internet services come in two basic flavors: one-way with terrestrial return and two-way. Because satellites providing service in most residential areas were designed to send data, the first Internet access over satellites involved downloading from the satellite, but data had to be uploaded via dialup modem. This transmission tied up phone lines, and upload speeds were rather slow. Two-way systems added technology to return a signal to the satellite. Speeds for uploads ran in the neighborhood of only 1 Mbps, but they did free up phone lines. Download speeds over satellite systems rival those of broadband services (such as ADSL and cable). Just like satellite television, satellite Internet is susceptible to the weather and elements.

Wireless

Wireless access to the Internet is provided through standard 802.11 (Wi-Fi) wireless networks, which are set up to provide coverage in prescribed areas. In some locations, wireless access is provided for free to customers of certain businesses, or by a municipal government like Fredericton, New Brunswick (www.fred-ezone.ca).

Sometimes, a company may set up access points in a wide range of locations, offering access through them as part of a subscription service. These wireless access points allow connectivity but only to the company's Web site to set up an account. After you set up and pay for an account, you can use any of the company's access points to access the Internet.

For more information about 802.11 networks, read Book VIII, Chapter 2.

Cellular

Sometimes called *wireless,* this system makes use of a cellular provider's wireless network (as opposed to 802.11 networking). To connect to a cellular network, you need a cellular modem for your computer or a cellular router for your network. The cellular modem may be built into your computer, or added as a PCMCIA card or a USB adapter; some phones may even be used as a cellular modem. The benefit of this technology is that you can access the Internet from anywhere your wireless provider has coverage. This is the same technology I cover in Book VIII, Chapter 2 when discussing WAN cellular.

Speeds will vary with each wireless carrier, but you will see rated speeds anywhere from 384 Kbps up to 4.9 Mbps. Speeds are dependent upon the provider providing service on EDGE (Enhanced Data for GSM Evolution), High Data Rate (HDR), EV-DO (Evolution-Data Optimized, or Evolution-Data Only) or 3G (Third Generation) networks. 4G networks can be expected to start emerging by 2010, driving data speeds to new levels.

Firewalls and Home Routers

When dealing with the Internet, remember that a lot of bad things are out there, and you need protection from the dangers of the world. All software firewalls have the inherent problem that they are software running on the system that they are trying to protect, which is considered bad because software (including firewalls) is more susceptible than hardware firewalls to breaches caused by Trojans or other viruses.

Home routers are typically NAT (Network Address Translation) gateways, which allow multiple computers to share one public IP address. This gives you a layer of additional security because only remote servers or computers are allowed to communicate with your computer after you initiate a connection to the remote computer. When you open the connection to the external server, a temporary channel opens to that server's IP address, allowing communication.

Some routers have more advanced firewall features to restrict the TCP and UDP ports that are allowed to be used between the two hosts, as well as the ability to filter or restrict access to URLs based on a series of rules. Figure 4-11 shows some of the security settings available on these devices.

Figure 4-11:
Typical
firewall
settings
on a home
router.

In addition to these hardware residential and SOHO (Small Office/Home Office) routers and firewalls, you can choose from various high-end hardware firewalls. Also, Linux firewalls are available that boot directly from CD-ROM, such as Linux Embedded Appliance Firewall (LEAF), IPCop, or SmoothWall. For many Linux firewalls, you need a low-end computer with two network cards and a CD-ROM drive. For a home or small office, even a Pentium or Pentium II processor (or lower if you can find one) will provide enough power for the job.

Getting an A+

This chapter provides a brief history of the Internet and how you connect to it. Other concepts that are covered include

✦ TCP/IP is the suite of protocols used on Internet.

✦ The TCP/IP suite of protocols is made up of other protocols such as FTP, HTTP, `telnet`, `ssh`, TCP, UDP, and IP.

✦ POP3, SMTP, and IMAP are the primary protocols used for e-mail.

✦ HTML is the formatting system used for Internet Web pages.

✦ Dialup, ISDN, T1, ADSL, and cable are the main methods used to connect to the Internet.

Book VIII
Chapter 4

Configuring Internet Access

Prep Test

1 **What is the governing body of the Internet?**

 A ○ W3.org

 B ○ DodNet

 C ○ IAB

 D ○ IABnet

2 **The TCP/IP networking protocol is composed of how many subprotocols?**

 A ○ 2

 B ○ 5

 C ○ 10

 D ○ Many, too numerous to list

3 **What purpose does MIME serve?**

 A ○ It is used as an encryption method for e-mail.

 B ○ It encodes binary data into ASCII data so that it may be sent through e-mail.

 C ○ It is used to convert HTML data into an e-mail format.

 D ○ It is used to trap people inside invisible boxes.

4 **What protocol is used to send e-mail?**

 A ○ POP3

 B ○ IMAP

 C ○ HTTP

 D ○ SMTP

5 **What protocols are used to read e-mail? (Choose two.)**

 A ❏ SMTP

 B ❏ POP3

 C ❏ IMAP

 D ❏ UDP

6 **Which of the following is used to format Web pages?**

 A ○ HTTP

 B ○ WWW

 C ○ SSL

 D ○ HTML

7 What protocol is used to transfer files to and from a remote server?

A ○ HTML

B ○ POP

C ○ FTP

D ○ SMTP

8 What is the first part of an Internet URL (for example, `http://`) called?

A ○ Pointer

B ○ Access method

C ○ Control source

D ○ Activation header

9 What system converts names you type in URLs into IP addresses?

A ○ Dual naming standards

B ○ Name resolution server

C ○ Name recognition system

D ○ Domain name system

10 Which of the following are ways to connect to the Internet? (Choose all that apply.)

A ❏ HSINet

B ❏ Cable

C ❏ Digital phone link

D ❏ ISDN

E ❏ Wire

F ❏ T1

G ❏ IAB

11 HTML files are what type of files?

A ○ Text/ASCII

B ○ Run-length encoded

C ○ Binary

D ○ Hyperlinked

Answers

1 **C.** The Internet Architecture Board (IAB) is the managing body of the Internet. *See "Understanding the Internet."*

2 **D.** Some subprotocols that make up TCP/IP include SMTP, POP3, SNMP, FTP, TFTP, and 500 to 1,000 other protocols. *Take a look at "Understanding Internet Protocols."*

3 **B.** MIME (Multipurpose Internet Mail Extensions) is used to convert binary files into something that can traverse the text-only e-mail system. *Peek at "E-mail."*

4 **D.** SMTP is used to send mail messages over the Internet. *Look over "SMTP."*

5 **B, C.** POP3 and IMAP are used to read mail that is on a mail server. *Study "E-mail."*

6 **D.** HTML (HyperText Markup Language) is the formatting language or standard for Web pages. *Refer to "HyperText Markup Language."*

7 **C.** FTP stands for File Transfer Protocol, which is the traditional method to transfer files to or from a server. *Examine "File Transfer Protocol."*

8 **B.** The first part of a URL represents the access method that is being used to connect to the server. *See "Using the Internet."*

9 **D.** The domain name system resolves requested names into IP addresses to allow you to connect to the named computer. *Review "Domain names and Web sites."*

10 **B, D, F.** Cable, ISDN, and T1 are methods of connecting to the Internet. *Check out "Ways to Access the Internet."*

11 **A.** HTML files are text or ASCII files. *Take a look at "HyperText Markup Language."*

Book IX

Securing Systems

The 5th Wave By Rich Tennant

"A centralized security management system sounds fine, but then what would we do with all the dogs?"

Contents at a Glance

Chapter 1: Fundamentals of Security

*O*ne of the most important skills to have if you are going to support networked systems or systems connected to the Internet is the capability of securing systems and networks. And even if you are not working in a networked environment, you can apply these same skills to your customers with home Internet machines. The bottom line is that you need a solid understanding of network security.

I remember when a close friend of mine had his Web site totally replaced by a hacker. My friend's Web site files were replaced with inappropriate content, and he wondered how on Earth someone had hacked his server. It seems amazing now, but back then (circa 1994), a lot of companies did not use firewalls because they were not aware of the risks involved in having a computer connected directly to the Internet. Back then, people thought, "I have a password on the administrator account, so I am secure."

In this chapter, I introduce you to the basic concepts and terminology used to help secure an environment. Be sure to read this chapter carefully and make sure you understand the topics as you will be tested on security topics on the A+ exams. Have fun with this topic area — it is very exciting!

Identifying Types of Attacks

To me, a hacker is someone with the technical expertise to bypass the security of a network or an OS. A hacker knows how to use features of a piece of software or hardware to gain access to restricted areas of a network and then how to use those features against you and your system. For example, most Web sites connect to a database behind the scenes so that you can get a list of products when you visit their site. A hacker knows how to input

data into the site to manipulate your database server into executing the code that the hacker wants to execute — and this happens because the hacker understands the technologies being used.

The two types of hackers are

+ **White-hat hackers,** who try to "hack" or break software or hardware so as to understand how to protect the environment from black-hat hackers. These are the good guys.

+ **Black-hat hackers** break into a system or network for malicious reasons or for personal gain. The reasons could be for financial gain, bragging rights, or revenge.

Hackers use a number of different types of attacks to hack into a network or an OS. Sometimes an attack lays the groundwork for a future or different type of attack: that is, the initial attack does not seem all that dangerous, but it is used in the future to gain unauthorized access.

This section outlines some of the most popular types of attacks that can happen in networking environments today.

Social engineering attacks

A *social engineering attack* occurs when a hacker tries to obtain information or gain access to a system through social contact with a user. Typically, the hacker poses as someone else and tries to trick a user into divulging personal or corporate information that allows the hacker access to a system or network.

For example, a hacker calls your company's phone number, listed in the phone book, and poses as a technical support person for your company. He tells the user who answers the phone that a new application has been deployed on the network, and for the application to work, the user's password must be reset. After the password is reset to what the hacker wants, he might "verify" with the user the credential that the user uses. A user who is not educated on social engineering might divulge important information without thinking.

A social engineering attack is an attack where a hacker tries to trick a user or administrator into divulging sensitive information through social contact. After the sensitive information is obtained, the hacker can then use that information to compromise the system or network.

This example might sound unrealistic, but it happens all the time. If you work for a small company, you might not experience a social engineering attack. In a large corporate environment, though, it is extremely possible

that a social engineering attack would be successful if the company does not educate its users. A large company usually has the IT staff or management located at the head office, but most branch locations have never talked to IT management, so those branch employees would not recognize the voices of the IT folks. A hacker could impersonate someone from the head office, and the user at the branch office would never know the difference.

There are a number of popular social engineering attacks scenarios — and network administrators are just as likely to be social engineering victims as "regular" employees, so they need to be aware. Here are some popular social engineering scenarios:

✦ **Hacker impersonates IT administrator.** The hacker calls or e-mails an employee and pretends to be the network administrator. The hacker tricks the employee into divulging a password or even resetting the password.

✦ **Hacker impersonates user.** The hacker calls or e-mails the network administrator and pretends to be a user who forgot her password, asking the administrator to reset her password for her.

✦ **Hacker e-mails program.** The hacker typically e-mails all the users on a network, telling them about a security bug in the OS and that they need to run the `update.exe` file attached to the e-mail. In this example, the `update.exe` is the attack — it opens the computer up so that the hacker can access the computer.

Educate your users never to run a program that has been e-mailed to them. Most software vendors, such as Microsoft, state that they will never e-mail a program to a person: Instead, they will e-mail the URL to an update, but it is up to the person to go to the URL and download it. A great book to learn more on the process a hacker takes to compromise a system is Kevin Beaver's *Hacking For Dummies,* 2nd Edition (Wiley).

Network-based attacks

A *network-based attack* uses networking technologies or protocols to perform the attack. Here are the most popular types.

Ensure that you are familiar with the different types of network-based attacks for the A+ exams.

Password attacks

There are a number of different types of password attacks. For example, a hacker could perform a *dictionary attack* against the most popular user accounts found on networks. With a dictionary attack, hackers use a program that typically uses two text files:

✦ One text file contains the most popular user accounts found on networks, such as administrator, admin, and root.

✦ The second text file contains a list of all the words in the English dictionary, and then some. You can also get dictionary files for different languages.

The program then tries every user account in the user account file with every word in the dictionary file, attempting to determine the password for the user account.

To protect against a dictionary attack, be sure employees use strong passwords that mix letters and numbers. This way, their passwords are not found in the dictionary. Also, passwords are normally case sensitive, so educate users on the importance of using both lowercase and uppercase characters. That way, a hacker not only has to guess the password but also the combination of uppercase and lowercase characters.

Also remind users that words found in *any* dictionary are unsafe for passwords. This means avoiding not only English words, but also French, German, Hebrew . . . even Klingon!

Hackers can also perform a *brute force attack*. With a brute force attack, instead of trying to use words from a dictionary, the hacker uses a program that tries to figure out your password by trying different combinations of characters. Figure 1-1 shows a popular password-cracking tool known as LC4. Tools like this are great for network administrators to audit how strong their users' passwords are.

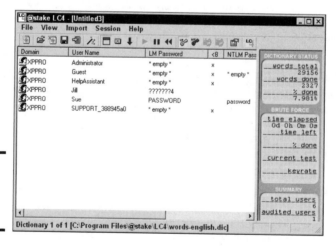

Figure 1-1:
Cracking
passwords
with LC4.

To protect against password attacks, users should use strong passwords, which is a password comprising of letters, numbers, and symbols with a mix of uppercase and lowercase characters and a minimum length of eight characters.

Denial of service

Another popular network attack is a *denial of service (DoS)* attack, which can come in many forms and is designed to cause a system to be so busy that it cannot service a real request from a client, essentially overloading the system and shutting it down.

For example, say you have an e-mail server, and a hacker attacks the e-mail server by flooding the server with e-mail messages, causing it to be so busy that it cannot send anymore e-mails. You have been denied the service that the system was created for.

There are a number of different types of DoS attacks: for example, the ping of death. The hacker continuously pings your system, and your system is so busy sending replies that it cannot do its normal function.

To protect against denial of service attacks you should have a firewall installed and also keep your system patched.

Spoofing

Spoofing is a type of attack in which a hacker modifies the source address of a network *packet,* which is a piece of information that is sent out on the network. This packet includes the data being sent but also has a header section that contains the source address (where the data is coming from) and the destination address (where the data is headed). If the hacker wants to change "who" the packet looks like it is coming from, the hacker modifies the source address of the packet.

There are three major types of spoofing — MAC spoofing, IP spoofing, and e-mail spoofing. MAC spoofing is when the hacker alters the source MAC address of the packet, IP spoofing is when the hacker alters the source IP address in a packet, and e-mail spoofing is when the hacker alters the source e-mail address to make the e-mail look like it came from someone other than the hacker.

An example of a spoof attack is the smurf attack, which is a combination of a denial of service and spoofing. Here is how it works:

1. The hacker pings a large number of systems but modifies the source address of the packet so that the ping request looks like it is coming from a different system.

2. All systems that were pinged reply to the modified source address — an unsuspecting victim.

3. The victim's system (most likely a server) receives so many replies to the ping request that it is overwhelmed with traffic, causing it to be unable to answer any other request from the network.

To protect against spoof attacks you can implement encryption and authentication services on the network.

Eavesdropping attack

An *eavesdropping attack* occurs when a hacker uses some sort of packet sniffer program to see all the traffic on the network. Hackers use *packet sniffers* to find out login passwords or to monitor activities. Figure 1-2 shows Microsoft Network Monitor, a program that monitors network traffic by displaying the contents of the packets.

Figure 1-2:
Using
Network
Monitor to
analyze FTP
logon traffic.

Notice in Figure 1-2 that the highlighted packet (frame 8) shows someone logging on with a username of `administrator`; in frame 11, you can see that this user has typed the password `P@ssw0rd`. In this example, the hacker now has the username and password of a network account by eavesdropping on the conversation!

To protect against eavesdrop attacks you should encrypt network traffic.

Man-in-the-middle

A *man-in-the-middle attack* involves the hacker monitoring network traffic but also intercepting the data, potentially modifying the data, and then sending out the modified result. The person the packet is destined for never knows that the data was intercepted and altered in transit.

To protect against man-in-the-middle attacks you should restrict access to the network and implement encryption and authentication services on the network.

Session hijacking

A *session hijack* is similar to a man-in-the-middle attack, but instead of the hacker intercepting the data, altering it, and sending it to whomever it was destined for, the hacker simply hijacks the conversation — a *session* — and then impersonates one of the parties. The other party has no idea that he is communicating with someone other than the original partner.

To protect against session hijacking attacks you should restrict access to the network and implement encryption and authentication services on the network.

Buffer overflow

A very popular type of attack today is a *buffer overflow attack,* which involves the hacker sending more data to a piece of software than what it is expecting. The information sent to an application is typically stored in an area of memory (a *buffer*). When more data than expected is sent to the application, the information is stored in memory beyond the allocated buffer. If the hacker can go beyond the allocated buffer, he can run their own code. This code executes in the context of the user account associated with the software that was hacked — normally an administrative account!

To protect against buffer overflow attacks you should keep the system patched and its applications.

Wireless attacks

There are a number of different attacks against wireless networks that you should be familiar with. Hackers can crack your wireless encryption if you are using a weak encryption protocol such as WEP. Hackers can also spoof the MAC address of their system and try to bypass your MAC address filters. Also, there are wireless scanners such as Kismet that can be used to discover wireless networks even though SSID broadcasting is disabled.

To protect against wireless attacks you should implement encryption proto-
cols such as WPA2 and use an authentication server such as a RADIUS
server for network access For more information on wireless check out Book
VIII, Chapter 2.

Software-based attacks

Just as there are a number of different types of network attacks, there are
a number of software attacks as well. As you can likely guess, a *software
attack* comes through software that a user runs. The most popular software
attacks are mentioned in the sections that follow, and you should be familiar
with them for the A+ exams.

SQL injection

A *SQL injection attack* occurs when the hacker sends `Transact SQL` state-
ments (statements that manipulate a database) into an application so that
the application will send those statements to the database to be executed.
If the application developer does not validate data inputted in the application,
the hacker can modify the data or even delete it. The hacker can potentially
manipulate the OS through the application that sends the input to the database.

Trojan horse

A *Trojan horse* is software that a user is typically tricked into running on the
system; and when the software runs, it does something totally different than
what the user expected it to do. For example, NetBus (an older attack) is
an example of a Trojan horse program sent as a file called `patch.exe`. The
user receiving the file, typically through an e-mail, believes that the file will
fix a security issue. The problem is that `patch.exe` is a Trojan horse, and
when that horse starts running, it opens the computer up to allow a hacker
to connect to the system.

The hacker then uses a client program, like the one shown in Figure 1-3, to
connect to the system and start messing with the computer. The hacker can
do things like launch other programs, flip your screen upside-down, eject
your CD-ROM tray, watch your activity, and modify or delete files!

Virus

A *virus* is a program that causes harm to your system. Typically, viruses
are spread through e-mails and are included in attachments, such as word
processing documents and spreadsheets. The virus can do any of a number
of things: delete files from your system, modify the system configuration, or
e-mail all your contacts in your e-mail software. To prevent viruses, install
antivirus software and do not open any file attachments that arrive in your
e-mail that you are not expecting.

Figure 1-3:
Using
NetBus
to control
a user's
computer.

Worm

A *worm* is a virus that does not need to be activated by someone open-ing the file. The worm is *self-replicating,* meaning that it spreads itself from system to system, infecting each computer. To protect against a worm, you should install a firewall. A *firewall* is a piece of software or hardware that prevents someone from entering your system.

Logic bomb

A *logic bomb* is malicious software that could run every day, but the soft-ware was designed to wreak havoc on your system on a certain date and time. The scary thing about logic bombs is that they seem like useful soft-ware until the day the programmer decides it will become malicious!

To protect against malicious software such as a virus, Trojan horse, worm, and a logic bomb you should use a firewall and keep your virus definitions up-to-date.

Understanding Physical Security

You should implement security in many places, and one of the most over-looked areas is physical security. *Physical security* has nothing to do with software; rather, it covers how you protect your environment and systems by making sure that a person cannot physically access the system. For example, many companies use a numeric keypad to secure entrance to a facility. To get into the facility, users must enter a valid combination to open the door.

Another example of physical security is the server room. Most server room doors are locked with a numeric padlock or a key. Higher-security server rooms sometimes even require fingerprint or retinal scans from anyone trying to enter the room. The benefit of locking your servers in the server

room is a hacker cannot boot off a bootable CD-ROM, which could bypass the OS entirely. After a hacker bypasses the OS, he typically can bypass a lot of the security by booting to a totally different OS.

You can apply enterprise security best practices to your home systems. For example, to help secure your home system, you might want to prevent booting from a CD-ROM so that an unauthorized person cannot try to bypass your Windows security.

BIOS settings

You can set a number of settings in your system BIOS to help control the security of the system. Be sure to investigate the BIOS settings on your system to see what security settings you can enable on the system. Here are some popular BIOS/CMOS settings to aid in physical security:

✦ **Drive lock:** Drive lock (a popular feature with laptops) is a hard disk specification used to protect access to the drive. To protect access to the drive, there are two drive lock passwords: a user password and a master password. The user password is used by the user wanting to access the system; the master password is used to reset the user password if the user forgets the password. Do not confuse drive lock passwords that prevent booting from the drive with the general CMOS passwords for the system. If the user password and master password are forgotten or lost, the drive is useless.

✦ **Passwords:** You can set a power-on password in CMOS to limit who can use the system. If the power-on password is forgotten, it can typically be erased via a jumper on the motherboard or by taking the battery off the motherboard and putting it back in.

✦ **Intrusion detection:** Most systems have intrusion detection features that can be enabled through the BIOS that will notify you if the cover is taken off the system. This is designed to alert you if someone opens the cover and takes internal components.

✦ **TPM:** The *Trusted Platform Module* (TPM) is a chip on computer hardware used to store cryptography keys that are typically used to encrypt data. A TPM chip can also be used to authenticate a device because it contains a unique key that identifies the chip, or hardware device. Most computers today have a TPM chip, and a number of software solutions (such as Windows Vista Bit Locker) can use the TPM chip to encrypt the contents of the drive.

Best practices

To protect your systems, follow these physical security best practices:

✦ **Secure server placement.** Lock your servers in a room for which only a select few individuals have the key.

✦ **Lock the workstation.** When you leave your system, get in the habit of locking your workstation. A locked workstation can only be unlocked by yourself or the network administrator. This will prevent other users from accessing the system while you are away.

✦ **Disable boot devices.** Dsable the ability to boot from a floppy disk or CD-ROM in the CMOS setup on the systems.

✦ **Set CMOS password.** Because most hackers know how to go to CMOS and enable booting from CD-ROM, make sure that you set a password on CMOS so that a hacker cannot modify your CMOS settings. Figure 1-4 shows a CMOS password being enabled.

Check out Book II, Chapter 4, to get the lowdown on reconfiguring your CMOS settings.

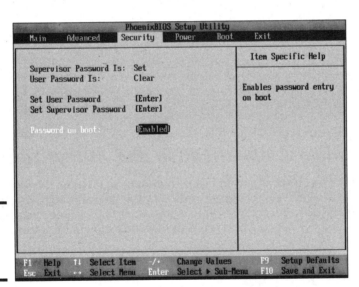

Figure 1-4:
Enabling
the CMOS
password.

✦ **Disable network ports.** To prevent a hacker from entering your office, plugging into the network, and performing a number of network attacks, ensure that network ports in lobbies and front entrances are disabled unless an administrator enables them.

✦ **Use a lockdown cable.** Use a *lockdown cable* to tether laptops, projectors, and other types of office equipment to a table or desk. Figure 1-5 shows a lockdown cable being used to secure a laptop. A lockdown cable usually connects to a special hole in the side of the computer equipment (look for a picture of a lock next to it).

Figure 1-5:
A lockdown
cable is
used to
secure
computer
equipment
to a desk.

Remembering ways to physically secure your systems will help you with the security portion of the A+ exam. Be sure to place critical systems in locked rooms and lock down equipment that is accessible by the public.

Understanding Authentication and Authorization

After you physically secure your environment, focus on the people who access your systems and network. The next step after implementing physical security is to ensure that persons who enter your server room or have a connection to a network port are authorized to log on to the network. Logging onto the network is *authentication*.

Authentication

Authentication is the process of proving one's identity to the network environment. Typically, authentication involves typing a username and password on a system before you are granted access, but you could also use biometrics to be authenticated. *Biometrics* is using one's unique physical characteristics, such as a fingerprint or the blood vessels in one's retina, to prove one's identity. Figure 1-6 shows a fingerprint reader used to scan your fingerprint when logging on.

Here is a quick look at what happens when you log on to your system with a username and password. When you type a username and password to log on to a system, that username and password are verified against a database —

the *user account database* — which has a list of the usernames and passwords allowed to access the system. If the username and password you type are in the user account database, you are allowed to access the system. Otherwise, you get an error message and are not allowed access.

Figure 1-6:
A fingerprint reader is an example of biometrics used for authentication.

The name of the account database that stores the usernames and passwords is different, depending on the environment. In a Microsoft network, the account database is the *Active Directory Database* and resides on a server known as a *domain controller* (shown in Figure 1-7).

Generating the access token

When you log on to a Microsoft network environment, the username and password you type are placed in a logon request message that is sent to the domain controller to be verified against the Active Directory Database. If the username and password that you typed are correct, an access token is generated for you. An *access token* is a piece of information that identifies you and is associated with everything you do on the computer and network. The access token contains your user account information and any groups of which you are a member. When you try to access a resource on the network, the user account and group membership in the access token are compared against the permission list of a resource. If the user account in

the access token or one of the groups contained in the access token are also contained in the permission list, you are granted access to the resource. If not, you get an access-denied message.

Figure 1-7:
Logging on to Active Directory in a Microsoft network environment.

If you do not have a server-based network environment and you are simply running Windows 2000 Professional or Windows XP, when you log on, the logon request is sent to the local computer — to an account database known as the Security Accounts Manager (SAM) database. When you log on to the SAM database, an access token is generated as well, and that helps the system determine what files you can access.

Smart card

Another type of logon supported by network environments today is the use of a smart card. A *smart card* is a small, ATM card–like device that contains your account information. You insert the smart card into a smart

card reader that is connected to a computer, and then you enter the PIN (personal identification number) associated with the smart card. This is an example of securing an environment by forcing someone to not only have the card but also know the PIN.

Strong passwords

It is really hard to talk about authentication without talking about ensuring that users create strong passwords. A *strong password* is a password that is very difficult for hackers to guess or crack because it contains a mix of uppercase and lowercase characters, contains a mix of numbers and letters, and is a minimum of eight characters long.

Authorization

After a user logs on and an access token is created, the user may start trying to access resources such as files and printers. To access a file, folder, or printer on the network, the user must be authorized to access the resource. *Authorization* is the process of giving a user permission to access a resource or the right to perform an OS task. Do not confuse authentication and authorization: You must be first authenticated to the network; then, after authentication, you can access the resources you have been authorized for.

Permissions

To authorize access to a resource, you set permissions on the resource. For example, if you want to allow Jill to access the accounting folder, you need to give Jill permission to the accounting folder, as shown in Figure 1-8.

Using strong passwords

A number of years ago, I had a co-worker who was always trying to get me to guess his passwords. He thought I had some magical trick or program that was cracking them, but all I was doing was guessing his passwords. I remember one time he changed it, and I could not guess it until one night when we were at a social function for work and all he talked about were the Flyers hockey team. I remember sitting there thinking, "I bet that is his password." Sure

enough, the next day at work, I tried `flyers` as his password, and it worked. Now the lesson here is that he should have at least mixed the case of the word *flyers* to make something like `flYeRs`, or even better, thrown a symbol in there by replacing the "s" with a "$." I would have had a much harder time trying to guess his password if he had used `flYeR$` instead. This is an example of a strong password.

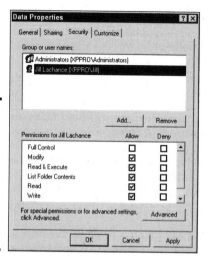

Figure 1-8:
Using
permissions
to authorize
which
users are
allowed to
access the
resource.

In Figure 1-8, you can see that the Administrators and Jill have access to the resource. No one else is authorized to access the resource. You find out how to set permissions in the next chapter, but for now, make sure you understand the difference between authentication and authorization.

Rights

In the Windows world, there is a difference between permissions and rights. As you can read in earlier sections, permission is your level of access to a resource. Comparatively, a right is your privilege to perform an OS task. For example, you can be assigned the right to change the time on the computer. Other examples of rights are the right to do backups or the right to log on to the system.

To learn more about how to set permissions and rights, check out Book IX, Chapter 2.

Methods of Securing Transmissions

After you authenticate users and authorize them to access certain parts of the network, you should then consider methods of securing information while it travels along the network cable.

Most network communication is sent along the network wire in *cleartext*, meaning that anyone connected to your network can read the information. But if the information is traveling across the Internet, anyone can view that information if it is passed in cleartext.

Most Internet protocols, such as HTTP, send information in cleartext, and it is up to the people who set up the servers that use these Internet protocols to encrypt the information before it is released to the Internet. *Encrypting* the information means that the information is run through a mathematical calculation that generates an altered version of the information: a *result*. For example, the words `Glen Clarke` could be encrypted to look like `7y3i s3fk4r`. If anyone intercepts such encrypted information and views it while it is traveling across the wire, the information would mean nothing.

Here is a real-world example. You type your credit card number on a Web site, but you certainly do not want that credit card number to be viewed while you send it from your client computer to the server. You want to be sure that the Web site where you enter the credit card number encrypts the traffic. You can tell by the lock icon that appears in the Web browser, as shown in Figure 1-9.

Figure 1-9: Identifying a secure site by locating the lock in Internet Explorer.

It is important for the A+ exam that you understand popular methods of encrypting traffic. You can use a number of technologies, such as

✦ **Secure Sockets Layer (SSL):** This protocol is used to encrypt different types of Internet traffic. For example, you could use SSL to encrypt HTTP traffic by applying a digital certificate to the Web site. The *digital certificate* contains the key that is used to encrypt and decrypt the traffic.

✦ **Internet Protocol Security (IPSec):** This protocol can encrypt all TCP/IP traffic between systems. As a network administrator, you configure IPSec on the server and the clients with the same key, which is used to

encrypt and decrypt network traffic. Because of the configuration, it is an unlikely solution for a Web site but is a great way to encrypt traffic on your network.

✦ **Virtual Private Network (VPN):** A VPN allows a user to connect across the Internet to a remote network, typically her office network, and send information between her system and the office network securely. The information is secured because the VPN technology used creates an encrypted tunnel between the user and the office network — any data that travels through the tunnel is encrypted.

The preceding sections touch on a number of places that require security. Here is a quick overview of the security steps that I have discussed so far:

✦ Secure your office environment first from physical access by unauthorized persons.

✦ Set up a system for authentication, which is the idea that users must log on to the network.

✦ After users log on to the network, they must be authorized to access resources.

✦ When you allow someone to access resources, make sure that you encrypt the traffic while it is in transit, especially if the information is transmitted outside your own network.

Do Not Forget about Data Protection

In this section, you find out about how to secure your data environment from a hacker or malicious user. When securing your systems, you want to protect the systems from a person who damages information or systems with or without intent. You want to be sure to secure your environment from hackers, but at the same time, you want to protect your systems from users on the network who may cause damage without meaning to. Accidents can happen, so be sure to prevent accidents from happening by following the best practices in the following sections.

Destroying data

Most office environments have strict policies in place to help secure confidential information. Shredding paper documents with personal or confidential information is a no-brainer, and computerized data should be no different. A company needs strict guidelines on how to destroy data that resides on computer hard drives.

Hard drive destruction

Destroying data that resides on a computer hard disk typically involves shredding the computer hard drive with a huge shredding machine, or destroying the drive another way, such as sanding the platters down to nothing.

I have talked to some customers who used to destroy drives by driving spikes through them, but what they found was that the data around the hole that the spike put in the drive could still be read! These customers now disintegrate the drive in a huge shredder. Other customers sand the drives right down to nothing. Either way, if securing the data is a concern, make sure to physically destroy the disk that contains the data.

Data wiping

Instead of destroying the drives with a traditional shredded, some companies use a *shredder application,* which writes a bunch of 1s to the drive, thereby overwriting the previous data. These applications typically overwrite the drive a number of times because hackers can retrieve the data from disk even after it has been overwritten a few times. When purchasing shredding software, be sure to investigate how many overwrite operations the software performs. I recommend using software that overwrites at least seven times.

Hard drive recycling

What do you do with your hard drive when you get an upgrade or replacement drive? Well, you could pass the hard drive on to someone else who needs the drive, or you could have the drive recycled. After all, a number of useful parts are on the drive, such as the hard drive platters and the magnets.

However, be aware of the risk of passing your drive over to someone! Companies concerned with corporate security and data privacy will likely opt to destroy the drive instead of recycling because of the risk of having private data lifted off the drive.

Backing up data

A big part of securing the data environment is not only setting the permissions but also ensuring that you create a good backup and restore strategy. Identify which files are critical to the operation of the business and should be backed up. You also want to be familiar with all types of information used by your company. For example, you might depend on e-mail, so make sure that you back up your e-mail server along with any files in shared folders. If your company stores important data in databases, make sure that you back up those databases as well.

Backup review

You can find out more about backups in Book VII, Chapter 3, but for the exam, here are some of the key points you need to remember.

When you perform a backup, the OS keeps track of which files have been changed since the last backup by setting the *archive bit.* The archive bit is an attribute of the file that tells the system that the file has changed. To view the archive bit within Windows XP or Vista, right-click the file and choose Properties. In the Properties dialog box, click the Advanced button.

The first option in the Advanced Attributes dialog box that appears — File Is Ready for Archiving — is the archive bit. (See Figure 1-10.) When this check box is selected, it means that the file needs to be backed up because it has changed.

Figure 1-10: Viewing the archive bit in Windows.

Before you perform a backup, decide what type of backup to perform. Each backup type deals with the archive bit a little differently. Here are the three major types of backup:

✦ **Full backup:** Copies any files that you select, whether the archive bit is set or not, and clears the archive bit on any file that is backed up — essentially recording the fact that the file has been backed up.

✦ **Differential backup:** Copies any files that have changed, but it does not clear the archive bit; thus, there is no record that the files have been backed up. The benefit is that the next time you do the backup, the files will be backed up again because the archive bit has not been cleared. As far as the OS is concerned, the file has not been backed up since it was changed.

✦ **Incremental:** Copies any file that has changed and then clears the archive bit on any files that are backed up. Thus, if a file is copied

during an incremental backup, because the backup process clears the archive bit, the file will not be backed up during subsequent incremental backups unless the file changes again.

Be familiar with the difference between a full, incremental, and differential backup. Also know which backup types clear the archive bit.

Tape rotation and offsite storage

Take the time to rotate tapes so that the same tape is not used all the time. You also want to make sure that you store a backup offsite in case of a disaster such as flood or fire. It is important that you are able to recover the system no matter what happens.

Test restore operations

As a last point with backup strategy best practices, you want to test restorations frequently to ensure that you can recover information from backup without any problem. You do not want to find out that the backups are bad when management is hanging over your shoulder waiting for the company network to come back online! Be sure to perform regular test restorations.

Implementing RAID solutions

To help secure your data, not only do you want to have good backups, but you also want to ensure that you are implementing some form of a RAID solution. RAID (Redundant Array of Inexpensive Disks) is covered in detail in Book II, Chapter 5, so in this section I review the different types of RAID volumes supported in Windows servers and ensure that you understand that RAID solutions are a way of helping secure data.

RAID is a way of storing duplicated data on multiple disks; if one disk goes down, the data is still available to the users because other disks in the RAID array have a copy of the data. The benefit of using RAID instead of backups is that with the RAID solution, the user never knows that a drive has failed because the other drive is supplying all the data. *Note:* You still need the backups, though, in case both drives fail, or some disaster happens, like a flood or fire, destroying the system and all of its drives.

A number of different types of RAID solutions are available. The ones provided by the Windows Server OSes are as follows:

✦ **RAID Level 0:** Also known as a *striped volume* in Windows, RAID Level 0 writes different parts of the data to different disks at the same time. The benefit of a striped volume is that you get a performance benefit

by writing the data at the same time to two different disks, essentially taking less time to read or write to the file. Note that the data is split between both drives, and there is no duplication — which means that this is not really a redundant solution.

✦ **RAID Level 1:** Also known as *a mirrored volume* in Windows. A mirrored volume duplicates the data stored on one disk to another disk. If one disk fails, the other disk has a copy of the data.

✦ **RAID Level 5:** Also known as a *RAID 5 volume* in Windows. A RAID 5 volume requires a minimum of three drives and writes to all drives in the solution like a striped volume. A RAID 5 volume is different than a striped volume in the sense that it does store redundant data — *parity data* — on one of the disks. The redundant data is used to calculate the missing data when a disk goes missing, ensuring that users can still retrieve the data without noticing a problem.

Be comfortable with the RAID levels when preparing for the exam. Check out Book II, Chapter 5, to see how to create volumes in Windows.

Data encryption

Encrypting data converts information to an unreadable format so that if folks gain access to the data, they cannot understand it. In the cryptography world, encryption is described as changing plain text to cipher text. As you can likely intuit, decryption converts cipher text to plain text.

There are a number of ways to encrypt data on the hard drive:

✦ **EFS:** The Encrypting File System (EFS) is a feature of NTFS and can be enabled through the file properties. After the file is encrypted, it can be read only by authorized persons. To read more about EFS, check out Book V, Chapter 4.

✦ **Bit Locker:** Instead of encrypting data at the file level with EFS, you can have Windows encrypt the entire partition or volume, which protects all data on the partition, including the Windows OS, the Registry, and the data. With Bit Locker, data is encrypted by using keys stored in a TPM chip or a USB drive, depending upon how Bit Locker has been configured.

✦ **Third-party software:** You can also use third-party software to encrypt data. For example, you can use the free program TrueCrypt (www.true crypt.org) to encrypt all your data into a TrueCrypt file and then copy the file to a USB flash drive.

Compliance and classification

Part of securing your computing environment is understanding how to protect the business from disclosure of information and by ensuring the business is compliant with government and industry regulations that surround computing and data.

Compliance

Data compliance is the concept of protecting the data from information leaks and ensuring recoverability of information by following government regulations and industry regulations. For example, if you are in the health industry, you must be compliant with the Health Insurance Portability and Accountability Act (HIPAA), which requires that health records and patient information be secured and kept private.

Companies are also required to protect customer information as outlined by to the Privacy Act. Companies are no longer allowed to share customer information with other businesses, including contact information such as e-mail addresses and phone numbers.

Another example of data compliance is ensuring that your company has taken the correct steps and implemented the correct controls to adhere to the Sarbanes-Oxley Act, which outlines that the company must be able to prove that adequate auditing controls have been put in place in case an incident requires review of internal information, such as company e-mails.

If you are the security manager for your company, be sure to spend time researching which government regulations and industry regulations your company falls under. With your list of regulations in hand, then you can determine the steps you need to take to be compliant.

Classification

Part of securing company information is through data classification, which assigns a level of sensitivity to information, such as Confidential or Top Secret. After the level of sensitivity is assigned to the information, the necessary controls are put in place to protect that classification of information.

Each data classification has specific security measures that need to be implemented to keep it secure. For example, a company might decide that top secret information cannot leave the "top secret" system — say, by disabling the ports on the system that typically would allow connecting a removable drive.

Data classification is assigned to the information based on the value of the information to the organization. Each classification level is designed to indicate whether the information is to be kept private or is available for public release. The following are examples of classification levels:

+ Top secret, secret, and unclassified

+ Confidential, official use only, and public

+ Highly confidential, proprietary, internal use, and public

Getting an A+

This chapter introduces you to a number of security-related terms that you need to understand before taking your first A+ exam. Here some key points to remember when preparing for the exam:

+ *Authentication* is the process of proving an identity to the network, but *authorization* is the process of determining whether accessing a resource is allowed after authentication takes place.

+ Hackers take many different approaches to compromise a system. Protect your environment from both network-based and software-based attacks, and make sure that physical security is in place.

+ A *denial of service* (DoS) is an attack on a system or network that prevents the system or network from performing its regular function.

+ *Social engineering* is a popular type of attack that involves the hacker compromising security by tricking an employee through social contact. The social engineer might entice the user to divulge confidential information or might trick the user into running a program that does harm to the system.

+ You secure network traffic by *encrypting* traffic between two systems by using technologies such as SSL and IPSec. Administrators typically use SSL to encrypt Web traffic and IPSec to encrypt internal or VPN traffic.

+ Securing your data involves not only protecting resources with permissions but also protecting your data by following proper data destruction procedures and backup strategies as well as creating redundant disk solutions.

Prep Test

1 What type of attack involves the hacker tricking a user through social contact?

A ○ Password attack

B ○ Eavesdrop attack

C ○ Man-in-the-middle attack

D ○ Social engineering attack

2 What type of attack involves the hacker using a packet sniffer and trying to view confidential information traveling over the network?

A ○ Password attack

B ○ Eavesdrop attack

C ○ Man-in-the-middle attack

D ○ Social engineering attack

3 What type of attack involves the hacker causing your system or network to become unresponsive to valid requests?

A ○ DoS attack

B ○ Eavesdrop attack

C ○ Man-in-the-middle attack

D ○ Password attack

4 What type of RAID volume duplicates the data fully on two disks?

A ○ Striped volume

B ○ Mirrored volume

C ○ RAID 5 volume

D ○ RAID Level 0

5 What should you purchase for each laptop to help protect it from theft?

A ○ Flash drive

B ○ Driver disk

C ○ A Doberman Pinscher

D ○ Lockdown cable

6 Which of the following are forms of biometrics? (Select all that apply.)

A ❑ Fingerprint scan
B ❑ Smart card
C ❑ Username and password
D ❑ Retinal scan

7 What type of backup copies the files that have changed but does not clear the archive bit?

A ○ Full backup
B ○ Incremental backup
C ○ Differential backup
D ○ Copy

8 What technology is typically used to encrypt traffic between a Web server and Web browser?

A ○ DoS
B ○ IPSec
C ○ Smart card
D ○ SSL

9 In high-security environments, what should you do with old hard drives?

A ○ Donate them to charity.
B ○ Recycle them.
C ○ Physically destroy them.
D ○ Drive a spike through them.

10 What type of attack involves the hacker modifying the source address of the packet?

A ○ Spoof attack
B ○ Eavesdrop attack
C ○ Man-in-the-middle attack
D ○ Social engineering attack

Answers

1 **D.** Social engineering is a type of hack that involves contacting victims through phone or e-mail and tricking them into doing something that compromises company security. *See "Social engineering attacks."*

2 **B.** An eavesdropping attack occurs when a hacker monitors network traffic to try to capture information that could be useful in another attack. *Review "Eavesdropping attack."*

3 **A.** A denial of service (DoS) attack is when a hacker consumes all the system's processing power or bandwidth so that it cannot to perform its normal job. *Check out "Denial of service."*

4 **B.** A mirrored volume is used to create a full duplicate of the data on two different disks. *Peruse "Implementing RAID solutions."*

5 **D.** A lockdown cable is used to secure the laptop to a desk to help prevent the laptop from being stolen. *Refer to "Understanding Physical Security."*

6 **A, D.** Biometric devices involve authenticating a user through the user's unique physical characteristics. Fingerprint scans and retinal scans are popular biometric authentication methods. *See "Authentication."*

7 **C.** A differential backup backs up only those files that have changed since the last full backup and then does not clear the archive bit. *Check out "Backup review."*

8 **D.** Secure Socket Layer (SSL) is used to encrypt Web traffic. You can identify whether you are on a secure Web site by looking for the lock icon at the bottom of the screen. *Peruse "Methods of Securing Transmissions."*

9 **C.** You want to make sure that you physically destroy the drives if securing data is critical to the business. *Take a look at "Destroying data."*

10 **A.** A spoof attack occurs when the hacker modifies the source address, trying to hide the origin of the packet. *Refer to "Spoofing."*

Chapter 2: Implementing Security

Exam Objectives

✔ Securing systems through BIOS

✔ Implementing users and groups

✔ Implementing permissions and rights

✔ Implementing auditing

✔ Implementing firewalls

✔ Implementing security best practices

*I*n this chapter, you find out how to implement security best practices on systems at home or at the workplace. The preceding chapter introduces terms such as *authentication* and *authorization;* this chapter demonstrates how to perform such tasks. You find out how to create a user account that can be used for authentication and how to authorize the user to access a folder or perform an action within the operating system. This chapter will ensure that you know how to perform basic security-related tasks!

When thinking about network security, understand that security is to be implemented at multiple layers, meaning that you cannot focus on just one security-related feature. You want to implement multiple security features to secure your environment. For example, a number of people feel that their systems are secure because they have a firewall. They don't realize that the firewall protects the system only from attacks coming across the network. What if the hacker is in the same room as the computer? The firewall is of no use at that point, so you need to ensure that you implement other security features to protect the system from all potential threats.

Securing Systems through BIOS

When securing systems, your first security concern is physical access. This involves ensuring that critical systems, such as servers, are in locked rooms that are not accessible to unauthorized users. Physically securing systems could also involve changing some of the CMOS settings, such as boot device order, power-on password, and CMOS password.

Changing these settings in CMOS is different for each type of system, but the first thing to do is enter CMOS. Normally, you press Delete, F1, F2, or F10 when the system is booting.

After the system is booted, you will find the following settings in the CMOS setup program to help secure the system:

✦ **BIOS Password:** Usually found in the security section of CMOS, you can set a power-on password (also known as a user password), which is a password that anyone who wants to use the system must type. You may also set an admin password, which is a password that must be known by anyone who wants to change CMOS settings.

✦ **Boot Devices:** In CMOS, you can control what devices the computer can boot from. Most computers today can boot from CD-ROM, floppy disk, hard disk, network, and USB removable drives. It is important to understand that if you allow a computer to boot from CD-ROM, a hacker can possibly boot from a CD and bypass all security enforced by your OS.

✦ **Intrusion Detection:** Most systems today have an intrusion detection option that will notify you if the computer case has been opened. This is important because instead of stealing the actual computer, a person could take the RAM or hard drive out of the computer, which is easier to hide and steal. Make sure that the intrusion detection option is enabled, and also be sure to lock the computer cases so they cannot be removed easily.

Implementing Users and Groups

In this section, you find out how to create user accounts that can be used to log on to the system and how to create groups to organize users together as a single object that permissions can be assigned to.

Creating user accounts

To secure the Windows OS from unauthorized access, you can create a user account for each person who is allowed to use the system. Anyone without a user account will be unable to log on to the system and, as a result, will not be able to use the computer. The other benefit of creating user accounts is that even if a person has a user account and logs onto the system, he might not be able to access a file because you have not given permission to that user to access the file.

To create a user account in Windows systems, use the Computer Management console. Right-click My Computer (Computer, in Windows Vista) and choose Manage. In the Computer Management console that opens, expand Local Users and Groups and select the Users folder (shown in Figure 2-1). In the Users folder, you will notice some user accounts on the right side. These user accounts are *built-in accounts,* meaning that they were built by the OS or by a piece of software you have installed.

Figure 2-1:
Creating
user
accounts
and groups
in the
Computer
Manage-
ment
console.

Two built-in accounts you should be familiar with for the A+ exam are

✦ **Administrator:** The *administrator account* is the built-in account in
 Windows that has full access to the system and can manage all aspects
 of the computer. During the installation of Windows, you were asked
 what you wanted to set as the password for the administrator account;
 you use that password to log on with the username of `administrator`.
 When you do log on as administrator, you can change any settings on
 the system. A normal user account cannot change major settings on
 the system such as the time, installing software, or any changes that
 affect the system. To make these types of changes, you need to log on as
 administrator to make changes.

✦ **Guest:** Users can use the *guest account* if they don't have an actual user
 account. When they try to access the system, they are authenticated as
 `guest`. The guest user inherits any permissions the guest account has
 on the system. There is one hook to this scenario, though. By default,
 the guest account is disabled, meaning that it is not available for use.
 Because of the security concerns of not requiring someone to log on,
 Microsoft has disabled the account. A disabled account appears with a
 red X on it and cannot be used.

Two default accounts are built in to Windows: administrator and guest. The
administrator account has full access to the system, and the guest account
is used for temporary access to the system. Also note that the guest account
is disabled by default.

Now that you have identified the two major built-in accounts, you can create your own user accounts. To create your own user accounts in the Computer Management console, right-click the Users folder and choose New User. The New User dialog box appears (shown in Figure 2-2). Fill in the following account details:

✦ **User Name:** This is the name that the user uses to log on to the system. Typically, it is a short version of the full name. For example, the full name Glen Clarke might get truncated to gclarke as the username. A username is also known as the *logon name*.

✦ **Full Name:** This is typically the person's first name and last name: for example, Glen Clarke as the full name.

✦ **Description:** This is a description of the user account. I typically put the person's job role here: for example, Accountant.

✦ **Password:** Type what you want for the user accounts password. The user needs to know this password to log on to the system. Be sure to use good practices with passwords, such as not using words found in the dictionary and using a combination of uppercase and lowercase letters, numbers, and symbols. See the preceding chapter for more information about strong passwords.

✦ **Confirm Password:** Type the password again in this box. This ensures that you typed what you thought you typed.

✦ **User Must Change Password at Next Logon:** Set this option if you want to force the user to change the password the first time he logs on. This ensures that you don't know the user's password because the password you originally set is overwritten.

✦ **User Cannot Change Password:** Set this option if you don't want the user to be able to change the password. This ensures that the password you set is the password that the user must use.

✦ **Password Never Expires:** In a password policy, you can specify that passwords must be changed every so many days. That policy applies to all users except for any accounts that have Password Never Expires activated. You might use this option if you have two employees sharing a user account.

✦ **Account Is Disabled:** If you want to disable an account at any time, you can set this option. A disabled account is unusable until you enable it again.

After you enter all the account information, click the Create button and then click Close to dismiss the New User dialog box. The user account has been created, and you can start using it right away to log on to Windows.

Figure 2-2:
Creating
a user
account in
Windows.

Creating groups

A *group* in Windows is a collection of user accounts. The benefit of using groups when managing access to resources is that you don't need to assign the same permissions multiple times. Instead, you assign the permission to the group, and anyone who is a member of the group receives the permission.

Like user accounts, Windows offers a number of built-in groups. A built-in group has predefined capabilities within Windows. For example, printer operators can manage all printers on the system, and anyone who is a member of the printer operators group will have that capability. The following is a list of some of the popular built-in groups found in Windows OS:

✦ **Administrators:** This group has full access to the system and can change any setting on the system. The administrator account is a member of this group by default, which is why the administrator account is allowed to change any setting on the system.

✦ **Backup Operators:** Members can perform backups and restores on the system.

✦ **Account Operators:** Members can create user accounts. This group is available on Windows servers. The benefit of using this group is that if you want someone to be able to manage user accounts, you can place that person in this group instead of in the administrators group and he or she will only be able to manage the user accounts — not the entire system.

✦ **Printer Operators:** Members can change any settings on the printers. Essentially, members of this group are trained to troubleshoot the printing environment and then assigned the task of managing all printing problems on the network.

✦ **Users:** All user accounts that are created are members of the users group. You can assign permissions to the users group knowing that all users will get the permission.

✦ **Power Users:** The power users group is the group on Windows client OSes that allows its users to create user accounts and manage the printing environment. Use this group if the desktop OS does not have an account operator or a printer operator group.

Be sure to know the default groups in Windows. Some of the more useful built-in groups are account operators, printer operators, and backup operators.

If the built-in groups do not satisfy your needs, create your own groups:

1. **Click Start; then right-click My Computer (Computer, in Windows Vista) and choose Manage.**

2. **In the Computer Management console, expand Local Users and Groups.**

3. **Right-click the Groups folder in Local Users and Groups and then choose New Group, as shown in Figure 2-3.**

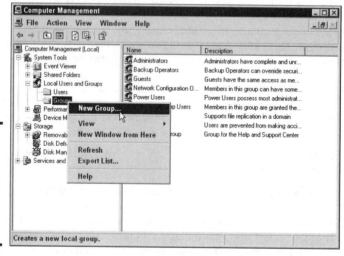

Figure 2-3: Creating a new group in Computer Management with Windows.

4. **In the New Group dialog box that appears, type the name you wish to use for the group.**

In this example, I use Accountants (shown in Figure 2-4).

Figure 2-4:
Fill in
information
for your new
group.

5. **Fill in a description for the group in the Description text box.**

6. **To begin adding members to the group, click the Add button.**

 The Select Users dialog box appears.

7. **Type the name of the user account you want to add and then click the Check Name button on the right side.**

 Windows should underline the account name, indicating that the user account exists and that you can add it to the group membership.

8. **Repeat Step 7 for each account you want to add to the group.**

9. **After you add all the accounts to the group, click OK and then click Create to create the group.**

After you create the users and place them into their appropriate groups, you are now ready to assign them permissions.

To practice creating users and groups take a look at Lab 2-1 in the Labs. pdf file in the Author directory of the CD-ROM.

Implementing Permissions and Rights

When controlling a user's access to the system, you typically modify the user's *rights* and *permissions*. Microsoft has made a huge distinction between a permission and a right.

✦ **Permission:** A user's level of access to a resource, such as a printer or file

✦ **Right:** A user's privilege to perform an OS task

In this section, you discover the difference between permissions and rights within the Windows OS and how to implement both.

Rights

If you were to log on to your Windows system as just a user account and then double-click the time in the bottom-right corner to change that time, you get an error message indicating that you do not have the privilege to change the time. This is an example of user rights. The user account that you are currently logged in with does not have the right to change the system time, which is an action that typically has to be performed by an administrative account.

There is a large list of user rights; some of the most popular ones are listed below:

+ **Access this computer from the network.** This right is needed by anyone who wants to connect to the system from across the network: for example, if you wish to connect to a shared folder on computer A, you need to this right on computer A.

+ **Back up files and directories.** This right is needed by anyone who wishes to back up files on the computer. For security reasons, not everyone should be able to perform backups on a system, so Windows controls who can perform a backup via this right.

+ **Change the system time.** To change the time on the computer, your user account must be given this right.

+ **Log on locally.** To log on to the system by pressing Ctrl+Alt+Delete, you need this right. Microsoft classifies *a local logon* as you sitting in front of the computer at the keyboard (versus a *remote logon,* where you connect from across the network, which is controlled by the first right mentioned in this list).

+ **Shut down the system.** To shut down the computer, you must have this right.

+ **Take ownership of files and other objects.** In Windows, the owner of the object, such as a file or folder, always has the ability to change the permissions of the resource. You might want to give selected individuals the take-ownership right so that they can take ownership of a resource and then change the permissions.

To change the user rights (for example, to assign Bob Smith the right to change the system time), you need to modify the user rights assignments in the local security policies of the Windows computer. The local security policy controls all security settings for the system. To change the local security policies in Windows XP, follow these steps:

1. **Choose Start⇨Control Panel.**

2. **In the Control Panel, choose Performance and Maintenance and then Administrative Tools, located at the bottom of the window.**

3. **In the Administrative Tools, double-click Local Security Policy to start the Local Security Policy console.**

4. **To modify the user rights within the local security policy, expand Local Policies and then highlight User Rights Assignments, as shown in Figure 2-5.**

When the User Rights Assignments node on the left side has been selected, you will notice the list of user rights on the right side of the screen in the Details pane.

Figure 2-5:
Configuring
user rights
within
Windows
allows you
to control
which
actions a
user can
perform.

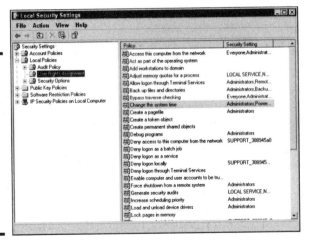

5. **To modify a user right, double-click the user right.**

You see a list of users or groups that have been assigned that right.

6. **To add a user or group to the list, click the Add User or Group button, type the name of the account you wish to add, and then click Check Names to ensure that Windows recognizes the user account.**

7. **Click OK to add the account to the right you chose (as shown in Figure 2-6) and then click OK to close the window.**

The steps used in Windows Vista to change the user rights are very similar after you access the Local Security Policy console. Choose Start⇨Control Panel⇨System and Maintenance⇨Administrative Tools and then double-click Local Security Policy.

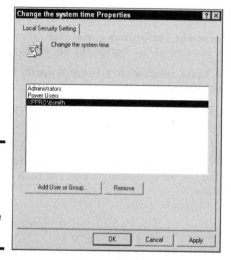

Figure 2-6:
Adding
Bob to the
change the
system time
user right.

User Account Control (UAC)

Windows Vista added the *User Account Control* (UAC) feature. When an administrative account logs onto Windows, that user is not initially given administrative access to the system. When the administrator launches a program to perform some administration, Vista prompts the user to raise the privilege level to the administrative level. If the administrator chooses Continue, the admin will be able to run the program.

Microsoft created the feature because over the last few years, a number of security incidents were caused by hackers that caused the user of the computer to run malicious software without the user's knowledge — and because the user logged on had admin access to the system, so did the program that the user did not know was running. This malicious software that now had admin access could do anything it wanted to the system.

In response, Microsoft created the UAC feature. Now if software runs without your knowledge and tries to manipulate the system, you are prompted to decide whether you wish to continue. Unfortunately, you also get prompted when you launch the software yourself, which is why most people get frustrated with the UAC feature. Still, it is a great feature from a security point of view.

You can modify the local security policy to get rid of the UAC prompt and automatically elevate the admin privileges. Locate the User Account Control: Behavior of the Elevation Prompt for Administrators in Admin Approval Mode setting in the Security Options section of the Local Policy. You can set the value of the policy to Elevate Without Prompting as shown in Figure 2-7.

Figure 2-7:
Modifying
the UAC
feature
within
the Local
Security
Policy.

Permissions

Permissions are different than rights: A right governs an action that can be
performed on the computer, but a *permission* is a user's level of access to a
resource. For example, you can give a user permission to read or modify a
file. Figure 2-8 shows the permissions you can set for a file.

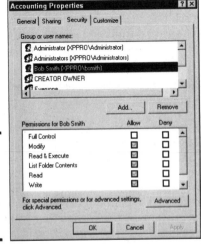

Figure 2-8:
Looking
at NTFS
permissions
in Windows
XP.

Permissions can be configured only on a partition formatted for NTFS. To obtain an NTFS partition, you can format the partition for NTFS (but lose all existing data), or you can convert the drive to NTFS by using the `convert` `driveletter: /fs:ntfs` command. When you convert, the existing data on the drive is preserved.

To modify the permissions on a folder or file in Windows, simply right-click the file or folder and choose Properties. In the properties window, choose the security page tab to set the permissions.

Here are the available permissions:

+ **Read permissions:** What I call the "read" permission is a combination of the three default permissions — Read, Read and Execute, and List Folder Contents. I personally classify all three as the read permission because at a minimum, this is typically what users need to read the file.

 • *Read:* Allows you read the contents of a file

 • *Read and Execute:* Allows you to read the contents of the file and execute a program

 • *List Folder Contents:* Allows you to see the file when you look in the folder

+ **Modify:** Allows a user to read, modify, and delete a file. When given the Modify permission to a folder, a user can also create new files or folders in that folder.

+ **Full Control:** Allows a user to do everything that the Modify permission allows, but the user can also change permissions on the resource or take ownership of the resource.

If someone can take ownership of the resource, that person can change the permissions. The Full Control permission should be used sparingly so that not everyone has the permission to change permissions on you.

+ **Write:** Used by the Modify permission to allow users to write to the file or folder. When you choose the Modify permission, you will notice that the Write permission is automatically selected.

The major difference between the Modify permission and Full Control permission is that Full Control allows a user to modify permissions and take ownership of the resource in addition to being able to modify and delete the resource.

Looking at Figure 2-8, you will notice a number of permissions with gray check boxes next to them. The gray check box means that you are not allowed to change the permission because the permission is being inherited from a parent level. *Permission inheritance* is a feature of Windows that is designed to minimize how much permission management you need to do.

With permission inheritance, when you set permission on a folder, that permission applies to all subfolders and files; you don't need to go to subfolders and files to set the same permission.

When you go to modify the permissions on a folder, however, you need to understand that the existing permissions are being inherited from the parent folder. To change the permissions, you need to break the permission inheritance feature on the folder by going to the properties of the folder, clicking the Security tab, and clicking the Advanced button. That invokes the Advanced Security Settings dialog box for the folder, where you can turn off the Inherit from Parent . . . option (see Figure 2-9).

Figure 2-9:
Disabling
permission
inheritance
in the
Advanced
Security
Settings
dialog box.

After you turn off the inheritance option and click OK to close that screen, you are presented with a dialog box asking whether you want to remove the existing permissions or copy the permission down from the parent folder so that you do not have to set all permissions again. Typically, I choose Remove and then add whoever needs to have access to the folder.

After you remove the existing permissions, you can add new users or groups to the permission list on the Security tab by clicking the Add button. You can type the name of the account or group you want to assign the permission to and then click the Check Names button. After you add all the users and groups to the permission list, you then choose which permission you want assigned to each user by selecting the user in the permission list and then choosing the permission. For example, in Figure 2-10, notice that the Accountants group has the Modify permission.

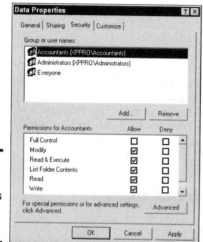

Figure 2-10: Giving the accountants the Modify permission.

To practice changing permissions and rights, take a look at Lab 2-2. Lab 2-2 can be found in the `Labs.pdf` file in the Author directory of the CD-ROM.

Copying and moving files

One last note: Permissions on a file can change as you perform file management tasks, such as moving and copying files. The following list shows the outcome if you move or copy a file that has permissions set on it:

✦ **Move on same partition.** When you move a file from one folder to another folder on the same partition, the file keeps its permissions.

✦ **Copy on same partition.** When you copy a file from one folder to another folder on the same partition, the new file inherits the permissions of the folder that it was copied to.

✦ **Move across partitions.** When you move a file from one folder to another on different partitions, the file inherits the permissions of the target folder and does not retain its original permissions. This is because when you move a file between partitions, Windows first copies the file and the deletes the original (if the copy was successful).

✦ **Copy across partitions.** When you copy a file from one partition to another partition, the new file inherits the permissions of the destination folder.

Remember the effect that copy and moving files has on the permissions of the destination file.

Implementing Auditing

After you set up security on a Windows system by setting permissions on the folders and files, configuring user rights, and placing users in the appropriate groups, make sure that the security of the OS is effective. To monitor what is happening on the system, you enable auditing, which notifies you when certain things happen on the system. For example, you might want to be notified if someone fails to log on to the system, using a correct username and password — this could be someone trying to guess the password of the account.

To effectively work with the auditing feature in Windows, there are two steps:

1. **Enable auditing**.

You must first enable auditing. Simply choose what events you wish to audit. The nice thing about auditing in Windows is that you choose which events you care to know about.

2. **Review the audit log.**

After you enable auditing, ensure that you monitor the log regularly for any security-related issues. For example, if you notice a failure to log on over and over for the same account, that is an indication that an account is being hacked.

The following sections offer more details about these two steps.

Enabling auditing

To enable auditing in Windows, modify the Local Security Policy:

1. **Choose Start⇨Control Panel.**

2. **In the Control Panel, choose Performance and Maintenance (XP) or System and Maintenance (Vista) and then Administrative Tools, located at the bottom of the window.**

3. **In the Administrative Tools, double-click Local Security Policy to start the Local Security Policy console.**

4. **In the Local Security Policy console, expand Local Policies and then highlight Audit Policy.**

On the right side of the screen (the Details pane) is a list of events that you can enable auditing for; see Figure 2-11:

- *Audit Account Logon:* Audit any remote users who are authenticated by this user account database. This is the event to enable auditing on a domain controller.

A *domain controller* is a server in a Microsoft network environment that holds all the user accounts for an entire network. In the corporate world, users log on to the network, not a particular machine, which means that the logon request is sent to the domain controller where the username and password are checked against a database. The database that holds the user accounts on a domain controller is known as the *Active Directory* database.

- *Audit Account Management:* Record an event in the log for any user account changes, such as any new accounts that are built, modified, or deleted.

- *Audit Logon Events:* Record the fact that the user logged on from this station regardless of whether the account was authenticated from this system.

- *Audit Object Access:* Audit access to a specific folder, file, or printer.

After you enable Object Access Auditing, you need to go to the Security page in the properties of a file, folder, or printer and click the Advanced button. Click the Auditing tab and choose which users and which permissions to audit for. You must perform this step on any folder, file, or printer you wish to audit.

- *Audit Policy Change:* Notification of any change to the security policy.

- *Audit Privilege Use:* Logs when a user takes advantage of any rights you have given that user. For example, if you give Bob the right to perform backups, you want to know when he actually performs a backup.

- *Audit Process Tracking:* Notification of when a process starts or exits.

- *Audit System Events:* Notification of system-related actions, such as restarting or shutting down the system. You might want to be aware when the system is restarted, especially on server OSes.

5. **To enable auditing on one of these events, double-click the event and then choose whether you want to audit the success of that event or the failure.**

For example, I do not care about the success of logons, so I would choose Failure for that event.

The steps in Windows Vista to enable auditing are very similar after you access the Local Security Policy console. Choose Start⇨Control Panel⇨ System and Maintenance⇨Administrative Tools and then double-click Local Security Policy.

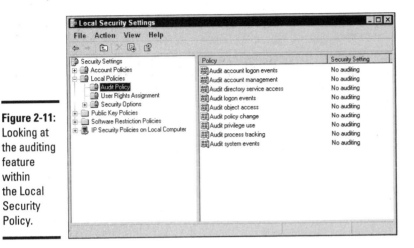

Figure 2-11:
Looking at
the auditing
feature
within
the Local
Security
Policy.

Reviewing the security log

After you enable auditing on the different events, you then need to view the
audited information in the security log of event viewer:

1. **Choose Start⇨Control Panel.**

2. **In the Control Panel, click Performance and Maintenance and then
 Administrative Tools, located at the bottom of the window.**

3. **In the Administrative Tools, double-click the Event Viewer to start the
 Event Viewer console.**

4. **Select the log that you want to view.**

 Note the events on the right side of the screen. If you select the security
 log, as shown in Figure 2-12, any events with a lock are failure events,
 and any events with a key are successful events. Figure 2-12 shows an
 account logon event with a lock, indicating a failure to log on.

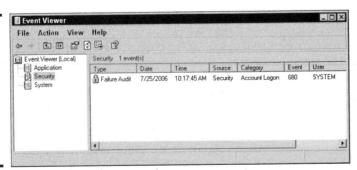

Figure 2-12:
Review the
security
log that is
populated
by the
auditing
feature of
Windows.

5. **(Optional) To view a description of a particular event, double-click the event.**

 Going back to the account logon failure example, you can see the date and time the logon was attempted. You can also view the username that was attempted and the computer that the person used to try to log on to the network.

The steps in Windows Vista to review the security log are very similar after you access the Event Viewer console. Choose Start⇨Control Panel⇨System and Maintenance⇨Administrative Tools and then double-click the Event Viewer icon. When the Event Viewer launches, expand the Windows Logs folder on the left and then choose Security.

After enabling auditing, review the security events by checking out the security logon event viewer.

Implementing Firewalls

A *firewall* is software or hardware designed to stop information from reaching your system unless you selectively choose certain pieces of information to pass through. This information is sent in the form of network packets (pieces of data) that are broken down into three parts:

+ **Header:** Contains address information, such as source and destination addresses.

+ **Body:** Contains the packet data, known as the *payload.*

+ **Trailer:** Contains checksum information, which is a value calculated off the data in the packet and helps ensure that the data has not been tampered with or damaged in transit. If the receiving system calculates a different value based on the data it receives, and that calculated value is different than the checksum value, the receiving system knows that the data has been altered in transit.

How a firewall works

A firewall is designed to look at the contents of the packet — specifically, the header information — to decide whether the data should be allowed into the system or discarded. The firewall uses the source and destination IP addresses from the header, as well as the port number, to help make this decision. A port number represents an application that runs on the system. For example, the Web server installed on my system runs at my IP address on port 80. The FTP server I am also running on my system uses my IP address but uses port 21 instead of port 80. If I want to allow the public to see my Web site but not my FTP site, I configure the firewall to allow information to reach

port 80 but not port 21. So each TCP/IP application that is running on your system uses a different port number, which is how data is sent to one application and not the other.

My point is that the firewall also uses the port number to decide whether the data should be allowed into your system. For example, I have a Web site at www.gleneclarke.com, so I had to configure my firewall to allow data destined for port 80 to be allowed in. Now, I don't have an FTP server, so I ensured that the firewall disallows data destined for port 21.

Understand that you don't need to open ports on the firewall unless you are hosting your own servers. For example, you don't need to open ports on the firewall to surf the Internet because most firewalls are built to allow responses to data you requested to come back through the firewall.

To enable the firewall feature in Windows XP, follow these steps:

1. **Go to your network properties by choosing Start⇨Control Panel⇨ Network and Internet Connections⇨Network Connections.**

2. **In the Network Connections window, right-click your LAN connection and choose Properties.**

3. **In the properties of the LAN connection, click the Advanced tab to view the advanced settings.**

4. **In the Windows Firewall section at the top of the screen, click the Settings button to enable the firewall (as shown in Figure 2-13).**

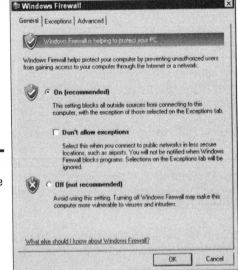

Figure 2-13:
Enabling the
Windows
firewall
feature in
Windows
XP.

5. **Make sure the firewall is set to On.**

6. **(Optional) You can also build exceptions for information that is allowed to pass through the firewall by clicking the Exceptions tab.**

 On the Exceptions tab, select which data is allowed to pass through the network card into the system. You may select an existing application from the list or add a program or port by clicking the Add Program button or Add Port button.

7. **Click the OK buttons to close the windows.**

The firewall concepts in Windows Vista are the same but the steps to locate the Windows Firewall in Vista are a little different.

1. **Choose Start⇨Control Panel⇨Windows Firewall.**

 You will notice a green check mark on the screen, stating that the Windows Firewall is turned on.

2. **If the firewall is not turned on, click the Change Settings link to open the Windows Firewall Settings dialog box.**

3. **You can then turn on the firewall by choosing the On option.**

Creating a DMZ

Most companies that want to publish their own Web sites or host other types of servers (such as FTP servers or e-mail servers) need to allow traffic to reach these types of servers. Placing public servers such as these alongside your private network servers is unrealistic because it means that you need to open the firewall to allow traffic into the network to reach these servers.

As a workaround, most network administrators create a *demilitarized zone* (DMZ) to hold these servers. A DMZ is a network segment between two firewalls where you have allowed selected traffic to reach the servers in the DMZ. The DMZ is different than your private network because you will not allow any content to come into your private network.

Figure 2-14 displays a typical DMZ setup. Note the two firewalls: firewall 1 and firewall 2. Firewall 1 connects the DMZ to the Internet and will allow only traffic destined for the three servers in the DMZ to pass through the firewall. The second firewall (firewall 2) is designed so that no systems from the Internet can pass through it, essentially protecting the private company network from outside access.

Servers that you wish to expose out to the Internet should be placed in a DMZ so that you can selectively choose which type of data is allowed to reach your servers.

Figure 2-14:
Identifying a
DMZ.

Hardware versus software firewalls

As I mention earlier, there are hardware firewall solutions that are physical devices placed on the network between the clients on the network and the Internet. The benefits of using hardware firewalls are that they typically outperform a software firewall, and you get the extra security benefit of having a separate security device between you and the Internet. Too, a hardware firewall solution typically protects the entire network and not just one system. Software firewalls have the benefit of being much cheaper than a hardware firewall.

Hardware firewalls

A number of vendors make hardware firewalls; for example, Cisco offers the Cisco PIX firewall device. You can also use your D-Link or Linksys home router as a firewall; both have firewall features that allow you to control what traffic is allowed to enter your network.

Software firewalls

Software firewalls are applications installed on your computer that protect only that computer. So-called *personal firewall software,* this kind of firewall protects only your personal computer: the one with the firewall software installed.

A number of different software firewall solutions are available. For example, Zone Alarm is a popular software firewall installed on a number of home computers. Each OS will typically have its own firewall software as well. For example, Linux has IPTables, and Windows has the Windows Firewall.

Port security and exceptions

When configuring the firewall, you typically specify rules that control which packets are allowed or not allowed to enter the network. A default rule that you typically set first states "Drop all packets" or "Accept all packets," and then you build a list of exceptions to that default rule.

For example, on my network, I have the default rule to drop all packets, but then I have an exception that says if traffic is destined for port 80, allow that traffic into the network. This way, people on the Internet can reach my Web site.

To configure exceptions in Windows Vista, follow these steps:

1. **Choose Start⇨Control Panel⇨Security⇨Windows Firewall.**

2. **Click the Change Settings link on the right side of the Windows Firewall dialog box. Then click Continue in the UAC query to give Windows permission to raise the level of security.**

3. **On the Exceptions tab, add exceptions for the type of traffic that can pass through the Windows Firewall. See some of your exception options in Figure 2-15.**

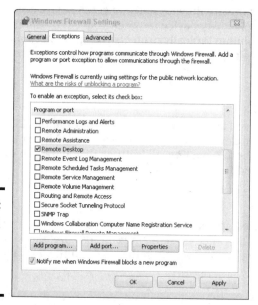

Figure 2-15: Configuring Windows Firewall exceptions in Vista.

I allowed Remote Desktop traffic to pass through the firewall by choosing it as an exception.

4. **(Optional) To add an exception for an application or a type of traffic not in the list, click the Add Port button.**

5. **In the Add a Port dialog box that opens (see Figure 2-16), define the port:**

a. *In the Name field, enter a descriptive name for the type of traffic that you are allowing entry.*

I am allowing FTP traffic, so I name my exception FTP Traffic.

b. *Enter the port number.*

I use 21, which is the port that FTP uses.

c. *Select a protocol: TCP or UDP.*

TCP is used for traffic that requires a connection to be established, and UDP is for connectionless. I want to go with TCP because FTP uses the TCP protocol.

6. **Click OK and click OK again.**

Figure 2-16:
Add a
port to the
exceptions
list in
Windows
Vista.

Adding exceptions to the firewall is similar in Windows XP but you locate the firewall exceptions a little bit differently. To locate the firewall exceptions in Windows XP:

1. **Go to your network properties by choosing Start⇨Control Panel⇨ Network and Internet Connections⇨Network Connections.**

2. **In the Network Connections window, right-click your LAN connection and choose Properties.**

3. **In the properties of the LAN connection, click the Advanced tab to view the advanced settings.**

4. **In the Windows Firewall section at the top of the screen, click the Settings button to enable the firewall.**

5. **Make sure the firewall is set to On.**

6. **(Optional) You can also build exceptions for information that is allowed to pass through the firewall by clicking the Exceptions tab.**

Implementing Security Best Practices

In the following sections, you discover some basic best practices that can help you secure your environment. These sections are designed to be a summary of features that I discuss throughout the chapters of this book.

Hardening a system

The first thing you can do to secure your system is to *harden* it: You remove any software that you are not using and disable any Windows services that are not needed. The concept of hardening comes from the fact that hackers compromise systems by leveraging software that is installed or running on the system. The less software you have running, the less likely you are to be hacked!

Patching systems

Regularly patching the system by running Windows Update is critical. As Microsoft finds out about security problems with its OS and software, its programmers fix the problem and deliver the fix through the Windows Update site. To ensure that you are getting the security fixes and patches, you must run Windows Update often. More on this topic in the next chapter.

 Microsoft changed Windows Update to Microsoft Update so that you can now get updates for more than just the Windows OS. You can download updates for a number of Microsoft products from the Microsoft Update site, such as Windows and Microsoft Office.

Firewalls

Make sure you turn on the Firewall feature in Windows. The firewall helps protect your system from network attacks, but it is not the be-all and end-all of network security. You also need to follow the other best practices presented in this chapter.

Password policies

Stress to your users the importance of using strong passwords. To enforce strong password usage, you can set a password policy in the Local Security Policies. To set the password policy, follow these steps:

1. **Choose Start⇨Control Panel.**

2. **In the Control Panel, click Performance and Maintenance. Then click Administrative Tools, located at the bottom of the window.**

3. **In the Administrative Tools, double-click Local Security Policy to start the Local Security Policy console.**

4. **Expand Account Policies and highlight Password Policy.**

5. **Ensure that users use strong passwords by double-clicking the Password Must Meet Complexity Requirements policy and then choose Enable (see Figure 2-17).**

 This setting ensures that users use passwords of a minimum of six characters, with a mix of uppercase and lowercase characters, numbers, and symbols. The password will also not contain any part of the username.

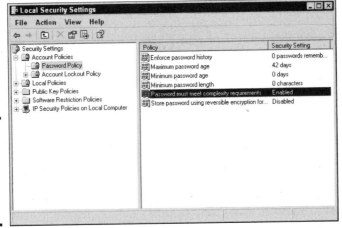

Figure 2-17:
Configuring
password
complexity
in Windows
XP.

Auditing

Make sure that you enable auditing on critical systems so that you will know (hopefully) when the system has been compromised. For example, if a hacker makes his way into the system and builds himself a hidden user account, you will know about it if you have enabled account management auditing.

Use switches instead of hubs

You can enable a number of security features when working with switches instead of hubs on the network. To begin with, switches filter traffic by sending only data to the port on the switch that the data is destined for. This can add to the security of the network because it is harder for a hacker to monitor network traffic when the port the hacker is using is not getting a copy of all data — just data destined for his system.

The second thing you could do to secure your environment with a switch is disable any unused ports on the switch. This way, if the hacker gets physical access to your network, she cannot simply plug into the switch to get access to the network.

The other thing you could do with more advanced switches is to configure a *virtual local area network* (VLAN), which is a grouping of ports on the switch that are allowed to communicate with one another but cannot communicate with other VLANs on the same switch. For example, I have a 24-port switch with two VLANs. The first VLAN comprises the first 12 ports, and the second VLAN comprises the last 12 ports. Any systems plugged into the first 12 ports cannot communicate with the systems on the second set of 12 ports and vice versa. Essentially, you have two networks — but only one switch.

Use antivirus software

Using antivirus software is another security best practice. Ensure you are using antivirus software on all your systems and keep the virus definition database up to date! Antivirus software is designed to protect your system against viruses. For more information on antivirus software, check out Book IX, Chapter 3.

Securing wireless

As a last note, I just want to add a few tips here to help secure your wireless environment. You can configure most of these settings on the wireless router by navigating to the administration site of the router, which involves starting a Web browser and entering either 192.168.0.1 or 192.168.1.1. If you have hit the Web administration pages of the wireless router, you will be asked to log on. Most routers have a default username of admin with no password that you will use to logon.

After you are logged onto the router, locate the following options in the administration pages:

✦ **Router password:** After you hook up your wireless router, be sure to connect to the router and change the admin password. Most wireless routers ship with no password, so be sure to protect your router by assigning one. Check the documentation that came with your router to find out how to set an admin password.

✦ **Setting the SSID:** The *Service Set Identifier (SSID)* is a name assigned to your wireless network. You should change the name of the SSID, but do not use your company name. When hackers are "*war driving,*" they pick up on a signal from a wireless network. Say the SSID says "BridgetsWidgets." Hackers then look for the building with the Bridget's Widgets sign. When they spot the sign, they then drive close to the building so that they get a stronger signal. Don't make it easy for them to figure out what building to get close to!

✦ **Disabling SSID broadcasting:** After you set the SSID, you also want to disable SSID broadcasting. The wireless router broadcasts the SSID so that anyone who gets close will know the wireless network is there. If you disable broadcasting, then to connect to the wireless network, a person has to know and input the SSID manually into his network client.

✦ **MAC address filtering:** If you check the administration pages on your wireless router, there is a place for you to enable MAC address filtering. This feature allows you to control which systems can connect to the wireless network by the MAC address of their network card. After MAC address filtering is enabled, only the MAC addresses listed can connect to the network.

✦ **Enable Encryption (WEP/WPA/WPA2):** Be sure to enable some form of encryption for your wireless network. You can use a number of protocols to encrypt traffic on your wireless network: WEP, WPA, or WPA2 depending upon what is supported by your wireless router. If you can use the more secure WPA2, use that.

For more information on Wireless networking check out Book VIII, Chapter 2!

Getting an A+

This chapter introduces you to a number of best practices for securing your Windows environment. Some of the key points to remember for the exam are to

✦ Create user accounts for each user of the system. Make sure that users use strong passwords for those accounts and understand to not share those passwords.

✦ Assign permissions to resources such as folders and files to ensure that unauthorized users don't get access to the resource.

✦ Enable auditing so that you are aware of any security-related events that happen on the system. Also be sure to review the security log often.

✦ Enable a firewall for the network and enable the Firewall on the Windows system.

✦ Secure your wireless router by disabling the wireless feature if you are not using the wireless components of the router. If you are using wireless, be sure to implement WEP or WPA and disable SSID broadcasting.

Prep Test

1 What security feature stops network packets from entering the system through the network card?

 A ○ Auditing

 B ○ Password policy

 C ○ Permissions

 D ○ Firewall

2 What is the network name assigned to the wireless network?

 A ○ WEP

 B ○ SSID

 C ○ SID

 D ○ WPE

3 What permission on a folder is assigned to allow a user to read, modify, create, and delete a file?

 A ○ Read

 B ○ Full Control

 C ○ Modify

 D ○ Deny

4 You have enabled auditing; where do you go to view the audit information?

 A ○ Local Security Policy

 B ○ Event Viewer

 C ○ LAN Connection Properties

 D ○ Firewall

5 A privilege to perform an operating system task is known as what?

 A ○ Permission

 B ○ Policy

 C ○ Right

 D ○ Firewall

6 **What permission allows a user to modify the permissions?**

A ○ Read

B ○ Full Control

C ○ Modify

D ○ Deny

7 **How would you allow Bob to change the time on his computer?**

A ○ Enable an Audit Policy.

B ○ Place Bob in the Administrators group.

C ○ Assign Bob the Change System Time permission.

D ○ Assign Bob the Change System Time right.

8 **Which security features might you enable through the system BIOS?**

A ○ Boot devices

B ○ Password policy

C ○ Permissions

D ○ Audit policy

9 **Which built-in group has full access to the system?**

A ○ Administrator

B ○ Power Users

C ○ Account Operators

D ○ Administrators

10 **Where do you go to enable the Firewall in Windows?**

A ○ Properties of the LAN connection

B ○ Local Security Policy

C ○ Event Viewer

D ○ Security tab

Answers

1 **D.** A firewall is designed to stop data from entering your system through the network card. *See "Implementing Firewalls."*

2 **B.** The SSID is the name assigned to the wireless network. *Review "Securing wireless."*

3 **C.** To allow users to read, modify, create, and delete a file, you assign the Modify permission. *Check out "Implementing Permissions and Rights."*

4 **B.** When auditing has been enabled, you view the auditing information by reviewing the security log in Event Viewer. *Peruse "Implementing Auditing."*

5 **C.** A right gives you the privilege to perform an operating system task. *Take a look at "Rights."*

6 **B.** The Full Control permission allows users to modify permissions on a file or folder. *Peek at "Permissions."*

7 **D.** You would assign Bob the Change System Time right. You could put Bob in the Administrators group, but that is not the best answer because you have given him a number of other capabilities at the same time. *Look over "Rights."*

8 **A.** The boot devices can be disabled through the BIOS, which controls whether someone can bypass your operating system by booting from a bootable CD or floppy. *Study "Securing Systems through BIOS."*

9 **D.** Administrators is a built-in group that has full access to the system. *Refer to "Creating groups."*

10 **A.** The Firewall can be enabled through the LAN connection properties. *Examine "Implementing Firewalls."*

Chapter 3: Viruses and Malicious Software

Exam Objectives

✔ **Understanding viruses**

✔ **Looking at malicious software**

✔ **Performing software updates**

*I*n this chapter, you find out about the different types of malicious software that you might encounter after you connect your system to the Internet or start sharing files with another system. As a service technician, you will spend most of your time trying to fix a computer that is polluted with viruses or other forms of malicious software.

Being able to protect your system from viruses and other forms of malicious software is an important skill to have. You also have to know how to perform a virus scan and remove viruses from your system.

My Computer Has a Virus!

A *virus* is a piece of software designed to do harm to the system in one fashion or another. The virus is typically associated with a file; and when that file is opened, the virus is activated and does its damage to the system. The damage could be disastrous in the sense that the system no longer starts up, or it might just create a faulty system that is annoying to work with. Either way, the virus has done its job — to cause pain and suffering in your computer's life, and yours!

Types of viruses

A number of different types of viruses can infect your system:

✦ **Boot sector:** A *boot sector* virus attacks the boot code contained in the boot sector of the disk. This type of virus loads every time the system boots up and sometimes may even prevent the system from booting.

✦ **File:** A *file* virus attaches itself to an executable file and is run, or activated, when the executable file is run. This has been one of the most popular forms of viruses for many years because the attacker simply has to trick you into running the executable.

✦ **Macro:** A very popular type of virus today is the *macro* virus. A few years ago, Microsoft was promoting the fact that you could program your own macros to customize Microsoft Office applications (such as Word, Excel, and Access). A *macro* is a set of Visual Basic for Applications (VBA) commands that performs a specific task. VBA can also be used to call other programs. For example, I created a macro in Excel that automatically starts Outlook and e-mails the contents of the spreadsheet to one of my business partners.

My point is that VBA is pretty much a full programming language. And the fact that VBA is a programming language is important because it can perform a lot of powerful actions, such as creating, deleting, and modifying files. Fear not, though. The following section explains how to keep yourself safe with the Office macro security settings.

You might also encounter worm viruses or Trojan viruses, but I save those for discussion in "Understanding Malicious Software," later in this chapter.

Office macro security settings

After the power of VBA became known, hackers started creating malicious macros in Word and Excel documents so that when you opened the documents, the macro would run and cause damage to your system. To prevent this from occurring, you could change the macro security settings in each Office application to control how to manage macros found in documents when the document is opened.

✦ **Office 2003 and earlier:** To change the macro security settings in these versions of Office, choose Tools⇨Macro⇨Security in your Microsoft Office program and then choose one of the following options (shown in Figure 3-1):

• *High:* Only macros from trusted sources are allowed to run; all other macros are disabled. This is the highest level of security because most macro code is not created from trusted sources.

• *Medium:* Office prompts you to decide whether to enable or disable macro support every time you open the file. This is a good setting because if you were unaware that a file had a macro, you could choose to disable macros while the file is open — knowing that if there is malicious code in the file, it won't run.

- *Low:* All macros run without your knowledge. If you have no worries about macro security, you may set this option — but never open a Microsoft Office document unless you know where it came from!

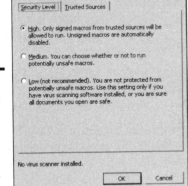

Figure 3-1:
Configuring macro security settings in Microsoft Office 2003.

✦ **Office 2007:** Choose Developer➪Code➪Macro Security. From the Trust Center window that opens, select one of the following radio buttons:

- *Disable All Macros without Notification:* Macros are disabled but you are not notified.

- *Disable All Macros with Notification:* Notifies you that macros have been disabled.

- *Disable All Macros Except Digitally Signed:* Signed code is code that is considered safe to run on your system. Choosing this option will only run macro code that has been signed.

- *Enable All Macros (Not Recommended):* Allows unsigned and signed macros to run.

Protection from viruses

To protect your computers and servers from viruses, it is essential that you have virus protection software installed. Simply, such software, such as the program shown in Figure 3-2, knows about the different viruses and can either remove the virus or remove files from your system that contain viruses.

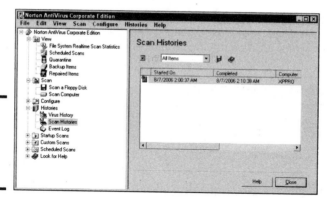

Figure 3-2:
Looking
at virus-
protection
software.

You can choose from many different name brands of virus-protection soft-
ware, each of which has its own benefits. Some of the popular names in
virus protection are

✦ **McAfee:** www.mcafee.com

✦ **Norton/Symantec:** www.symantec.com/norton/index.jsp; www.
symantec.com/index.jsp

✦ **Panda Security:** www.pandasecurity.com

✦ **F-PROT:** www.f-prot.com

Each antivirus software product has its own benefits and features. For
example, you might prefer the interface or usability of one product over
another. Still, each product should offer similar features. When shopping for
antivirus software, you should look for software that offers at least the fol-
lowing features:

✦ **Scheduled virus scans:** This is a great feature because you can have
the virus scanning software scan the system in the middle of the night
(when the system is not being used), and you do not have to physically
perform the scan yourself. You may also choose what happens when a
virus is found: say, attempt to remove the virus from the file, place the
file in a quarantine area, or delete the file.

✦ **Real-time protection:** The virus protection software runs in memory all
the time and scans any file that you open. The benefit of real-time pro-
tection is that you are protected from viruses between scan times. Be
sure to have software that supports real-time protection and have the
feature enabled (Figure 3-3)!

Figure 3-3:
Enable
real-time
protection
within
antivirus
software.

✦ **Scheduled definition updates:** Virus definitions are what virus protection software uses to update its knowledge of viruses. Your virus protection software should have a feature that allows the definitions to be downloaded from its vendor site.

✦ **Scanning e-mail:** Many virus protection software versions support scanning e-mail messages as they arrive in your inbox. This is typical of virus protection software that runs on an e-mail server and you usually pay an annual subscription fee for the service.

Updating virus definitions

When you perform a virus scan, your virus protection software knows only about the viruses as of the creation time of the software. This is a huge problem because new viruses appear every day.

So, to keep your software valid and to allow it to still be useful years after you purchase it, manufacturers use virus definitions as a way for the software to know the current list of viruses. The virus definitions can be updated online. So, even though your software might be two years old, you can keep it current.

It is critical that you update your virus definitions regularly, or your virus protection software won't know about any new viruses that are developed.

To update the virus definitions in my Norton AntiVirus, after I start the software, I see a LiveUpdate button on the main screen, as shown in Figure 3-4. To update my virus definitions, I simply click the LiveUpdate button; updating virus definitions should be this simple in most other antivirus programs as well. It is also important to notice that the antivirus software also displays how up to date the virus definitions are. In my example, I have not run LiveUpdate yet, so my software only knows about viruses developed before August 2001. I really need to run the update!

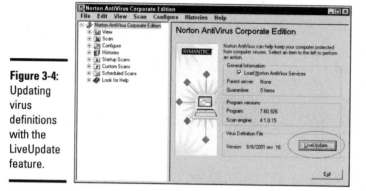

Figure 3-4:
Updating
virus
definitions
with the
LiveUpdate
feature.

Understanding Malicious Software

Other types of malicious software, outside of your typical viruses, attack
systems every day. The following sections outline other types of malicious
software — but understand that they are all considered types of viruses.

Trojan horses

Trojan horses are special programs that do something totally different than
what the user who runs it thinks it does. For example, NetBus is a very
popular Trojan virus that ships as a file called `patch.exe`. A hacker e-mails
the file called `patch.exe` and explains in the e-mail that this is a security
patch you need to apply to make sure your system is secure. Unfortunately,
`patch.exe` is the security hole! When you run `patch.exe`, it opens your
system up to the hacker by opening a port so that the hacker can connect to
the port at any time and control your system.

Trojan viruses are normally loaded on your system by the hacker tricking
you into running the program on the system, typically through an e-mail
message. You can remove the Trojan with virus protection software.

Worms

A *worm* is a self-replicating virus: The worm doesn't need to be activated
by the user opening the file. Rather, a worm is a virus that runs on a system
and also tries to infect other systems on the network. The Nimda virus is an
example of a worm virus.

Worms are loaded on your system by connecting to your system across
the Internet. The worm is usually designed to infect the system by connect-
ing through a specific piece of software. For example, Nimda was designed
to infect any system running Microsoft Web server software (Internet
Information Services; IIS).

To prevent a worm from infecting your system, be sure to have a firewall and make sure that you are up to date with patches. For more information on firewalls, check out Book IX, Chapter 2. For more about staying up to date, read the "Preventing Problems by Staying Up to Date" section in this chapter. To remove a worm from your system, you can try your antivirus software, or you may have to download a removal tool specific for that worm. For example, Microsoft offers a malicious code removal tool that you can download from www.microsoft.com/downloads.

Spyware and adware

Spyware is software that loads on your system and then monitors your Internet activity. *Adware* is software that creates pop-ups from time to time advertising a particular product or service.

Both types of viruses infect your system when you surf the wrong Internet site. Spyware and adware have become a huge negative result of the Internet, so a number of products are available to eliminate spyware and adware. The most popular products used to eliminate spyware and adware are

+ **Spybot Search & Destroy:** http://spybot.search-destroy 2009.com

+ **Ad-Aware:** www.lavasoft.com

+ **Microsoft Windows Defender:** www.microsoft.com/windows/ products/winfamily/defender/default.mspx

 You can download Defender for free and install it on your Windows XP SP2 system. (See Figure 3-5.) Defender is installed by default on a Windows Vista system.

When selecting which software to use for spyware or adware removal, be sure to go with a product that supports features similar to good antivirus software, such as real-time protection and scheduled spyware scans.

Pop-ups and phishing

To help protect your system from malicious activity when surfing the Internet, newer versions of Internet Explorer (IE) have built-in pop-up blockers and prevent phishing attacks. Windows Vista has these features enabled by default, protecting you from malicious content on the Web!

A pop-up blocker prevents additional windows from launching when you are surfing a Web site. Web sites and adware often have pop-ups appear to promote products. With a pop-up blocker enabled, though, you are notified by a yellow bar at the top of the browser indicating when a pop-up is blocked. Click the yellow bar to allow the pop-up.

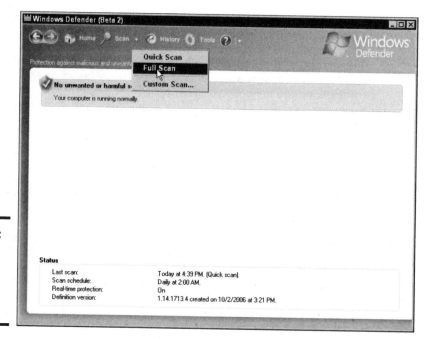

Figure 3-5:
Remove
spyware
with
Windows
Defender.

Windows Vista and newer versions of IE (7 or greater) have built-in phishing protection that allows you to check the authenticity of a Web site to ensure that it is not a known "phishing" site. If the site is a known phishing site, the browser will block the site.

Identifying Hoaxes

It is important to understand that some malicious code that you hear about is a *hoax!* For example, I remember a few years back, I was playing an elf bowling program that everyone was e-mailing around at Christmas time. After weeks of playing this game, it was said that the program should be removed from your system because on a certain date it would do damage to your system. I removed the program from my main computer, but I ran the program on a test system after that date, and it did no harm.

You typically receive hoaxes about viruses through your e-mail system. The e-mail you receive is acting as a virus alert, but unfortunately, there is no actual virus to report — it is a hoax. The benefit of such hoaxes is for the creators of the *actual* viruses; hackers hope that you receive so many hoaxes that you eventually ignore true virus alerts.

If you receive an e-mail or other form of notice about a virus, check it against a virus hoax list to see whether the warning message is a hoax or has merit. Most virus protection software manufacturers keep an up-to-date list. For example, McAfee lists hoaxes at `http://vil.mcafee.com/hoax.asp`. You can also go to a generic hoax site like Hoaxbusters, which is found at `http://www.hoaxbusters.org`.

Preventing Problems by Staying Up to Date

One of the most popular techniques hackers use to compromise systems is to find vulnerabilities in the software we use day in and day out. For example, hackers quickly figured out a way to perform the "dot dot" attack on Windows 2000 systems after IIS was installed. With the "dot dot" attack, hackers navigate the folder structure of a Web server and delete files — a serious security flaw. After Microsoft got wind of the mistake, its programmers created a fix. It is your responsibility as a network administrator to download all the fixes to problems in the software you use.

Windows Update

To make it easier for you to get security fixes (patches) and updates for Microsoft software, use Windows Update feature within the operating system. If you choose the Windows Update command from the Start menu, you are automatically connected to the Microsoft Windows Update site, where your system is scanned for which updates are needed.

Windows Update allows you to do an express update where all critical updates are installed on your system, or a custom update (see Figure 3-6) where you get to select which updates to install (see Figure 3-6). From the Windows Update site, you install all the updates or patches that your system needs. Performing a Windows Update is a critical step to securing your systems — be sure to do it regularly. You can access Windows Update in Windows XP and Vista by choosing Start⇨All Programs⇨Windows Update.

Microsoft has started using the term Microsoft Update instead of Windows Update because you can now update all the Microsoft software, not just the Windows operating system.

SUS and WSUS

Most companies have thousands of systems on the network, which would make it impossible to visit each system individually and run Windows Update. To solve the problem of deploying updates to thousands of systems at a time, Microsoft created Software Update Service (SUS). The SUS

software is loaded on a server and gets all of the updates from the Windows Update site. After the SUS server downloads all the updates, you review and approve the updates. The SUS software then sends the updates to the other systems on your network. This means that you don't have to run Windows Update on every system on your network — saving you time and money!

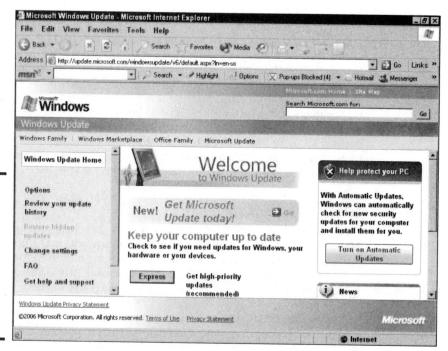

Figure 3-6:
The Windows Update site allows you to do an express update or a custom update.

The software update service was improved a few years later to create Windows Software Update Services (WSUS). WSUS solves a number of problems that existed in the original SUS. Some of the benefits of WSUS over SUS are

✦ **Synchronization:** In this context, *synchronizing* involves download-ing updates from the Microsoft Update site to the SUS server. When you synchronize the SUS server with Windows Update, it takes hours because all the updates on the Windows Update site are downloaded to your SUS server. This makes no sense because you receive updates for software you don't use, thus wasting time and space on your system. WSUS downloads a listing of updates when you choose to synchronize the WSUS server. After you get the listing of updates, you then select which updates to download — saving space and time!

✦ **Product selection:** With WSUS, you can select which Microsoft products you use so that you get a listing of updates for only those products. For example, if you aren't using Microsoft Exchange server, it doesn't make sense to get updates for that product. With WSUS, you can specify that you are not using that software, and the updates for that software do not appear in the list.

✦ **Computer groups:** With WSUS, you can deploy updates to selected groups of systems. This is a big improvement over SUS because with SUS, when you approve the update, the update gets sent to all the systems. With WSUS, you can create groups of computers, and when you approve an update, you assign it to a group. For example, you could create a group called Accounting and then place all the accounting computers in that grouping, which allows you to approve updates for just the accounting systems if you like.

Antivirus

A big part of keeping your system up to date is making sure that you download security fixes from the Windows Update site or from the WSUS server, but you also need to be sure that you update the virus definitions for your virus protection software. You want to make sure that you investigate how to update the virus definitions with your antivirus software. The virus protection software should also give you the opportunity to schedule virus definition updates.

Other security software

In addition to virus protection software and Windows Update, you should be aware of a number of other software products.

Microsoft has malicious software removal utilities that you can download from www.microsoft.com/downloads. The malicious software removal tool is updated the second Tuesday of every month and is designed to remove the most recent list of viruses from a system. This is a great utility to use when trying to clean an infected system. It is important to note that this is virus removal software — not virus protection software. You should always run your virus protection software, but if you need to remove a virus from an infected system you can use the malicious software removal tool!

One of the most beneficial types of software out there for network administrators is *vulnerability assessment software,* which can scan all the systems on your network and alert you to any missing security patches or whether you are breaking any major security best practices, like not having a password on your administrator account. The Microsoft vulnerability scanner is Microsoft Baseline Security Analyzer (MBSA) (shown in Figure 3-7), which you can download from www.microsoft.com/downloads.

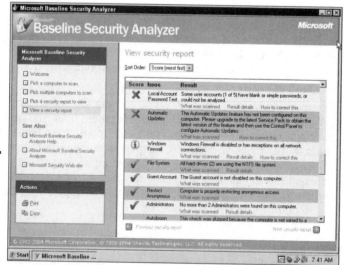

Figure 3-7:
MBSA
identifies
any security
issues with
your system.

The MBSA identifies a number of issues surrounding the security of your system. A few examples of the types of information you will be presented with are

✦ **Windows vulnerability checks:** MBSA verifies that your current system is up to date with operating system patches. It also identifies any security best practices that have been broken.

✦ **Weak passwords:** MBSA ensures that all the user accounts have strong passwords.

✦ **IIS and SQL server vulnerabilities:** MBSA verifies that any IIS and SQL servers you are using are up to date with security patches specific to those products.

Another example of a vulnerability scanner that I use quite often is the LAN guard network security scanner from GFI (`www.gfi.com/lannetscan`). LANguard is very similar to MBSA but offers much more detail with regard to the overall picture of the network and how secure the systems are. LANguard (shown in Figure 3-8) has the benefit of logging the information to a Microsoft Access database or an SQL server so that you can create your own reports on the information collected. LANguard collects vulnerability information but also reports the following information:

✦ Information on the password policy

✦ Existing groups

✦ Existing user accounts

✦ Running services

✦ Existing shares

✦ NetBIOS name information

Figure 3-8:
Use
LANguard
to identify
security
issues with
an OS.

To practice performing a Microsoft Update to your system, check out Lab 3-1. To practice using the Microsoft Baseline Security Analyzer (MBSA), check out Lab 3-2. Lab 3-1 and Lab 3-2 can be found in the Labs.pdf file in the Author directory of the CD-ROM.

Getting an A+

This chapter introduces the concepts of viruses and malicious software. Some key points to remember when you take the A+ Certification exam are

✦ A *virus* is a program that does harm to your system.

✦ Popular types of viruses are file, boot sector, and macro viruses.

✦ Other types of malicious software are Trojan horse viruses, worms, and spyware.

✦ You may use antivirus software to remove viruses from your system and antispyware software to remove spyware from your system.

✦ Be sure to update your virus definitions on a regular basis so that your virus protection software can protect your system against the most popular viruses.

Prep Test

1 **What must be updated in your antivirus software?**

 A ○ Virus software

 B ○ Virus definitions

 C ○ Patches

 D ○ Trojans

2 **What type of malicious software does something totally different than what the user expects?**

 A ○ Virus

 B ○ Virus definitions

 C ○ Worm

 D ○ Trojan virus

3 **What type of virus can prevent the system from booting?**

 A ○ File virus

 B ○ Macro virus

 C ○ Boot sector virus

 D ○ Trojans

4 **What type of virus might occur in a Microsoft Office document?**

 A ○ File virus

 B ○ Macro virus

 C ○ Boot sector virus

 D ○ Trojans

5 **What type of malicious software monitors your Internet activity?**

 A ○ Adware

 B ○ Worm

 C ○ Spyware

 D ○ Trojans

6 What type of malicious software creates pop-ups on your system?

 A ○ Adware

 B ○ Worm

 C ○ Spyware

 D ○ Trojans

7 What is the best way to ensure that your system is up to date with security patches?

 A ○ Virus protection software

 B ○ Virus definition update

 C ○ Spyware

 D ○ Windows Update

8 What software allows the network administrator to deploy patches to all the systems on the network after they are downloaded to a central server?

 A ○ Virus protection software

 B ○ Virus definitions

 C ○ WSUS

 D ○ Trojans

Answers

1 **B.** Virus definitions are needed to ensure that your virus protection software knows about recent viruses. *See "Updating virus definitions."*

2 **D.** A Trojan virus is a piece of software that does something totally different than what the user expected when he installed the application. *Review "Trojan Horses."*

3 **C.** A boot sector virus prevents a system from booting because it corrupts the boot sector. *Check out "Types of viruses."*

4 **B.** A macro virus is created in a programming language like VBA, which exists in the Microsoft Office suite. *Peruse "Types of viruses."*

5 **C.** Spyware is the type of malicious software that monitors Internet activity. *Take a look at "Spyware and adware."*

6 **A.** Adware is the type of malicious software that is responsible for creating pop-ups on your system. *Peek at "Spyware and adware."*

7 **D.** You should perform a Windows Update regularly to download current patches to your system. *Look over "Windows Update."*

8 **C.** WSUS can deploy updates to all systems on the network. *Study "SUS and WSUS."*

Appendix A: About the CD

On the CD-ROM

✔ **System requirements**

✔ **Using the CD with Windows and Mac**

✔ **Quick Assessment tests to help you gauge your strong and weak areas of knowledge**

✔ **Prep Test with hundreds of sample questions to make sure you're ready for the A+ Certification exam**

✔ **Lab exercises to help you practice and hone your skills**

✔ **Troubleshooting**

This appendix is designed to give you an overview of the system requirements for your system in order to run the software found on the accompanying CD. I also include a description of what you can find on the CD that will help you prepare for your A+ certification exams.

System Requirements

Make sure that your computer meets the minimum system requirements shown in the following list. If your computer does not meet most of these requirements, you might have problems using the software and files on the CD. For the latest and greatest information, please refer to the ReadMe file located at the root of the CD-ROM.

◆ A PC running Microsoft Windows 2000 or later

◆ A Macintosh running Apple OS X or later

◆ An Internet connection

◆ A CD-ROM drive

If you need more information on the basics, check out these books published by Wiley: *PCs For Dummies,* 11th Edition, by Dan Gookin; *Macs For Dummies,* 10th Edition, by Edward C. Baig; *Windows XP For Dummies,* 2nd Edition, *Windows 7 For Dummies,* and *Windows Vista For Dummies,* all by Andy Rathbone.

Using the CD

To install the items from the CD to your hard drive, follow these steps.

1. **Insert the CD into your computer's CD-ROM drive to bring up the license agreement.**

 Note to Windows users: The interface won't launch if you have AutoRun disabled. In that case, choose Start⇨Run. In the dialog box that appears, type **D:\start.exe**. Replace D with the proper letter if your CD-ROM drive uses a different letter. If you don't know the letter, see how your CD-ROM drive is listed under My Computer (XP and earlier) or Computer (Vista and 7).

2. **Click OK.**

 Note for Mac Users: The CD icon will appear on your desktop. Just double-click the icon to open the CD and then double-click the Start icon.

3. **Read through the license agreement and then click the Accept button to use the CD.**

 The CD interface appears, from which you can install the programs and run the demos with just a click of a button (or two).

What You Will Find on the CD

The following sections are a summary of the software on the CD-ROM included with this book.

Quick Assessments

The Quick Assessment tests are designed to help you get comfortable with the A+ testing situation and pinpoint your strengths and weaknesses on the topic. These tests are located within the Quick Assessments folder in the Author directory. There are tests for the individual chapters of each book, and taking these tests before reading the chapter will help you determine what areas you should spend extra time on when studying for the exams.

To use this tool, click the document for the chapter you are about to read. You can choose to answer the questions as you read them onscreen, or you can print the document and answer on paper. After you take the Quick Assessment test, you will know which answers you got right and which ones you got wrong because immediately after the questions is a section with the answers. Included with the answer to each question is a cross-reference to the specific section in that chapter where you can find the text that answers the question.

Prep Test

The Prep Test is designed to simulate the actual A+ test — a question with multiple choice answers. The Prep Test on the CD-ROM is not adaptive, though, and it is not timed, so you might want to time yourself to gauge your speed. After you answer each question, you find out whether you answered the question correctly. And if you answered correctly, you are on your way to A+ success! If you answered incorrectly, you are told the correct answer with a brief explanation of why it is the correct answer.

The Prep Test includes all the Prep Test questions from the end of each chapter in the book as well as hundreds of additional questions. If you perform well on the Prep Test, you're probably ready to tackle the real thing.

Lab exercises

The lab exercises included on the CD-ROM are designed to give you hands-on experience executing specific A+–related tasks. Doing these labs will help you become comfortable with the tasks you will be performing on the job, and they will also allow you to hone your skills. These labs are located within the Author directory in the `Labs.pdf` file. The labs in this document are organized by minibook and chapter so that you can easily locate them.

As you read through the chapters within this book, you will come across text marked with an On The CD icon. To access the labs referenced by the text, click the `Labs.pdf` file and then locate the minibook, chapter, and lab you are looking for using the file's Table of Contents. You can choose to execute the labs as you read them onscreen, or you can print the entire `Labs.pdf` file — and that is not a bad idea because many of the labs require you to record information on a piece of paper.

Troubleshooting

I tried my best to compile programs that work on most computers with the minimum system requirements. Alas, your computer may differ, and some programs might not work properly for some reason.

The two likeliest problems are that you don't have enough memory (RAM) for the programs you want to use or you have other programs running that are affecting installation or running of a program. If you get an error message such as `Not enough memory` or `Setup cannot continue`, try one or more of the following suggestions and then try using the software again:

✦ **Turn off any antivirus software running on your computer.** Installation programs sometimes mimic virus activity and might make your computer incorrectly believe that it is being infected by a virus.

✦ **Close all running programs.** The more programs you have running, the less memory is available to other programs. Installation programs typically update files and programs; so if you keep other programs running, installation might not work properly.

✦ **Have your local computer store add more RAM to your computer.** This is, admittedly, a drastic and somewhat expensive step. However, adding more memory can really help the speed of your computer and allow more programs to run at the same time.

If you have trouble with the CD-ROM, please call the Wiley Product Technical Support phone number at 1-877-762-2974. Outside the United States, call 1-317-572-3994. You can also contact Wiley Product Technical Support at `http://support.wiley.com`. Wiley Publishing will provide technical support only for installation and other general quality control items. For technical support on the applications themselves, consult the program's vendor or author.

To place additional orders or to request information about other Wiley products, please call 1-877-762-2974.

Appendix B: CompTIA A+ Exam Reference Matrix

*Y*ou can use this chart to identify which chapters to study in preparation for the CompTIA A+ Certification Exams. Because the topics for each exam have a number of overlapping areas, this matrix can be used to point you to correct chapters for each exam. Since you need to take two exams, then it is still best to read this entire volume because there is a great deal of overlap between the Essentials exam and all of the other exams.

After reading the entire volume, you can use this chart as part of your review. If you go through the objectives and find any area you don't think you know, you can immediately turn to the appropriate chapter for in-depth review.

The exams covered in the matrix and their column key identifiers are:

✦ **220-701 Essentials (E)**

✦ **220-702 Practical Application (P)**

2009 Examination Objectives

Domain/Objective/Description	E	P	Book-Chapter
1.0 Hardware			
1.1 Given a scenario, install, configure, and maintain personal computer components	✓		
Storage devices such as HDD (SATA, PATA, Solid state), FDD, Optical drives (CD, DVD, RW, Blu-Ray), Removable, External	✓		2-5
Motherboards, related items such as Jumper settings, CMOS battery, Advanced BIOS settings, Bus speeds, Chipsets, Firmware updates, Socket types, Expansion slots, Memory slots, Front panel connectors, I/O ports (Sound, video, USB 1.1, USB 2.0, serial, IEEE 1394 / Firewire, parallel, NIC, modem, PS/2)	✓		2-1
Power supplies such as Wattages and capacity, Connector types and quantity, Output voltage	✓		2-6
Processors such as Socket types, Speed, Number of cores, Power consumption, Cache, Front side bus, 32bit vs. 64bit	✓		2-2
Memory	✓		2-3

Domain/Objective/Description	E	P	Book-Chapter
Adapter cards such as Graphics cards, Sound cards, Storage controllers (RAID cards, eSATA cards), I/O cards (Firewire, USB, Parallel, Serial), Wired and wireless network cards, Capture cards (TV, video), Media reader		✓	3-1, 3-2, 3-3, 3-6
Cooling systems such as Heat sinks, Thermal compound, CPU fans, Case fans		✓	1-4, 2-2
1.2 Given a scenario, detect problems, troubleshoot and repair/replace personal computer components		✓	
Storage devices such as HDD (SATA, PATA, Solid state), FDD, Optical drives (CD, DVD, RW, Blu-Ray), Removable, External		✓	2-5
Motherboards, related items such as Jumper settings, CMOS battery, Advanced BIOS settings, Bus speeds, Chipsets, Firmware updates, Socket types, Expansion slots, Memory slots, Front panel connectors, I/O ports (Sound, video, USB 1.1, USB 2.0, serial, IEEE 1394 / Firewire, parallel, NIC, modem, PS/2)		✓	2-1
Power supplies such as Wattages and capacity, Connector types and quantity, Output voltage		✓	2-6
Processors such as Socket types, Speed, Number of cores, Power consumption, Cache, Front side bus, 32 bit vs. 64 bit		✓	2-2
Memory		✓	2-3
Adapter cards such as Graphics cards, Sound cards, Storage controllers (RAID cards, eSATA cards), I/O cards (Firewire, USB, Parallel, Serial), Wired and wireless network cards, Capture cards (TV, video), Media reader		✓	3-1, 3-2, 3-3, 3-6
Cooling systems such as Heat sinks, Thermal compound, CPU fans, Case fans		✓	1-4, 2-2
1.3 Given a scenario, install, configure, detect problems, troubleshoot and repair/replace laptop components		✓	
Components of the LCD including inverter, screen, and video card		✓	3-7
Hard drive and memory		✓	3-7
Disassemble processes for proper reassembly such as Document and label cable and screw locations, Organize parts, Refer to manufacturer documentation, Use appropriate hand tools		✓	4-2
Recognize internal laptop expansion slot types		✓	3-7
Upgrade wireless cards and video card		✓	3-7
Replace keyboard, processor, plastics, pointer devices, heat sinks, fans, system board, CMOS battery, speakers		✓	2-1, 2-2, 2-3, 2-4, 3-7
1.4 Given a scenario, select and use the following tools		✓	
Tools would include Multimeter, Power supply tester, Specialty hardware / tools, Cable testers, Loop back plugs, Anti-static pad and wrist strap, Extension magnet		✓	4-2

Domain/Objective/Description	E	P	Book-Chapter
1.5 Given a scenario, detect and resolve common printer issues		✓	
Symptoms such as Paper jams, Blank paper, Error codes, Out of memory error, Lines and smearing, Garbage printout, Ghosted image, No connectivity		✓	3-4
Issue resolution such as Replace fuser, Replace drum, Clear paper jam, Power cycle, Install maintenance kit (reset page count), Set IP on printer, Clean printer		✓	3-4
1.6 Categorize storage devices and backup media	✓		
Such as FDD, HDD (Solid state vs. magnetic), Optical drives (CD / DVD / RW / Blu-Ray), Removable storage (Tape drive, Solid state, thumb drive, flash, SD cards, USB), External CD-RW and hard drive, Hot swappable devices and non-hot swappable devices	✓		2-5
1.7 Explain motherboard components, types, and features	✓		
Form Factor such as ATX / BTX, micro ATX, NLX	✓		2-1
I/O interfaces such as Sound, Video, USB 1.1 and 2.0, Serial, IEEE 1394 / Firewire, Parallel, NIC, Modem, PS/2	✓		3-1, 3-2, 3-3
Memory slots such as RIMM, DIMM, SODIMM, SIMM	✓		2-3
Processor sockets	✓		2-2
Bus architecture and Bus slots such as PCI, AGP, PCIe, AMR, CNR, PCMCIA	✓		2-1
Hard Drives such as PATA (IDE, EIDE), SATA (eSATA)	✓		2-5
Contrast RAID (levels 0, 1, 5)	✓		2-5
BIOS / CMOS / Firmware such as POST, CMOS battery	✓		2-4
Riser card / daughterboard	✓		2-1
1.8 Classify power supplies types and characteristics	✓		
Such as AC adapter, ATX proprietary, Voltage, wattage and capacity, Voltage selector switch, Pins (20, 24)	✓		2-6
1.9 Explain the purpose and characteristics of CPUs and their features	✓		
Identify CPU types such as AMD, Intel and examine technologies such as Hyper threading, Multi core (Dual core, Triple core, Quad core), Onchip cache (L1, L2), Speed (real vs. actual), 32bit vs. 64 bit	✓		2-2
1.10 Explain cooling methods and devices	✓		
Technologies such as Heat sinks, CPU and case fans, Liquid cooling systems, Thermal compound	✓		2-2
1.11 Compare and contrast memory types, characteristics, and their purpose	✓		
Types such as DRAM, SRAM, SDRAM, DDR / DDR2 / DDR3, RAMBUS as well as technologies such as Parity vs. Non-parity, ECC vs. non-ECC, Single sided vs. double sided, Single channel vs. dual channel	✓		2-3
Speed such as PC100, PC133, PC2700, PC3200, DDR3-1600, DDR2-667	✓		2-3

Domain/Objective/Description	E	P	Book-Chapter
1.12 Distinguish between the different display devices and their characteristics	✓		
Technologies such as Projectors, CRT and LCD, LCD technologies (Resolution (XGA, SXGA+, UXGA, WUXGA), Contrast ratio, Native resolution), Connector types (VGA, HDMi, S-Video, Component / RGB, DVI pin compatibility), Settings such as Refresh rate, Resolution, Multi-monitor, Degauss)	✓		3-3, 3-7
1.13 Install and configure peripherals and input devices	✓		
Technologies such as Mouse, Keyboard, Bar code reader, Multimedia (Web and digital cameras, MIDI, microphones), Biometric devices, Touch screen, KVM switch	✓		3-2, 3-6
1.14 Summarize the function and types of adapter cards	✓		
Technologies such as Video (PCI, PCIe, AGP), Multimedia (Sound card, TV tuner cards, Capture cards), I/O (SCSI, Serial, USB, Parallel), Communications (NIC, Modem)	✓		2-1, 3-2, 3-3
1.15 Install, configure, and optimize laptop components and features	✓		
Technologies such as Expansion devices (PCMCIA cards, PCI Express cards, Docking station).	✓		2-1, 3-7
Communication connections (Bluetooth, Infrared, Cellular WAN, Ethernet, Modem)	✓		3-7, 8-2,
Power and electrical input devices (Auto-switching, Fixed input power supplies, Batteries)	✓		2-6
Input devices (Stylus / digitizer, Function keys, Point devices. touch pad, point stick / track point)	✓		3-2
1.16 Install and configure printers	✓		
Technologies such as Differentiate between printer types (Laser, Inkjet, Thermal, Impact), Local vs. network printers, Printer drivers (compatibility), Consumables	✓		3-4
2.0 Operating			
2.1 Select the appropriate commands and options to troubleshoot and resolve problems		✓	
Tools such as MSCONFIG, DIR, CHKDSK (/f /r), EDIT, COPY (/a /v /y), XCOPY, FORMAT, IPCONFIG (/all /release /renew), PING (-t –l), MD / CD / RD, NET, TRACERT, NSLOOKUP, [command name] /?, SFC		✓	5-5, 6-4, 8-3
2.2 Differentiate between Windows Operating System directory structures (Windows 2000, XP and Vista)		✓	
Directories such as User file locations, System file locations, Fonts, Temporary files, Program files, Offline files and folders		✓	5-2

Domain/Objective/Description	E	P	Book-Chapter
2.3 Given a scenario, select and use system utilities / tools and evaluate the results		✓	
Tools such as Disk management tools (DEFRAG, NTBACKUP, Check Disk), Disk Manager (Active, primary, extended and logical partitions, Mount points, Mounting a drive, FAT32 and NTFS, Drive status)		✓	2-5, 5-3, 6-3, 6-4
Tools such as System monitor, Administrative tools (Event Viewer, Computer Management, Services, Performance Monitor), Devices Manager, Task Manager, System Information, System restore, Remote Desktop Protocol (Remote Desktop / Remote Assistance), Task Scheduler, Regional settings and language settings		✓	5-2, 5-3, 6-3, 6-4
2.4 Evaluate and resolve common issues		✓	
Issues such as Operational Problems (Windows specific printing problems, Auto-restart errors, Bluescreen error, System lock-up, Devices drivers failure (input / output devices), Application install, start or load failure, Service fails to start), Error Messages and Conditions (Boot, Startup, Event viewer (errors in the event log), System Performance and Optimization)		✓	6-4, 7-1, 7-2
2.5 Compare and contrast the different Windows Operating Systems and their features	✓		
OSes such as Windows 2000, Windows XP 32 bit vs. 64 bit, Windows Vista 32 bit vs. 64 bit	✓		5-1
Features such as Side bar, Aero, UAC, minimum system requirements, system limits	✓		5-1
Windows 2000 and newer — upgrade paths and requirements	✓		5-1, 5-3
Terminology (32 bit vs. 64 bit – x86 vs. x64), Application compatibility, installed program locations (32 bit vs. 64 bit), Windows compatibility mode	✓		5-1
User interface, start bar layout	✓		5-1
2.6 Given a scenario, demonstrate proper use of user interfaces	✓		
Technologies such as Windows Explorer, My Computer, Control Panel	✓		5-2
Command prompt utilities (telnet, ping, ipconfig), Run line utilities (msconfig, msinfo32, Dxdiag, Cmd, REGEDIT), My Network Places, Task bar / systray	✓		6-4, 8-3
Administrative tools (Performance monitor, Event Viewer, Services, Computer Management), MMC, Task Manager, Start Menu	✓		6-3, 6-4
2.7 Explain the process and steps to install and configure the Windows OS	✓		
Technologies such as File systems, Directory structures, Files, Verification of hardware compatibility and minimum requirements, Installation methods (Boot media such as CD, floppy or USB, Network installation, Install from image, Recover CD, Factory recovery partition), Operating system installation options (File system type, Network configuration, Repair install), Disk preparation order (Format drive, Partition, Start installation)	✓		5-3

Domain/Objective/Description	E	P	Book-Chapter
Device Manager (Verify, Install and update devices drivers, Driver signing)	✓		6-4
User data migration — User State Migration Tool (USMT)	✓		5-3
Virtual memory, Configure power management	✓		5-6
Demonstrate safe removal of peripherals	✓		2-5, 3-3, 4-2
2.8 Explain the basics of boot sequences, methods, and startup utilities	✓		
Technologies such as Disk boot order / device priority, Types of boot devices (disk, network, USB, other), Boot options (Safe mode, Boot to restore point, Recovery options)	✓		2-5, 7-1, 7-3
3.0 Networking			
3.1 Troubleshoot client-side connectivity issues using appropriate tools		✓	
Technologies such as TCP/IP settings (Gateway, Subnet mask, DNS, DHCP (dynamic vs. static), NAT (private and public)), Characteristics of TCP/IP, Mail protocol settings, FTP settings, Proxy settings, Tools (Ping, Tracert, Nslookup, Netstat, Net use, Net /?, Ipconfig, telnet, SSH), Secure connection protocols, Firewall settings		✓	
3.2 Install and configure a small office home office (SOHO) network		✓	
Technologies such as Connection types Dialup, Broadband, Wireless, Routers / Access Points, LAN (10/100/1000BaseT, Speeds), Bluetooth (1.0 vs. 2.0), Cellular, Basic VoIP (consumer applications), Basics of hardware and software firewall configuration, Physical installation (Wireless router placement, Cable length)		✓	8-1, 8-2, 8-3, 8-4
3.3 Summarize the basics of networking fundamentals, including technologies, devices, and protocols	✓		
Technologies such as Basics of configuring IP addressing and TCP/IP properties (DHCP, DNS), Bandwidth and latency, Status indicators, Protocols (TCP/IP, NETBIOS), Full-duplex, half-duplex, Basics of workgroups and domains, Common ports (HTTP, FTP, POP, SMTP, TELNET, HTTPS), LAN / WAN, Hub, switch and router, Identify Virtual Private Networks (VPN), Basics class identification	✓		8-1, 8-3, 8-4
3.4 Categorize network cables and connectors and their implementations	✓		
Technologies such as Cables (Plenum / PVC, UTP (CAT3, CAT5 / 5e, CAT6), STP, Fiber, Coaxial cable), Connectors (RJ45, RJ11)	✓		8-1
3.5 Compare and contrast the different network types	✓		
Technologies such as Broadband (DSL, Cable, Satellite, Fiber), Dial-up, Wireless (All 802.11 types, WEP, WPA, SSID, MAC filtering, DHCP settings), Bluetooth, Cellular	✓		8-2, 8-4

Domain/Objective/Description	E	P	Book-Chapter
4.0 Security			
4.1 Given a scenario, prevent, troubleshoot, and remove viruses and malware		✓	
Technologies such as Use antivirus software, Identify malware symptoms, Quarantine infected systems, Research malware types, symptoms and solutions (virus encyclopedias), Remediate infected systems, Update antivirus software (Signature and engine updates, Automatic vs. manual), Schedule scans, Repair boot blocks, Scan and removal techniques (Safe mode, Boot environment), Educate end user		✓	9-1, 9-2, 9-3
4.2 Implement security and troubleshoot common issues		✓	
Technologies such as Operating systems (Local users and groups: Administrator, Power Users, Guest, Users, Vista User Access Control (UAC), NTFS vs. Share permissions, Shared files and folders, System files and folders, Encryption (Bitlocker, EFS), User authentication), System BIOS security		✓	9-1, 9-2, 9-3
4.3 Explain the basic principles of security concepts and technologies	✓		
Technologies such as Encryption technologies, Data wiping / hard drive destruction / hard drive recycling, Software firewall, Authentication technologies (User name, Password, Biometrics, Smart cards), Basics of data sensitivity and data security (Compliance, Classifications, Social engineering)	✓		9-1, 9-2
4.4 Summarize the following security features	✓		
Technologies such as Wireless encryption (WEPx and WPAx, Client configuration, SSID)	✓		8-2
Malicious software protection (Viruses, Trojans, Worms, Spam, Spyware, Adware, Grayware)	✓		9-3
BIOS Security (Drive lock, Passwords, Intrusion detection, TPM), Password management / password complexity, Locking workstation (Hardware, Operating system), Biometrics (Fingerprint scanner)	✓		9-1, 9-2
5.0 Troubleshooting, Repair, and Maintenance			
5.1 Given a scenario, explain the troubleshooting theory	✓		
Processes to Identify the problem, Establish a theory of probable cause (question the obvious), Test the theory to determine cause, Establish a plan of action to resolve the problem and implement the solution, Verify full system functionality and if applicable implement preventative measures, Document findings, actions, and outcomes	✓		1-2, 4-1
5.2 Given a scenario, explain and interpret common hardware and operating system symptoms and their causes	✓		
Technologies such as OS related symptoms (Bluescreen, System lock-up, Input/output device, Application install, Start or load, Windows specific printing problems), Hardware related symptoms (Excessive heat, Noise, Odors, Status light indicators, Alerts, Visible damage (cable, plastic)), Use documentation and resources (User / installation manuals, Internet / Web based, Training materials)	✓		1-2, 4-1

Domain/Objective/Description	E	P	Book-Chapter
5.3 Given a scenario, determine the troubleshooting methods and tools for printers	✓		
Technologies such as Manage print jobs, Print spooler, Printer properties and settings, Print a test page	✓		3-5
5.4 Given a scenario, explain and interpret common laptop issues and determine the appropriate basic troubleshooting method	✓		
Technologies such as Issues (Power conditions, Video, Keyboard, Pointer, Stylus, Wireless card issues), Methods (Verify power (LEDs, swap AC adapter), Remove unneeded peripherals, Plug in external monitor, Toggle Fn keys or hardware switches, Check LCD cutoff switch, Verify backlight functionality and pixilation, Check switch for built-in WIFI antennas or external antennas)	✓		3-7, 4-1, 4-2
5.5 Given a scenario, integrate common preventative maintenance techniques	✓		
Technologies such as Physical inspection, Updates (Driver, Firmware, OS, Security), Scheduling preventative maintenance (Defrag, Scandisk, Check disk, Startup programs), Use of appropriate repair tools and cleaning materials (Compressed air, Lint-free cloth, Computer vacuum and compressors), Power devices (Appropriate source such as power strip, surge protector or UPS), Ensuring proper environment, Backup procedures	✓		4-1, 4-2
6.0 Operational Procedure			
6.1 Outline the purpose of appropriate safety and environmental procedures and given a scenario apply them	✓		
Technologies such as ESD, EMI (Network interference, Magnets), RFI (Cordless phone interference, Microwaves), Electrical safety (CRT, Power supply, Inverter, Laser printers, Matching power requirements of equipment with power distribution and UPSs), Material Safety Data Sheets (MSDS), Cable management (Avoiding trip hazards), Physical safety (Heavy devices, Hot components), Environmental — consider proper disposal procedures	✓		1-3
6.2 Given a scenario, demonstrate the appropriate use of communication skills and professionalism in the workplace	✓		
Technologies such as Use proper language — avoid jargon, acronyms, slang, Maintain a positive attitude, Listen and do not interrupt a customer, Be culturally sensitive, Be on time, Avoid distractions, Dealing with a difficult customer or situation, Set and meet expectations / timeline and communicate status with the customer, Deal appropriately with customers' confidential materials	✓		1-2

Index

1

U

W